पुरातत्त्व
पुरातत्त्व
PURĀTATTVA

Bulletin of the Indian Archaeological Society

No. 8 1975-1976

Editor
B.K. Thapar

Assistant Editor
B.M. Pande

D.K. Printworld (P) Ltd.
New Delhi

Cataloging in Publication Data — DK
[Courtesy : D.K. Agencies (P) Ltd. <docinfo@dkagencies.com>]

Purātattva : bulletin of the Indian Archaeological Society, no. 8, 1975-1976 / editor, B.K. Thapar ; assistant editor, B.M. Pande.
p. cm.
Includes bibliographical references.
ISBN 8124602840

1. Archaeology — India — Periodicals. 2. India — Antiquities — Periodicals. 3. India — Civilization — Periodicals. I. Thapar, B.K. II. Indian Archaeological Society.

First Published in 1978
First Reprinted in 2005
ISBN 81-246-0284-0
Price for volume 8 (1975-1976): Rs. 800 US $ 40

Reprint authorised by
Indian Archaeological Society
New Delhi - 110 016

The Editors are not responsible for the opinions expressed by the Contributors.

Purātattva is published annually.

Manuscripts (whether in the form of articles or notes or book reviews) offered for publication should be sent to the Editor, Purātattva, Indian Archaeological Society, B-17, Qutab Institutional Area, New Delhi - 110 016.

Published and printed by:
D.K. Printworld (P) Ltd.
'*Srikunj*,' F-52, Bali Nagar
New Delhi – 110015
Phone : (011) 2545 3975, 2546 6019 Fax : (011) 2546 5926
E-mail : dkprintworld@vsnl.net
www. dkprintworld.com

PURATATTVA

NUMBER 8, 1975-1976

CONTENTS

PAGE

Editorial 1

ARTICLES

Metrical Analysis of Handaxes from Chirki-on-Pravara
R.V. JOSHI 3

The Acheulian Industry of Rock Shelter III F-23 at Bhimbetka, Central India : a Preliminary Study
V.N. MISHRA 13

Use of Caliche as a Chronological and Environmental Tool in the Study of Late Quaternary Formations in Gujarat and Rajasthan
K.T.M. HEGDE 37

Settlement Archaeology of Inamgaon
M.K. DHAVALIKAR 44

Ancient Plant Economy at Inamgaon
VISHNU-MITTRE and R. SAVITHRI 55

ARCHAEOLOGY AND TRADITION: THEME PAPERS

The Later Vedic Phase and the Painted Grey Ware Culture
R.S. SHARMA 63

Indian Archaeology and the Epic Tradition
B.D. CHATTOPADHYAYA 67

Prehistoric Colonization in India : Archaeological and Literary Evidence
H.D. SANKALIA 72

Puranic Lineages and Archaeological Cultures
ROMILA THAPAR 86

Archaeology and Indian Tradition : Some Observations
M.C. JOSHI 98

Harappan and Rigvedic Inter-relations
MALTI J. SHENDGE 103

Archaeology and Tamil Literary Tradition
R. CHAMPAKALAKSHMI 110

PRESIDENTIAL ADDRESSES

At Random
A. GHOSH 123

Problems of Indian Archaeology : Planning Ahead
B. B. LAL 126

NOTES AND NEWS

Technology and Social Change in Early Indian History : a Note Posing a Theoretical Question
NIHARRANJAN RAY 132

Ancient Gold Workings : Some New ^{14}C Dates
D.P. AGRAWAL AND C. MARGABANDHU 139

Comments on Subsistence Pattern of an Early Farming Community of Western India
Y.M. CHITALWALA 140

A Note on the Antiquity of Seal
P.K. AGRAWAL 141

Origin of the Form of Harappan Culture : a New Proposition
S.P. GUPTA 141

A Note on Cross Contacts of Vedic India with West Asia and Iran
S.B. ROY 146

Bibliographical Aids for the Study of the Indus Civilization : a Critical Survey
ASKO PARPOLA 150

Inscribed Harappan Material from Kalibangan : Some Remarks on Methodology and Approach
B.M. PANDE 156

On the Conquest of Meluhha by Rimus (2315-2307 B.C.) : a Hypothesis
H. SARKAR 157

Reserved Slip Ware in the Harappan Context
DILIP K. CHAKARABARTI 158

A Channel Spouted Vessel from Hissar
PARVEEN MOGORDAM and DILIP CHAKRABARTI 164

The Heliodorus Pillar at Besanagar
JOHN IRWIN 166

Comments
M.D. KHARE 176

A Note on the Excavation at Bhagwanpura
J.P. JOSHI 178

A Note on the Excavation at Virbhadra
N.C. GHOSH and R.P. SHARMA 180

Fallacies of Archaeological Interpretation
A. M. THAKKAR 182

Sociological Framework for Archaeological Research
GOPALA SARANA 183

Greek or Yavana Donors in Ancient India
S.D. DOGRA 185

BOOK REVIEWS

H.D. Sankalia : *Prehistory and Protohistory of India and Pakistan, New Edition* (Poona, 1974)
S.C. MALIK 191

Sashi Asthana : *History and Archaeology of India's Contacts with Other Countries from Earliest Times to* 300 *B.C.* (Delhi, 1976)
H.D. SANKALIA 193

Purshottam Singh : *Neolithic Cultures of West Asia* (London, 1974)
D. P. AGRAWAL 194

K. Paddayya : *Investigation into the Neolithic Culture of the Shorapur Doab* (Leiden, 1973)
H. SARKAR 195

M. Hanumantha Rao and S. Nagaraju : *Excavations at Hemmige* (Mysore, 1974)
AMARENDRA NATH 197

A. V. Narasimha Murthy : *The Coins of Karnataka* (Mysore, 1975)
B. D. CHATTOPADHYAYA 198

M. K. Dhavalikar ; *Ajanta : a Cultural Study* (Poona, 1974)
S. P. TEWARI 198

D. Desai : *Erotic Sculptures of India* (Calcutta, 1975)
D. P. AGRAWAL 199

PURATATTVA

NUMBER 8 1975-1976

Editorial

READERS of the previous issue of the *Puratattva* would recall that in the editorial notes we had pointed out, without being critical, the imbalance in the development of archaeological studies in our universities. It is gratifying to learn that the University Grants Commission has recently set up an Expert Committee 'to draw upon a scheme for developing expertise in the field of archaeology and museum in the universities. In anticipation of the recommendations of this Committee, however, it may be necessary to recognize that without field-work and museum-and laboratory-studies, teaching of archaeology is as meaningless as medicine without hospital duties. In fact, without excavation there can be no systematic development of the subject. It is not asked that any university which decides to offer course of archaeology may take to the spade and undertake excavation, to vindicate perhaps the inclusion of the course in the curriculum. That would amount to justifying means with ends. Archaeological excavations are afterall not as much easy; an adequately trained and experienced field staff is a prerequisite for any field-work—not 'the senile play-boys of science rooting in the rubbish heaps of antiquity', but persons with a good measure of comprehension of the causative relation of things, and properly equipped with the latest methodology. Some of the qualities cannot be initiated but can be developed only by training. Overall training, therefore, is needed for this increasingly complex discipline, and its necessity must be fully appreciated.

WITH a view to bridging up some of the gaps in our cultural history, the Central Advisory Board of Archaeology, at its meeting held in November 1974, had approved of a list of twenty-five problem-oriented national projects, which are required to be undertaken during the Fifth Five Year Plan (1974-79) as collaborated works by the Archaeological Survey of India, the universities, and Research Institutes and the State Departments of Archaeology. Among these, only nine projects (four belonging to the Stone Age Period, two to the Historical Period and three to the Medieval Period) have so far been taken up, six being under operation since the last four years or so. It is time, therefore, that their progress is reviewed. For any appraisal of the work done so far, it is perhaps desirable at this stage to ascertain the extent to which the objectives set forth for each of these projects have been realized. Meanwhile, it may be relevant to add that in respect of the projects of the Historical Period the conclusions that the archaeological data would pesmit are likely to be found at variance with those indicated by the materials of literary or mythical genre. It is often hazardous to assume that accounts of preliterate events have survived in traditional encapsulated form. The approach has to be contextual rather then textual. To highlight the problem, a series of seven articles dwelling on the theme—Archaeology and Tradition—have been included in this issue, which, it is hoped, would provide a proper perspective to the readers.

A reference to the list of the national projects would show that in the absence of any priorities, some of the important projects still remain uninitiated. Of these, one, relating to the Indus Civilization studies, has an extra Indian scope and as such needs our continuous attention. In addition to the immense increase in the available data relating to this Civilization over the past three decades, there have also been broad qualitative changes in the context of the enquiry—a shift to a new paradigm and a new framework of thought. The Harappan monolith in terms of chronology, geographical distribution and homogeneity of the cultural equipment now stands broken up. Although specific stages of the origin and growth of the Indus Civilization still elude us, a process of its transmutation or transformation into successor cultures is being identified both in western India and in Punjab and Haryana. Specific investigations are now needed to ascertain the nature and extent of the post-urban Harappan or sub-Harappan settlements in these regions.

During the last three decades many cultures in these regions have been labelled by research workers, often by the excavators themselves, as Late Harappan, even though they are found to be different in their cultural content, represented largely by ceramic tradition. This tends to add confusion to both the temporal and spatial aspects of the Harappa Culture. For example, Lothal B, Rangpur III, Prabhas and Mehgam in Gujarat, Diamabad II in Maharashtra, Mitathal IIB, Bhagwanpur, and Daulatpur in Haryana and Sanghol, Dadheri, Nagar and Katpalon in Punjab have all been classed as Late Harappan. To this may be added the Jhukar Culture in Sind which has also been now ascribed to this phase. And, we all know that they do not mean the same thing. For affording precision to the term, it would be necessary, therefore, to enquire, in the first instanee, whether the phase Late Harappan corresponds to the terminal part of the Culture in terms of time-bracket, representing an effete stage of a sub-Indus variant in an evolutionary or developing sequence or is the transmuted manifestation of the Culture, representing an amalgam, includlng some distant Harappan and even pre-Harappan tradition. The percentage of the classical Harappan elements should be worked out in both cases. Against the background of this enquiry it would not perhaps be appropriate to designate cultures represented by the latter elements as Late Harappan. In the same context may perhaps be viewed the recently-identified overlap of the Painted Grey Ware Culture with that represented by the latter constituent elements. The overlap of the two cultures provides us an occasion for pause and reflection. The initial end of the temporal bracket of this overlap has to be determined with some measure of certainty. Did the Painted Grey Ware in this region come into use during the latter half of the second millennium B.C.? Or, did the amalgam culture of Harappan and Pre-Harappan elements stagger on till the first two centuries of the first millennuim B.C.? Equally important will be to ascertain the real continuity between the two cultures in their material equipment. The archaeologist need not overestimate the importance of the evidence nor be unrealistic in his explanation for its occurrence, keeping in view the circumstances and the archaeological background; his approach should be not to look at a particular tree but to visualize the wood.

* * * *

It is heartening to note that as a befitting tribute to the memory of Sir Mortimer Wheeler. the Archeological Survey of India has instituted the Wheeler Memorial Lectures, to be delivered every alternate year. The first series of Lectures, (i) The impact of Mortimer Wheeler cn archaeology and (ii) Archaeology in India since Wheeler, were delivered in January 1978 by Professor Grahame Clark, a distinguished archaeologist of international repute and at present Master of Peterhouse, Cambridge, U.K. It is hoped that the Survey would publish these lectures at an early date for a wider public.

B. K. THAPAR

Metrical Analysis of Handaxes from Chirki-on-Pravara (Western Maharashtra, India)

R. V. Joshi and A. R. Marathe

Deccan College Postgraduate and Research Institute, Pune

[*Received on the 7th March,* 1976]

AFTER the publication of the treatise by Bordes[1] on the Typology of the Lower and Middle Palaeolithic, metrical study of Stone Age tools has become more or less standardized. The utility of such experiments on tools has now been clearly understood. They can be very conveniently applied for the study of a homogeneous as well as mixed collections of tools from a single site and for the comparison of collections from different localities. Clark,[2] who applied matrix analysis to British Beaker Pottery, had suggested that this method could be used for comparing the tools from different areas. Roe[3] has suggested a system of metrical analysis for handaxes not dissimilar to that of Bordes, but involving parameters including the weight of a tool and indices concerned with shape and refinement.

In the experiments concerned with manufacturing handaxes Newcomer[4] has defined the stages, first subjectively and then quantitatively, by counting and weighing flakes in the order of their removal. David Gilead's[5] work on the handaxe industries in Israel and the Near East, in which the metrical analysis of the tools was included, has shown that in that area the mean length of handaxes diminishes with time. He has, however, admitted that he could not claim that the descending order follows exactly the chronological sequence of the handaxe assemblages. A large number of research papers (Ph. D. theses) on the Stone Age industries of India have been contributed by scholars from the Deccan College, Pune,[6] in which some statistical data have been presented in a very limited way. In these the most recent publication is by Lele and Koti[7]. These authors have worked out the relation between different characters of handaxes from three different sites and presented the data in the form of equations. According to them if at any site several hundred tools are found, then such laws can be established on the basis of about 50 observations simultaneously for all the characters, length, breadth and thickness. Only one character, say length, need then be observed on the remaining hundreds of tools and no time need be spent for observations on breadth and thickness, which can be estimated from the established laws[8]. It is indeed a time saving device. But we feel that such statistical studies should not have only limited aims; their utility should rather be directed towards solving problems which otherwise could not be tackled by normal studies. Yet another attempt

[1]Francois Bordes, *Typologie du Paleolithique: Ancien et Moyen,* Universite de Bordeaux, Mem. no. 1 (Bordeaux, 1961).

[2]D.L. Clarke, 'Matrix analysis and archaeology with reference to British Beaker Pottery', *Proceedings of the Prehistoric Society,* vol. 28 (1962), pp. 371–82.

[3]D.A. Roe, 'The British Lower and Middle Palaeolithic; some problems, methods of study and preliminary results', *Proceedings of the Prehistoric Society,* vol. 33 (1964), pp. 245–67.

[4]M.H. Newcomer, 'Some quantitative experiments in handaxe manufacture', *World Archaeology,* vol. 3, no. 1 (1971), pp. 85–93.

[5]David Gilead, 'Handaxe industries in Israel and the Near East', *World Archaeology,* vol. 2, no. 1 (1970).

[6]H.D. Sankalia, *Prehistory and Protohistory of India and Pakistan,* Poona, 1974.

[7]V.S. Lele and N.N. Koti, 'Statistics in Archaeology', *Indian Antiquary,* vol. IV, nos. 1–4 (1970), pp. 64–74.

[8]*Ibid.*, p. 67.

is by Ghose[1] who conducted technological study of the cleavers of Mayurbhanj. In this the authors have measured the length, breadth, thickness and weight of cleavers with the aim to find out whether there was any norm by which the cleavers of Mayurbhanj could be defined and also the variations within them in respect of these parameters. Joshi[2] has tried to establish the significance of cleavers in Indian Acheulian industries, taking into consideration the raw material, environment and distributional pattern of cleaver-bearing industries but he has not dealt with the parameters of the tools concerned.

The last fifty years' explorations have brought to light scores of Stone Age sites in this subcontinent[3] and the stratigraphical horizons of these industries have also been fixed. Yet the evolutionary or other cultural sequence within every industry has not been successfully worked out, for we often come across handaxe industries apparently showing varied chronological and typological characteristics within the same collection from the same site obtained from the same stratigraphic horizon. Even the excavations at Adamgarh have not solved these problems.[4] In carrying out metrical studies of handaxes in India our aim was to standardise these experiments and to find out their applicability in solving the cultural and chronological problems of Stone Age industries.

It is always advantageous if all the tools under study are made of the same raw material and preferably obtained from one known stratigraphic horizon, as determined by excavation. These precautions avoid complexities arising from mixing up of tools or of varieties of rocks, and from imprecise knowledge of provenance. For this purpose, Sankalia very kindly allowed us to carry out our experiments on the Lower Palaeolithic collection from Chirki.

Chirki is a small stream, draining into the Pravara, a tributary of the Godavari, near Nevasa, a place known for its rich Stone Age sites.[5] Here Gudrun Corvinus[6] carried out systematic excavation of the palaeolith-bearing gravel, and exposed an Acheulian workshop yielding a large number of tools comprising handaxes, cleavers, scrapers, knives, borers, flakes and cores together with a quantity of waste material derived in the manufacture of the implements. She has described[7] the typology of tools but has not yet published the statistical data of the individual tools.

All the tools recovered from Chirki are made of the Deccan Trap (basalt) and are of 'Acheulian' character. The single Acheulian horizon is situated directly on the bed-rock and is covered by gravel in which some Upper Palaeolithic artifacts occur. Typical later Acheulian handaxe forms are absent and on techno-typological considerations the tools may be placed in Early to Middle Acheulian stages.[8] There is no stratigraphic division of the horizon, so that no subdivision of the occurrence into successive cultural phases would be justifiable.

We have carried out the present study on 88 handaxes and 100 cleavers from Trench VII.[9] This paper deals with the data on the handaxes. The material on the cleavers is being processed for enlarging the results obtained on the study of Indian cleavers.[10] The complicated analysis of the data on the handaxes, an immense task, if done by hand, was quickly achieved with the aid of a computer. The data was processed on CDE 3600-160A Computer System at Tata Institute of Fundamental Research (TIFR), Bombay, a special programme being prepared for the analysis of the data.

In the Lower Palaeolithic Cultures, the handaxe and cleaver are the two most standardized tool-forms. They are made of various types of rock, sometimes as core tools and sometimes on large flakes. In any assemblage of this kind a variety of shapes and sizes of these tool types is met with but their uses in the life of Stone Age man have not yet been well understood. Surely every specimen of a handaxe or a cleaver must have been put to a specific use otherwise it is difficult to see why there should be such a variety of shapes.

[1] Reena Ghose and Gautamsankar Ray, 'A technological study of the cleavers of Mayurbhanj", *Man in India*, vol. 40, no. 1(1964), pp. 50–74.

[2] R.V. Joshi, 'Significance of cleavers in Indian Acheulean industries', *Archeocivilization* (Antiquites Nationales et Internationales, Nouvelle Series, Paris), nos. 7–8 (1970), pp. 39–46.

[3] Sankalia, *op. cit.*

[4] R.V. Joshi, 'Acheulian succession in India', *Asian Perspectives*, vol. VIII, no. 1 (1964), pp. 150–63.

[5] Sankalia, *op. cit.*

[6] Gudrun Corvinus, 'An Acheulian occupation floor at Chrirki on Pravara, India', *Current Anthropology*, April-June, 1968, pp. 216–18; 'Stratigraphy and geological background of an Acheulian site at Chirki-on-Prawara. India' *Man*, vols. 63–64, (1968), pp. 921–40; and 'The Acheulian workshop at Chirki on the Pravara river, Maharashtra', *Indian Antiquary*, vol. IV, nos. 1–4 (1970), pp. 13–22.

[7] Corvinus (1968 and 1970), *ibid.*

[8] Corvinus (1968), *ibid.*

[9] Corvinus (1970), *op. cit.*

[10] Joshi *op. cit.* (1970)

We may suppose that these tools were generally used in the naked hand. A few of them, of smaller sizes, could have been used with the help of some handle. In use, the weight of such tools must have been a very important factor, followed by a particular shape. There are obvious limitations in the case of handling a tool of certain weight. A very large specimen cannot be used with one hand. Besides, physical strength will differ from person to person. Perhaps the age of an individual will also have to be considered, for an adult can manipulate bigger specimens than that could be handled by a child. The shape of a tool will be the next important factor. It will determine whether the tool is a pointed specimen or one having a convex edge. Thus, the weight and shape of any tool will control its function. The technological features such as the nature of flaking, the symmetry of the tool, etc., perhaps indicate the evolutionary stages in manufacturing techniques; the cruder flaking and symmetrical forms of implements point to an earlier stage in the history of their development, while finer flaking and symmetrical outlines of the tools clearly show evolved character and suggest a higher cultural stage. It may, however, be mentioned here that when the tool is made to discharge a specific function, careful symmetry may not necessarily be a requirement.

In a tool collection, where all the specimens are made of the same raw material, the physical qualities of the tools are the same. Thus, the volume and size of a tool can be obtained from the known values of specific gravity and its actual weight. If the tools are made on tabular or rectangular blocks or flakes, the volume obtained from the LxBxT gives approximate maximum

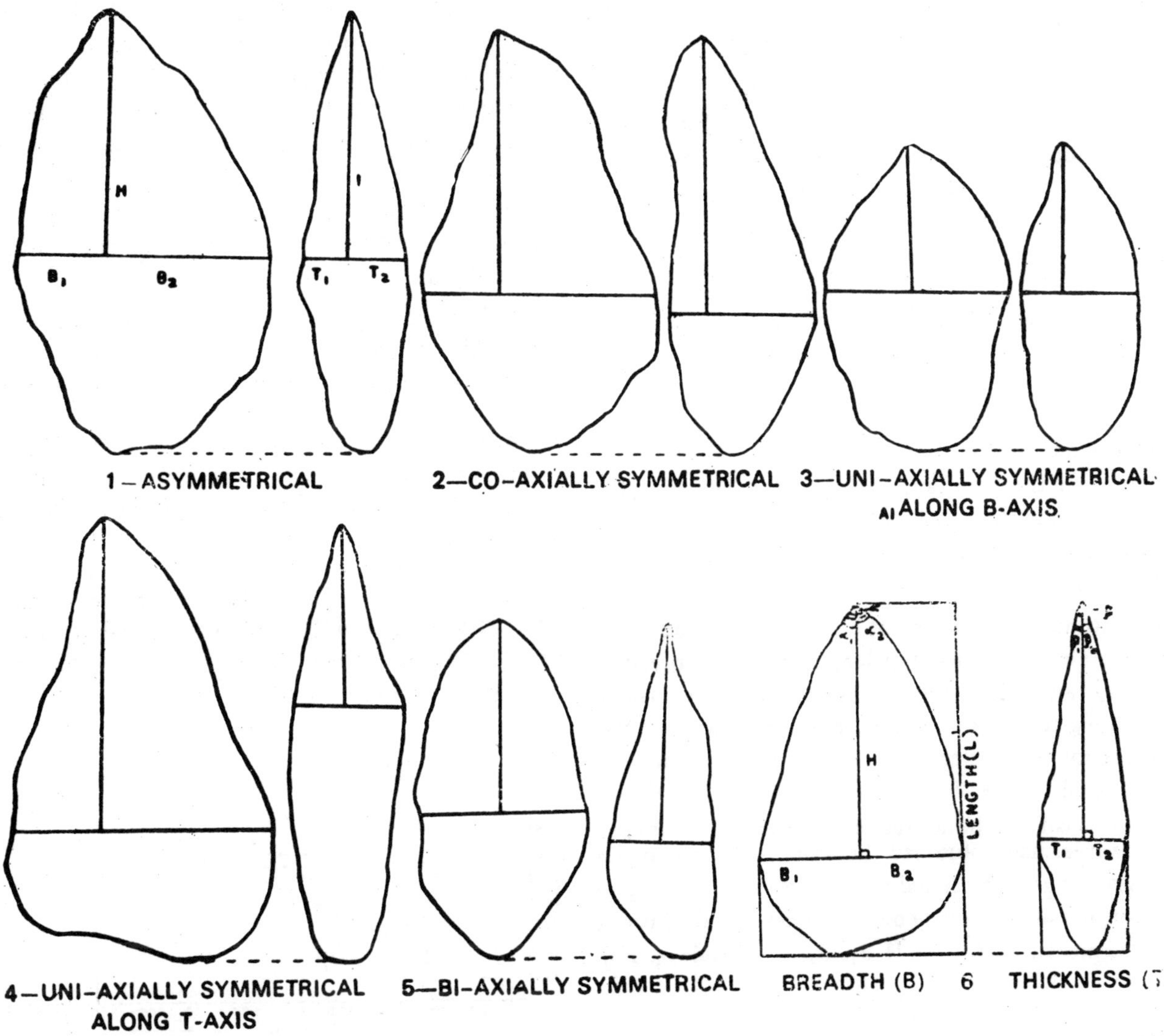

FIG. 1. *Proposed parameters and the classes*

size of the original raw material on which a tool is made (V_I). The volume calculated from its weight and density gives the actual volume (V_A). During the process of manufacture from the original block of raw material there is always a reduction in weight and volume. The ratio V_I/V_A is thus a measure of the wastage of raw material in the manufacturing work. In the present study of the handaxes from Chirki, this ratio gives a mean of 3·304 indicating nearly 2/3 wastage of raw material. In the experiment carried out by Newcomer

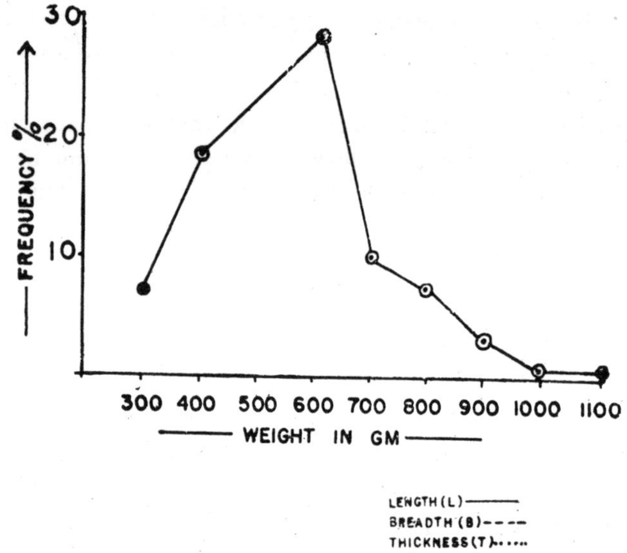

FIG, 2. *Frequency distribution of length (L) breadth (B) and thickness* (T)

a handaxe was prepared out of a flint block weighing 2948 gm and the resultant tool weighed 230 gm . In this case the manufactured tool is of an advanced Acheulian type and, therefore, involves a higher wastage of the raw material.

For estimating the shape of a tool, Bordes had used the measurements of maximum length, maximum breadth, thickness, and other measurements taken at specific points along the length. He had, however, discarded the consideration of angles at the convergence of the two sizes of tool. Roe[2] followed broadly similar procedure for classifying handaxes into their various shapes. We, however, have obtained the values of these angles as shown in figs. 1 and 2 and plotted in fig. 3. The angles were not measured directly but obtained by calculations from the measurements of H B_1, B_2. I, T_1 and T_2. For this purpose, the tool was oriented first along its maximum breadth and a perpendicular He was dropped from

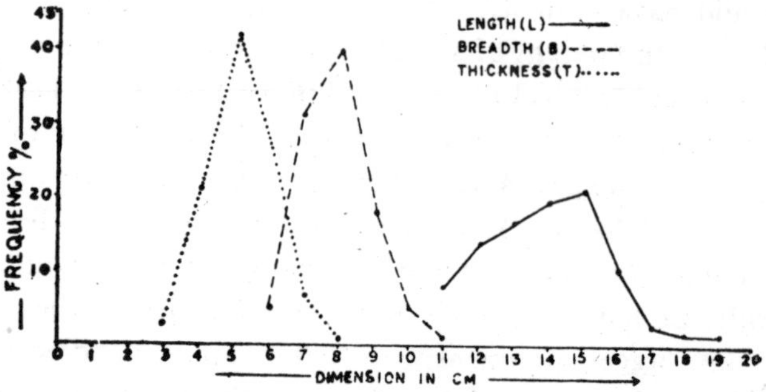

FIG. 3. *Frequency distribution of weight*

the apex of the tool on the line of breadth (B). The same procedure was followed on the line of maximum thickness (T) with a perpendicular (I) from the apex of the tool. The majority of tools in the present collection have triangular or sub-triangular forms. The error due to curvatures along the two sides converging on the apex would, therefore, be uniformly distributed. This method would not be useful if the tools have varied forms, particularly those having strongly curved convergingt sides, as in such cases angular measurement would no be meaningful.

While these angular measures do not throw much light on the shape of a tool they can give a useful indication of its degree of symmetry. Generally, the more asymmetrical forms are found in earlier or lower cultural stages, while the tools of advanced stages are more symmetrical. This symmetry may be worked out along two axes B and T by reference to two media H and L. The results give the following classes: biaxially symmetrical, uniaxially symmetrical; coaxially symmetrical and asymmetrical (fig. 1.). The relative occurrence at Chirki of asymmetrical types (62 %) and symmetrical types (38 %) perhaps indicates earlier Acheulian stage of the present collection (of Table 4d)

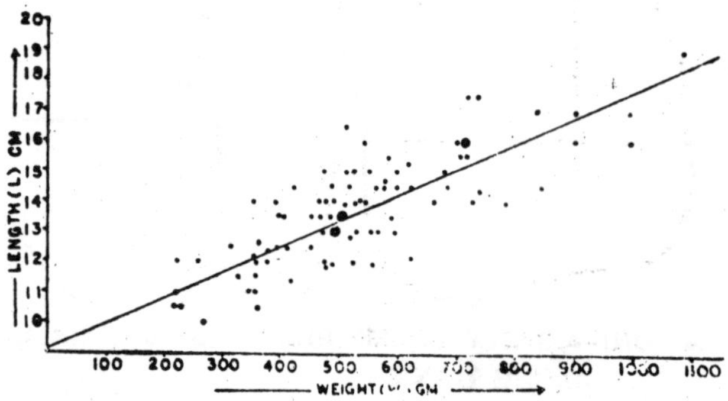

FIG. 4. *Regresasion of length* (L) *on weight* (W)

[1]Newcomer, *op. cit*
[2]Roe, *op. cit.*

TABLE 1
ANALYSIS OF VARIATION IN EACH PARAMETER AND RATIOS

	L	B	T	(B/T)	(T/B)	(B+T)	(V_1/V_A)	W
Mean	13·8	7·6	4·88	1·582	0·6398	12·66	3·304	539·23
Standard deviation	3·7	0·3	1·26	0·0382	—	0·203	0·148	171·43
Coefficient of variation	27·0	4·0	25·13	0·0199	—	1·603	4·489	31·77

TABLE 2
REGRESSION ANALYSIS

	Equation	Slope	% error	coefficient of correlation
Length on weight	$L = 0{\cdot}0086\ W + 9{\cdot}1246$	0·0086	0·8840	0·7910
Breadth on weight	$B = 0{\cdot}0044\ W + 5{\cdot}2886$	0·0044	0·9687	0·7315
Thickness on weight	$T = 0{\cdot}0030\ W + 3{\cdot}3573$	0·0030	1·5415	0·5767
(B/T) on weight	$(B/T) = (-0{\cdot}0001)\ W + 1{\cdot}6234$	0·0001	2·1511	0·0389
(B+T) on weight	$(B+T) = 0{\cdot}0074\ W + 8{\cdot}6459$	0·0074	—	—
(B+T) on length	$(B+T) = 0{\cdot}8604L + 0{\cdot}7959$	0·8604	—	—
V_A on V_1	$V_A = 0{\cdot}2639\ V_1 + 212727$	0·2639	1·4047	0·9097

For determining an index of refinement, Roe[1] used the ratio of thickness/breadth (T/B). He considered this as a more convenient ratio than thickness over length, because where implements are broken, length is the measurement most often affected by the damage. According to him a high value of T/B usually indicates refined tools while low values of T/B show refined forms. He has, however, further stated that the refinement could not be allowed to depend solely on the index T/B as sometimes it gives misleading high values. To avoid this confusion he devised a further index, T_1/L, where T_1 is the thickness at a point one-fifth distance on L from the tip.

The collection under study gives generally high values of T/B, thus suggesting unrefined forms, which is true in this case as the industry shows Early to Middle Acheulian characters. This ratio is also more or less constant (i.e. the standard deviation is small for the sample) as the entire collection is from the same cultural stage. If these tools had been hafted as lance points, the thickness should be much less, and the index T/B would give low values. The tools under consideration are fairly thick and do not seem to have been used this way.

In a subsequent article, Roe[2] presented various groupings among 38 British handaxe assemblages, some of which include cleavers. In this the groups that emerge are clusters of sites where industries are similar in terms of the morphological range and usual degree of refinement of their handaxes. In his statistical summary tables, Roe[3] has given mean and standard deviation figures for T/B for all his 38 samples. Most of the sites yielded low mean values lying between 0.408 and 0.595. Only four sites show values over 0.6. The handaxes from Chirki gave a mean value of T/B as 0.66.

If we assume that these tools from Chirki are hand tools, i.e. used in the hand, the holding capacity (or presence of a grip) is equally important. Assuming normal holding capacity of a hand of an adult to be about 15 cm, if the tool is to be used as a missile for throwing, it need be encircled by the hand only to about 1/3 of its periphery, but if it is to be held for use in the hand, the grip should cover 2/3 of the tool's periphery. To a certain extent there is some relation between L and (B+T) of a tool. The values of (B+T) are remarkably constant showing a very small coefficient of variation. The variation in T is more (25.13%) but in (B+T) it is far less (1.603%). The variation in (B+T) which represents the transverse section of a handaxe in a vertical plane to the L-axis, is also far less (0·01991%).

The variation in the values of weight is maximum (1·77%) which is as a result of variation in L, B, and T. The variation in L and T is substantial (26·98% and 25·13% respectively). But the variation in B is far less

[1] *Ibid.*
[2] *Ibid.*

[3] *Ibid.*, p. 28.

(3·974%). The scope to increase in T is far less, as indicated by means of standard deviation ($\pm$ 1·265). Therefore, the increase in weight is mainly achieved by increasing the length. This may be shown by regression analysis (slope=0·0086 and coefficient of correlation = 0·7910). Table[2]

According to the laws of Physics, the work done while digging with or throwing an implement (handaxe or any other tool) is proportional to the loss of kinetic energy (L.K.E.) during the impact or collision. The loss of K.E. is given by —

$$L.K.E = \frac{M_1M_2(U_1-U_2)^2 \ (1-e)^2}{M_1+M_2}$$

where, M_1 : mass of the tool

M_2 : mass of the object (i.e. at which it is thrown or on which it is used).

U_1 & U_2 : their respective velocities

e : coefficient of restitution

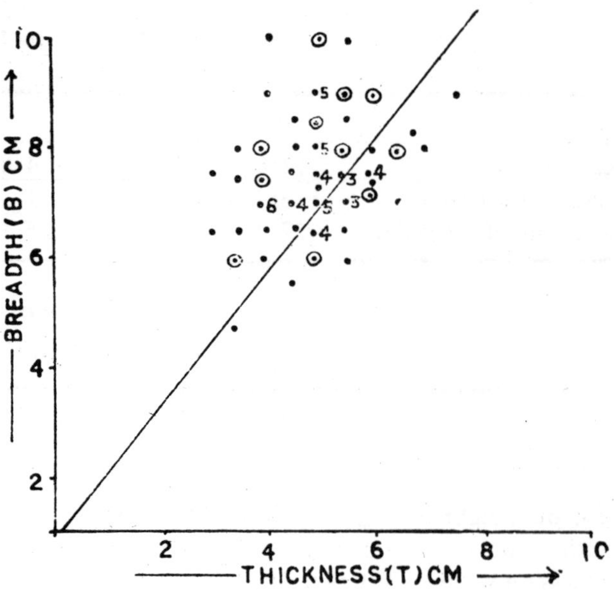

FIG. 7. *Regression of breadth* (B) *on thickness*

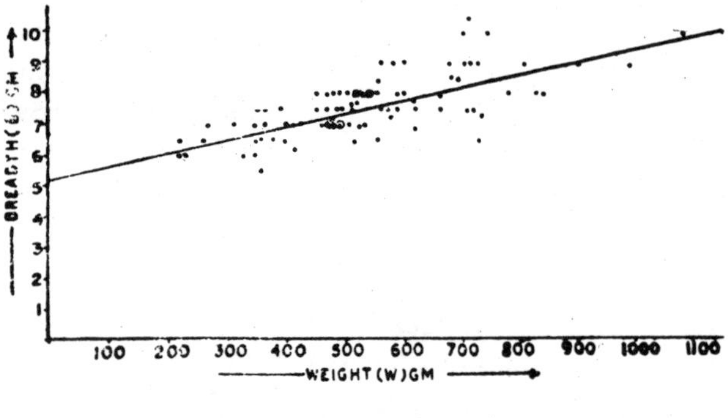

FIG. 5. *Regression of breadth* (B) *on weight* (W)

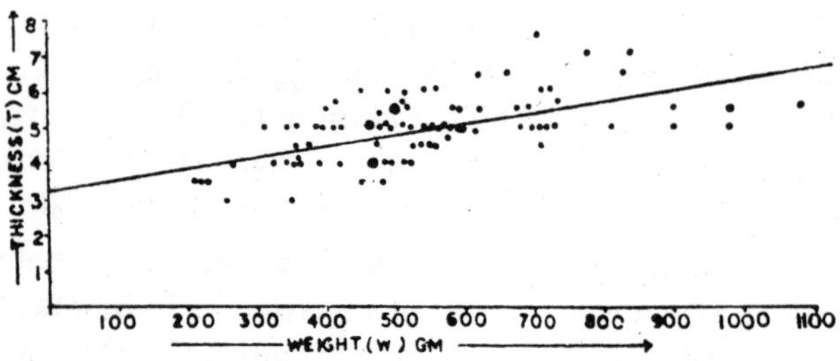

FIG. 6 *Regression of thickneas* (T) *on weight* (W)

The principle of 'Total Energy' suggests that the system must remain constant; hence, the kinetic energy which appears to be lost must get converted into other forms and must be used in doing certain work. In the case of collision between two bodies the loss of kinetic energy is used in redistribution of molecules of the colliding bodies, and part of the energy is used in producing heat and sound, etc. In our experimental work for testing the effectiveness of the tools, only the mass of the concerned tool and its velocity (i.e. the momentum of the tool) can be controlled. Since a heavy hammer with slow velocity works better than a light hammer with more velocity, the weight of a tool is of prime importance.

The Binfords[1] have tried to identify groups of tools that were used for various kinds of jobs by using statistical analysis of the implements found at palaeolithic sites. Their hypothesis is based on the data from Mousterian sites. The authors state that 'in technologically simple societies, we can distinguish two broad classes of artifacts, extraction and maintenance. Base camps are chosen primarily for living space protection from elements and central location with respect to resources. We would expect the archaeological assemblages of base camps to reflect maintenance activities, the preparation and consumption of food and manufacture of tools for use in other less permanent sites. Another settlement type would be a work camp, a site occupied

[1]S.R. Binford and L.R. Binford, 'Stone tools and man behaviour', *Scientific American*, vol. 220 (1969), pp. 70 48–hu·

TABLE 3

THE "T" TEST

Coefficient correlation	Degrees of freedom	"t"	Level of significance	Table value*of "t"
$r_{LW} = 0.7910$	86	11·9899	0·001	3.46
$r_{DW} = 0.7315$	86	9·9491	0·001	3.46
$r_{TW} = 0.5767$	86	6·5464	0·001	3.46
$r_{V_AV_2} = 0.9097$	86	20·3120	0·001	3.46

*From R.A. Fisher and F. Yates, *Statistical Tables*, Oliver and Boyd, London.

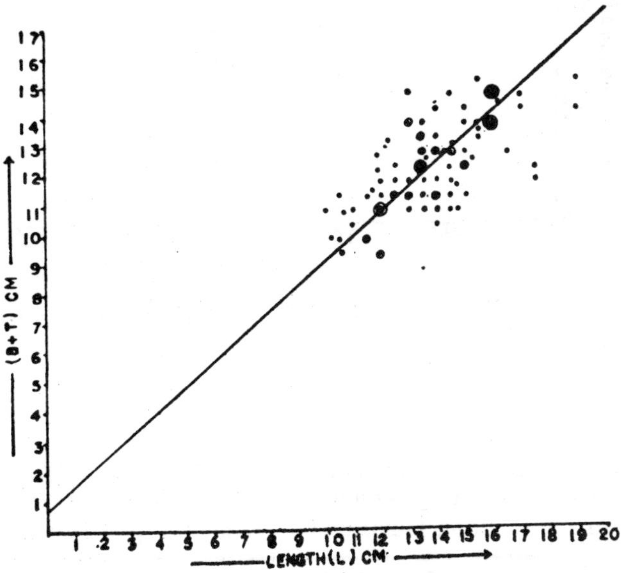

FIG. 8. *Regression of* B+T *on* L

while smaller social units were carrying out extractive tasks. Archaeologically, these would appear as kill sites collecting stations and quarries for extracting flint to be used in tool making.

It is difficult to distinguish between base camp and work camp at Chirki. Perhaps, both such activities were carried out at the same place or in close proximity to each other. It was definitely a factory site as well as a camp site of a more or less permanent nature. There was no possibility of intense climatic variation during the year compelling the inhabitants to change their camps seasonally. A variety of Lower Palaeolithic tools have been located at other sites on the nullah at Chirki. In these, handaxes and cleavers are the only standardised tools having definite form, while the choppers, scrapers, etc., do not possess well defined repetitive shapes. A variety of shapes and sizes is found in the handaxes and cleavers and each seems to have discharged a specific function. It is, however, difficult to attempt evaluation of their functions such as for killing, meat extracting, skinning, etc., from the metrical studies of the tools alone.

The site of Chirki is in western Maharashtra and the handaxes, as mentioned previously, are all made of the basalt rock (Deccan Trap). It is interesting to compare the metrical data for the tools from this site with that from the few other series for which such information is available. The handaxes from Rajasthan[1] are made of quartzite, those from Gujarat[2] (Saurashtra) are on quartzite and dolerite, while cleavers from Mayurbhanj are on quartzites. Some metrical details are given in table No. 5 for comparative purposes. The following deductions can tentatively be made from them.

1. The mean weights of handaxes and cleavers from Chirki are 539·23 gm. and 562·22 gm. respectively while the cleavers from Mayurbhanj have 521.66 gm. This shows that the raw material makes little difference as far as weight of tools denoting comparable cultural stages is concerned.

2. The L, B and T measurements of tools from Rajasthan and Chirki bringout the difference between these industries. The Chirki industry shows early to Middle Acheulian forms while the Rajasthan industry indicates Late or Advanced Acheulian characters. Since the weights of the tools from Rajasthan are not known further comparison is not possible at this stage.

3. The tools from Saurashtra also show advanced Acheulian characters.

[1]V.N. Misra, *Pre-and Proto-history of Berach Basin, South Rajasthan*, Ph. D. Thesis-(1967) (unpublished), Deccan College, Pune.

[2]Lele and Koti, *op. cit.*

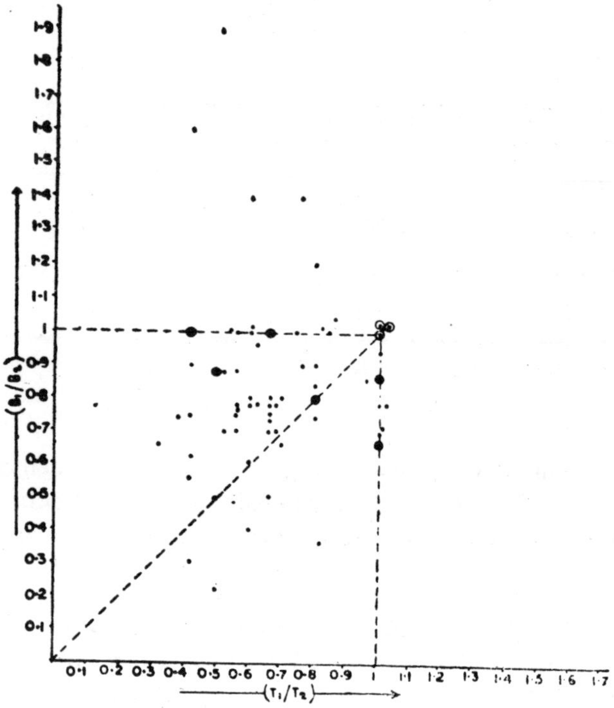

FIG. 9. *Frequency distribution in different classes.*

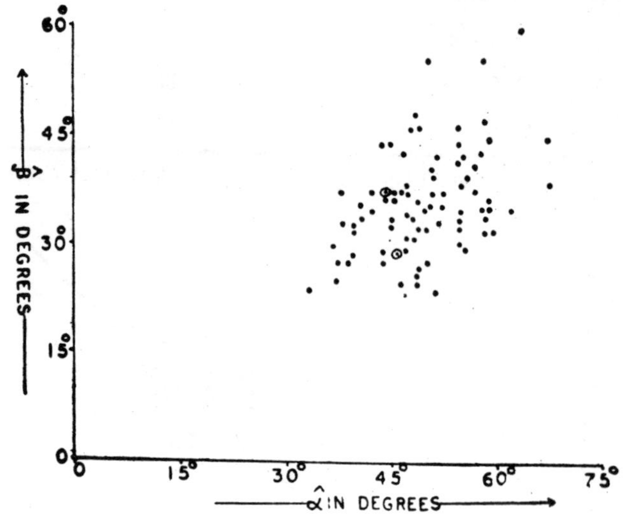

FIG. 10. *Relationship of L and B*

TABLE 4(a)

DETAILS OF SPECIMENS REPRESENTING THE CLASS

No.	Register no.	Class term	Index of symmetry along B-axis (u_1)	Index of symmetry along T-axis (u_2)	Coefficient of symmetry(u_1) = (u_1/u_2)
1.	CHIR-VII 23/783	Asymmetrical	0·5625	0·4517	1·2195
2.	CHIR-VII 31/1002	Co-axially sym.	0·50000	0·50000	1·0000
3.	CHIR-VII 53/197	Uni-axially sym. (along B-axis)	1·0000	0·6000	2·3333
4.	CHIR-VII 58/542	Uni-axially sym. (along-T-axis)	0·6007	1·0000	0·6667
5.	CHIR-VII 45/178	Bi-axially sym.	1·0000	1·0000	1·0000

TABLE 4(b)

PERCENTAGE OF HANDAXES IN DIFFERENT CLASSES

No.	Class	$U_1=(B_1/B_2)$	$U_2=(T_1/T_2)$	$\mu=(\mu_1/\mu_2)$	Percentages	
1.	Biaxially symmetrical	=1	=1	=1	03·409	
2.	Uniaxially symmetrical	1	=1 or	=1	31·100	37·918
3.	Co-axially symmetrical	=1	1	1	03·409	
4.	Asymmetrical	1	1	1	62·082	
				Total	—100·00	

TABLE 5

DATA ON HANDAXES AND CLEAVERS FROM DIFFERENT LOCALITIES

SITE	Tool type (and no.)	Raw Material	gms Weight (W)		cm Length (L)		cm Breadth (B)		cm Thickness (T)		(B/L)		(T/B)		(T/L)	
					M	S	M	S	M	S	M	S	M	S	M	S
Rajasthan	Handaxes	Quartzite														
Berach	(22)		—	—	11·63	2·15	8·05	1·74	3·91	1·09	0·68	0·081	0·49	0·093	0·34	0·070
Gambhiri	Handaxes (25)	Quartzite	—	—	13·38	2·91	8·05	1·74	4·58	1·31	0·68	0·081	0·49	0·093	0·38	0·080
Wagan	Handaxes (35)	Quartzite	—	—	10·60	1·95	7·10	1·42	3·80	0·98	0·67	0·120	0·54	0·120	0·36	0·060
Kadmali	Handaxes (8)	Quartzite	—	—	12·20	—	7·70	—	4·40	—	0·63	—	0·52	—	0·35	—
Saurashtra	Handaxes (3)	Quartzite-2	—	—	11·47	—	6·93	—	3·67	—	0·62	—	0·53	—	0·32	—
		Dolerite-1	—	—												
Mayurbhanj	Cleavers (60)	Quartzite	521·66	—	13·90	—	—	—	—	—	—	—	—	—	—	—
Chirki	Cleavers 100	Quartzite	562·22	—	—	—	—	—	—	—	—	—	—	—	—	—

M—Mean
S—Standard Deviation

It should be mentioned in passing that these industries, representing early to late Acheulian stages, do not show much variation in their composition of tool types.

Using the same data as worked out by Roe,[1] Graham[2] presented another scheme of classification of British handaxes. While commenting on the results thus obtained by Graham, Roe has shown a reasonably good agreement between these schemes. Roe's remarks in this context are very pertinent. He states that: But ultimately, if there is to be a real understanding of which handaxe industries lie closest to each other in the British sequence, such metrical and statistical studies as these cannot be regarded as a complete substitute for the filling of the appalling gaps in our knowledge of the relative chronology of the assemblages under discussion. To propose a pattern of morphological likes and unlikes is not necessarily to solve problems of chronological and cultural relationships. The need for more information about the Pleistocene geology of the British Palaeolithic sites is only too obvious, and there are many other problems requiring investigation.[3] This statement holds good for the palaeolithic studies in India as well.

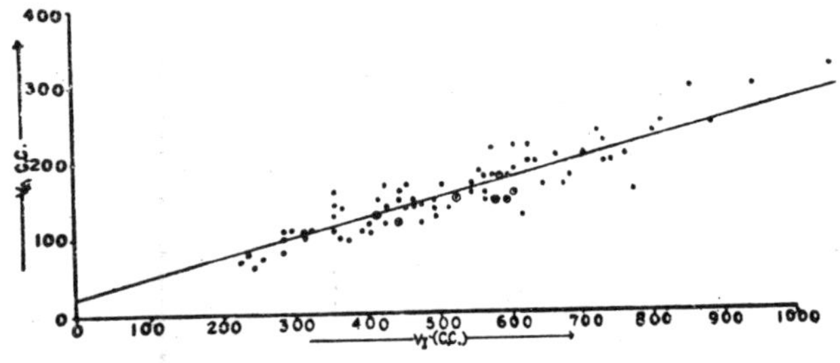

FIG. 11. *Regression of* (V_A) *on* (V_1)

ACKNOWLEDGEMENTS

We would like to express our grateful thanks to Dr H.D. Sankalia for permitting us to work on the Chirki collection stored at the Archaeology Department of the Deccan College, Pune and encouraging us to take up such problems. Our sincere thanks are due to Kumari Purohit who helped us in computer analysis and mathematical deductions and Shri S. Chakravarty who undertook the measurements of the tools along with the second author. We are extremely grateful to Dr D.A. Roe, University of Oxford, Oxford, U.K., for reading the manuscript of this paper and offering useful suggestions.

This work was carried out as one of the projects approved by the University Grants Commission under the programme of Special Assistance to the Archaeology Department of the Deccan College, Pune, and we express our thanks to the U.G.C. authorities.

[1]Roe, *op. cit.*

[2]J.M. Graham, 'Discrimination of British Lower and Middle Palaeolithic handaxe groups using canonical variates', with a note by Derek Roe, *World Archaeology*, vol. 3, no. 1 (1970), pp. 322-42.

[3]Roe in Graham, *ibid.*, p. 342.

The Acheulian Industry of Rock Shelter III F-23 at Bhimbetka, Central India: a Preliminary Study

V. N. Misra

Poona University, Pune

[*Received on 4 August 1975*]

INTRODUCTION

IT was over a century and a decade ago that the first Acheulian implement—a cleaver—was found by Robert Bruce Foote in a lateritic gravel pit at Pallavaram near Madras.[2] During the following three decades Acheulian finds were made from many sites in peninsular India, mainly by Foote himself but also by some other amateur archaeologists. In the last three and a half decades, systematic exploration of many regions in the country for Palaeolithic remains has been carried out by research workers from several institutions. majority of them from the Deccan College, Pune, working under the inspiration and guidance of Professor H.D. Sankalia. Acheulian industries have been found almost all over the country except the Indo-Gangetic plains and the western coast. As a result of these studies the geographical distribution of Acheulian industries is now fairly satisfactorily known.[3]

But that is almost all that we know of the Acheulian culture. We know virtually nothing of the way of life of Acheulian man. Even our knowledge of the real nature of the Acheulian industries and consequently of their technological evolution and relative chronology is negligible. The main reason for this state of affairs is that until very recently Palaeolithic research has been confined, with the exception of one early attempt at excavation,[4] to the exploration of secondary sites like riverine sediments, stream beds and surface occurrences of artefacts. The artefact collections have, in the circumstances, of necessity been selective and heavily weighted in the favour of finished and large tools. The artefactual material obtained from such contexts is naturally mixed both in time and space, and gives only fragmentary and distorted picture of Acheulian industries. In the last few years there is beginning to emerge a welcome shift of attention to the excavation of Palaeo-

[1]Professor H.D. Sankalia, who first conceived the idea of excavation at the site, has all along provided encouragement and valuable guidance. Dr V.S. Wakankar who discovered the site in 1958 readily welcomed the idea of joint excavation at the site. During the three seasons of digging at Bhimbetka I have been assisted, at various stages, by Shri P.K. Tewari, Shri P.K. Thomas, Shri S.C. Nanda, Shri S. Prasad, Shri Y.D Mathpal, Shri D.P. Sharma, Km. N. Boga, Shri O.K. Singh, Shri P.M.C. Forbes Irving, Shri C.G. Padval, Shri P.R. Kulkarni, Shri S.K. Kulkarni, Shri R.B. Sapre, Shri V.K. Nagpure, Shri S.R. Prabhu, Shri J.S. Jairaj and Shrimati S. Nayak. Shri M.D. Khare, Superintending Archaeologist, Archaeological Survey of India was helpful in many ways. In the analysis of the cultural material I have received valuable help from Dr D.K. Bhattacharya, Shri S.C. Nanda and Shri P.K. Thomas. Dr S.N. Rajaguru who is studying the palaeo-environment of Bhimbetka helped me in the sedimentological and colour identification of stratigraphy at the site. Drawings have been prepared by Shri C.G. Padval and photoprints by Shri V.K. Nagpure. Financial support for the excavations has been received from Poona University, Deccan College, University Grants Commission and the Archaeological Survey of India. To all these persons and institutions I express my warm thanks.

[2]Robert Bruce Foote, *The Foote Collection of Indian Prehistoric and Protohistoric Antiquities: Notes on their Ages and Distribution* (Madras, 1916), p.v.

[3]For a very comprehensive treatment and extensive bibliography, see H.D. Sankalia, *Prehistory and Protohistory of India and Pakistan* (Poona, 1974).

[4]N.K. Bose and D. Sen, *Excavations in Mayurbhanj* (Calcutta, 1948).

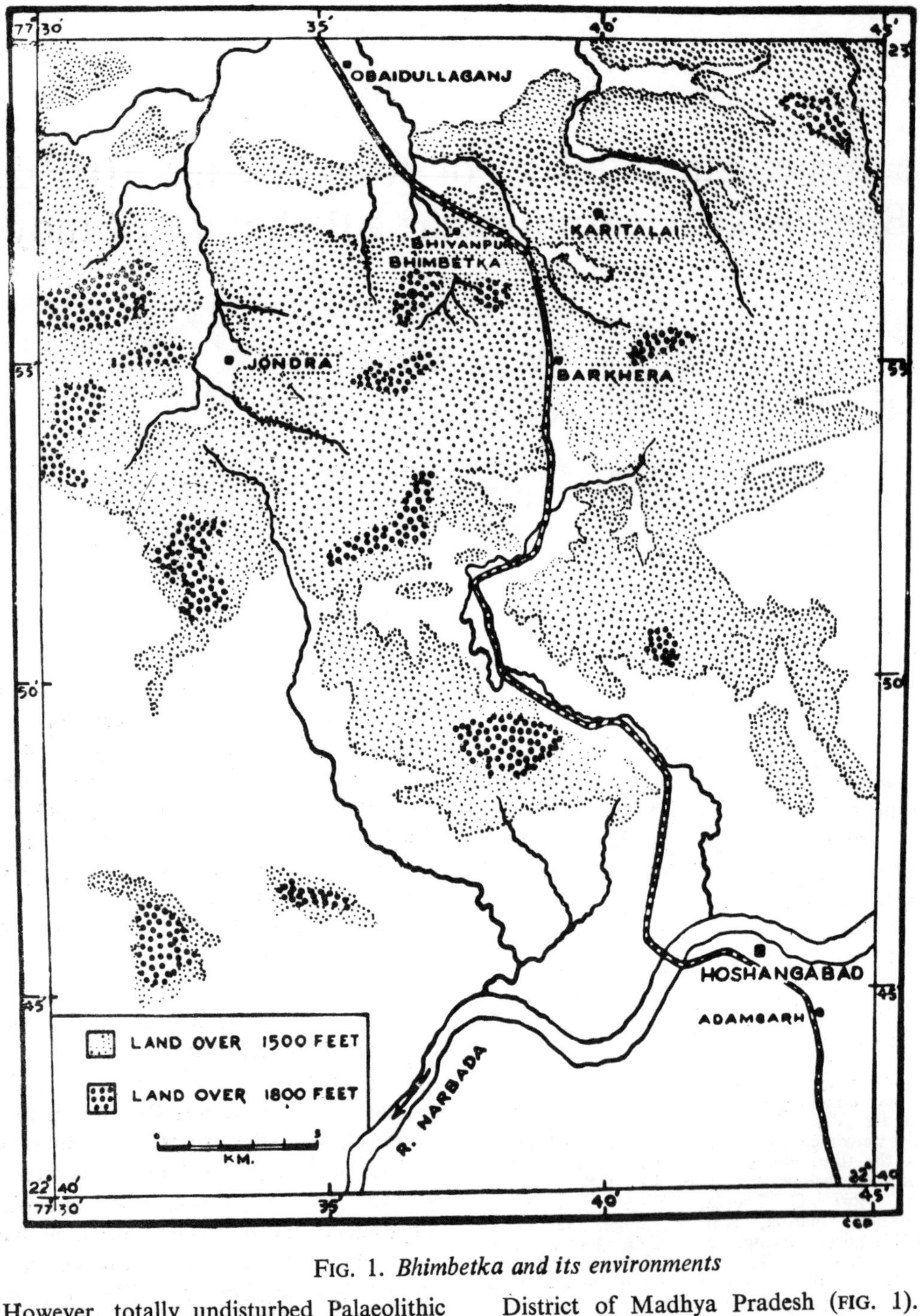

FIG. 1. *Bhimbetka and its environments*

lithic sites. However, totally undisturbed Palaeolithic sites are as yet very scarce. In this context, the discovery and excavation of thick, undisturbed Acheulian occupation-deposits in the caves and rock shelters at Bhimbetka promises to add substantially to our knowledge of the Acheulian culture.

THE SITE AND ITS ECOLOGICAL SETTING

The site of Bhimbetka (77° 37′ E ; 22° 50′ N) is located on the northern margin of the Vindhya Hills in Raisen District of Madhya Pradesh (FIG. 1). The Vindhyas run parallel to the Narmada river on its northern side. Though in the main they consist of Deccan Lavas, between Bhopal and Itarsi they are essentially composed of sandstones and quartzites. The hills form a great scarp overlooking the Narmada valley and rarely exceeding a height of 610 m (2000 ft.).[1] Near Bhimbetka, the hills recede to the sides to form

[1]O.H.K. Spate and A.T.A. Learmonth, *India and Pakistan : Land, People and Economy* (London, 1967), pp. 22-23.

a broad, extensive valley through which runs the Bombay-Delhi line of the Central Railway. The hills at this point also form a watershed. The drainage to the north flows into the Betwa river, to ultimately join the Ganga valley, while drainage to the south goes into the Narmada river. There is no perennial stream close to Bhimbetka, the nearest such stream being Narmada, some 25 km to the south and the Betwa, about 20 km to the north.

Bhimbetka (corrupted form of Hindi name Bhimbaithka, meaning the sitting place of Bhima, one of the heroes of the epic *Mahābhārata*) is the name applied to a hill about one kilometre long (east-west), half a kilometre broad (north-south) and over a 100 m high from the plain level (and 650 m above mean sea level). The hill lies about two km south of the tiny tribal hamlet of Bhianpur (original form Bhīmapura, meaning the village of Bhīma) which lies close to the southern side of the railway line and the Itarsi-Bhopal highway running parallel to it. It can be approached on foot or by jeep from the village. The village is situated 45 km south of Bhopal and 30 km north of Hoshangabad and is almost midway between the towns of Obaidullaganj in the north and Barkhera in the south (FIG. 1). A very obtrusive feature of the hill is the presence on its top of a chain of discontinuous monolithic rocks which give from a distance the appearance of a fort. Many of these rocks have been weathered to form caves and rock shelters of various sizes. Some of the caves and the rocks in which they are formed are of enormous size, the largest cave (III F-24 or Auditorium Cave) being 40 m long, 4 to 12 m broad and 6 to 15 m high. Possibly because of this factor the caves have become associated, in folk tradition, with Bhīma, one of the Pāṇdava heroes, celebrated for his prodigious strength. Apart from Bhimbetka and Bhianpur other features in the local geography, recalling association with the epic story, are the ruins of an old settlement at Pandapura (meaning Pāṇḍavapura or the village of the Pāṇḍavas) and a spring known as Banganga (the spring created by an arrow).

The top and northern and western slopes of the Bhimbetka hill contain over two hundred caves and shelters. Another hill to the west of Bhimbetka, known as Lakha Juar, and a third to the east known as Bhaunrewali are almost equally rich in caves and shelters. Altogether in a stretch of over 10 km between the villages of Kari Talai in the east and Jondra in the west, the hills contain over 750 caves and shelters:[1] the shelters have been divided into seven groups, designated by Roman numerals, from east to west. Each of these groups has been further divided into sub-groups which have been designated by letters of the Roman alphabet. Finally, individual shelters within each subgroup have been differentiated by Arabic numerals. These three-tiered numbers (example, III F-23) have been put in black India ink on the inner walls of the shelters.

Over 500 of the shelters contain paintings on their walls and ceilings, the number of paintings in a single shelter varying from one or two to well over a hundred. On the basis of superimposition, subject matter, style and correlation with finds from excavations the paintings are seen to range from Mesolithic to Medieval times. Bhimbetka and its neighbouring hills thus have the largest known concentration of prehistoric paintings in India, and perhaps in the world. A smaller but indeterminate number of shelters also contain on their floors occupation deposits of variable thickness covering the period from Acheulian to late Mesolithic times.

Bhimbetka region receives an annual rainfall of over 120 cm which is largely concentrated in the three monsoon months of July-September. The hills are thickly covered by deciduous forest vegetation. Though increasing population and consequent growing demand for timber and fuel are taking a heavy toll of vegetation, the forest cover on hills, away from human settlements, is still fairly well preserved. At least thirty species of trees and plants in the forest have edible flowers, fruits and seeds and several plants have edible roots and tubers. Among the former, the more important are: Mahua (*Bassia latifolia*), Achar (*Buchanania latifolia*) Tendu (*Diosphyros tomentosa*), Bel (*Aegle marmelos*), Bhandara (*Erytherina indica*), Jamun(*Eugenia jambolana*), Am (*Mangifera indica*), Gular (*Ficus glomerata*), Aonla (*Phyllanthus emblica*), Ber (*Zizyphus jujuba*), Imli (*Tamarindus indica*), Ghathor (*Zizyphus xylopera*), Papda (*Gardenia latifolia*), Khajur (*Phoenix sylvestris*), Sitaphal (*Anona squamosa*), Kakhera or Kankher and Menar. Among tubers the more common are Semal Kand, Safed Musli, Potia Kand, Karhari Kand and Khalula. Even today the local population for many kilometres around Bhimbetka extensively exploits the forest foods, especially Mahua and Achar. From March to May every year almost the entire population of the region descends on the forest to collect Mahua and Achar. During lean periods many tribal families depend almost exclusively on forest foods to ward off starvation.

Wildlife in the forests used to be plentiful within living memory, but clearing of forests and indiscriminate hunting have largely exterminated it. However, even today a number of species are present in small numbers and during our four seasons of camping in the forest we were able to sight several of them. They include

[1]The classification and numbering of the shelters has bee, done by Dr. V.S. Wakankar with the help of Dr. S.K. Arya Shri Narayan Vyas, Km. Daljeet Kaur Gill, Shri J.C. Joshi and Shri N. Bhati. Shri Y.D. Mathpal has numbered many shelters which were missed in the earlier countings.

Sambar (*Cervus unicolor* Kerr), Chital (*Axis axis* Erxleben), blackbuck (*Antilope cervicapra* Linn.), Nilgai (*Boselaphus ragocamelus* Pallas), wild boar (*Sus scrofa cristatus* Wagner), hyena (*Hyaena hyaena* Linn.), leopard (*Panthera pardus* Linn.), wolf (*Canis lupus* Linn.), sloth bear (*Melursus ursinus* Shaw), porcupine (*Hystrix indica* Kerr), hare (*Lepus nigricolis* F. Cuvier), fox (*Vulpes bengalensis* Shaw), jackal (*Canis aureus* Linn.), and common langur (*Presbytis entellus* Dufresne). However, hunting as a source of food is now practically non-existent. Fish are caught in the streams and ponds by professional castes and sold to other communities. There are several natural perennial springs close to Bhimbetka and these constitute the only source of water for local human and animal populations. Ecologically thus Bhimbetka region is ideally suited for supporting hunting-gathering populations. And judging from the thick occupation deposits in numerous caves and shelters spanning the period from Acheulian to late Mesolithic it would appear that this favourable ecological situation has existed all through prehistoric times.

EXCAVATION AND STRATIGRAPHY

Excavations at Bhimbetka were begun in 1972 by V.S. Wakankar. He dug a trench each in III F-24 and II B-33 and found Acheulian materials in the former and Mesolithic materials in the latter. In subsequent years he found Acheulian materials in two other shelters, namely, III A-29 and III A-30. We started digging in III F-23 (FIG. 2) in 1973. During the three seasons (Jan.-April, 1973; Feb.-April, 1974; Feb.-May, 1975) digging has been done over a period of 235 days in an area of 52 sq. m inside the shelter.

Shelter III F-23 is one of the largest shelters on the Bhimbetka hill and among the excavated shelters it has yielded the maximum thickness of occupation deposit. The shelter opens to the south on a level plateau which overlooks an extensive panoramic green valley. It has a broad and high open frontage and another small opening on the left corner of the back side. The latter has to some extent been enlarged

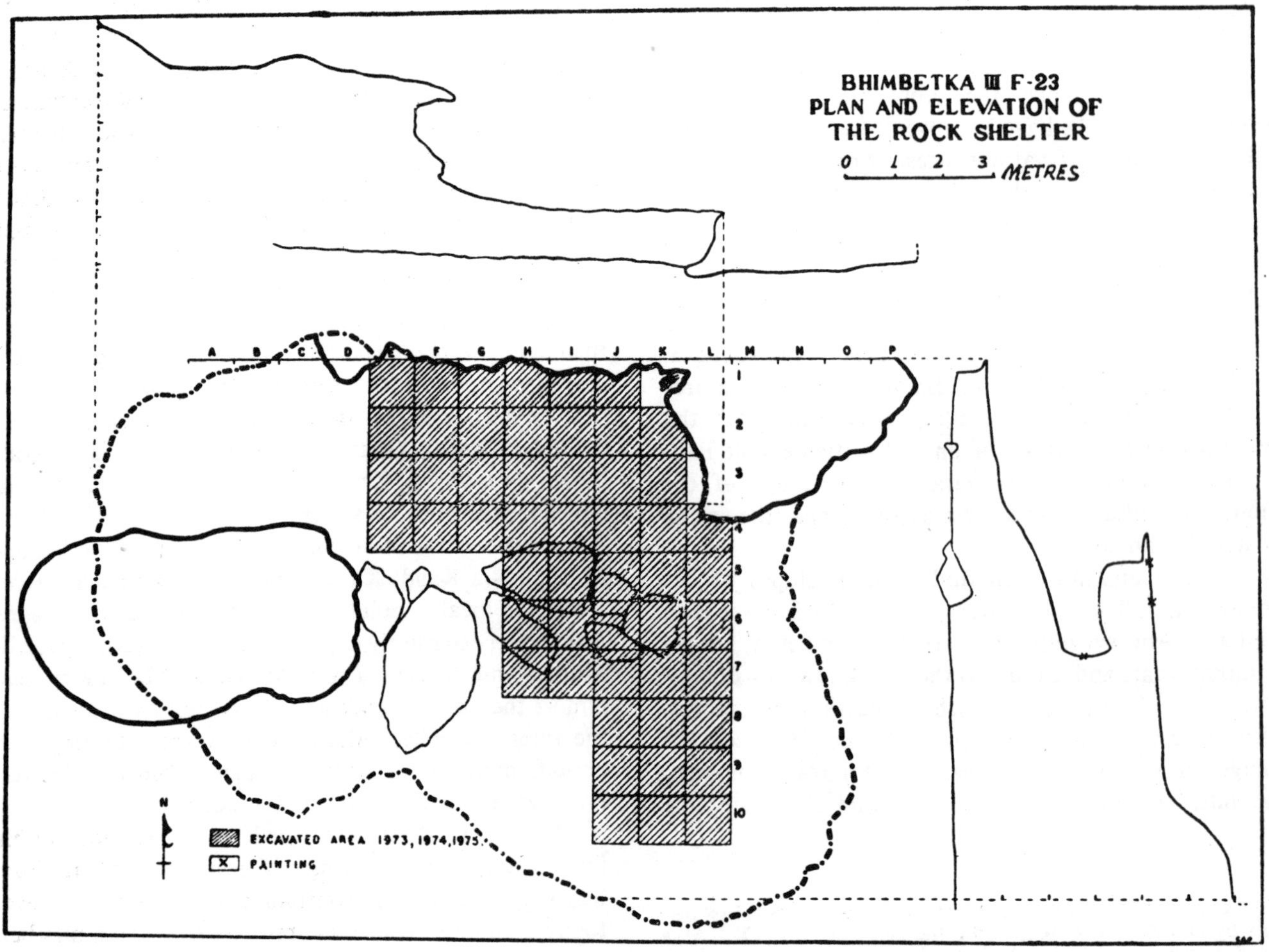

FIG. 2

by rockfall in post-Mesolithic times. An area of about 32 sq. m is enclosed by side walls and can be called cave proper while the massive rocky overhang extends forward and to the left over an additional area of nearly 80 sq. m. (FIG. 2). By late Mesolithic times the shelter had been filled to a height of less than 1 m from the ceiling and would appear to have been abandoned for occupation only when movement inside it became all but impossible. Its surface is remarkably even and has a gentle slope towards the outside. Before starting the dig the entire shelter was put under a 1 sq. m grid with permanent markings on the walls and ceiling. Digging was done in one sq. m at a time and in depths of 5 or 10 cm. All earth was sieved—in the case of fine and soft débris by 1 mm mesh sieves and in the case of coarse and compact débris by 2 mm mesh sieves. Every piece that showed human workmanship—whatever its size—was carefully sorted out of sieved débris, washed and recorded immediately on the spot.

The maximum deposit encountered so far is 3·90 m. This was found only in squares J2–J5. In different squares of trenches G, H and I bedrock was encountered at much less depth—between 1·40 m and 2·85 m (Table 1). The original floor of the shelter was thus very uneven. The high level of the bed rock in squares G3, H3–4 and I3–4 left only narrow channels —a little over 1 m wide—for early Acheulian occupation on the eastern and northern sides of the shelter. More level and broader areas were, however, available for occupation on the western and southern sides of the shelter.

In all, eight layers were recognized in the deposit. Their physical and cultural characteristics are briefly as follows (FIGS. 3 and 4):

Layer 1: 5–10 cm thick; dull yellowish brown (10 YR 5/3); soft silty sand, poor in clay content; occasional angular stones; geometric microlithic industry made on chalcedonic silica and a small quantity of quartzite flakes, blades and microblades associated with hammers, grinders and querns of basalt, occasional stone beads, small quantities of highly fragmentary sherds of plain red and grey ceramics and rare bone pieces.

Layer 2: 10–25 cm thick; dull yellowish brown; slightly darker in colour than (1) (10 YR 4/3); finer in composition than (1); sandy silt and clayey silt; cultural material as in (1) but without pottery and beads; stone industry richer than in (1).

Layer 3: 10–20 cm thick; brown (7·5 YR 4/3); more sandy than (2) but not as sandy as (1); sandy silt; a characteristic feature of this layer is the presence of thin weathered reddish stone chips almost all over the excavated area. However, in the inner part of the cave the colour of the earth becomes lighter and the quantity of stone chips declines. There is a decline in the quantity of microlithic industry.

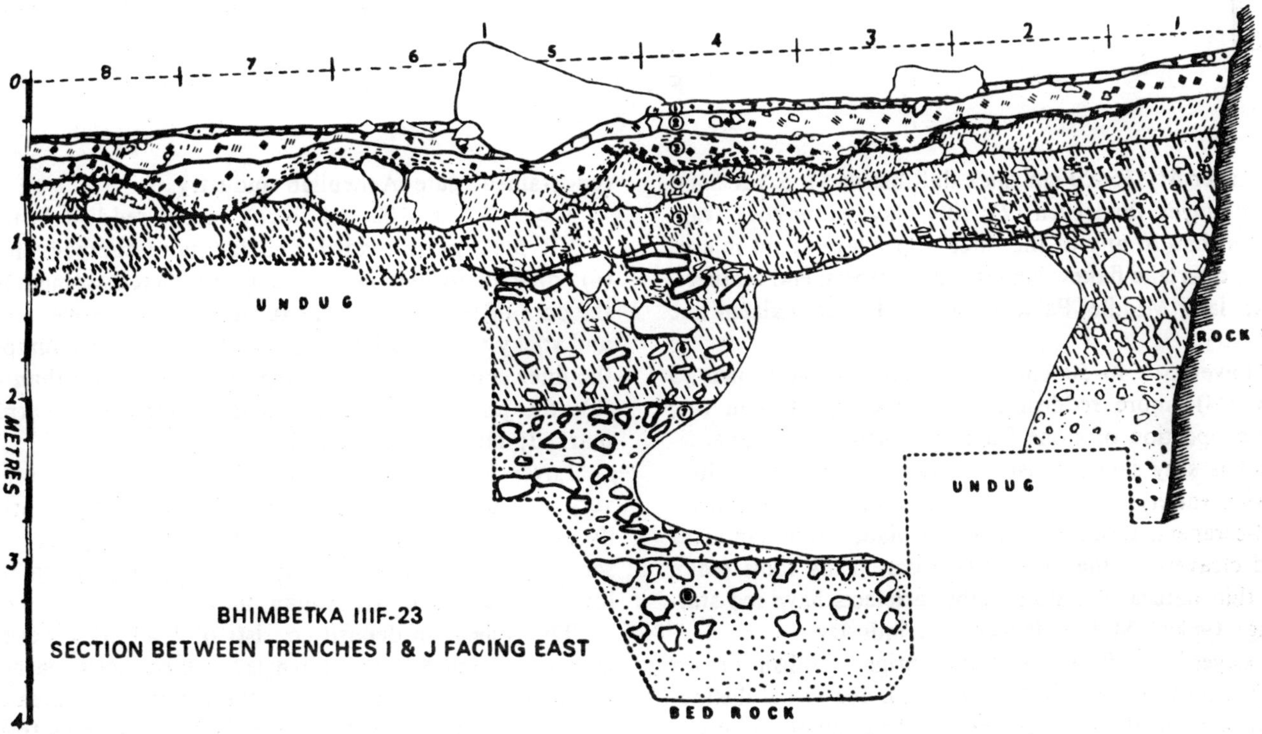

FIG. 3

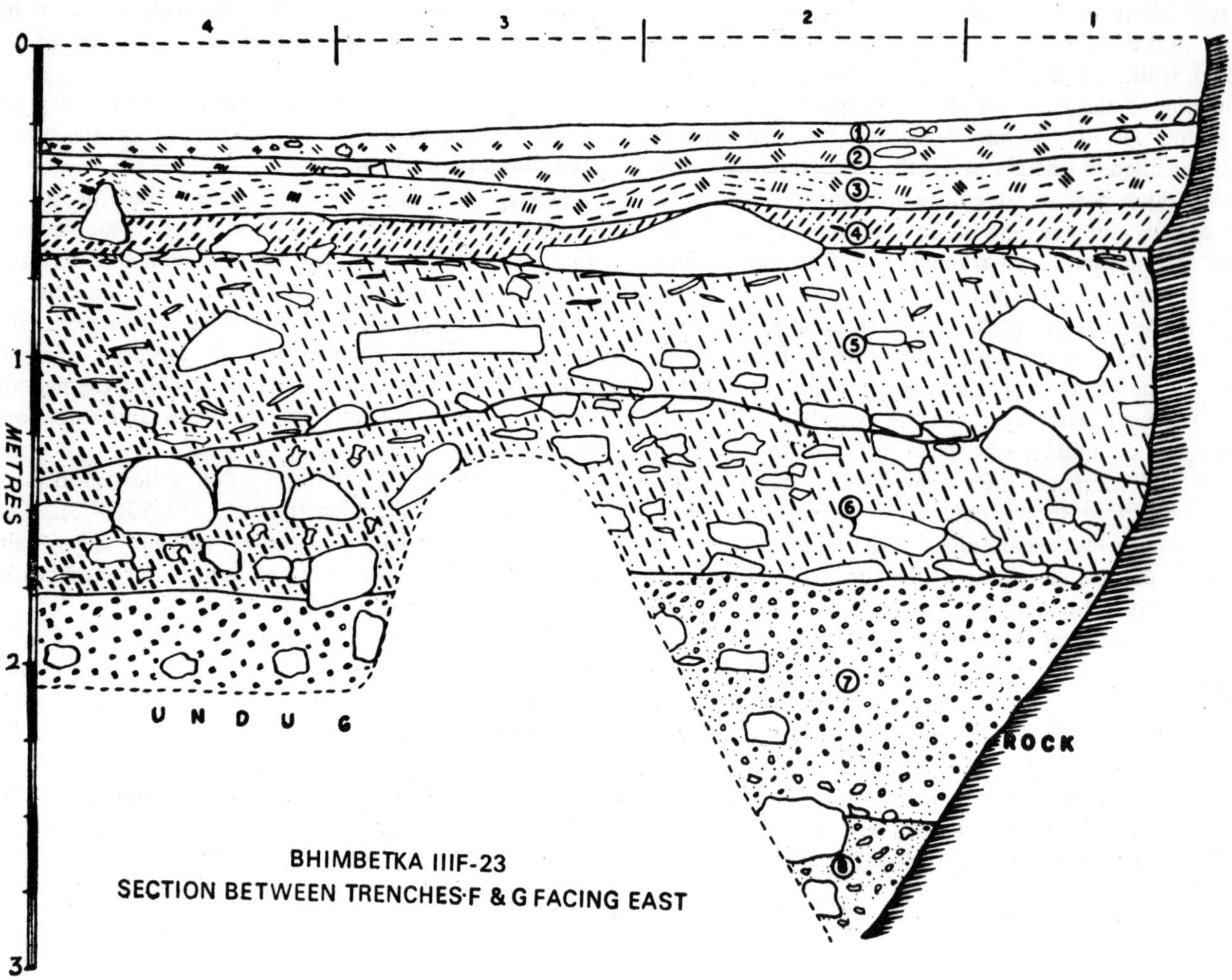

FIG. 4

Layer 4: 15–20 cm thick dull brown (7·5 YR 5/4); more clayey than even (2); silty clay; more rock fragments than in any of the three upper layers; no microliths; quartzite flakes, blades, side scrapers, end scrapers, etc.; late Middle Palaeolithic or Upper Palaeolithic industry.

Layer 5: 40–50 cm thick; dull reddish brown (5 YR 5/4); more reddish and more compact than (4); the proportion of stone fragments increases; finer sediment is silty sand; moist and sticky when freshly dug; a wide variety of side scrapers, less common but typical end-scrapers, Levallois flakes and blades, rare handaxes and cleavers in the lower 10–15 cm; many tools made on thin natural flat stone slabs; artefacts have red staining; typical Middle Palaeolithic industry.

Layer 6: 80–90 cm thick; bright reddish brown (5 YR 5/6); essentially similar to (5), and visual distinction between the two not very marked; siltier and more compact than (5); size of stone blocks larger; artefacts red stained; late Acheulian industry.

Layer 7: 90–100 cm thick; bright reddish brown (5 YR 5/8); more reddish and far more compact than (6); difficult to dig; more deeply weathered, sometimes the core of the stone blocks turning to grey; very moist and sticky when freshly dug; comes out in large lumps; the finer component of the deposit is more silty than in (6); the junction between this layer and (6) is sharply marked; late Acheulian industry.

Layer 8: 80–90 cm thick; orange (5 YR 6/6); very little of fine transported sediment; consists essentially of heavily weathered chips and blocks of argillaceous sandstone; mottled colour; no cultural material in the lower 30 cm, late Acheulian industry.

The Acheulian deposit consists of 2·40 m, covering layers 6, 7 and 8. Acheulian levels have been reached so far only in the inner part of the shelter in an area of 26 sq. m. However, only the artefactual materials from 1973 and 1974 digs covering an area of 18 sq. m in trenches G, H, I, J and K has been analyzed, and the present report is based on this analysis only.

There was no evidence of the use of fire, and no organic remains have survived, probably because of the highly acidic nature of the deposit. However, there are other positive indications that the shelter was used not only for manufacturing tools but also for habitation. During the 1975 season in trenches E and F covering an area of 8 sq. m a series of five stone-paved floors, showing intentional structural activity, were encountered at different depths. A number of cleavers and handaxes show tell-tale signs of use in the form of edge damage, and many others survive only as fragments. The latter must have been used in and near the shelter for broken fragments seem to have been discarded within the shelter. The main evidence of Acheulian occupation consists of stone industry alone.

THE ACHEULIAN INDUSTRY

In most squares of trenches G, H, I and K bedrock was encountered at fairly high but varying levels. Deep digging was possible only in squares J1–5 and to a less extent in squares G2, H2 and I2 along the back wall of the cave. It is not, therefore, easy to see a clear trend in the incidence of artefacts according to depth (TABLE 1). However, from the limited data available it can be said that below 2·10 m depth the incidence of artefacts suffers a sharp decline and this trend persists till the end. In squares G2, H2 and I2 several digs between 1·95 m and 2·45 m gave no artefacts at all (TABLE 1). Therefore in this part of the cave occupation in the earlier stages was less intense. The reason for this appears to be the non-availability of a sufficiently large living area, for in the trenches E and F where there was no obstruction there is no decline in the incidence of tools in corresponding levels. No noticeable typological change is seen in the material from the three layers. Therefore all the material is treated as a homogeneous assemblage rather than separately for each layer. The methodology followed for the classification and analysis of non-biface tools is that elaborated by Professor Francois Bordes for Lower and Middle Palaeolithic tools, and this appears to serve well for the Bhimbetka material. The present analysis is partial only as some of the technological indices remain to be worked out, and metrical analysis of tools, especially of the bifaces, remains to be completed.

The artefact assemblage all through the deposit consists of shaped tools as well as cores, flakes and chips, showing that the tools were manufactured inside the shelter. The raw material used was, with the exception of rare pieces of chalcedony and chert, throughout orthoquartzite—partially metamorphosed sandstone. A very clear choice was, however, made in the type of quartzite used for handaxes and cleavers, on the one hand, and for the rest of the artefacts on the other. The former, with a few exceptions, are all made of a purple or dark grey quartzite which is richer in iron content, is more intensely metamorphosed and is consequently tougher and more resistant to weathering than the light-coloured quartzite. These tools have suffered little weathering even in levels where other tools have been heavily weathered. The rest of the tools are made of a yellowish quartzite which has undergone only moderate metamorphism. These tools have suffered heavy weathering in the lowermost levels and tend to crumble into powder. To a certain extent they have been affected in upper layers as well. Except in layer 8 all tools, irrespective of the type of quartzite used, have a shining mint-fresh look.

The yellowish quartzite used for the majority of the tools was available in abundance right in and around the shelter in the form of fallen blocks and thin weathered slabs. The purple-coloured quartzite is less plentiful though veins of it occur in the rocks on the hill. It was apparently quarried from a spot or spots some distance away from the shelter, and the tools were manufactured at or near the source of raw material. This inference is based on the observation that the ratio of cores and flakes to finished tools in purple quartzite is much lower than in the case of artefacts of yellowish quartzite. The tools in the lighter material were for the most part manufactured within the shelter as there is plenty of manufacturing débris in this material in the deposit.

The detailed typological analysis of the industry is presented in Tables 2–6. The main typological and technological observations are summarized below.

1. The industry consists of 4705 artefacts. Of this 31·90 per cent (1501 pieces) are tools and 68·10 per cent (3204 pieces) are waste products. The horizontal and vertical distribution of tools in relation to waste materials is fairly uniform, and in this part of the shelter at least no area or areas appear to be specifically marked off for tool manufacture.
2. The very high proportion of flakes (29·29%) 1378 pieces), chips[1] (26·78%; 1260 pieces), cores (3·29%; 155 pieces) and débris (3·89%; 183 pieces) clearly shows that most of the tool making activity took place inside the shelter.

[1]All flakes that appear to be too small, thin and irregular for any possible use have been classified as chips. They generally do not exceed 3 cm in length.

3. Among flakes and blades[1] (1378 pieces) 14·20 per cent (228 pieces) are blades, 22·48 per cent (361 pieces) side-struck flakes, 43·71 per cent (702 pieces) end-struck flakes, and 19·61 per cent (315 pieces) indeterminate flakes.

[1]This figure does not include Levallois flakes and blades.

4. Among cores the majority (41·29%; 64 pieces) are of amorphous shape. The next common types are bifacial (29·03%; 45 pieces) and discoidal (16·77%; 26 pieces) forms. Levallois cores account for only 7·10 per cent (11 pieces) of the collection. The remaining 5·81 per cent (9 pieces) are of diverse shapes.

TABLE 1

SQUARE AND DEPTH-WISE DISTRIBUTION OF THE ARTEFACTS OF ACHEULIAN INDUSTRY IN ROCK-SHELTER III F-23 AT BHIMBETKA

Depth in cms B.D.	G_1	G_2	G_3	G_4	H_1	H_2	H_3	H_4	I_1	I_2	I_3	I_4	J_1	J_2	J_3	J_4	J_5	K_2	Total	%
121–125	5	28	30	11	6	20	12	9	7	19	21	11	21	30	34	37	13	20	334	7·10
126–130	10	41	11	11	5	18	3	14	4	29		15	27	17	56	57	35	33	386	8·20
131–135	20	112	22	13	3	18	8	26	8	33	2	7	32	33	28	34	37	20	456	8·90
136–140	6	11	15	44	3	35	14	7	4	71		8	16	9	23	21		15	302	7·20
141–145	20	18		14	7	46	9	7	6	24		0	12	25	35	6	11	17	257	5·46
146–150	10	8		6	8	25		2	5	10		25	25	30	27	27	10	26	244	5·19
151–155	15	10		3	5	17		2	2	49			9	27	25	31	35	16	246	5·23
156–160	11	36		8	12	1		9	6	18			1	24	52	39	17	23	257	5·46
161–165	19			12	0	12		3	3	4			29	21	12	12	17	13	229	4·87
166–170	7	72		21	5	23		2	0	13			7	11	19	14	9	9	140	2·98
171–180	47	60		41	19	61			3	48			21	13	19	35	6	16	389	8·27
181–190	16	28		37	19	14				15			29	13	27	36	38		272	5·78
191–195	8	5		8	4	7				5			15	12	1	77	49		191	4·06
196–200	3	0		4	4	0				0			32	25	11	41	28		148	3·15
201–210		0	13			0				70			25	10	30	43	19		210	4·46
211–220		0		13		12				14			8	6	5	30	8		96	2·04
221–230		3				11				6			8	4	9	8	21		70	1·49
231–235		0				0				3			3	3	1	13	9		32	0·68
236–240		0				9				0			1	16	8	13	8		55	1·17
241–245		0				0				1			0		0	2	8		11	0·23
246–250		29				13				6			0		3	4	4		30	0·74
251–255						13				12			3		0	1	7		65	1·27
256–260		8				2				20			14		0	2	13		59	1·25
261–265		5				4				6			10		1	5	7		38	0·81
266–270		5				8				3			3		1	5	10		32	0·68
271–275		3				2				3			3		0	0	7		18	0·38
276–285		3								4			2		1	4	2		16	0·34
286–295													0		0	9	4		13	0·28
296–305															5	7	19		31	0·66
306–315															1	4	8		13	0·28
316–325															0	4	0		4	0·08
326–335															1	14	2		17	0·36
336–345															1	8			9	0·19
346–355															1	13			14	0·30
356–365															4	17			21	0·45
Total	197	485	78	259	100	371	46	81	48	483	23	66	356	329	441	673	461	208	4705	

TABLE 2

DEPTH-WISE DISTRIBUTION OF MAIN CLASSES OF ARTEFACTS OF ACHEULIAN INDUSTRY IN ROCK-SHELTER III F-23 AT BHIMBETKA

Depth in cms	Flake tools	Handaxes	Handaxe fragments	Cleavers	Cleaver fragments	Flakes	Cores	Debris	Total
121–125	94	—	1	—	1	222	5	11	334
126–130	97	2	1	—	—	270	4	12	386
131–135	108	2	—	3	2	278	10	16	419
136–140	102	4	—	4	3	206	12	8	339
141–145	79	—	1	6	1	156	7	7	257
146–150	61	1	—	1	3	159	8	11	244
151–155	55	—	—	5	—	175	4	7	246
156–160	67	—	1	2	2	175	3	7	257
161–165	46	1	1	5	1	165	8	2	229
166–170	35	1	—	—	1	97	2	4	140
171–180	98	2	2	7	4	263	4	9	389
181–190	86	6	—	8	8	131	21	12	272
191–195	55	4	—	5	3	109	8	7	191
196–200	56	2	—	9	4	60	10	7	148
201–210	69	—	—	3	7	105	14	12	210
211–220	35	—	2	2	2	48	3	4	96
221–230	24	1	1	2	3	38	—	1	70
231–235	15	2	—	2	—	8	4	1	32
236–240	17	—	—	2	1	25	2	8	55
241–245	5	—	—	—	—	5	—	1	11
246–250	13	—	—	2	—	11	1	8	35
251–255	16	—	—	—	1	34	3	6	60
256–260	10	—	—	2	—	41	4	2	59
261–265	14	—	—	2	—	16	1	5	38
266–270	12	—	—	3	—	13	2	2	32
271–275	7	1	1	—	—	7	—	2	18
276–285	7	1		—	1	5	1	1	16
286–295	4	—		4	1	4	—	—	13
296–305	7	1		3	2	10	5	3	31
306–315	6	—			1	3	3	—	13
316–325	2	—			—	1	1	—	4
326–335	6	1			1	7	—	2	17
336–345	3	—				3	2	1	9
346–355	3	—				9	1	1	14
356–365	8	1				7	2	3	21
Total	1322	33	11	82	53	2866	155	183	4705
%	28·10	0·70	0·23	1·74	1·12	60·91	3·29	3·89	99·98

TABLE 3

TYPE- AND DEPTH-WISE DISTRIBUTION OF FLAKES AND CORES OF ACHEULIAN INDUSTRY IN ROCK-SHELTER III F-23 AT BHIMBETKA

Depth in cms B.D. \ Type	1	2	3	4	5	6	7	8	9	10	11	12	13	14	15
121–125	10	39	56	21	96	11	—	—	—	1	—	1	—	—	3
126–130	16	44	81	30	99	12	—	—	—	1	—	—	—	—	3
131–135	27	36	64	44	107	16	—	1	—	1	—	—	1	—	7
136–140	11	18	47	19	111	8	1	—	—	2	—	—	4	—	5
141–145	14	21	41	17	63	7	1	—	—	1	—	—	2	—	3
146–150	9	16	39	18	77	11	2	—	—	2	—	—	1	—	3
151–155	12	28	40	16	79	7	—	—	—	2	—	1	—	—	1
156–160	14	16	39	18	88	7	1	—	—	—	—	—	1	—	1
161–165	9	17	45	12	82	2	1	—	1	1	—	—	3	—	2
166–170	9	11	15	10	52	4	1	—	—	—	—	—	—	—	1
171–180	20	21	57	20	145	9	1	—	—	1	—	—	1	—	1
181–190	13	19	30	10	59	12	—	—	—	5	1	—	10	2	3
191–195	9	13	17	10	60	7	—	—	—	2	—	—	5	—	1
196–200	9	13	17	5	16	7	—	—	—	2	—	—	5	—	3
201–210	14	19	28	9	35	12	—	—	—	1	—	—	4	—	9
211–220	6	7	11	4	20	4	—	—	—	2	—	1	—	—	—
221–230	6	3	12	8	9	1	—	—	—	—	—	—	—	—	—
231–235	1	1	5	—	1	1	1	—	—	—	—	1	2	—	—
236–240	1	1	6	7	10	8	—	—	—	—	—	—	1	—	1
241–245	—	—	2	2	1	1	—	—	—	—	—	—	—	—	—
246–250	3	2	—	5	1	8	—	—	—	—	—	—	—	—	1
251–255	1	7	5	6	15	6	—	—	—	—	—	—	1	—	2
256–260	5	1	13	5	17	2	—	—	—	1	—	—	—	—	3
261–265	2	—	4	4	6	5	—	—	—	—	—	—	—	—	1
266–270	—	1	6	4	2	2	—	—	—	—	—	—	—	—	2
271–275	3	1	—	1	2	2	—	—	—	—	—	—	—	—	—
276–285	1	1	2	—	1	1	—	—	—	1	—	—	—	—	—
286–295	—	—	2	1	1	—	—	—	—	—	—	—	—	—	—
296–305	—	1	4	3	2	3	—	—	—	—	—	—	2	—	3
306–315	1	2	—	—	—	—	—	—	—	—	—	2	—	—	1
316–325	—	—	1	—	—	—	—	—	—	—	—	—	—	—	1
326–335	—	—	5	2	—	2	—	—	—	—	—	—	—	—	—
336–345	1	1	1	—	—	1	—	—	—	—	—	—	2	—	—
346–355	1	1	6	—	1	1	—	—	—	—	—	—	—	—	1
356–365	—	—	1	4	2	3	—	—	—	—	—	—	—	—	2
Total	228	361	702	315	1260	183	9	1	1	26	1	6	45	2	64

Key to artefact types

1. Blade
2. Side flake
3. End flake
4. Indeterminate flake
5. Chips
6. Débris
7. Levallois flake core
8. Levallois blade core
9. Levallois point core
10. Discoidal core
11. Globular core
12. Prismatic core
13. Bifacial core
14. Pyramidal core
15. Amorphous core

TABLE 4

TYPE– AND DEPTH-WISE DISTRIBUTION OF HAND AXES AND CLEAVERS OF ACHEULIAN INDUSTRY IN ROCK-SHELTER III F-23 AT BHIMBETKA

Depth in cms B.D.	1	2	3	4	5	6	7	8	9	10	11	12	13	14	15	16	17
121–125											1						1
126–130								1	1		1						
131–135	1				1									3			2
136–140		1		1		1	1				1			2		2	3
141–145											1	1		5			1
146–150									1					1			3
151–155												4		1			—
156–160											1	1		1			2
161–165							1				1			3	2		1
166–170					1									—			1
171–180				1				1			2	1		5		1	4
181–190			1			1	1	1	2			1		6	1		8
191–195			1				1		2			2		2		1	3
196–200							1			1		1		6		2	4
201–210														1	2		7
211–202											2	1	1				2
221–230				1							1				2		3
231–235	1					1								2			
236–240														1	1		1
241–245																	
246–250													1	1			
251–255																	1
256–260															2		
261–265														2			
266–270												1		2			
271–275									1		1						
276–285							1										1
286–295													1	2	1		1
296–305					1							1		2			2
306–315																	1
316–325																	
326–335				1													1
336–345																	
346–355																	
356–365									1								
Total	2	1	2	4	3	3	6	3	8	1	11	13	4	48	11	6	53

Key to artefact types

1. Lanceolate handaxe
2. Ficron
3. Triangular handaxe
4. Sub-triangular handaxe
5. Elongated cordiform handaxe
6. Sub-cordiform handaxe
7. Oval handaxe
8. Limande
9. Miscellaneous
10. Discoid
11. Handaxe fragment
12. V-butt and transverse edge cleaver
13. V-butt and oblique edge cleaver
14. U-butt & transverse edge cleaver
15. U-butt & oblique edge cleaver
16. Miscellaneous cleaver
17. Cleaver fragment

TABLE 5

FREQUENCIES OF NON-BIFACE TOOL TYPES IN THE ACHEULIAN INDUSTRY OF ROCK-SHELTER III F-23 AT BHIMBETKA

		Real Count		Essential Count	
Type	No.	%	Cumulative %	%	Cumulative %
1	88	6·66			
2	73	5·52	12·18		
3	3	0·23	12·41		
5	10	0·76	13·17	0·97	0·97
9	23	1·74	14·91	2·23	3·20
10	99	7·49	22·40	9·59	12·79
11	51	3·86	26·26	4·94	17·73
12	1	0·07	26·33	0·10	17·83
13	3	0·23	26·56	0·29	18·12
15	9	0·68	27·24	0·87	18·99
16	5	0·38	27·62	0·48	19·47
17	5	0·38	28·00	0·48	19·95
18	1	0.07	28·07	0·10	20·05
19	3	0·23	28·30	0·29	20·34
20	7	0·53	28·83	0·68	21·02
21	16	1·21	30·04	1·55	22·57
22	8	0·60	30·64	0·78	23·35
23	21	1·59	32·23	2·04	25·39
24	13	0·98	33·21	1·26	26·65
25	57	4·31	37·52	5·52	32·17
26	28	2·12	39·64	2·71	34·88
27	2	0·15	39·79	0·19	35·07
28	4	0·30	40·09	0·39	35·46
29	12	0·91	41·00	1·16	36·62
30–31	107	8·09	49·09	10·37	46·99
32–33	1	0·07	49·16	0·10	47·09
34–35	14	1·06	50·22	1·36	48·45
36–37	86	6·50	56·72	8·33	56·78
38	75	5·67	62·39	7·27	64·05
39	9	0·68	63·07	0·87	64·92
40	87	6·58	69·65	8·43	73·35
41	3	0·23	69·88	0·29	73·64
42	111	8·40	78·28	10·76	84·40
43	78	5·90	84·18	7·56	91·96
44	5	0·38	84·56	0·48	92·44
45	18	1·36	85·92		
46–49	108	8·17	94·09		
52	2	0·15	94·24	0·19	92·63
54	15	1·13	95·37	1·45	94·08
55	1	0·07	95·44	0·10	94·18
56	9	0·68	96·12	0·87	95·05
59	2	0·15	96·27	0·19	95·24
61	1	0·07	96·34	0·10	95·34
62	48	3·63	99·97	4·65	99·999

TYPE-AND DEPTH-WISE DISTRIBUTION OF NO

	1	2	3	5	9	10	11	12	13	15	16	17	18	19	20	21	22	23	24
121-125	—	5	—	—	3	8	3	—	—	—	—	1	—	—	—	—	—	1	—
126–130	3	1	—	—	1	6	5	—	—	4	1	—	—	—	—	1	—	1	—
131–135	2	4	—	1	3	10	7	—	—	—	1	—	—	—	1	1	—	4	1
136–140	15	5	1	1	3	6	4	—	1	1	1	—	—	—	1	3	—	1	1
141–145	5	6	—	1	—	8	3	—	—	2	1	—	—	—	—	1	2	2	1
146–150	5	2	—	1	1	1	5	—	—	—	—	1	—	—	—	1	—	—	—
151–155	6	3	—	—	2	4	1	—	—	1	—	—	—	—	1	1	1	1	—
156–160	3	4	1	—	1	6	6	—	—	—	1	—	—	1	—	1	—	—	—
161–165	8	2	—	—	—	—	1	—	—	—	—	—	—	—	—	1	—	—	2
166–170	2	3	1	—	—	3	2	—	—	—	—	—	—	—	—	1	—	—	—
171–180	3	5	—	2	3	6	2	1	1	1	—	1	—	1	2	2	—	5	2
181–190	5	3	—	1	4	6	5	—	—	—	—	1	—	—	—	—	1	3	—
191–195	6	2	—	1	—	10	1	—	—	—	—	—	1	—	—	—	1	—	—
196–200	6	9	—	1	—	1	—	—	—	—	—	—	—	1	1	1	—	—	2
201–210	4	7	—	1	1	6	3	—	—	—	—	—	—	—	1	1	—	—	2
211–220	3	2	—	—	—	1	1	—	—	—	—	—	—	—	—	—	1	1	—
221–230	2	2	—	—	—	—	—	—	—	—	—	—	—	—	—	—	1	1	1
231–235	3	2	—	—	—	1	—	—	—	—	—	—	—	—	—	—	—	—	1
236–240	—	2	—	—	—	1	1	—	—	—	—	—	—	—	—	—	—	—	—
241–245	—	—	—	—	—	—	—	—	—	—	—	—	—	—	—	—	—	—	—
246–250	3	1	—	—	—	4	—	—	1	—	—	—	—	—	—	—	—	—	—
251–255	2	1	—	—	—	1	—	—	—	—	—	—	—	—	—	—	—	—	—
256–260	—	—	—	—	—	1	—	—	—	—	—	—	—	—	—	—	1	1	—
261–265	—	—	—	—	—	—	—	—	—	—	—	—	—	—	—	—	—	—	—
266–270	1	—	—	—	—	2	—	—	—	—	—	—	—	—	—	1	—	—	—
271–275	—	—	—	—	1	1	—	—	—	—	—	1	—	—	—	—	—	—	—
276–285	—	—	—	—	—	2	—	—	—	—	—	—	—	—	—	—	—	—	—
286–295	—	—	—	—	—	1	—	—	—	—	—	—	—	—	—	—	—	—	—
296–305	—	—	—	—	—	1	1	—	—	—	—	—	—	—	—	—	—	—	—
306–315	—	1	—	—	—	2	—	—	—	—	—	—	—	—	—	—	—	—	—
316–325	—	—	—	—	—	—	—	—	—	—	—	—	—	—	—	—	—	—	—
326–335	—	—	—	—	—	—	—	—	—	—	—	—	—	—	—	—	—	—	—
336–345	—	—	—	—	—	—	—	—	—	—	—	—	—	—	—	—	—	—	—
346–355	—	—	—	—	—	—	—	—	—	—	—	—	—	—	—	—	—	—	—
356–365	1	—	—	—	—	—	—	—	—	—	—	—	—	—	—	—	—	—	—
Total	88	73	3	10	23	99	51	1	3	9	5	5	1	3	7	16	8	21	13

KEY TO TOOL TYPE NUMBERS IN TABLES 5 AND 6

1. Typical Levallois flake
2. Atypical Levallois flake
3. Levallois point
5. Pseudo-Levallois point
9. Single straight side scraper
10. Single convex side scraper
11. Single concave side scraper
12. Double straight side scraper
13. Double straight-convex side scraper
15. Double convex side scraper
16. Double concave side scraper
17. Double concave-convex side scrap
18. Convergent straight side scraper
19. Convergent convex side scraper
20. Convergent concave side scraper
21. Dejété (offset) side scraper
22. Straight transverse side scraper
23. Convex transverse side scraper
24. Concave transverse side scraper
25. Side scraper on ventral face
26. Abrupt retouched side scraper
27. Side scraper with thinned back

TABLE 6

N BIFACE TOOLS IN THE ACHEULIAN INDUSTRY OF ROCK-SHELTER III F-23 AT BHIMBETKA

					30	32	34	36									46								
25	26	27	28	29	31	33	35	37	38	39	40	41	42	43	44	45	49	52	54	55	56	59	61	62	Total
4	3	1	—	—	11	—	—	—	1	—	8	—	15	13	—	1	13	—	1	—	—	—	—	1	94
1	2	—	—	1	9	—	2	1	3	—	14	—	13	8	—	1	17	—	1	—	—	—	—	1	97
7	2	—	1	2	17	—	2	3	4	2	6	—	7	9	—	1	6	—	—	—	1	—	—	3	108
8	1	—	—	1	9	—	—	6	5	1	3	—	10	6	—	1	3	—	2	—	—	—	—	2	102
3	3	—	—	2	9	—	1	3	4	—	2	1	8	3	—	1	4	—	3	—	—	—	—	—	79
3	1	—	—	—	2	—	1	2	7	1	4	—	6	3	—	2	7	—	3	—	1	—	—	1	61
2	1	—	—	—	3	—	1	5	4	2	4	—	3	4	—	—	2	—	—	—	—	—	—	3	55
5	1	—	1	—	5	—	2	3	5	—	3	—	8	4	1	1	2	—	2	—	—	—	—	—	67
1	—	1	—	—	3	—	—	5	2	—	7	—	4	3	—	—	2	—	—	—	—	—	—	4	46
2	1	—	—	—	1	—	—	3	1	1	2	—	5	2	1	2	1	—	1	—	—	—	—	—	35
2	2	—	—	1	10	—	—	6	6	—	4	1	8	5	—	1	10	1	—	—	—	—	—	4	98
4	2	—	—	—	12	1	2	5	3	1	7	—	4	5	—	1	4	—	—	—	1	—	—	5	86
4	1	—	—	1	2	—	2	4	5	—	—	—	7	1	—	1	3	—	1	1	—	—	—	—	55
3	—	—	—	—	1	—	—	7	2	—	6	—	4	3	—	—	6	—	—	—	—	—	—	2	56
1	2	—	1	1	5	—	1	5	6	—	4	—	4	3	—	—	4	—	—	—	1	1	—	4	69
2	1	—	1	—	1	—	—	3	2	—	3	—	—	2	1	1	5	—	—	—	—	—	—	4	35
—	2	—	—	1	1	—	—	2	3	—	1	1	—	—	—	1	3	—	—	—	—	1	1	—	24
—	—	—	—	—	1	—	—	1	1	—	1	—	1	—	—	—	2	—	—	—	—	—	—	1	15
1	—	—	—	—	—	—	—	2	2	—	3	—	—	—	—	—	3	—	—	—	1	—	—	1	17
—	—	—	—	—	—	—	—	—	—	—	1	—	1	—	—	1	—	1	—	—	—	—	—	1	5
—	—	—	—	—	—	—	—	3	—	—	—	—	—	—	—	—	1	—	—	—	—	—	—	—	13
—	—	—	—	—	—	—	—	4	2	—	1	—	2	—	—	1	—	—	1	—	—	—	—	1	16
—	—	—	—	—	—	—	—	1	1	1	—	—	—	2	—	—	—	—	—	—	1	—	—	1	10
1	1	—	—	—	2	—	—	5	2	—	1	—	—	1	1	—	—	—	—	—	—	—	—	—	14
—	—	—	—	—	—	—	—	—	2	—	2	—	1	—	1	—	2	—	—	—	—	—	—	—	12
1	—	—	—	—	—	—	—	—	—	—	—	—	—	—	—	—	3	—	—	—	—	—	—	—	7
—	—	—	—	1	2	—	—	2	—	—	—	—	—	—	—	—	—	—	—	—	—	—	—	—	7
—	—	—	—	—	—	—	—	2	—	—	—	—	—	—	—	—	—	—	—	—	—	—	—	1	4
1	1	—	—	1	—	—	—	—	—	—	—	—	—	—	—	—	1	—	—	—	—	—	—	1	7
1	—	—	—	—	—	—	—	—	—	—	—	—	—	—	—	—	1	—	—	—	—	—	—	1	6
—	1	—	—	—	—	—	—	1	—	—	—	—	—	—	—	—	—	—	—	—	—	—	—	—	2
—	—	—	—	—	—	—	—	1	1	—	—	—	—	—	—	—	2	—	—	—	1	—	—	1	6
—	—	—	—	—	—	—	—	—	1	—	—	—	—	—	1	—	—	—	—	—	—	—	—	1	3
—	—	—	—	—	1	—	—	—	—	—	—	—	—	—	—	—	—	—	—	—	1	—	—	1	3
—	—	—	—	—	—	—	—	1	—	—	—	—	—	—	—	1	1	—	—	—	1	—	—	3	8
57	28	2	4	12	107	1	14	86	75	9	87	3	111	78	6	18	108	2	15	1	9	2	1	48	1322

er

28. Side scraper with bifacial retouch
29. Alternate retouched side scraper
30-31. End scrapers
32-33. Burins
34-35. Borers
36-37. Backed knives
38. Naturally backed knife
39. Raclette
40. Truncated blade and flake
41. Mousterian tranchet
42. Notch
43. Denticulate
44. Alternate retouched beak
45. Retouches on ventral face
46-47. Abrupt and alternate retouch (thick)
48-49. Abrupt and alternate retouch (thin)
52. Notched triangle
54. End-notched piece
55. Hachoir
56. Rabot (Pushplane)
59. Chopper
61. Chopping tool
62. Miscellaneous

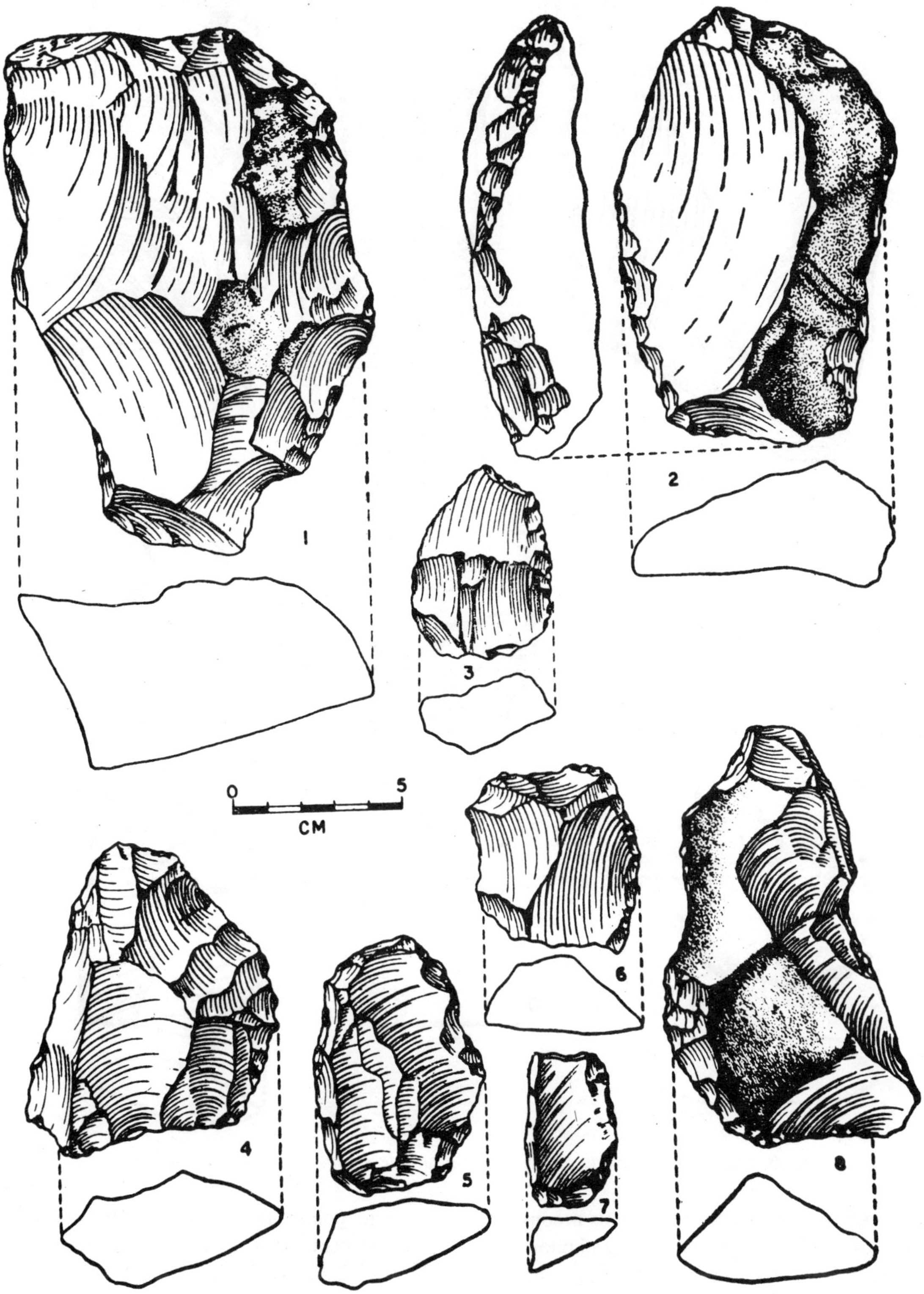

FIG. 5. *Simple convex scrapers*

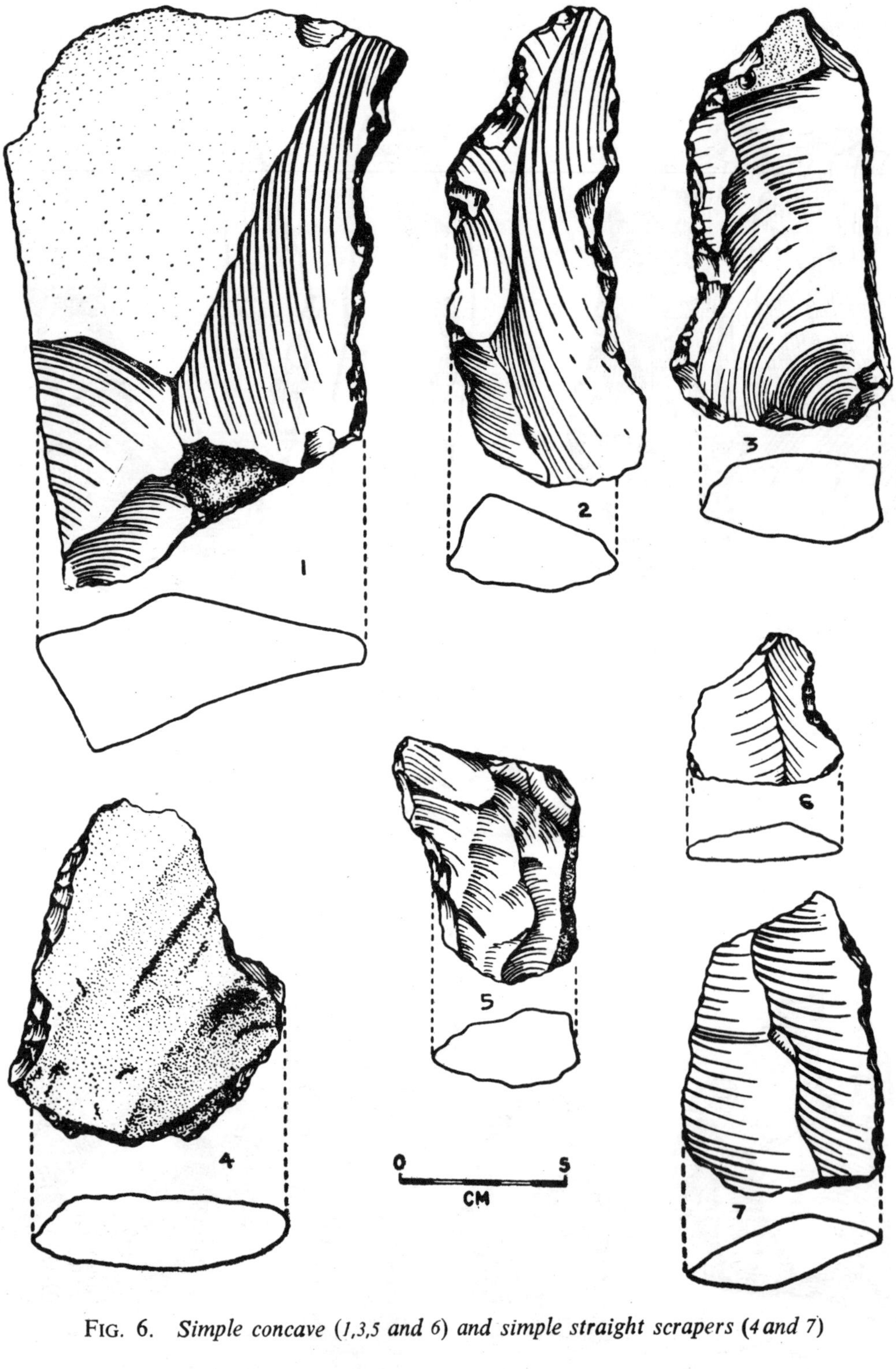

FIG. 6. *Simple concave (1,3,5 and 6) and simple straight scrapers (4 and 7)*

5. Side scrapers and other non-biface tools account for 28·10 per cent (1322 pieces) tools, and bifaces (handaxes and cleavers, including their fragments) for the remainder 3·80 per cent (179 pieces). The biface element therefore plays a minor role in the Bhimbetka Acheulian industry.
6. Unretouched Levallois flakes (including blades and points) (PL. IIIa and IᴵIb) constitute 12·41 per cent (164 pieces) of the assemblage. The Levallois typological element is therefore fairly large.[1]

[1]The percentages under paras 6–10 are worked out of the total of non-biface tools (1322 pieces). See Table 5.

7. Side scrapers constitute the biggest class of tools (27·83%; 368 pieces) and display the total range of types (except one, viz. No. 14) recognized by Bordes in Lower and Middle Palaeolithic assemblages. In this class the most common types are simple convex (7·49 %; 99 pieces; FIG. 5), ventrally retouched (4·31%; 57 pieces; FIG. 7), simple concave (3·86%; 51 pieces; FIG. 6, *1–3*, *5–6*), simple straight (1·74 %; 23 pieces; FIG. 6, *4*,*7*), abrupt retouched (2·12 %; 28 pieces), transverse convex (1·59 %; 21 pieces) and dèjète (offset) (1·21 %; 16 pieces).
8. End-scrapers constitute 10·37 per cent (107 pieces) of the tool assemblage. The high percentage of end-scrapers—a type that is characteristic of Upper Palaeolithic—is indicative of an evolutionary late stage of the industry.
9. Prepared back and naturally backed knives account for 15·60 per cent (161 pieces) of the assemblage.
10. Other common tool types are truncated flakes and blades (6·58 %; 87 pieces), notches (8·40 %; 111 pieces) and denticulates (5·90 %; 78 pieces). The presence of these tool types has rarely been noted in Indian Acheulian industries.
11. There are only 2·20 per cent (33 pieces) intact handaxes and 5·46 per cent (82 pieces) intact cleavers, together accounting for 7·66 % (115 pieces) of the finished tool group.[1] Taken together with their fragments (handaxes 11 pieces, cleavers 55 pieces) they constitute 2·93 per cent and 8·99 per cent of the industry respectively, the combined percentage of both types being 11·93. The large proportion of broken bifaces, particularly cleavers, shows that these types were used inside and in the close vicinity of the shelter.
12. The proportion of cleavers to handaxes is 3:1. Thus, the biface element is clearly characterized by the predominance of cleavers.
13. The handaxe sample being small does not lend itself to the perception of any clear typological preference. However, it may be stated that nearly half (15 pieces) of the intact specimens belong to cordiform(PL. IB, *1*) and oval (PL. IB, *2,3*) shapes. The rest are of narrow elongated (PL. IA) and other shapes. Most of the handaxes are made on flakes, have a symmetrical outline and thin section, and are characterized by shallow, even flake scars.
14. The cleavers are all made on end-flakes. While the upper surface is extensively worked, on the ventral face secondary work is confined to bulbar end and the sides. The most common type of transversal cross-section is parallelogrammatic which lends itself ideally to hafting. The cleavers are regularly characterized by a symmetrical form and even surfaces. The most preferred shape is one with rounded butt and transverse edge (48 pieces; PL. IIA), the next being one with pointed butt and transverse edge (13 pieces; PL. IIB, *2*). Other shapes are rounded but and convex edge (PL. IA, *2*) rounded butt and oblique edge(PL. IA, *3*),pointed butt and convex edge(PL. IB, *1*,) and pointed butt and oblique edge(PL. IB, *3*).

To summarize, the Bhimbetka Acheulian industry is characterized by a very low percentage of bifaces, high proportion of cleavers to handaxes, a remarkably high standard of workmanship in bifaces, especially cleavers, predominance and great diversity of non-biface tools, high percentages of end scrapers and Levallois flakes, and complete absence of chopper-chopping tools. All these features unequivocally show the closeness of this industry to the Mousterian facies of Acheulian tradition; it is to be noted that layer 5 which overlies the Acheulian deposit is stratigraphically and culturally a continuum of the Acheulian culture except for the disappearance of the biface element and a certain decline in the standard of workmanship. Thus there can be no doubt that the Bhimbetka Acheulian industry represents the terminal phase of the Acheulian tradition.

The principal typological indices are given below:

REAL TYPOLOGICAL INDICES AND CHARACTERISTIC GROUPS

Typological Levallois index: 12·41. Scraper index: 27·83. Unifacial Acheulian index: 6·50. Handaxe index: 11·93 (including fragments) and 7·66 (excluding fragments).

Levallois group (I): 12·41. Mousterian group (II): 27·83. Upper Palaeolithic group (III) : 23·30. Denticulate group (IV): 5.90.

ESSENTIAL TYPOLOGICAL INDICES AND CHARACTERISTIC GROUPS

Typological Levallois index: O. Scraper index: 35·65. Unifacial Acheulian index: 8·33. Handaxe index: 14·78 (including fragments) and 10·03 (excluding fragments).

Levallois group (I): O. Mousterian group (II): 35·65. Upper Palaeolithic group (III): 28·59. Denticulate group (IV): 7·56.

[1]These percentages are calculated out of the total of biface and non-biface tools (1501 pieces). See Tables 4 and 5.

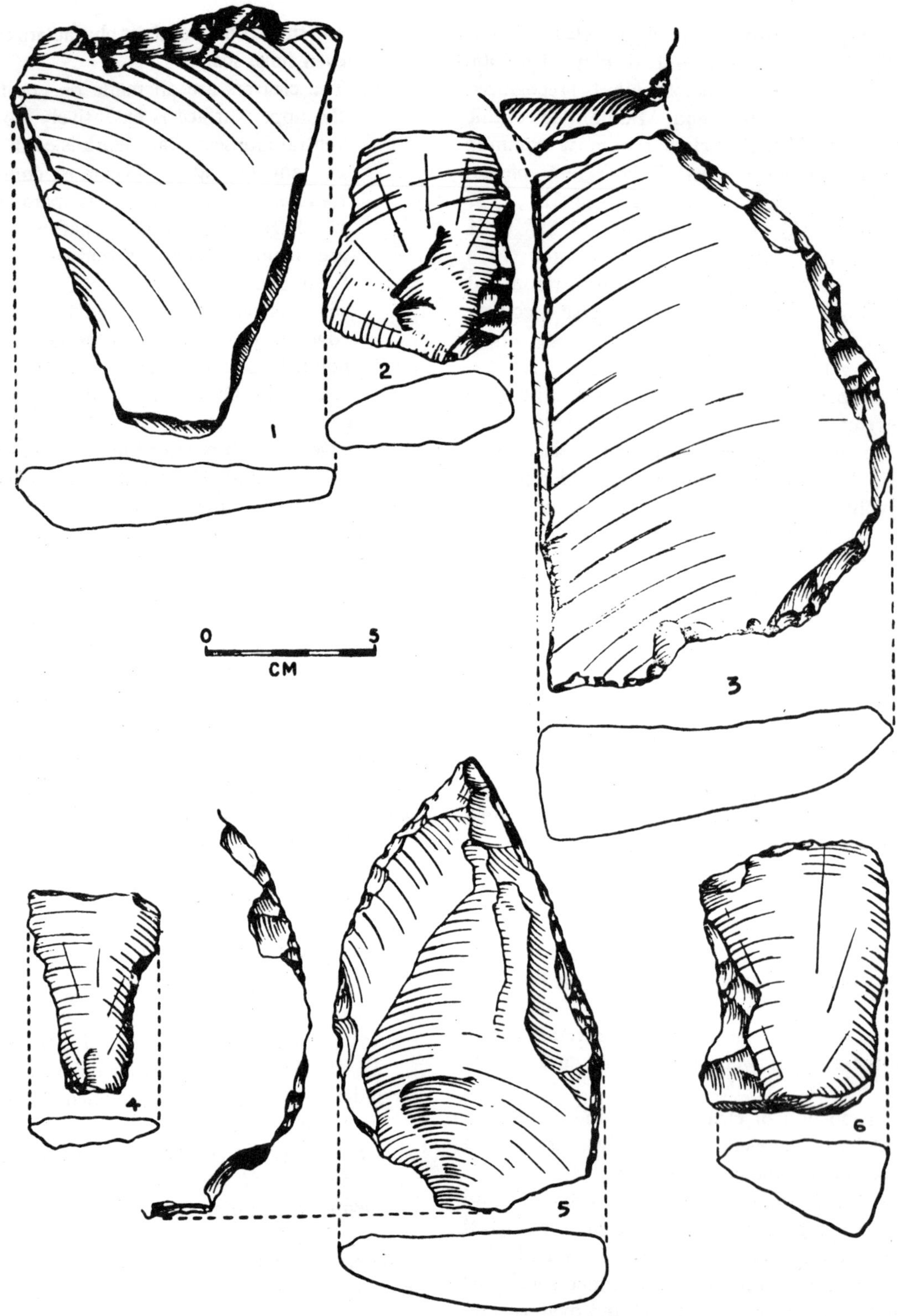

FIG. 7. *Ventrally retouched scrapers*

COMPARISON WITH OTHER SITES

With the present evidence it is not possible to date the industry in actual years with any degree of precision. It might, however, be instructive to compare the Acheulian industry of rock shelter III F-23 with other Acheulian industries in the country, known from stratified sites. So far stratified material is available only from twelve other sites. Of these material from only five sites can be compared; from the remaining sites cultural material is either too small or not yet published. The five sites are: (1–2) Trenches I and II from Cave IIIF-24 at Bhimbetka, (3) Lalitpur in Uttar Pradesh, (4) Chirki-Nevasa in Maharashtra, and (5) Anagawadi in Karnataka.

The cultural material from these sites and Bhimbetka III F-23 is presented in Tables 7 and 8. Table 7 lists the frequencies and percentages of main artefact classes and Table 8 those of principal classes of finished tools from these sites. To achieve comparability the frequencies and percentages of artefacts from Bhimbetka III F-23 have been reworked by excluding Levallois flakes and utilized flakes from the finished tool group and by including bifaces in the latter. In the ensuing pages we shall give a brief summary of the geographical setting and stratigraphy of these sites and then comment on the comparability of the cultural material from each of them with that of Bhimbetka III F-23.

BHIMBETKA III F-24

At Bhimbetka, Acheulian material has been found in three other localities, all excavated by V.S. Wakankar. These are Cave III F-24(also known as Auditorium cave) and Rock shelters III A-29 and III A-30. In the two latter contexts only a thin Acheulian layer was found, and the artefactual material is very small and not yet published. In Cave III F-24, located within a few metres of III F-3, three trenches have yielded Acheulian material; of these preliminary reports are available for trenches I and II.[1] Both these are primary archaeological contexts, and there is little possibility of any significant disturbance. In Trench I (3×2 m) the topmost layer yielded Mesolithic remains, and below it occurred an industry predominantly of scrapers and made of quartzite. The lowest horizon was Acheulian. It is 1·20 m thick and is composed of a very tough breccia which appears to have been formed by the precipitation of calcium carbonate derived from water percolating from the ceiling and walls of the cave. Tools could be extracted with great difficulty and they were thickly encrusted with calcium carbonate.

The Acheulian layer yielded a total of 469 artefacts of which four are made of chalcedony and the remainder of quartzite. There is evidence that a certain amount of artefacts, especially those of smaller size, got discarded with the débris. The collection consists of 35·82 per cent finished tools and 64·12 per cent cores and flakes. In this respect the difference from Bhimbetka III F-23 is not very marked. The percentage of flakes at the two sites is fairly close, but the percentage of cores in Trench I is appreciably higher. Among the finished tools in Trench I handaxes and cleavers both account for 39·88 per cent each,[2] and side scrapers for 17·26 per cent. The remaining 2·98 per cent tools are accounted for by a solitary borer and 4 discoids. Blades and Levallois flakes seem to have been grouped with ordinary flakes, for I had seen excellent examples of both these types in the collection. The absence in this trench of other tool types, noted in III F-23, is partly at least due to the different typological scheme followed by Wakankar and the preliminary nature of his classification. The other significant difference between the two industries is the very high percentage of bifaces in Trench I of III F-24. Technologically, however, the assemblage from Trench I displays the same high standard of craftsmanship as seen in III F-23.

In Trench II (3×2 m) of III F-24, located at the other end of the cave, some 20 m away from Trench I, the cultural material was broadly similar but there was no brecciation of the deposit. Below the Acheulian layer there was a 60 cm thick sterile layer, and underneath it a lateritic deposit yielded a few highly weathered chopper-like pebble tools. The Acheulian horizon is 1·0 m thick. Though artefacts occurred all through, on two levels, one near the bottom and the other near the top, they were found scattered over large boulders and are therefore indicative of working floors.

The assemblage from Trench II is bigger, consisting of 1029 artefacts. They are all made of quartzite and are very fresh in appearance. Finished tools constitute 22·93 per cent. It is surprising that while there are 789 (76·68 per cent) big and small flakes, there are only 4 (0·39 per cent) cores. Among finished tools bifaces account for 52·12 per cent and side scrapers for the remaining 47·88 per cent. The ratio of cleavers (30·93%) to handaxes (21·19%) is roughly 1·5: 1. In this respect the assemblage from Trench I presents a less marked contrast than Trench I from that of Bhimbetka III F-23. The absence of blades, Levallois flakes and non-biface tools (other than side-scrapers) in Trench II is probably due to the same factors as mentioned in the case of Trench I. In spite of these marked typological differences my limited first-hand examination of the material from Trench II shows it to be technologically fairly similar to that from III F-23. It seems unlikely that there was a significant time gap between the Acheulian occupations of the two shelters.

LALITPUR

The site of Lalitpur (78° 25′ E ; 24° 42′ N) is located in open plain ground about 1·5 km north-west of Lalitpur railway station on the Central Railway in Uttar Pradesh. In 1962 R. Singh carried out a small dig in an area of 6×3 m (20×10 ft) on the edge of a cultivated field about 200 m south of a small stream known as Biana

[1]V.S. Wakankar, 'Bhim-Betka Excavations', *Journal of Indian History*, Vol. LI, pt. 1 (1973), pp. 23–33.

[2]I have included Wakankar's 'points or lanceolates' (9·52%) among handaxes because during discussions with him in the field I had found that he uses these terms for pointed handaxes.

TABLE 7

FREQUENCIES OF MAIN ARTEFACT CLASSES AT SIX EXCAVATED ACHEULIAN SITES

Artefact class	Bhimbetka III F-23		Bhimbetka III F-23 Tr. I		Bhimbetka III F-24 Tr. II		Lalitpur		Chirki (Nevasa)		Anagawadi	
	No.	%	No.	%	No.	%	No.	%	No.	%	No.	%
Finished tools	1219	25·19	168	35·82	236	22·93	121	11·55	1510	62·73	94	44·13
Cores	155	3·29	36	7·68	4	0·30	55	5·25	95	3·95	61	28·64
Blades	238	5·06	—	—	—	—	—	—	—	—	—	—
Flakes/big flakes/large waste	1650	35·07	128	27·29	232	22·55	497	47·42	444	18·45	28	13·15
Chips/waste/ small waste	1260	26·78	137	29·21	557	54·13	340	32·44	358	14·87	30	14·08
Débris/angular fragments	183	3·89	—	—	—	—	35	3·34	—	—	—	—
Total	4705	100·00	469	100·00	1029	100·00	1048	100·00	2407	100·00	213	100·00

TABLE 8

FREQUENCIES OF MAIN CLASSES OF FINISHED TOOLS AT SIX EXCAVATED ACHEULIAN SITES

	Bhimbetka III F-23		Bhimbetka III F-24 Tr. I		Bhimbetka III F-24 Tr. II		Lalitpur		Chirki (Nevasa)		Anagawadi	
	No.	%	No.	%	No.	%	%	No.	%	No.	No.	%
Handaxes	44	3·61	67	39·88	50	21·19	88	72·73	516	34·17	27	28·72
Cleavers	135	11·07	67	39·88	73	20·93	22	18·18	382	25·30	13	13·83
Side scrapers	368	30·19	29	17·26	113	47·88	2	1·65	66	4·37	12·	12·77
End scrapers	107	8·78	—	—	—	—	—	—	—	—	—	—
Knives	161	13·21	—	—	—	—	—	—	—	—	—	—
Denticulates	78	6·40	—	—	—	—	—	—	—	—	—	—
Notches	111	9·10	—	—	—	—	—	—	—	—	—	—
Truncated flakes	87	7·14	—	—	—	—	—	—	—	—	—	—
Choppers	—	—	—	—	—	—	4	3·31	546	36·16	33	35·11.
Chopping tools	—	—	—	—	—	—	5	4·13	—	—	—	—
Other tools	128	10·50	5	2·98	—	—	—	—	—	—	9	9·57
Total	1219	100·00	168	100·00	236	100·00	121	100·00	1510	100·00	94	100·00

nala.[1] Gully erosion of the field had earlier exposed Acheulian tools in the section. Commercial limemaking quarries nearby had revealed that the tool bearing layer was covered by a 15 cm thick deposit of brown earth. In the excavated area, however, this layer had been completely washed away. The archaeological layer was 30 to 45 cm thick and was composed of "a large number of angular fragments of quartz, small quartzite pebbles, factory débris, flakes and tools in extremely fresh condition".[2] This layer rested on a slightly sloping granite rock. Quartz fragments, small quartzite pebbles and many chips were discarded from the excavated débris. Despite this the collection contains over 80 per cent flakes of various sizes. This, taken together with the freshness of the artefacts, suggests the site to be a real working floor and eliminates the possibility of any significant disturbance of the original deposit.

In a collection of 1048 artefacts 40 (3·82 per cent) are made on quartzite pebbles and the remainder on granite and quartz blocks, presumably quarried from exposed rocks. Finished tools account for less than 12 per cent of the collection. Among finished tools 91 per cent are bifaces, and less than two per cent are scrapers. The ratio of handaxes to cleavers is 4:1. From Singh's description it appears that most of the handaxes and cleavers are made on end-struck flakes. Of the 88 handaxes as many as 36 are worked on only one face. Cleavers are rarely worked on the ventral face. The near absence of retouched flake tools is probably due, partly at least, to the difficulty of executing retouch on coarse-grained rocks like granite and quartz. Among 497 large flakes 47 (9·46 per cent) are described as prepared flakes for handaxes and 51 (10·26 per cent) as prepared flakes for cleavers.

The Lalitpur industry presents a marked contrast to Bhimbetka III F-23 industry. In the latter, bifaces account for only 14·68 per cent of the finished tools against 90·91 per cent in Lalitpur and scrapers and other non-biface tools account for 85·32 per cent against 9·09 in Lalitpur. The ratio of handaxes to cleavers at Bhimbetka is 1:3 against 4:1 at Lalitpur. The complete absence of Levallois flakes at Lalitpur is another significant feature. The Lalitpur industry therefore represents a typologically and technologically different and much earlier stage of Acheulian tradition than the Bhimbetka industry.

CHIRKI—NEVASA

The site of Chirki is part of the larger site of Nevasa (74° 50′ E; 19° 30′ N) in Ahmednagar District, Maharashtra, well-known for over two decades for its wealth of Palaeolithic and palaeontological remains.[3] The site is located on the confluence of a small nullah, Chirki with the Pravara river, 3 km down stream from Nevasa. Excavations were carried out here for three seasons (1966–1968) by Gudrun Corvinus.[4] Though a number of trenches were dug, the main evidence for the Acheulian culture was found only in one trench, namely No. VII. This trench (its precise size is not clear from descriptions) is located close to the southern bank of the Pravara river. The topography of the area consists of alluvial badlands. The rocky land surface, now buried beneath thick alluvial deposits, slopes from south toward the river. Acheulian artefacts were found on and within a colluvial bouldery rubble deposit of 20 to 40 cm thickness. This bouldery rubble, formed of grey and red basalts, provided the raw material to the Acheulian man for manufacturing his tools. Fine-grained dolerite used for the best tools was probably brought from trap dykes some kilometres away from the site. Chalcedony and quartz were also used to a limited extent.

Many tools are angular and sharp, and this shows "that no transport could have taken place."[5] Other artefacts are, however, rounded in varying degrees, but this rounding is said to be due to exposure and not to transport and rolling. The sharpness of the tools, their large number, presence of many unfinished tools and of many flakes and cores are regarded as showing that Trench VII represents a workshop or factory of Acheulian man.

The bouldery rubble is filled in and sealed by an alluvial gravel which in places reaches a thickness of 8 m. This alluvial gravel is believed to have sealed the bouldery rubble soon after the Acheulian occupation as there is no hiatus between the two deposits. Occasionally Acheulian tools are found in the alluvial gravel as well. But the more common industry in the gravel consists of scrapers, borers and points made of chalcedony, jasper, etc. This assemblage was long ago recognized by Sankalia as an independent and post-Acheulian industry, termed initially as Series II and later as Nevasian.

[1]R. Singh, *Palaeolithic Industries of Northern Bundelkhand*, Ph.D. Thesis, 1965 (unpublished), Deccan College Library, Pune, pp. 66–79.

[2]*Ibid.*, p. 67.

[3]H.D. Sankalia, 'Animal Fossils and Palaeolithic Industries from the Pravara Basin at Nevasa, District Ahmednagar', *Ancient India*, no. 12 (1956), pp. 35–52.

[4]G. Corvinus, 'An Acheulian Occupation Floor at Chirki-on-Pravara, India', *Current Anthropology*, vol. 9, no. 2–3 (April-June, 1968), pp. 216–18; 'The Acheulian Workshop at Chirki on the Pravara River, Maharashtra', *Indian Antiquary* (Third Series), vol. IV, nos. 1–4 (1973), pp. 13–22; 'Excavations at an Acheulian Site at Chirki-on-Pravara in India', in (ed.) N. Hammond, *South Asian Archaeology* (New Jersey, 1973), pp. 13–28.

[5]Corvinus, *op. cit.* (1970), p. 16.

[6]H.D. Sankalia, *op. cit.* (1956).

While Corvinus had earlier agreed with this position,[1] in her more recent publication she is inclined to view the Nevasian as a component of the Acheulian, "a light duty industry made of jasper and other siliceous material, accompanying a heavy duty industry made of basalt."[2]

The assemblage from the workshop (presumably entirely from Trench VII) consists of 2407 artefacts. Of this 62·73 per cent are finished tools, 3·95 per cent cores and 33·32 per cent flakes of various sizes.[3] Among the flakes 18·45 per cent (444 pieces) are large waste, 9·89 per cent (238 pieces) small basalt flakes and 4·98 per cent (120 pieces) small silica flakes, the last of the kind found in the gravel sealing the Acheulian layer. Corvinus concedes that the "great difference in the percentage of tools to waste, specially to the small waste ....would be very unusual for an undisturbed workshop".[4] She explains this anomaly by assuming that the occupation floor must have been disturbed in its original context. The water of the rising river, which brought the alluvial gravel sealing, must have washed away most of the smaller components of the factory site, leaving all the larger artefacts and only a small percentage of the smaller ones. Many of the light duty flakes seem to have been washed into the river and got subsequently deposited into the gravels in the down stream vicinity of Chirki.[5]

The explanation leaves two questions unanswered. First, in so far as silica flakes are more numerous in the gravel, the floods must have acted selectively in removing more of silica flakes and less of small basalt flakes. Secondly, why should the action of the river water start only from the workshop and not from the higher ground beyond? Elsewhere Corvinus says: "No trace has been found of a camp site. It might be possible that the strong erosional forces have destroyed everything which might have been present on the valley flats. These flats, now barren and rocky in many places and covered at other places with a thin black soil on which millet grows, must have carried at the time of Early Man an extensive, though thin forest. The finding of calcified wood, and a few tree trunks and branches, which have been washed into the alluvium proves the existence of such a forest even at the time to the sealing of the occupational level."[6] Surely the floods that could transport tree trunks and branches should have been capable of transporting stone artefacts as well, and thereby depositing them in the depressions at the margin of the sloping landscape. The conclusion seems inescapable that erosional forces contributed to the disturbance of the "workshop" not only by removing material from it but also by adding material to it.

Leaving aside the question of the extent of the disturbance of the Acheulian deposit at Chirki, the differences between the Chirki and Bhimbetka Acheulian industries are very marked indeed. And these are not confined to the highly contrasting ratios of tools to waste. Of the 1510 finished tools at Chirki as many as 876 (58·00 per cent) are made on pebbles, among them 330 (37·67 per cent) handaxes and 546 (62·33 per cent) choppers, chopping tools, polyhedrons, etc. This latter group of tools is entirely absent at Bhimbetka, and handaxes there are nearly all made on flakes. Again, handaxes and cleavers together account for 59·47 per cent of the tools at Chirki as against only 14·68 per cent at Bhimbetka, and the ratio of cleavers to handaxes is 1 : 1·4 at Chirki as against 3 : 1 at Bhimbetka. Among handaxes at Chirki there are many pick-like forms—a type completely absent at Bhimbetka. Though data on the relative thickness of handaxes are not available, my personal observations on the Chirki material suggest the relative thickness of handaxes there to be far greater than at Bhimbetka. Further, the percentage of scrapers and other flake tools at Chirki is only 4·37 whereas at Bhimbetka it is over 80. Thus, altogether the Chirki industry represents a much earlier technological stage than Bhimbetka industry, and is probably the most primitive and possibly the earliest of all the Acheulian industries known so far.

ANAGAWADI

The site of Anagawadi (75° 40′ E; 16° 15′ N) is in a nala bed joining the Ghataprabha river, some 13 kilometres north-west of the town of Bagalkot in Bijapur District of Karnataka. The implementiferous deposit consists of a well cemented pebbly gravel exposed in the bed and on the sides of the nala. The gravel has a thickness of 45 to 60 cm, and it rests over a 1·0 m to 1·50 m thick layer of detrital laterite. In the nala cliffs the gravel is covered by a dark brown silt of up to 3·0 m thickness. In the nala bed, which has a width of about 35 m, the pebbly gravel bed is exposed for a length of 85 m. In 1965 R.S. Pappu dug ten trenches, each of 1·50 × 1·50 m in the gravel.[7] The artefacts occurred

[1]Corvinus, *op. cit.* (1970), p. 17.
[2]Corvinus, *op. cit.* (1973), pp. 22–23.
[3]These figures are compiled from Corvinus, *op. cit.*, 1970 and 1973.
[4]Corvinus, *op. cit.* (1973), p. 23.
[5]*Ibid.*, p. 23.
[6]Corvinus, *op. cit* (1970), p. 16.

[7]R.S. Pappu, *Pleistocene Studies in the Upper Krishna Basin* (Poona, 1974), pp. 32–33 and 56.

all through the 50 cm thickness but were more frequent in its upper part. The gravel is made up of rounded to sub-rounded pebbles of quartzite and occasionally of chert. The context of the artefacts here is essentially geological.

The dig yielded 213 artefacts. Of these 94 (44·13 per cent) are finished tools and 119 (55·87 per cent) waste. Of the tools 35·11 per cent are choppers, 28·72 per cent handaxes, 13·83 per cent cleavers, and 12·77 per cent scrapers. The Anagawadi assemblage is thus considerably close to Chirki industry, and has very little in common with Bhimbetka industry.

Four other excavated Acheulian sites deserve discussion even though no detailed comparison between them and Bhimbetka is possible. These sites are Adamgarh and Mahadeo Piparia in Madhya Pradesh, Kuliana in Orissa and Hunsgi in Karnataka.

ADAMGARH

The site of Adamgarh is located on a low, isolated quartzite hill in the midst of an alluvial plain, about two kilometres south of the town of Hoshangabad (77° 43′ E;22° 45′ N) and some 30 km south of Bhimbetka. Though today the alluvial plain is all cultivated and presents a treeless aspect, in Pleistocene times whenever it formed a land surface, it must have been covered with thick vegetation. The Narmada river which must have flown in close vicinity as it does today, was a perennial source of water. There are a number of rock shelters on the hill which contain Mesolithic and later paintings and several of them habitation deposits of Mesolithic and, less frequently, Palaeolithic periods.

As early as 1935 de Terra had found Palaeolithic implements on the hill in lateritic soil 1·0 m to 1·25 m below the surface.[1] In 1964 R.V. Joshi and M.D. Khare excavated a number of trenches on the hill within and outside the shelters. Acheulian material was found in several trenches but figures for artefacts found are available only for two trenches, namely, ADG-6 and ADG-7.[2] The Acheulian artefacts occur in a fragmentary talus or débris which rests on and is partly enclosed in a sticky red clay. In the upper part of the talus artefacts of a post-Acheulian flake industry are found. The talus is covered by a thin layer of red silty clay which yields microliths. The sticky red clay layer rests on a lateritic gravel of detrital origin which in turn lies on the Vindhyan sandstone.

[1]H. de Terra and T.T. Paterson, *Studies on the Ice Age in India and Associated Human Cultures* (Washington, 1939), pp. 313–23.

[2]R.V. Joshi, 'Acheulian Succession in Central India', *Asian Perspectives,* vol. VIII, no. 1 (1966), pp. 150–63.

The archaeological deposit in the two trenches was 1·80 m. thick. Within this Acheulian artefacts occurred in Trench ADG-6 in the lower 1·20 m thickness and in Trench ADG-7 in the lower 1·0 m thickness. The main horizon in ADG-6 was between 1·0 m and 1·60 m depths and in ADG-7 between 0·80 m and 1·20 m. The number of Acheulian artefacts found in the two trenches is only 93; of this 70 were found in ADG-6 and 23 in ADG-7. The frequencies of different artefact types in the two trenches are given below.

TABLE 9

FREQUENCIES OF ARTEFACT TYPES IN TRENCHES ADG-6 AND ADG-7 AT ADAMGARH

Artefact type	ADG-6 No.	ADG-7 No.	Total
Handaxes	8	—	8
Cleavers	6	—	6
Scrapers	1	3	4
Points	3	2	5
Choppers	22	10	32
Discoids	8	4	12
Flakes	21	4	25
Cores	1	—	1
Total	70	23	93

Nearly all the tools are made on quartzite or fine-grained sandstone which were obtained in the form of blocks and chunks of rocks from the talus or from well jointed rocks exposed on the hill or as pebbles derived from the river bed. Nearly half the assemblage consists of choppers. Handaxes and cleavers were completely absent in ADG-7. The very small number of artefacts shows that the site was only occasionally frequented by Acheulian hunters. And the very low proportion of flakes and cores shows that most of the tools were made outside the shelters.

MAHADEO PIPARIA

Mahadeo Piparia (79° 16′ E ; 23° 06′ N) is a small village on the left bank of the Narmada river in Narsimhapur District of Madhya Pradesh. The alluvial deposits of the Narmada in Narsimhapur District have been known to be rich in mammalian fossils and Palaeolithic implements for several decades. S.G. Supekar carried out two small digs near Mahadeo Piparia in 1963 and 1965.[1] In 1963 a trench of 10 × 10 ft (3 × 3 m) was dug in the cemented bouldery gravel midway between the cliff section on the left bank and the present river channel. Below the depth of 7 ft (2·15 m) the trench was narrowed down to an area of 2 × 2 ft (0·60 × 0·60 m) to cope with the increasing quantity of sub-soil water, and digging had to be closed down at 10·6 ft (3·20 m) depth without reaching the bottom of the gravel. The gravel was pebbly and bouldery, well cemented and devoid of any fine sediment and stratification. Except for the last two digs which were of 21 inches (52 cm) each, all other digs were of 6 inches (15 cm) each. The distribution of artefacts in various digs was fairly uniform.

A total of 1025 artefacts were found in the gravel. Following the then current ideas about the nature of Lower and Middle Palaeolithic industries Supekar divided the artefactual material into two groups: Lower Palaeolithic (802 artefacts) and Middle Palaeolithic (223 artefacts).[2] Artefacts of both these cultures were represented in all the digs. Since according to earlier explorations the bouldery gravels were everywhere thought to be the basalmost deposit in river sections and the horizon of Lower Palaeolithic industries, Supekar's observations from his excavations came to him and to other prehistorians as a disappointment. To check the cultural and chronological position of the bouldery gravel Superkar decided to dig into this gravel where it was buried under a thick alluvium in the cliff section. Accordingly in 1965, he dug two trenches into the cliff—one of 10 × 10 ft (3 × 3 m) and the other of 2 × 2 ft (0·60 × 0·60 m) at right angles to the first. The stratigraphy revealed by the dig was as follows from top downwards:

1. Yellow brown sandy silt:	0·75 m
2. Pebbly sandy gravel, at times cross-bedded with intercalations of sand and silt:	5·65 m
3. Red brown silty sand with a lenticular pocket of pebbly gravel:	3·0 m
4. Yellow brown silt:	3·0 m
5. Boulder conglomerate:	1·20 m

The boulder conglomerate was dug to a depth of of 1·20 m without reaching its bottom. It yielded 173 artefacts. This collection too was taken by Supekar to be mixed and divided into Lower Palaeolithic (36 artefacts) and Middle Palaeolithic (137 artefacts).

[1]S.G. Supekar, *Pleistocene Stratigraphy and Prehistoric Archaeology of the Central Narmada Basin,* Ph.D. Thesis, 1968 (unpublished), Deccan College Library, Poona.

[2]Following the terminology then current Supekar hudwedL the terms 'Early Stone Age' and 'Middle Stone Age' for asoer' Palaeolithic' and 'Middle Palaeolithic', respectively.

While it is certain that the bouldery gravel, being an unsorted fluviatile deposit of immense thickness and extent, must have been laid down by powerful stream current and most contain archeaological assemblages of different spatial and temporal locations, the division of the artefact collection into Lower and Middle Palaeolithic on the basis of assumed typology, size and raw material is arbitrary and unwarranted. Whatever the extent of disturbance we consider it more advisable to treat the collections as single entities.

The 1963 (river bed gravel) dig yielded 1025 artefacts. The vast majority of them are made of quartzite (94·44 per cent; 968 pieces), the remainder being made of chert (3·51 per cent; 36 pieces), quartzitic chert (1·46 per cent; 15 pieces) and chalcedony (0·58 per cent; 6 pieces). As regards state of preservation 45·85 per cent (470) artefacts are rolled in varying degrees and 54·15 per cent (550 pieces) are fresh. Finished tools account for 32·78 per cent of the collection, and cores, flakes, etc. for the remaining 67·22 per cent. The two major classes of finished tools are choppers (49·11 per cent) and side scrapers (37·50 per cent). Handaxes (5·06 per cent) and cleavers (4·17 per cent) occur in small proportions.

The 1965 dig (cliff gravel) yielded only 173 artefacts. These are made of chert (60·12 %; 104 pieces), quartzite (29·48 per cent; 51 pieces), chalcedony (4·62 per cent; 8 pieces) and quartzitic chert (2·31 per cent; 4 pieces), the material of six artefacts remaining unspecified. Ninenty-one (52·60 per cent) artefacts are more or less rolled and 82 (47·40 per cent) fresh. The collection comprises 39·89 per cent finished tools, 45·35 per cent flakes, 2·89 per cent cores and 13·87 per cent chunks. Among finished tools the most common class is that of side scrapers (39·13 %) followed by end scrapers (17·39 per cent) and points (17·39 per cent). Handaxes and cleavers account for only 4·35 per cent and 2·90 per cent of the assemblage respectively.

Even though the assemblages from the two excavations come from the same geological horizon, there are very marked differences between them. To begin with, while the vertical distribution of artefacts in the river bed gravel was fairly uniform, in the cliff gravel as many as 60·69 per cent (105) artefacts occurred in the first dig (top 30 cm) and only 39·31 per cent (68 pieces) in the next two digs (60 cm). Secondly, the proportion of tools made on chert is much higher in the cliff gravel (60·12 %) than in the river bed gravel (3·51 %). Thirdly, the composition of finished tool group differed very markedly in the two collections. For example, in the river bed gravel the proportion of pebble tools is as high as 49·11 per cent while in the cliff gravel it is only 11·59 per cent.

TABLE 10
FREQUENCIES AND PERCENTAGES OF ARTEFACTS IN THE TWO EXCAVATIONS AT MAHADEO PIPARIA, MADHYA PRADESH

	1963 excavation		1965 excavation	
Artefact type	No.	%	No.	%
Finished tools	336	32·78	69	39·89
Flakes	589	57·47	75	43·35
Cores	89	8·68	5	2·89
Chunks	11	1·07	24	13·87
Total	1025	100·00	173	100·00

TABLE 11
FREQUENCIES AND PERCENTAGES OF FINISHED TOOL TYPES IN THE TWO EXCAVATIONS AT MAHADEO PIPARIA, MADHYA PRADESH

	1963 excavation		1965 excavation	
Tool type	No.	%	No.	%
Handaxes	17	5·06	3	4·31
Cleavers	14	4·17	2	2·90
Side scrapers	126	37·50	27	39·13
End scrapers	4	1·19	12	17·39
Points	7	2·08	12	17·39
Borers	2	0·59	3	4·35
Burins	—	—	2	2·90
Knives	1	0·30	—	—
Choppers	165	49·11	8	11·59
Total	336	100·00	69	100.00

Again, in the former end scrapers and points account for 1·19 per cent and 2·08 per cent respectively, while in the latter they account for 17·39 per cent each. Finally, the proportion of tools made on flakes is far higher in the cliff gravel. One explanation for these differences possibly is that while the cliff gravel after it was sealed by overlying alluvium remained undisturbed, the river bed gravel, being exposed, is likely to have been repeatedly reworked and the archaeological material got more and more mixed. Whatever the explanation, it is clear that the two assemblages are unlikely to be contemporaneous. The cliff gravel assemblage has a late Acheulian character and several features in common with Bhimbetka. However, in view of the very small sample of the Mahadeo Piparia assemblage the comparison cannot be closely pressed. The river bed gravel assemblage, on the other hand, has little in common with Bhimbetka.

KULIANA

The site of Kuliana (86° 39′ E ; 22° 04′ N) is located in Mayurbhanj District of Orissa. Here palaeoliths were known to occur on surface and in the sections of road metal quarries and tanks dug in lateritic deposits. N. K. Bose and D. Sen of Calcutta University dug here several pits (of unspecified size) on the margins of two existing tanks and one quarry in the late thirties and early forties of this century.[1] The stratigraphy of these pits consisted of a layer of yellowish earth (up to 55 cm thick) at the top and pisolitic laterite (of indeterminate thickness) below. The upper part of the laterite (30 to 90 cm in thickness) was less compact and yielded stone artefacts. Unfortunately, actual figures and classification of artefacts is not available; only selected implements have been described and illustrated. This precludes any comparison of the Kuliana material with Bhimbetka. The artefact bearing laterite is of detrital origin and the tools may have undergone a certain amount of dislocation. The assemblages consist of choppers, handaxes, cleavers, knives, scrapers and flakes. The excavators are inclined to see a succession from choppers through irregularly worked handaxes to neatly worked handaxes and rather crude cleavers. However, in the absence of adequate primary data nothing more can be made of the Kuliana industry.

HUNSGI

The site of Hunsgi (76° 31′ E ; 16° 27′ N) is in Gulbarga District of Karnataka. It is located on the edge of a narrow seasonal stream known as Hunsgi nala which joins the Krishna river about 35 km downstream. The stream has a width of about 35 m and has cut to a depth of 2 to 3 m in the sub-recent alluvium. The stratigraphy of the alluvium is as follows:

1. Black soil with a maximum thickness of 50 cm;
2. Loose secondary gravel with a thickness of up to 1·25 m and resting on and held together by disintegrated whitish granite; and
3. Granite bed rock.

Acheulian artefacts occur sparsely on the eroded surface of the gravel as also in the gravel itself. Several trial digs in the gravel by K. Paddayya eventually led

[1] N.K. Bose and D. Sen, *op. cit.*

to the discovery at its base of a thick concentration of Acheulian artefacts which from its characteristics can be described as an Acheulian working floor.[1]

The floor was exposed over an area of 22·75 sq. m in a trench 8·75 m long and (at its maximum) 4·0 m broad, and it has a thickness of 20 to 35 cm. It is made up of sub-angular to sub-rounded limestone pebbles, cobbles and rubble. While the pebbles and cobbles were laid down by the ancient stream, the angular blocks must have been brought by man from the plateaux 2 to 3 km away. Strewn amidst the gravel are numerous granite blocks measuring from 5 to 30 cm and occasionally up to 1·0 m in length. These blocks when viewed in relation to others in the unexcavated vicinity of the trench suggest an oval structural feature covering an area of about 40 sq. m The Acheulian man occupied the boulder strewn gravelly surface. In contrast to the overlying gravel the Acheulian layer is very well consolidated and could be excavated only with the aid of heavy picks and chisels.

The floor has yielded over 300 artefacts the detailed study of which is yet to be made. Limestone is the principal raw material used for tools. It was obtained in the form of pebbles from the gravel bed and as angular blocks from the plateaux. The artefacts retain sharp edges and show no traces of rolling. Neither pebbles nor artefacts show any specific orientation. The proportion of waste is nearly twice of the finished tools. There are several rounded limestone and granite pieces with battered surfaces, suggesting their use as hammerstones. All these characteristics point to the archaeological horizon having been an Acheulian working floor. The principal tool types in the assemblage are handaxes and cleavers, the other types being picks, points, scrapers and backed knives. Most of the artefacts appear to have been made by the use of the stone hammer technique. Though choppers and chopping tools are rare and any judgement on the nature of the industry at present must be tentative, paucity of non-biface flake tools and the extensive use of stone hammer technique suggest the Hunsgi industry to belong to the general group which may include Lalitpur, Chirki and Anagawadi industries.

Acheulian assemblages have also been found in the excavations of open air sites at Gudiyam in Trivellore Taluk[2] and at Attirambakkam,[3] both in Chingleput District of Tamil Nadu and at Gupteshwar near Gwalior in Madhya Pradesh.[4] However, adequate details of these have not yet been published to make comparison with Bhimbetka possible.

CONCLUSION

This brief review of excavated Acheulian sites highlights the scanty nature of the material available for finding out the typlogical and technological variability among the Acheulian industries, and for building up a relative chronology of them. Outside the caves and rock shelters which are few and far between, all material comes from sites located in or along the stream channels where it must have been affected by flowing water in varying degrees. Also, excavated assemblages are sometimes too small to present a reliable picture of the industry and for comparison with other industries. And finally, standardized typological framework and analytical procedures have to be applied to all of them to make any comparative study significantly meaningful.

However, even with these limitations we can see that the Acheulian industries known from excavated sites reveal a considerable diversity and must encompass a long period of time. At least two clear phases of the Acheulian culture can at present be recognized. To the first and earlier phase we can assign the industries from Lalitpur, Adamgarh, Kuliana, Mahadeo Piparia (river bed gravel), Chirki-Nevasa, Anagawadi and Hunsgi. These are characterized by all or most of the following features: high percentage of chopper-chopping tools and bifaces, low percentage of non-biface tools made on flakes, high ratio of handaxes to cleavers, low incidence of blades and Levallois flakes and predominance of stone hammer flaking technique. Among these industries themselves there no doubt exist considerable typological and technological variability and temporal differences, but the data available at present are not sufficient, both in quantity and quality, to bring these out clearly. To the second and later phase can be assigned the industries from rock shelters III F-23 and III F-24 at Bhimbetka and cliff gravel at Mahadeo Piparia. These, especially the industry from Bhimbetka III F-23, are characterized by the absence of chopper-chopping tools, low percentage of bifaces, high ratio of cleavers to handaxes, very high percentage of, and great diversity among non-biface flake tools, high incidence of blades and Levallois flakes and greater use of soft hammer technique.

Now that there is a welcome shift of emphasis in Palaeolithic research to the excavation of sites, especially primary sites, we can reasonably hope that in the coming years there will be considerable improvement and addition to our knowledge of the Acheulian cultures in India.

[1]K. Paddayya, 'Acheulian Occupation site at Hunsgi, Gulbarga District Karnataka—a preliminary report', *Bulletin of the Deccan College Research Institute*. vol. 35 (1975) (in press).

[2]*Indian Archaeology 1963-64—A Review*, p. 19.

[3]*Indian Archaeology 1964-65—A Review*, p. 20-22.

[4]B.B. Lal and K.P. Nautiyal, 'Lower and Middle Paloaelithic Industries in Gwalior', Paper presented to the Seminar on Indian Prehistory, Deccan, College Pune, June 1974.

Use of Caliche as a Chronological and Environmental Tool in the Study of Late Quaternary Formations in Gujarat and Rajasthan[1]

K. T. M. Hegde

Maharaja Sayajirao University of Baroda

[*Received on 6 May 1975*]

THE term caliche was originally used to denote rich sodium nitrate deposits, popularly known as saltpetre, that occur in extensive beds in the rainless districts, between the ridges on the Tarapaca plateau and Antofogasti in Chile. More recently, the term has also been used to denote calcium carbonate concentrations.[1,2] In this paper, we are concerned with the calcium carbonate concentrations found in the late Quaternary alluvial and aeolian stratigraphy of Gujarat and Rajasthan.

The late Quaternary formations in Gujarat and Rajasthan are made up of alluvial and aeolian deposits. The plain of Gujarat is built up of the coalescing alluvial fans brought down by rivers flowing from the hills of central India and Rajasthan. The northern part of this plain and the south-western part of Rajasthan are covered with fossil aeolian sand dunes (FIG. 1).[3]

During the last five years, a Cambridge-Baroda team has been working in this area, investigating the evidence for the chronology of late Quaternary stratigraphy, climatic change and their relationship to the culture of early man. This team-work has yielded interesting

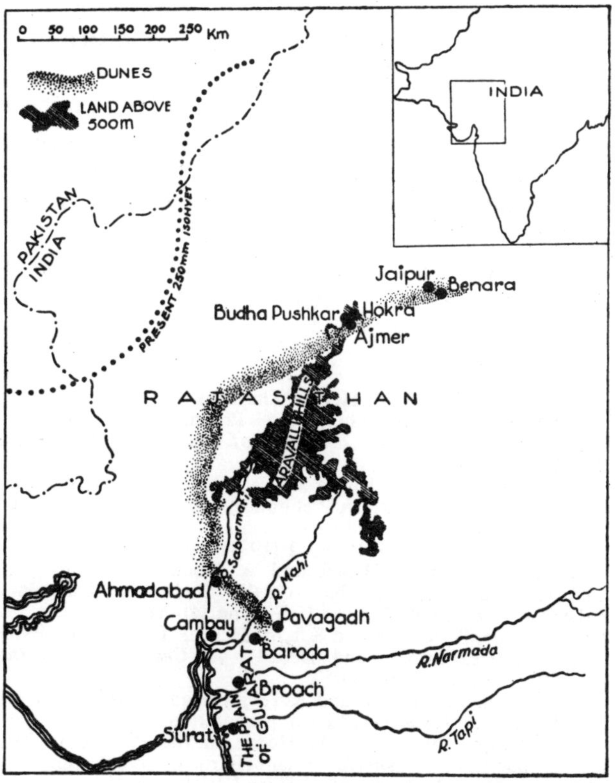

FIG. 1

[1]This work is a part of the Cambridge-Baroda Project. I wish to acknowledge the part played in this research by my colleagues, Dr B. Allchin and Dr A. Goudie. Radiocarbon dating of the caliche samples was very kindly done by Dr V.R. Switsur. My grateful thanks are also due to Professor R.N. Mehta and Dr R.G. West, for their kindness and encouragement, to the Master and Fellows of St. John's College, University of Cambridge, for electing me a Fellow of the College and giving me all facilities to work in Cambridge for a year in 1972 and 1973.

[2]K.W. Butzer, 'Climatic-Geomorphic interpretationof Pleistocene Sediments in the Eurafrican Sub-tropics', Viking Fund Publication No. 36 (New York, 1963), pp. 1–27.

[3]K.W. Butzer, *Environment and Archaeology* (London, 1972), p. 190.

results.[1-5] These results are briefly summarized here with a view to putting the caliche concentrations in the alluvial and aeolian stratigraphy into proper perspective.

The Narmada, Mahi and Sabarmati and their tributaries, flowing through the plain of Gujarat, cut vertically and deeply into the alluvium. In some parts of these valleys, the sections measure more than 40 m and show clear signs of recent stream rejuvenation. In all these river-valleys there are two clearly defined terraces. The upper terrace corresponds to the general level of the plain. The lower terrace is contained within the valley cut by the upper terrace.

ALLUVIAL STRATIGRAPHY

Examination of the sections exposed by the rivers indicates that the main features in their stratigraphy occur fairly regularly in the same sequential order. Near the bottom of the sections, up to a metre or two above the winter water level, they consist of hard clay. In the proximity of the hills, the clay is overlain by an indurated gravel layer.

Above the gravel is a series of laminated silts, weathered at the top to form a black soil, popularly referred to as the black cotton soil. About 30 km down stream from the hills, the gravel gradually disappears and silts lie directly on the basal clay. Within the silts there is a predominant disconformity in the form of a buried land surface. It is prominently seen in the sections of all the rivers and their tributaries, as a three to four-metre deep reddish-brown band, about 10 to 12 m below the surface of the plain (FIG. 2). Chemical analysis of samples obtained from this deposit has shown that it is a mature pedocal soil profile, a product of deep weathering of the alluvial silt *in situ.*[6]

The gravel deposit has yielded a number of handaxes, cleavers, choppers and crude flakes, the tools of Early Palaeolithic man.[7-9] Some of these tools do not appear to be rolled. The gravel deposit is therefore either contemporaneous with or immediately post date the tools. On the black cotton soil numerous Mesolithic sites have been found.[10,11,12] The tool assemblages of these sites consist of blades and composite points like triangles, trapeziums and lunates. At a number of these sites we found a large number of the microliths on the surface of the soil while a small number of them were found embedded deeply within the soil. Chemical analysis of the black cotton soil revealed that it is rich in clay and humus.[13,14] It

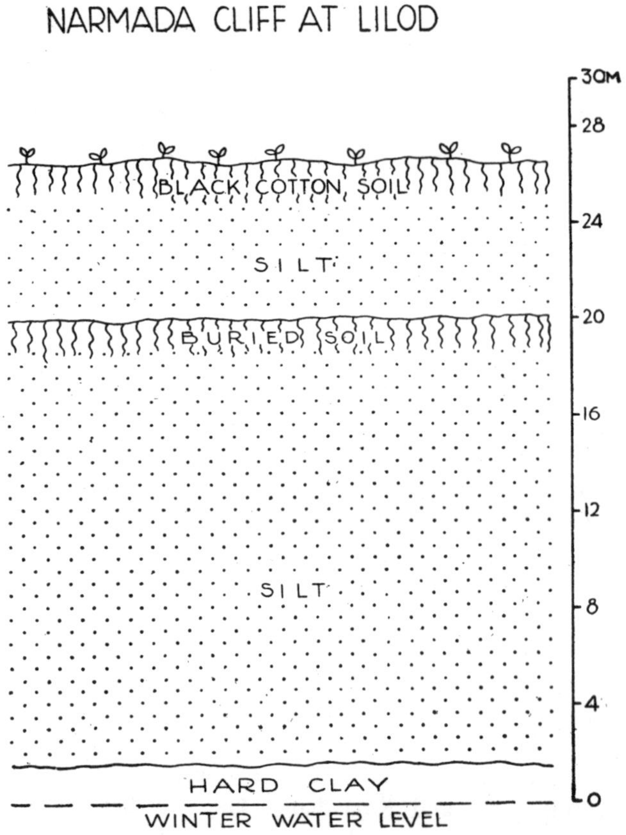

FIG. 2

therefore develops deep polygonal fissures when it dries up and hardens during the summer months. Evi-

[1]B. Allchin and K.T.M. Hegde, 'The Background to Early Man in the Narmada Valley, Gujarat: A Preliminary Report of the 1969 Season's Field Work', *Journal of the M.S. University of Baroda*, vol. 17, no. 1, pp. 141–45.

[2]B. Allchin, K.T.M. Hegde and A. Goudie, 'The Background to Early Man in Gujarat: A Preliminary Report of the Cambridge-Baroda Expedition, 1970–71 season', *Journal of the M.S. University of Baroda*, vol. 19, no. 1 (1971), pp. 15–33.

[3]B. Allchin, K.T.M. H egde and A. Goudie, 'Prehistory and Environmental Change: a Note on the Budha Pushkar Basin, Rajasthan', *Man*, vol. 7, no. 4 (1972), pp.541–64.

[4]A. Goudie, B. Allchin and K.T.M. Hegde, 'The Former Extension of the Great Indian Sand Desert', *The Geographical Journal*, vol. 139, pt. 2 (1973), pp. 243-57.

[5]B. Allchin, A. Goudie and K.T.M. Hegde, *Environment and Early Man in Western India* (in preparation).

[6]G.J. Wainwright and K.T.M. Hegde, in *The Pleistocene Deposits of the Lower Narmada River* (Baroda, 1964), pp. 13–45 and figs. 9,10 and 11 and pls. VII and VIII.

[7]B. Allchin, K.T.M. Hegde and A. Goudie, *op. cit.* (1971), p.18.

[8]B. Subbarao, *Personality of India* (Baroda, 1958), p. 62 and fig. 15.

[9]H.D. Sankalia, *Investigations into Prehistoric Archeology of Gujarat* (Baroda, 1946), pp. 13–48.

[10]B. Allchin and K.T.M. Hegde, *op. cit.* (1970), pp. 141–45.

[11]B. Subbarao, *op. cit.*, p. 75.

[12]R.N. Mehta, 'Stone Age Sites in the Valia Taluka and Mangrol Taluka of Broach and Surat Districts', *Journal of the Oriental Institute, Baroda*, vol. 17, no. 2 (1967), pp. 142–48.

[13]G.J. Wainwright and K.T.M. Hegde, *op. cit.*, pp. 16–20.

[14]K.T.M. Hegde, 'Laboratory Studies in Jokha Midden Soil Samples' *Puratattva*, no. 3 (1969–70), pp. 9–14.

dently, the artifacts had found their way into the interstices of the soil through the fissures. It is therefore possible to observe that the black cotton soil was formed before the Mesolithic hunters came into the plain.

In the Narmada valley we have observed a black soil, similar to the black cotton soil of the plain, now being formed on the freshly deposited alluvium. For example, at a number of meander bends of the river, the current strikes the north bank and is turned back. This produces a helical flow of much higher potential, which enables the river to cut deeply into the alluvium. As on the opposite edge of the stream there is less turbulence, the silt eroded from the north bank is deposited near the south bank, first in the form of a point bar. The bar gradually grows in the downward direction of the stream. As vegetation begins to grow on the bar it becomes stabilized and attracts more silt and gets extended in all directions. The trough between the bar and the south bank is gradually filled. On such recently deposited alluvium, we have observed the development of veneer of a black soil, whose eluvial and illuvial characteristics are comparable to that of the black cotton soil of the plain. On the banks of the Jorvan river, near Champaner(70° 35′ E, 22° 29′ N), we have found a mature black cotton soil, that was formed during the last 400 years.[1] Therefore it is possible to observe that the black cotton soil of the plain of Gujarat was formed in a climate comparable to that of the present, under the natural vegetation cover of coarse grass and brush wood, which can still be seen here and there on the plain.

AEOLIAN STRATIGRAPHY

In the northern part of the plain of Gujarat and south-western part of Rajasthan, on the windward slopes of the Aravalli Hills, we have seen, from Pavagadh near Baroda to Benara near Jaipur, over a stretch of 700 km sand dunes (FIG. 1). These dunes are large continental sand shields formed under a sparse vegetation cover which will permit extensive sand movement over a wide area. There is little sand movement within these dune fields now. They are covered with kankar, above which grow acacia scrub and grass. They are all deeply gullied. These features indicate that they are fossil sand dunes.[2,3] Our investigations in western Rajasthan show that sand-dunes are now being formed only in those areas where the mean annual rainfall is less than 250 mm and when the land is covered with inadequate vegetation[4] (FIG. 1). The mean annual rainfall from Pavagadh to Benara at the present, ranges from 900 to 600 mm. It is therefore possible to observe that when there was large scale sand movement in this area and the dunes were being formed, the mean annual rainfall was less than 250 mm.

The surface of the dunes is covered with kankar. It is a form of caliche. It appears as a crust of sand grains cemented together by a concentration of calcium carbonate. On a number of these dunes we have found Mesolithic sites on their kankarized surface.[5,6] It appears therefore that on these dunes sand movement of any great intensity has been absent since the formation of kankar on them. On the stabilized dune tops Mesolithic hunters came and camped.

On some of these dunes, particularly those close to the villages, we have noticed reactivated sand crests formed due to over grazing. However, where such crests have not been recently disturbed, we have also noticed re-formation of a thin crust of kankar on them. This is significant. It shows that the process of calcification of the surface sand on the dunes has taken place continuously from pre-Mesolithic times to the present day.

Buried within the dunes in a 75 to 80 cm deep 7·5 YR 4/4 reddish-brown grading into 10 YR 5/8 yellowish-brown soil profile (FIG. 3). This soil is exposed in the rain gullies and sometimes on the degraded surface of the dunes. At some places it is seen to stand out like compact stumps or knolls. Sometimes the entire profile of the soil is thus exposed. Chemical analysis of the soil samples obtained from sites near Pavagadh, Budha Pushkar and Benara has yielded interesting results (TABLE 2). The data is discussed below in some detail. It may suffice to mention here that this soil stretching from Pavagadh to Benara was formed under the same climatic condition at the same time. The illuviation characteristics of the soil show that this climate was significantly wet and the soil supported abundant flora. It was therefore of great interest to the Cambridge-Baroda team to see if this soil was associated with any of the Palaeolithic cultures. There are a number of perennial fresh water and salt water lakes close to the western slopes of the Aravalli Hills. Some of those are shown as surrounded by sand dunes in the survey sheets.

[1] K.T.M. Hegde, 'A Recently Formed Black Cotton Soil in Gujarat', *Journal of the M.S. University of Baroda*, vol. 19, no. 1 (1971), pp. 41–43.

[2] B. Allchin, K.T.M. Hegde, and A. Goudie, *op. cit.* (1971), p.18.

[3] A. Goudie, B. Allchin and K.T.M. Hedge, *op. cit.* (1973), p.245.

[4] *Ibid.*, pp. 248–49.

[5] B. Allchin, K.T.M. Hegde and A. Goudie, *op. cit.* (1971), pp. 23–24.

[6] B.Allchin, K.T.M. Hegde and A. Goudie, *op. cit.* (1972), pp. 544–45.

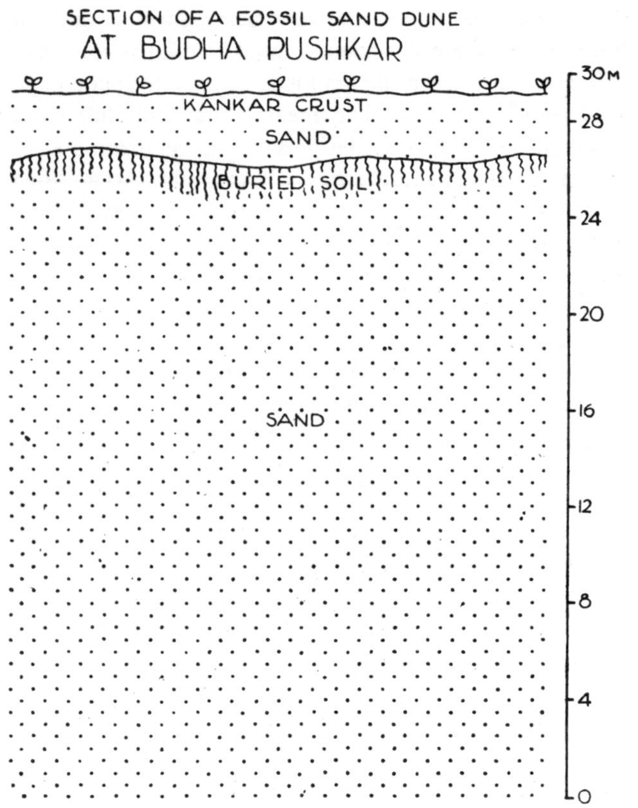

FIG. 3

These dunes, particularly those parts of these dunes that were deflated and where the buried soil is exposed, were, therefore, systematically explored. This study brought to light a number of Middle Palaeolithic and Upper Palaeolithic sites in association with the soil at Budha Pushkar and Hokara (FIG. 1).[1,2]

Thus we have stone tools at the beginning, in the middle and at the end of the sequence of events responsible for the geomorphic features seen in the area. But these tools are silent. They do not tell us dates of these events nor do they tell us about the intensity of climatic fluctuations during the late Quaternary period. Unfortunately, these alluvial and aeolian deposits do not contain fossil bones. Our recent palynological study on the samples obtained from the alluvial buried soil in the Narmada, Mahi and Sabarmati valleys has shown only fragmentary, unidentifiable pollen grains. Therefore we attempted the construction of a temporal framework for the alluvial stratigraphy by radiocarbon dating of the caliche nodules found concentrated in the illuvial zone of the buried soil in the alluvium.

[1]B. Allchin, K.T.M. Hedge and A. Goudie, *op. cit.* (1972), pp. 547–53.
[2]B. Allchin and A. Goudie, 'Pushkar: Prehistory and Climatic change in Western India', *World Archaeology*, vol. 5, no. 3, (1974), p.361.

RADIOCARBON DATING OF CALICHE

We have noted above that the buried soil in the alluvial stratigraphy of the plain of Gujarat is a product of deep weathering of the alluvial silt *in situ*. Chemical analysis of samples collected from this soil has shown that there has been considerable leaching in the upper part of the soil indicative of heavier precipitation when this soil was in formation.[3] The deep profile of the soil indicates that this climate remained steady over a long period of time. During this period, the soil forming processes were not interrupted by inundation. It is therefore possible to observe that the heavier precipitation came down as evenly distributed rainfall over a prolonged rainy season each year. Among the minerals redeposited in the illuvial zone of the soil is calcium carbonate precipitated as nodules. The following observations indicate that the radiocarbon assay of these nodules could indicate approximate formation time of the buried soil:

1. The soil is a product of silt weathered *in situ*.
2. The silt was derived from basalt. Therefore, the minerals that weathered to yield calcium carbonate were calcic feldspars like anorthite, zoisite, etc.
3. The following reactions illustrate hydrolysis and carbonation of anorthite, $CaOAl_2O_32SIO_2$.

$$CaOAl_2O_32SiO_2+3H_2O=Ca(OH)_2+Al_2O_3SiO_2H_2O$$
$$H_2O \quad +CO_2=H_2CO_3$$
$$Ca(OH)_2 \quad +H_2CO_3=Ca(HCO_3)_2+2H_2O$$

$Ca(HCO_3)_2$ is calcium bicarbonate. It is stable in the presence of carbonic acid. From the eluvial zone of the soil, where it is formed, it percolates down into the illuvial zone where, the available carbonic acid being insufficient, it decomposes into calcium carbonate and gets precipitated of nodules.

$$Ca\ (HCO_3)_2 = CaCO_3 + CO_2 + H_2O$$

The carbon in this carbonate represents the soil atmosphere carbon dioxide of the time at which this soil was formed.

As this soil profile is buried underneath 10 to 12 m of alluvium, it is not likely to be affected by the percolating calcium bicarbonate formed in the black cotton soil at the top. It is found precipitated as calcium carbonate within 2·5 m from the surface of this soil.[4]

To collect caliche samples for this study, the lower Narmada valley between Dhegam and Sinor was divided into four segments. Similarly the Mahi valley was divided into three segments and the Sabarmati valley

[3]G.J. Wainwright and K.T.M. Hedge, *op. cit.* (1964), p.28.
[4]G.J. Wainwright and K.T.M. Hegde, *op. cit.* (1964), pp. 16–20.

into two. From each of these segments, one site was chosen to collect the soil samples. These sites were close to the following villages: Dhegam, Lilod, Deroli and Sinor in the Narmada valley; Dabka, Vasad and Ahima in the Mahi valley and Hirpura and Pethapura in the Sabarmati valley. At all these sites, the river sections were first explored to locate the most suitable position of the vertical profile of the soil, free from talus or vegetation. Then this selected position of the soil was reached from the bottom of the section by cutting steps out into the alluvium. The profile of the soil was then scraped to a depth of 15 to 20 cm. From the cleaned profile, soil samples were collected in the form of a column, beginning from the bottom, at an interval of 20 cm.

In the laboratory, carbonate content of each of these samples was determined using schrotter flask. The samples yielding the highest carbonate value was used for radiocarbon dating. The results are given in table 1.[1]

TABLE 1
RADIOCARBON DATES OF THE CALICHE NODULES OBTAINED FROM THE BURIED SOIL IN THE ALLUVIUM

Site	Latitude/Longitude	Laboratory number of the sample	C^{14} date in years B.P.
Dhegam	21°42′N/72°55′E	Q - 1104	22,450 ± 550
Lilod	21°52′N/73°14′E	Q - 1106	21,650 ± 500
Deroli	21°55′N/73°15′E	Q - 1107	24,478 ± 700
Sinor	21°55′N/73°20′E	Q - 1108	17,426 ± 400
Dabka	21°54′N/72°56′E	Q - 1109	22,600 ± 550
Vasad	22°28′N/73°07′E	Q - 1110	18,250 ± 400
Ahima	22°36′N/73°12′E	Q - 1111	22,150 ± 600
Pethapura	23°36′N/72°41′E	Q - 1112	20,400 ± 550
Hirpura	23°11′N/72°50′B	Q - 1113	21,500 ± 500

The dates suggest that this soil was formed over a long period of time extending from 17000 to 24000 B.P. The results are consistent within this bracket of time. Yet, at the present stage of our research, these dates are considered here only as an indication of the approximate time of formation of the soil. Further work on radiocarbon dating of more calcihe samples obtained from the entire profile from a number of sites is now planned. These studies may reveal a much broader bracket of time for the formation of the site.

[1]K.T.M. Hegde and V.R. Switsur, 'Radiocarbon Dating of the Buried Soil in the Lower Narmada Valley,' *Current Science*, vol. 42, no. 17 (1973), pp. 607–9.

CALICHE INDICATES CLIMATIC CHANGE

The buried soil within the dunes separates two phases of aridity and represents an interval of significant wet climate. Results of the chemical analysis of the soil samples obtained from Pavagadh, Budha Pushkar and Benara are given in Table 2 (see below, p. 42)

From the data given below in Table 2, it is possible to observe the following:

1. In all the three profiles, the eluvial zone of the soil appears to be eroded away. And what is left of the illuvial zone of the soil, in the three profiles, measures 75 to 100 cm. It is a deeply weathered profile. During the last three decades much field and experimental data bearing on soil weathering rates have been collected. A review of these data indicates: (a) the rate of soil formation depends mainly on climate; (b) the increase in depth of weathering is an exponential function of time. Under humid tropical climate the rate of weathering in sandy deposits is indicated as 10 to 30 cm in 1000 years. This weathering rate decreases with the increasing thickness of the soil profile.[2] The buried soil under discussion is bereft of its eluvial zone. Nevertheless, it measures 75 to 100 cm. It is therefore possible to observe that this soil took a long time to form.
2. In all the three profiles the soil is faintly acidic and completely free from caliche deposits. This decalcified nature of the soil is very interesting. Calcic feldspars in the dune sand weather in the same manner as in the alluvium. They undergo hydrolysis and carbonation. But in this dune soil, calcium carbonate was not precipitated. All the calcium bicarbonate that was formed was leached away from the soil profile. For this to happen, there must have been abundance of moisture and carbon dioxide in the soil atmosphere, which form carbonic acid and in whose presence, calcium bicarbonate is leached away. The abundance of moisture within the soil atmosphere indicates a significantly wet climate when this soil was in formation. Abundance of carbon dioxide in the soil atmosphere indicates that the soil supported plentiful flora and fauna. Carbon dioxide in the soil atmosphere is formed by root respiration and oxidation of decaying organic matter. Thus, the absence of caliche in this soil is an evidence of high precipitation when this soil was in formation.

To visualize how much wet this climate was, we may compare the illuviation characteristics of this soil

[2]Z. Kukla, *Geology of Recent Deposits* (Prague, 1971).

TABLE 2

ILLUVIATION CHARACTERISTICS OF THE BURIED SOIL WITHIN THE DUNES

Site	Sample	Depth in cm	P H	Carbonate %	Humus %	Iron %	Phosphate
Pavagarh	1	Top of the Profile	7·2	1·40	0·81	0·889	0·332
	2	15	6·8	0·80	0·88	0·826	0·324
	3	30	6·8	Nil	0·56	0·724	0·289
	4	45	6·2	Nil	0·24	0·731	0·262
	5	60	6·2	Nil	0·20	0·628	0·251
	6	75	6·4	Nil	0·12	0·609	0·248
	7	90	6·7	Nil	0·06	0·548	0·230
	8	105	6·9	1·50	Nil	0·346	0·221
	9	120	7·1	4·20	Nil	0·337	0·222
	10	135	7·3	5·90	Nil	0·342	0·210
Eluvial zone of the soil is indicated as eroded away. Samples 1 to 8 constitute the illuvial zone of the soil. Samples 9-10 are from the parent material.							
Budha Pushkar	1	Top of the Profile	7·1	2·30	0·73	0·678	0·268
	2	15	6·9	1·80	0·86	0·621	0·264
	3	30	6·6	Nil	0·41	0·605	0·257
	4	45	6·5	Nil	0·42	0·604	0·238
	5	60	6·2	Nil	0·21	0·428	0.221
	6	75	6·4	Nil	0·16	0·431	0·208
	7	90	6·8	2·08	0·18	0·298	0·204
	8	105	6·9	4·01	0·06	0·296	0·200
	9	120	6·9	4·08	0·07	0·287	0·196
Benara	1	Top of the Profile	6·7	2·02	0·62	0·762	0·310
	2	15	6·6	1·09	0·63	0·754	0·318
	3	30	6·4	Nil	0·48	0·726	0·286
	4	45	6·5	Nil	0·42	0·561	0·264
	5	60	6·6	Nil	0·21	0·538	0·257
	6	75	7·0	3·04	Nil	0·361	0·203

with those of the kankarized surface of the dunes. The weathering characteristics of the kankarized surface of the dunes is given in Table 3.

The above results show a rich accumulation of caliche on the surface of the dunes. This calcium carbonate has been derived from the weathering calcic feldspars in the sand. Its concentration at the surface indicates inadequate moisture and carbon dioxide in the weathering horizon. There is so little of carbonic acid formation in the weathering horizon that it is incapable of moving the calcium bicarbonate down. It is therefore decomposed at the surface. The resulting accumulation of calcium carbonate cements the sand grains to form the kankar crust.

We have noted above that the process of kankar formation on the surface of the dunes has been continuous from pre-Mesolithic times to the present day. We have also noted that the kankar crust and scrub vegetation on the dunes indicate stabilization of sand and more precipitation in the region than that prevailing at the time when the sand beneath the kankar crust accumulated.

TABLE 3

WEATHERING CHARACTERISTICS OF THE CALCIFIED (KANKAR) SAND ON THE SURFACE OF THE DUNES

Site	Sample No.	Depth in cm	P H	Carbonate %	Humus %	Iron %	Phosphate %
Pavagarh	1	Top of the crust	7·7	42·00	0·06	0·342	0·226
	2	15	7·2	28·00	Nil	0·338	0·194
Budha Pushkar	1	Top of the crust	7·5	38·20	0·04	0·286	0·221
	2	10—15	7·4	21·60	Nil	0·284	0·194
Benara	1	Top of the crust	7·4	35·60	Nil	0·364	0·206
	2	10—15	7·2	23·00	Nil	0·348	0·204

The mean annual precipitation from Pavagadh to Benara, at the present, ranges from 900 to 600 mm and the mean annual rainy days vary from 45 to 30 days. This rainfall is producing kankar on the dune surface. It is therefore possible to observe that the mean annual precipitation and the number of mean annual rainy days necessary for the formation of the deeply weathered, decalcified, buried soil in the dunes must have been considerably higher than the present mean annual precipitation and the number of mean annual rainy days. We have noted above that this soil is associated with the Middle Palaeolithic artefacts. The Middle Palaeolithic Age therefore was a wet phase.

This is supported by the observations in the Central Luni Valley where, the Middle Palaeolithic artefacts have been found associated with the coarse gravel deposits of the river.[1] The valley was subsequently choked up with sand. At the time when the Middle Palaeolithic man was active in this area, the Luni was a freely flowing river, with a current strength that was competant to transport pebble and gravel.

Summing up, it is possible to observe:

(1) There has been a relatively moist climate in Gujarat and Rajasthan in the Recent period. During this period, the black cotton soil of the Gujarat plain was formed. In the northern part of the plain and south-western part of Rajasthan the sand dunes were stabilized under kankar and vegetation. Radiocarbon dates of the lake sediments in Rajasthan indicate that this relatively moist climate began in the region about 9000 B.P.[2] Sometime during this period the Mesolithic hunters became active in the area.

(2) The period preceding the Recent was arid. The rivers in the plain were aggrading; they appear to have flowed in broad shallow channels as braided streams. In the northern part of the plain and south-western part of Rajasthan the mean annual precipitation was less than 250 mm. There was an inadequate flora carpet. This resulted in sand movement and its accumulation on the dunes.

(3) The period preceding was humid. The deeply weathered soil buried within the alluvium of the plain of Gujarat was formed in this period. Stratigraphic position of this soil and that of the buried soil in the dunes suggest that they were coeval. We have seen above that the illuviation characteristics of both these soils suggest that when they were in formation, there was much heavier rainfall in the region than that there is at the present time. Middle Palaeolithic Man was active on the soil in the dunes. Radiocarbon assay of caliche nodules in the buried soil of the alluvium suggests that this soil was in formation about 24000 to 17000 years ago. Further radiometric dating of the soil samples is planned to determine the beginning and the end of the period when this soil was in formation.

(4) The period preceding was arid. The rivers in the plain were aggrading at this time and in the north, sand dunes were in formation.

(5) During the period preceding, the rivers in the plain carried a much stronger current than they do at the present time. The rivers then brought down cobble, pebble and gravel. Early Palaeolithic man was a contemporary of this period.

Thus using caliche, we have been able to construct a chronological framework for the alluvial stratigraphy of the plain of Gujarat. We have also obtained an inkling of the climatic fluctuation during the late Quaternary period in Gujarat and Rajasthan.

[1] V.N. Mishra, 'Middle Stone Age in Rajasthan', in *La Prehistoire: Problems et tendencies* (Paris, 1968), p. 298.

[2] G. Singh, R.D. Joshi and A.B. Singh, 'Stratigraphic and Radiocarbon Evidence for the Age and Development of Three Salt Lake Deposits in Rajasthan, India', *Quarternary Research* vol. 2, no. 4 (1972), pp. 496–505.

Settlement Archaeology of Inamgaon

M. K. Dhavalikar

Deccan College Postgraduate and Research Institute, Pune 6

[*Received on 6 May 1975*]

THE excavations at Inamgaon (District Pune, Maharashtra) have brought to light an extensive chalcolithic settlement which began in 1600 B.C. and came to an end around 700 B.C. The ancient site is situated on the right bank of the Ghod, a tributary of the Bhima, which, in its turn, belongs to the Krishna system (FIG.1). The ancient site is spread over an area of five hectares and is thus probably one of the largest chalcolithic sites so far discovered in Maharashtra. The semi-arid climate of the region in which the site is situated has, to a considerable extent, been responsible for the survival of the evidence, more particularly of the mud houses of the people. Our aim in excavating the site for six seasons from 1968-75 was to recover the house plans and expose, as far as possible, the ancient settlement. In retrospect we feel that our work, albeit circumscribed by time and money, has been amply rewarded. We have been able to lay bare about sixty houses of different periods with the result that it is now possible to study the ancient settlement pattern at the site.

CULTURE SEQUENCE

The excavations revealed a sequence of three cultures: the Malwa, the Early Jorwe and the Late Jorwe. The first settlers at the site were the people from Malwa who occupied the site about 1600 B.C. Their occupation came to end around 1400 B.C. when a new culture, termed as the Early Jorwe Culture appeared on the site. Both these cultures remained overlapped for some time. It may, however be stated that elsewhere in Maharashtra the Jorwe Culture begins around 1300 B.C. but it appears to have come into being at Inamgaon earlier by a century or more as indicated by radiocarbon dates.[1]

The Early Jorwe Period (*circa* 1400-1000 B.C.) ushered in an era of prosperity. The Jorwe Culture, which has been found in different parts of Maharashtra actually represents the Early Jorwe phase. At Inamgaon, besides the Early phase, tangible evidence for a Late phase of the Jorwe Culture has also been found. So far only a few late Jorwe sites have been discovered in the Bhima valley.[2] Elsewhere in Maharashtra, the Jorwe habitation comes to an abrupt end around 1000 B.C. the reason for which may possibly be the marked deterioration in the climate which became more arid. The climatic change is represented stratigraphically in the weathered layer at Nevasa.[3] Although the Jorwe farmers deserted their habitations in the Tapti and the Pravara-Godavari valleys about 1000 B.C., they continued to survive in the Bhima valley where the climatic change may not have been very drastic. None the less, they too were affected by these environmental changes and had to face poverty which is so well reflected in their cultural equipment at Inamgaon. On the basis of

[1] M.K. Dhavalikar' 'Development and Decline of the Deccan Chalcolithic', in D. P. Agrawal and A. Ghosh (eds.), *Radiocarbon and Indian Archaeology* (Bombay, 1973), pp. 139–41.

[2] A. Sundara, 'Protohistoric sites in the Bhima valley, *Journal of the Karnatak University* (Soc. Sc.), vol. 4 (1971), pp. 2–23.

[3] G.G. Mujumdar and S.N. Rajaguru, Comments on Soils as Environmental and Chronological tool, in V.N. Misra and M.S. Mate (eds.), *Indian Prehistory: 1964* (Poona, 1965), p. 152.

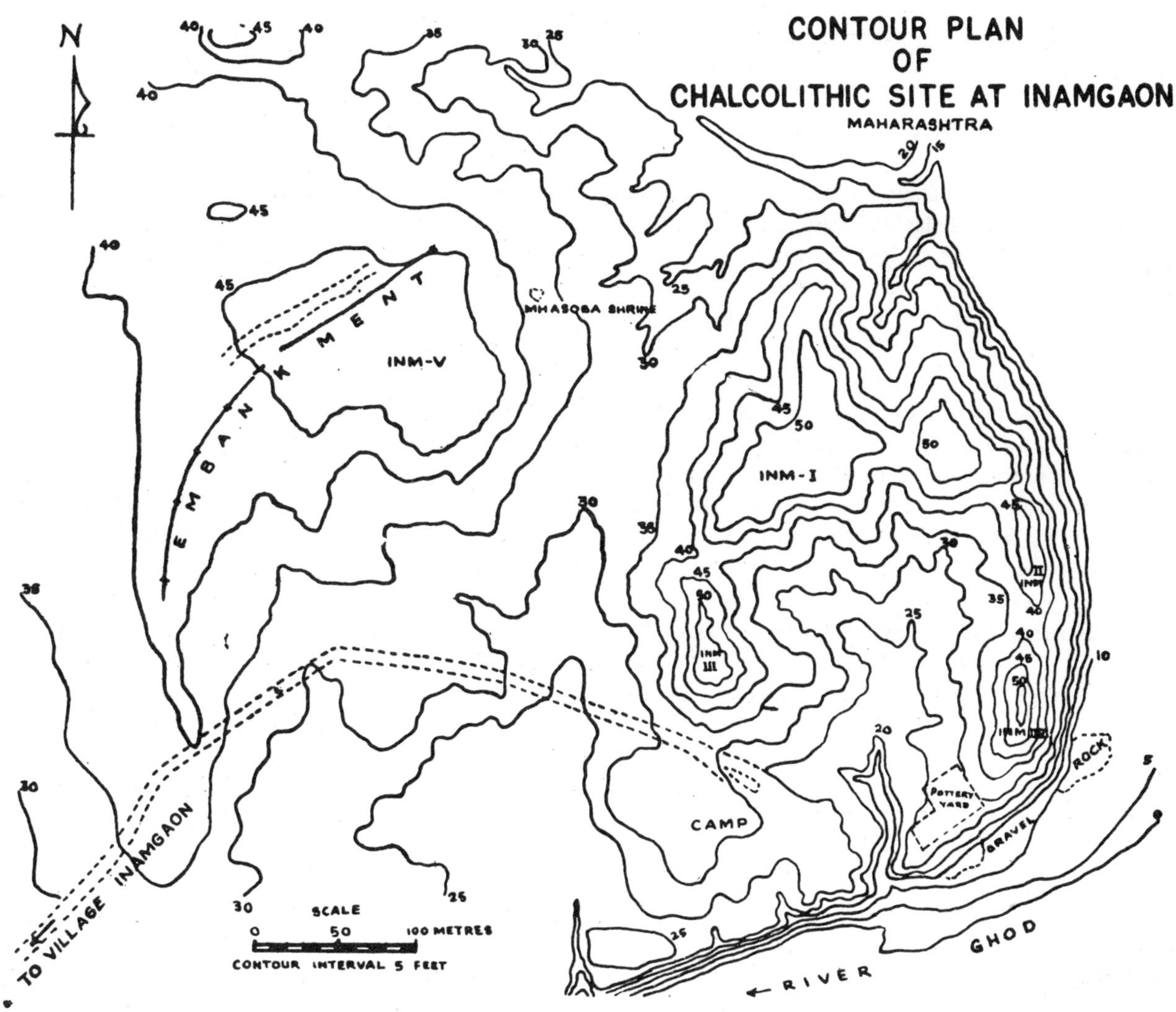

FIG. 1

stratigraphical evidence the Late Jorwe phase can be dated to *circa* 1000-700 B.C.

ECOLOGY

Geologically, the region around Inamgaon forms part of the Deccan trap and the outcrop of the columnar basalt is to be seen on the other bank of the river opposite the ancient habitation. The region consists of stony uplands and rugged valleys, but towards its river boundaries slope into more open plains. The uplands have, in some cases, rich tracts of black cotton soil which is very productive even with a scanty rainfall. The area along the river up to its confluence with Bhima has a fair share of rich black soil but for which the soil cover is very thin. Consequently the region is throughout sparsely wooded, and the vegetation cover is Xyrophytic : *acacia, caparis,* tamarind etc. It was, however, more wooded; some fifty years ago wild boar and deer roamed here. But in recent times a serious depletion of vegetal cover has taken place as a result of felling trees and clearing land for agriculture and overgrazing which, in its turn, has affected the fauna. The region is now classed as semi-arid because of scanty rainfall which averages 40-42 cm. The picture, however, is now changed because of the construction of a dam on the Ghod some 20 km upstream at Chinchani which irrigates large tracts of land on either bank of the river at Inamgaon and the surrounding region. The principal crops today are *Jowar* (*Sorghum vulgare*), *Bajra* (*Penicillar spicata*), pulses, *Kulith* (*Dolichos biflorus*) and oilseeds such as *til, kardi* and *alshi* while wheat and very rarely rice is also grown in small carefully tended plots which are irrigated.

SETTLEMENT PATTERN

As already observed, the ancient site at Inamgaon is one of the most extensive chalcolithic sites in Maharashtra, and is also the only site of its kind where excavations have been carried out on such a large scale (FIG. 1). In the course of six seasons' work we have been able to lay bare sixty houses of different periods. Of these obviously, a majority (39) belong to the final phase (III) of occupation whereas a few ones are of the Early Jorwe (II) and the Malwa Period (I). The earliest settlers at the site first chose a spot quite close to the river, just on the right bank as the location of INM II shows. Nevertheless, the Malwa habitation was quite extensive for the remains of this period have been found in all localities except on INM V. In all likelihood the pioneering farmers came from Malwa in different waves from *circa* 1600 B.C. onwards. They seem to have been attracted by large tracts of black soil and the perennial source of water in the Ghod. Another important factor is the large pool of water in the river where the massive columnar basalts on the left bank at the site form a sort of barrier to the flow of the river. Even now when the region, time and again, is in the grip of famine as a result of scanty rainfall, the water in the pool at the site is always sufficient for the surrounding villages.

There does not appear to be any proper planning in the Malwa settlement, for the houses, though large and spacious, were situated close to each other and even dwelling pits were dug by the side of mud houses. The pit houses, however, disappear in the succeeding period (II). The Early Jorwe houses were large rectangular structures and there appears to be some modicum of planning of the settlement during this period (FIG. 2). The houses were situated about a metre and half from each other, the intervening space forming a sort of road or lane as at present. The Early Jorwe settlement was very extensive: it was spread over the whole of the site, save INM II which was occupied only during Period I. The alignment of the houses suggests that it was probably a linear settlement which is also corroborated by the rectangular shape of all the mounds except INM

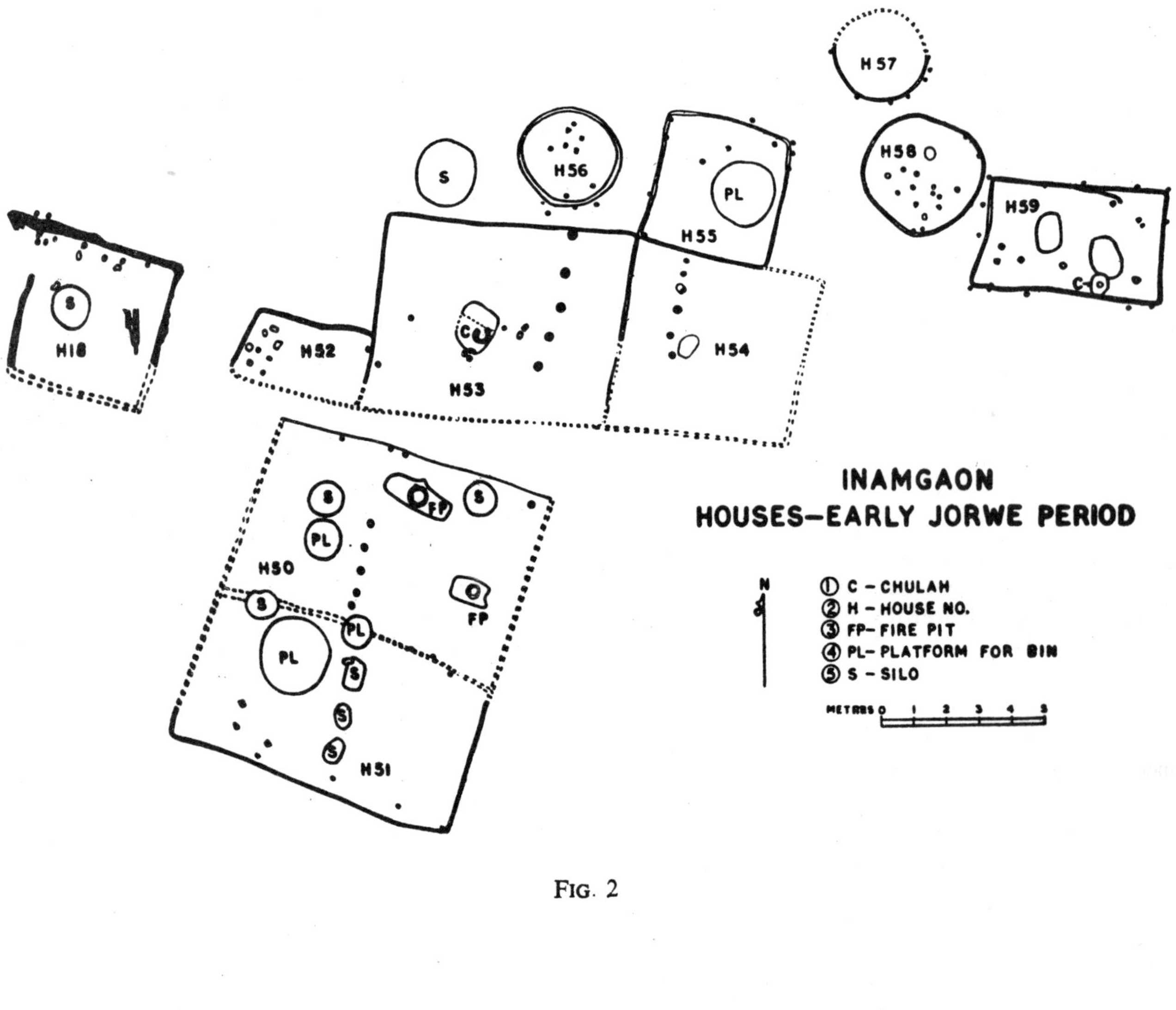

FIG. 2

V which is some what circular. With the increase in population which must have crossed one thousand mark during Period II (Early Jorwe) the habitation extended all over the present site except on INM II which is a relatively low lying mound and may have served as a passage for going to the river and also may have constituted the eastward extension of the road passing through the gap between INM I and INM IV. INM V which is located at a distance of 150 m west of the settlement came to be occupied only during the Early Jorwe phase and was also abandoned after it. It is indeed enigmatic that some people of this period should have chosen to be away from the main habitation area. The shape of INM V is rather circular and indicates that it was a nucleated settlement composed of closely spaced units. The occupants of this area were no doubt the men of means because the embankment on its west was constructed to protect their habitation from the river floods. Unfortunately much of the area has been dug out by local people for earth and our excavation in the small undisturbed area on the periphery also did not yield anything significant.

The size of the settlement shrunk during the Late Jorwe period (III) possibly owing to the adverse conditions caused by a gradual decrease in the rainfall pattern[1] and INM II and V remained unoccupied. The house plan now undergoes a drastic change; the large rectangular houses of the preceding period are no more to be seen; they are replaced by small round huts (FIG. 3). The Late Jorwe habitation was a nucleated settlement with clusters of round houses and the entire habitation from above would have looked like a veritable beehive. The huts were tightly spaced units, almost nestling with each other and the open space in between the two huts was hardly a metre. Considering the fact that in a traditional Indian house the most important part is not the house but the courtyard where most of the family's life is lived, it is surprising that only a few Late Jorwe houses have a courtyard. It therefore seems highly likely that each cluster of huts had a common courtyard which was used for private as well community purposes.

EMBANKMENT

A huge diversionary embankment wall (240 m long and 2·25 m wide) was constructed during the Early Jorwe Period (FIG. 1). It was built near the INMV mound, in a south—north-east direction. A channel 4 m wide and 3·50 m deep was dug almost parallel to it. The wall was constructed of rubble, set in mud mortar at the base, whereas the upper part may have been earthen for which the earth dug from the channel may have been

[1]Dhavalikar, *op. cit*, pp. 143–44.

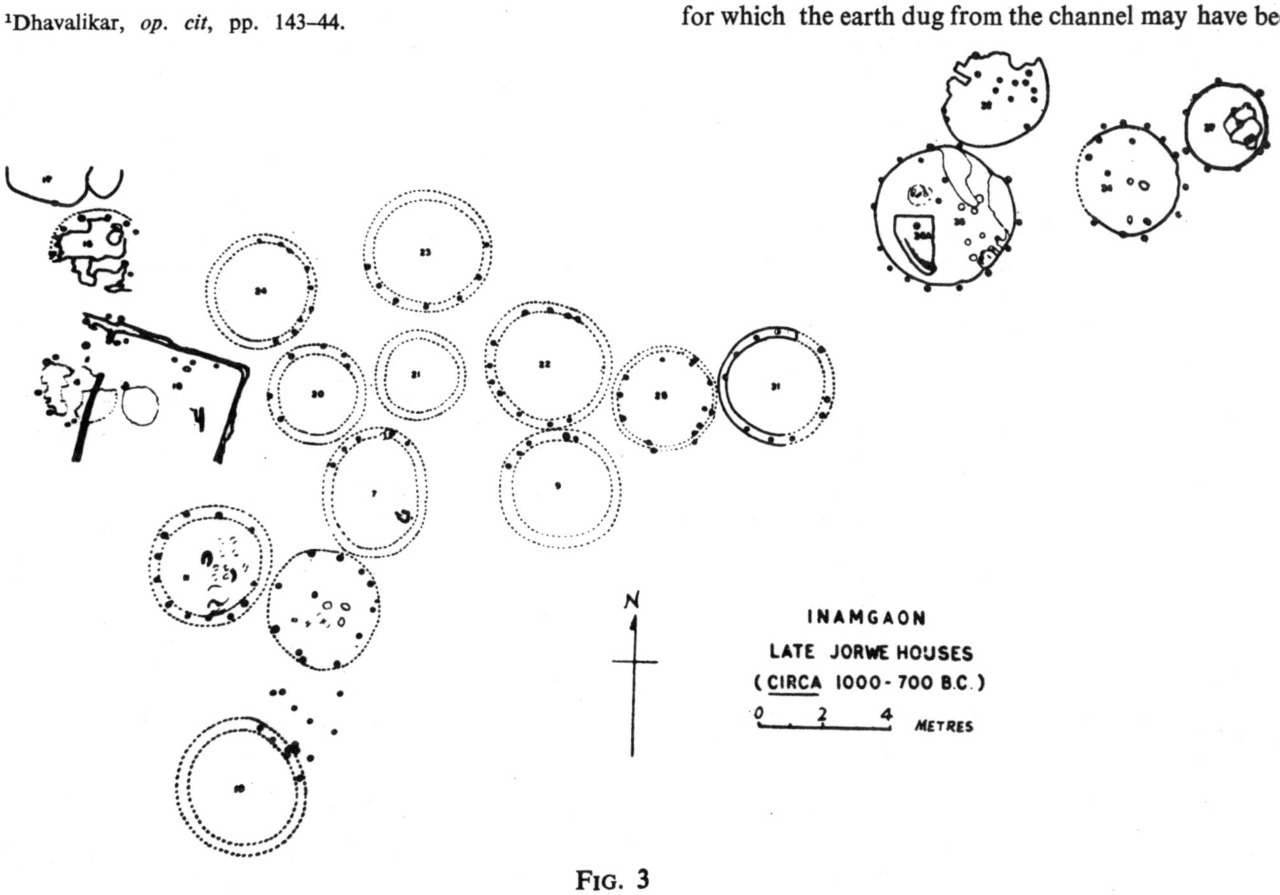

FIG. 3

used. The channel in its southern end almost joins the large feeder stream of the right bank of the river so that flood water from the river could be easily siphoned through the channel. In all probability, the water from the channel was used for irrigating the low lying fields nearby, or else it could have been drained through another stream near the southern end of the channel.

SOCIAL STRATIFICATION

A distinguishing feature of the pattern of the chalcolithic settlement is the location of the craftsmen's quarter on the periphery of the habitation. Our excavations have been confined mostly to the western periphery and to a part of the central area of the main mound (INM I): they have brought to light a number of houses which, on the basis of their contents, can be identified as those of craftsmen. The periodwise distribution of these houses is as follows: Period I (Malwa period), (i) Potter, (ii) Ivory carver; Period II (Early Jorwe), (i) Potter, (ii) Coppersmith; and Period III (Late Jorwe), (i) Goldsmith, (ii) Lime-maker, (iii) Wine distiller, (iv) Potter, (v) Coppersmith.

All the above houses were recovered in a small area of about 200 sq. m which we have so far excavated, and it is surprising that no structure from the other excavated area adjacent to the craftsmen's quarter can be identified as that of a craftsman. It is clear that right from the beginning, the craftsmen's houses were situated on the western periphery of the main habitation area on INM I just to the left of the entrance to the settlement and the same pattern continued in the subsequent periods. It is interesting to note that the same pattern prevails even today in the villages in central Maharashtra. Tradition dies hard, more so in a country like India!

A unique feature of the houses uncovered in the craftsmen's quarter is that a majority of them have pit silos which have not been found in the houses in other parts of the habitation with a solitary exception from INM II. The pit silos were found to have been dug into the house-floor. They had perfectly vertical sides and flat bottom and were plastered with lime which obviously served as an insecticide. The pit–silos first appear in Period I and continue in Period II, but their number decreases in Period III. An average pit-silo is a metre and a half deep and has a diameter of one metre. In one of the pit-silos the base was covered with grass. Some of the pit-silos of the Late Jorwe period contained a huge storage jar which was handmade and unbaked, and have a bulging belly and a wide, outcurved mouth.

The occurrence of pit-silos in the houses in craftsmen's quarter is indeed interesting and is suggestive of the fact that their need to store grain was perhaps greater than their fellowmen living in other parts of the settlement. This must have been a full time job for the craftsmen and the community must have paid them in exchange for their services in kind. They naturally must have been paid in the form of grain once or twice a year, and hence the need to store it properly.

It reminds us of the *Baluta* system which was in vogue till recently in some parts of central Maharashtra and according to which the craftsmen such as the potter, cobbler, blacksmith, carpenter and others were paid in kind at the harvest time for their services. Traditionally there are twelve such *Balutedars*. The chalcolithic craftsmen in all probability received coarse grain such as barley and *kulith* which they stored in silos. The absence of mud platforms for storage bins save in the potter's house of Period I shows that they usually did not consume wheat.

A few trenches laid at the centre of the main mound (INM I) revealed a different story. Here only Early Jorwe and Late Jorwe levels were dug. Of the few large rectangular houses of the Early Jorwe Period the most complete and intact was a house (No. 38) which had successively repaired floors and arrangement for draining out rain water. The house contained three burials of which two were extended ones and the remaining one was of urn type. Both the extended skeletons are interesting since one of them which was found by the side of the western wall of the house was kept in a crouching posture in a pit while the other lay north-south in a large pit. The latter was of inordinate height (1·83 m or 6 ft) and its lower extremities were intact in sharp contrast to the normal practice of chopping them off. It is therefore not unlikely that here was a person to whom normal rules of the community were not applied and he may therefore be an important person in the settlement.

Not far from the priest's house, but in an earlier building level, was found a large but disturbed house which has yielded the mother goddess in a clay receptacle, the goddess without head and a bull, her mount.[1] A very large house of Period II was also laid bare in the same area. It is by far the largest house of the Late Jorwe Period and may have belonged to some rich man of the settlement. The Late Jorwe Period houses in this area usually had a set of four flat stones supporting a storage jar, but the large house referred to above had two such storage jars, one of which rested on four flat stones and the other was plastered to the ground

[1]M.K. Dhavalikar, 'Chalcolithic Religion' a paper read at the *Seminar on Post-Harappan Chalcolithic Cultures*, Kurukshetra University, Nov. 1972 (in press).

with mud. The evidence, therefore, suggests that the central part of INM I was occupied by the elite as against its western end where the houses of the artisans stood.

GRANARY (SHRINE?) (FIG. 2, PL. VA)

A unique structure was encountered close to the craftsmen's quarter, not far from the elite area which is located in the centre of the principal mound (INM I). It is a squarish structure (10·50 × 9·15 m), partitioned into two rooms by a reed screen which, however, appears to have been removed later to make room for storage bins. The structure had low mud-walls, may be not more than 30 cm high, over which was the mud plastered bamboo screen. The structure contained a number of pit-silos (6) and round mud platforms (7) for storage bins of various sizes, all disposed in a very orderly fashion for storing different kinds of grains. In some cases the sides and the bottoms of the pits were lined with lime whereas in case of others, the bottom was full of sand. No remains of grains, however, were found in the pits. The structure is open on south and partly on east where only post-holes are to be seen.

In the southern half of the structure there were two large fire pits, one (42 cm × 77 cm—2·18 m deep) near the southern edge and the other (1·30 m × 72 cm—35 cm) near the eastern periphery where there was no wall. Both the pits were of much larger dimension than the ordinary *chulas* which have been found in several houses at the site. In the centre of the bottom of both of them there was a large flat round clay lump possibly for keeping a receptacle which, however, was missing. But a similar fire pit unearthed in the Malwa levels had the broken base of a huge storage jar well embedded in the centre of the pit. The sides and bottom of both the pits were completely burnt hard indicating that they were in use over a long period. It may be noted that such fire-pits are dug today for community cooking when the whole village is to be fed.

The identification of the structure is not as easy as it appears to be. It is pertinent to note in this connection that very little pottery and other articles of domestic use were recovered from within the structure, thus suggesting that it was not used for residential purposes. We are therefore inclined to identify it as a public building, very probably of a religious character for the simple reason that no sane person will have such large fire pits in his house; and secondly, if the pits were meant for community cooking, as is done now, they could not have been inside the house but in the open. These fire pits recall to the mind the *agnikuṇḍa* from Navda Toli[1] and the Malwa people may therefore be justifiably credited with the introduction of the fire worship in Maharashtra which, as the Inamgaon evidence shows, was later adopted by the people of the Jorwe Culture.

The existence of a number of pit-silos and mud platforms for bins suggests that the structure could have been a granary, for there is very little or no living space inside. With the identification of the structure as a temple for fire worship, the existence of so many of pit-silos and platforms for bins can be explained easily. The people must have paid tribute and made offerings in the form of grain which was stored in the silos and bins. This, in its turn, is to be taken as evidence of organized religion with a priest chief. It may not be out of place here to state that there is convincing evidence in the archaeological record which demonstrates the transition from temple to 'palace' because "the increasing wealth in the temples offered vastly greater inducements to military activity".[2]

HOUSE OF THE RULING CHIEF (FIG. 2)

Just to north of the granary and almost adjoining it was found a large house consisting of five rooms of which one was a kitchen and the other a store-room. The house had a well plastered floor and it covered an area of 25 × 10 m. In the courtyard of the house was found a symbolic burial consisting of one full and the other half four-legged, unbaked urns which contained a Jorwe Ware painted jar covered with a lid. In the same area was found a similar four-legged urn containing a human skeleton which belonged to the beginning of of the Late Jorwe Period. Hence the one in question can be identified as a symbolic burial since it did not contain any mortal remains. The elaborate burial and the multi-roomed house can be identified as that of the ruling chief since all other houses so far discovered are single room units. Morever, its proximity to the granary also indicates that he collected the taxes from the members of the community in the form of grains and stored it in the granary by the side of his house.

POPULATION

It is not an easy task to compute population of an ancient settlement fairly accurately purely on the basis

[1]H.D. Sankalia, S.B. Deo and Z.D. Ansari, *Chalcolithic Navda-Toli* (Poona, 1971), p. 49, pl. IV b.

[2]Robert M. Adams, 'Some hypotheses on the Development of Early Civilizations, in Mark P. Leone (ed.), *Contemporary Archaeology* (Carbondale and Edwardville, Ill, 1972), p. 361.

of the size of its area. However, attempts have been made in recent times to calculate population of a given site. One such satisfactory estimate which was developed for south-west Asia is of a population of 200 persons per hectare[1] while the other is by Fairservis[2] however, computes the population of Mohenjo-daro to 800 sq. feet per person or 133 persons per hectare. Hole[3] has arrived at a figure of 60 to 80 persons per acre or 150 to 200 persons per hectare. Each of these estimates has accounted for open spaces, roads, public architecture and other non-habitational areas. We may, therefore, not be far off the mark if we calculate the population of Inamgaon on the basis of 200 persons per hectare.[4] The size of the habitation at Inamgaon during the Malwa, the Early Jorwe and the Late Jorwe Periods was respectively five, five and two hectares and the population therefore can be taken to be 1000 during the Malwa and the Early Jorwe Periods and 400 in the Late Jorwe Period. It is not unlikely that our computation for the final phase of occupation at the site is not very near the truth. This is, in the main, due to the fact the size of the house, as will be seen later, becomes smaller reflecting the general decline in the standard of living. But all the same, the number of houses might not have been less than that in the Early Jorwe phase, a large number of houses could have been squeezed in a much smaller area and consequently the population would not have been less. It is therefore reasonable to assume that the population of Inamgaon would have been in the neighbourhood of a thousand souls figure which qualifies it as a considerably large settlement of the Jorwe Culture.

DOMESTIC ARCHITECTURE

The earliest inhabitants of Inamgaon lived in large rectangular houses which had thin, dwarf mud walls over which the framework was of split bamboo, plastered over with clay and cowdung. One complete house of the Malwa period which was exposed measures 6·64 m long and 4·42 m wide; its dwarf walls were flimsy and extremely thin (13 cm thick) and their extant height is 60 cm (PL. VA). There were a number of postholes outside the walls and some inside the walls also. The house was divided into two compartments by a dwarf wall over which probably rested the reed screen. In the northeastern corner of the house was circular mud platform, 1·9 m in diameter and its height was 10 cm. Such circular mud platforms are still constructed in the houses in the surrounding region for supporting a large cylindrical storage bin made of wickerwork. The mud platform contains thorny branches of *ber* (*Ziziphus*) and sand in order to prevent rodents from destroying grain in the bin. It should be noted that the mud platform from the Malwa house also contained sand.

In the northern corner of the house was a *chulah* which was rectangular in shape and had a disc-shaped clay stem in the centre, in which was also embedded a flat rectangular stone. This was covered with mud in order to support the cooking vessel. In one case a clay pan was found plastered to the central clay disc obviously for baking the dough. The rectangular *Chulah* in each case was full of ash, charcoal and lumps of burnt earth. The central clay support recalls to the mind those in West Asia which, however, were circular.[5]

Some people also lived in pit-houses. It is noteworthy that pit-houses occur only in Period I and not in later periods. But even in the early levels they are quite few in number. One such pit-house lay to the south and adjacent to the Malwa house described above. It was roughly circular on plan (maximum dia. 3 m) and its sides were perfectly vertical, and since the pit was considerably deep (1·23 m), a step was provided on the southern side for descending into it. The floor and the sides were plastered with lime. There were several postholes along the periphery at the top for supporting the roof and on the east the ground was provided with a gradual slope for draining out rain water, thus preventing it from getting into the dwelling pit. On the north-east was found a double *chulah* which belonged to the occupants of the pit, thus indicating that cooking was done outside in the open. Two more pit-houses, which were considerably shallow and may therefore be described as sunken floors, were also found. They were smaller (dia. about 1·50 m) than the preceding one. The discovery of a twin urn burial in one of them shows that they were used for dwelling purposes for at Inamgaon burials have always been found under the house floor. It is worthy of note that even today such sunken floors and pit-houses are constructed in and around Inamgaon. This is obviously

[1]Robert M. Adams, *Land Behind Baghdad* (Chicago, 1965), pp. 23–25 and 123–25.

[2]Walter A. Fairservis Jr., 'The origin, character and decline of an early civilization', *American Museum Novitates*, No. 2302, (New York, 1967).

[3]Frank Hole, 'Evidence of Social Organization from Western Iran, 8000–4000 B.C.', in Binford and Binford (eds.), *New Perspectives in Archaeology* (Chicago, 1968), p. 252.

[4]M.K. Dhavalikar and Gregory L. Possehl, 'Subsistence pattern of an early farming Community of Western India,' *Puratattva*, no. 7, (1974), p. 40.

[5]Donald P. Hausen, 'Al-Hiba, 1970–71: A Preliminary Report', *Artibus Asiae*, vol. XXXV, nos. 1–2 (1973), p. 66, fig. 5.

due to the short lengths of *Babul* (*acacia*) posts and in order to obtain sufficient height for the structure the pit houses are dug into the ground.

EARLY JORWE HOUSES

The Jorwe people adopted the house plan of their predecessors at the site but their houses are slightly of smaller dimensions, about 5 m × 3 m. One of the houses (No. 38) had a channel dug outside in the courtyard for draining out water from the roof. The floor was made with due care and plastered with mud and lime. The houses in the centre of the locality had no pit-silos and the grain was stored in handmade storage jars supported by four flat stones on the floor. Terracotta lamps have been found inside the houses and our experiment shows that the boat-shaped lamps, if filled with oil, can burn the whole night. Men of means probably had squarish lamps with pedestalled bases; they could accomodate four wicks at a time. Oil for the lamp might have been of *karadi*, charred grains of which have been found in the excavation. Pit-houses were not in use during the Early Jorwe phase, but round houses begin to occur in the last phase of the Early Jorwe period.

There is a striking change in the house plan in the Late Jorwe phase; instead of large rectangular houses, there are small round huts of modest dimensions which was possibly due to the influence from the southern Deccan (PL. VB). The overall economic degeneration is visible in every field of human activity. The houses are small, built close to each other in a haphazard manner, giving the appearance of a slum. They have dwarf walls with bamboo screen which were plastered over with mud and cowdung; the roof was probably conical and was supported on wooden posts. Every house had a set of four flat stones for supporting a four-legged storage jar. The floors were well made and even the outside area around the hut was in some cases rammed with murum and plastered with mud. Their diameter varies from 2·50 to 4·25 m. The floor of the house was no doubt relaid at regular intervals, may be every alternate year as is done now; the maximum number of relaid floors counted by us in the section at one place was fourteen, the average number being between five to eight. This would show that a house was occupied from 15 to 25 years or for a generation or so. The largest house of this period was found in the central part of the mound INM I. About forty houses of this period have so far been exposed.

SUBSISTENCE

The mixed economy of the chalcolithic farmers of Inamgaon was based on farming and hunting-fishing. They raised a number of crops such as wheat, barley, rice and pulses and lentil and also collected fruits like *ber* (*Ziziphus*) charred seeds of which have been found. A number of perforated stones from all the three cultural periods shows that they were used for hafting on digging sticks. Our estimates for population and the food requirements lead us to believe that the farmers of Inamgaon must have cultivated the black cotton soil which abounds in the region.[1] The most important cereal was barley which was cultivated right from the beginning of the occupation. It is a crop of short duration and can be easily raised in a semi-arid environment. It is, however, not grown today but our inquiries revealed that it was cultivated on a large scale some fifty years before.

The next important crop was wheat which however begins to be cultivated only from the Early Jorwe period and it is conspicously absent in the Malwa levels. It is indeed surprising that the people of the Malwa culture should not have grown wheat at Inamgaon. But wheat is rabi crop which requires winter rains. The region around Inamgaon lies in the rainshadow zone, and it has consequently become a semi-arid region which does not receive even its normal quota of the monsoon, let alone the winter rains. Wheat is presently grown in the area which has an assured supply of water from wells or the regular canal irrigation. The Early Jorwe farmers must have faced tremendous difficulties in growing wheat. In all probability cultivation of wheat became possible because of the supply of water diverted by the embankment which also was built only during Early Jorwe Period. Rice was cultivated possibly in small, carefully tended plots as is done now.

CRAFT SPECIALIZATION

As already stated, a number of houses belonging to craftsmen have been laid bare. Among these, potter occupies an important position. A potter's house (Period I) and two potter's kilns, one each of Period II and III have been found in the excavation. While the identification of the potter's house in the earliest levels is based on circumstantial evidence, potter's kilns of the subsequent period have been uncovered. The kiln of Period II is like a huge trough made of clay and embedded in the ground on stone foundation (PL. IVB). It appears to have been built *in situ*. Its maximum diameter is 1·75m, and at a depth of 60 cm from the top were found clay cushions in the kiln placed over the fire chamber down

[1]Dhavalikar and Possehl, *op. cit.*, pp. 42–44.

below. These cushions are oval in shape and have a hole in the centre and a groove on the middle of each side; the holes in the centre served as outlets for the hot gas. In the base of the kiln were flues or air ducts radiating from the centre. To the north-east of the kiln was the fire passage lined with stones and reaching below the bottom of the kiln where an andiron or firedog of clay was placed. It is rectangular in shape with projecting corners and curved upper sides for supporting firewood. At the time of baking pottery the firewood on the andiron was lit and the resulting hot gas would be passed above through the flues and holes and grooves in the clay cushions. It is thus a unique kiln which has so far no parallel within the country or even beyond. But in principle it is akin to those from Indus cities which were brick built and were provided with several holes for hot gas.

The clay andiron from the kiln, however, has parallels in West Asia where they have been dated to *circa* 2700-2000 B.C.[2]

Another kiln, belonging to the Late Jorwe Period, was also found. It was an open type of kiln consisting of a shallow pit dug in the ground. The pit, when exposed was found to be full of potsherds and ash.

IVORY CARVING

Another house of Period I which unfortunately was in much disturbed condition yielded a piece of an elephant tusk buried carefully in a small pit in the house floor. We do not know whether this was done with a view to preserving the piece of ivory. One end of the ivory is nicely cut flat, thus indicating that the owner may have been an ivory carver. Disc beads of ivory have been found at the site in all the periods and we may therefore safely conclude that they were manufactured at the site. It may also be stated that a bone fragment from the site has been identified tentatively as that of elephant (*Elephus indicus*). Ivory could also have been obtained from southern Karnatak which even today supplies ivory to the country.

COPPER SMELTING

Copper objects have been recovered from all the occupational phases of the site, and the remains of a furnace for smelting copper have been found in the middle levels of Period II and besides, a lump of copper ore came from the late levels of Period III. This shows that the ore was smelted at the site and that the objects were fashioned locally. It should be noted in this connection that native copper has been reported from Rashin (Taluka Karjat, District Ahmednagar, Maharashtra) which is about 65 km SE of the site and chalcopyrite is also available in areas around Sirur, not far from Inamgaon itself. Lumps of native copper were obviously heated and then beaten into the desired shape but copper must have been extracted from chalcopyrites for which furnaces were specially built. One such structure which can be identified as a furnace for smelting copper has been unearthed (FIG. 4). It lay just to the west of the pottery kiln in Period II. It is a boat-shaped structure built of clay on stone foundation and by constant use it has been completely baked. An oval clay cushion, similar to that from the kiln, was found in the centre of the furnace possibly for keeping the ore. It, however, had no perforations. Stylistically, the structure bears family resemblance with the bronze age furnaces in Israel which are dated to the middle of the second millennium.[3]

GOLDSMITH

Gold ornaments were found only in the shape of beads (long barrel, circular), and they too, were confined to the Late Jorwe (III). It is significant that the goldsmith's crucible and a pair of tongs of copper were also recovered in the Craftsmen's quarter from the Late Jorwe levels. The only source of gold was the Karnatak region and there is clear evidence of cultural contact with south, for the black-and-red ware occurs only in the Late Jorwe levels.

LIME-MAKING

Lumps of finely made lime, in the shape of balls, have been found mostly from the Late Jorwe levels. Sometimes these have been found carefully stored in pots whereas in one of the Late Jorwe houses a large number of lime balls were found. All this clearly shows that some people were actively engaged in the manufacture of lime. The house of lime maker was exposed in the upper levels of Period III. A number of lime balls were recovered from this house whereas in his courtyard was what appears to be a lime kiln.

[1]H.D. Sankalia, *Some Aspects of Prehistoric Technology in India* (New Delhi 1970), pp. 13–15, figs. V-VII.

[2]Robert J. Braidwood, *Excavations in the Plains of Antioch* (Chicago, 1960), pp. 371–73, figs. 290 and 291, A and B.

[3]R.F. Tylecote, *Metallurgy in Archaeology* (London, 1962), pp. 25–27, fig. 3a.

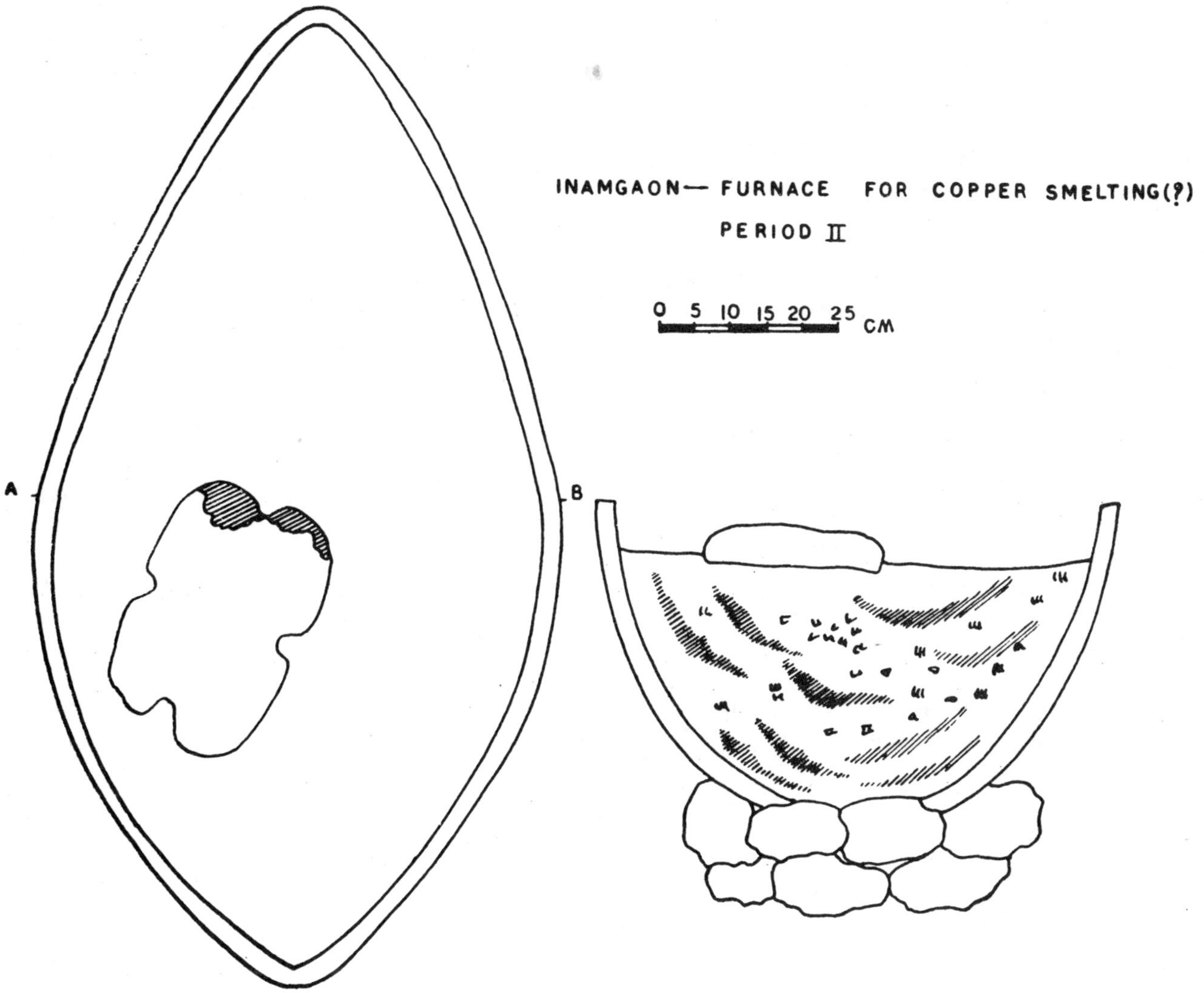

FIG. 4

It consisted of a number of stones rammed in a circular fashion (maximum dia. 60 cm) over which was placed a large flat stone. It is significant that a heap of shells was noticed near the house but not far from the kiln. This would suggest that lime was made by burning shells just as they do today in Tamilnadu and Kerala. But *kankar* (calcified grit) which is available around the site abundantly, may also have been used for preparing lime as is done today.

Lime must have been required in large quantities by the chalcolithic inhabitants of Inamgaon for frequently plastering the pit-silos and walls and floors of their houses. Lime making may have therefore become a specialist's job. Small balls of lime which have been recovered from many houses appear to have been so kept for serving as an insecticide. Lime is also sometimes applied to soils for correcting acidity and as a source of calcium but we do not know whether the early farmers at Inamgaon used lime for this purpose.

DISTILLATION

From a Late Jorwe house, which unfortunately was much disturbed, was recovered a tall cylindrical vessel with flat base and slightly outcurved rim. Near the mouth it had three holes, obviously for suspension. The vessel was found to have been carefully kept in a deep, narrow pit; only the mouth of the vessel was seen jutting out of the pit. It is obviously unsafe to keep a vessel of such height above ground as it could tumble any moment and hence it was kept in the pit. It was probably tied with string at the mouth through the holes in order to facilitate lifting it out of pit as and when required for pouring out the liquid that it must have contained. It could have contained either oil or wine, but no trace of oil has been found in it and there was no need to store oil in such a manner below ground. In all probability, therefore, it must have contained wine which may have been some sort of beer made out of barley which is reported from all the levels. The jar appears to be too large to be in the house of a common man and the house can therefore be plausibly identified as of a wine merchant who obviously must have been the distiller also. Incidentally, it may be stated that two graceful jars with narrow tubular neck like that of a wine flagon were found in a Late Jorwe burial; they must have been wine jars which formed part of the burial goods.

The huge wine vessel from Inamgaon is the only of its kind in India, but is paralleled at Mundigak in Afghanistan where it comes from Period III which is dated to mid-third millennium B.C.[1]

CONCLUSION

The foregoing account of the excavations at Inamgaon shows how the large-scale horizontal excavation helps us in the understanding of the settlement archaeology of a chalcolithic community. What we have tried to make out is not the settlement pattern in the accepted sense of the term, but rather the community pattern.[2] The concentration of the houses of the craftsmen along the western periphery of the settlement and the location of the houses of men of means in the central part demonstrate that it was a class structured society and that we have here the beginning of the *varna* system which later becomes the distinguishing feature of the Hindu society.

The excavated evidence also throws light, to some extent on the administration during the chalcolithic period. The discovery of the multi-roomed house (consisting of nos. 52-56) with a symbolic burial in the courtyard[3] and the granary (house nos. 50-51) adjoining it is indeed significant. Our identification of this house as that of the ruling chief of the settlement is no doubt borne out by the evidence. To this should be added the evidence of the diversionary embankment and the channel for draining out water which could have been used for irrigating fields. It implies the control excercised by a central authority who would see to the equitable distribution of water, the periodical silt clearance of the channel and its normal repairs. All this is bound to remain hypothetical, howsoever plausible it may be. But it should be emphasized in the end that our excavations have been confined to a small part of the principal mound (INM I) and much more area remains to be dug. The site requires some more seasons of planned work and there should be little doubt that it will prove fruitful.[4]

[1]Jean-Marie Casal, *Fouilles de Mundigak* (Paris, 1961), vol. I, p. 227; vol. II, fig. 130, i.

[2]K.C. Chang, *Settlement Patterns in Archaeology* (Reading, Mass., 1973), p. 24.

[3]M.K. Dhavalikar and Z.D. Ansari, 'Chalcolithic Burials of Inamgaon', *World Archaeology* (in press).

[4]The present paper represents a modified version of that read at the Seminar on Indian Prehistory held at the Deccan College, Pune, in June 1974.

Ancient Plant Economy at Inamgaon

Vishnu-Mittre and R. Savithri
Birbal Sahni Institute of Palaeobotany, Lucknow

[*Received on 12 April 1975*]

INTRODUCTION

Inamgaon is a chalcolithic site situated along the right bank of the Ghod River, a tributary of Bhima River, about 88 km from Pune, Maharashtra. It has been excavated by Prof. H.D. Sankalia and his colleagues. While some archaeobotanical materials from this site were given to the senior author by Prof. Sankalia during the former's visit to the site, in 1971, the bulk material was sent by Dr. Z.D. Ansari together with detailed information on the archaeological provenance of the samples.

We have the pleasure to record our gratitude to Prof. Sankalia and his colleagues for placing this interesting material at our disposal and for providing us with the important information on the archaeobotanical provenance of the samples. We are thankful to Dr. Uttam Prakash of Sahni Institute for the identification of some charcoals from this site. The results of our investigation[1] are presented in this paper.

The plant materials recovered from this site consist of carbonized cereals (rice, wheat, barley and *Sorghum*), legumes, fruit and seed remains of edible plants and charcoals. A large variety of the plant remains from this site suggests a wide choice and intensity of cultivation and provides us with important information on the cultural contacts of ancient peoples at Inamgaon with the neighbouring peoples in western India.

The stratigraphical and archaeological provenance of all the 78 samples and the plant remains therein are set out in Table 1, which is based upon the information sent to us of the concordance and correlation of various trenches at the site. As is apparent from Table 1, the plant remains belong to two distinct periods, viz. Period I (layers 1-12) comprising the Late and Early Jorwe cultures and Period II (layers 14, 15) comprising the Malwa culture. The samples, representing the overlap between these cultures are also included in the Table. Whereas the bulk of samples belongs to Phase I i.e. INM-I, a sample each comes from Phase II i.e. INM-II and Phase III i.e. INM-III.

All the samples sent to us were suitably packed in match boxes and plastic containers. Stratigraphy at this site reveals that the virgin soil was colonized first by the Malwa culture which in course of time was replaced first by the Early Jorwe culture and subsequently by the Late Jorwe. In terms of absolute dates the Malwa culture is dated to about 1600 B.C. and the Late Jorwe to about 1000 B.C., disregarding the erratic dates.[2] Thus, the site has been under occupation for nearly 600 years or so—a pretty long time indeed. Elsewhere, the absolute dates for these two cultures are believed to be synchronous (The Malwa culture, 1600 B.C.—1300 B.C.; The Jorwe culture, 1600 B.C.—1300 B.C.)[3]

[1]A brief report of the samples was published in *Indian Archaeology 1968-69—A Review*.

[2]*Indian Archaeology 1970-71—A Review*.

[3]D. Mandal, *Radiocarbon Dates and Indian Archaeology* (Allahabad, 1972).

although at Chandoli the end of the Jorwe culture is indicated at 1200 years B.C.

Most match boxes contained a mixture of remains of cereals, legumes, fruits and oil yielding seeds though a few contained only fruit remains of Indian Jujube. The morphological details were studied by usual methods i.e. examination under the low power binocular microscope.

In one of the samples, viz. sample no. 514, recovered from Tr. $D_2(_7)$ B. No: 12, D ? impressions of grains and spikelets were observed on small clay masses. On splitting open these clay masses, it was possible to recover five complete and some fragmentary grains. The impressions on the clay masses were of two kinds; (i) oblong to elongate ones, perhaps of rice, (ii) small ovoid cavities with membranes preserved in them and caused by the presence of ovoid grains. Besides, some fragments of spikelets reduced to ash were also observed. The chess-board pattern on them looked very much like that of rice spikelets. The charred grains and seeds were critically examined under the microscope to obtain as much information as possible on their morphology.

The charcoals were first examined by the snapping method under the binocular low power microscope, which did not give much information beyond the large and small pores which looked probably pitted, spiral or annular vessels. The sections of the charcoals were cut by adopting Johansen's method which involved Dehydration, Clearing, Infiltration and Embedding. The sections were cut in three planes, viz. the transverse, the tangential longitudinal and radial longitudinal with the help of a microtome knife. The charcoals being very brittle, a large number of slides had to be prepared to reconstruct the original material.

DESCRIPTION OF THE PLANT REMAINS

A. Cereal Grains

(i) Rice (*Oryza sativa* L. *var sativa* Bor)

A single broken rice grain has been recovered from one sample only, viz., sample no. 1156, Tr. $I_8(_6)$ belonging to the Late Jorwe period. Charred spikelets reduced to ash have however been recovered in sample no. 514 from Tr. $D_2(_7)$ belonging to an overlapping period between the Late and Early Jorwe cultures. The elongated shape of the latter together with its well preserved chess-board pattern are highly suggestive of its belonging to *Oryza* spps. The single broken rice grain is somewhat oblong, flattened on the sides and strongly ribbed. The hilum scar is not very well preserved. From the above data this grain in all probability belongs to *Oryza sativa* Linn. var. *sativa.* Bor

(ii) Wheat

Wheat in the collection is represented by carbonized grains only. Present only in six samples the number of wheat grains recovered from both the Malwa and Jorwe cultures is only 7, out of which 6 are complete and one broken. All the seven wheat grains are short, oblong, grooved and thick with their ends broad and blunt and devoid of hump and measure 3–5 mm×2–3·75 mm×2·2–2·3 mm in dimensions and look like those of *T. compactum*. They differ from grains of *Triticum vulgare* in not being long and with pointed ends and from *Triticum sphaerococcum* in not being rounded and devoid of a hump on their dorsal side. Modern grains of the latter though usually characterised by a hump on their dorsal side are also without it. In their size indices particularly in their L/B, L/T, B/L and T/L indices they compare with those of *T. sphaerococcum* rather than with those of *T. vulgare* and *T. compactum.*[1] The amount of reduction on carbonisation has however not been determined. The dimensions of wheat grains are shown in Table 2.

TABLE 2

Dimensions (in mm) of seven Wheat Grains

L	B	T	L/B	L/T	B/L	T/L	T/B
3·00	2·00	2·25	1·50	1·33	0·66	0·75	1·12
4·00	2·50	2·00	1·60	2·00	0·63	0·50	0·80
4·00	3·25	2·25	1·23	1·77	0·81	0·56	0·69
4·25	2·75	2·20	1·13	1·70	0·88	0·58	0·66
5·00	3·00	2·25	1·66	2·20	0·60	0·45	0·75
5·00	3·00	3·00	1·66	1·66	0·60	0·60	1·00
5·00	3·75	2·25	1·33	2·20	0·75	0·45	0·60
Av. 4·32	3·00	2·36	1·40	1·80	0·69	0·54	0·78

[1]Vishnu-Mittre, 'The beginnings of agriculture: palaeobotanical evidence from India', in Prof. Sir Joseph Hutchinson (ed.), *Evolutionary Studies in World Crops: Diversity and Change in the Indian Subcontinent* (Cambridge, 1974), pp. 3-33.

TABLE 3

DIMENSIONS (IN MM) OF SIXTY-ONE HULLED BARLEY GRAINS

No. of grains		L	B	T
1		4·00	3·00	2·00
1		4·00	2·75	2·00
1		4·00	2·75	1·75
1		4·00	3·50	2·50
1		4·00	3.25	2·25
1		4·25	3·25	2·25
1		4·25	2·50	1·75
1		4·50	3·25	2·00
1		4·50	3·25	2·25
1		4·50	3·50	2·50
1		4·50	3·75	2·25
2		4·75	3·25	2·75
1		4·75	3·00	2·50
1		4·75	3·50	2·00
3		5·00	4·00	2·75
3		5·00	3·00	2·00
1		5·00	3·00	2·50
2		5·00	3·25	3·00
3		5·00	4·00	3·00
2		5·00	3·50	2·00
1		5·00	4·00	2·00
1		5·00	3·25	2·75
1		5·00	3·75	2·25
1		5·00	3·50	2·75
1		5·00	3·75	2·50
1		5·00	3·50	2·50
1		5·00	3·25	2·50
1		5·00	3·50	2·25
1		5·00	4·00	1·50
1		5·25	4·00	3·00
1		5·25	3·50	2·50
1		5·25	4·00	2·75
1		5·25	4·00	2·25
1		5·25	3·75	2·25
1		5·25	4·25	2·75
1		5·25	3·25	2·25
1		5·50	3·00	2·50
1		5·50	2·50	1·50
1		5·50	3·25	2·50
1		5·50	3·00	2·00
1		5·50	4·00	2·50
2		5·75	3·25	3·00
2		5·75	3·00	2·25
1		5·75	4·00	4·00
1		6·00	3·50	2·75
1		6·00	3·25	2·50
1		6·00	3·75	3·00
1		6·00	4·00	3·00
1		6·00	3·75	2·50
1		6·00	3·50	2·50
61	Av.	5·02	3·00	2·50

(iii) Barley (*Hordeum* spp.)

Barley grains are found in samples right from the Malwa to the Late Jorwe periods. The spike parts being partly or completely absent, the identification is based completely upon the kernels. There are in all 66 complete grains of barley in addition to several broken ones.

Hulled Barley—Most kernels are of hulled type as in cross-section they are angular and furnished with longitudinal ridges and grooves impressed by the palea veins, clearly visible along the ventral furrow. Besides, the coarse wrinkling of the paleas is present in some carbonised barley grains and the transverse rippling characteristic of naked barley is lacking in most of these kernels.

A few barley grains have traces of palea bases preserved, resulting probably from tar exudation, and these lead us to think that the kernels might have been derived from both the nodding and erect spike types. A soft bevel characteristic of the nodding spike is noticeable in some, whereas a few display a deep transverse furrow corresponding to the erect spike. The narrow angle between the kernel and the axis in a few grains with palea bases preserved highly suggests their belonging to six-rowed spike of *Hordeum vulgare;* some grains showing a wider angle to the axis resulting in a sharp furrow, across the palea base seem to correspond with the six-rowed vaiety of *Hordeum hexastichum.*

Naked Barley—Being devoid of the imprint of paleas (surface characters caused by closely adpressed paleas in hulled forms) a few barley kernels appear to be naked or hull-less and exhibit transverse rippling in the fruit shell under the microscope.These kernels are further evenly rounded in cross-section except towards the ventral and dorsal sides because of depression caused by the furrow on the ventral side and a slight longitudinal depression on the dorsal side.

The hulled forms (92 per cent) in the Inamgaon material outnumber the naked ones (7 per cent).

The dimensions of hulled and naked barley grains are given in Tables 3 & 4.

(iv) *Sorghum vulgare*, Pers.

Sorghum remains, recovered from a single sample no. 514, from Tr. D2, layer 7 representing the overlap between the Early and the Late Jorwe periods, comprise burnt grains, burnt and ashy spikelets and impressions of grains on clay masses. Their fixiform impressions are in the form of cavities which are ovoid, sub-rotund to orbicular in shape and slightly compressed and pointed at one end. Some cavities are broader in the middle, narrower and pointed towards the ends which might probably be the lateral views of the ovoid grains.

TABLE 4

DIMENSIONS (IN MM) OF FIVE NAKED BARLEY GRAINS

	L	B	T
	4·25	2·75	2·25
	4·25	3·00	2·00
	4·25	3·25	2·50
	4·50	2·50	2·00
	4·50	3·00	2·25
Ad.	4·35	2·90	2·20

Splitting open the clay masses did damage the cavities but it was possible to recover 5 complete grains and several crushed or broken ones. The complete grains are biconvex, ovate to rotundate, sub-rotundate to orbicular and compressed, ranging in size from 2—2·50 × 1—1·50 mm with a thickness of 1 mm.

There are large number of varieties of sorghum cultivated in India. Snowden[1] in his account of the Indian varieties of the grain Sorghum has divided the genus *Sorghum* into two sections *Sorghum* and *Para-Sorghum*.

The grains in section *Sorghum*, being obtuse, elliptic or subelliptic, acute and acuminate differ in size and shape from the carbonised grains recovered from Inamgaon. In sub-section *Arundinacea* of section *Sorghum* the grains are oblong, lanceolate or elliptic acute or acuminate which also do not compare with our carbonised grains. The biconvex, ovate to rotundate, subrotund to orbicular and compressed grains in this section are very much similar to those of the carbonised grains. In size, the grains are 3-6 × 2·5-6 mm, rarely above 10mm in length and belong to *Sorghum vulgare* Pers. Smaller grains than these are found in *Sorghum milliforme* (Hook) Snowden var. *milliforme* of which the grains rarely exceed 3x3 mm in dimensions. The modern grains of *Sorghum vulgare* Pers. (Jowar or Cholam) examined in the laboratory were found to measure 3x3x1 mm Giving allowance for the reduction of size on carbonisation, the Inamgaon grains would appear to belong to *Sorghum vulgare* Pers. Dimensions of five carbonised Sorghum grains are shown below in Table 5

TABLE 5

DIMENSIONS (IN MM) OF FIVE SORGHUM GRAINS

No. of grains		L	B	T
2		2·00	1·50	1·00
1		2·25	1·00	1·00
1		2·25	1·50	1·00
1		2·50	1·50	1·00
5	Av.	2·20	1·40	1·00

B. LEGUMES

(i) *Lens esculenta* Moench (Lentil)

With the exception of a few samples, lentil has been found abundantly and in a better state of preservation than the remains of other legumes in most samples from both the Malwa and the Late Jorwe periods. Apart from several broken fragments as many as 60 complete seeds of lentil have been recovered. They show considerable variation in size, some of them are of extremely small size. The dimensions of lentil grains are shown in Table 6.

[1]J.D. Snowden, *The Cultivated Races of Sorghum* (London, 1936.)

TABLE 6

DIMENSIONS (IN MM) OF GRAINS OF *Lens esculenta* MOENCH

No. of grains	Diameter	Thickness
2	2·50	1·50
2	2·75	2·00
1	2·75	1·25
3	2·75	1·50
1	2·75	1·00
4	3·00	1·50
3	3·00	1·25
4	3·00	1·75
4	3·00	2·00
1	3·00	1·00
8	3·25	2·00
2	3·25	1·75
1	3·25	2·25
2	3·25	1·25
1	3·25	1·50
3	3·50	2·00
1	3·50	2·25
1	3·50	1·00
1	3·75	2·25
1	3·75	1·75
2	3·75	2·00
1	3·75	2·50
1	3·75	1·25
7	4·00	2·00
3	4·00	2·25
2	4·25	2·25
1	4·75	1·25
63 Av.	3·37	1·17

The lentil seeds have retained their lenticular shape and the keeled edge and in some even the seed coat and hilum are well preserved.

(ii) *Dolichos biflorus* L. (Kulthi)

Carbonized seeds of *Dolichos biflorus* have been recovered in samples from both the Malwa and Jorwe cultures. The seeds 3-5·25 × 1·75-4 × 1-2 mm are kidney shaped and compressed with a small hilum scar towards the convex or the inner side. In all, 20 complete seeds and a few fragmentary ones are recovered. The dimensions of 20 complete grains are shown in Table 7.

TABLE 7

DIMENSIONS (IN MM) OF GRAINS OF *Dolichos biflorus* L.

No. grains		L	B	T
1		3·00	2·00	1·00
1		3·25	3·00	2·00
1		3·50	2·25	1·00
2		3·75	2·50	1·00
1		4·00	2·50	1·00
1		4·00	3·00	1·00
1		4·00	3·00	1·75
3		4·00	3·00	2·00
1		4·25	3·25	2·00
1		4·75	3·00	1·75
1		5·00	3·00	1·50
1		5·00	1·75	1·25
1		5·00	4·00	1·50
1		5·00	3·00	2·00
1		5.25	3·50	2·00
1		5·25	3·75	2·00
1		5·25	3·75	1·50
20	Av.	4·30	2·94	1·59

(iii) *Dolichos lablab* Linn. cf. var. *typicus* Prain

The typically bean-shaped or kidney shaped thick and compressed somewhat flattened seeds measure 4·25-8 mm × 3-5·25 × 1-3·75 mm in dimensions. Only in some carbonized seeds the funicle and hilum are very well preserved though the seed coat is well preserved in most of them. As many as twentyone complete seeds and nine broken ones have been recovered from almost all the samples from both the Malwa and Jorwe cultures. The dimensions are shown in Table 8.

(iv) *Pisum sativum* L.

The carbonized seeds, 2.75-5 × 1·50-4 mm, have been recovered from both the Malwa and Jorwe cultures. The seeds are spherical in shape with smooth seed coat wherever preserved. Hilum scar is not well preserved. Considerable variation has been observed among the five complete seeds recovered. The dimensions are shown in Table 9.

TABLE 8

Dimensions (in mm) of Grains of *Dolichos lablab* Linn

No. of grains		L	B	T
1		4·25	3·00	1·75
2		5·00	3·25	2·25
1		5·00	3·00	1·75
1		5·00	3·25	2·00
1		5·25	4·00	3·00
1		5·50	3·50	3·00
1		5·50	3·75	2·50
1		5·50	4·50	3·00
1		6·00	4·00	2·75
1		6·00	4·00	1·00
1		6·00	4·25	3·25
1		6·00	4·25	2·00
1		6·75	4·25	3·75
1		6·75	5·00	3·00
1		6·75	4·50	3·25
1		6·75	5·00	3·75
1		7·00	4·50	3·25
1		7·25	5·00	3·00
1		7·75	5·00	3·00
1		8·00	5·25	3·25
21	Av.	6·10	4·16	2·73

TABLE 9

Dimensions (in mm) of Five Seeds of *Pisum sativum*

No. of grains		D	T
1		3·50	2·50
1		3·50	3·75
1		4·00	3·50
1		4·00	3·75
1		4·50	4·00
5	Av.	4·00	3·50

(v) *Phaseolus radiatus* Willd (Moong)

The carbonized seeds are derived from the Malwa, the Early Jorwe and the deposit representing the overlap between the Early and Late Jorwe cultures. The seeds are small and round about 3·75-4·50 × 2-3 × 1·50-2 mm in size. The seed-coat is not preserved and the tiny linear hilum scar as seen in a few of them occurs on the somewhat raised edge. The dimensions of the twelve complete seeds are shown below in Table 10.

TABLE 10

Dimensions (in mm) of Seeds of *Phaseolus radiatus*

No. of grains		L	B	T
1		3·75	3·00	2·00
2		4·00	2·00	1·50
2		4·00	3·00	2·00
1		4·00	2·75	2·00
1		4·00	2·50	2·00
1		4·25	3·00	1·75
1		4·25	3·00	1·50
1		4·25	3·00	2·00
1		4·25	2·75	1·50
1		4·50	3·00	2·00
12	Av.	4·12	2·80	1·82

(vi) *Lathyrus sativus*. L. (Kesari)

Only four seeds have been recovered in samples from the Malwa, the Early Jorwe and the deposit representing the overlap between the Early and Late Jorwe cultures. The seeds are squat and wedge shaped and measure about 4-5·50 × 3-4·50 × 2-4 mm in size. The hilum is not clearly visible.

(vii) *Vicia* sp.

A single seed spherical in shape and with a linear hilum scar towards one side and with the seed coat preserved measures about 3 × 2 mm in size. In the sample it has been found together with seeds of barley, *Lathyrus, Dolichos* spp and *Phaseolus radiatus* and from the Malwa culture only.

C. Oil Seeds

(i)*Buchanannia* sp. (Chiraungi)

Complete seeds and some fragments referred to this species have been discovered in sample nos. 1298, Tr. $G_{8(15)}$ 1132; Tr. H $_{8(8)}$ and 1156 Tr. I $_{8(6)}$ from both the Malwa and Jorwe Cultures. The seeds are lenticular and two-valved with a bony seed-coat, and gibbous acute at one end. The seeds measure 5 × 3·25-3·75 × 2-2·50 mm in size. In overall morphology, the carbonized seeds approach very closely the modern seeds of *Buchanannia* and their size compares with that of *Buchanannia angustifolia*. *Buchanannia angustifolia* is believed to be a native of the south end of the Peninsula of India.

D. Fruit Remains

(i) *Zizyphus nummularia* W. & A.

Fruit stones ranging from 4·50-8·50 mm in diameter, globose, rounded in shape are met with in almost all the samples right from the Malwa period to the Late Jorwe period. The fruit stones are woody or bony, rugose, and rough on the outside and are 1-2 celled. In most samples, the fruit stones are broken, and complete seeds have been observed only in a few of them. The seeds are solitary affixed at the base and planoconvex. The dimensions are given below in Table 11.

TABLE 11

Dimensions (in mm) of Fruit Stones of *ZIZYPHUS NUMMULARIA* W. & A.

No. of Fruit stones		Diameter
1		4·50
1		5·00
3		6·00
1		6·25
1		6·50
1		6·75
1		7·00
1		7·25
1		7·50
1		7·75
4		8·00
1		8·50
17	Av.	7·00

(ii) *Phoenix sylvestris* Roxb.

The two fruit stones measuring about 12-16·50mm × 8 mm × 5·8 mm, one from the Malwa culture and the other from the deposit representing the overlap between the Early and Late Jorwe, are oblong in shape and rounded at the ends with a deep longitudinal groove on the ventral side.

E. Charcoals

Most charred fibres belong to Bamboo, though it is not possible to ascertain their genera or species. The following plant genera have been identified for us by Dr Uttam Prakash from Charcoals in the following samples :

Sample No.	Botanical identity
441	*Sapindus?* (Sapindaceae), *Dalbergia* sp.
409	*Zizyphus* sp.
366	*Acacia* sp.
386	Rubiaceae
456	*Acacia, Zizyphus, Anogeissus, Terminalia*
1314	Bamboo probably *Dendrocalamus* sp.

In the last sample from INM-I Tr. G9 (7) H No. 39, it has not been possible to precisely identify the charcoals of Bamboo to the known genera but marked resemblance with the bamboo of *Dendrocalamus* is the basis of the probable identity cited above. Of all the identifications from charcoals, *Zizyphus* is one of which fruit stones occur commonly in many samples. Post holes caused by the use of bamboo posts occur profusely at the site, and in some charred bamboo fibres have also been found.

F. Unidentified Plant Remains

It has not been possible to identify the following plant remains.

1. A rounded fruit, measuring about 7 mm in diameter, with shining reticulate type of ornamentation over the fruit wall from sample no. 511, Tr. $C_{3(3)}$.

2. Four oval-shaped seed-like structures, measuring about 7-8·50 mm long, 5·6 mm broad, 4-5 mm thick, with a conical or beaked apex from sample no. 1220, Tr. $G_8(_{11})$.
3. Two oval-shaped seed-like structures measuring about 8-8·50 mm × 5 × 5 mm from sample no. 1220, Tr. $G_8(_{11})$ and one measuring 6 × 4 × 4 mm from sample no. 1280, G ( ) D–2-95 M.
4. Three oval seed-like structures measuring about 7·50-9 mm × 5-5·75 mm x 3·50 -4·25 mm in sample no. 1227, Tr. $G_8(_{12})$.
5. One full and a half seed probably of a legume measuring about 5.50 mm × 3×2 mm in sample no. 1256, Tr. $G_9(_8)$.
6. Two cotyledons of a legume (?) measuring about 12 mm × 6 mm × 7mm in sample no. 1272, Tr $G_9(_9)$ D-2·20 M.
7. Several broken pieces of a nut-shell of a fruit (?) in sample no. 1092, $G_8(_7)$ D-1·75 M.
8. Broken fragments of a legume (?) in sample no. 1205, Tr. $H_8\text{-}_9(_7)$.
9. An oval shining object in sample no. 1863 Tr : I_5 D-1·50 M.
10. Mass of fungal hyphae intertwined to look wiry thread-like structures in Sample 517, $C_3(_5)$.

CONCLUSION

The present investigation brings out rich and varied plant economy at Inamgaon both during the Malwa and the Jorwe cultures. The food plants common to both the cultures comprise barley, wheat, lentil, *Dolichos biflorus* D. *lablab, Pisum* sp., *Zizyphus nummularia* and *Buchanannia.* The remains of *Phaseolus radiatus and Lathyrus sativus* have not been discovered from Late Jorwe. The stones of *Phoenix sylvestris* are absent from Early and Late Jorwe though present during the period of overlap between them. These discontinuous records do not necessarily mean that there was a break in the consumption or use of these food plants. Perhaps their remains are not preserved.

A significant feature observed is the use of rice during Late Jorwe and of *Sorghum* during the overlap between the Early and Late Jorwe. These together with some legumes and the other plants as yet unidentified are distinct additions to food economy during the Jorwe period. One would be led by this to conclude that the new cultural waves during the Jorwe period introduced these food plants at Inamgaon or else the widening cultural contacts of the Jorwe peoples had resulted in the import of these new food elements at Inamgaon.

In regard to rice, particularly, a similar situation is observed at Navdatoli-Maheshwar,[1] an important Malwa culture site in Madhya Pradesh, where the impact of Jorwe culture in Phase II is accompanied by the beginning of rice at this site with wheat-based plant economy[2] Sorghum has earlier been known at Ahar in Rajasthan and the palaeobotanical evidence discussed above very strongly brings out influences from Ahar peoples at Inamgaon. Wheat was earlier known at another Malwa site Kayatha in Madhya Pradesh and at the Jorwe site Sonegaon in Maharashtra.

The presence of Barley at Inamgaon during the Malwa culture is intriguing so far as it is not known from the other sites where this culture has been discovered. A re-examination of carbonized wheat from Navdatoli Maheshwar and other sites is highly desirable to solve this mystery.

Rice at Inamgaon has indeed been diffused from the North and Northeast as records known from south India are not pre-Iron Age.

The superimposition of the two cultures, the Malwa and the Jorwe, at Inamgaon is very clear and the influx of the Jorwe culture at Navdatoli, where the Malwa culture persisted in spite of this influx, immediately suggests that the Malwa and Jorwe cultures could by no means have been synchronous as upheld by Mandal.[3] It may indeed be difficult to explain that these two cultures existed between 1600 and 1300 B.C. as opined by Mandal.[4] May be this was the case at certain sites, but cannot hold true for the cultures as a whole. The Inamgaon C14 dates would have us believe that the Jorwe culture at this site is later than 1300 B.C. and continued up to 1000 B.C.[5] More work is indeed necessary to straighten out the jumble created by C14 dates in relation to stratigraphy for the important bearing it has upon the cultural evolution in relation to diffusion of cultivated plants.

[1]H.D. Sankalia, S.B. Deo and Z.D. Ansari, *Chalcolithic Navdatoli* (Poona-Baroda, 1971).

[2]Vishnu-Mittre, *Plant Economy in Ancient Navdatoli*, Technical Report on Archaeological Remains, Deccan College, Poona, 1961, pp. 13-52.

[3]Mandal, *op. cit.*

[4]*Ibid.*

[5]*Indian Archaeology 1970-1971—A Review.*

Archaeology and Tradition

The Later Vedic Phase and the Painted Grey Ware Culture

The later Vedic texts, comprising the collections of the *Yajus* and *Atharvan*, the *Brāhmaṇas,* and the *Upanishads* were composed in the land of the Kurus and Pañchālas.[1] This coincides with the major portion of western Uttar Pradesh, almost the whole of Haryana, and the neighbouring parts of Punjab. From the climatic point, along with the eastern portions of Rajasthan, this whole area constitutes one unit having the same kinds of plants and trees. We may list a few trees which are mentioned in the Vedic texts and are at present found in the region. *Udumbara*[2] (Hindi *gūlar*) is found in this region and also in other parts of the country. *Karīra,* a leafless shrub, is found along the banks of the Yamuna in the Mathura area.[3] *Pīlu,*[4] a tree on the fruits of which doves fed, is found in the same region. The *jujube* (Hindi *ber*), trees such as *karkandhu,*[5] *kola,*[6] *kuvala,*[7] and *badara*[8] are found in good numbers in the whole area. *Pītūdāru*[9] or *putudru,*[10] a name for *devdār*, is found in the foothills of the Himalayas. *Plaksha*[11] (Hindi *pākar*), a waved leaf tree with small white fruits, is found in this region as well as in eastern India. *Varaṇa*[12] (Hindi *varanā*) is found in Haryana in good numbers. *Vikankata,*[13] identifiable with *kaṭāī,* and *śāmī,*[14] identifiable with *chonkar,* are found in the region of our study. So far the plant remains of the levels belonging to the first half of the first millennium B.C. have not been impressive, and hence an integrated study of the later Vedic plants on the basis of archaeology and geographical provenance cannot be pursued far. But there is considerable evidence to show that the flora of the later Vedic texts is identical with that of the *doab* and the adjacent areas.

The Painted Grey Ware sherds have been found in the same areas as are represented by the later Vedic texts. Although the PGW wares have been noticed in eastern UP and even in Bihar, their epicentre seems to be the upper Ganga and Sutlej basins. However, there is nothing like an exclusive PGW culture because other wares such as black-and-red ware, black-slipped ware, red ware, and plain grey ware are also associated with them. Although very distinctive both in form and fabric at Atranjikhera, where the PGW covers an area of about 650 square metres, its incidence ranges between three and ten per cent of the total pottery complex.[15] Even where their number is fairly large, the PGW sherds may not exceed fifteen per cent of the total pottery recovered from the PGW levels. Thus, the PGW horizon represents a composite culture just as the culture revealed by the later Vedic texts represents an amalgam of Sanskritic and non-Sanskritic, Āryan and non-Āryan elements.

The dating of the PGW levels coincides with that of the later Vedic texts. Although some enthusiasts would like to push back the date of both the PGW and iron on the basis of a single carbon dating from Atranjikhera, the overall picture comprising both the origin and the diffusion of the PGW covers a period of less than five centuries from *circa* 800 B.C. This also seems to be the case with the compilation of the later Vedic texts. Keith would like to place all the *Brāhmaṇas* between 800 and 600 B.C.,[16] but Louis Renou is possibly right to extend the period of the later Vedic texts including the *Upanishads* up to 500 B.C.[17] The dates of the Vedic texts were fixed by Sanskritists on the basis of linguistic considerations, the appearance of Vedic names in inscriptions of about the fourteenth century

[1]A.A. Macdonell and A.B. Keith, *Vedic Index of Names and Subjects*, vol. I (London, 1912), pp. 165–69.
[2]*Ibid.*, p. 86.
[3]*Ibid.*, p. 139.
[4]*Ibid.*, p. 535.
[5]*Ibid.*, p. 139.
[6]*Ibid.*, p. 189.
[7]*Ibid.*, p. 173.
[8]*Ibid.*, Vol. II, p. 59.
[9]*Ibid.*, Vol. I, p. 534.
[10]*Ibid.*, Vol II, p. 11.
[11]*Ibid.*, p. 54.
[12]*Ibid.*, p. 205.
[13]*Ibid.*, p. 294.
[14]*Ibid.*, p. 355.

[15]R.C. Gaur, 'The Painted Grey Ware at Atranjikhera—An Assessment', *Potteries in Ancient India,* ed. B.P. Sinha (Patna, date not mentioned), pp. 185–86.
[16]*Cambridge History of India*, vol. I (Cambridge, 1922), 131–32.
[17]Louis Renou, *Vedic India* (Calcutta, 1957), p. 38.

B.C. in western Asia and on the basis of the appearance of the Indo-European speaking people in western Asia and Europe. The coincidence that the later Vedic texts seem to have been compiled in the age of the PGW can be rendered meaningful by a comparison of the material cultures revealed by these two sources.

The PGW mud-brick walls found at Hastinapura[1] remind us of later Vedic references to bricks in connection with the construction of altars; seven brick names are found in the *Taittirīya Saṁhitā,* nine in the *Kathaka Saṁhitā,* and eleven in the *Maitrayanī Samhita.*[2] In the *agnichayana,* the stacking of the bricks for the fire altars which is made obligatory in the *mahāvrata* and optional in other *soma* sacrifices, the building of the *uttaravedi* involves five courses of bricks, making 10,800 bricks in all in prescribed patterns often in the form of a bird with outstretched wings.[3] But neither the PGW archaeology nor the later Vedic texts know of fire-baked bricks. Of course a battered facing of brick on the mud ramparts of Kauśāmbī has been discovered, but it cannot be pushed beyond 550 B.C.[4] In fact, the find of a cast copper coin may bring down its date to around 300 B.C. Therefore, the bricks mentioned in the Vedic texts were not baked in the fire. A potter's kiln of the PGW level has been discovered in Atranjikhera.[5] Such a kiln is known by *āpāka* (Hindi *āvā*) in the Vedic texts, but no term for brick kiln is found in the Vedic sources. The old Vedic practice of using unbaked bricks for religious purposes continues in Maharashtra and possibly in other parts of the country. The total picture of PGW settlements does not warrant their characterization as urban, as has been done by Wheeler;[6] towards the end of the PGW period they can be called proto-urban at best. The later Vedic texts do not know of urban life. Kāmpila,[7] the capital of Pañchāla, may have been an administrative settlement. The term *nagara* occurs in an *Āraṇyaka*[8] and the *nagarin,*[9] in two *Brāhmaṇas* which are not earlier than 600 B.C.

Technologically the PGW period is distinguished by the use of iron implements comprising spears, arrowheads, hooks, etc. Consistent C^{14} datings do not make them earlier than *circa* 850 B.C. The use of iron in the later Vedic texts is indicated by several terms. Iron objects recovered from Atranjikhera implies advanced knowledge including the use of the bellows. *Bhastrā,* which became a common term for bellows in post-Vedic times, is interpreted as leather container in the *Śatapatha Brāhmaṇa,*[10] but it may imply the acquaintance of the people with the bellows towards the end of the Vedic period.

Several terms for iron are found in the late Vedic texts. The term *śyāma* occurs in the *Vājāsaneyi Saṁhitā,*[11] the youngest of the *Yajus* collection, which might belong to about 800 B.C., for it is later than the *Taittirīya Saṁhitā.*[12] The term *śyāmena* is found in *Atharva Veda,* IX.5.4. and *śyama ayas* in XI.3.1, 7; but these books are part of the priestly literature rather than of "popular poetry", and are possibly later in time.[13] Since in its present form the *AV* is certainly the latest of the four *Saṁhitas,*[14] these references cannot be attributed to a period earlier than 800 B.C. The terms *krishṇāyas, kārshṇāyas* occur in *Jaimini Upanishad Brāhmaṇa,* II. 90, which is later than the *Śatapatha Brāhmaṇa* and *Aitareya Brāhmaṇa,*[15] and may be later than 600 B.C. Curiously enough the Egyptian word for iron is black copper from heaven,[16] which is almost the same as *krishṇāyas.* Similarly glass beads and bangles found in the PGW levels[17] have their counterparts in the term *kācha* in the Vedic texts.[18]

On the basis of the iron objects that have been discovered so far in Punjab, Haryana, western UP and the adjoining areas of Rajasthan in the levels belonging to *circa* 800–500 B.C. we cannot postulate their use in handicrafts and agriculture on any considerable scale. In this phase only arrowheads and spearheads supplemented by nail[19] have been encountered; axes, hoes and sickles are rare, and ploughshares are completely absent. It was therefore primarily an age of iron weapons and not of iron tools. Since the Upper Gangetic basin

[1] B.B. Lal, 'Excavation at Hastināpura and other Explorations in the Upper Gangā and Sultej Basins 1950–52'', *Ancient India,* nos. 10 & 11 (1954 & 1955), p. 13.

[2] G.R. Sharma, *The Excavations at Kauśāmbī (1957–59) The Defences and the Śyenaciti of the Puruṣamedha,* (Allahabad, 1960), p. 101.

[3] Renou, *op. cit.,* pp. 110–11.

[4] Sir Mortimer Wheeler, *Early India and Pakistan* (London, 1959), p. 130.

[5] *Indian Archaeology 1963–64—A Review,* p. 49. In subsequent pages abbreviated as *IAR* followed by the year.

[6] *Civilizations of the Indus Valley and Beyond* (Cambridge, 1966), p. 102.

[7] *Vedic Index,* I, p. 149.

[8] *Ibid.,* p. 432.

[9] *Ibid.*

[10] I. 1.2.7 ; 6.3.16 quoted in *Vedic Index,* II, p. 99

[11] XVIII. 13.

[12] B.K. Ghosh, 'Vedic Literature—General View', in (ed.) R.C. Majumdar, *The Vedic Age,* History and Culture of the Indian People, Vol. I (London, 1957), p. 232.

[13] Renou, *op. cit.,* pp. 20-21.

[14] Ghosh, *op. cit.,* 232.

[15] Wilhelm Rau, *Staat und Gesellschaft im alten Indien* (Wiesbaden, 1957), p. 27.

[16] Charles Singer, E.J. Holmyard and A.R. Hall (eds.), *A History of Technology,* vol. I (Oxford, (1954), p. 594, f.n.1.

[17] Lal, *op. cit.,* pp. 91, 94. In addition to Hastinapura, glass objects from the PGW levels have also been reported from some sites in Punjab.

[18] *Kapiṣṭhala-Kaṭha Saṁhita,* XXXI.. 9 ; *Ś Br.,* XIII. 2.6.8; *Taittiriya Br..,* III. 9.4. 4-5; all these references are quoted in M.G. Dikshit, *History of Indian Glass* (Bombay 1969), Appendix II, p. 162.

[19] *IAR 1958-59,* pp. 54-55; *1962*-63, pp.31-34; *1971-72*

does not have any rich iron mines, and since the evidance for the use of bellows seems to be doubtful,[1] the number of weapons was limited, and most probably they lay in the sole possession of princes and nobles.

The PGW deposits, which are at several places four to five metres deep, leave no doubt that these settlements lasted for at least three to four centuries. Their relative stableness, their richer context indicating increase in population suggest that they were inhabited by agricultural communities. The late Vedic texts speak of four, six, eight, twelve and even of twenty-four oxen being yoked to the plough[2] which may indicate the yoking of more than two oxen to break the hard soil. The importance of field agriculture was realised, and the ploughshare made of *khadira* was asked in prayer to confer cows, goats, children and grain on the people.[3] It seems that the ploughshare made of *khadira* or *katthā*, which is called very hard and compared to bones in the *Śatapatha Brāhmaṇa,*[4] was used on a considerable scale. But in the *Atharva Veda* the plough is described as *paviravant*[5] or *pavarivam,*[6] which is interpreted as having a metal share like that of lance;[7] this was possibly an iron share. Similarly in recitation an instrument called *kuśī,* which was an article made of metal or wood, was used for marking.[8] In later times the term came to mean an iron ploughshare and is still used in that sense in the dialects of western U.P., Punjab and Haryana. But we do not get any iron ploughshare in the PGW levels. In the age of the *Ṛig Veda* ploughshares of *khadira* and *udumbara* were used. The practice continued in later Vedic times, and the ritual is still observed in the Banaras area. According to it before the start of ploughing a small piece of land is furrowed with the wooden share attached to the plough.

A few implements found at Atranjikhera[9] appear like reaping hooks, but no iron sickles have been found in the PGW levels. The terms for sickle are not found in the family books of the *Ṛig Veda. Dātra* appears in its late portions,[10] and is used for both a reaper and a sickle meant for cutting purposes. Its derivative *dā, dāu,* etc., means a large agricultural cutting tool in north-eastern India, but in Haryana and the neighbouring regions its derivative *dārāntī* means a sickle for reaping. *Sṛṇī* is another term for reaping sickle found in the late portions of the *Ṛig Veda,*[11] and also in the *Atharva Veda,* [12]but the term is not widely used. It is significant that the later Vedic texts specifically use the term *lavitra*[13] for reaping hook or reaping the crops. But we have no exact idea of the material of which these sickles were made. All told the PGW/later Vedic people practised field agriculture, but iron does not seem to have played any role in it.

In the age of the *Ṛig Veda, yava* or barley was produced. Barley ripens quickly and does not require much rain. Therefore the sole dependence of people on it suggests that they lived from hand to mouth because of the lack of the knowledge of the other crops. But besides barley, rice and wheat[14] have been found in the PGW levels at Atranjikhera. All these are attested by later Vedic texts which know of barley, rice (*vrīhi*), bean-pulse(*māsha*), and sesamum (*tila*); millet (*śyāmaka*)[15] is also mentioned.[16] In the Vedic texts, another name for paddy crop is *saṣṭika,* which ripened in sixty days.[17] An inferior type of rice, it survives now as *sāṭhī* in almost the whole of northern India.[18] The fact that this variety is used in Hindu rituals in preference to the other varieties shows that it was the earliest type of cultivated rice. *Godhūma* or wheat found in the PGW levels appears in several later Vedic texts,[19] but so far bean, sesamum and millet have not been discovered in the PGW levels. However, besides wheat, barley and rice, lentil, black gram (*urd*), green gram (*mung*), grasspea and linseed have been reported from chalcolithic levels in Madhya Pradesh.[20] The cultivation of rice in western UP might be explained by the fact that in ancient times this area had a heavier rainfall and much waterlogging. The continued use of rice in Vedic rituals[21] is also explained by this fact; on the other hand it is significant that wheat has no place in these rituals.

[1]The term *bhrastra* is used in the *SBr.*, I.1.2.7;6.7.16. in the sense of leather container (*Vedic Index*, II, 99).

[2]All the references from the *AV*, *TS*, *KaS*, *MS* and *SBr.* are quoted in *Vedic Index*, II, 451.

[3]*AV*, X. 6.23.

[4]XIII. 4.4.9.

[5]*AV*, III.17.3 & *VS*, XII. 71 quoted in *Vedic Index*, I, 509.

[6]*TS*, X.2.5.6 ; *MS*, II.7, 12 ; *KS*, XVI. quoted in *Vedic Index*, I, 509.

[7]*Vedic Index*, I. 509.

[8]*Ibid.*, p. 173 ; R.L. Turner, *A Comparative Dictionary of Indo-Aryan Languages* (Oxford, 1966), no. 3367.

[9]*IAR, 1965-66*, plate XXXC; several of the objects illustrated in this plate appear to be sickle or reaping hooks, but they have not been identified.

[10]VIII. 78.10 ; *Nirukta*, II. 1 in *Vedic Index* I. p. 384.

[11]I.58.4 ; X.101.3 ; in *Vedic Index* II, 471.

[12]III.17.2 quoted in Rajchhatra Mishra, *Atharvedā men Sāṁskritik Tattva* (Allahabad, 1968), p. 147, fn. 3.

[13]*Lunāti* in the sense of 'reaps' in *TBr.*, *lavana* in the sense of reaping in *Kāty. Śr.*, and *lavitra* in the sense of sickle in Pāṇini; all quoted in Turner, *op. cit.*, nos. 10986-10988.

[14]G.M. Buth & K.A. Choudhury, 'Plant Remains from Atranjikhera Phase III (1200-600 B.C.)', *The Palaeobotonist*, XX, no. 3 (1971), 286.

[15]*vrihimattam yavamatho māshamatho tilam*, *AV*, VI.140.2

[16]*AV*, XX. 135, 12.

[17]*Vedic Index*, II, 345.

[18]Turner, *op. cit.*, no. 12806.

[19]Monier-Williams, *A Sanskrit English Dictionary*, p. 365, col. 1.

[20]H.D. Sankalia, *Prehistory and Protohistory of India and Pakistan* (Poona, 1974), *pp.* 460-61.

[21]s.v. *purodās*, *Vedic Index*, II, p. 4 ; Monier-Williams, *op. cit.*, *AV*, VI. 140.2.

Animal remains from Atranjikhera include bones of cattle and other animals bearing cut marks and leave no doubt that they were used for food. Animal bones from Hastinapura show that young cattle were used for food purposes.[1] Sacrifices prescribed in the later Vedic texts indicate the killing of cattle and other animals on a large scale, and animal food is an important item in the life of the Vedic people. Sacrificial altars have not been discovered so far, although such a claim is made for Kauśāmbī in connection with the *purusha-medha.*

Although the remains of horse have been found at Hastinapura,[2] it is not clear whether the animal was used for food. So far the remains of horse have not been recovered from any other PGW site. Horse goods belonging to about *c.* 900 B.C. have been reported from the Gandhara graves.[3] In any case the importance of horse and chariot is attested by the *RV* and more so by subsequent Vedic texts which prescribe place for horse in the *aśvamedha, rājasūya, mahāvrata,* etc.

To the PGW levels belong a good number of pots. It is thought that they were used for eating by members of the upper classes, but some of them may have been used for cooking; of course the point can be established only if marks of soot are noticed on them. Others may have been used in rituals which formed a striking feature of the later Vedic religion. It is not possible to produce corroborative evidence from the Vedic texts regarding the colour and fabric of these pots, but something can be said about their types. The two typical PGW pots are bowls and dishes; we do not meet with *hāṇḍīs,* which became a widely prevalent cooking pot in subsequent times. It is remarkable that the later Vedic terms *ambarīsha,*[4] *ukha,*[5] *kandu,*[6] *sthālī,*[7] *bhrashṭra,*[8] stand for frying pans, resembling broadly the dishes that have been discovered. These recall to our mind the pots in the red ware found in the PGW levels. *Kumbha*[9] was meant for storing water and *kośa*[10] for storing grain; these again may have been non-PGW pottery. *Kuṇḍa* seems to be the term used for bowl,[11] and the term *kuṇḍa-payin,*[12] drinker from the bowl, is used as a proper name. *Śarāva* is another name for bowl,[13] which was also used for measuring corn. According to the *Kātyāyana Śrautasūtra* (II.4.27–34) a small bowl or cup was indicated by the word *kapāla,* because of its resemblance to skull;[14] sacrificial offerings were placed in it. Many of the PGW bowls may have been used for ritualistic purposes', and they remind us of the later Vedic *kapālas* meant for offering sacrificial cakes to the gods.

The terms for cooking pots in later Vedic texts suggest that frying was an important form of cooking, and this purpose was served by the dishes that have been discovered. Some inference regarding the use of the PGW and other dishes can be made from the size of the ovens that have been discovered. The Atranjikhera PGW level hearths are half-oval in shape and 25 to 30 cms in height.[15] An oval-shaped hearth, partly underground, was found in the PGW level at Kaseri in the district of Meerut.[16] The hearths from Achichchhatra belonging to the earliest phase of the NBP period, into which the PGW shades off at this place, are underground ovens.[17] In the case of both Kaseri and Ahichchhatra we should find out whether the size of the PGW level pots matches with the PGW ovens.

The rows of hearths discovered at Atranjikhera in the PGW levels as well as the sets belonging to post-PGW levels at Ahichchhatra show that these were meant for communal feeding or for cooking the food of large families. A hearth showing one mouth and three openings was found in Atranjikhera besides another hearth on a kitchen floor belonging to the period of overlap of the Painted Grey and the NBP Wares.[18] Obviously these hearths were meant for feeding a large family. In the case of the hearth at Ahichchhatra[19] as many as three cooking pots can be placed at a time on the multiple ovens. The multiple hearths with baked brick wall from Purana Qila from the 'Maurya' levels[20] can take four pots at a time. A row of four hearths has been found at Ahar,[21] but these are rectangular and above the ground, and not oval and underground, as is the case with the Kaseri and Ahichchhatra hearths as well as the 'Maurya' hearths from Purana Qila. The term

[1]Lal, *op. cit.*, pp. 107-20.
[2]*Ibid,*. p. 109.
[3]B.K. Thapar, 'The Aryans: A Reappraisal of the Problem', *India's Contribution to World Thought and Culture,* ed. Lokesh Chandra *et al.* (Madras, 1970), p. 150.
[4]Ambarīsha is the name of a person in *RV*, I.100. 17 ; *Vedic Index*, I, 31 ; (in the sense of frying pan see Monier-Williams, *op. cit.*, s.v. *ambarisha.*)
[5]Used in the sense of saucepan or cooking pot in *AV*, XII.3.23, *TS*, etc., quoted in Monier-Williams, *op. cit.*, s.v. *ukha* : cf. *Vedic Index*, I, 83.
[6]Monier-Williams, *op. cit.*, s.v. *kaṇḍu* ; cf. Turner, *op. cit.* nos. 2726 & 2728.
[7]Monier-Williams, *op. cit.*, s.v. *sthālī* ; *Vedic Index*, II, 487.
[8]Monier-Williams, *op. cit.*, s.v. *bhrāṣṭra* ; Turner, *op. cit.*, no. 9656.
[9]*Vedic Index,*, i, 163; Shivaji Singh, 'Vedic Literature on Pottery', *Potteries in Ancient India*, p. 304.
[10]In the ritual *kośa* appears as a large vessel to hold *soma*, as opposed to *kalaśa, VI*, i, 189 ; *kusūla* appears as a storage jar in Pāṇini IV.3.56 (*Potteries in Ancient India*, p. 267).

[11]For the sense of bowl-shaped vessel see Monier-Williams, *op. cit.*, s.v. *kuṇḍa* ; Turner, op. cit., no. 3264.
[12]*Vedic Index*, I, 160-61 .
[13]*Vedic Index*, II.
[14]Singh, *op. cit.*, p. 304 & fn. 60.
[15]*IAR, 1963-64*, p. 49.
[16]*IAR., 1969-70*, p. 43.
[17]*IAR., 1963-64*, p. 44, plate XXVII.
[18]*IAR, -196566*, p. 47, plate XXXIIIA.
[19]*IAR, 1963-64*, plate XXVIIA.
[20]Picture of 47/70-71 PQ (Kindly shown to me by Dr M.C. Joshi).
[21]Sankalia, *op. cit.*, p. 407 and fig. 117.

bhrashṭra or *bhrāshṭra* in the Vedic texts[1] throws some light on the communal character of the later Vedic hearths. This term is interpreted in the sense of frying pan,[2] but it might mean a large cooking fire, for almost in the whole of western U.P., Haryana and Punjab its derivation *bhaṭṭhī* stands for ovens meant for cooking food on the occasion of communal feasts, although *bhaṭṭhī* or *bhaṭṭhā* is also used for brick-kilns. My inquiry shows the traditional *bhaṭṭhī* erected for communal feeding in western U.P. is invariably underground and is half oval in shape. This may be a survival of the PGW hearth corresponding to the Vedic *bhrashṭra/bhrāshṭra*.

The later Vedic phase is marked by the predominance of sacrificial rituals, conducted by priests and mainly meant for tribal chiefs and princes, in which laying fire invariably plays an important part and is also prescribed for the vaiśyas or peasants. Archaeological evidence for this practice is thin in the PGW levels. 'Fire-altars' in the form of shallow oval or rectangular pits have been reported from Amri, Lothal and Kalibangan,[3] and possibly they continued in some form in subsequent centuries. Circular firepits discovered at Atranjikhera in the PGW levels[4] may have served sacrificial purposes. Horizontal excavations are likely to expose more of the firepits, which may have been borrowed by the PGW people from the preceding cultures.

All told the stage of the material equipment of the PGW phase, called so because of the distinctive character of this pottery, is comparable on many counts to the material culture of the later Vedic texts. We notice beginnings of territorial state formation, advent of social stratification, and the emergence of administrative machinery, in the later Vedic texts; all these presuppose a full-fledged agrarian society, not typical of the *RV* phase. Although a good portion of the geographical areas covered by the *RV* overlaps the area covered by the later Vedic texts and the PGW culture, the fact that the RV people were mostly pastoralists, used neither iron nor glass, and cultivated only barley, rules out the possibility of their being equated with the users of the PGW culture. On the other hand we have a good case for using the PGW archaeology for the study of the later Vedic culture. If this position is accepted, the combined method can help us to form an integrated picture of society and economy in the first half of the first millennium B.C. in the Sutlej and upper Gangetic basins.

[1]Turner, *op. cit.*, no. 9656 ; Monier-Williams, *op. cit.*, s.v. *bhraṣṭra*.
[2]Turner, *op. cit.*, no. 9656.
[3]Sankalia, *op. cit.*, p. 350.
[4]*IAR, 1963-64*, p. 49.

Department of History,
University of Delhi, Delhi-110007

R.S. SHARMA

Indian Archaeology and the Epic Traditions

Archaeological work on sites mentioned in the epics is not new. While a number of them were covered in the surveys of Alexander Cunningham,[1] more recently two such sites, Takshaśilā and Ahichchhatra, have been excavated with a high level of stratigraphic precision.[2] What is, however, new is an effort to correlate archaeology with the epic evidence and to reconstruct the epic milieu in the light of archaeology. The present note aims to review the work already done as also the work proposed to be done in this direction, with an initial reference to the *Rāmāyaṇa* tradition. It will, in the process, examine the assumptions which have led to the highlighting of epic tradition in the context of archaeology and attempt a purely personal assessment of what contributions such assumptions are likely to make towards the progress of Indian archaeology.

Perhaps the first work in the way of correlating epic tradition with the archaeology of north India was by B.B. Lal who explored a number of sites mentioned in the *Mahābhārata*, excavated an important '*Mahābhā-*

[1]*Archaeological Survey of India, Report for the year 1971–72*, Vol. IV (Delhi and Agra) (reprinted, Varanasi, 1966), p.3, *ibid*, 1871–72 and 1872–73 (Report of tour in Eastern Rajputana), Vol. VI, p. 91 ff; *ibid*, Vol. I, Archaeological Report for 1862–63, pp. 320–322. See also A. Cunningham, *The Ancient Geography of India* (reprinted, Varanasi, 1963) pp. 153, 303 ff. etc.
[2]See A. Ghosh 'Taxila (Sirkap), 1944–45', *Ancient India*, No. 4, p. 41 ff; A Ghosh and K.C. Panigrahi, 'The Pottery of Ahichchhatra, District Bareilly, U.P.', *ibid*, No. 1, p. 37 ff.

rata'[1] site,[2] and initiated digging at Purana Qila, the site which is believed, by tradition, to represent Indraprastha of the *Mahābhārata*.[2] Talk about the archaeology of the *Rāmāyaṇa* is more recent. H.D. Sankalia who made a brief exploration of Ayodhya and collected PGW sherds there seems to be of the opinion that an excavation at the site is likely to shed considerable light on the *Rāmāyaṇa* mystery.[3] A more comprehensive justification is worked out by B.B. Lal[4] who has already completed the first season's excavation at Ayodhya.[5]

I

Both these pleas and what else has been mentioned above imply an archaeology of the epics. Let us try to grasp its meaning in relation to the *Rāmāyaṇa* to begin with. What Sankalia attempts broadly is to indicate the archaeological range which can correspond to the growth history of an original *Rāmākathā*, apart, of course, from an analysis of the internal evidence. Archaeologically, the final dates are suggested to him by the description of such cities as Ayodhyā, Kishkindhā and Laṅkā 'which were built between the Kushāṇa and Gupta periods' (alternatively, he suggests a third-fourth century B.C. date for the description of Ayodhyā).[6] While the timespan which the descriptions of the *Rāmayaṇa* cities can cover is thus as broad as eight hundred years, the position with the early stratum of the *Rāmakathā* is no better. One item in the cultural equipment of this stratum, namely weapons, is taken to indicate Iron Age, suggesting 800 B.C. as the earliest possible date.[7] If one were to draw comparisons with Homer's allusion to an already lost Mycenaean civilization,[8] reference to iron weapons may have been a case of transferred value—from bronze to iron—in an age which had grown used to iron. And indeed Sankalia thinks also in terms of the foundation of Ayodhyā 'about 1500 B.C. or latest 1000 B.C'.[9]

The position would really not be simple even if one were to assume that the core of the *Rāmakathā* related to the Iron Age. In terms of the archaeology of the Ganga valley this may imply, although it has not been clearly spelt out by Sankalia, the period of the PG Ware Culture or that of the NBP Ware. Sankalia's ingenious finding that the earliest stratum of the *Rāmāyaṇa* portrays an Ayodhyā in which the houses were made of mud[10] does not help, because burnt brick houses did not come to be constructed on a large scale in this region before about the second century B.C. anyway.[11] And the least one can hope for in the protohistoric sites of the area is the evidence of single culture occupation which may recognizably correspond to any of the layers of the *Rāmāyaṇa*.

What also has been totally ignored by the advocates of *Rāmāyaṇa* archaeology is the total spatial dimension of cultures. If one accepts the findings of D.R. Chanana's research—of which incidentally neither Sankalia nor Lal seems to be aware—the '*Rāmāyaṇa* society' incorporates two types of culture, one tribal, represented by that of the *vānaras* and *rākshasas* and the other agrarian, that of the kingdom of Kośala.[12] This differentiation on the basis of the traits available in the *Rāmāyaṇa* should have helped not only to recognize the nature of the additions made subsequently to the traits (such as the account of the city of Lāṅkā which will have no archaeological correspondence, if it is supposed that the *rākshasa* society represents a tribal stage of culture, a supposition subscribed to by Sankalia too in his characterization of Rāvaṇa as a Gond chief[13]), but should have had several archaeological implications as well. First, it will have involved a search for an archaeological correspondence to the geographical distribution of two types of cultures, assuming of course, that the original stratum of the *Rāmāyaṇa* did in fact represent these two types. The archaeology of the *Rāmāyaṇa* would in such a case not simply have covered

[1]B.B. Lal, 'Excavation at Hastināpura and other Explorations in the Upper Ganga and Sutlej Basins 1950–52: New Light on the Dark age between the end of the Harappa culture and the early Historical Period,' *Ancient India*, nos. 10–11, (1954 & 1955) p. 5-151.

[2]See *Indian Archaeology 1954–55—A Review*, pp. 13–14; *IAR 1969–70*, pp. 4–5.

[3]*Ramayana: Myth or Reality ?* (New Delhi, 1973), p. 45.

[4]B.B. Lal, 'Archaeology and the two Indian epics,' *Annals of the Bhandarkar Oriental Research Institute*, Vol., LIV, pts. I–IV (1973), pp. 1–8.

[5]See the report in *The Statesman*, Delhi, 1 April, 1975, p.8.

[6]Sankalia, *op. cit.*, p. 46. The internal evidence alone of the *Rāmāyaṇa* on the city of Ayodhyā, as available in the *Bālakāṇḍa*, gives a crucial clue for a dating which may correspond to its description:

Sāmantaıā asarighaiścha Bālikarmābhirāvritāṁ/Nānādeśanivāsaischa vanigbhirupaṇobhitām/Rāmāyaṇa, 1.5.9, Baroda Oriental Institute edition, I, 1960. Here more than the description of the city, it is the expression *Sāmantarājasaṅgha* which is important. The expression *sāmanta* in the sense it has been used here cannot be earlier than the Gupta period.

[7]Sankalia, *op. cit.*, p. 16.

[8]See M.I. Finley, *The Ancient Greeks* (Harmondsworth, 1966), p. 21.

[9]Sankalia, *op. cit.*, p. 45.

[10]*Ibid.*, p. 46.

[11]A. Ghosh, *The City in Early Historical India* (Simla, 1973), pp. 68–70.

[12]D.R. Chanana, *The Spread of Agriculture in Northern India (as depicted in the Rāmāyana of Vālmīki)* (New Delhi, 1963), *passim*.

[13]Sankalia, *op. cit.*, pp. 48–49.

a few select sites of the *Rāmāyaṇa* but would have demanded a study of the relationship in which the archaeology of U.P. and northern Bihar stood with reference to the regions in which the *rākshasas* and the *vānaras* may be supposed to have been located. And all these suppositions in an apparent chronological void would have indicated the kind of problems a not-too-comprehensive coverage of *Rāmāyaṇa* archaeology was likely to confront.

The spread of settled agriculture is a part of the problem of Indian archaeology in general, but the relative advance made in different periods is supposed to be indicated in the two epics—an indication which, if it were dependable, would have led to important assumptions regarding the chronology of the completion of the two epics.[1] Archaeologists like B.B. Lal have already speculated upon their relative chronology from a different perspective, partly on the basis of an already worked out literary synchronism and partly on the basis of an attempted correlation between archaeology and the evidence of local tradition. Basing himself on the synchronism worked out by H.C. Raychaudhuri who, on the strength of a passage in the *Bṛihādāraṇyaka Upanishad*, showed Janaka to be later than Parikshit and possibly contemporaneous with Nichakshu[2] Lal remarks,[3] although with some reservations,

> It may incidentally be recalled here that it was in the time of Nichakshu that Hastināpura was washed away by the Gaṅgā and the capital was shifted to Kauśāmbi where a devolved form of the Painted Grey Ware has been encountered at the lower levels.

Lal seems to be little aware that he contradicts himself in the next paragraph by depending on a local tradition at a '*Rāmāyaṇa*' site, which identifies the harpoons of the Copper Hoard complex as arrows of Lava and Kuśa thus, favouring the claim of the Copper Hoard culture as being that of the *Rāmāyaṇa*.[4] As Lal himself associates the Copper Hoard culture with the OCP on the basis of circumstantial evidence,[5] the contradiction involved here in believing the *Rāmāyaṇa* to represent both a late phase of the PGW and the Copper Hoard culture is obvious. It is not at all being suggested here that the *Rāmāyaṇa* cannot cover the timespan of two cultures, but then such an admission would clearly recognize the difficulty of approaching the archaeology of the epic sites in terms of any ill founded assumptions regarding their relative chronology.

Let us probe this point about relative chronology a little further in literary and archaeological terms. If, as assumed by Sankalia, the *Rāmāyaṇa* does not represent a pre-Iron stage and if, along with the already cited evidence of the *Bṛihadāraṇyaka Upanishad*, the story of the colonization of Videha, as narrated in the *Śatapatha Brāhmaṇa*,[6] is considered in this context, then the *Rāmāyaṇa* story and consequently the archaeological sequence at least of northern Bihar would appear to have been later than that of the Kuru-Pañchāla region, perhaps the locus of the *Bhārata-Kathā*. A comparative economic study of the two epics, however, does not seem to bear this out; Chanana who made such a study sums up his conclusions in the following words:[7]

> .... a comparison of these few pockets of cultivation in the valley of the Ganges with the area of cultivation as described in the *Mahābhārata* (taking only those regions of the Ganges valley, which were ruled by the princes belonging to the *Kaurava* and *Pāṇḍava* families) shows us that during an intervening period, cultivation has spread further.

There can in fact be no unanimity regarding the relative chronology of the two epics. Their growth process, spread over a number of centuries, presupposes a considerable degree of overlapping in time, and it may be too much to expect that the chronology of a few 'epic' sites, even after they are correctly ascertained archaeologically, will settle the problem of relative dating. To reiterate a point made earlier, the advocates of the archaeology of the epic sites do not speak of the entire range of places mentioned either in the *Māhābhārata* or in the *Rāmāyaṇa:* the first phase of the five year project on the archaeology of the *Rāmāyaṇa* sites does not even include Mithilā or Videha in north Bihar.[8] The explanation for the selection of sites may be that the initial focus ought to be on the core sites of the epics, but such an explanation gives rise to the problem of another type of selection: the criteria for the selection of literary data for correlation with archaeological evidence.

This perhaps brings in a bigger question of the relative reliability of different categories and strata of literary tradition; one need not go into any details here but point to only what is strictly relevant to the context of the archaeology of the Ganga basin. As a preface to what will be said later on we quote V. Gordon Childe:[9]

[1]How difficult it is to make an assessment of the relative advances made by different areas will be clear from a look at the agricultural regions of India around the middle of the second millennium B.C. Agricultural practices in central and eastern India are certainly not later than in the upper or central Ganga basin.

[2]H.C. Raychaudhuri, *Political History of Ancient India,* sixth edition (University of Calcutta, 1953), pp. 8–49.

[3]Lal, *op. cit.* (1973), p. 7.

[4]*Ibid.*

[5]B.B. Lal, 'Further copper hoards from the Gangetic Basin and a review of the problem,' *Ancient India,* 7, pp. 20–37.

[6]I.4.I. 14–17.

[7]Chanana, *op. cit.*, p.19.

[8]See the handout 'Archaeology of the Ramayana sites published by the Archaeology of the Ramayana Sites Project, Gwalior, March, 1975.

[9]V. Gordon Childe, *The Aryans* (London, 1926), p. 32.

> .... the *Kṣatriya* (i.e., the Epic and Puranic) tradition....is hardly an unpolluted source of history. The orthodox view is not really based on the priestly tradition, as embodied in epexetical works, but rather on the internal evidence of the Veda itself. The latter carries conviction precisely because the historical and geographical references in the hymns are introduced only incidentally.... The same cannot be said of the *Kṣatriya* tradition, which in its recorded form dates from an age (perhaps as late as 200 A.D.) when myth-making had had many centuries to work in, and which might serve dynastic ends.

Several other reasons, apart from these general features of the internal evidence of several categories of literary sources, compel one to turn to Vedic rather than epic and Puranic data for correlation with archaeological evidence. It is widely admitted now that the stages in the societal evolution of the Ganga basin and its peripheries are indicated in the Vedic tradition[1] and chronologically at least the PGW and NBP Ware phases in the archaeology of this region broadly coincide with the period generally known as the later Vedic.[2] As has been shown by Raychaudhuri, many traditions are common between the Vedic and the Epic sources (in fact this is the basis of many synchronisms worked out by him),[3] and while the epics continued to grow, thus making it practically impossible to isolate their different strata from one another, their early milieu may be believed to have been preserved in the Vedic tradition.

Why the Epics and not the Vedic or early Buddhist sources have been the concern of the archaeologists is another matter, but the point just made leads us on to another dimension of the Vedic evidence which is of crucial importance so far as the archaeology of the Ganga basin is concerned. The Vedic texts show an unmistakable shift from tribe to territory,[4] a common enough corollary to the transition to an agrarian economy. Areas of settlements—their names associated with various groups—are mentioned throughout the later Vedic texts, and the list of sixteen *mahājanapadas* as given in the Buddhist *Aṅguttara-nikāya*[5] was anticipated in such later Vedic references.[6] The 'epic' sites of the Ganga basin and its peripheries, which have so far been shown to be of any archaeological potential, are in fact subsumed in these settlement areas or *janapadas* which provide the territorial milieu of the early strata of both the epics. By the sixth century B.C. different types of settlements such as *grāma*, *nigama* and *nagara* had emerged within the framework of the *janapadas*,[7] and this literary classification has two important bearings on an analysis of the archaeological data: (1) the archaeological culture of a region ought not to be considered as monolithic; the culture assemblage at rural, commercial or urban sites is likely to have varied considerably, (ii) the process of the formation of *janapadas*, if understood in literary terms alone, implies the evolution of a composite type of culture,[8] and as such it should be considered risky, if not at times totally futile, to single out any particular archaeological cultural trait for correlation with literary evidence. This point may be a little elaborated by reference to the archaeology of the PGW phase at Hastinapur. The PG Ware itself has often been understood in terms of the Aryans[9]; the distribution of the PG Ware sites tallies excellently with that of the Pūru-Bharatas leading to D.D. Kosambi's identification of PGW with 'Pūru-Kuru ceramics'.[10] And yet wheel-made pottery is, so far as the Vedic evidence is concerned, post-Ṛigvedic, and in view of its association with the Asuras, probably a non-Aryan craft.[11] Two other cultural traits of this phase, namely rice and such domesticated animals as pig and buffalo are shown to have had an 'eastern cultural bias.'[12]

The point of this rather lengthy digression was to show that traditional evidence—here represented by the evidence of literary texts—and that of archaeology can perhaps meet only at certain points. For the protohistoric cultures of the Ganga basin, neither the genealogical accounts of royal families nor the distribution or movements of individual tribal groups are likely to provide such common meeting grounds. The point may perhaps be reached by undertaking a total structural study of society and the major trends of societal change in terms of both archaeology and literary tradition.

[1]See D.D. Kosambi, *An Introduction to the study of Indian History* (Bombay, 1956), Chapters 4 and 5; for stages in the evolution of economy see R.S. Sharma, *Light on Early Indian Society and Economy* (Bombay, 1966), pp. 55–66.

[2]See R.S. Sharma, 'The Later Vedic Phase and the Painted Grey Ware culture,' paper presented at the 35th session of the Indian History Congress, Jadavpur, 1974. See above, pp. 63-67.

[3]Raychaudhuri, *op. cit.*, Chapter II.

[4]Ghosh, *op. cit.*, pp. 4, 34.

[5]Raychaudhuri, *op. cit.*, Chapter III.

[6]*Ibid.* p. 58. The list of countries which Raychaudhuri has compiled for the age of Janaka includes many of the Buddhist *mahājanapada* list. That the brāhmanical sources perhaps relate to an earlier tradition may emerge from the substitution of Vajjian confederacy for Videha in the *Aṅguttara-nikāya* list.

[7]See N. Wagle, *Society at the time of the Buddha* (Bombay, 1966), Chapter II.

[8]Kosambi, *op. cit.*, Chapter 4.3; 4.4; for an analysis of the linguistic evidence see Romila Thapar, Presidential Address, Section I, Indian History Congress, Varanasi, 1969.

[9]The hypothesis, first put forward by B.B. Lal, *op. cit.*, (1954 & 1955) 10–11, pp. 150–151 has been extensively discussed among others by Dilip Chakrabarti, 'The Aryan Hypothesis in Indian Archaeology', *Indian Studies: Past and Present*, Vol. IX, 4 (1969), pp. 349 ff. and B.K. Thapar, 'The Aryans: A re-appraisal of the problem' in Lokesh Chandra *et al.*, (ed.) *India's contribution to World Thought and Culture* (Madras, 1970), pp. 156–158, 160–161.

[10]D.D. Kosambi, *The Culture and Civilization of Ancient India in Historical outline*, Indian Edition (Delhi, 1972), p. 91.

[11]S.R. Das, 'The Mahabharata and Indian Archaeology,' in D.C. Sircar (ed.), *The Bhārata War and Purānic Genealogies*, (University of Calcutta, 1969), pp. 73–75.

[12]Chakrabarti, *op. cit.*

Secondly, the roots of both the epics in so far as they are embedded in any organized literary material have to be traced in the process of the formation of the early *janapadas*. Hastināpura and Indraprastha were two important centres of the Kuru *janapada*, Ayodhyā of the *janapada* of Kośala and Mithilā of Videha.[1] The neglect of this type of correlation, beyond which it is perhaps not possible to go at this stage, explains why the PGW has been sought to be understood both in terms of the Aryans and the *Mahābhārata* tradition.[2] The archaeology of the epic sites of the Ganga basin can thus at best be the archaeology of its *janapadas* and nothing more.

II

We finally come to the examination of the plea for the archaeology of the Epics from a different perspective—from the perspective of a 'consumer'[3] to whom such pleas are vitally related to the overall archaeological planning in the country. It is historiographically interesting to note that this plea has emerged over the years from an initially crucial archaeological understanding 'to bridge...(the) vast gap of nearly twelve centuries'[4] between the Harappan and the early historical cultures. The possibility that what was put forward as a hypothesis might develop into an axiomatic truth in Indian archaeology was foreshadowed by A. Ghosh in his editorial notes on the Hastinapur excavation report :[5]

> The following report often refers to the *Mahābhārata* and the place-names mentioned in it and brings into prominence the fact that the Painted Grey ware is found at the sites associated with the story of that epic. Such references are easily understandable and even unavoidable, for was not Hastināpura the focus of the epic-tale ? But a word of caution is necessary, lest the impression is left on the unwary reader that the Hastināpura excavation has yielded archaeological evidence about the truth of the story of the *Mahābhārata* and that here at last is the recognition by 'official archaeology' of the truth embodied in Indian traditional literature. Such a conclusion would be unwarranted. Beyond the facts that Hastināpura, the reputed capital of the Kauravas, was found to be occupied by a people whose distinctive ceramics were the Painted Grey ware in a period which might roughly have synchronized with the origin of the nucleus of the *Mahābhārata* story, that this occupation came to an end with a heavy flood and this ware is found at many early sites, some of which are connected, either in literature or by tradition, with the epic-heroes, the excavation has no bearing on the authenticity or otherwise of the epic tale. It is indeed tempting to utilize archaeological evidence for substantiating tradition, but the pitfalls in the way should be guarded against, and caution is necessary that fancy does not fly ahead of facts.

And yet the case for the archaeology of the *Rāmāyaṇa* sites is apparently based on the 'success' of the PG ware archaeology in unravelling the *Mahābhārata* mystery. Besides, the arguments given above to show that no particular archaeological phase can correspond to the *Mahābhārata* or for that matter *Rāmāyaṇa* times—because the span of 'epic' times can cover several archaeological phases—the backbone of the entire PG Ware—*Mahābhārata* correlation, namely the confirmation of the Puranic flood legend and the legend relating to the transfer of the Kuru capital to Kauśāmbi, may not be as strong as it looks.[6] And what kind of material remains have Hastinapura and Indraprastha revealed to provide points of comparison with the epic evidence? Admittedly, here archaeology can serve as a corrective to the exaggerated accounts of the epics, and the fact that there cannot be any one to one correlation between archaeology and tradition comes out clearly from a statement regarding Troy, supposedly one of the best sites served by tradition: 'There is something wrong either with Schliemann's Troy or with Homer's.'[7] On the other hand, the spade digging at the epic sites in India has been expected to cover such an enormous range of questions as, one would suspect, take a Delphic oracle to answer: 'When did Rama live? Where is Laṅkā? ....and what about the *Mahābhārata?* Is it a fact or a fiction? How about the mighty palaces mentioned in this epic? And the weapons wielded by the heroes at the battle of Kurukṣetra?'[8] Questions such as these or whether 'any traces of Rāma and Krishna'[9] have been found have, in the final analysis, led to the emergence of 'epic' archaeology as a serious archaeological undertaking, because as one scholar admits, 'When questions like these cannot be answered, people, including scholars, think that we—archaeologists—are wasting our time and nation's money.[10] It is precisely these considerations which have made the author of the present note feel wary: One would have expected archaeological planning and expensive excavations to rest on serious academic considerations and on the current state of research in archaeology and not on a decision to resolve certain emotional hang-ups regarding a particular epic hero or an archaeological site.

Methodologically too the 'epic' archaeology could produce important repercussions on

[1]Raychaudhuri, *op. cit.*, Chapter III, Section I.
[2]Lal, *op. cit.* (1954 & 1955), pp. 147–151.
[3]For the sense in which the term is being used here see Barun De, 'Encapsulation as an alternative to the difficulties of periodising Indian history', in S.C. Malik (ed.), *Indian Civilization: The First Phase* (Problems of a Source Book) (Simla, 1971), pp. 83–84.
[4]Lal, *op. cit.* (1954 & 1955), p. 6.
[5]A. Ghosh, 'Notes,' *Ancient India*, nos. 10 & 11, pp. 2–3.

[6]Das, *op. cit.*, pp. 56–58.
[7]Rhys Carpenter cited by M.I. Finley, *Aspects of Antiquity: Discoveries and Controversies* (Harmondsworth, 1972), p. 36.
[8]Lal, *op. cit.*, (1973), p. 1.
[9]Sankalia, *op. cit.*, p. 1.
[10]*Ibid.*, p. 2.

archaeology elsewhere in the country. The *Mahābhārata* and the *Rāmāyaṇa* are not the only two literary compositions in India which can provide a case for correlation with archaeological evidence. If a fresh digging at Kaverippumpattinam is undertaken, and if its excavator wishes to model his assumptions on the archaeology of the *Mahābhārata* and the *Rāmāyaṇa*, he may no longer be excavating a site in the littoral region of the *Sangam* sources but may rather be searching for Kovalan and Kannaki, respectively the hero and heroine of the *Silappadikaram*.

Jawahar Lal Nehru University B.D. CHATTOPADHYAYA
New Delhi, 110057

Prehistoric Colonization in India : Archaeological and Literary Evidence

Before proceeding to examine our literary and archaeological data let me define colonization as a stage when a group of people, united either by race, religion, trade or profession, migrates to a new place, region or country and establishes its way of life, to which it was accustomed, making such changes as are or become necessary, owing to environmental, ecological and other reasons.

ARCHAEOLOGICAL EVIDENCE

Our literary data are preserved in the Vedic and Purāṇic literature. These describe, very incidentally indeed, how certain regions of India came to be occupied by Vedic tribes or chiefs and Purāṇic dynasties. Neither do the Vedic texts and the Purāṇas tell us about the earlier inhabitants of the places occupied or colonized; nor do we get a detailed or intimate picture of the way of life of either the original inhabitants or the new settlers. Something about the political, social, religious and economic conditions, however, may be gathered by putting together the scraps of evidence from these sources.

As opposed to this we have a number of chalcolithic and neolithic cultures recently, identified in different parts of India during the last thirty years or so. Since 1955, I have several times pointed out as to how one may try to identify these cultures with the Vedic and Purāṇic tribes or dynasties; the thesis put forward therein has been enlarged here in this paper.

Now, each of these cultures has to be regarded, on the principle explained above, as a kind of colonization. But, colonization from where? In our present knowledge, from Iran and countries further westwards. For, in every case, we have no earlier deposits, except on sites like Anjira and Rana Ghundai, and even there, the pottery of each sub-phase is found to be quite different and distinct from the earlier and later cultures. We do not have much evidence for local development and, therefore, Ross was compelled to describe these cultures as colonization by newcomers.

Thus, in Baluchistan, in the absence of any other evidence of a local, indigenous development , we have got to postulate arrival of different groups of people at various times and settling down on the same site or different sites in a region divided by hills and valleys. The scene changes a little when at one time, about 2500 B.C., we find not at one place but at many places, from north to south and east to west, not only pottery, but relics like seals, figurines and even brick-made houses with sanitary arrangements as found at Mohenjo-daro. Thus, the Indus Civilization spread not only in Baluchistan but also in the whole of Punjab, Sind, Saurashtra and even the borders of Afghanistan or the North-West Frontier Province. Though as yet we do not know who the authors of the Indus Civilization were, there is little doubt that it was one of the largest and widespread colonizations or an empire. For, wherever we go, either at Gumla or Kulli or Mehi and Dabarkot in Baluchistan or Ropar in East Panjab,

Kalibangan in north Rajasthan, or Lothal in Saurashtra,[1] we behold an almost uniform, identical way of life.

Such a uniformity in material culture or objects of daily life has never been witnessed in the cultural history of India including the British, the Mughal, the Gupta, Maurya or the Roman empires. In all these examples, we have had, no doubt, the exercise of political hegemony from Delhi or Patna or from Rome. But no one can call it, by any stretch of imagination, a colonization. But it was different with the Indus Civilization. The Harappans had probably spread out from Sind, in about 2500 B.C. or even earlier, and gradually occupied the regions mentioned above, and established everywhere their way of life. This could have been made possible only when the authorities at Harappa and Mohenjo-daro had sent out trained architects, engineers, masons, potters, bead-makers, etc.

Of course, with more careful excavations and study of finds from each site, some differences will be found, but these are not expected to be of a major kind in such a far-flung "Cultural Empire".

As far as we know, this was the most widespread attempt in the colonization of India. But it now appears that it was not the first. From the small probings made by Sir Mortimer Wheeler at Harappa, and from those by the Pakistani archaeologists at Kot Diji and recently at Gumla and those at Kalibangan, the existence of a culture earlier than the Harappan is indicated. This culture has been called pre-Harappan, but Rafique Moghul[2] would prefer to call it "Early Harappan". To me the name is not of much relevance, as the fact that a few centuries before the mature Harappan was established all over Sind, the Punjab, Baluchistan, Kutch, Saurashtra and Gujarat coast, there was an equally extensive culture covering these regions. Whoever the authors might have been, a uniform kind of daily life was witnessed, a few centuries before the Harappans, over a wide area. It had no *visible roots* in the earlier indigenous culture. So, according to the definition of colonization we have adopted, we have to describe this phenomena, and phenomenon it was, as colonization.

From where did these colonizers come? At the moment the answer is from Iran, and further afield. For, in the pottery fabrics and designs found among the pre-Harappan deposits at Kalibangan, at Kot-Diji and at Gumla there are a majority which are identical with those from Baluchistan and Iran. Unless, therefore, we can show that these too have developed on the Indian soil, these have got to be regarded as imports or objects made by a group of people who had come from Iran and Western Asia through the Bolan and Gomal passes in Baluchistan and Afghanistan.

According to the latest information received from Rafique Mughal of Pakistan Directorate of Archaeology, the nucleus of the pre-Harappan and post-Harappan or the Cemetery-H Culture, or as he prefers to call the Early, Mature and Late Harappan Culture—was the central Indus Valley.[3] This region, it would appear on the present showing, had received a series of impacts from Iran and Western Asia. These, acting on or mixing with the indigenous element, flowered into the Indus Civilization. There is no denying the fact, that as now, or throughout the known historical periods or phases, beginning with the Irano-Mauryan, Indo-Greek, Saka, Kushan, Roman and Gupto-Sassanian, the number of foreigners or colonizers must have been biologically always small indeed, though the actual number and their depth of penetration into India would depend upon a number of other circumstances. Foreign objects, however, such as the Roman amphora had reached even the heart and forested regions like Devnimori in northern Gujarat.

As is now understood, owing to several causes the Indus Civilization began to decline and disappear both in the nuclear and in the peripheral regions by about 1700 B.C. Even in Saurashtra, at Rangpur and Somnath, not only the brick-built houses are replaced by the mud or the lime-stone houses but the pottery also gradually changed. The chert and flint blades went out of use. Among the new pottery shapes and fabrics were the footed cups or goblets[4] of the Lustrous Red Ware. Since I first saw this I have been reminded of Iranian parallels, viz., the goblets at Sialk and Hissar, though I must admit that the Rangpur goblets are not the exact copies of any Iranian originals.

What was the source of these cultures?

At Navdatoli, the culture appears already in a fully developed form, in about 1600 B.C. There is no change whatsoever in the house plans, though the use of lime becomes infrequent. The blade industry also shows no change. The only change one witnesses is in pottery forms, fabrics and decorations. These show a profusion in phases II and III and seem to decline in phase IV.

1. E.J. Ross, 'A chalcolithic site in Baluchistan'. *Journal of Near Eastern Studies* Vol. V (1946), no. 4, pp. 284-317; H.D. Sankalia, *The Prehistory and Protohistory of India and Pakistan* (Poona, 974), p. 325.

2. Mohammad Rafique Mughal, *The Early Harappan Period in the Greater Indus Valley and Northern Baluchistan* (*C.* 3000-2400 B.C.) Ph.D. Thesis, University of Pennsylvania, 1970 (Xeroxed Copy, Michigan, 1976).

3. Mohammad Rafique Mughal, *Exploration in Northern Baluchistan* (Cyclostyled Copy, 1973).

4. Not less than eight such goblets with flared bases in the orwe fabric have been found in the recent excavations at Daimabad, JDistrict Ahmednagar.

Among all these, the only indigenous elements are no doubt the house plans and methods of construction. These may still be seen at Navdatoli itself or anywhere on the Narmada from Amarkantak to Maheshwar.

But nowhere among the indigenous inhabitants, which are largely Bhils in the central Narmada Valley, and Gonds in the upper, does one see such wine-cups, champagne-and brandy-cups as Sir Mortimer Wheeler christened them on first seeing them in 1959 at Navdatoli. Nor can one see anywhere, the now-familiar large, channel-spouted bowl. In fact, it was the discovery of such a channel-spout in the excavations at Navdatoli in 1953-54 and its occurrence in Iran, as brought to my notice by A.V. Naik, one of my first pupils, that led to the large-scale excavation at Navdatoli. These excavations brought to light not only rich pottery-complex and equally rich stone blade industry but also charred grains of wheat, rice, barley, mung, beans and also oil seeds like flax.

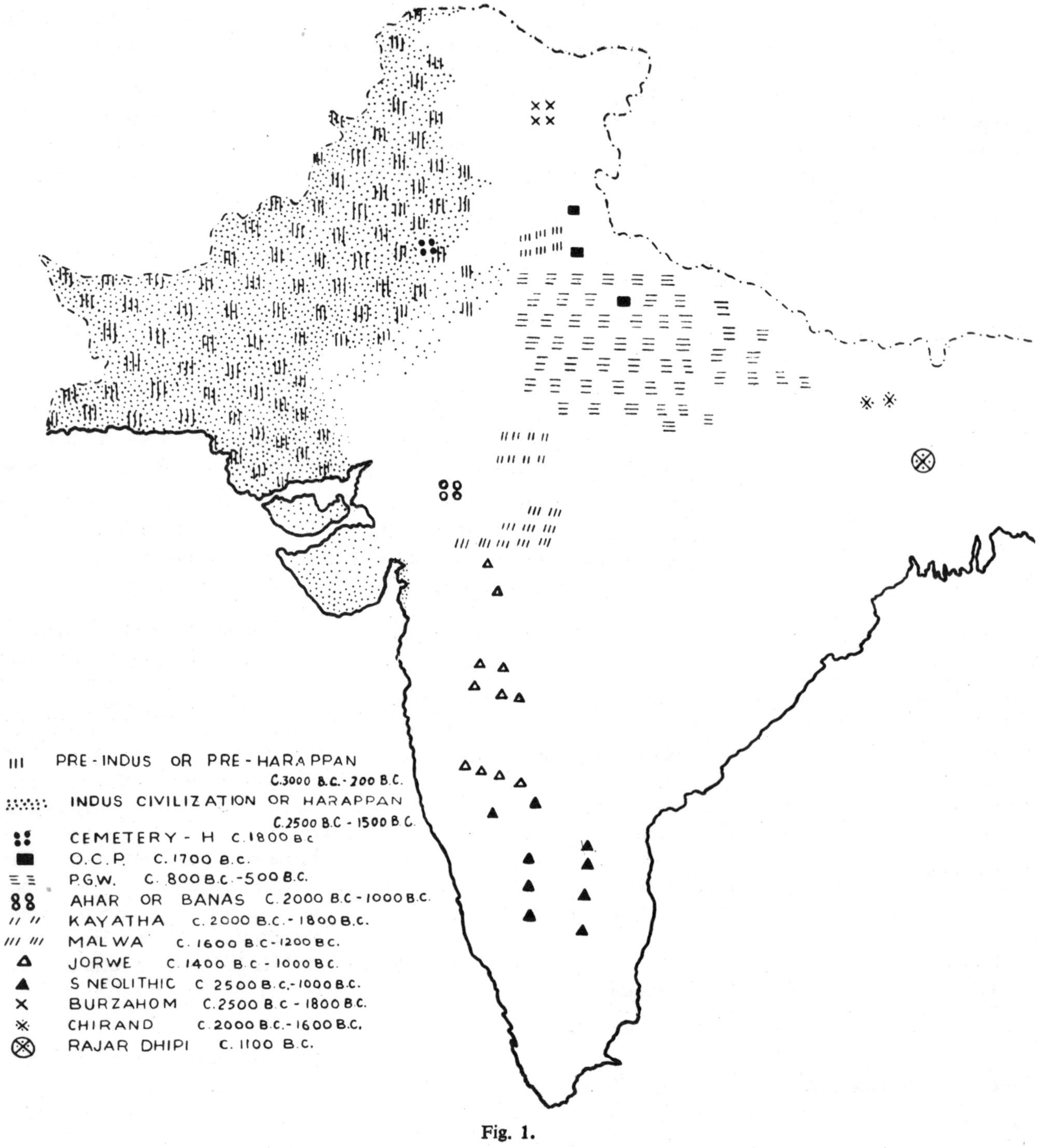

Fig. 1.

Now this was the first time that so many cereals were found at one site. They are all grown today in and around Navdatoli and in Madhya Pradesh. Thus, the antiquity of the food habits of the people or of food production has been taken back to at least 3500 years. But when and where did it begin? In Madhya Pradesh or outside? On this point the palaeobotanists tell us that at least three of the grains viz., wheat, lentil and barley, and the oil seed, viz., flax, have had a much earlier origin in Western Asia, at Catal Huyuk in Turkey. All these have been found there as early as *circa* 6000 B.C. There are many other sites as well, as can be seen in the accompanying map.

All the available data as known upto August 1974 has been listed in the chart published in my book.[1] This shows an unmistakable eastward diffusion of such important grains as wheat, barley and lentil and the oil seeds like flax and sesamum.

Some ten years later, V.S. Wakankar discovered Kayatha, the ancient Kapitthaka of Varāhamihira, near Ujjain. Excavations here have yielded the genesis of an earlier culture called the Kayatha Culture and superimposed by that of Ahar and Navdatoli.

The Ahar or the Banas Culture reveals a similar story. No antecedent stages are found in the 15·24 m deposit at Ahar, a site now part of Udaipur city. The ancient Aharians were well conversant with the smelting of copper from the beginning, i.e., when we first meet them settling on the banks of the Ahar river in about 2100 B.C. They made an altogether different kind of pottery, very little of it was painted, and the inhabitants used no stone tools, except huge saddle-querns and pounders for grinding or crushing grains. Their houses were large, built on the locally and easily available schist stone plinth, with walls of mud and mud-brick. These houses were furnished with huge storage jars, built-in silos and large two-mouthed *chūlās*.

These house-remains, provided with abundant pottery, saddle-querns and *chūlās*, contained little else, so that contacts and connections with other sites in India, even Rajasthan and Madhya Pradesh are difficult to establish. But among the thirty-eight terracotta beeads bering incised decorations, eight beads show designs which are identical with those from Troy, while one recalls that from Anau in Central Asia. This is indeed insufficient evidence to warrant any legitimate conclusions regarding the foreign origin of the Ahar Culture. But, on the other hand, we have none at all for indigenous origins either. Detailed study by one of my former pupils, Malti Nagar, of the Bhils in and around Dhulkot at Udaipur and in south-east Rajasthan showed no more evidence of the local origins than the house-plan, which I had first noticed in 1962. Thus my view that the Bhils might have been once the original authors of the Ahar Culture remains unproved.

Thus though there is evidence, albeit insufficient, to say that the Ahar and the Navdatoli Cultures (cf map on p. 74) were colonizations from outside India, still it is necessary to point out the general reaction, practically all over the world, among scholars and others, against such an attempt to seek an explanation for cultural changes at a site, to foreign-influences, be it as diffusion, or actual biological contact, invasion, migration or trade. Several authors have shown by various kinds of study, such as spectography, detailed analysis of techniques, that many of the earlier views based on general resemblances between objects, say in England and Europe, or Egypt and Crete, were based on very insecure foundations. And very often the explanation, or the understanding of the origin of prehistoric cultures might be found in the archaeological record itself. This has been shown by Graham Clark, Walter Adams and Lewis Binford.

Thus, the old views of Elliot Smith, Gordon Childe and even Braidwood (who tried to seek the origins of agriculture and domestication of animals and the beginning of civilization in the supposed nuclear area of Western Asia) are no longer regarded as sacrosanct. It is, therefore, possible that when further work is done in India, we may find the origins of the various regional-prehistoric-cultures discovered during the last 25 years within India itself. Though my personal belief—or call it a hunch—is that what has happened during the historical times had also happened during the various prehistoric periods. And it is by the interaction of these foreign (outside) forces and those within the country that the various chalcolithic cultures were born. These regional cultures, at present known by very prosaic names after the type-sites or the pottery fabric such as Ahar or Banas, Navdatoli, Jorwe-Nevasa and the PGW. do not represent only distinct pottery groups or functional needs of the respective groups of people but these are probably distinct ethnic and linguistic entitles and these are possibly the forerunners of the linguistic units in which India is divided today. Of course, in these Andhra, Karnataka and Tamilnadu would form one large ethno-linguistic group or block, Jorwe-Nevasa might be proto-Marathi, Navdatoli would be proto-Malwa and Ahar proto-Rajasthani. Similar would be the story in Saurashtra, and the Harappans would thus form a large culture-linguistic group.

It should be one of the main goals of the archaeologists and culture historians in the next decade to try to understand how far this view or prophecy is correct.

[1]Sankalia, *op. cit.*, p. 560.

LITERARY EVIDENCE

On the fundamental question of colonization there are two schools of thought. Not only orthodox scholars of Sanskrit and Hinduism, but even the late K.M. Munshi once thought that the view that the Aryans came to India from Iran had no basis whatsoever. And one argument they put forward was that these people who had migrated had always remembered the fact that they had once belonged to another country or region. They cited the example of the Parsis, among comparatively recent migrants, and the ancient Egyptians and Sumerians among the prehistoric peoples. But no such statement, even a hint, is found either in the Vedic or Puranic literature. Hence Munshi said that if the Aryans had ever come from outside, it was such a long time ago, that they had lost memory of it.

Other arguments have also been advanced to controvert the theory of Aryan migration based on the nature of the language of the *Ṛigveda* and its close affinity to the *Avesta,* the occurrence of the names of Vedic gods, Mitra and Varuṇa in the fourteenth century B.C. Boghazkuei inscriptions and the non-mention of the tiger in Vedic literature.[1]

As opposed to this, not only foreign scholars, but champions of Hinduism and Independence like Tilak and modern scholars like the late A.S. Altekar, A.D. Pusalkar, S.N. Pradhan, and Bhargava have accepted the view that the Aryans had come from outside and gradually settled in India. The question is from where, when and how. Unfortunately, none of these scholars ever cared to pose these questions. This was natural. They were primarily Sanskritists, and not historians; or if so, they never worried to examine, except Altekar to some extent, what would be the effect of their theory of colonization, if we were to accept it. Secondly, when scholars like Pargiter wrote there was no archaeological evidence at all. The great Indus Civilization was still buried under the womb of the earth.

I have been interested in this problem since long, and have tried to correlate the archaeological evidence with the literary tradition, as evidence began to come forth from our excavations at Nasik and Navdatoli in 1950-53.

Since then I have discussed this problem thrice; first at the Seminar on Indian Prehistory, held at Poona in 1964, then in the first and second editions of my book *Prehistory and Protohistory of India and Pakistan* and recently in an international journal, *World Archaeology*.[2] For I believe that this question cannot be solved single-handed, either by archaeologists, or Sanskritists, ethnographers or culture-historians. The problem is indeed complex, and we are likely to be side-tracked, whereas the problem, as I will show, needs all the time an open mind.

Among the scholars who accept the view that the Aryans had come from outside, and who have relied on a careful comparative study—called synchronisms —between the Vedic and Purāṇic evidence, there is no complete unanimity of views. Both the groups of scholars, however, believe that whereas the Vedic evidence is far more trustworthy, the Puranic can or should be accepted, when and where it is corroborated by the Vedic. One major point of difference is the probable date of the Mahābhārata War. Whereas Pradhan and Pusalkar have placed it in *circa* 1400 B.C., Pargitar and Bhargava would do so in about 1000 B.C. Though this does make some difference as to the identity of the people, or tribes in about 1000 B.C. or 1400 B.C in the Punjab and U.P. and elsewhere too, still it does not affect the basic fact that there was a gradual colonization of India by the Aryans from the north-west, who later proceeded eastwards, and then in the heart of India.

Let us now see what would be the nature of the political set up according to these scholars and then examine it in the light of what we know about these regions archaeologically.

The *Ṛigveda* only incidentally mentions the names of tribes which had settled or existed at the time of its latest composition. It is not a historical account in the modern sense. So a careful consideration of it shows that the whole of the territory known to the Vedic settlers was divided into a number of tribal principalities ruled normally by kings.[3] To quote Pusalkar (cf. map on page 77).[4]

> "The extent of the country as reflected in the hymns is, Afghanistan, Punjab, parts of Sind, and Rajputana, the North-West Frontier Province, Kashmir and Eastern India up to the Sarayu. The Vedic people had not yet penetrated into the swampy jungles of Bengal, as would appear from the absence of the mention of the tiger in the *Ṛigvada*. Roughly speaking the extreme north-west was occupied by the Gandhāris, Pakthas, Alinas, Bhalānases and Vashānins, some of whom probably contained the non-Aryan elements. In Sind and the Punjab were settled the Śivas, Parśus Kekayas. Vṛichīvants, Yadus, Anus, Turvaśas, and Druhyus. Further east towards the region of the Madhyadesa were the settlements of the Titsus, Bharatas, Pūrus, and Śṛiñjayas, the easternmost part being in the occupation of the Kīkaṭas. The Matsyas and Chedis were settled to the south of the Punjab in the region of

[1]Those views have been summarized in an Appendix in R.C. Majumdar (ed.), *The Vedic Age* (Bombay, 1971).

[2]H.D. Sankalia, 'Prehistoric colonization in India', *World Archaeology,* vol. 5 (1973), no. 1, pp. 86-91.

[3]A.D. Pusalkar, 'Aryan Settlements in India', in R.C. Majumdar (ed.), *The Vedic Age*, p. 245

[4]*Ibid*, pp. 244-50

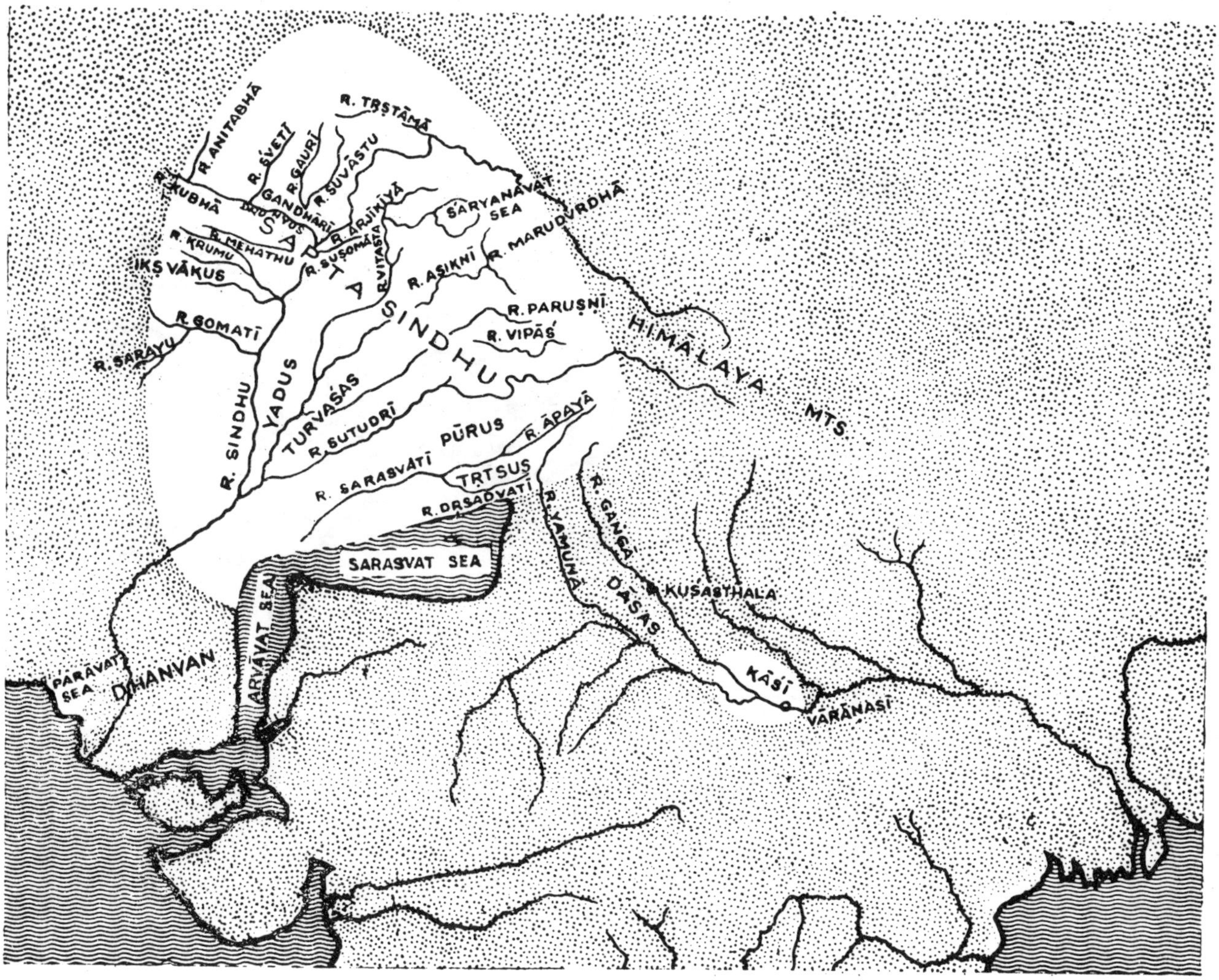

Rajputana and Malwa. The Aryan settlements during the period of the *Ṛigveda* were practically coterminous with the extent of the geographical knowledge of the period, as mentioned above.

During the period of the Later Saṁhitas, Brāhmaṇas. Upanishads, and Sūtras, more areas were colonized, Pusalkar[1] characterizes this period as the one of

"a spirit of adventure and expansion, and the advancing, Aryans were spreading in every direction, colonizing the east south and north. The Gangetic *Doab* was completely occupied by the Aryans and the adventurous Bharatas and Videghas led expeditions along the Yamunā, the Sarasvatī and the Sadānīrā. Towards the east Kosala, Videha, Magadha, and Aṅga came under Aryan occupation during this period. In the north and the north-west, we come across the Uttarakurus and the Uttaramadras, Bāhlīkas, Mahāvṛishas and Mūjavants, showing the expansion along Kāshmir and the Himālayas. Towards the south the Vindhya appears for the first time in the *Kaushitaki Upanished* (11.8), and the Kuntis and Vītahavyas seem to have penetrated further south, and the Narmada and Vidarbha also were within the Aryan fold."

The geographical (topographical) politico-cultural changes during this period should be noted or emphasized, as these might have some bearing from the archaeological point of view. First the Sarasvaṭi is said to have disappeared, according to the *Pañchaviṁśa Brāhmaṇa* (XXV.10.6). "The main centre of the life of the period is Kurukshetra in the country of the Kuru Pañchālas, bounded by the Khāṇḍava on the south, Tūrghna on the north, and Pariṇaḥ on the west."[2] The centre of civilization gradually shifted eastwards, and became localized in the modern Haryana region around

[1] *Ibid.*, 261.

[2] *Ibid.*

Delhi. The Punjab and the west not only decline in importance, but the tribes of the west are looked upon with disapproval in the *Śatapatha* and *Aitareya Brāhmaṇas*. There has been a change and re-grouping of tribes of the Ṛigvedic period, and many new tribes emerge during this period. The Bharatas merge with the Kurus, who, with their allies, the Pañchālas, are the tribe *par excellence*.

The Vasas and Usinaras, the Kuru-Pañchālas occupy the Madhyadeśa.

The Uttarakurus and Uttaramadras lay to the north beyond the Himalayās, and Satvants to the south.

To the east, come up Kosala, Videha, Magadha and Aṇga. Non-Aryan, or not fully Brahmanized tribes, mentioned are the Āndhras, Puṇḍras, Mūtibas, Pulindas and Śabaras as also the Nishādas (cf. map above).

Thus, at the end of the Upanishadic period the whole of India to the north of the Narmada, and some region even to the south of this river had been Aryanized, or had come under the Aryan influence.[1]

[1]*Ibid*.

Pusalkar, unlike Bhargava and Pradhan, reconstructed the traditional history from the Purāṇas and the epics, separately, relying also upon the Purāṇic accounts when they are corroborated by the Vedic texts.[1] There is also the fact, stressed by Altekar and Pusalkar before, to which I would subscribe, that all the Purāṇic genealogy cannot be a figment of imagination of the Sūtas, though there is certainly much repetition of names. Secondly, these names are so characteristic of the Vedic and Purāṇic periods that they rarely occur later. So had all or many of the proper names of persons, as those of places, rivers and mountains, definitely some physical existence. What is most likely is the overlapping of names and dynasties or contemporaneity and not chronological succession. Thus, the period, as worked out by the Purāṇas, would be very much reduced.

Dynastic or political history according to the Purāṇas broadly falls into two main periods: (I) Dynasties before the Flood; (II) Dynasties after the Flood.

The Flood is calculated to have occurred somewhere in the north, about 3100 B.C. The ruler at that time was Manu Vaivasvata. He is said to be the originator of the human race and all the dynasties mentioned in the Purāṇas sprang from him. Of his 9 sons, 4 were important, as they were the founders of the four kingdoms and dynasties.

1. Ikshavāku at Ayodhyā
2. Śaryāti in Ānarta
3. Nābhāgodishṭa at Vaiśālī in north Bihar
4. Karūsha occupied the Karūsha country around Rewa.

From Ilā married to Buddha started the Aila dynasty. From this sprang up the various dynasties such as the Kānyakubjas. Yādavas (Haihayas, Andhakas, and Vṛishṇis, Turvasus, Druhyus, Ānavas, Pañchālas, Barhadrathas, Chedis, etc. From Ilā, transformed into a Kiṁpurusha named Sudyumna, sprang the Sudyumnas—his three sons Utkala, Gaya and Vinatisva, who respectively ruled over the Utkala country, Gaya and the eastern regions. Pusalkar has then divided the entire post-Flood era into several periods, according to the chief or important king. Thus we have the Yayāti Period (*c.* 3000–2750 B.C.). Yayāti's five sons—Yadu, Turvasu, Anu, Druhyu and Puru, carved out several small kingdoms, the main being at Pratishthāna (Allahabad). Yadu ruled over the region of the south-west, embracing the country watered by the rivers Charmaṇāvati (Chambal), Vetravatī (Betwa), and Suktimatī (Ken), Turvasu ruled around Rewa, Druhyu's kingdom was situated west of the Yamuna and north of the Chambal. Anu received the north, i.e., the northern portion of the Ganga-Yamuna *doab*.

The Yādavas (from Yadu) destroyed the Rākshasa power in Gujarat-Kathiawar. They later branched into the Yādavas and Haihayas. In the Solar dynasty at this period, Ikshvāku, the eldest of the Manu's sons, ruled Ayodhyā, the capital of Madhyadeśa. From his other son Nimi, also known as Videha, and named after his son Mithi, we have Mithilā and Videha, whereas one of Manu's grandsons Viśāla founded Viśāla or Vaiśāli.

Śāryati, another of Manu's sons, was succeeded by his son Ānarta, after whom a part of Gujarat-Saurashtra came to be known. The dynasty was short-lived, and was destroyed by the Puṇyajana Rākshasas.

In the next sub-period called "The Māndhātri *c.* 2750–2550 B.C." Māndhātri and his son Purukutsa conquered the Druhyus and Ānvas in the north-west and the Mauneya Gandharvas, and the Nāgas gave him their princess Narmada.

"This shows," says Pusalkar "the extension of the Aryan Culture towards the river Narmada and the land of the Nagas." Later Māndhātri's son Muchukanda built and fortified a town on the Narmada between Paripatra and Riksha mountains. This was later conquered by the Haihaya king Mahishmant who named it Mahishmatī. Later, the Haihayas under Bhadraśrenya marched eastwards and conquered Kāśi which was sometime still later conquered by the Kshemaka Rākshasas, and recovered by Durdama of the Haihayas.

Descendents of Anu, of the Puru or the Aila Lunar Dynasty, extended their sway towards the east(?) and the Punjab (cf map on p. 78). Later Usinara established a kingdom on the eastern border of the Punjab which was divided among his five sons. Of these, Sibi is well known and ruled at Multan, whereas from Nriga sprang the Yaudheyas who ruled parts of Bikaner and the present Montgomery district. Later Sibi is said to have conquered the whole of the Punjab, and established through his sons four kingdoms, the names of which are important for our purpose. These are: (i) The Sibis (or Vrishadarbhas) in the home province of Multan; (ii) the Sauviras of Sind; (iii) the Kekayas in the modern district of Gujrat and Shahpur between the Jhelum and the Chenab; (iv) the Madrakas, with their capital at Sakala (modern Sialkot) in the Lahore division of the Punjab, and Jammu province in Kashmir.[2]

Titikshu is credited with the foundation of "the Kingdom of the East," after having crossed Videha and Vaiśālī. This later developed into the five kingdoms of Aṅga, Vaṅga, Kalinga, Puṇḍra and Suhma, said to be five sons of Bāli.

[1] *Ibid.*

[2] *Ibid.*

The Dṛhuyus are said to have been pushed out from Rajasthan into the Punjab, where these settlements came to be known as Gandhara after one of Aṅgāraś successors. Later they are said to have crossed the borders of India and founded many principalities in the Mlechchha countries.

This expansion of the Aryans from the Madhyadeśa, first into the Punjab, and then beyond India's north-west frontier is palpably unbelievable. And hence, one has to say that the Purāṇas have deliberately tried to invent the explanations of the various divisions of the Punjab and even Sind. We shall see later what would be the significance of this Aryan expansion *vis-a-vis* archaeology.

The next period, according to Pusalkar's interpretation of the Purāṇic and Vedic data is "The Paraśurāma Period (*c.* 2550–2350 B.C.)." The events though skillfully summarized by him appear most bizzare. These 200 years were taken up by the conflict between the Bhṛigus and the Haihayas. Interestingly enough, both these are said to be originally friendly, the former being priestly Brāhmaṇas, and the latter Kshatriya rulers, and both originally belonged to western India. From here the Haihayas, with the help of the Bhṛigus, conquered Māhishmatī on the Narmadā and later carried their expedition eastwards up to Ayodhyā. Ultimately after the long and bitter struggle between the Bhṛigus and the Haihayas, Rāma of the Solar dynasty once again established the supremacy of the Kshatriyas, and Paraśurāma retired to the west, where the entire coast from Broach to Kanyakumari is said to have been reclaimed by him from the sea. From our point of view, what is important are the conquest of Māhishmatī by the Haihayas, their alleged conquests of the east up to Ayodhyā, the survival of the Kshatriya kingdoms, of Ayodhyā, Magadha, Aṅga, and Kāśī from the universal destruction by Paraśurāma, and the emergence of the west coast.

If there is any truth in these Purāṇic accounts, we should find some evidence of the cultural influence from western India into the eastern. For instance, the echoes of the Navdatoli-Maheshwar Chalcolithic Culture can be seen in the recently discovered Ganga Chalcolithic. Also, there is some evidence of the Central Indian Chalcolithic on the west coast. But far more interesting would it be, if we can correlate the alleged rise of the Haihayas in the west, and the belief that the Bhārgavas were some foreigners—westerners—who initially helped the Haihayas in establishing a kingdom on the Narmada at Māhishmatī. The Purāṇas also tell us that the Haihayas had attacked Ayodhyā with the help of the Ṣakas, Yavanas, Kāmbojas, Pāradas and Pahlavas from the north-west.[1] Later, of course, Sagara with the help of the Bhārgavas, retrieved much of the lost kingdom.

The history of the Solar dynasty at Ayodhyā under Sagara, his conquests of the Haihayas, and their allies the Śakas, Yavanas, would be likewise significant, were we to get some archaeological evidence of the eastern cultural influences in the west.

Anyway, Ayodhyā when excavated, should give us thick deposits and the earliest should go back to at least 2500 B.C. The deposits at Champāpurī, near Bhagalpur in east Bihar, is said to have been built by Champa, grandson of Harīśhchandra.

According to the Purāṇas, with the wars of Paraśurāma and Sagara, the Kṛitayuga came to an end. As a result of these wars "The Rāmachandra Period" (*c.* 2350–1950 B.C.), is notable for the appearance of the Gaṅgā and Bhagīratha.

Of the various kings, Raghu gave his name to the family, whereas under Daśaratha, because of his conquests, Ayodhyā once again came into contact with the Yādava kingdom at Mathura, founded by Madhu, whereas in the Doab there were Paurava states of which north Pañchāla was prominent. To its east lay Videha, Vaiśali and Aṅga, and the Vatsa country which formed part of Kāśī, lay to its south. The region south from the Yamuna up to Gujarat and beyond the Vindhya and the Satpura mountains was under the Yādava emperor Madhu.

Pusalkar[2] (as well as Bhargava) believes that the story of Rāma is important because it brings south India definitely into view for the first time. This, as has been pointed out by me elsewhere,[3] is based on wrong interpretation of the Rāmāyaṇa data as well as evidence which is interpreted incorrectly. However, let us proceed to narrate the epic and Purāṇic evidence as to what happened afterwards.

We are told that Lakshamaṇa's two sons Aṅgada and Chandraketu were assigned the Karapatha-deśa near the Himalayas, and Bharata's two sons Taksha and Pushkara, conquered Gandhāra from the Gandharvas and founded respectively Takshaśilā and Pushkalāvatī. Satrughna defeated the Satvata-Yādavas on the west of the Yamuna, killed Madhava Lavaṇa, and established his capital at Madhupuri (Madhura) or Mathura. Rāma's two sons Kuśa and Lava ruled in Ayodhyā and Śrāvastī respectively.

However, very soon, all these were lost, the Ikshvākus, or the Rāghavas are heard of no more and the Pandavas, and Yādavas become the most important dynasties in northern India.

[1] *Ibid.*

[2] *Ibid.*

[3] H.D. Sankalia, *Ramayana: Myth or Reality* (Delhi, 1973).

In the Lunar Dynasty, according to the Purāṇas, Dushyanta's son Bharata was a famous king. The capital was transferred from Pratishṭhāna to the city called later Hastināpura, while his dominions stretched from the Ganges to the Sarasvatī, and some Purāṇas attribute the name Bhāratavarsha to this Bharata.

Later, under Bharata's descendents the 'empire' was split up; Ṛiksha ruled at Hastināpura, while the eastern territory was divided into northern and southern Pañchāla. Further south, Bhīmaratha, the father of Damayanti, of the main Yādava line ruled in Vidarbha, whereas Bhīma Sātvata regained Mathura from Satrughna's son Subāhu.

With Rāma's coronation ended, the Tretā Yuga (Age) and Dvāpara started. This coincides with the Kṛishṇa Period (*c.* 1950–1400 B.C.)."

Until the Bhārata War, three families—the Pañchalas, Pauravas and Yādavas, dominated the scene. Sometimes, there were fights among each of these families, as between the north and south Pañchāla, or between the Pañchāla, and Pauravas. Kuru, of the latter dynasty is said to have sacrificed at Prayāga, and it was after him that Kurukshetra and Kurujangala, that is the cultivated and uncultivated land or country, came to be so called, and the family named after him.

Sudhanvan, Kuru's youngest son gave rise to two branches of the family, known as the Chedi and the Magadha. Later Vasu, the fourth successor of Sudhanvan conquered the Chedi kingdom from the Yādavas. His capital Suktimatī was on the river of the same name, now known as the Ken. Later, he conquered Magadha and possibly Matsya. His five sons established separate kingdoms: Bṛihadratha in Magadha, Kuśa at Kauśāmbī, Yadu at Karūsha and Pratyagraha at Chedi. Later the Bārhadratha dominated the history of Northern India. First under Jārasandha they drove out the Yādavas and Bhojas from Mathura.

The large Yādava kingdom ruled over by Bhīma Sātvata with his four sons; Bhajamāna, Devavṛidha, Andhaka and Vṛishṇi. It is these, with the earlier Yādava families of the Yadavas, still known as Satvatas and the branches and sub-branches of the Pauravas mentioned earlier, which ultimately figure in the Bharata war. It is not necessary to follow their fortunes separately. Suffice if we know as to who were the principal participants on the side of the Kauravas and Pāṇḍavas.

The whole of eastern Magadha, Videha, Aṅga, Vaṅga, and Kaliṅga which were under Karṇa joined the Kauravas. But Sahadeva, a son of Jarāsandha ruling in Western Magadha was on the side of the Pāṇḍavas.

The Kirātas under Bhagadatta of Pragjyotisha, supported the Kauravas. So also Bṛihadbala, king of the Kosalas. The various rulers in Madhyadeśa of Vatsa, Kaśī, Chedi, Karusha, Daśārṇa and Pañchāla were on side of the Pāṇḍavas.

The large Yādava family was divided in their allegiance; Yuyudhana and Sātyaki among the Vṛishṇis and Yādavas, came to the Pāṇḍavas while Nīla of Māhishmatī, Vinda and Anuvinda of Avanti, Kṛitavarman of the Bhoja-Andhaka-Vṛishṇis, Vidarbha, Nishāda and Śalva supported Duryodhana, the Kaurava chief.

The Punjab and the north-west were wholly with the Kauravas, Jayadratha of Sindhu-Sauvīra, Śakuni Gandhāra, Suśarmā Trigarta, Kekaya, Śibi, Śalya of Madra, Vahlīka, Kshudraka, Mālava, Sritaya of the Ambashṭhas, Sudakshina of the Kambojas. Only Abhisara, said to be forming southwestern part of Kashmir, had joined the Pāṇḍavas. In short, broadly speaking the Madhyadeśa and Gujarat stood for the Pāṇḍavas; while the rest, viz. east,, north-west and western India opposed them.

Pusalkar's is a balanced treatment of the Vedic and the Purāṇic, including the epic evidence Hence we shall discuss it *vis-a-vis* the archaeological evidence, and simply reproduce the maps from Bhargava and Pargiter which give respectively graphic pictures of the Vedic and Purāṇic and the Purāṇic only.

Before entering into a discussion regarding the nature of the colonization, or the significance of the Vedo-Purāṇic settlements and the Chalcolithic settlements, we must cite and endorse Pusalkar's views about the reliability of the Purāṇic evidence. As he has rightly pointed out there is nothing like the Brahmanic tradition (as represented by the Vedas), and the Kshatriya tradition (as represented by the Purāṇas and epics), for the latter do hold the Brāhamaṇas in high esteem. At the same time it is equally true that whereas the Vedic texts are comparatively less tempered with, and hence the interpolations are few, the Purāṇas and the epics contain quite a number of interpolated. At the same time they alone contain something like a continuous historical narrative, and it is absurd to suppose that the elaborate genealogies were all merely figment of imagination or a tissue of falsehoods. For these people (*sūtas*) did not know that we in the twentieth century after Christ would not believe them. They wrote or recited for their readers and audience, which certainly was in a much better position to judge about the veracity of the accounts they were reading or listening to than what we can do. But while granting this, we must also point out that such recitations, repeated over centuries, did give an opportunity to a poet (story teller) to add or subtract a few things or incidents or names. Under these circumstances, what we propose to do is to rely on the archaeological data, chronology, culture data, etc., as given by the recent excavations rather than date the archaeological evidence by the Purāṇic data. Thus years ago, some scholars sought to date the Maheshwar-Navdatoli Culture to *c*. 3000 B.C. and credited it to the Haihaya emperor Sahasrārjuna.

While one might do this one must also be prepared to accept the implications of this attribution. The most unwelcome result is that we shall have to imagine that the mightly Sahasrārjuna fought with arrows and spears tipped with tiny microliths! But this is a thing we cannot escape. We shall therefore, examine the implications of a likely correlation between the archaeological data and the traditional data from the point of view of colonization, as well as the technological and cultural development in India.

In the first place, neither the Vedic nor the Purāṇic accounts are against the idea of colonization. While they do not specifically use any expression for this "western" concept, they do maintain that in the remote past, before the Flood, India was more or less an empty land and gradually settled by the sons and grandsons of Vaivaśvata Manu. This process lasted for nearly 2000 years, if we place the Flood, about 3500 B.C. and the Bhārata war in about 1,400 B.C. But by the fifteenth century or 1000 B.C. if we accept Bhargava's and Pargiter's dating of the Bharata war, then the political geography of the whole of Northern India had assumed the form that we witness about the fifth century B.C. However, in this picture we have to note two things. Though during Rāma's time south India is supposed to have become known for the first time, there is no mention of any kingdom except Vidarbha, south of the Vindhya and the Narmada, either in Andhra, Maharashtra or Karnataka, let alone Kerala and Tamil Nadu. Thus, south India had still remained outside the Aryan impact. In fact, we do not know, nor are we told as to who the rulers of this large mass of land were !! Secondly, the Vedic and the Purāṇic data is not specific enough about the cultural differences, if any, between the various Aryan kingdoms, either in the Kṛita, Tretā and Dvāpara Yugas or the various Ages or Periods named by Pusalkar. No doubt, there is the occasional mention of the acquisition of new *astras*—not *śastras*, by Arjuna or Karṇa, but no reference to the development in town-planning, agriculture, domestication of animals, and the daily life led by the people—their food, dress and ornaments, even their religion!!

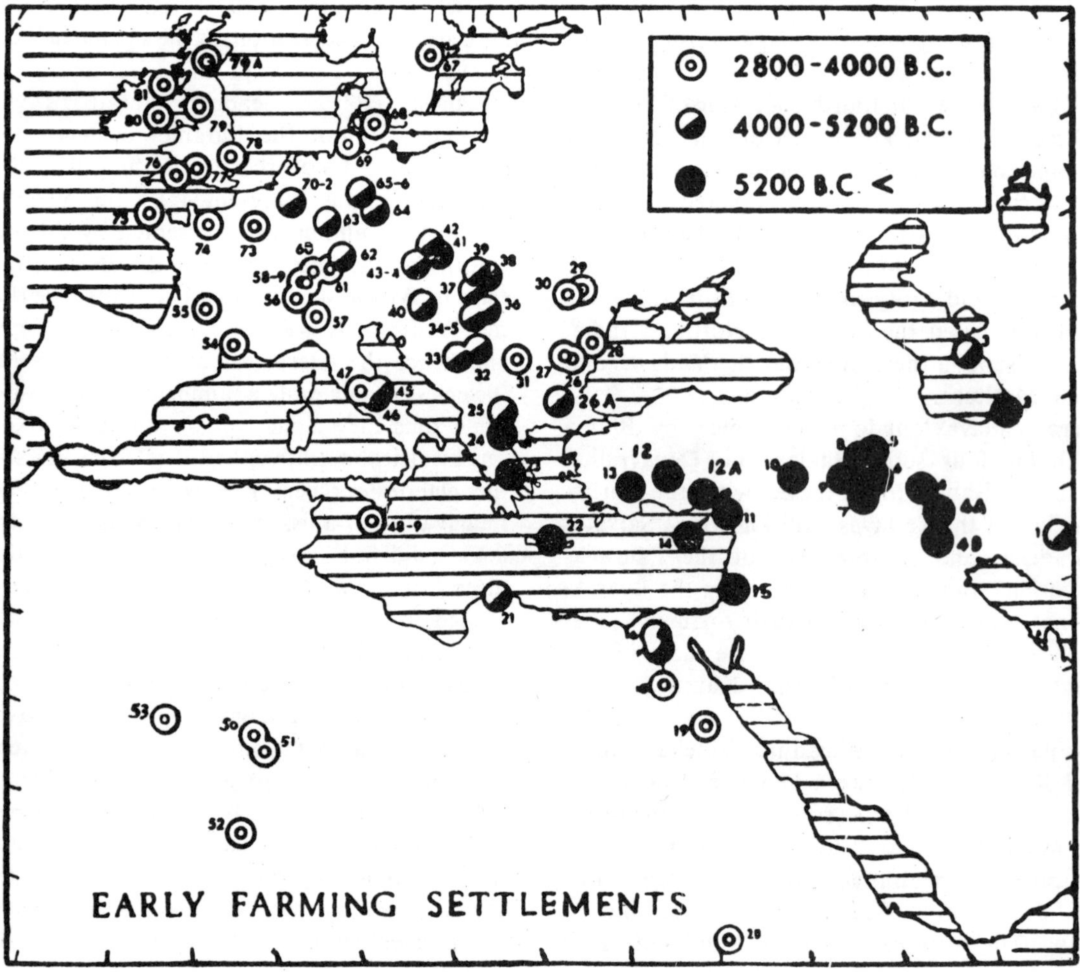

As against this traditional picture, the picture reconstructed by archaeology during the last 25 or 50 years is certainly more detailed, though we sorely miss the identity of the authors of the various regional and sub-regional cultures.

Two or three things are however remarkable to which renewed attention is drawn. If we leave out the various Baluchi cultures known so far by their pottery, fabrics or site names only, then we find that by about 3000 B.C., a culture known at present as pre-Harappan or Early Harappan, or by the site names, Harappa-1, Kalibangan-1, Kot Diji-1, Gumla-2 had come into existence. The C-14 dates suggest a period of 500 years or more for this expansion. As far as known, except for some differences in pottery fabrics and forms between the various excavated sites, there is no vital difference in the use of lithic equipment. But it is noteworthy that at no site, chert or the Sukkur-Rohri flint was used. Though a ploughed field of this period is known from Kalibangan, we do not know whether wheat, barley and seasamum were eaten. And the settlers, as shown by Kot Diji-1 and Kalibangan-1 were not simple villagers, but early town folk having mud brick fortification round their settlement.

Who were these people? We do not know. But they could be from Iran or were a people who had greater affinity with those from Iran, as shown by the designs and some forms and techniques at Kalibangan-1. If we now think in terms of the literary data, the pre-Harappans might be equated with the Early Aryan expansion, according to the purely Vedic data, or even according to the Vedic-Purāṅic data as interpreted by Bhargava.

If we are not inclined to accept this correlation, then shall we equate the Harappan itself with the Vedic Aryan? Mind you, except the fact that the Harappan Culture shows a great uniformity, even in its wide expanse, as does the Vedic at the end of the first phase of its expansion, we have no data for a detailed comparison.

Equally significant is the fact that just as during the next phase Madhyadeśa, that is the Ganga-Yamuna *doab* became all important, and the west gradually sank into insignificance, so much so that it was looked down upon by the Aryans of the Madhyadeśa! Of course, this inference or interpretation of the archaeological evidence is at present based on the slender data from Haryana and east Punjab, and some reports from Sind and West Punjab in Pakistan. But even in the latter, according to the latest information received from Rafique Moghul, several sites of Cemetery-H have been discovered in West Punjab. However, the widespread existence of this culture after the Harappan does not necessarily prove its continuance, say, after *c.* 1500 B.C. Hence, as the Late Vedic texts tell us, the Early Vedic Culture was disappearing after a lapse of nearly 1000 years from the west, north-west. The Saraswati which was known for its *ghee* and milk was drying up. Thus there is a *superficial correspondence* between the Vedic evidence as interpreted by Pusalkar, or both the Vedic and Purāṅic as interpreted by Bhargava and the available archaeological evidence. At present, there is real dearth of archaeological evidence, because no site of this period (Cemetery-H) is excavated either in India or Pakistan. And the long gap, say of 500 or 700 years between *c.* 1500 B.C. and 800 B.C. cannot be filled up by the Painted Grey Ware, for the simple reason, that we know really little about it, and secondly it does not seem to go back beyond *c.* 800 B.C. at the most. Thus, the period between *c.* 1500 B.C. and *c.* 800 B.C. is archaeologically unknown in northern India.

Anyway, let us see how the presence of the PGW may be explained traditionally. Soon after its discovery, B.B. Lal (now Professor) ascribed this Ware and the associated culture to the Early Aryans, because according to him, the then dating of this Ware fitted in very well with the supposed arrival of the Aryans in India by *c.* 1200 B.C. Lal also attributed this ware to the Mahabharata war period. Since then, several C-14 dates from Hastinapur and elsewhere have firmly placed the PGW between *c.* 800 B.C. and 400 B.C. It has also been shown convincingly by Dr. G.G. Mujumdar[1] that the PGW is essentially a local produce of the Gangetic *doab*, and in no way foreign-oriented. Further, it heralds as far as the associated objects are concerned, as I have shown, the dawn of the Early Historic period.

Accepting the majority view that the PGW has to be dated between *c.* 800 and 400 B.C. , let us see how its wide distribution—from the borders of Bihar in the east to Bikaner in northern Rajasthan in the west, and from Ujjain in the south to Ropar in the north—may be interpreted according to the Purāṅic view of colonization.

Accepting the Purāṅic view that the Aryans originated somewhere in midwestern U.P. around Praṭishṭhāna or Allahabad, and spread in all directions, we find that this view fits in surprisingly with the present known origin and distribution and nature of the PGW and the associated Early Iron Age Culture. Though we do not know the names of the various rulers at this time, except through the Purāṅas and late Vedic texts, like the Brahmanas and Upanishads, we *might say that the Purāṇas had* probably *in view* the rise and spread of the PGW culture and its authors. Though it is not proper nor legitimate to infer about the social characteristics of the users or authors of the PGW and the associated objects, still it is not impossible that *at least* the ruling

[1]Personal Communication; also see, H.D. Sankalia, 'Functional significance of the O.C.P. and P.G.W. shapes and associated objects, *Purātattva*, no. 7 (1974).

families, if not the ruled, belonged to one racial stock, as the Purāṇas tell us.

If this view is accepted then it would show that the Purāṅic tradition, though true to some extent, is late, and does not or cannot go beyond a few centuries before the Christian era. All the early accounts, purporting to go back to 3000 B.C. are imaginary.

Secondly, even if this corollary is accepted it would show that even according to this view of Aryan expansion, the Deccan proper or Maharashtra and the south lay outside the pale of Aryan occupation, or influence, though Pradhan's interpretation of the Vedic and Purāṇaic evidence does show some Aryan colonies in the Deccan by the Rig Vedic period. This statement is quite vague.[1] But, according to Bhargava, Pargiter and Pusalkar the Deccan and the south were not penetrated by the Aryans or people from the north until very late, that is the beginning of the early historical period.

We may tabulate the various hypotheses as follows:[2]

I. *Colonization according to Bhargava*

A. Aryans entered India after the Flood in *c.* 3000 B.C. and spread in the Saptasindhu.	Archaeologically Baluchistan, NWFP culture up to 3000 B.C. would be pre-Aryan
B. Harappan Culture pre-Aryan. But we have still to discover what was the material culture of the invading Aryans.	

On the contrary, if we regard the Harappan Culture as Aryan, then the various Baluchi and pre-Harappan as pre-Aryan, then we can explain very well the subsequent spread of the Harappan Culture in the Punjab, U.P., NWFP, Gujarat, and Saurashtra, and its subsequent decay or disappearance by about 1700 or 1500 B.C. This would be traditional drying-up of the Sarasvati.

Thus we arrive at a novel way of interpreting the Harappa Culture as far as its authorship is concerned. The question is will the decipherment of the script bear this out? Though the majority view is against its Aryan ascription, both the Raos—Krishna and Surya—from their reading of the script have concluded that the script is proto-Brāhmī and its contents Purāṇo-Vedic. So also is the recent interpretation by Hajra.

II. *Colonization according to Pusalkar*

This is not quite different from that of Bhargava, as far as the interpretation of the purely Vedic evidence is concerned. Even Pradhan also thought that the Aryans had colonized Kāśī, Videha and even Aṅga.[3] However, we may add that if we regard the Harappan as Aryan, then both at Kot-Diji and Gumla, and possibly at many other sites, there are signs of destruction of the pre-Harappan occupation by fire. Thus, there is some archaeological evidence, *if required*, for the destruction of the pre-Aryan by the Aryan, though at Kalibangan, a peaceful co-existence of both the cultures is postulated.

III. *Colonization according to Pargiter (and Pusalkar)*

A. Origin or beginning in mid-eastern India, and spread in north, south, east and west.

This view is against the present archaeological evidence in its entirety, for as far as we know, all the earlier cultures are so far found from Baluchistan and Afghanistan and soon after in Sind, the Punjab and northern Rajasthan.

But as explained before, Pargiter's view would very well suit the likely origin and spread of the Painted Grey Ware Culture, and the various other pottery cultures, such as the black-slipped and the black-and-red ware found at various sites in U.P. , Bihar and West Bengal, might be regarded as antecedent cultures belonging to various indigenous peoples, particularly the Sudyumnas or the Easterners which even the Purāṇas find it difficult to explain and have invented an interesting story of Ila's transformation to male/female forms.[4] While the culture flourishing before the Great Flood might be the Ochre Coloured Ware or that of the Copper Hoards, there is increasing evidence from Saipai, Lal Quila and Atranjikhera excavations, as well as numerous sites in the various western districts of U.P.—Kanpur, Lucknow, Meerut, Saharanpur, Muzaffarpur—that this culture was washed away by a flood. Thus if we accept this line of thinking then both the Pre-Flood and Post-Flood Purāṅic dynastic accounts find corroborations in archaeology. Though the dates of the accounts do not tally, it does not matter much. For, in the first place, we have no exact dates, so far, for the various pottery cultures, while some exaggeration, or high dating in Purāṅic accounts is expected. Pargiter's further argument that his theory of Madhyadeśa (Midland) around Allahabad as the original home of the Aryans (the Ailas) no way goes against Grierson's theory of the "Outer and the Inner Band" of Aryans,[5] might also be corroborated by this interpretation of the archaeo-

[1]S.N. Pradhan, *Chronology of Ancient India* (Calcutta, 1927), p. 202

[2]In this no dates have been given except the first, viz., *c.* 3000 B.C., because whether we accept the view of Cunningham School, c. 1400 B.C. or *c.* 1000 B.C., according to Pargiter; for date of the Bhārata War, no fundamental difference will take place regarding the rest.

[3]Pradhan, *op. cit.*, p. 208

[4]Other explanations are similar and it would be interesting if all these are gathered together and examined ethnoarchaeologically.

[5]P.E. Pargiter, *Ancient Indian Historical Tradition* (London, 1922) ,p. 296.

logical evidence. The present interpretation of the archaeological and literary evidence fully answers point no. 5 of Pargiter.[1]

However, if any one wants to corroborate it fully then he has to dig at Kauśāmbī or some other site, and these are numerous and to show stratigraphically, culturally and chronologically that the first steps in the birth and development of civilization were taken in this part of the Indian sub-continent and not in the north-west!! This is indeed a challenge, and the Universities in U.P. should take it up.

I think, we have had enough of this speculation. Those scholars who are interested in the further follow-up of any particular interpretation might name the various regional and sub-regional cultures after the Vedic or Purāṅic tribes, as the late Dr. Kosambi proposed to name the Painted Grey Ware at Hastinapur as "Puru Culture".

Before we close this discussion we must again draw the attention of the scholars that however much we may distrust the traditional accounts, and not rely much on speculation based on it, one has to recognize that this is an ancient land, where the traditions have survived in a distorted form, and therefore the traditional accounts—both Vedic and Purāṇic—do contain a grain of truth which we must endeavour to discover by long and continuous sieving.

Since the subject of this symposium is "Archaeology and Tradition", I would also draw attention to two of my papers where I have shown how our excavations at Dwarka and Tewar (Tripuri) beautifully illuminate the epic and Purāṇic accounts of these cities.[2]

In the wake of these excavations and their significance, comes the discovery of the Naga temple and sculptures, by Dr. Haertel at Sonkh near Mathura. These discoveries should be understood in a much larger context.

The Purāṇas and the Mahābharata contain accounts of small and large Naga settlements all over North India from Taxila and Pushkalāvatī to Gwaḷior or Padmavāṭī in Madhya Pradesh. The Sarpayajña performed by Janamejaya and the ouster of the Kaliya Nāga from Mathura by Krishṇa is well known. The late K.P. Jayaswal had already postulated the existence of a Naga empire before the Vākāṭaka-Gupta empire in the fourth century A.D. during the so-called "Dark Period" of Indian history of, viz. 2nd-3rd century A.D.

The discovery at Sonkh gives a new edge to this view, affording further proof of a once flourishing Naga cult and its patrons in many parts of northern and central India.

[1] *Ibid.*, p. 302

[2] H.D. Sankalia, 'Archaeology and Tradition', *Indica,* vol. I, no. 1, pp. 3-16.

It would appear that both the Sakas, and Kushanas had occasionally to fight with these people, until all were absorbed in the resulting Purāṇic or Hindu Culture.

As far as Mathura and its environs are concerned, it would appear that it was Krishṇa who was responsible for ousting the Nāga Cult or rule from that region. For, as far as we know, the rising Krishṇa cult had no difficulty or quarrel with the existing Jaina and Buddhist cults in Mathura. For there is hardly any reference to these in the epics and the Purāṇas. Probably, the Krishṇa-Vishṇu cult achieved one further success. It fully absorbed the Nāga cult by accepting Samkarshaṇā and Ananta, though in each case, these got a slightly lower position than Krishṇa. It is due to this compromise, that we owe the grand conception of Vishṇu lying on Śesha or Ananta, and its rendering in sculpture by the 4th century A.D. The earliest image we have so far is at Deogarh in central India, once the heart of the Nāga empire.

It is difficult to say as to who these "Nāgas" were. A study of the personal names in an early inscription of northern India and the Deccan had shown that it was a general practice to add the suffix the *datta, gupta, mitra, pālarakshita* to the proper name of a man or woman, thus showing what god the person worshipped. In the case of persons bearing Nāga or Sarpa as the first or second part of the name, we do not find such suffixes though we do find a name like Nāgapālita.[3] Thus it is not clear whether they were former devotees of a Nāga or Sarpa. But if we assume that since considerable time had elapsed when these people or families were worshippers of Nāga, and hence the suffixes have been dropped, then such names as Gaṇapatināga, and Kuberanagara which appear in the inscriptions of the 4th-5th century A.D., show that these are indeed the remnants of a once flourishing and popular Nāga cult.

That this Naga cult was very ancient has been realized by Jitendranath Banerjea[4] from the references in the Ṛigveda, Yajurveda and Atharvaveda. This antiquity now finds confirmation in the discovery of numerous figurines of snake goddess in terracotta from Gumla and other sites in NWFP in Pakistan, though so far no such figurines have been found from the classical Indus Valley sites, nor from the newly found sites in India. Those from Gumla are said to be pre-Harappan that is at least before *c.* 2500 B.C. Thus a long period of symbiosis seems to lie before the principal Nāga families were absorbed in the ever expanding Hindu fold. And the peculiar flexibility of the latter is best revealed by the

[3] H.D. Sankalia, 'Cultural significance of the personal names in the early inscriptions of the Deccan', *Bulletin of the Deccan College Research Institute*, vol. III (1941), p. 381.

[4] Jitendra Nath Banerjea, *The Development of Hindu Iconography* (Calcutta, 1956), p. 345.

observance of the Nāgapañchamī during the month of Śrāvaṇa (bright half) of (August-September) every year, when Nāgas are worshipped and fed with milk. Thus one of the most ancient folk cult lives with the most advanced philosophies about God and then othe world in India, and the symbiosis—action, reaction and interaction—can be understood by a study of Indian traditions and archaeology.

Deccan College Post-Graduate and Research Institute, Pune-411006

H.D Sankalia

Puranic Lineages and Archaeological Cultures

At a seminar in Poona in 1964, Prof. Sankalia initiated discussion on the subject of Traditional Indian Chronology and C^{14} dates of excavated sites, by stating that his paper was an essay in speculation. The speculation continues. In the absence of contemporary written records or deciphered scripts, any attempt to co-relate archaeological material with traditional accounts of the past becomes a venture into speculation. This is particularly so as the literary sources represent accretions over a period of many centuries and the archaeological evidence is partial, supported more by exploration than excavation and ultimately based on vertical rather than horizontal excavation. It is, therefore, again very much as a speculative enterprise that an attempt is being made here to compare the excavated material with the historical tradition in the general time bracket of the second and early first millennia B.C The attempt arises not from a need to insist on a co-relation of tradition and archaeology but more in the nature of an investigation of the tradition which may perhaps be carrying an element of historical memory for which archaeology might provide some evidence.

Earlier attempts to co-relate archaeology and the literary sources have in the main focussed on the question of identifying the Aryans (and inevitably the Dravidians as well), and trying out a variety of archaeological cultures—perhaps the most plausible identification being with the Painted Grey Ware Culture.[1] But the term 'aryan' covers a wide range of groups and geographical distribution, quite apart from its ethnic connotation or its distinctiveness as a geographical culture being ambiguous in the texts.[2] Nor are we clear about the nature of 'aryanisation' at this time and the channels through which it proceeded. More recently, the focus has been narrowed to that of examining particular cultures in the light of a single literary text. Here, the use of epic literature raised some fundamental problems, since epic literature in particular in all societies is the survival of many encrustations in the form of events and locations introduced through interpolations. If ever higher criticism and textual analyses manage to unravel the original *Rāma-kathā* and *Bharata-kathā* the result may be somewhat startling to those who take even the critical editions of the *Rāmāyaṇa* and the *Māhabhārata* as the earliest, original epics.[3] A more promising investigation has been the attempt to co-relate some aspects of the Painted Grey Ware Culture with the Later Vedic Literature where the emphasis has not been so much on the identity of the geographical distribution as on the co-relation of the social and economic data from both the literary and the archaeological sources.[4]

The attempt in this paper will be to narrow the literary focus still further although the framework of archaeological cultures relates to virtually the whole of northern India. It has been suggested in the past that some of the archaeological cultures may be linked to the major lineages of the early tradition, and in this connection the Painted Grey Ware (hereinafter referred

[1]B.B. Lal, 'Excavations at Hastināpura and other explorations in the Upper Ganga and Sutlej basins', *Ancient India*, nos. 10 & 11 (1954 & 1955), H.D. Sankalia, 'Traditional Indian Chronology and C-14 Dates of *Excavated* Sites' in V.N. Misra and M.S. Mate (eds.), *Indian Prehistory : 1964* (Poona, 1965), pp. 219-235; B. and R. Allchin, *The Birth of Indian Civilisation* Penguin Books (Harmondsworth, 1968), p. 144 ff. D.H. Gordon, *The Prehistoric Background of Indian Culture* (Bombay 1958), pp. 59ff, 83ff.

[2]H.W. Bailey, 'Iranian *Arya* and *Dahā*', *Transactions of the Philological Society*, 1959, pp. 71-115

[3]C. Bulcke, *Rāma-kathā*. (in Hindi). V.S. Sukthankar, *On the Meaning of the Mahabhārata* (Bombay , 1957).

[4]R.S. Sharma, 'The Later Vedic Phase and the Painted Grey Ware', Paper read at the Indian History Congress, Calcutta, 1974 ; See above, pp.

to as the PGW) has been associated with the Pūrus and the Chalcolithic Black-and-Red Ware (hereinafter referred to as the BRW) with the Yadus Yādavas.[1] The suggestions have largely been casual and there has been little attempt to use the history of the lineages and see to what extent it tallies with the archaeological data. The *vamśānuchrita* sections of some of the major *Purāṇas* give a fairly detailed listing of lineages which would suggest that they carried some importance in the tradition. Societies which stress social organisation (as did the ancient Indian society) usually place a heavy accent on the preservation of some memory of lineages. In this case, the details appear to be confused since personal names are often mixed with tribal names and geographical place-names. This may be due to the compilation of the texts dating to a period much later (mid-first millennium A.D.) than that to which the events apparently relate: also that the concern of the compilers was not so much to record the actual descent of kings but perhaps more appropriately the distribution of tribes and peoples. As such the genealogies are not apparently factual information on history and chronology but can be taken as records of a general pattern of settlements and migrations. In this paper I am not, therefore, concerned with the chronology of the lineages since that is an almost insurmountable problem. The reliability of Puranic chronology *per se* has yet to be proven.[2] This paper is an attempt to investigate other types of evidence which lineage records can supply and which can perhaps be examined in the light of archaeological data.

The *vaṣmānuchrita* sections, describing as they do the two major descent groups—the Ikshvaku/Sūryavamśa and the Aila/Chandravaṁśa—and the fanning out of these groups, include as their geographical framework the whole of northern India.[3] The archaeology of the Ikshvāku areas, essentially Ayodhya, Videha and Vaiśāli, is substantially unknown as yet for this period. This paper will therefore be concerned only with the Chandravaṁśa lineages; and in that too the discussion will be limited to the obviously more significant lineages, that of the Pūru and the Yādava, which also happen to relate to the area where fairly substantial archaeological material is available.

The lineage commences with Ilā the daughter of Manu born from a sacrifice performed by Manu, which in some texts is associated with the termination of the Great Deluge from which Manu was saved by the Matsyāvatāra of Vishṇu.[4] Ilā gives birth to Purūravas whose great grand-son is Yayāti. Of Yayāti's five sons, the eldest is Yadu and the youngest is Pūru, the middle ones being Anu, Druhyu and Turvaśa. Yadu "the rightful successor, displeases his father and is banished to the south/west, and Pūru the youngest inherits the *madhya-deśa*. The descent of the Paurava line is geographically concentrated and relates to the Indo-Gangetic divide and the Ganga-Yamuna *doab* and its environs, whereas the Yādavas spread out over the Aravalli region, Gujarat, Malva, the Narmada valley, the northern Deccan and the eastern Ganges valley. The descent groups of the three middle sons are relatively unimportant according to the texts. The line of Turvaśa merges with the Pūru fairly early and that of Druhyu associated with Gandhāra and the extreme north-west is referred to as producing the *mlechchhas* after a few generations. The descendents of Anu survived in central Punjab and Sind and one branch is said to have migrated to the extreme east, Aṅga, Vaṅga, Pundra, etc. Only the lineages of Pūru and Yadu are listed in detail and at great length.

The Flood is in many historical traditions a time-marker, clearing away the past as it were and initiating a new era. It need not therefore refer to an actual flood.[5] It is, however, a useful point for our purposes since it also provides a possible archaeological co-relation with the decline of the major cities of the Indus civilization. The attempted co-relation here will, therefore, be with the archaeological cultures which succeed the Harappan. Until recently the Flood would have been acceptable as a useful starting point for the cultures of the western Ganga valley as well; but now there is a debate on this question involving the explanation for the peculiar characteristics of the Ochre Coloured Pottery (OCP).[6] Even if one of the theories regarding the possibility of a flood in the upper *doab* is accepted, it could still not be co-related with the legend, for, in order to do this, the flood would have to be dated to the end of the third millenium B.C. and have occurred prior to the OCP culture, whereas the argument is that

[1]D.D. Kosambi, *Introduction to the Study of Indian History* (Bombay, 1956), p. 139 ; H.D. Sankalia, *op. cit*.

[2]Many attempts have been made to work out the chronology and perhaps among the most detailed are those of S.N. Pradhan, *Chronology of Ancient India* (Calcutta, 1927), and P.L. Bhargava, *India in the Vedic Age* (Lucknow, 1956).

[3]*Vishnu Purāṇa IV*.I am using this text as the basic text for the lineage co-relations. In many ways it is the most standard of the *Puranas*.

[4]. *Matsya Purāṇa*, I. 11-34 : *Śatapatha Brāhmana* 1.8.1 1-10 ; *Mahābhārata* III. 185 (All references to the *Mahābhārata* are to the Critical Edition.) The *Śatapatha Brāhmana* describes how Manu was saved from the Flood by the fish and how a daughter was born to him. The Puranic lineages trace descent back to Manu and his children including Ilā. Thus there is a link, albeit indirect, of the Flood with Manu Vaivasvata, the progenitor of the lineages.

[5]Mircea Eliade, *The Myth of the Eternal Return* (London, 1955).

[6]B.B. Lal, 'A Deluge ? which Deluge?.... *American Anthropologist*, 1968, vol. LXX, pp. 857-63. Dr. B.B. Lal, 'The Ochre-Coloured Pottery—a Geochronological Study', *Purātattva*, No. 5 (1971-72) pp. 49-58. R.L. Raikes, 'Kabangan: death from natural causes', *Antiquity*, No. 42, 1968, pp. 286-91.

GENEALOGICAL TABLE

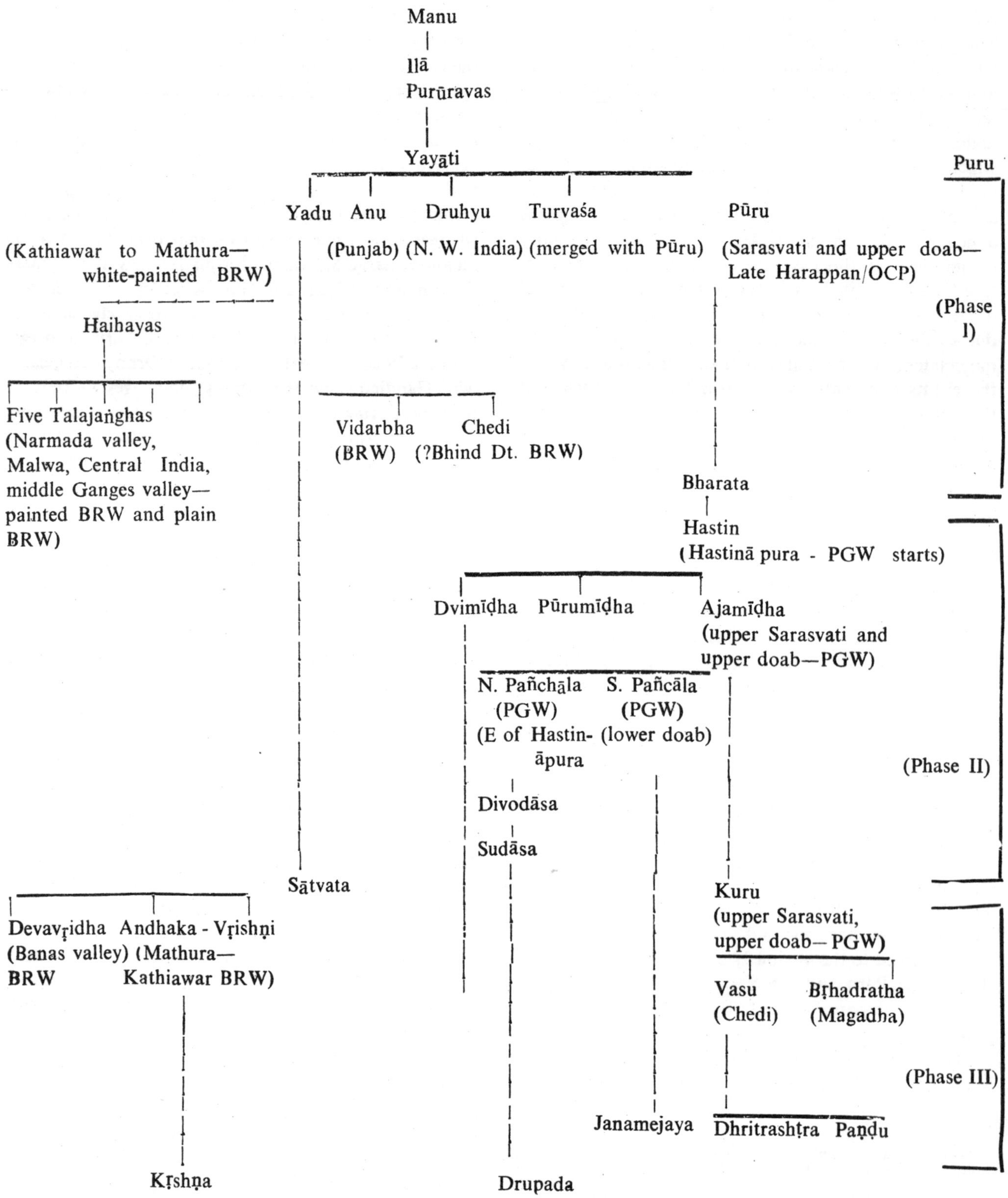

There is some variation in the *vaṁśānucharita* sections of the *Purāṇas* which makes a uniform genealogical table impossible. The above table is based on Pargiter's attempt at collating the lists. (F.E. Pargiter, *The Ancient Indian Historical Tradition* (London, 1922 pp. 144–149.)

the rolled condition of the OCP sherds is due to the settlements suffering from a flood in the mid-second millennium B.C. However, whether or not there was a massive deluge, there seems to have been a major disturbance in the river systems of the Indo-Gangetic divide and this may have taken the form of flooding in some areas and dessication in others. The two predominant cultures of the post-Harappan period (during the second and early first millennia B.C.) are quite unmistakably the PGW and the BRW. The antecedents and evolution of these two will therefore have to be considered. The keeping of lineages and genealogical records (in howsoever garbled a form) is also associated generally with societies at a stage which would be regarded as chalcolithic in archaeological terms, since the motivation for maintaining lineage records stems from kinship organisation and property relations, both of which would become more complex in chalcolithic societies as compared to earlier societies.

Evidence of the Late Harappan culture in the northern area is available at sites along the river-bed of the Sarasvati (especially in Ganganagar District), in the water-shed between the Indus and Ganga systems and in the Upper Doab (in Saharanpur, Meerut, Bulandshahr and Gurgaon Districts). The latter two regions are areas of relatively uniform elevation (200–500 m) and suggest a movement generally along the river lines. The suggested C14 dates for the peripheral sites of the late Harappan are 2200-1700 B.C.[1] It is also in these two regions that there is now growing evidence of other cultures, either co-existent with the Harappan or else continuing into the post-Harappan period. Of the first there appears to be a continuity of pre-Harappan cultures into the second millennium B.C. at sites in the Sutlej valley which it is said were largely uninfluenced by the mature Harappan Culture and the upper Sarasvati (e.g., Bara and Siswal A).[2] Of the second, the OCP begins during the Harappan period and continues into the post-Harappan, with a mean date of 1880 B.C. Variations in the OCP culture suggest some affinities with the Harappan (as at Bahadrabad) with a noticeably more independent development in sites further south in the *doab* (as at Atranjikhera, Lal Qila and Saipai).[3] However, the concentration of the OCP is strikingly heavier in the upper *doab* in Saharanpur District. This would suggest a more cohesive geographical settlement in the upper *doab* with a diffused movement southwards, thinning out towards the southernmost site at Noh. Eastwards it extends to Saheth-Maheth but the region to the east of the Ganga has not so far produced much evidence of the OCP. The recent excavations at Lal Qila, Mitathal and Saipai indicate fairly settled peasant communities.[4] If the Copper Hoards are to be associated with the OCP then the Chalcolithic nature of this culture would be well-established. Furthermore, since the OCP was in contact with the Harappan settlements some survivals of the latter into the OCP culture are possible even if the OCP was not a degenerate form of the Harappan culture.

With the termination of the OCP in the late second millennium B.C. there appears to be a hiatus between it and the succeeding PGW culture. This is evident from those sites where the PGW settlers occupied the earlier OCP sites and which register a break in occupation between the two cultures. The earlier date for PGW, *c.* 1100 B.C. would have indicated a short break in occupation, but the more recent date of *c.* 800 B.C. suggests a longer period. If the contention is correct that the weathering of the OCP sherds is due to extended exposure then a long hiatus between the OCP and the PGW will be further supported. It does, however, seem unlikely that there should be a uniform date for the PGW, considering the extensive area over which the culture is distributed, an area which includes the Ravi and Satluj valleys, the erstwhile Sarasvati valley, the Indo-Gangetic divide and the entire *doab* and its environs extending eastwards to the Gomati (Bahraich and Varanasi Districts) and westwards to Rohtak, Hissar, Ajmer and Jaipur Districts. The distribution of PGW sites in the *doab* tends to adopt a pattern of settlement closely following the banks of rivers and their tributaries.[5] It may well turn out that the Ravi and Satluj valley PGW is a little earlier and that of the *doab*, associated with iron, a little later. The sites along the southern fringes of the *doab* appear to be of a later date than those of the upper *doab*, and places still further south (e.g. Ujjain, etc.) register the arrival of the PGW even later as an immediate prelude to or in association with iron and the Northern Black Polished

[1] D.P. Agrawal and Sheela Kusumgar, *Prehistoric Chronology and Radiocarbon Dating in India* (New Delhi, 1974), p. 103.

[2] Y.D. Sharma, 'Value of Common painted Ceramic designs.. in D.P. Agrawal and A. Ghosh (eds.), *Radiocarbon and Indian Archaeology* (*Bombay*, 1973), pp. 222-30. Suraj Bhan, 'The Sequence and Spread of Prehistoric Cultures in the upper Sarasvati Basin' in *ibid.*, p. 252 ff.

[3] Y.D. Sharma, Comments on OCP Seminar. *Purātattava*,, no. 5 (1971-72), p. 21.

[4] It would be worth plotting the OCP sites on a topographical map to see whether they reflect at all one of the modern characteristic uses of the flood plain in the upper *doab*, namely, the partial transhumance between the *khādar* and the *bhangar* where the flood-plain is used as grazing ground by pastoral communities such as the Gujars. If the sites are substantially in the flood-plain it might explain in part the condition of the pottery as well as what superficially appears to be the nomadic nature of the culture. R. Ramachandran and S.C. Thakur, 'Human Perception and Adjustment to Flood Hazard in the Ganga Flood Plains', paper presented at the Twenty-second International Geographical Congress, 1972.

[5] Information based on a map of the sites prepared by Roshan Dalal.

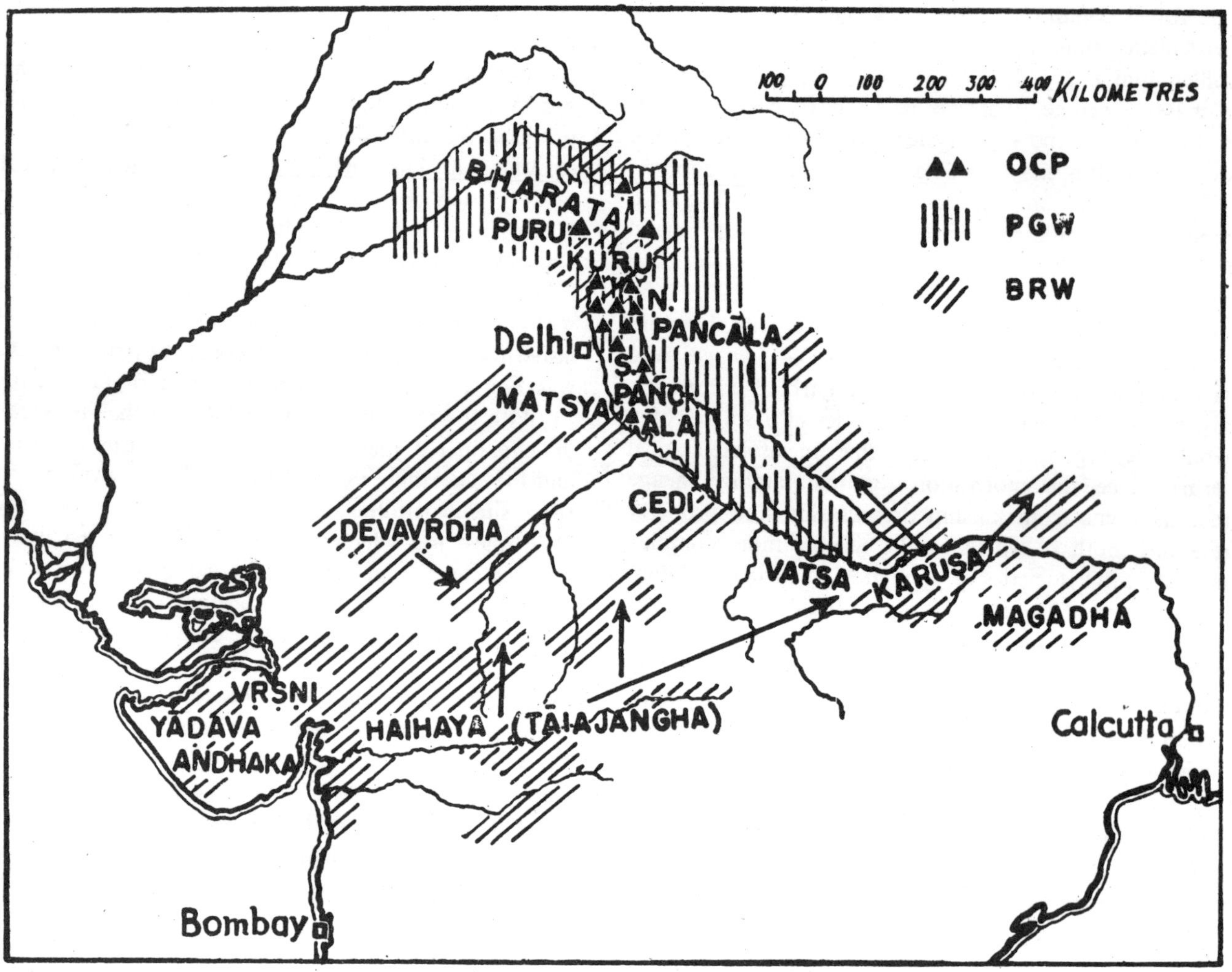

Ware[1] (see map above). The predominance of the PGW over theOCP is based not merely on the substantially larger area of distribution, but also on individual settlements being larger with a well-defined material culture and the increasing use of iron technology. The latter appears to have been introduced gradually with a shift from copper to iron.[2]

The association of PGW sites and the places mentioned in the *Mahābhārata* has been discussed at length.[3] But the events of the *Mahābhārata* focus on the last part of the Pūru lineage. Taken as a whole the Pūru lineage seems to have three distinct phases.[4] The first phase is from Pūru to Bharata; the second sees the segmentation of the main lineage into four groups with a consequent expansion of the territory held by the lineage; and the third is the descent from Kuru to the period of the *Mahābhārata* war. (See Genealogical Table, p. 88.)

The first phase is probably reflected in some of the hymns of the *Ṛig-Veda* where the Pūrus are described as a tribe dwelling on the two grassy banks of the Sarasvatī and associated both in war and friendship with the Bharatas.[5] There is the curious use of the epithet *mṛidhra vāch* for the Pūrus in the *Ṛig Veda* suggesting that they spoke insultingly or discordantly; and the *Śatapatha Brāhmaṇa* refers to Pūru as an ancient king who was an Asura Rākṣasa and was overthrown by the Bharata.[6] This could be a reference to the famous Daśarajña battle described in the *Ṛig-Veda* or else to the coalescing of the Pūrus and the Bharatas to from

[1]N.R. Banerjee, 'The Iron Age in India', in V.N. Misra and M.S. Mate *op. cit.*, (ed.) p. 177ff.

[2]This is indicated by a comparative study of copper and iron finds from Hastinapur, Atranji khera and Noh.

[3]Lal, *op. cit.* (1954 & 1955).

[4]The phasing of the Puarava lineage is suggested by F.E. Pargiter, *Ancient Indian Historical Tradition* (London, 1922), p. 110, but my preference is to take the first phase from Pūru to Bharata rather than Ajamīdha as Pargiter suggests because of the myth associated with the succession after Bharata to be discussed further in this paper.

[5]*Ṛg Veda* VII. 96.2 ; VII. 8.4 ; VII. 18.3.

[6]The phrase *jesma pūrum vidathe mṛidhravācam*, occurs in *Ṛig Veda* VII. 18.13. and is sometimes understood to mean hostile or scornful speech an/on other occasions speech which is alien or incorrect and therefore grating on the ears, The *dasyūs* jeṣma pūrum vidathe mṛidhravācan.

the Kuru-Pañchāla. In terms of the Pūru lineage these events would relate to the last part of the first phase of the lineage just prior to the segmentation.. It is interesting that the inclusion of Bharata in the Puranic genealogy is immediately followed by a curious story. We are told that Bharata was dissatisfied with his own sons and therefore adopted the son of Bharadvāja to succeed him. Could adoption be the mythological symbol of the amalgamation of tribes ? The etymology of the name Bharadvāja is explained as 'one who is borne (*bhara*) by two progenitors (dva—ja)'.[1] The archaeological association of the first phase of the Pūru lineage i.e., from Pūru to Bharata, could be with either the OCP or may have been carried as part of the surviving tradition into the early PGW. At the end of this phase there was a break represented by Bharata adopting sons in the genealogy, after which there was a commencement with the PGW co-related in the genealogy with the second phase of segmentation after Hastin.

At the start of what we have called the second phase the city of Hastinapura is said to have been founded by Hastin and thereafter the Pūru lineage divides into segments with each segment controlling a distinct area of territory. The segmentation is in effect an augmentation of the lineage and would reflect an increase in numbers which required migration into the neighbouring areas. What appears to have been the main line continued at Hastinapura. The other segments consisted of the line established in North Pañchāla, South Pañchāla and the successors of Dvimīḍha whose geographical base is not clear.[2] What is interesting about the distribution of these segments is that the Pūru lineage now covers a wider geographical area and this area tallies fairly closely with that of the distribution of PGW sites. The watershed region and the upper *doab* would constitute what later came to be known as the land of the Kurus. North Pañchāla (north of the Ganga and east of the upper *doab*) with its capital at Ahichchhatrā has produced PGW sites as has to an even greater degree, South Pañchāla (south of the Ganga as far as the junction of the Chambal and the Yamuna) with its capital at Kāmpilya. The Dvimīḍha line may have been located in the Rohtak and Hissar region which is also associated with PGW. The break in descent after Bharata and the segmentation may well indicate a new cultural element in terms of the lineage record.[3] The ceramic tradition of the PGW is from every point of view—fabric, firing, shape, design and function—a new feature and does not have any connections with the earlier ceramic tradition of this region. The associated wares and other artefacts from PGW sites suggest a materially far more prosperous people than the authors of earlier cultures of the *doab*. It would seem feasible that this material culture provided the base for the emergence of states with a monarchical system of government in which the control of agricultural land and rights to succession would play a major role. The excavation at Hastinapura shows an OCP occupation followed by a break and then the very substantial PGW occupation. It is clear that the potentiality for urbanization came with the PGW culture and not the earlier. The segmentation and consequent migration of the lineage would coincide not only with the diffusion of PGW but also the consolidation of the emergent kingdoms beginning to exploit the newly introduced iron technology.

The third phase of the genealogy is marked by the name of Kuru in the descent list. By now relations between the Kurus and the Pañchālas were established both through lineage connections as well as the occasional rivalry of neighbouring kingdoms. We are told that soon after this one of the Kuru kings Vasu branched off and conquered Cedi (on the southern fringe of the Yamuna) and Magadha (southern Bihar), both areas said to be previously in the hands of the Yādava tribes.[1] If the Bhind District can be identified with the Cedi kingdom there is some evidence of the intermixture of PGW and BRW from surface collections; but the stratigraphical sequence is yet to be established through excavation.[2]

In Magadha, however, although BRW is known, PGW is absent. We are further told that Vasu's five sons carved out new kingdom, with Bṛhadratha founding a dynasty at Magadha, Kuśa ruling the territory of Vatsa from Kauśāmbī and the other three ruling the kingdoms of Cedi, Karūsha and possibly Matsya. The sequence at Kauśambī from the excavator's reports suggests that the earliest levels show an affinity with pottery from Navdatoli and western India and that the PGW marks the second cultural phase.[4] The date suggested for the founding of Kauśāmbī by the

are generally characterized by the epithet *mridhravāch.*) The comment of the *Śatapatha Brāhmaṇa* on this specific verse of the *Rig Veda* suggests the latter meaning.

[1] *Vishṇu Purāṇa*, IV.19. The same text clarifies in another section (II.1.) that the Bharata after whom Bhāratavarṣha was named was Bharata the son of Risabha.

[2] Pargiter, *op. cit.*, p. 146. *Vishṇu Purāṇa* IV. 19.

[1] Pargiter, *op. cit*. p. 118.

[2] *Indian Archaeology—A Review*, 1958-59, p. 26, 1961-62, p. 98 (sites at Barata and Akoda). Chedi is sometimes identified with the Suktimati river but this seems too far from the Yamuna with which Chedi had connections. B.C. Law, *Historical Geography of Ancient India* (Paris, not dated), p. 313.

[3] Pargiter, *op. cit*. p. 118

[4] G.R. Sharma, *The Excavations at Kauśāmbī* 1957-59 (Allahabad 1960), pp. 6-7 ; V.D. Misra, 'Pottery of Kausambi' in B.P. Sinha (ed.), *Potteries of Ancient India* (Patna, not dated), p. 203 ff.

excavator has been questioned as being too early.[1] The important point for our purposes however is that the PGW should post-date the BRW however small the evidence may be. A late date would fit better with the lineage account. Karūsha, generally identified with the Shahbad District of Bihar, provides evidence of a BRW settlement but no PGW. The Matsyas, often located in the Alwar-Jaipur region, may be indicated by the mixed BRW and PGW evidence but the stratigraphy is not clear,[2] although the arrival of the PGW at Noh in the adjoining area appears to be late.[3] If the lineage co-relations with archaeological cultures referred to so far have any validity then these kingdoms should relate to the period just prior to the NBP since they are mentioned late in the lineage.

The suggested co-relation of the Yadava lineage with Chalcolithic BRW[4] also needs to be examined closely. BRW, unlike PGW, had a much earlier start in *c.* 2000 B.C. and in some of the sites in Saurashtra and Kutch is associated with the late Harappan (e.g. Surkotada, Amra, Bhatiravdi). If the white-painted BRW is of the same genesis as the plain BRW, then the BRW can be said to have travelled from western India in two directions. One was along the Aravalli Hills with a base in the Banas Valley (*c.* 2000-1800 B.C. at Ahar.) continuing in the direction of the Ganga-Yamuna *doab* where plain BRW dates to *c.* 1200 B.C. or later (Atranji-khera, Noh). At sites in this region, where the BRW and the PGW occur mixed in the same stratum, either the BRW date will have to be made later or else the PGW date somewhat earlier than *c.* 800 B.C. In the few sites in the *doab* itself where BRW occurs it is generally mixed with PGW.[5] An unpainted, plain BRW is also found along the Yamuna as far north as the Indo-Gangetic divide and dating to the end of the second millennium B.C. The second direction in which the BRW appears to have travelled was along the Narmada valley and into Malwa and central India, largely following the river valleys and finally going eastwards to Bihar, the middle Ganga valley and ultimately to the eastern Ganga valley (*c.* 1650 B.C. at Navdatoli, *c.* 1500 B.C. at Eran and *c.* 1200 B.C. at Mahisdal and Chirand). That there was a diffusion of the technique seems apparent. The further southward extension of the BRW *via* the west coast and through Vidarbha seems to have occured later. The BRW therefore essentially skirts round the *doab* and the substantial concentrations of this culture occur in Kutch, Kathiawar and in the districts of Udaipur, Bhilwara, Bharatapur, Indore, Bhind, Ghazipur, Mirzapur and Varanasi.[6]

This geographical distribution in terms of the traditional lineages would evidently point to the Yādavas. The association of the Yādavas with Kathiawar is mentioned more than once. The *Purāṇas* state that Raivata, the grandson of Anarta was established at Kuśasthali (Dvārakā as it came to be called later) but on having to be away at the court of Brahmā he returned to find that many centuries had passed.[7] In the interval Kuśasthali had been conquered by a Rākṣhasa and Raivata's brothers had fled in various directions. The Andhaka-Vṛishṇi were now ruling at Dvarakā. This story which suggests an original dispersal in various directions from the Kathiawar region would agree with the archaeological pattern. But the story of Yadu in the *Purāṇas* suggests that he came from the *madhya-deśa* although he finally established himself in western India.

The *Ṛig Veda* refers to Indra helping the Yadus across the flood.[8] In one hymn they are said to have come from across the sea and in another from afar. This could be explained as their having come from Gujarat near the sea. The *Ṛig Veda* also associates them with wealth in cattle and horses and it is significant that among the earliest evidences for the horse are the remains from Surkotada.[9] The *Harivaṁśa* states that Yadu had his capital at Ānarta (Kathiawar) and that his maternal grandfather was the Rākshasa Madhu whose territory, which extended from Ānarta to Mathura, was conquered by the Yadavas.[10] This would suggest a movement along the Aravallis towards the *doab*. It would also imply that the Yadus had control over a part of the *madhya-deśa,* namely Mathura, which control in the *Puraṇas* is suggested as being of a late period

[1]A. Ghosh, *The City in Early Historical India* (Simla, 1973), pp. 11, 62, 80-81. K.K. Sinha, 'Stratigraphy and Chronology of Early Kausambi' in *Radiocarbon and Indian Archaeology*, pp. 231-239.

[2]*IA*, 1958-59 p. 45

[3]B. and R. Allchin, *op. cit.*, p. 211

[4]D.P. Agrawal, 'Protohistoric Chronology and Technology and Ecological Factors....', *Puratattva,* no. 1 (1967-68), pp. 17-23. D.P. Agrawal and Sheela Kusumgar, *op. cit.*, pp. 103-113 give the revised dates for the Chacolithic BRW from the sites discussed here.

[5]*IA*, 1962-63, p. 30 (site at Bharatpur, Aligarh District), *IA*, 1965-66 p. 41 (site at Khalaua, Agra District), *IA*, 1965-66, p. 47 (site at Bishnupur, Farrukhabad Dt.), *IA*, 1958-59, p. 50 (site at Alamgirpur, Meerut District), IA, 1969-70, p. 43 (site at Kasu, Meerut District).

The excavation at Atranji-khera however does not conform entirely to this pattern. Here the BRW occurs as a distinct cultural level on the south side lying between OCP and PGW levels. But on the north side it is the earliest occupational deposit. R.C. Gaur, 'An appraisal of the Protohistoric Problems of the Ganga-Yamuna Doab', *Puratattva,* no. 4, (1970-71) p. 42 ff.

[6]Information collated from *Indian Archaeology—A Review*.

[7]*Vishnu Purāṇa*, IV. 1.

[8]*Rig Veda*, I.174.9, ; IV. 30.17 ; V. 31.8 ; VI.20.12 ; VI. 45.1.

[9]*Rig Veda* VIII. 6.46. J.P. Joshi, 'Excavati on at Surkotada' in D.P. Agrawal and A. Ghosh (eds.), *Radiocarbon and Indian Archaeology*, p. 181.

[10]*Harivaṁśa*. 54

with the emergence of the Andhaka—Vṛshṇi segments. One of the important segments of the Yādava lineage was that of the Satvata from whom were descended three major clans—the Andhaka, the Vṛshṇi and the Devavṛidha. The emergence of these clans occurs fairly late just prior to the third or Kuru phase of the Pūru lineage which, on the basis of the archaeological co-relation suggested with the PGW, would date it to approximately *c.* 1000 B.C. or a little later. The Andhaka and Vṛshṇi are closely linked with the Mathura region from where they are said to have fled when attacked by Jarāsandha of Magadha and finally settled in Dvārakā. For this there is little archaeological confirmation since the presence of BRW is, so far at least, virtually absent at Mathura (barring a small amount at Sonkh), and the excavations at Dvārakā have not as yet reached possible BRW levels.[1] The lineage of Devavṛidha is said to have been connected with the Parnāśā river (the modern Banas) and the Mt. Abu region.[2] In terms of archaeological co-relation, the occupation of the Banas region by the Yādavas should have occurred earlier.

The more adventurous group of Yādava lineages are those which come under the title of the Haihaya clans. These were in the main, five, all of whom called themselves Talajaṅgha (perhaps with the palm tree as totem ?).[3] Among these were included the Saryāta (whose ancestors had fled from Kuśasthali), Bhoja, Vītihotra, Avanti and Tuṇḍikera. The Haihayas moved along the Narmada and are believed to have captured Mahishmati from the Karkoṭaka Nāga and fortified it as an important settlement.[4] According to the tradition the Haihayas are credited with attacking Kāśī, presumably making their way through central India to the Son-Yamuna *doab*. The BRW presence is attested to in these areas often at the earliest level. The Haihayas are also said to have over-run Ayodhyā and to have come into conflict with Vaiśālī and Videha.[5] From all these places as from Kāśī, the Haihayas are said to have been driven back. The evidence of BRW is not as yet available from Ayodhyā and Vaiśālī but the extension of BRW to eastern Uttar Pradesh and Bihar is of a later date than its occurence in Rajasthan and Madhya Pradesh. It was also a Yādava prince who is said to have wandered in the upper reaches of the Narmada and finally settled in the hills where the Ken rises. His son Vidarbha went in a southerly direction and established the kingdom of Vidarbha. The BRW from sites in Vidarbha (e.g. Paunar and Kaundanpur) is later than that from sites along the Narmada.[6]

Thus, the Yādava lands were Kathiawar and the areas drained by the Banas, Chambal, Betwa, Ken, Narmada and pockets along the Yamuna, all of which are areas associated with the migration of the BRW people, provided that the north Indian variants in the BRW ceramic type can all be said to belong to one cultural foundation. The record of the Yādava lineage in the *Purāṇas* virtually terminates with the events of the *Mahābhārata* war. The association of the Yādavas with Kathiawar however continued as late as the seventh century A.D. with the epigraphical reference to a Yādava family ruling at Siṁhapura[7]. The medieval period sees a revival of the seeking of connections with the Yādava lineage. This is perhaps most insistent in the thirteenth century A.D. with the reference in the south Indian tradition to the eighteen Yādava clans who are believed to have migrated from the north to the Deccan and further south under the leadership of Agastya [8] The date for this 'event' has been calculated to the eighth century B.C. The Yādavas are said to have settled initially mainly along the west coast as far south as Kerala. It has been argued that the eighteen clans of the Veḷir of the Sangam period were Yādavas.[9] A number of medieval dynasties of the western half of the peninsula—the Tulūvas, Rashṭrakūṭas, Hoysalas, Yādavas of Devagiri—claim Yādava descent. The Āy chiefs of Āykkudi of the ninth century A.D. claim to be of the Vṛshṇi-*kula* as also the Mūshaka kings who link themselves with Haihaya origins.[10] Is this sheer fantasy, or is it an attempt to acquire status, or does it reflect the persistence of descent (or supposed descent) even in very changed historical circumstances? The interest in this tradition lies in the coincidence of the diffusion of BRW associated with the megalithic culture in the peninsula during the first millennium B.C., an association which is a new feature. A detailed technical and comparative investigation of the BRW ceramic industry associated with the northern Chalcolithic and the southern Megalithic would go a long way towards clarifying the problem. As it stands there is at least a superficial similarity between the two ceramic industries

[1] M.S. Mate and Z.D. Ansari, *Excavations at Dwarka* (Poona, 1966).

[2] Pargiter, *op. cit.*, pp. 279

[3] *Vishnu Purana*, IV. 1.

[4] Pargiter, *op. cit.*, p. 266

[5] *Viṣhṇu Purana*, IV 3.

[6] S.B. Deo and M.K. Dhavalikar, *Paunar Excavation* (1967) (Nagpur, not dated), p. 6 : *IA*, 1961-62 pp. 29-30.

[7] The Lakkha-maṇḍala prasasti. *Epigraphia Indica*, I, pp. 11-12

[8] B. Saletore, *Ancient Karnataka* (Poona, 1936), pp. 245, 247

[9] M. Raghava Aiyangar, *Veḷir Varālaru* (third edition, Madras, 1964). (This reference was mentioned to me by Dr R. Champakalakshmi.)

[10] P.B. Desai, *Ancient History of Karnataka*, pp. 112-3, 305.

[11] Gopinatha Rao (ed.), *Travancore Archaeological Series*, No. 1. p.191

but this may not be found viable on further analysis.

The Yadu lineage has a greater tendency to branch off into segments and this process takes the segmented lineages over a larger geographical area than that of the Pūrus. The branching off starts earlier in the Yadu lineage with the Haihayas emerging in the eighth generation whereas the first segmentation of the Pūrus takes place as late as the fifty-first generation.[1] This may in part be accounted for by the fact that the alluvial plains of the *doab* could contain a larger population and the exploitation of agricultural resources could be confined to a more limited area as compared to Rajasthan and Madhya Pradesh where movement along the river valleys would be necessary for a growing population and demands on agriculture. The Yādava lineages do subscribe to a higher degree to one of the chief functional purposes of segmentary lineages, namely, predatory expansion.[2] In a pastoral-*cum*-agrarian society pastoralism would be more conducive to movement and would also provide the motive in the search for new grazing lands. The ability to segment suggests political flexibility and an economy not too deeply embedded in sedentary plough agriculture. Political flexibility and the absence of the social hierarchy of monarchical systems are reflected in the seemingly more egalitarian inter-clan relations of the Yādava lineage. Their pastoral economy is frequently referred to. Possibly the bull cult, evident from some sites linked with the BRW (Kayatha, Eran, Banas) may also have been a part of this.[3] In the movement from Kathiawar and Kutch *via* the Banas valley to the edge of the *doab* the migration might have been along the copper producing areas of the Aravallis, especially as the Ahar copper artefacts appear to have been produced from local ore.[4] The culture may have lost its momentum when it arrived in areas already familiar with copper technology such as the Ganga-Yamuna *doab*. The search for new settlements would also have brought them into conflict with microlithic and neolithic cultures already occupying these lands, such as the Bagor culture or the earliest phase of the Malwa culture. These would be food-gathering and herding groups or agriculturalists at a pre-metal stage. Can these be identified, as has been suggested, with the Nāgas and Pulindas, etc.; which occur in the literary sources?[5] The archaeological remains of these would be difficult to locate as most of them would have been absorbed into the Chalcolithic culture.

The ecological context of most BRW sites, barring those of eastern India, suggests a more generalized reliance on a subsistence economy with pockets of a more advanced economy. There appears to be a tendency to remain within a similar ecological bracket with settlements on elevated plateau regions of lightly wooded vegetation cover, huts with post-holes and wattle-and-daub walls, large-sized or multiple hearths and a substantial meat diet. This would in part explain the gradual succumbing of the BRW Chalcolithic to the iron-using PGW in the mid-first millennium B.C., and it would be worth investigating whether the extension of the BRW into a new ecological area in the eastern Ganga valley was due to association with iron technology. Indeed it might also explain, in reverse, how the more advanced iron technology of the peninsular megalithic cultures (whatever may have been their origin) withstood for a considerable period the advance of the northern cultures. Was the migration of the Yādava clans into the peninsula (if the tradition is correct) carried out on the backs of the newly emergent megalithic culture, or can the continuity of the Yādavas and their traditions be explained by assimilation into the existing megalithic culture?

The attempt to link the Pūru and Yādava lineages with certain archaeological cultures as examined in this paper has resulted in some echoes of identification, but nothing more definite than that can be said at this point. The identification remains speculative and requires both more information and more analysis before anything conclusive can be stated. Even this suggested identification raises a number of problems. The first of these is the problem of chronology. The start of the lineage is indirectly connected with the Flood. If the flood referred to is to be related to the only known major flood of the protohistoric period, the flood on the Indus, then it would date to *c.* 2000 B.C. and even assuming a MASCA correction for Indian sites can, at most, be taken back to 2400 B.C. This is still very much later than one of the dates which is associated with the start of the lineages, 3102 B.C. Was the flood in the lineage records mythical and borrowed perhaps from the Sumerian king-lists where the flood plays a dominant role and is archaeologically not entirely speculative ?

Further, if the Kuru section or the third phase of the Pūru lineage is to be identified with the PGW then the date of the Mahābhārata war cannot be earlier than *c.* 800 B.C. and was probably later. This would again conflict with the traditional chronology where the minimum time-span between Mahāpadma Nanda

[1] Pargiter, *op. cit.* p. 146.

[2] Marshall D. Sahlins, 'The Segmentary lineage: an organisation of predatory expansion', *The American Anthropologist*, vol. 63, (1961) No. 2. pp. 332–45.

[3] M.K. Dhavalikar, 'Some Aspects of the Chalcolithic Cultures of Central India', *Purattva*, No. 4. (1970–71), pp. 24–30.

[4] K.T.M. Hegde, 'Early Stages of Metallurgy in India' in *Radiocarbon and Indian Archaeology*, p. 401 ff.

[5] H.D. Sankalia, *op. cit.* p. 223

and Parikshit is 1050 years which would place Parikshit in approximately the fifteenth century B.C.[1] This lack of fit between chronology, archaeology and genealogy can perhaps be partially resolved if it is assumed that the listing of the generations was not meant to be a precise time-reckoning (in which case regnal years would have been mentioned), but rather a means of providing an approximate notion of the chronological framework. This is also indicated by the fact that not all the names listed in the genealogies are personal names (or even used in later times as personal names): some are quite clearly geographical place names and others are tribal names. Furthermore, it is as well to keep in mind that the tradition was compiled as a conscious attempt to record the past many centuries after the events referred to. As in all such records there would be a strong element of reorganizing the material to suit contemporary needs. The tradition itself therefore needs to be looked at more analytically. Many scholars have pointed out that the tradition is the end result of a series of encrustations and until these can be prised apart the tradition cannot be accepted as an entity. With reference to the Mahābhārata war one view among scholars maintains that the original war was fought between the Kurus and the Pañchālas.[2] It is not impossible that the original *Bhārata* referred to in Vedic literature[3] and differentiated from the *Mahābhārata* may have concerned an earlier section of the Pūru lineage and may have referred to a battle fought some time in the second millennium B.C. and that this *kathā* may have been appropriated by a later epic concerning the Kuru-Pāṇḍava conflict. Sukthankar's analysis of the Bhṛiguization of the *Mahābhārata* for example, shows clearly that attempted synchronisms from traditional sources are not as simple as they may seem at first glance[4]. There is also the inexplicable fact that the two protagonists in the epic, the Kauravas and the Pāṇḍavas are not related by blood with the Pūru lineage, both Dhritarāshṭra and Pāṇḍu being born of parents not directly descended from the Pūrus (In terms of blood ties Bhiṣhma is the last of the Pūrus). The link with the lineages seems very forced. This is strange, coming from a society where so much stress was laid on kinship relations.

The second major problem raised by the identifications examined in this paper is the inevitable question of identifying the Indo-Aryan speakers. Undoubtedly the simplest solution would be to say that all the archaeological cultures were Indo-Aryan speaking: yet the contradiction is that the language of the *Ṛig Veda* shows evidence of non-Aryan elements which evidence grows stronger in the later Vedic literature suggesting that the substratum cultures were non-Aryan speaking.[5] The older Pūrus (whom we have tried to identify with the OCP) are described as Asura Rakṣasa, yet it is their descendents (if the lineage is correct)—the Kuru-Pañcalas—in whose land the best Sanskrit is spoken.[6] If Pūru was a distant figure of the past as he appears to have been to the later Vedic literature and there was a break in the lineage after Bharata, then Pūru may well have been called an Asura Rakṣasa by more recent cultural groups such as the people of the PGW. The PGW could well reflect the arrival and settlement of a new group such as the Indo-Aryan speakers since there is a hiatus between the OCP and the PGW and the latter is technologically and otherwise more advanced. This could be a neat hypothesis but for two problems; firstly, the *Ṛig Veda* would have to be dated to the start of the PGW period (*c.* 800 B.C. unless an earlier period can be suggested for the Punjab river valleys) which would seem late for the *Ṛig Veda* and secondly, the origin of the PGW culture would have to be traced and this remains an enigma. Links with Iran suffer from an absence of any well-defined migratory route. So far, the possible link seems to be *via* the Swat Valley Grave cultures (Ghaligai V and Timargarha II and III),[7] and that too assuming that there was a major change in pottery type and other cultural facets on arrival in the Punjab, a change conditioned by local needs. This remains very tentative evidence at best. (In tracing such migrations or cultural continuities it might be worth-while to examine the substratum pottery such as the grey ware and the red ware which occur as associated wares with the more noticeable ceramic types).

If the *Ṛig Veda* is sought to be equated with the post-Harappan cultures of the second millennium B.C. with a geographical focus in north-western India conforming to the *sapta-sindhava* of the text, there is a striking absence of uniformity in any of the cultures variously identified as 'Aryan', *i.e.* the Jhukar, Cemetery

[1]D.C. Sircar, *The Bharata War and Puranic Genealogies* (Calcutta, 1969), p. 19 ff.

[2]N.N. Bhattacharya, 'The Kurukshetra War and the Pandavas' in D.C. Sircar (ed.), *The Bharata War and Puranic Genealogies*, p. 37 ff, argues in support of the earlier theories of Lassen, Weber and Monier-Williams that the original war was a Kuru-Pañchāla war.

[3]*Aśvālayana Griha Sūtra*, III.4.4.

[4]V.S. Sukthankar, 'Epic Studies', *ABORI*, XVIII, pp. 1–76. P.K. Gode (ed.), *Sukthankar Memorial Edition*, Vol. I.

[5]T. Burrow, *The Sanskrit Language* (London, 1965), pp. 373–388. B.M. Emeneau, *Collected Papers* (Annamalainagar, 1967), pp. 148, 155.

[6]*Satapatha Brāhmana*, III. 2.3.15.

[7]G. Stacul, 'Exacavation near Ghaligai (1968) and chronological sequence of protohistorical cultures in the Swatv alley,' *East and West*, 1969, vol. 19, pp. 44–92. A.H. Dani, 'Timargarha and Gandhara Grave Culture', *Ancient Pakistan*, III, 1967, p. 1 ff.

H and the Gandhara Grave Culture.[1] Apart from lack of uniformity there is also an absence of any group of common traits—settlement patterns, artefacts, weapons, burial customs—which could be said to indicate a related culture. There are only isolated artefacts suggesting connections with West Asia. On the question of the diffusion of the Indo-Aryan language there are two other possibilities which merit attention. One is the very useful distinction drawn by Hawkes between primary diffusion and secondary diffusion.[2] The first refers to the physical entry of a new people bringing an assemblage of new cultural traits. The second refers to the assimilation of the cultural traits of one group by another contiguous group without the first physically imposing itself on the second. The assimilation of cultural traits can be the adoption of the material culture where artefacts would register a difference, or the adoption of selected items such as language where the difference would not be easily recognizable from material remains, or both. In such an understanding of diffusion the element of invasion could be quite limited and it would be some aspect of dominance through technology, trade or some similar feature which would lead to the acquisition of new cultural traits. Another possibility is that the diffusion of Indo-Aryan in India followed a pattern similar to that of Hittite and Phrygian. The Hittites adopted the higher material culture of the people whom they conquered but kept their own Indo-European language.[3] Thus the material culture of Anatolia during this period does not declare the arrival of a new people to the extent that the cuneiform inscriptions indicate the arrival of a new language.

From recent work in linguistics it is clear that invasion is not the only method of accounting for the spread of a language. On the diffusion of Indo-European, for instance, the earlier model of Indo-European replacing the existing languages in many parts of west Asia is now giving way to the notion of there being periods of bilingualism and relationships between the various languages of a particular language area. Thus it has been suggested that Uralic is cognate with Indo-European and also with Dravidian and more recently the theory has been put forward that Elamite is cognate with Dravidian.[4] if these relationships can be finally established then the nature of the diffusion of Indo-European will undergo a change and it may not be necessary to look for uniform, superimposed cultures in the archaeology of north-western India to identify the arrival of Indo-Aryan speakers.

If language diffusion is seen in these terms then it would be possible to argue that there could have been small nucleii of Indo-Aryan speakers prior to the PGW who may have adopted the material culture of the previous settlers but retained their own language thus initiating a period of bilingualism.[5] The continuity of cultures contemporary with the Harappan, such as the OCP and the white-painted BRW indicate that elements of survival from the Harappan have to be conceded. Against this background the introduction of the new technology of iron if controlled by the Indo-Aryan speakers would have provided this group with the required political and economic edge reducing the need for extensive conquest. However, the epicentre of iron in India is as yet uncertain although the area of distribution is known.) Some of the religious rituals and practices of the indigenous culture would be Sanskritized and the new rulers would seek social legitimization by being incorporated into the earlier elite lineages (a process which incidentally occurs repeatedly in later centuries of Indian history). The lineages would then be recorded as continuing in an unbroken line of descent from the earlier to the later period (which is again a characteristic of the *vaṁśāvalis* of the historical period). New ruling groups would thus 'latch-onto' the existing lineages and become socially acceptable as well. The archaeological culture of the PGW and its literary counterpart the later Vedic Literature would then be an evolved culture reflecting both the indigenous as well as the later elements,[6] and 'aryan' would refer not to an ethnic group but to a social group identified by status, language and conformity to a particular cultural pattern, which certainly seems much closer to the connotation of the word '*ārya*' as it occurs in Vedic literature. The heartland of the PGW where it had the maximum impact, *i.e.* the *doab* and its fringes would remain the *ārya-varta*.

This process of acculturation can perhaps be more clearly visualized with reference to the BRW cultures. The association of BRW sherds with late Harappan levels in the same site and its subsequent diffusion would have made it a carrier of Harappan survivals to a far greater extent than the cultures contemporary with the Harappan in the upper Sarasvati and upper *doab*.

[1] D.H. Gordon, *op. cit.* pp. 59, 83. A.H. Dani, *op. cit.*

[2] C.F.C. Hawkes, *The Prehistoric Foundations of Europe to the Mycenean Age* (London, 1940).

[3] H. Hencken, 'Indo-European Languages and Archaeology', *American Anthropological Association*, Dec. 1955, Vol. 57. No. 6, Part 3, Memoir No. 4, pp. 2 ff, 41 ff.

[4] S.A. Tyler, 'Dravidian and Uralian: the lexical evidence', *Language*, 1968, No. 44, pp. 798–812. D.W. McAlpin, 'Elamite and Dravidian: Further evidence of Relationship', *Current Anthropology*, March 1975, Vol. 16 No. 1., p. 105 ff.

[5] Emeneau, *op. cit.*

[6] I have discussed the possible mechanism of such a cultural evolution in the Presidential Address—Section I of the Indian History Congress, Varanasi, 1969. See Proceedings.

In the case of the BRW there was no hiatus either. The movement of the white-painted BRW culture along the copper route in Rajasthan may further suggest that despite the decline of the Harappan cities there may still have been a modicum of the copper trade with west Asia of which the BRW culture of Rajasthan and Kathiawar was the inheritor. The movement into the Narmada valley may also have been in continuation of an earlier source of timber and carnelian for the west Asian trade.[1]

However should the identity of the Chalcolithic BRW with the Yādava lineage be acceptable, it raises its own problem, namely, that the Yādavas were unlikely to have been Indo-European speakers. The occurrence of the black-and-red ware in the ancient middle east is generally not associated with Indo-European speakers. Similar pottery is found in Egypt and Nubia (going back to the fourth millennium B.C.) and some traces in the Arabian peninsula have been suggested.[2] Archaeologically there is uptil now no connection between Egypt Nubia and the west coast of India apart from some traits in the first millennium B.C. megalithic culture of the peninsula. It is also not certain that the black-and-red of Egypt/Nubia is of the same ceramic type as the Indian megalithic counterpart. It has been suggested that references to the Land of Punt in the Egyptian sources may be to trade connections with India but even these were very sporadic with long time intervals and the maximum contact was during the fifteenth century B.C.[3] A variety of what seems to be the black-and-red ware, the Khirbet Kerak Ware, reported from Palestine, northern Syria and Anatolia, has been under discussion as a possible ware associated with Indo-European speakers.[4] But the dates of this ware, *c.* 2600–2400 B.C. precede the earliest indications of the arrival of possible Indo-Europeans in Anatolia, the Luwians in *c.* 2300 B.C. In any case the distribution of this ware ceases east of the Euphrates. Once again the links between the BRW in India and in west Asia remain enigmatic. There is, however, a single shape which might indicate some connection and that is the channel-spouted bowl which occurs in white painted BRW and resembles in form a type from Sialk, Tepe Hissar and Tepe Giyan.[5] But this is again tenuous evidence.

Even from literary evidence the Yādavas are clearly not a primarily Indo-Aryan speaking group. The Vrishṇi and Andhaka are referred to as *vrātyas*.[6] The inhabitants of Ānarta and Surāṣṭra are described as belonging to the *sankīrṇa jātis*.[7] The Yādava kinship system shows traces of a matrilineal structure which is alien to the Indo-European kinship system.[8] If the *nīla-lohita* referred to in the *Atharvaveda* is to be taken as BRW as suggested, then it is evident that the text disapproves of the practises of those who use this pottery.[9] It would seem that the continuity and survival of cultures going back to the early second millennium B.C. in Gujarat would not only have preserved more of the third millennium culture but would also have modified the impact of linguistic and cultural Sanskritization in these areas. It is significant that the survival of the Harappa script in the form of a few recognizable pictograms, occurs, so far as is known to-date, painted on some Chalcolithic pot sherds and as graffiti on the black-and-red pottery of the peninsula megalithic.[10] It is also curious that Gujarat is listed as one of the *pañcha-drāviḍa* lands in a late Buddhist text.[11]

Attempts at co-relating Puranic lineages and archaeological cultures are beset with speculation and suppositions. It would seem that the identification of the Yādava lineage on the whole appears to fit the archaeological evidence better, provided that the white-painted and plain Chalcolithic BRW cultures can be said to

[1]Romila Thapar, 'A Possible Identification of Meluhha, Dilmun and Makan', *Journal of the Economic and Social History of the Orient*, vol. XVIII (1975), Part 1, p. 30ff.

[2]S.P. Gupta, 'Gulf of Oman: The Original Home of Indian Megaliths', *Puratattva*, no. 4, 1970–71, p. 7

[3]M.Murray, *The Splendour That was Egypt* (London, 1949), pp. xxi, 20, 49, 98.

[4]I am grateful to Mr B.K. Thapar for drawing my attention to this discussion. E. Anati, *Palestine before the Hebrews* (London, 1963), p. 101 ff and L.C. Woolley, *A Forgotten Kingdom*, Pelican Books (Harmondsworth, 1953), p. 32 ff, both associated the ware with barbarian invasions. More extensive excavation has modified these views B. Maisler, *et al.*, 'The Excavation at Beth Yerah, *Israel Exploration Journal*, 1944–46, 1952. Vol. 2. Nos. 2, 3, 4,. In the same journal, Ruth Amiran, 'Connections between Anatolia and Palestine in the Early Bronze Age'. R. Braidwood, *Mounds in the Plain of Antioch* An Archaeological Survey (Chicago, 1937) p. 55. S. Hood, 'Excavations at Tabera al Akad, 1948–49', *Anatolian Studies*, 1951, Vol. I., pp, 113 ff. More recent views on this discussion are given in brief in the *Cambridge Ancient History*, Vol. I. Part 2, p. 213 ff.

[5]K.V. Soundara Rajan, 'The Iron Age Cultu e Provinces of India', *Bharatiya Vidya* 1963, vol. XXIII, nos. 1–4, pp. 1–21.

[6]*Mahābhārata*, VII. 143.15.

[7]*Baudhāyana* L.1. 32–33

[8]The main feature is the mention of cross-cousin marriages which is particularly prohibited in the Indo-Aryan kinship system. For a discussion of this see T.R. Trautman, 'Cross-cousin mariage in Ancient North India', in T.R. Trautman (ed.), *Kinship and History in South Asia*. For Indo-European kinship structure see P, Friedrich, 'Proto-Indo-European Kinship', *Ethnology*, 1966, vol, V. pp. 1–36.

[9]*Atharvaveda* IV. 17.4 and cf. V.31.1. The reference is discussed in A. Ghosh, *The City in Early Indian History*, p. 6 and Shivaji Singh,' Vedic Literature on Pottery' in B.P. Sinha, *op. cit.*, p. 305 ff. The reference to *sūtra nīla-lohita* in the Paippalāda text can perhaps be explai ed as a late recension in a distant land (Kashmir) being totally unfamiliar with black and red pottery associating the colours with *sūtra*.

[10]B.B. Lal, 'From the megalithic to the Harappa: tracing back the graffiti on the pottery' *Ancient India*, o, 16, 1960, pp. 4–24.

[11]*Khuddakanikāya*, Apadāna, II, p, 359

emanate from a common source or at least are closely related. The identification of the Pūru lineage is far more complex owing to the more pronounced changes in the archaeological cultures of the OCP and PGW. With the literary sources there is not only the problem that the Puranic texts were compiled many centuries, after the events referred to, and even in the most meticulously maintained oral tradition chronological discrepancies are bound to enter thereby changing the concordance of the event and its record; but also, that the Vedic and Puranic texts are sometimes in serious disagreement even with regard to the order of succession of the various descent groups. For example, Divodāsa and Sudās are mentioned in the *Ṛig Veda* as approximate contemporaries of Purukutsa and Trasadasyu. Yet, in the Puranic genealogies the latter two occur fairly early in the list of kings of Ayodhyā and the former two are listed late as kings of North Pañchala, thus indicating a substantial time difference between the two.[1]

If archaeological evidence suggests that the Aryan speaking people settled in India in the post-Harappan period then a more fundamental question connected with the historical tradition has to be posed. Does the tradition record personalities and events related only to Aryan culture or has it assimilated into its own tradition those names and events which might refer to non-Aryan and pre-Aryan times. In a period of bilingualism for instance, it could be assumed that non-aryan names from an earlier tradition would be rendered into Sanskrit. If there is evidence of archaeological survivals from the Harappa culture then some survivals within the tradition must also have persisted and these may not have been confined only to religious practices.

Perhaps at this stage it would be best to work towards a more precise definition of the evolution of archaeological cultures through more intensive excavation in an attempt to give greater clarity to the chronology, distribution and socio-economic structure of the various groups of people who were the authors of these cultures. Once the archaeological picture is more clearly defined and the information arrived at placed on a firmer footing, then the co-relation with the historical tradition from literary sources might be more meaningful.

ROMILA THAPAR

Jawahar Lal Nehru University,
New Delhi.

[1]*Ṛig Veda,* I.63.7; IV.42.8; VI. 61. ff; VI. 16.4; VII.18.25; VII.191.3. Pargiter, *op. cit.* pp. 145–46.

Archaeology and Indian Tradition—Some Observations

Hoary, colourful, varied and vast Indian tradition has attracted the attention of scholars for over a century. The traditional accounts of kings, heroes, saints or events are mainly found in the Brahmanical, the Buddhistic and the Jaina texts, and include, to a considerable extent, even mythical or supernatural elements. There are, however, some traditions which are not purely of a religious nature. It is widely known that the historians of India have reconstructed the early history of India including the lives of Mahāvīra and Buddha and the dynastic lists from traditional accounts. In some cases, the epigraphical material has been found to be in conformity with the traditional records. At the same time, it must be realized that whatever is recorded as a part of tradition is not necessarily correct, for it lacks (a) the objectivity and (b) the contemporaneity.

Attempts have been made in the recent decades, by some eminent archaeologists, to substantiate archaeological evidence with data embodied in the tradition. The classic example is by Wheeler[1] who equated Cemetery-H culture with Aryans to prove the theory of Aryan invasion and consequent destruction of the centres of the Indus civilization. In his enthusiasm to establish the theory of Aryan conquest he could neither critically examine the archaeological evidence nor the literary data. He tried to connect the so-called massacre of Mohenjo-daro with the Cemetery-H material without

[1]R.E.M. Wheeler, 'Harappa 1946', *Ancient India,* No. 3 (1947) p. 82.

adequate proof. Lal[1] has convincingly refuted him more than once showing the weak points of his hypothesis, especially the absence of a cultural overlap between the Harappan and Cemetery H levels at Harappa. G.F. Dales[2] and Romila Thapar[3] too have advanced arguments against Wheeler's surmise.

However, we are presently concerned with the literary aspect of Wheeler's contention which too does not appear to be sound. There is no relevance of *āyasī-puras* (forts of metal or iron) or *śatbhujī-puras* or forts with hundred walls in the Harappan context. None of Harappan fortifications known to us bear any trace of metallic appearance or multiple walls to justify the appellations *āyasī* and *śatabhujī*. Even if the latter is supposed to refer to a defence-wall with hundred angles we cannot apply the term in question to any of the fortified Harappan settlements. It would not be out of context to note that in a few hymns of *Ṛigveda* (I. 58.8, I.166.8 and VII-15.13–14) metallic and *śatabhujī* castles are also associated with the Aryan gods, Agni and Maruts.

Thus, the so-called forts of metal were perhaps nothing but a natural phenomenon. Similarly, the term *śāradī-pura* (autumnal forts) cannot be applied to Harappan settlements, for these do not seem to be seasonal townships. Many scholars including Wheeler, feel that *śaradī-puras* were places of refuge during heavy floods or rains, but in that case these would have been named as monsoonal forts and not autumnal ones, because in north India rivers normally remain flooded during the rainy season. Moreover, so far no remains of any such seasonal fort have come to light. Perhaps a *śāradī-pura* represented the brilliant battlemented cloud castle of the autumnal months as suggested by Muir.[4]

As regards the principal enemy of Indra, i.e. Vṛitra is concerned, it is doubtful whether he represented any human being, for hymns refer to him distinctly as a serpent (*ahi*) and some time as an Asura. He is often accused of stopping the flow of waters which were released by Indra.

Similarly, Śambara who has been called a dweller of the hills (*Rv.* I.130.7, II.12.13, IV.30.14 and VI.26.5) cannot be identified as a Harappan chief. As regards the identification of Harappa with Hariyūpīyā, it may be affirmed that by sheer name it cannot be understood to be a city of the non-Vedic people, for the literal meaning of the term Hariyūpīyā would be a place with golden *yūpas* (sacrificial posts). Recently S. B. Roy[5] has proposed another name i.e. Yavyāvatī (a city of grains or granary) for Harappa, but the name itself is of Sanskritic origin, hence cannot be applied to a settlement of non-Aryan tribes. It is unlikely that the conquerors would change the name of a settlement which was destroyed by their armies. The *Ṛgvedic* hymn (V.I29.5) referring to the Harīyūpīyā reads as under:–

Vadhīdindro Varaśikhasya śesho
bhyāvartine chāyamānāya śikshan |
Vṛichivato yaddhvariyūpīyāyāṁ
han purve ardhe bhiyasaparo-dart ||

The race of Varaśikha and the descendants of Vṛichivat referred to in the above hymn do not seem to be non-Aryans; further, the attack on Hariyūpiyā according to the hymn in question was from the east, and not from the west. This would not have been the case if Harappa (Hariyūpiyā) would have been sacked by the invading Aryan armies as suggested by Wheeler. Allchins,[6] who have also supported the invasion theory, cite another reference from *Ṛigveda* (I.149.3) to a *pura* called Nārminī burnt by fire. The meaning of the hymn is hardly specific; according to Sāyaṇa it contains a reference to fire altar, while some modern translators, including Griffith, find in it a mention of lighting up (not destruction) of joyous castle by Agni.[7]

The adversaries of the Aryan deities and Vedic people are referred to as Dasyus and Asuras and sometimes as both. But taking into account the Indian tradition we cannot separate Asura and Deva or Sura (the so called Aryans) origins, and in case the Asuras are identified as the Harappans, as suggested by Roy,[8] they can be regarded originally to be of the same stock as the Aryans. Yet, without positive proofs, even this speculation would be subjective.

A more serious attempt was made by Lal[9] in interpreting, in the light of the tradition, the culture-sequence obtained through excavations at Hastinapura. In the cutting across the ancient mound, he identified traces of a huge flood, making the end of the Painted Grey Ware period (Period II). He felt that this flood represented the one which destroyed the city of Hastinapura

[1]B.B. Lal, 'Protohistoric Investigations', *Ancient India*, no. 9 (1953), p. 88; also, Lal, 'Excavātion at Hastinapura and other explorations in the Upper Gaṅgā and Sutlej Basins 1950–51' *Ancient India* nos. 10 & 11 (1954 & 1955), p. 151.

[2]G.F. Dales, 'The Mythical Massacre at Mohenjo-daro', *Expedition*, vol. VI, no. 3 (1964), pp. 36 ff.

[3]Romila Thapar, Presidential Address, Section 1, Indian History Congress, Thirty-fifth Session, Dec. 28–30, 1969 (Varanasi), pp. 5 and 19.

[4]Quoted by Ralph T.H. Griffith, *The Hymns of the Rigveda* (Translation), Vol. I, (Second ed. Benares, 1896), p. 183.

[5]S.B. Roy, Chronological Infrastructure of Indian Protohistory, '*Journal' of the Bihar Research Society*, Vol. LVIII, pts 1–4 (Jan-Dec. 1972), pp. 70–72.

[6]Bridget and Raymond Allchin, *Birth of Indian Civilization* (Harmondsworth, 1968), p. 155.

[7]Griffith, *op. eit.* p. 203.

[8]Roy, *op. cit.* p. 73.

[9]Lal, *op. cit.* (1954 & 1955) p. 147 ff.

during the reign of Nichakshu, according to the *Purāṇas,* and as a result of which the Kuru capital was shifted from Hastināpura to Kauśāmbī. He further tried to substantiate his postulate on the ground that the Painted Grey Ware had been found in a number of sites associated with the *Mahābhārata* story including Tilpat, Indraprastha, Mathurā, Ahichchhatrā, Barnawa, Kampil, Kurukshetra, etc. He writes:–[1]

> Now, when the archaeological data are viewed against the background of literature, some obvious questions begin to pose themselves. Is it a mere chance—
>
> (i) that a large number of sites associated with the Mahābhārata story contain the same ceramic industry, viz. the Painted Grey Ware, in their lower levels ?
>
> (ii) that the date of the *Mahābhārata* battle falls within Period II at Hastināpura ?
>
> (iii) that the people who appeared in the Ghaggar-Sutlej valleys in a post-Harappan context—a period which synchronizes with the arrival of the Aryan-speaking people in that area, as per literary and inscriptional evidence, cited above—used the Painted Grey Ware ?
>
> Further, may not the archaeological evidence be taken to indicate that the Purāṇic tradition regarding the washing away of Hastināpura and the subsequent shifting of the capital to Kauśāmbī may have some historical basis ?
>
> If it is believed that all these coincidences are nothing more than mere chances, the questions wind themselves up. Otherwise, a conclusion that would appear to force itself on us is: that the sites of Hastināpura, Mathurā, Kurukshetra, Barnāwā, etc., are identifiable with those of the same name mentioned in the *Mahābhārata.* If that be so, the Painted Grey Ware would be associable with the early settlers on these sites, viz. the Pauravas, Pañchālas, etc., who formed a part of the early Aryan stock in India. Such an association may also explain the synchronism between the appearance of the Painted Grey Ware in the Ghaggar-Sutlej valleys and the probable date of the arrival of the Aryans in that area. *May it, however, be emphasized that the evidence is entirely circumstantial and until and unless positive ethnographic and epigraphic proofs are obtained to substantiate the conclusions they cannot but be considered provisional*[2]

It is interesting to note that Lal's view on this issue was differently interpreted by different writers. By one group of scholars the Painted Grey Ware at Hastināpura and elsewhere was taken to be an evidence of the Aryan settlements and by others a proof of Mahābhārata tradition. Lal, it appears, is not very clear on this point, for, according to the Indian tradition, the people and heroes connected with the principal events of the *Mahābhārata* are much different from their Vedic ancestors, culturally and chronologically. The founder of the Paurava (Kuru) line according to the *Purāṇas* was Pururavas, who is also mentioned in the *Ṛigveda* (I.31.4). Should we, therefore, connect him with the Painted Grey Ware settlements ? Yet there is another difficulty, i.e. the gap of over ninety-two generations between Pururavas and Pāṇḍavas.

If we take 950 B.C. or 850 B.C. as the date of *Mahābhārata* battle then the early Pauravas are to be placed somewhere before 2000 B.C. or so. But, unfortunately, nowhere in any of the known sites the Painted Grey Ware or the culture associated with it shows an early beginning.

The C^{14} dates on the other hand in most cases suggest a shorter and later date-bracket viz., 800 B.C. to 350–400 B.C.[3] for the Painted Grey Ware levels, which further makes the association of this Ware with the great epic doubtful.

Besides, Hastināpura, which has invariably been mentioned as a city in ancient texts, cannot be called an urban settlement in Period II. Non-availability of the Painted Grey Ware in the upper Punjab and further north-west (Madra and Gandhāra regions) creates difficulty in accepting the view proposed by Lal. Lastly, Lal has explained the *Mahābhārata* tradition only in isolated contexts without taking into account the contemporary cultures in other regions connected with various tribes and events of the main story of the great epic. In other words, if some one interprets the culture associated with the Pāṇḍavas at Hastināpura and other places in archaeological terms, he should also be in a position to explain similarly the cultures of the Yādavas (of Dvārikā), Chedis, Magadhas, etc., with positive proofs, so that the tradition covering a large part of India could be examined in its entirety.

Lately Sankalia and Lal have taken up the problem connected wi h the archaeology of the *Rāmāyaṇa.* According to Sankalia, the *Rāmāyaṇa*, as a story in its present well-known form, is a pure fancy or fiction, but its core contains germs of truth.[4] After studying the *Rāmāyaṇa* critically and employing archaeology in all its aspects, he draws[5] the following inferences:–

> "(i) there is no doubt about the existence of Ayodhya and other cities mentioned in the Rāmāyaṇa such as Kausambī, Mithila, Kanyakubja at least by 1000 B.C.;
>
> (ii) whether these cities, now called by these names, were at that time respectively known by their names and were ruled by dynasties called Iksvaku and others is very likely but can be proved, only when the sites of these cities are excavated;
>
> (iii) the core of the Rāmayana story—viz. Rama, Sita, Lakshmana and the exile of Rama with Sita and her being kidnapped by Ravana—was true and was known at this time;
>
> (iv) Ravana was a dark-skinned man who had not more than two hands and one head and he had carried away Sita in his arms;
>
> (v) Ravana belonged very probably to the Gond tribe;
>
> (vi) Lanka of this Ravana was in the Chota Nagpur plateau in and most probably near Jabalpur. All this area, Ramayana expressly tells us, was included in Rama's kingdom, i.e. (Southern) Kosala;
>
> (vii) Rama and Lakshmana and the Gonds fought with bows, arrows and swords, and spears, whereas the Vanaras who were other aboriginal tribes fought with missiles like trees and stones;
>
> (viii) All the places occurring in the Dandakaranya can be satisfactorily identified in this region, south of Prayag.

[1] *Ibid.*, pp. 150–51.
[2] F.E. Pargiter, *Ancient Indian Historical Tradition* (London, 1922), pp. 144–48.
[3] D.P. Agrawal and Sheela Kusumgar, *Prehistoric Chronology and Radiocarbon Dating in India* (New Delhi, 1974), p. 132.
[4] H.D. Sankalia, *Rāmāyaṇa—Myth or Reality* ?(New Delhi 1973), pp. v-vi.
[5] *Ibid.* pp. 62–63.

> Thus, in the original Ramayana, the entire episode took place in a compact geographical area. There is nothing unnatural about it—either the persons or the places.
>
> It was this nucleus which the poet named Valmiki, supposed to be himself a hunter, turned into a heroic poem—*adikavya*.

It is apparent from Sankalia's conclusions that he has not been able to date the episode or to put Rāma or Ikshvākus in a chronological frame, although he feels that Ayodhyā could at least be as old as 1000 B.C. It is highly doubtful whether excavation at Ayodhyā would in any way be helpful in establishing the truth about the Ikshvākus rule or Rāma's existence. He does not specify the grounds on which he thinks Rāma, Lakshmaṇa, Sītā etc. to be historical figures. To treat Rāvaṇa as a Gond of the Chhota Nagpur area is something that is basically against the strong epic tradition. A Gond, traditionally, could be called a Śabara and not a Rākshasa. And Rāvaṇa was not an ordinary Rākshasa but a Brahma-Rākshasa well-familiar with the Vedic lore. Hence *Rāmāyaṇa* tradition has to be explained in relation to the Vedic tradition and associated archaeological data, if any. Lastly, the identification of the region or site of Rāvaṇa's Laṅkā proposed by Sankalia is unsupported by an archaeological evidence.

Lal, it seems has simplified the whole issue. He proposes to solve the problem by excavating some important sites locally associated with the *Rāmāyaṇa,* such as Ayodhyā, Sṛiṅgverapura, Bhardvāja-āśrama, Chitrakuṭa, Bithur and Parihar and by connecting the earliest cultures in these spots, in case these are identical.[1] He sees the probability of getting either the Copper Hoard Culture or the Painted Grey Ware culture or some other hitherto-unknown culture in the lowest levels at these sites. It is surprising as to how with this kind of approach, Lal would be able to prove or disprove the Rāmāyana episode or the associated culture, for it is definite that he is not going to find any inscribed material. Then how to ascertain the exact Ramayaṇic character of the cultural assemblage, which may also be of pre-Rāma or post-Rāma period or may not have any association with the Ikshvākus. Secondly, if the tradition is to be taken into account, the Ramayaṇic cultures of Ayodhyā, Bharadvāja-āśrama, Sṛiṅgverapura and Parihar should differ from each other, for, the character of these places was not identical according to the story in question. Lal, following H.C. Ray Chaudhury, is inclined to place the *Rāmāyaṇa* events later than that of the *Mahābhārata* on the basis of the following statement in the *Bṛihadāraṇyaka Upanishad* made in the court of Janaka of Mithila '*Kva Pārikshitāh abhavan*' i.e. 'where have the descendants of the Parikshit gone' ? 'The simple implication of this story,' in the words of Lal, 'is that Janaka was later than Parikshit. According to Ray Chaudhury, the possibility is that Janaka was a contemporary of Nichakshu. It may, incidentally be recalled here that it was in the time of Nichakshu that Hastināpura was washed away by the Gaṅgā and the capital was shifted to Kauśambī where a developed form of the Painted Grey Ware has been encountered in the lower levels. However, it would be desirable to go deeper into the literary evidence itself in order to make sure that Janaka, referred to in this incident, is none other than the father-in-law of Rāma.[2] This is something which goes basically against the strong Indian tradition placing Pāṇḍavas and Kṛishṇa later to Rāma. Besides, there were more than one Parikshita and one Janaka. At least one Parikshita who was seventieth in descent from Pururava, lived many generations before the Pāṇḍavas. Janaka was a title of the rulers of Videha (Mithilā) as late as the time of Buddha according to early Pali texts.

Both Sankalia and Lal appear to be absolutely sure about the identification of ancient Ayodhyā with the modern town of the same name, but an early refrence to this city gives a different picture. The original text is as under[3]:-

Ashṭachakrā navadvārā devānāṁ purayodhyā I
Tasyām hiraṇmayaḥ-kośḥa svargo loko jyotishāvṛtaḥ II
Yo vai tām Brahmaṇo veda amṛtenavṛtām-purīm I
Tasmai brahmā cha Brahmā cha āyuḥ kīrtim prajām daduḥ II
Vibhrājamānām harinīm yaśasā samparivṛtām I
Puran Hiraṇmayīm Brahmā vivesāparājitām II
(*Taittirīya Āryaṇyaka,* I, 27.)

Tvashtṛīm māyām vaisravaṇah ratham sahasrabandhuram.
Puruschakram sahasrāśvam āsthāyāyāhi no balim
(*Taittirīya Araṇyaka.*, I, 37.)

"Ayodhyā (impregnable), the city of the gods, consists of eight circles (also cycles) and nine entrances; within it there is the golden treasure-dome, the celestial world, ever-illuminated with light (north pole). Whoever knows it as the Creator's city ever surrounded with nectar will have long life, fame, and offspring bestowed on him, by Brahmā (the sun), and Brahma (the moon). Into this city ever shining, moving, and pervaded with Yaśas (fame and lustre), the Creator has entered."

[1] *Rama-kathānaka sambandhī sthalon kā Purātātvik aṇveshaṇ*, a Hindi pamphlet issued in March 1975 in connection with excavations at Ayodhyn by Prof. Braj Basi Lal and others (Gwalior, 1975).

[2] B.B. Lal, Archaeology and the two Indian Epics' *Annals of the Bhandarkar Oriental Research Institute*, Vol. LIV,pts. I-IV, (1973), pp. 7-8.

[3] R. Shamasartry, 'Ayodhya, The city of the Gods', *D.R. Bhandarkar Volume* (Calcutta, 1940), p. 17.

Shamasastry[1] says that Ayodhyā is described in the above mentioned verses in both microcosmic and macrocosmic terms. He feels that the *Rāmāyaṇa* episode has evolved out of zodiacal myth. To quote him:-

"Expressed in terms of time the eight Chakras represent the cycle of 20 years made up of eight minor cycles of 2½ years with one intercalary month each (see the Vedāṅajyautisha on 2½ years cycle). The seven months were regarded as being presided over by seven Adityas and eight Aditya named Mārtaṇḍa (born of lifeless egg) is cast out. The seven Adityas who are the lords of the seven intercalary months occurring in the cycle of 20 years reduced to 19 years are distinct from the sun or suns presiding over the ordinary months.

'The whole of the above twelve intercalary month-circles evidently forms a cycle of 33 years divided into two parts, one part of 19 years with seven intercalary months and a second part of 13 years with 5 intercalary months called Rākshasaloka as contrasted with name of Devaloka given to the division of 19 years. Thus 19 + 13 years + 12 months make up 33 years. The intercalary year is called Adhi-samvatsara in the Taittiriya. Araṇyaka. The cycle of 20 years which is one-third of the 60 years cycle beginning with Prabhava and ending with Akshaya is also referred to there in the very beginning of the work.

'Rāma, the son of Daśaratha, the friend of Indra, is an incarnation of Vishṇu, the sun-god. He lives in Ayodhyā which is formed by the seven intercalary month-circles and becoming 19 years old, he leaves it at the behest of his father for the forest world of Daṇḍaka and Laṅkā. He wanders there for 14 years. Reaching Laṅkā on or near the equator, he destroys the Rākshasa and Rāvaṇa, their chief, and returns at the completion of 33 years to Ayodhyā of the Devaloka. The same work is repeated in every cycle of 33 years. This is the original real Kalpa which the authors of the Purāṇas and the Siddhāntas magnified into 43,20,000 years. The word Zodia or Zodiac seems to be philologically akin to Ayodhyā. Accordingly the story of the Rāmāyaṇa appears to be a development of an early Zodiacal myth ?

One may accept or reject Shamasastry's surmise, but it is certain that the time when the *Taittarīya Āraṇyaka* was composed the memory of the Āyodhyā of the mortals was wholly forgotten, if it existed at all. Ayodhyā with nine portals, eight circular enclosures and a surrounding pool of nectar appears to be purely a mythical city which could be compared to some extent with Samavasaraṇa and Nandīśvara-dvīpa (central part) of the Jaina mythology. Thus, it is probable that modern Ayodhyā and its association with Rāma is of a later origin.

It is clear from what has been discussed above that Indian tradition Vedic or Purāṇic is not likely to help much in the interpretation of archaeological data. The theories propounded by reputed archaeologists are laboured ones and based on pre-conceived notions. Most scholars have twisted the traditional accounts or invented their own legends to suit their interpretations because it is utterly difficult to apply the tradition as a whole to the field of pure archaeology involving one or more material cultures.[2] When the excavations at Maheshwar (ancient Māhshmatī) could not unfold the mystery of the great Haihaya monarch Kārttavīrya Sahasrārjuna, a contemporary of Parasurama and Rāvaṇa, how digging at Ayodhyā will solve the problems of *Rāmāyaṇa*. Majority of Indian traditions are unhistoric and coloured and therefore none of their archaeological interpretation would prove to be free from subjectivity.

The *Rāmāyaṇa* and the *Mahābhārata* were not written for the simple aim of recording the past happenings, but these were composed with the specific purpose for expounding the message of *dharma* through the stories, in the tradition of Aśokan *dhamma* which itself was an outcome of the problems growing out of the Iron Age Urbanization.

Even the later and secular Indian tradition connected with Vikramāditya or Ālhā-Udal cannot be explained in archaeological terms. Hence tradition and archaeology should not be mixed together in any form at least as far as Indian protohistory is concerned.

Archaeological Survey of India M.C. JOSHI
New Delhi

[1] *Ibid.*, p. 18.

[2] Lately Sankalia has revised his views on the location of Lanka [Hindustan Times, Feb 23, 1976] He feels that it was either in the south eastern Madhya Pradesh or in the adjoining areas of Orissa and Andhra. But he has not referred to any archaeological evidence in the terms of a specific pottery (showing Rākshasa association) or strictural remains to support his surmise.

Harappan and Rigvedic Inter-relations[1]

As far as the protohistory of the Indian sub-continent is concerned, a vast amount of archaeological and also literary material, probably of a slightly later date, is available. Both the types of material, however, present serious difficulties in creating a coherent picture of the past events. In the archaeological material, the Indus civilization and at certain sites, the pre-Indus stratum are the earliest. Little is known about the ethnic and linguistic identity of the people who created the extensive, well-organized and literate Indus civilization with planned urban centres, and much less about their predecessors. The sum total of the contribution made by this civilization to the subsequent developments is still unestimated, as on most of the sites, the continuity of occupation is broken and the sites are abandoned for some centuries. Amongst the literary material the *Ṛigveda,* the oldest literary compositions of the Indo-Aryan language, precious enough to have been preserved intact for more than thirty centuries, is, at the present stage of our knowledge, no more than an account of wars waged by the gods and demons, intermingled with some misty mysticism and of late some patches of historical events. A clear picture of events or the life of the people in the centuries intervening between, roughly speaking the Indus civilization and Aśoka, is still enveloped in darkness except for religious life despite the mass of literature that exists by way of Vedic and Buddhist literature, the epics and the identifiable archaeological cultures such as the Painted Grey Ware and Black-and-Red Ware. It is obvious that the source material of the two types referred to above, when used singly, does not help to create a coherent and self-sufficient picture and the gaps in our knowledge can hardly be filled with any one of them.

Despite the handicaps from which *Ṛigveda* at present suffers, it must be conceded that as far as the literary material is concerned, it is the closest in time to the Indus civilization and as such may be expected to retain traces of the older tradition represented by the Indus civilization. It would thus be worthwhile to re-examine the Ṛigvedic material from the point of view of throwing light on the problems faced by the archaeologists. In doing this, the events described in *Ṛigveda* will be automatically verified on the basis of archaeological findings. Thus, it promises to be a weapon which cuts both ways.

In the following pages is demonstrated a new approach and some of the results it yields. The approach consists in showing that the so-called mythology in the *Ṛigveda* (RV) is a later superimposition of the times when the Aryans sought to create religion out of the events which actually took place. Thus, originally the hymns which sang the praises of the Aryan hero Indra, referred to his battles with the pre-Aryan population of the Indus valley and not the demons. In the process, the Ṛigvedic material is automatically denuded of the layers of the so-called mythology of gods and demons, clouds and cows, lightening and thunder, sun and rain, which was the outcome of the wholesale applicātion of the myth of rain-making, etc. from whose shackles it has been found difficult to free RV. This approach commends itself on the following grounds: (a) It treats the material rationally considering its literal meaning which is also preserved and has come down to us. (b) It can be applied almost universally to RV and related literature at least in the particular context of the wars of the Aryans and pre-Aryans, thus creating a harmonious picture out of what is now a mass of chaotic mythology. The picture that emerged may be verified in the light of the archaeological findings.

The material presented here is extremely limited and selected, as the article is meant as a pre-publication, communication of a larger and detailed study which has been ready for press since August, 1973. It is hoped that the selection and choice of material presented here does not hamper the understanding.

A few words about the genesis of this work may not be out of place here, as they have a direct bearing on the basic assumption. While investigating the origins of Buddhist Tantric ideology, it was observed that many names of the Tantric female deities like Vetālī, Śavarī, Pukkasī, Ḍombinī, Parṇaśavarī, Gaurī, Chaṇḍālī, etc. were identical with the names of castes belonging to the group called *saṁkīrṇayoni,* mixed castes, by the Hindu lawgivers and with the names

[1]This paper was read at a meeting organized by the Indain Archaeological Society on December 26, 1973. I am profoundly indebted to Prof. R. D. Wadekar. His contribution to the work went to the extent of filling gap created by the lack of institutional support both in personal and academic life. Through his good offices, library facilities in Vaidic Saṁśodhana Maṇḍala. Deccan College Post-graduate and Research Institute, and other institutions in Pune became available. I must also express my deep sense of gratitude to Shri M.N. Deshpande for extending to me library facilities and all other help during this work. I should like to acknowledge with thanks the keen interest shown by Professor Satish Chandra, Vice-Chairman of University Grants Commission. It has been possible to get the work ready for press through a generous grant given by Indian Council of Historical Research.

of tribes mentioned in the various lists of peoples in Mahābhārata (MBh), *Bṛihatsaṁhitā* of Varāhamihira, etc. This was confirmed by M.N. Srinivas' observation that the names of gods and goddesses of the lower castes in Coorg are identical with the castes propitiating him or her.[1]

In another context I came across a passage in an unpublished Buddhist Tantric text *Śriguhyasiddhi*;

prāpya mudrāṁ parām divyām śuddhāsarvaguṇlayām
vicitrarūpasaṁpannāṃ śokamṛtyuvivarjitām
asurin nāgin tatha yakshim surim vātha kinnarim
gandharvim rūpasaṁpannām athavā siddhayoginīm
etā divyastriyoginyaḥ samākshṛyā prapūjayet

. . . .

yadi vātha na śhaknoti ākṛṣṭām divyayoshitām

pīḍyate chaiva kāmena tadā seveta mānushīm Chapter 7). "Having got hold of an extremely gracious *mudrā* (woman partner) pure and endowed with all the virtues, extraordinarily beautiful, devoid of grief and death, an Asurī, a Nāgī, or a Yakshī or a Surī or else a Kinnarī or a Gandharvī with a beautiful form or a Sidhdayoginī, these divine female yoginis should be attracted and worshipped.........If it is not possible to catch hold of these divine ladies, and if the practicant is troubled by desire, he should propitiate a *Mānushī*, i.e., a woman."

But for the reference to the mythic females, the passage is realistic enough. Considering the findings in the case of deities, there was room for doubting their mythic character. As the work progressed it became apparent that these mythic beings and especially those in whom the tradition invested the powers of evil were originally communities whose names were derived from those of their gods leading to the identity of the two. The loss of their human, social and cultural identity was the result of the stubborn resistance they put up to the attempts at permanent settlement by the Aryans on their entry in India from the north-west. Asura, Gandharva, Rakshas, Yaksha and Pisācha were the five peoples originally designated as the *pañchajana*, the five peoples. Later the Aryans interfered in this tradition leading to the confusion already noticed in the epics. These peoples later came to represent the powers of evil. The process of this transformation also unfolds itself during the course of the study.

To these peoples belonged the Indus civilization with the ruins of which the Aryans were well acquainted and in fact a place mentioned as Vailasthana in RV has been identified with Mohenjo-daro by Burrow. As will be shown subsequently, archaeological findings about the material culture of the people of the Indus civilization are confirmed in the literary evidence. Further, literary sources seem to preserve detailed information about the various aspects of life in the Indus empire which may not be obtainable from the excavated remains, on account of the absence of written records of appreciable length. From this point of view, the seals may not prove to be of much use. However, on the basis of the literary material, it is possible to get a glimpse of the domains of the Indus empire, its form of government, its religious life, etc.

Besides the five peoples mentioned above, there were no doubt many others. But these five constituted the prominent ethnic groups. The regions of the Indus empire extended from the Indo-Gangetic plain upto the borders of Iran. Over these regions were spread the peoples whom the Aryans considered their enemies who could not be matched with equal physical and moral strength. Even after the Aryans settled down, the memories of the struggle were fresh in their minds. The RV is replete with the episodes as narratives of the heroic deeds of their chief Indra, and they have permeated into the Brāhmaṇas and their rituals. Through these rituals the Aryans mimicked these battles of the age bygone. After centuries the meaning was forgotten but the ritual preserved the stereotype action. It was performed without a thought as to its propriety as for example the propriety of hitting a blade of grass four times with a wooden sword and then casting it on to a heap of rubbish.[2] This particular rite commemorates the destruction of Asura Araru. In the sacrificial rites are used chariots, wooden swords and other weapons, etc. Are these not rather strange instruments of worship?

ASURA AND DEVA AS TITLES

A peculiar feature of the usage of the terms Asura, Yaksha, Gandharva and Deva is that they appear both in singular and plural. It seems probable that when used in singular, these terms denoted the divinity worshipped by the people and at times individuals of whose names the name of the divinity formed a part; when used in plural, they denoted the peoples.

The term asura is ancient. It is preserved in different traditions. The three traditions—the Ṛigvedic and later Indian tradition as preserved in MBh, etc. the Assyrian

[1] M.N. Srinivas, *Religion and Society among Coorgs of South India* (Bombay, 1965), p. 186.

[2] *Satapathabrāhmana*—I.2.4.8-21.

and the Avestan—furnish plenty of evidence indicating that originally it was the name of a god of people who called themselves after him. It thus formed a part of the names of individuals and that its meaning was lord, master. In fact in Assyria it preceded the name of the king. In Avesta it forms part of the name of the chief deity viz., Ahura Mazda, in which Ahura is an equivalent of Skt. Asura. The Ṛigvedic usage is similar. Asura as god is mentioned in RV X. 177.1 and in several other places and Sāyaṇa for once has given the correct interpretation. Asura is also called Dyaus Asura which is perfectly in consonance with the Assyrian and Avestan tradition where Ashur and Ahura Mazda are conceived as the sky and sun-gods. Asura as title of individuals also appears in several cases.

In the same way, Deva even in the classical times was used as a title of honour. In the *Ṛigveda* the literal meaning of the term is shining and probably prominent but there is no element suggesting the divine, imperishable nature of god. The Devas probably traced their origins to Div of which the term Deva is cognate, their god being Dyaus Pitar. Moreover, not all the Aryans were called Devas. The ordinary Aryan folk were known as *visas*.

In ṚV X.53.10, the Devas are said to have acquired immortality which means that they were not naturally so. SB II. 2.2.8 calls both the Devas and the Asuras mortals. In *Atharvaveda* (AV) XI.5.19, IV.11.6 and SB X.4.3.3 ff. the Devas are said to have been originally mortals and immortality was bestowed on them by Agni, Soma or Savitri. This may mean that they were deified either in their own life time as a result of their deeds or after death as was the custom in the ancient world.

Asuras also can claim to be mortals from a different angle: the struggle between the Devas and the Asuras has been treated as a struggle between the Aryans and some others, some of them being Dāsas, Dasyus, Paṇis, etc. But for some reasons the Asuras have never been considered the legitimate opponents of the Aryans. The epithets Dāsa and Asura have been applied many times to the same individuals interchangeably; even the Paṇis are called Asuras in *Jaiminīyabrāhmaṇa* (JB) 2.440. This probably denotes that these epithets were indicatory of ethnic origin or social or professional hierarchy. Later just as the term Asura came to denote demon, likewise the terms Dāsa and Dasyu and Paṇi lost their original significance and came to be used in the derogatory sense. It seems probable that originally dāsha, as is found in the term *purodāsh* in *Ṛigveda* and the Brāhmaṇas, meant a mariner, sailor, fisherman, though at a later stage, it came to be derived from *dāś*, to give, to hurt of late origin and meant fiend demon. If the first meaning of dāsa is applied to Ṛigvedic passages, it would mean that those who were described as dāsas were mariners or fishermen.[1]

Further, the current meaning of *dasyu* is enemy of the gods and impious, barbarian, robber, etc. and is derived from √ *das*. It is also said to be cognate of *dasma* and *dasra* which are derived from √ *daṁs*. *Ḍasma* has antithetical meanings: accomplishing wonderful deeds, wonderful, extraordinary and thief, robber, etc. the context being the decisive factor. Now the Avestan word *daxyu*, equivalent of Skt. *dasyu*, is derived from √*danha* (Skt. *J daṁs*) and is semantically equivalent of Skt. *grāma*. *Daxyu* means land or *province*, often coterminous with the inhabitants, multitude, etc. *Grāma* means common inhabitants of a place, community, race. It is not unlikely that *dasyu* was also derived from√*daṁs* like its cognates *dasra* and *dasma* and even in Indian context had the same meaning as its Avestan equivalent *daxyu*. But at a certain stage along with other words it obtained a bad meaning and was tagged on to another root to suit the new significance. Since the original meaning of these terms is preserved more often than not, it may be surmised that originally they were used in that sense but later when the villification of the pre-Aryan tradition started the bad sense was superimposed on them. This seems to be a plausible explanation of this phenomenon of words having antithetical meanings. It may be noted that when the original meaning of the terms is restored, the so-called mythology disappears and what remains is a rational account of events. The narratives in the Brāhmaṇas support this process, and the meaning it yields.

As has been pointed out above, the Paṇis are called Asuras. In RV V.34.5–7 and AV V.11.6, Paṇis are styled as Dāsas and elsewhere as Dasyus. Kosambi traces the descendents of Paṇis in the present Baṇias. Paṇi is derived from√*apaṇ*, to barter—a word of doubtful origin. It is not impossible that the Paṇis were traders as are a large percentage of the Bania community. The present associations with the Paṇis, viz. miser, niggard, demon, etc. are indicatory of their defeat and slaughter described in many places in RV (V.34.7, VI.13.3, etc.) and their subsequent antagonism towards the gift-seeking Aryan priesthood which emerged with the system of sacrifices.

It is characteristic that the Devas are said to have fought with all those who were later designated as mythic beings and also those who are recognised even in later tradition as human beings, though pushed down the ladder of social hierarchy.

[1]Monier-Williams M., *A Sanskrit-English Dictionory* (Oxford, 1951), p. 476, col. 3.

THE CONFLICT BETWEEN THE DEVAS AND THE ASURAS

In the RV Indra has been praised sky-high for his Asura-exploits, which have won him two epithets, viz. *Purabhid,* the destroyer of the fortresses, and Vṛtrahan, the killer of Vṛtra. Indra is said to have destroyed several other Dāsas or Dasyus who are also at times called Asuras, as for example, Pipru (VIII.32.2, X.138.3), Namuhī (V.30 7-8, X.131.4, etc.), Varchin (VI.47.21, VII.99.5). In the case of Shambara, Dāsa and Dasyu have been used interchangeably (VI.47.21, VI.31.4, etc.). RV refers to many Asuras. Most of these Asuras and Dāsas are said to be possessing fortresses and by breaking these, Indra won the treasures and defeated and destroyed the foes. Indra killed Vṛtra and conquered the waters, made them flow freely. Practically everywhere the waters are described as *tastabhyāṁsam,* banned (RV II. 11.5), *Vavrīvāṁsam,* imprisoned, captivated, (RV III.32.6, IV.16.7, VI.20.2) *parishthā* obstructed (RV IV 72.3). In ṚV 1.32.11, Indra is said to have "opened that mouth of the waters which was covered, after killing Vṛtra" (*apām bilam apihitam yadāsit vṛtram jaghanvān apa tad vavāra*). The imagery in this connection is significant: opening of the hole as compared to the piercing of the belly of the mountain (RV V.32.1-2).

Vṛitra is derived from √ *vṛi* meaning to cover, conceal, hide, obstruct, but also used in the sense of to ward off, check, prevent, etc. It seems likely that if Vṛitra is taken in the latter sense, he was really speaking warding off or preventing Indra from going near the *bila,* i.e. the hole or the sluice valve of the dam, the latter being referred to in the imagery as the mountain. The dam is also referred to in *kṛitrimāni rodhāṁsi,* the artificial barriers, and in several other places. Briefly it may be said that the possibility of the existence of a dam with a sluice valve which Vṛitra was guarding cannot be ruled out. In fact some of the archaeological findings become meaningful when considered in the light of this interpretation, as will be seen below.

The excavated cities of Harappa and Mohenjo-daro, along with several smaller settlements divided into a fortified citadel and the lower town, reflecting advanced stages of urban life, are a well-known fact, and it is unnecessary to go into the details. However, an interesting observation in connection with the interpretation of the dammed waters may be cited here. The archaeologists have noted 'the intermittent recurrence of abnormal and devastating floods' which could be detected in the form of deep deposits of silty clay which is said to be 'of still-water origin, as distinct from those of the freely flowing seasonal floods normal to the river systems.' This finding when considered in the light of the above literary evidence about the opening of the hole through which water could flow, may only mean that it was probably a dam which was protected by Vṛitra and his troops which are described as the Vritras in several places in the RV. Indra by killing Vṛitra allowed the waters to flow so that the cities which were situated on the banks of the Indus were inundated in untimely floods, resulting in chaos and destruction.

It is possible to have a better idea of the conflict from the Brāhmaṇas, where mainly Asura, Rakshas and other so-called mythic beings are mentioned. The conflict seems to have been a long drawn out affair (JB I.107, 125 etc.). Initially the Asuras vanquished the Devas. But ultimately the Devas succeeded in defeating the Asuras first in the north-east and later in other quarters. When the Devas realized that it may not be possible to defeat the Asuras in a straight fight, they decided to defeat them through cunning, reflected in the story of Vishṇu taking the three steps and the strategy which was evolved. It seems that the original version of the latter event is related in ŚB I.2.5.1--5 where the devas beg from the Asuras space enough for the dwarf Vishṇu to lie down. Later modifications reflect the reversals of fortunes: the defeat of the Asuras and the complete victory of the Devas is in fact celebrated in the version of the *Aitareyabrāhmaṇa* VI.15 and is narrated with tongue in cheek. The dwarf Vishṇu could cover the three worlds in his three steps. Briefly the story goes like this: Indra and Vishṇu defeat the Asuras. The fight is concluded in a treaty the main condition being to allow Vishṇu to take three steps. Whatever is not traversed byVishṇu's steps may belong to the Asuras. Vishṇu traverses the three worlds, the three Vedas and the space which all belonged to the Asuras. Investigations show that the traverses of Vishṇu are really the three incursions into Asura-territories under disguise after which a strategy was evolved. The strategy was to bribe the high officials of the Asura empire for which their discontent, envies and jealousies were exploited. Having won them over, taking possession of the dam which Vṛitra and his troops were defending was the most important task as Vṛitra could not be bribed. Indra fought with him and killed him and subsequently inundated the cities situated on the southern banks. In fact Indra's supremacy was established only when he took possession of the dam.

The subtle device used by the Aryans was to bribe the prominent Asuras and to render assistance to them against each other as for example, Rijiśvan was assisted against Pipru, Namī Sāpya against Namuchī, etc. Kavi Uśanā who seems to have occupied the key position as the priest-adviser of the Asuras was bribed by the Aryans with wealth and the life of his grandson who was ultimately killed by Indra. Uśanā presented a vajra, thunderbolt, to Indra with which he killed Vṛitra, (RV I.121.12, V.34.2). He assisted Indra to destroy Shuṣhṇa. Uśhanā also played an important part in the defeat of the Asuras, according to the tradition of JB II.125–127. Later tradition identified him with Śukra who was well versed in military strategy as well as diplomacy.

Besides these, agni assisted Indra in defeating the Asuras by which is meant that the Aryans used fire in their conflict with the Asuras. In appreciation of this, when they created religion out of wars, agni was installed as the receiver of all oblations The innumerable hymns addressed in *Ṛigveda* ask him to burn the foes of the aryans especially the Rakshas, Very realistic descriptions of the burning fire are found in *Ṛigveda.* The titles of Agni as *dasyuhantama,* the killer par excellence of the dasyus (RV VI.16.15 & VIII.39.8), *rakshohā,* the killer of the rakshas are also significant and refer to the use of the fire by the Aryans in the war. The Brāhmaṇas also mention the siege of the Asura towns. Thus the Aryans acquired better weapons probably of Asuric make through the good offices of Uśanā and others. They practised *paurumadga*, i.e. inundation of cities & also laid siege.

The flooding of the cities, especially those situated on the lower Indus, has been noted by the archaeologists. But not many traces of conflagrations are discovered, especially in the northern cities of Indus civilisation. In the western regions in Rana Ghundai III phase contemporary with Harappa are found pockets of ashes as though great conflagrations have taken place. At Dabar Kot and Nal, the conflagrations have left lasting impressions. In the first case the upper six feet of the tell showed no less than four thick ash-ayers. In Nal, the site got the name Sohr Damb, the Red Mound, from its fire reddened soil.[1] Piggott considered these as the signs of trouble outside the Indus valley proper. At Harappa, no great conflagrations have been noticed by the archaeologists. But indications of local fires, especially in Mohenjo-daro have been noted by Marshall. Baked wall-plaster, large block of carbonized wood, charred wheat, seasamum, straw, etc. have been discovered. G.F. Dales in his 1964 excavations has found five sprawling skeletons between walls of the latest period in a thick accumulation of collapsed brick, ash, and broken pottery. The position of the skeletons suggests that they might have been sheltering there. The local fires may not have been accidental, as is usually conjectured, but were probably used to evict people who were sheltering there or as is explicitly said in RV to burn them to death as happened to those unfortunate five. At Lothal the superstructure of the great granary which might have been of timber had been burnt and baked clay sealings of normal Indus type were discovered. Not much information is available about the destruction of other sites.

There are definite indications of the struggle between the Aryans and the Rakshas, the Gandharvas, the Yakshas, and the Piśāchas. It is also clear that after their defeat during the campaign of villification, these peoples came to represent the forces of evil. Taken literally there is nothing in their names indicating connections with evil. But either through misrepresentation or through the intermingling of the traits of the people and those of the divinity they worshipped, a confusion was probably deliberately created so that these peoples who were really human beings became either demoniac creatures or something to be warded off because of the evil powers attributed to them, e.g. Yakshas are said to live in trees and possess innocent people. The literary sources give us the following information. The Yakshus as a people are mentioned in the RV VII.18.6 as fighting against Indra in the Gaṅgā-Yamunā Doab. In RV-Yaksha is used first as an appellation and secondly, as something intimately associated with the body but distinct from it, having a transferable quality. In AV and the Upanishads, Yaksha is associated with Brahman, with Virāṭ. It is said to be one, the Essence, the Spirit of everything, the Centre of the world. It is described as lying on the surface of the water, the refuge of the gods. Yaksha as Paśupati Rudra resides in the waters. He is associated with trees and mountains. In short, the concept of Yaksha is that of the all-pervading Force which is the essence of everything. It may be compared with the later concept of Brahman. In fact, in *Kenopanishad* the concept of Brahman which was not yet clearly formep is explained with the help of Yaksha, which denotes acquaintance with it. In *Bṛihadāraṇyakopanishad*, the *mahadyaksha,* the great yakṣa is said to be the first born. Thus Yaksha might be considered the proto-type of the later concept of Brahman.

In RV VII.18.6 Yakshu Turvasha is referred to as former *dāsha*, i.e. mariner. Considering the close connections of the Yaksha with the waters it is likely that the clan of Yakshus, by profession mariners, might have worshipped Yaksha as a water-god, i.e. the Essence of waters. The later conception of Yakshas as living in trees refers to the Yaksha the unseen Force or Essence of the tree which makes it grow. This during the villifi-

[1]S. Piggott, *Prehistoric India*, Penguin edn. 1950, p. 215.

cation period became transferred to the people and the Yakshas in general became the evil spirits who live in tree and possess men.

The case of Gandharvas is slightly different from that of others. Gandharva as god is men ioned in RV X.122 and also in *Atharvaveda* in the hymn to Bhuvanaspati. Obviously after the initial struggle in which they were deprived of *Soma*, they yielded and joined the Devas. This is ultimately recognized in their being appointed as the musicians of the gods, but all the same it has not prevented their becoming mythic beings inferior to the devas which in this connection means the loss of human identity. The Gandharvas are said to possess women which is probably the distortion of the trait of excessive fondness of women referred to in several places.

The root *raksh* in the word Rakshas has two antithetical meanings: to guard, watch, protect (RV) and to ward off, to guard against injure (AV), etc. As is obvious, in the *Ṛigveda*, the term was used in the good sense and seems to have acquired the 'bad' meaning only later. Thus Rakshas taken in the earlier sense may probably represent that stratum of population which mainly supplied the armed guard of the kingdom. This interpretation may be supported by the fact that the Rakshas fought alongside the Asuras and later probably went southwards and settled there as is indicated in the tradition of *Rāmāyaṇa*. In the ṚV, *yātu* is usually associated with the Rakshas and *yātudhāna* is interpreted as magic, sorcery. But literally *yātu* may be derived from causal of *J yāt, yāta, yātu* being its nominal formation and as such may mean (caused) fight. *Dhāna* mây be from *J dha*, to exhibit, show, etc. Thus *yātudhāna* may mean the exhibition or shows of (caused) fights (of animals, birds, etc.). The *yātus* of birds like owls, eagles, vultures, etc. are mentioned in the RV. Bull-fights, cock-fights, etc. have been a means of entertainment until medieval times all over the world. Sealings depicting bull-fights are found on Harappan sites.

Piśhācha is usually said to be a ghoul thriving on the flesh of the dead bodies. Literally, *piśa* (or *piśaṅga*) means yellow, red, reddish; √ *piś* means to form, fashion, mould, carve. In either senses there is no trace of flesh eating or cannibalism. Paiśāchī as a language exists in the north-west of the Indian sub-continent, though now it is called Dardic on account of the unpleasant associations with the word Piśācha. Incidentally it may be of interest to note that this language is said to retain traces of its affinities with the Eranian family of languages. Even Grierson found favourable evidence to consider Piśāchas as human beings.[1]

[1]Paiśāci, Piśācas and modern Piśāca, *Zeitschrift der Deutschen Morgenlandischen Gesellschaft*, Vol. 66, pp.49–86.

Piśācha as noted above could be derived either from piṣa, (*piśaṅga*), yellow or from √ *pish*, to mould, carve, form, etc. or may be a mixture of both. In a solitary and obscure reference to RV I.133.5, a piṣā is called *piśaṅgabhṛṣhṭı*. The word is extremely obscure, but in its general sense, as has been accepted by Macdonell,[2] it may point to the yellowish complexion of the piśāchī. The latter trait of carving, moulding, etc. derived from √ *pish*, is emphasized in the later Vedic and non-Vedic literature but obviously in a distorted manner. The Piāśchas are said to eat raw flesh from the dead bodies. It is not impossible that these people called Piśāchas ate raw meat as is customary in some parts of the civilized world even now. Or more probably the Piśāchas from √ *pis* to mould, carve were sculptors, i.e. carvers of human figures which was combined with the consumptionof raw meat and distorted into cannibalism. As has beennoted by Inayat-ur-Rahman, an anthropologist, the tradition of wood-carving has flourished since ancient times amongst these people. The fact that later the Gandhara school of art flourished in this area may add to the significance of the derivation of piśācha from √ *pis*. Besides this, according to the MBh tradition the piśāchas were the Khashas, identified with the modern Khasias, who were sons of Kāśyapa by his wife Krodha. The present Khasias are located in the north-eastern Himalayan regions. But as is pointed out by Grierson they might have travelled there from Hindukush, that is from the north-western region. The Khasias are short-statured with Mongoloid features.

This short discussion of the traits attributed to the so-called mythic beings shows that these were not their inherent qualities in the Ṛigvedic period but were attributed to them by later tradition. The process of transformation has also been discussed briefly. Thus it is plausible that these so-called mythic beings originally formed communities who resisted the Aryan advance in the Indo-Gangetic plain. It may be possible to identify the ethnic types by an examination of the human skeletal remains excavated from Harappa and Mohenjodaro. The following types, besides the round-heads which supposedly said to represent the Aryan type, are said to be common to the places: (i) Proto-Austroloid, (ii) Mediterranean or Caspian, (iii) Alpine variant (iv) Mongolian. Proto-Austroloid type of skull may correspond with the Rakshas who are traditionally ascribed dark complexion. In the RV, the foes of the Aryans are said to be dark-skinned. Linguistic evidence also supports the one-time existence of the Dravidian speaking population in north India and especially in Baluchistan. The dancing girl statuette recovered from Mohenjodaro bears features of the proto-Austroloid type and

[2]*Vedic Mythology*, Strasburg, 1897, p. 164.

similar to those found in the tribal populations of southern hilly areas. With *yātus*, which was probably a nickname for the Rakshas, is associated the phallic worship in RV. It is also significant that the tradition of Rāmāyaṇa makes Rakshasa Rāvaṇa, the villian of the story, a devotee of Śiva. Mediterranean or Caspian type may belong to the Asuras. This type is widespread over the western Asian and coastal tracts of Europe. The third type is minority element in the Indian population and was represented at Sialk in Iran as is pointed out by Piggott. This element probably represents the Gandharvas. The Mongolian type represents the Piśāchas and the Yakshas as both are said to be subtribes of the Khasas. The material describing these types is extremely scanty and the above classification and identification may be indicatory of the lines of approach.

THE BURIAL RITES OF THE ASURAS

The burial rites of the Asuras are described in ŚB XIII 8.1.5 etc. where there is clear reference to the practice of inhumation in oval graves. The Asuras and others are said to separate their dead (from the earth) "either on the basin or some such thing". This is how *chamū*, pot, vessel has been interpreted by Eggeling in his translation of the passage. But taken literally it may mean that pot burial and inhumation were common customs among the Asuras, the principle being to separate the dead from the earth. Inhumation was the common custom in the Indus civilization and in some cases graves are also found. In one case the skeleton wrapped in a shroud of reeds has also been recorded. In Kalibangan graves with oval pits and pot burials were excavated. At Lothal a bricklined grave was discovered, whereas at Rupar, the cemetery has revealed several burials, one very much looking like a clay coffin or a basin of clay in which the skeleton rests. Other graves appear to be oval in shape.

Chāndogyopanishd 8.8.5 lays down in no unclear terms the description of the burial rites of the Asuras as well as the belief on which they were based: This is the secret doctorine of the Asuras. They perform the funeral rites by leaving food by the dead body, by clothing it properly and by decorating it. They believe that the next world will be conquered by such funeral. This is exactly in keeping with the observations of the Archaeologists. Practically in all the graves of the Harappan period in most of the sites of the Indus Civilization vessels and pots of different sizes have been noticed. In some cases even the ornaments have been found on the skeletons and, as has been mentioned above, in one case a shroud of reeds has been recorded.

The Asura *patras*, vessels, were made on the wheels, according to the *Śrāddhatattva* of the *Chāndogyppaiṣiṣṭa.* Their use during the later Vedic period in the religious rites of the Aryans was strictly prohibited whereas the unbaked pots were supposed to be Aryan, *daivi*. The Indus civilization pottery is all wheel made and is decorated with distinctive designs which were painted in black on a red background.

In the literary sources two species of cows are mentioned—*gavaya* (bos gavacus) and *gaura* (bos gaurus). The latter has been identified on the seals found in the excavations.

The Asuras and others were obviously agriculturists as is reflected on the epithet *pañcha-charṣaṇi* as found in the RV. It is applied to *pañchajanas*. *Charṣphaṇi* denotes men as cultivators, distinct from nomads. A number of terms associated with agriculture seem to be of non-Aryan origin. Later the meaning of some terms was changed to denote something demoniac, probably a sign of their non-Aryan origin. As examples may be cited *kīnāṣka*, a farmer, *kīnāra*, a cultivator, a demon.

The Asuras were also well versed in navigation which is indicated by the common epithet of the Asuras viz., Dāśa meaning mariner. Seals with the impressions of ships have been discovered in the excavations. Sutkagen-dor, Bala-kot and Sotkakoh have been identified as coastal stations of Indus Civilization by G.F. Dales in his excavations of 1964.

They were skilled engineers and architects as is reflected in another epithet invariably accompanying Asura, viz. *māyāvī* usually interpreted as magical power. *Māyā* is derived from *mā* to build, to construct, to create. *Māyāvin* may thus mean endowed with the creative power, the power to construct, to build, etc. as is the case in the Avesta. The tradition of the MBh also ascribes such skills to the Asuras as for example Mayāsura is said to have built the palace full of wonders and illusions for Draupadi's wedding. As another tradition goes, the Yakṣas constructed a palace for Aśhoka. The skill in building the great granary and the bath in Mohenjo-daro and the systematized nature of town planning, etc. corroborate this speciality of the Asuras whose Veda is called the Māyāveda in ŚB.

The evidence appears to be sufficient enough to conclude that the Indus Civilization belonged to the five peoples: the Asuras, the Rakṣas, the Gandharvas, the Yakṣas and the Piśācas. These are some of the findings and a more detailed work will be published soon.

Thus it is possible to verify the literary tradition through archaeological findings and the literary tradition may also be used to throw light on the archaeological remains without which they may best be described as artefacts which do not seem to breathe life on their own. As the above evidence indicates this is no longer an impossible task. Further archaeological excavations could pin down the literary evidence to earth. It is apparent that if a coherent picture is to be drawn both literary and archaeological evidence have to go hand in hand.

1603 Sadashiva Peth
Poona 411030
MALATI J. SHENDGE

Archaeology and Tamil Literary Tradition

Archaeological excavations in the Tamil country have been generally aimed at finding material evidence of some kind for the existence of early cultures. The choice of sites has been mostly determined by references, in the Sangam anthologies, to historically known sites, and by the common belief that early settlements would invariably occur in the river valleys. These deterministic criteria have, in recent years, led to a more intensive exploration of the Kaveri Valley and to problem-oriented excavation of sites identifiable with "Sangam." Yet, with the exception of Kāverippūmpaṭṭiṅam, Uṟaiyur and Karūr, the other excavated sites, like Tirukkampuliyūr and Aḷagarai, have no apparent relation to early Tamil traditions as recorded in the Sangam works, the earliest extant stratum of Tamil literature. The occurrence of Black-and-red Ware (BRW) at the last two sites during explorations, would perhaps have influenced their choice for excavation. Apart from the Kaveri Valley, some other sites have also been excavated in the Peninsula: Korkai, Kāñchīpuram, Arikamedu, Śaṇūr, Kunnattūr, Amrithamangalam and Perumbair, Śengameḍu and Adichanallur. The west coast remains comparatively less known through excavations. with the exception of Porkalam (Megalithic site) and Koduññallūr (medieval habitation site).

The aim of the present paper is to examine the nature of these excavations, to attempt to relate the evidence to literary tradition, to check the reliability of historical tradition through excavated data or to indicate such possibilities. The problem of correlating literary evidence with archaeological material would require a thorough investigation into and proper handling of the literary sources. The results of such an investigation for the Tamil region seem to be neither too promising nor too discouraging to be utterly discarded. The basic need seems to be a systematic indexing of names of places, people and regions mentioned in the concerned literature, identifying and mapping them out geographically and extending the assistance of archaeology to such areas, which can be recognised as potentially rich in archaeological remains. A historical atlas of early sites known from literature would be the first essential step towards such attempts at correlation of literary and archaeological evidence.

In this context, it is necessary to point out, at the outset, that no useful results can at present be obtained by analysing archaeological data from pre-historic sites in this region. The proto-historic sites, on the other hand, possess great significance for the evolution of early settlements with uniform cultural traits such as iron, common pottery (BRW) and evidence of large-scale agriculture based on irrigation and other related crafts. This uniformity makes its appearance in the Tamil country, as elsewhere in South India, with the megalithic folk.

It is proposed to take up the main theme of this paper in two parts, the first being a critical account of the excavations carried out so far and the attempted correlations with literary evidences and the second, a general appraisal of the situation in relation to the spread of BRW and its probable associations with early movements of people to the south from the north.

KAVERI VALLEY

1. Karur (Karuvūr), District Tiruchirappalli Karūr, the ancient Cēra capital is known to all the Sangam classics and to the epics *Śilappadikāram* and *Maṇimēkalai*.[1] It is also called Vañji and Vañji muṟṟam.[2] The river Ān Porunai flowed along this place, which was the capital of the Cēra Kōdai.[3] The river now goes by the name of Amarāvati on which modern Karūr is situated.

Archaeological explorations and excavations have helped in the correct identification of this city. The earlier identification of Vañji with Tiruvañjaikkalam on the west coast, by S. Krishnaswami Iyengar and K.G. Sesha Aiyar, was based on the similarity of the names Vañji and Tiruvañjaikkalam and the occurrence of a place called Karūr near the former. The identification subsequently proposed by K.A. Nilakanta Sastri and M. Raghava Iyengar, viz that it is the inland town of Karūr the District Tiruchirappalli has been confirmed by the explorations and excavations in this area. Foreign notices by Ptolemy would also show that Korura (Karūr) was an inland town.[4] In the *Padiṟṟuppattu,* Cēran Śenguṭṭuvaṉ is compared to Kūḍal i.e. the confluence of the rivers Āṉ Porunai, Kuḍavan Āru (Kudaṟṟānāṟu) and the Kaveri[5] and this place may be equated with Kūḍal which is about 9 km from modern Karūr. A number of references from the *Puṟam, Padiṟṟuppattu* and the epics may be cited to show that Karuvūr and Vañji were identical.[6]

The Pugalūr Tamil Brahmi inscription, giving the names of Cēra rulers of the Sangam age[7], is only 12 km from Karūr. Later hero-stone inscriptions from Karūr, datable in the eighth century A.D. refer to the place both as Karūr and Vañji.[8]

Archaeological explorations in this area have yielded a fairly large number of Roman coins. It is relevant to add that the majority of the hoards of Roman coins discovered in South India come from the adjacent district of Coimbatore, although some Roman coin hoards also come from the West coast.[9]

The excavations at Cranganore on the west coast (Kaduññallūr—for Tiruvañjiakkalam) by the Archaeological survey of India have revealed that the earliest occupational levels here go back only to the 8th century A.D. On the other hand excavations at Karūr, by the Tamil Nadu Department of Archaeology, have provided positive clues to its location, in the form of Roman amphorae pieces, local Rouletted ware, a Roman copper coin in one of the lower strata, BRW, some with graffiti marks.[10] Thus, it would seem that archaeological evidence has to a considerable extent proved helpful in locating or identifying ancient sites like Karūr mentioned in Sangam literature. Wherever conflicting opinions and interpretations have tried to fog the issue, archaeology may be able to clear up the situation, if undertaken systematically.

If ancient Vañji or Karūr is the modern Karūr in District Tiruchirappalli, the question is one of migration of the names of this inland town to the West coast in the post-Sangam era and hence Tiruvañjaikkalam and Karūr on the West coast.

The evidence of the epics, which appear to be chronologically later than the Sangam anthologies, would again point to the development of Karūr into a larger urban complex and the inclusion in it of Buddhist and Jain establishments. It is in this context that the location of Kuṇavāyir Koṭṭam, where Iḷango Aḍigal the author of the *Śilappadikāram* is said to have retired, assumes considerable significance.[11] Again the conflict revolves round locating it in Karūr or in the West coast.

2. Uraiyūr, District Tiruchirappalli— At present a part of Tiruchirappalli, Uraiyūr represents the site of the old capital of the Cōḷas of the Sangam period. It was also known as Koḷi and Vāraṇam.[12] It was a strongly defended city and its outskirts (outside its defences) had burial grounds which were full of stones, and hence "there were many obstacles to easy movement".[13] This description is strongly suggestive of the existence of the megalithic burials such as cairn circles, dolmens etc.

The Cōḷa Karikāla is said to have enlarged this town, fortified it and enriched it with beautiful buildings.[14]

[1] *Puram* : 5 Col; 11, 32, 33 etc.
Paḷamoḷi : 62 : 1.

[2] *Puṟam* : 373 : 24; *Śilappadikāram* : xxv : 9, 34.

[3] *Aham* : 93 : 2; *Puṟam* : 36; *Silap*., Vāl., 4; *Naḍukal.*, 125.

[4] See K.K. Pillay, *A Social History of the Tamils*, (Madras, 1969). p. 269.

[5] *Padiṟṟuppattu*, 50 : 7

[6] R. Nagaswamy, "Karuvur—Vañji, the Capital of the Sangam Ceras, *Journal of Kerala Studies*, Vol. I, Pt. IV, Dec. 1974, pp. 395-402.

[7] I. Mahadevan, "Tamil Brahmi Inscriptions of the Sangam Age," *Second International Conference of Tamil Studies*, (Madras, 1968).

[8] R. Nagaswamy, *op. cit.*

[9] Eyyal Hoard. *Annual Report of the Archaeological Department* for 1945-46 to 47-48.

[10] An initial report in the Hindu of 26-6-73 carried a reference to potsherds with Brahmi letters but Mr. Nagaswamy told the present writer that no Brāhmi letters have been found on pottery.

[11] M.G.S. Narayanan "New Light on Kuṇavāyir Kottam and the Date of Cilappadikāram", *Journal of Indian History*, XLVIII, 1970, pp. 691 ff.

[12] *Sila* : *Uraiperukaṭṭurai* . 4 ; X : 248; XI ; 11.

[13] *Aham* ; 122 ; 21.

[14] *Paṭṭiṇappālai*, p. 285; *Sirupāṇ āṟṟuppadai* ; 83.

Several poets of the Sangam period hailed from Eṇicceri, a suburb of Uraiyur.[1] The descriptions in the Sangam classics would show that it was a big city, as important as Kaverippumpattinam, the port-capital of the Colas, and had a large number of structures, religious and secular, and was well fortified.

That is was one of the foremost urban centres of the Sangam period is not only known from the Sangam works, but also from the references made by classical writers who describe the place as noted for its cotton textiles—Argaritic derived from Argaru or Uraiyūr.[2]

Two major seasons of excavations, conducted here by the Department of Ancient History and Archaeology, University of Madras, have established a cultural sequence of three periods. Period I[3] is represented by BRW, the Russet coated Painted Ware, the Rouletted[4] and Arretine Wares, together with the associated red and all-black wares. Sherds with graffiti marks and Brāhmī inscriptions assignable to 1st-2nd centuries A.D. have also been met with. Period II[5] shows a gradual disuse of BRW and the emergence of a red-slipped ware. A rectangular cistern,[6] which the excavators describe as a dyeing vat, also belongs to this period. Evidence of flood and waterlogging has been attested in one of the cuttings. The floods are assigned to the second half of the 1st millennium A.D. An inscription from Allūr about 5 km from Uṛaiyūr, datable in A.D. 944, refers to a flood in the Kaveri which caused destruction in Allūr and the surrounding areas.[7] Period III in Uraiyūr has been assigned to the eighth-fourteenth century A.D. as it is represented by a crude ill-fired red ware and Celadon Ware besides terracotta figurines and beads of semi-precious stones.

It is obvious that the Uṛaiyūr excavations have not been able to confirm the literary descriptions of the place. The problems that confront the archaeologist here are related to the continuous occupation of the site and disturbance caused by it and the evolution of a large urban complex into the present Tiruchirappalli, of which Uṛaiyūr is now only a part. Apart from the remains of a dyeing vat, which confirms the literary evidence on the famous textile industry of Uraiyūr (which it continues to manufacture even today) and the fact that the earliest occupation of the site belongs to the BRW level, the excavations have been much less significant than they were expected to be.

3. TIRUKKAMPULIYUR, DISTRICT TIRUCHIRAPPALLI

Tirukkāmpuliyūr is hardly known to early literature, nor is there any evidence of it from later inscriptions in the vicinity. Yet, a huge mound in its neighbourhood held out great promise of hidden archaeological evidence. Surface indications also pointed to its antiquity. The excavations at Tirukkāmpuliyūr brought to light a habitation site (with an urn burial site nearby) of the Megalithic and subsequent periods, comparable to other sites in the Kaveri Valley and perhaps of greater archaeological significance as indicated by thick deposits of BRW and Russet coated Painted Ware. A conservative estimate would assign this stratum to a period between the third century B.C. and third-fourth century A.D.[8] An earlier date (c. 500–400 B.C.) for the beginnings of this settlement would also find favour with some scholars.[9] Period II, according to the excavators, would fall between third-fourth century A.D. and ninth-tenth century A.D. The last period (III) ranges from ninth-tenth century A.D. to fourteenth-fifteenth century A.D.

The chronology is admittedly tentative and no precise dates are available for this site. However, the site belongs to one of the few habitational sites of the Megalithic phase excavated till now. The Russet-coated Painted Ware, along with BRW, and red ware occurs here for the first time in a habitational site, although it has been known from burial sites in Coimbatore. Some potsherds carry graffiti marks, some of which have been described as "totemic" and "religious" symbols.[10] A comparative study of these symbols with those occurring on the chalcolithic pottery in Western and Central India and those on the Harappan seals might prove highly interesting and useful as it has been pointed out that at least two of the symbols from Tirukkāmpuliyūr occur in exactly the same order as on Harappan seals.[11] It is unfortunate that the report on the excavations does not take this factor into consideration and merely lists the symbols separately.

The excavators have shown an understandable

[1] *Puṛam* ; 13, 127, 128 etc. Eṇicceri means a suburb or "quarters on the border"

[2] See K.K. Pillay, *op. cit.*, p. 198.

[3] The excavators assigned this cultural deposit to a period between 3rd century B.C. and 1st, 2nd centuries A.D. *Indian Archaeology, a Review, 1964-65*, p. 25. (Subsequently referred to as IAR followed by the year.

In a subsequent report they have given a different time bracket i. e. 1st century B.C. to 4th century A.D. *IA*. 1965-66, para 37.

[4] *I.A.R.* 64-65, pl. XIX

[5] At first dated between 2nd century A.D. and 5th century A.D. and later assigned to 4th—7th centuries A.D.

[6] *I.A.R.* 64-65, pt. XX A.

[7] There is an earlier literary tradition about floods in the Kaveri. *Aham* : 376 : 4.

[8] T. V. Mahalingam, *Report on the Excavations in the Lower Kaveri Valley*, University of Madras, 1970, pp. 14-16.

[9] B. K. Gururaja Rao, *The Megalithic Culture in South India*, Mysore, 1972, p. 315. Also 4th or 5th century B.C. B. K. Gururaja Rao, "Megalithic Culture in the Tiruchirapalli district" *K. A.Nilakanta Sastri 80th Birthday Felicitation Volume*, (Madras 1971), p. 203.

[10] T.V. Mahalingam, *op. cit.*, 46-49.

[11] These symbols are the "Ujjain" symbol, and the arrow or three pronged symbol.

eagerness to connect the site with literary evidence of the Sangam period as seen in their attempt to relate it to Sittalavāi, the nearest Railway Station, which they identify, with Śīttalai, a place to which Śīttalai Sāttanār, the author of the Buddhist work *Maṇimekalai*, is said to have belonged.[1] Another significant factor seems to be the location of Madukkarai, about 1.6 km west of the site, which is believed to represent the meeting point of the three kingdoms, viz. the Cōḷa, Cēra and Pāṇdya.[2] The urn-burial site[3] is located about 200 m from the main site at Tirukkāmpuliyūr.

4. ALAGARAI, DISTRICT TIRUCHIRAPPALLI. On the opposite bank of the Kaveri (north), is situated Alagarai, another habitation-cum-burial site of the Megalithic phase. Variously derived from Alai + Karai = banks or Aikarai or five Karais meaning 150 *kāṇis* of land, Alagarai's occupational deposit is in conformity with that of Tirukkāmpuliyūr and has been divided into three periods, the earliest being the Megalithic, with BRW and Russet-coated Painted Ware in the lowest levels. It is unknown to Sangam literature but mentioned in inscriptions from ninth century A.D. onwards.

The Alagarai graffiti is considerably more interesting and greater in number (49) and show a great deal of similarity with the Harappan and Chalcolithic.

Explorations in the region between Karūr and Tiruchirappalli in the Kaveri Valley have shown that the area is studded with Megalithic habitation and burial sites and the two excavated sites seem to confirm the early literary descriptions of the Cōḷa country as "marked by rows of settlements of numerous clans (families?), who showed no enmity among them selves".[4]

5. KAVERIPPUMPATTINAM, DISTRICT THANJAVUR Kāverippūmpaṭṭiṇam was one of the capitals of the Sangam Cōḷas and a chief port on the east coast down to about the fifth century A.D. The Sangam anthologies abound with references to the port. The *Paṭṭiṇappālai* is devoted wholly to its description, while the epics *Śilappadikāram* and *Maṇimekalai* contain numerous references to the town, its religious and secular buildings and various quarters. Its development into a huge urban complex is evident from the *Paṭṭiṇappālai*, while the epics would show that it included Buddhist and Jain institutions apart from a number of temples to Brahmanical deities.

Kāverippūmpaṭṭinam was also known as Puhār (harbour),[5] Kākandi[6] and Sampāpati (or Sampati).[7] The last name seems to be preserved to this day in the name of the Sampapati temple, believed to be the temple of the tutelary deity, where the Archaeological Survey of India carried out trial diggings.

No less than forty odd sites may be located near the present Kāverippaṭṭiṇam, which once formed parts of the city.[8] The more important among them are Neidavāsal[9], Vānagiri, Vellaiyaniruppu (the abode of the white men—Yavana settlement?) Sāyāvanam,[10] Maṇigrāmam and others, where archaeological digging has brought to light occupational debris belonging to a period ranging from c. third century B.C. to A.D. fifth century. It would hence be more fruitful to make an extensive survey of this area, locate tentatively the different parts of this complex and follow it up with excavations at selected sites for archaeological evidence in a stratified context marking successive levels of occupation.

The city had two main parts, the Paṭṭinappakkām and Maruvūrppākkam (the residential area and the coastal area with its harbour)[11]. The residential area is also referred to as Ahanagar (internal city)[12], where there were buildings of brick i.e. houses of Vēḷālas, feeding houses, market places, gardens, tanks and religious structures, while the coastal area contained the harbour, customs offices with the tiger emblem on their doors, storehouses, godowns, merchant's quarters and fishermen's colony.[13] People of different tongues including foreigners lived there.[14]

Public meeting places, resting places with public baths, gardens with artificial ponds, filled with hot water for bathing are also mentioned in the epics.[15]

The Nāḷangāḍi and Allangāḍi (the morning and evening bazaars) met in the spacious open space between the two main divisions of the city on the east and the west.[16]

[1] *Ibid.* p. 112.
[2] *Ibid.*, p. 11.
[3] *Ibid.*, pp. 100-101.
[4] *Paṭṭiṇappālai*, pp. 27-28.

[5] *Aham* : 110 : 4 ; *Puram*. 30; 12; *Padirruppattee* 73 : 9 ; *Pattinappalai* : 173 *Silap*. XVII ; *Manimekalai* : V : 109.
[6] *Mani*, xxii : 37.
[7] *Mani* Padiham : 8, 13.
[8] That it was a huge town is indicated by references like Perūr and Mānagar-*Mani* : VI : 26, 37 ; XXII : 63, 68.
[9] Neidalangānal—*Puram* : 10. 203 col. — *is a town* associated with another Cola king Ilamcetcenni and seems to have been on the Coromandel coast. It is also the name given to the beach in Kaverippattinam—*Śilap*. VI : 150, IX : 78.
[10] *Aham* : 220 : 18 ; *Narrinai* : 73 : 9.
[11] Was Marungurpattinam mentioned in *Narrinai* 258 : 10 and *Aham* : 227 : 20 also part of Puhar?
[12] *Mani* : I : 72 : This was evidently the prosperous section of the city where the richer classes lived. *Mani* : XIX : 54 : *Śilap* : V 213 ; VI : 127.
[13] ll. 40-50 ; 59-74 ; 116-171 ; 183-212.
[14] *Pattinappalai*. pp. 213-18.
[15] *Silap* : V : 117, 121 ; X : 31 and *Mani* III : 45
[16] *Aham* : 73 : 10 ; *Silap* : V : 63, 196.

The various temples of the city included those of the God of Love (Kāma), Sun, Moon, Indra and Balarāma. The public square had its guardian deity—in the market place—the Catukkattu Būtam. Sāttan, a folk deity, had a temple outside the city.[1] Buddhist and Jain structures also existed and one of the Buddhist monasteries was called Indra vihāra.[2]

The cemetery and the burial ground situated in the outskirts of the city, also had their guardian deities such as the deity in the pillar.[3] *Maṇimekalai* devotes a whole chapter (VI) to the description of the different types of burial in the outskirts of the city, which conforms closely to the Megalithic.

Remains of .. brick structure have been unearthed in Kīḷaiyūr identified as a wharf, where boats were anchored with the help of wooden pegs.[4] The bricks of this structure are compared in size with those of the Ikṣvāku period in Nāgārjunakoṇda. The radiocarbon date for the wood sample from this structure being c. 315 B.C.,[5] would indicate a fourth—third century B.C. date for the wharf, apart from the evidence of the contemporary BRW deposits. The size of this structure would also show that it was probably an anchoring site in the backwaters, with wooden pegs, to which boats bringing paddy in exchange for salt were tied.[6] Evidence of the harbour with docking facilities for big ships from foreign countries is, however, lacking. This could perhaps be explained by the tradition that Kāverippaṭṭiṇam was submerged in the sea on account of a curse on the city due to the failure of a Cōḷa ruler to conduct the Indra festival.[7] This tradition seems to be confirmed by a survey conducted on the beach about 6 metres from the edge of the water, which is reported to have shown indications of buried archaeological remains under the sand. Under water archaeology has also been suggested for this area, in the hope of finding evidence of possible ship wrecks, the contents of which can be analysed and archaeologically studied.[8] As late as 1849 encroachments of the sea on this coast are believed to have washed away part of the ancient town.

It is surprising that no relics of such magnitude and grandeur as described in literature, have been revealed by the excavation.

The semi-circular brick structure with an internal diameter of 8 meters unearthed at Vānagiri may represent a water reservoir and seems to have been fed by a 83 cm. wide inlet channel from the Kaveri. The channel has a corbelled roof and shows evidence of moulding, chamfering and rounding off of the edges. Associated deposits yielded BRW and Rouletted ware. As such a first-second century A.D. date is indicated.[9] It could be one of those public tanks or baths mentioned in literature.

The most striking remains are those of a Buddhist *Vihāra* found at the site of Pallavaneśvaram consisting of a full wing of cells and a long veranda on the south,[10] confirming the evidence of the epics. A subsidiary structure, identified as part of an apsidal *caitya* together with other Buddhist objects, was also revealed at the same site and has been assigned to a later phase i.e. fourth—fifth century A.D. with reconstructions of a still later phase.[11]

Trial pits laid in Maṇigrāmam revealed deposits of BRW and Rouletted Ware of different fabrics, in addition to terracotta figurines and square copper coins of the Cōḷas, all assignable to the beginning of the Christian era.[12] The name Maṇigramam was later borne by a famous merchant guild of South India. Thus it would appear that the urban complex of Kaveripattinam included in it an important colony of merchants, which provided the background for the story of the *Śilappadikāram*.[13]

The diggings at Vellaiyaniruppu have, contrary to expectations, not revealed any early Yavana settlement but only show a deposit going back to about the ninth century A.D.[14]

6. KORKAI, DISTRICT TIRUNELVELI. Korkai was the most famous of the Pāṇdya ports of the Sangam period. Located on the south eastern coast and at the mouth of the Tāmraparṇi river, it also served as one of the Pāṇdya capitals. The present site of Korkai lies 3 km north of the Tāmraparṇi. It is now 6 km interior due to the recession of the sea in recent times. The urn-burial site of Ādichanallūr, also on the banks of the Tāmraparṇi, is about 15 km west of this village (west) and Sawyerpuram, the microlithic site, (Teri) is only 3 km away. Altogether, the area is rich in archaeological

[1] *Silap* : V : 128 ; IX : 23 *Mani* : VII : 78.
[2] *Silap.*, X : 14 ; XXVII : 92 ; XXVIII : 70 ; *Mani* XXVI : 55.
[3] *Mani* : XXII : 2, 91 etc. *Silap* : IX : 12.
[4] *I.A.R.* 62-63, p. 13.
[5] *Ibid* ; 65-66, R.C. dates—10.
[6] *Kaḷi*—Backwaters, See N. Subrahmanian, *Pre-Pallavan Tamil Index*, (Madras, 1966), *Anai*—woodenpeg—*Pattinappalai*, 29 ff.
[7] *Pre-Pallavan Tamil Index*, p. 105.
[8] *The Hindu*, 28th Feb. 71.
[9] *I.A.R.* 63-64, p. 20.
[10] *Ibid.*, 64-65, para 42, 65-66, para 35.
[11] *Ibid.*
[12] *Ibid.*, 63-64, p. 20. The coins bear the figure of the standing tiger on one side and elephant on the other.—1st century A.D.
[13] The Nattukkottai Chettiars and the Twelfth Chettis of Tiruchirappalli claim that their ancestors orginally belonged to Kaveripattinam.
[14] *I.A.R.* 62-63, p. 13.

remains and represents an important group of proto-historic sites in the Tamil country.

While it would be difficult to establish any direct connection between Korkai and the microlithic sites of this region, there seems to be a possible link with the Ādichanallūr urn-burial sites provided by the urn-burials, two of which have been revealed in the early levels of Korkai. The previous excavations (in the Korkai area and at Kāyal and Ilañji), by Dr R. Caldwell brought to light a number of giant size urns one of which contained a perfect skull among other human skeletal remains.[1] The excavations by the Tamil Nadu Department of Archaeology[2] yielded two burial urns of the megalithic phase. The lowest levels of occupation at Korkai are, on the basis of a radiocarbon determination, dated to c. 785 B.C. This would indicate an early occupation of the site by the urn-burial folk, earlier than other dated sites of the megalithic phase in the Tamil country. The proximity of Ādichanallūr is hence not without significance.

The occurrence of Black-and-red Ware, Roman Ware (also Rouletted ware of local origin), sherds with graffiti marks, inscribed potsherds with Tamil Brahmi characters of the period from second century B.C.—A.D. second century and also a few sherds possibly of Northern Black Polished Ware (or are they a special fine variety of Rouletted ware?) is consistent with the results so far obtained from all other excavated sites in the Tamil country.[3]

Korkai, according to Sangam literary tradition, was reputed for its pearl fisheries where the *Paradavar* (fishermen) dived for pearls.[4] It had a famous harbour (Muṇ-Tuṛai).[5] Kāyal, (meaning salt pans), which is located not far from Korkai, was famous for its salt pans.[6] The *Periplus Maris Erythrae* talks of Colchi (Korkai) and its pearl fisheries worked by condemned criminals.[7].

The occurrence at various levels of pearl oysters confirms the literary evidence that Korkai was a centre of pearl fisheries and trade in pearls.[8]

OTHER SITES

7. KANCHIPURAM, DISTRICT CHINGLEPUT. The far famed city of Kanchi is well known to history as the capital of the Pallavas, whose occupation of Kañci is clearly attested at least from A.D. 350.[9] The earliest excavations in the city were undertaken at a site locally known as Pallavamēḍu, obviously in the hope of establishing its Pallava associations with the help of archaeological evidence, apart from the innumerable Pallava monuments of the seventh-ninth century A.D.

The trial digs at Pallavamēḍu[10] have brought to light an early urn burial site with ring wells indicating the megalithic phase. The subsequent phases showed a mere superposition of structures with no difference in pottery. Later digging at the same site have also not led to any conclusive results except that the excavators seem to think that the river Vēgavatī once flowed very near the site and is at present 2.5 km away.[11]

The second important season of excavations was that undertaken by the Archaeological Survey of India in the premises of the Sankara *matha*.[12] Three major periods of occupation were established with a subdivision of Period I into IA and IB. To Period IA belong the Black-and-red Ware, and black slipped ware and to the upper levels of IA are assigned the sherds of Rouletted Ware, conical jars[13], a Sātavāhana coin of Rudra Sātakarṇi of the second century A.D., terracotta figurines of a cult goddess, royal head and part of a lady dancer. Period IB is said to be that of the Pallavas i.e. assignable to fourth-ninth century A.D. represented by a bright red slipped ware and lead coins.

Period II is said to belong to the medieval, times with a thick dull red pottery, glass beads bangles and a copper coin of Rājarāja Cōla I.

The last period (III) is said to represent the modern occupation.

Consecutive seasons of digging at Kañchi were undertaken by the Department of Ancient History and Archaeology, University of Madras, from 1969-70. The digs centered round the area near the Kāmākṣi temple and the Ekāmreśvara temple.

The choice of the Kāmākṣi temple site was apparently influenced by the references in Tamil literature (the *Maṇimekalai*, in particular) and in the accounts of Hiuen Tsang to the Buddhist associations of the place

[1] *Indian Antiquary*, 1887, pp. 81-83 "Sepulchral turns in southern India."

[2] "Excavations at Korkai", *Damilica*, (Madras, 1970), No. 1. pp. 50 ff.

[3] Apart from the charcoal sample, a piece of wood at 3.17 m. depth in KRKI has given an R.C. date of 805 B.C. *I.A.* 69-70, p. 68.

[4] Aham : 350 : 13

[5] *Ibid.* 27 : 9 ; *Aingurunūru* : 185 : 1 & 188 : 2; *Mani.* XIII : 84.

[6] *Aham* : 366 : 5.

[7] See *Pre-Pallavan Tamil Index* for Korkai.

[8] *Aham* : 27 ; *Maduraikkanji* : 134, 135, 138 ; *Narrinai*, 25.

[9] T.V, Mahalingam, *Kāñcīpuram in early south Indian History*, (Bombay, 1969), p. 19.

[10] *I.A.R.*., 1953-54, p. 12.

[11] *Ibid.*, 1970-71, para 5.

[12] *Ibid.*, 1962-63. p. 12.

[13] *Ibid.*, pl. XXXVIII A.

and also due to popular belief that the Kāmākṣi temple was originally a Buddhist site later converted into a Hindu one at the time of Śankarācārya's establishment of Kāmakoṭi piṭha in the ninth century A.D.

The excavators claim to have brought to light three major cultural periods—what they call Pre-Pallava (I), Pallava (II) and Cōḷa and Vijayanagar (III).[1]

Under period I, a subdivision into IA and IB is also made, on the basis of the occurrence in the lower levels of fine Black-and-red ware and painted ware with lattice designs assignable to the period from third century to 1st century B.C. Period IB, which the excavators have assigned to a period from first century B.C. to fourth century A.D., shows megalithic affiliations with the typical Black-and-red Ware, Rouletted Ware, Arretine ware, beads, terracotta objects and iron objects. In addition the remains of a baked brick structure, identified by the excavators as a Buddhist shrine, have also come to light. The identification has been made evidently on the occurrence of a greyware sherd with Brahmī letters read by them as *Pu ta la ti sa* in characters of the first-second century A.D. and also on the basis of the discovery of other terracotta objects of a Buddhist nature.

To period II (fourth-ninth century A.D.) have been ascribed amphorae (?) jars, said to be local imitations (they are really only conical jars), fine bright red and orange slipped wares (with some of them painted black) glass and other objects. To the same period was assigned remains of a small circular structure which the excavators chose to describe as a votive *stūpa*.[2]

Period III (ninth-sixteenth century A.D.) is represented by a polished red ware with incised and impressed designs and a dull coarse red ware, both slipped and unslipped varieties and Celadon Ware.

The excavations were continued for the second season in order to ascertain Kāñcī's Buddhist associations and is said to have confirmed the sequence established in the previous season. Besides three coin moulds,[3] one of them bearing a short legend in Brahmī and another the 'Ujjain' symbol, amulets and pendants of various designs and potsherds with Brahmī letters are also reported.

But the identification of the remains of a brick structure, a few courses of which were found in a somewhat curved outline, as a *stūpa* is rather doubtful as further extensions of the trench on either side have failed to reveal the nature and shape of the structure, although the bricks are of considerable size (50 x 22 x 6 cm.) and comparable to those of other Buddhist sites like Nagarjunakonda. The dating of this structure is unfortunately not without doubt.

Traditions regarding the Buddhist associations of Kāñcī are late and cannot be taken back to the second century B.C. In the Sangam anthologies, there are no specific indications of Kāñcī having become an important Buddhist centre. It is only in the *Maṇimēkalai* (a post-Sangam work of about the fifth century A.D.) that references to the Buddhist settlements and monuments in Kāñcī occur. Once again, it is only in the accounts of Hiuen Tsang that Kāñcī's Buddhist associations are stressed and the Chinese pilgrim suggests great antiquity for the Buddhist structures. Mahendravarman in his *Mattavilāsa prahasana* gives additional proof of the existence of a Buddhist *vihāra* in Kāñcī in the early part of the seventh century A.D.[4]

Even granting the early associations of Buddhism with Kāñcī the ruins discovered in the above excavation have not been conclusively established as those of a *stūpa*. Furthermore, datable evidence for the spread of Jainism and Buddhism in this area (Toṇḍaimaṇḍalam) does not go back to a period before fourth-fifth century A.D.[5]

To Tamil literature, Kāñcī is known as Kacci,[6] Kaccimurram[7] and Kaccippeḍu.[8] Kaccippedu may have been a suburb of Kāñcī, from where a number of early Tamil poets hailed.[9] Kāñcī[10] and Kañcinallūr[11] may also be the same as Kāñcīpuram.

The *Perumbaṇārruppadai* gives a graphic description of the city of Kacci, calls it an old city (Mūdūr), formed by a number of small settlements. It was full of tall buildings of bricks and fortified by high walls. The palace of Iḷamtiraiyan is described with poetic fancy, however, marked by occasional glimpses into realism.[12] The river Vēgavatī, on which the city stood, comes in for elaborate treatment[13] and its Vaiṣṇava associations are highlighted. Curiously enough, Buddhism is hardly spoken of in this work as an important part of the religious life here.

[1] *Ibid.*, 1969-70, p. 34.

[2] The same structure is assigned to 2nd—1st centuries B.C. in a subsequent report. See *I.A.* 1970-71, para 50. The reports of the two seasons are confused on this point.

[3] *I.A.R.*, 1970-71, pl. XLIX A.

[4] T.V. Mahalingam, *op. cit.*, (1969) pp, 74-5.

[5] The Jain work *Lokavibhāga* (5th c. A.D.), Tirunatharkuṇrn epitaph 4th—5th c. A.D. and Pallankōyil Copper Plate. c. 550 A.D.

[6] *Perumbāṇārrupadai*, 420 ; *Mani*. Padiham. 90 ; XXVIII heading and subheading 152.

[7] *Mani*. XXI : 174.

[8] *Narrinai* : 266.

[9] *Kuruntogai*, 30, 172 ; *Narrinai*, 144, 213 & 266.

[10] *Kuruntogai*, 10 : 4; *Mani*. XXI : 148 and 154.

[11] *Kainnilai, Marudam*. 10 : 1.

[12] ll. 405 ff.

[13] Tiruvehkā or Vegavati, ll. 371-76.

What really poses a serious problem in excavating such sites is the fact that Kāñcī, like Madurai, Uṟaiyūr, etc. has been under continuous occupation and no systematic archaeological excavation seems possible in the face of a total lack of potential areas for digging. Archaeology can provide, only through trial diggings, an occasional insight on the antiquity of the settlement. There is little doubt however that the earliest levels of occupation in Kāñcī have been taken back, by these excavations, to the Megalithic phase or the Black-and-red Ware period.

8. ARIKAMEDU, PONDICHERY. The excavations carried out at this site in 1945 have brought to light the remains of an Indo-Roman trading station on the east coast, apart from providing 'a firm datum-line from which the classification of pre-medieval South Indian cultures can begin'. The associated BRW at this site has been dated with greater precision on the basis of the occurrence of the Arretine and Rouletted Wares and Roman amphorae.[1] These excavations have confirmed the literary evidence from Sangam works of the close trade contacts of South India with the Roman world. It has been further established that the ancient name of Arikamedu was Vīrai. (modern Vīrāmpaṭṭiṇam near the site), which was one of the Vélir strongholds known to Sangam literature.[2]

Vīrai, described as a harbour, belonged to the Vēlir.[3] It was probably one of the coastal towns, like 'Śopaṭṭiṇam (modern Marakkāṇam), of the Oy clan of Vēlir. It was also the capital of the Velir chieftain Virai Veliyaṇ Veṇman.[4] Names of poets who hailed from Virai would also suggest the Vēlir associations of the port. Archaeological evidence in support of the Vēlir connections with this centre has also been recognised in a potsherd of BRW, containing some Brahmi letters read as Yaḍu Balabhūti-y or Balabhūti of the Yaḍu (Iḍai-cowherd) clan. The characters are assigned about the first century A.D.[5] The Vélir claimed descent from the Yādavas.[6] A possible derivation of the Podouke of Ptolemy and the *Periplus* is interesting in this connection. Podouke may be derived from Podikai, a meeting place, where the members of a settlement met. Such Podikais or Podyil were common among the Vēlir settlements.[7]

9. VASAVASAMUDRAM (NEAR SADRAS) Situated at the mouth of the river Pālār, this site is about 13km south of Māmallapuram. A chance discovery of some pieces of amphorae, while digging for lime shell, led to some salvage excavations at the site. The 1.92–m deposit indicated a single period of occupation belonging to the first-third century A.D. Apart from pieces of amphorae, Rouletted ware and two ring wells and other important discoveries were also made at this site[8]. Evidence of brick structures, contemporaneous with this deposit has also been noticed.[9]

The location of Vasavasamudram is significant. Kāñcī, the Pallava capital, has been spoken of as a port by Hiuen Tsang[10]. Kāñci, situated on the banks of the Vegavatī, a tributary of the Pālār, has access to the sea only through the Pālār and hence some early port at the mouth of Pālār may well have served as the ancient port of the Tiraiyar, the earliest known rulers of the region. The subsequent development of Mamallapuram as the leading port of the Pallavas may also be thus linked up with the earlier port at the mouth of the Pālār.

The *Perumbāṇarruppaḍai,* one of the Sangam works, which contains interesting descriptions of Kāñci and other places in the Toṇḍaimaṇḍalam region, refers to a port called Nīrppeyaṟṟu. It had a lighthouse in the days of Toṇdaimān Ilamtiraiyan (contemporary of the Coḷa Karikāla of the Sangam period). The relevant lines in *Purumbāṇarruppadai* describe the port as a big one with broad streets, tall houses (of merchants), fishermen's quarters, godowns guarded by professional men and with a harbour full of ships bringing white horses and precious stones. The tall light house on the shore guided the ships[11]. U.V. Swaminatha Iyer identified the place with Nīrppēr in the Madurantakam taluk of the Chingleput district. M. Rajamanickam was inclined to identify it with Māmallapuram and derived the word thus—Nīr+peyal+tū[12]. Yet another derivation of the name is given by P.V. Somasundaranar,[13] according to whom, the original name was Nīrppāyaṟṟuṟai which was later corrupted into Nīrppeyaṟṟu. He would hence support the identification with Māmallapuram. Yet, it may also be suggested that with the evidence provided by the Roman pottery and pieces of amphorae, the site at the mouth of the Pālār was probably the early port known to *Perum-*

[1]Mortimer Wheeler, "Arikamedu, an Indo-Roman Trading Station", *Ancient India,* No. 2, pp. 17 ff.

[2]I. Mahadevan, "The Ancient Name of Arikamedu", *Surya Narayana Sastri Centenary Volume, Ed.* N. Subrahmaniam (Madurai, 1970), pp. 204 ff.

[3]*Aham* : 206 : 13-14.

[4]*Narriṇai* : V, 58.

[5]I. Mahadevan, "Arikamedu Graffiti : A Second Look", *Damilica,* II, (Madras, 1973), pp. 62 ff.

[6]*Infra,* p. 120.

[7]For the meaning of Podikai, see *Pre-Pallavan Tamil Index.*

[8]*I.A.R.* 1970-71, p. 33.

[9]R. Nagaswamy, "Archaeology and Epigraphy", *Proceedings of the III International Conference Seminar, Tamil Studies* (Pondicherry, 1973) p. 60.

[10]Mahalingam, *op. cit.,* (1969), pp. 5-6.

[11]11. 319 ; 346-51.

[12]Pre-Pallavan Tamil Index. p. 501.

[13]Ed. *Perumbānārruppadai,* Saiva Siddhanta Publication, 1967, 11. 319-27.

bānarruppaḍai and that it was very soon (probably in fourth-fifth century A.D.) superseded by Māmallapuram to the north of it, and hence the occupational deposit at Vasavasamudram indicates a single period.

THE BLACK-AND-RED WARE AND MEGALITHS

The uniform occurrence of the BRW in the lowest levels of all the excavated sites and the density of the distribution of megaliths with the dominant BRW would show that the BRW levels represent the earliest settlements of a widespread agrarian population and as such form the earliest archaeological culture of importance in this region. Habitation and burial sites located side by side would also indicate that the basic elements in the evolution of the Tamil socio-economic organisation as presented in the Sangam works were provided by the authors of this culture.

It is now well known that the BRW is quite independent of the Megalithic idea as seen from its occurrence in Megalithic and non-Megalithic contexts. B. Subba Rao repeatedly emphasised the need for separating the pottery from the Megalithic idea and ritual and the necessity for studying the grave goods, which are most crucial, in relation with other archaeological sites with BRW as in East Rajasthan, stratigraphically linked with central and West Indian proto-historic (chalcolithic) cultures of the early-second millenniun B.C.[1] He considered the pottery and other elements like iron as the diagnostic traits which can be linked up with the Dravidian. Hence he stressed the need for large scale excavations of the habitation sites of the Megalithic folk. A comparative study of the symbols occurring as graffiti marks on the megalithic pot-sherds with those of a non-megalithic context (Harappan and post-harappan) has also indicated the significance of such a study for the expansion of Proto-Indian cultures.[2]

The material element for the movements of people in the proto-Indian context is thus provided by the BRW. Its origin and distribution in space and time within the subcontinent takes it back to c. 2000 B.C. in East Rajasthan, to other Chalcolithic cultures in Gujarat and it continues with the Painted Grey Ware in places like Bikaner.

The PGW sites in the Gangetic region have been most plausibly linked with evidence from the later Vedic literature. It seems now possible and necessary to recognise other archaeological cultures such as those represented by the Ochre Coloured Pottery and BRW and, attempt, however tentative, to link them with people known from literary traditions in a proto-Indian context has already been made.[3]

The sudden emergence and affluence of megaliths in the south would point to a fusion of several elements, the BRW and iron, which came together to South India, and the Megalithic idea and cult, which were probably picked up during the course of the BRW movement from the north to the south. Or it may be argued that the BRW and iron were adopted by an already established Megalithic culture. The dominance of the intruding BRW culture was due to its advanced iron technology and hence its widespread and uniform character.

Problems involved in the study of the Megaliths relate to the types of burials and the pattern of their distribution in South India, particularly in Tamil Nadu. The factors determining the types may either be geological or social. The distribution of the types needs to be plotted out on a map and the direction of movements traced, wherever possible, if the factors determining the types are to be recognised. However, the common traits that link them together being BRW and iron, it becomes more important now to identify the authors of the BRW in general and the immigrant folk, who brought it to the south. How and where the Megalithic idea gets mingled with it does not seem to be of immediate importance, once it is accepted that the significance of BRW and its distribution is basic to an understanding of cultural expansion in the South.

The dichotomy of an 'Aryan' and 'Dravidian' India and its racial implications has cast a red-herring around all historical analyses and has influenced proto-Indian studies to a considerable extent. Even those who recognise in these terms a linguistic and cultural basis would hasten to identify the Megalithic culture either with the Dravidian or with the Aryans and to suggest probable routes of their movement to the subcontinent.[4]

[1]B. Subba Rao, "Some Problems in the Archaeology of South India", *Transactions of the Archaeological Society of South India*, 1956-57, pp. 63-78. and "Megalithic Problem of South India and the Dravidian Languages" *TASSI, Silver Jubilee Volume*, 1962 pp. 132-147.

[2]See B.B. Lal, "From the Megalithic to Harappa : Tracing back the graffiti on pottery", *Ancient India*, No. : 16, pp. 4 ff.

[3]Dr. Romila Thapar, has pointed out (above, pp. 72 the probable associations of the Yadavas with the BRW based on her study of the lineages contained in the *Purānas* and the archaeological evidence of BRW sites in the north and the pattern of their distribution.

[4]Asko Parpola in his work "*Arguments For an Aryan origin of the South Indian Megaliths*, Madras 1973, associates them with the Vrātyas (including the Andhaka—Vṛṣṇis) who, according to him, belonged to waves of Aryans earlier than the Rg Vedic Aryans and were the perpetuators of the traditions of the BRW people. They arrived, he says, much earlier than the later waves of Aryans, introduced iron and gave an impetus to the abutting of Aryans to South India.

It would perhaps be a more useful exercise to look for evidences of the BRW people in the earliest known traditions of the south and to trace them backwards with the help of archaeologically related sites in the other parts of India.

References to the megalithic burials and practices are found in the Sangam anthologies (first-third century A.D.) and in the *Maṇimekalai,* An exhaustive collection of such references and popular beliefs about the Megaliths has been made by K.R. Srinivasan.[1] Urn burials and cairn circles are largely mentioned in the earlier collections like *Puṟanāṇūṟu, Naṟṟinai* and *Padiṟṟuppattu,* while all practices such as inhumation, burial pits, urns, subterranean cells and cairn circles (*Karkiḍai*) are known to the *Maṇimekalai,* apart from cremation. Even kings of the Coḷa and Cera dynasties followed the practices of urn burial[2] and were entombed in *tāḷis* (urns). Of considerable interest is a reference to a Vēḷir chieftain being buried in the burial ground, "where the 'red eared' cock and *poguval* (a bird) sit on the heap (of stones) outside the lid that covered the red burial urn."[3] N.R. Banerjee pointed out fragments of crushed or broken pots in a cairn filling in Sāṇūr and suggested that they are the relics of a ritual, probably of pot breaking, connected with the entombment.[4] Such a ritual is actually referred to in the *Maṇimekalai.*[5] All these literary references would show that the Sangam period represented at least the last phases of the Mgealithic culture in this region.

It may also be reasonable to look for some clues in the Sangam works to the authors of this culture or their descendants. The Megalithic builders in the South are archaeologically the earliest known large-scale agricultural community, who introduced cultivation and sedentary agrarian settlements with tank irrigation. Hence their choice of hilly areas, the slopes providing the burial ground, and the low lying plains, arable lands. Their burials never encroached on arable lands.

Looking for evidence of such large-scale agricultural communities, the references in the Sangam works to the Vēḷir (Chieftains) and the Vēḷāḷas, who represented the peasantry would appear to provide the necessary clues to the Vēlir and their people (Vēḷāḷar) as the folk who introduced BRW and iron, which revolutionised the earlier primitive farming known to the neolithic people. In Paiyampalli (North Arcot district), the Neolithic phase is followed by the Megalithic with indications of a brief transition and in places like Brahmagiri, a slow infiltration of the Megalithic is seen.[6] Śengamedu is another important site providing evidence of the Neolithic and Megalithic phases of occupation in succession, especially in the light of the recent discovery of a Neolithic site at Nallur near Śengamedu.[7]

A survey of the references to the Vēlir settlements, traditions regarding their migration provides a useful index to their probable association with the BRW or Megalithic sites. A table showing the Vēḷir settlements among other sites mentioned in the Sangam works and the corresponding Megalithic sites, burial and habitational, is given at the end.

The term Veḷir, plural of Veḷ, has been interpreted variously as deriving from 'Veḷvi' or 'sacrifice' and 'Veḷ' meaning 'bright' 'desire' (beloved of the people)[8]. A more interesting derivation, however, is that from 'Vēl' meaning earth (or mud) or land.[9] Apart from Vēḷāḷar the terms Vēḷān kuḍi and Vēḷān māndar are used to refer to the peasantry.[10]

While the Vēḷir were the chieftains, the Veḷāḷar[11] were of two categories, the landowners and landless

[1]K.R. Srinivasan, "The Megalithic Burials and Urn fields of South India in the light of Tamil literature and Tradition", *Ancient India,* No. 2 July 1946, pp. 9-16 and "The Megalithic Monuments of South India—Literature and Tradition" *TASSI,* 1958-59, pp. 7-13.

[2]*Padiṟṟuppattu,* 44, ll. 22-23 ; *Puram.* 228 ll. 1-15.

[3]*Puram,* 238, ll. 1-5.

[4]N.R. Baner jee, "The Megalithic Problem of Chingleput in the light of recent exploration", *Ancient India,* No. 12, 1956 p. 31.

[5]Ch. VI : ll. 90 ff. *Manimekalai,* Ed. U.V. Swaminatha Iyer, p. 75 :

[6]It may be mentioned here that attempts have been made to find clues in the Sangam anthologies to the pre-history of Tamil nadu and to establish links between the late stone age people of the coastal *teri* sites with the people of the *neidal* (coastal) region and the neolithic cattle keepers with the pastoral people of the *mullai* (pastoral) region. See K. Sivathamby "Early South Indian Society and Economy : The Tinai Concept," *Social Scientist,* December 1974, No : 29, p. 34. The author analyses the *Tinai* concept relating to different ecological regions and considers it to be a geographical reality which is highly useful and interesting. But his attempts to find evidence of pre-history are premature as the neolithie complex of the Tamil country has not yet been systematically studied, althongh stray occurrences of neolithic polished stone tools have been reported from a number of places such as Salem (Shevoroy hills), Krishnagiri, Sēṇgamēdu the lower Kaveri Valley and even further south.

[7]Report of A. Swamy's discovery of "Late Stone Age Man in the Neighbourhood of Nattur", The Hindu, 26-12-74.

[8]M.A. Dorai Rangaswamy, *The Surnames of the Cankam Age, Literary and Tribal* Madras, 1968 pp. 153-56.

[9]R. Nagaswamy, *Yāvarum Kēlir,* p. 162. Also S. Sambasivan, "Pillai Inapperumai", *7th Conference of the Indian universities Tamil Teacher's Association.* part II, 1975, p. 677 for 'Vel' meaning 'earth' or 'land'.

[10]*Tolkāppiyam ,Poruladikaram*: 635 : 1 ; *Tirikadugam,* 42: 4 etc.

[11]The Vēḷāḷar followed six professions important for colonisation of new areas, such as cultivation, Smithy (iron), pottery, weaving, domestication of animals and hospitality-M. Ragahva Iyengar, *Velir Varalāṟu.* 3rd edition, 1964, pp. 27-28. With slight variations similar professions are listed in the *Divākara Nigaṇḍu* See R. Nagaswamy, *Yāvarum Kelir,* p. 161. The *Tolkāppiyam* (*Poruladikāram*) talks of the six professions of Velālas and Naccinarkkiniyar the medieval commentator, gives a slightly different list which includes cultivation, domestication of animals and trade.—*Poruḷādikarām,* Saiva Siddhanta Publication, 1971, pp. 214–15.

agricultural workers. The landowning Veḷāḷas were usually referred to by their place names with the suffix Kiḷān or Kiḷār, meaning one who possesses rights (in land).[1] The chieftains held large tracts of land and the others belonged to lesser categories controlling land. Veḷvi may hence mean any ritual, the performance of which was connected with land rights and by extension came to include the performance of any religious rites, including *Yajña* or sacrifice. It is in the last sense that the word is used in the Sangam works when referring to the Cōḷa, Cera and Panḍya rulers performing Vedic sacrifices. It may be noted here that no Veḷir chieftain is known o have performed Vedic sacrifices.

The Veḷir are known to the Sangam works as the ancient Veḷ and their old capital Tuvarai as the 'old house' (*Mūdil*).[2]

The *Purananūru* verse 201 contains the most interesting reference to their old capital. It says that the Veḷir were the descendants of those who ruled over Tuvarai for 49 generations, after appearing from the sacrificial pot (or pit?) (*taḍavu*) of a northern sage. Naccinarkkiniyar, a commentator of the fourteenth century A.D. identified it with Dvaraka[3]. Commenting on the *Toḷkāppiyam* Naccinarkkiniyar states that Agastya led a group of kings, eighteen clans of Vēḷir and the Aruvāḷar from Dvaraka to the south, destroyed the forests and made them habitable and cultivable and that the Vélir belonged to the lineage of Kṛṣṇa, the lord of Dvaraka.

Agastya is often described as the harbinger of "Aryan" civilisation in the south. While legends about him are known to Sanskrit literature, he is better known from Tamil traditions and is celebrated as the father of Tamil, who organised the Second Tamil Sangam and composed the *Agattiyam* (not extant), the earliest grammar for the Tamil language. The name Agattiyar is itself derived from a Dravidian root.[4] The Kāveri flowed from his pitcher[5] and he brought the river Taṉ Porunai (Tamraparṇi) down the Podigai hill (which was his abode) to the eastern sea.[6]

Tamil tradition has glorified and deified Agastya and the cult of Agastya became a prominent feature of Tamil religion and even spread to the South East Asian countries.[7] Would these traditions point to an early colonisation of the south and the Tamil country, in particular, by a Dravidian speaking people, who brought with them an advanced agricultural technology and hence their rapid colonisation of the south? The migration probably followed the western coastal regions and branched off from Maharashtra towards the east into the Andhra region and southwards to Karnaṭaka, Konkaṇa, Kéraḷa and to the Tamil regions, that section branching off from Kéraḷa to the Tamil areas moving gradually down the river valleys and northwards to the region of Kāñcipuram (Toṇḍaināḍu). It would be highly useful to work out the chronological position of the megaliths of different regions to see if the megaliths follow this movement in the order suggested above. The available dates for megalithic settlements take them back to the third century B.C. (Brahmagiri) and if the dates of Hallūr[8] are dependable even to the tenth century B.C. More recently Koṛkai has given as early a date as eighth century B.C. for the BRW levels[9] and this would lend additional evidence for an early spread of this culture in the extreme south. From the

The term Vel or Vela survives in other Dravidian languages also such as Tulu and Telugu e.g., Tuḷuva—Veḷāḷa for cultivator in Tuḷu and Golla Velama for blacksmiths in Telugu and Velama in general for land owners. *Veṭko* in early Tamil meant potter i.e. one, who worked with mud or clay.—See *Pūranāmuru,* 288 : 1, 4, 256 : 1. The potter in early Tamil country discharged important social functions. He forecast festivals and wore the special *Nocci* (flower) garland while doing so in the *manram* or meeting place of a settlement. He also fed the crows and the Gods in the *Maṉram.—Naṛṛiṇai* 200:4,293 : 2.

[1]M.A. Dorai Rangaswamy, *op. cit,* p. 151. e.g. Maiyūr Kiḷāṉ, Kunrūr Kiḷār etc.
"Veḷ Muḍumakkal" "Ton Mudir Veḷir"—*Aham* 372 : 3,4 ; Muḍukudi'—*Puram* : 166; Puram 289: 5.

[2]N. Subrahmaniam would however equate it with Dvārasamudra—*Pre-Pallavan Tamil Index,* p.445. Dvārasamudra, however is a later adoption of the earlier Dvāraka for the capital of the Hoysalas who traced their descent from the Yādavas. Dvārasamudra is also called Halebīdu or "Old House".

[3]M. Raghava Iyengar argues convincingly in support of the reliability of this tradition and links the Yādavas (Vṛṣṇis) with this migration. One of the Veḷir families ruled in the region of the Podigai hill—Bettigo of Ptolemy—the abode of Agstya and the region later came to be called Veṇād (Veḷ nāḍu) and Nāṉjil-nāḍu (the land of the plough) and was considered to be one of the areas of Koḍum Tamil—difficult or pure? Tamil. See *Veḷir Varalāru,* pp. 5 ff. Raghava Iyengar also points out the *Mahābhārata* references to the 18 clans of Yādavas, who on account of Jarasandha's opposition, migrated to Dvāraka. The Ays of Veṇādu claimed descent from the Yādavas. Copper plate records of Kokkarunanda ḍakkan of 9th century A.D.—T.N. Subrahmaniam ed. *Ten Pandya Copper Plates,* p. 8 in section on Ay Copper Plates.

[4]Agastya is derived from Agatti and hence Agattiyar in Tamil. T. Burrow *Collected Papers on Dravidian Linguistics,* Annamalainagar, 1st edition p. 179.

[5]*Manimekalai* : Padiham : 11; XXII : 35.

[6]*Taṉ Poruṇai* as the ancient name of Tāmraparni occurs in early literature and also "later Pāṇḍya inscriptions. See Annual Report on South Indian Epigraphy, 1916-17 Inscription No: 334 of 1916.

[7]If the Brahman—Kśatriya or priest—ruler tradition is pre-Aryan and a survival of Proto-Indian priest rule, as has been suggested, then Agastya would be a proto-Indian product. See I. Mahadevan, "Method of Parallellisms in the Interpretation of the Proto-Indian Script" *Proceedings of the III International Conference Seminar, Tamil Studies,* p. 52. Also D.D. Kosambī, *The Culture and Civilisation of India in Historical Outline* (1970), p. 83. The myth of the miraculous birth from a jar shared by families which were both Brahman and Ksatriya by tradition is specially associated with South India. All important South Indian dynasties associated themselves with jar legends.I. Mahadevan *op. cit.*, p. 52.

[8]See K.S. Ramachandran, "Chronology of the Indian Megaliths —Some Considerations" *Puratattva* No. 3, 1965-70 p. 108. *Supra*, p.

[9]*Supra*, p. 115.

purely archaeological context of the occurrence of BRW in Chalcolithic levels and subsequent occurrence in megalithic levels, B. Subba Rao suggested a date not earlier than 500 B.C. (or 600 B.C.) for the southward movement of BRW in the Megalithic context.

Now we have a number of habitational sites in Tamilnadu apart from Koṛkai with dates ranging from fifth-fourth century B.C. to the first-second century A.D. (Arikamēḍu). The Sangam works may be said to represent a stage of expansion of this culture, when the people who inherited it had progressed towards a more sophisticated cultural phase, with developed urban centres, maritime towns carrying on external trade and a more developed socio-political organisation in which the Vēndar (crowned kings) and the Vēḷir (lesser rulers—Kuṛunilamannar —ruling over smaller territories) were at the top of the social organisation. Simultaneously, Brahmanical or Sanskritic influences had introduced the Varṇa-jāti concept in social division in which the early tribal elements were gradually relegated to the lowest ranks and even to the position of outcastes. The Vēlāḷa had become in this process the fourth category. After a fairly long process of evolution, Tamil developed into a literary language, and preserved in its earliest literature some memories of the past relating to certain folk migrations. A time lag of at least three or four centuries may be suggested for the beginnings of this culture in Tamilnadu and the emergence of the three crowned monarchs in the river valleys of Kāvēri, Vaigai (and Tāmraparṇi) and Periyāṛu, "the areas of attraction."

The following brief survey of Vēḷir settlements where megaliths are found in fairly large numbers represents a preliminary investigation into the nature of the evidence literary and archaeological.

Some of the Vēḷir territories described in the Sangam works can be identified with the help of other evidences, mostly from later inscriptions referring to them and from persistent associations of certain areas with these chieftains. The Vēlir of old are said to have belonged to Kuṉṟūr which may be identified with modern Coonoor on the Nilgris.[2]

The Āys, one of the important Vēḷir families, ruled in the region now represented by South Travancore i.e. the border of Tamil Nadu and Kerala, which came to be known as Vēnāḍu (Vēḷ+nāḍu). Their settlement is called the Āy Kuḍi, Āy being short for Āyar—cowherds. They claim to have belonged to the Yādava clan. Āy Āṇḍiraṉ was a great agriculturist and ruled from Āy Kuḍi near the Podiyil hills. Āy Eyiṉaṉ son of Veḷiyan Vēṇmāṉ was another of these chieftains and was also known as Adihan.[3] A family of chieftains known as Adigaimans (or Adihans) is known to have ruled in the region of Dharmapuri (Ancient Tagaḍūr). The region of Vēṇādu needs to be more thoroughly investigated for Megalithic remains.

The Palaṉi hills were occupied by another Vēḷir clan *viz.* the Āviyar[4]. The Kōḍai hills were in the hands of a chieftain called Porunaṉ. Pāri of Paṛambu nāḍu was a famous Vēḷir benefactor and was the greatest of the last seven *vaḷḷals* (benefactors).[5] His generosity and his encounter with the three crowned monarchs of Tamilaham forms the main theme of several verses in the Sangam anthologies[6] Paṛambunāḍu is located in the Ramanathapuram district and the region south of Madurai which is known in later inscriptions from eigth-ninth century A.D. as Parambunādu.

The Vēl of Koḍumbai or Koḍumbālūr (near Pudukkottai), known as the Irungovēḷs (Irukkuvēḷs), represent another branch of the Vēḷir, who played an important role in Tamil history from the Sangam age down to late thriteenth century A.D. A verse in the *Puṛanāṉūṛu* refers to the chief Irungovēḷ as a descendant of the rulers of Tuvarai. Kapilar, the poet, who addresses the chief refers to him as Pulikaḍimāl[7] meaning "the great man who killed a tiger". Scholars, who identify Tuvarai with Dvarasamudra, are influenced by the late legend of the origin of the Hoysalas, which alludes to the foundation of the Hoysala kingdom by one Sala, who killed a tiger to save an ascetic.[8] On the other hand, the identification of Tuvarai with Dvaraka seems to be more plausible, for in later inscriptions found in temples dedicated to Kṛṣṇa (and sometimes to the Pañcavīrās or Vṛṣṇi heroes) Tuvarai is the Tamil form used for Dvaraka.

Irungovēḷ is said to be one of the five great Vēḷir.[9] The number of the Vēḷir families as mentioned in the Sangam collections range from 5,—7—11 to 14.

[1]The term Kuṛumbu which at one time formed the basis of Kuṛunila mannai or feudatories ruling over smaller tracts of land is used to mean nuisance or mischief or insubordination —vide *Kuṛal.* 735 : 2 *Puṛam* : 97:4, 9; 293:2. Did this influence later popular belief that the megaliths were Kuṛumbarkudi? K.S. Ramachandran, *Bibliography of Indian Megaliths*, p. 165

[2]*Naṛṛiṇai* : 280 : 8. There is, however a reference to this place as situated near the eastern sea—*Kuṛuntogai* 164 : 3, which makes the identification somewhat difficult.

[3]*Puram* 129: 5; 240 :3; col.375; *Aham* : 142 : 13; 148 : 7 etc.

[4]Palaṉi is called *Podiṉi* in *Aham*: 1 : 3; 61 : 16. Aviyar or Avinankudi was the same as Aykuḍi—*Puṛam* : 147 : 7.

[5]*Pre-Pallavan Tamil Index, pp.* 337–8.

[6]e.g. *Aham.* 78 : 22; 303 : 10 : *Puram,* 105,106, 107 etc.

[7]Puṛam 201 : 15 and 202 ; 10

[8]*Pre-Pallavan Tamil Index,* p. 445.

[9]*Aham* : 36 : 19.

In the Kaveri Valley, where the Cōḷas became powerful, a number of Vēḷir strongholds are known to have existed, such as Aḷundūr[1] near Mayavaram, Nāngūr and Piḍavūr[2] near Uraiyūr. With the Vēḷirs of Aḷundūr and Nāngūr, the Coḷas had matrimonial relations. Even Uṟaiyūr was held by a Vēḷir chieftain at one time[3] and some connection (father and son?) is sought to be established between him and the Coḷa king Poravaikkoperunaṟkiḷḷi, who fled to Āmūr in the North Arcot district due to his father's hostility.[4]

The Cengam (Śeṇgaṇmā) region in the North Arcot district was another Vēḷir territory ruled by Naṇṇan of the *Malaipaḍukaḍām* (colophon). Coins bearing the name of Nannaṇ have been recently unearthed in Cengam and have been assigned to the second-third centuries A.D.

The Oviyar ruled in the region around modern Tindivanam, known as Oymā ṇāḍu in the Sangam works. Their capital was Māvilangai, located in the Chingleput district[5]. Oymān Nalliyakkoḍan, a leading member of this family controlled places such as Āmūr, Kiḍangil and Eyiṟpaṭṭiṇam.[6] Āmūr seems to have been a very important centre of this Vēlir family and is described as a well guarded town with a moat surrounding it.[7] Subsequently, it became the centre of an important administrative division, Āmūr Koṭṭam in the Pallava times.[8] Eyiṟpaṭṭinam is the same as Śopatma identified with Marakkaṇam, a coastal site—north of Pondichery. Vēlūr, another important town in Oymānādu, may be the modern Vellore in the North Arcot district. The territory of the Oviyar possibly included Vīrai, which was a port belonging to the Vēlir,[9] and its identity with Vīṟampaṭṭiṇam (Arikamēḍu) south of Pondichery is now established.[10]

A number of other chieftains are also known from the Sangam works (though not specifically called Veḷir). The Kāris or Malayamāṇs of Tirukkovalūr (South Arcot district) on the banks of the river Peṇṇai[11] the Oris of Kolli hills in Kongunāḍu,[12] and other chieftains such as those of Kudirai hills and Tagaḍūr (modern Dharmapuri near Salem) are some of them.[13]

The frequent references to the Vēḷir and their strongholds as overflowing with rice and prosperity and their generosity to learned men would favour their identification with the founders of the earliest agrarian settlements in this region. The table given above would show the occurrence of megaliths at all important Veḷir sites and occasionally both burial and habitational sites.

The tentative nature of the hypothesis put forward in this paper is due in the main to the inherent difficulties in utilising a corpus of literature, which is highly composite, presenting a varied picture of socio-economic life in early Tamilaham. The inadequacy of the data relating to the chronological position of the various megalithic sites, burial and habitational, adds to the problems by forcing reliance upon a few R.C. dates.

Jawaharlal Nehru University R CHAMPAKLAKSHMI
New Delhi

[1]Aḷundūr—*Aham* : 24 : 4; 196 : 11.
[2]Piḍavūr—*Puṟam* : 395 : 20.
[3]*Naṟṟiṇai* : 58 : 5. This Vēḷir was called Viṟāi Veḷiyan Vēṇmān Tittan, who also ruled at Virai.
[4]M.A. Dorai Rangaswamy, *op. cit.*, p. 148. Also *Aham* 6:4; 15:5;226: 14; *Naṟṟinai, 58:5.*
[5]Nanmāvilangai—*Siṟupāṇāṟṟuppaḍai.* 120.
[6]*Puṇam* : 176: 6; *Śiṟupān*, 152:3; 160.
[7]*Śīrupān*, 187-188.
[8]T.V. Mahalingam, *op. Cit*; (1969), p. 4
[9]*Aham:* 206:13-14.
[10]*Supra*, p. . As late as the beginning of the 11h centu y A.D. we hear of a Hovya (Oviya) family, who composed the royal charter of the Coḷa Rājarāja I *viz.* The Larger Laiden Grant —*Epigraphia India*, Vol. XXII. The five Composers of this grant bore Vaiṣṇava names.
[11]*Aham* : 35:14.
[12]*Aham* : 33 : 14, *Kuṟuntogai*, 100:5; *Naṟṟiṇai*, 185:7; *Puṟam*: 22:28 and *Padiṟṟuppattu*, 73.9.
[13]*Puram* 168:14; 158:26.
Padiṟṟuppattu ; VIII : Ten Padiham 9; 78: 9; *Puram*: 50 Col; 230.

At Random[1]

A. Ghosh

WHEN, earlier this year, one of the organizers of the Prehistoric Society of India told me that it was its earnest desire that I should be the President of its next Conference, I was really taken aback, for my contribution to prehistory has been practically nil. While I have always tried to take interest in the subject, I cannot even claim that that interest has always been intelligent. In spite of my limitations, of which you are as well aware as I am, I accepted the invitation, as I regarded it as an honour not to me personally but to the fillip that prehistoric researches received in the country during my active days. And I dutifully thank you today but do not congratulate you on your choice. In these circumstances you would certainly not expect to hear any original discourse from me, as you heard from my predecessors-in-office. If, during the next few minutes, I make a few banal observations, you have only yourselves to blame for having chosen me to this office.

It is the privilege of old persons like myself to recall the good old days. I may, therefore, be pardoned if I indulge here in some reminiscences. Long ago, when I was trying to carve out for myself an archaeological career, archaeology was not exactly what it is now. It has been my good fortune to see and even take part in all the stages that Indian archaeology has gone through since then. When I began, an Indian archaeologist was not expected to know much of the Stone Ages. We all knew that Bruce Foote had discovered the first palaeolith in India in 1863. We were acquainted with his catalogues of prehistoric objects in the Madras Museum, as also with Coggin Brown's catalogue of such objects in the Indian Museum and had seen the prehistoric collections in these and other museums. We had read of the discoveries of Cammiade in the Kurnool area, interpreted by Burkitt, and of Todd in the Bombay region, both in the early thirties. Hardly anybody in the Archaeological Survey of India and only few Indians outside it could grasp the significance of the work of De Terra and his associates in the north-west and elsewhere, though we were vaguely aware that some great discoveries had been made. But thereafter things began to change. In the late thirties, the University of Calcutta started its work in the Kuliana valley in Orissa, and shortly after that the Archaeological Survey organized an expedition to the Sabarmati valley in Gujarat. Incidentally, the latter, though the first of its kind organized by the Survey, did not include any person from the Survey itself; this fact is its own commentary on the prevailing technical limitations of the Survey to undertake this type of work. Somehow, neoliths and microliths seemed nearer to our heart than palaeoliths. In 1940, I collected bagfuls of microliths from the rock-shelters of Pachmarhi.

The 1939-recommendation of Sir Leonard Woolley that there should be a 'protohistorian' on the staff of the Survey to deal with Stone Age archaeology materialized only in 1946 with the appointment of V.D. Krishnaswami, who, however, was assigned only the duty of listing the megalithic monuments of some Districts of the south—a work which he accomplished with his usual thoroughness. It was only the mid-fifties that the Survey could have a real Prehistoric Branch. By then prehistory had become a progressive branch of Indian archaeology, thanks to the activities not only of the Archaeological Survey but of other institutions, particularly the Deccan College under the leadership of Sankalia, and other institutions did not lag behind. Indeed, year after year, I had to face the criticism of the Central Advisory Board of Archaeology that I was encouraging prehistoric research to the detriment of other branches of archaeology. I regarded the criticism as unjustified.

The subsequent developments of prehistoric studies in the country are well–known to you of the younger generation, and many of you have actively contributed to them. A historical review is, therefore, uncalled for. I think nobody will now agree that Indian prehistory is obsessed with the typological classification of tools.

[1]Presidential address to the Prehistoric Society of India, Third Annual Conference, Chandigarh, 22 to 24 December 1975.

If find that our young colleagues are harnessing whatever other disciplines can give them, and I do not hesitate to add that some of these disciplines go over my head. And there is no end to disciplines and subdisciplines these days. For example, I find that blood-typing has been done on human skeletal remains from neolithic and later cemeteries in various parts of Eurasia and conclusions on blood-grouping at individual and ethnic levels have been drawn.[1] You, who are actually engaged in the work, have no doubt to ensure that you are equipped to deal with the developments abroad, develop them further and evolve your own methods to solve your problems. From what has been done during the last thirty years, I am sure that all will be well and even better with you in future. At the same time, archaeologists of the older generation like myself may well have reasons to lament, as others have done before me, that much that is being written on new archaeology and the relationship between archaeology and the new sciences is in the phraseology of the new sciences,[2] and this tendency is bound to grow in future. It seems that in days to come digging alone will remain the preserve of the archaeologist and that too to a limited extent. Fire is a good servant, but if left uncontrolled, it can kill its master, or, at least, leave him homeless.

What I have said above relates almost exclusively to Stone Age archaeology, which may be taken to be the minimum definition of prehistory. But it is generally agreed that prehistory includes something more than the Stone Age. What that something is does not seem to be clearly defined. Not knowing what the initiators of this Society had in mind when they started it, whether they liked its deliberations to be confined only to the Stone Age, I refrain from making observations on the non–I and post-Stone Age fields. At the same time, I would like to be clear on how one should define prehistory. According to Childe, prehistory deals with the period before the earlier written documents begin in Egypt and Babylonia.[3] The same seems to be the tenor of the periodization of cultures by Albright.[4] At the same time, writing has been regarded by most, including Childe himself, as one of the criteria of civilization.[5] Taken together, these would mean that all civilizations, including the Egyptian and west-Asian ones, would belong to the historical period; in other words, there was and could not be, any prehistoric civilization. Yet, these very civilizations have sometimes been called prehistoric.[6]

Applied to Indian conditions, the confusion becomes worse confounded, with the literate Indus Civilization followed by several non-literate cultures, till we come to the third century B.C., perhaps a couple of centuries earlier, whence we have written records.

During the last thirty years or so, as if to obviate the difficulty, it has been the fashion to introduce a period called 'protohistoric', as a buffer between the ill-defined prehistoric and the fairly well-defined historical. I admit I was largely responsible for the popularization of the term in the publications of the Archaeological Survey, without ever attempting to define it clearly. I may repeat what I have said earlier that no less an authority than Woolley would have liked a 'protohistorian' to take charge of Indian Stone Age archaeology. Protohistory has been defined as 'the period of human history between prehistory, when no written sources existed, and history *sensu stricto*, when written sources are a main source; the time when history can be written only from an appraisal of many sources—archaeological, literary, linguistic and oral.[7] This does not solve the problem, for here again the emphasis is on writing, which, according to others, distinguishes history from prehistory. Why then another term? Further, what is history in the strict sense? With the fast-changing concept of historiography, which Indian historians have not been slow to catch up, history is no longer a chronicle of kings and dynasties.

The same emphasis on writing has led Sankalia, in his recent *magnum opus,* to retain the term 'protohistory' to cover the motley of cultures that followed his Holocene Mesolithic. While admitting that it is not a precise definition, he has adopted the minimum definition of prehistory as comprising the various Stone Ages, but not including the Neolithic, which he has classed as protohistoric.[8]

I placed the same problem in 1972 before a gathering in which many of you were present. At that time some agreed with me that the term 'protohistory' be dropped, while others differed. The main speaker on the occasion, however, turned down the proposal, laying stress on

[1]L.A. Lengyel, *Palaeoserology,* Publishing House of the Hungarian Academy of Sciences, Budapest, 1975.

[2]Henry Hodges in *The Antiquarian Journal,* LIV, part II, 1974. p. 310. Jacquetta Hawkes in *Antiquity,* XLII, no. 168, December 1968, p. 257 : 'It is difficult not to feel that the longing to participate in the prestige of the natural sciences has led archaeologists to put up a scientific facade far too grandiose for the modest historical building behind it.'

[3]V. Gordon Childe, *Man Makes Himself,* 4th edition, Fontana Library, 1965, p. 4.

[4]W.F. Albright, *From the Stone Age to Christianity,* 2nd edition, Baltimore, 1946, pp. 82-83.

[5]V. Gordon Childe, *Progress and Archaeology,* London, 1944, p. 8. For other references, see A. Ghosh, *The City in Early Historical India,* Simla, 1973, p. 26.

[6]In the past the term 'prehistoric' was used in diverse senses, many of them now obsolete. See Glyn Daniel, *A Hundred Years of Archaeology,* London, 1950, pp. 86-87.

[7]*Ibid.* p. 8.

[8]H.D. Sankalia, *Prehistory and Protohistory of India and Pakistan,* Poona, 1974, pp. 7-8 and 15.

the long tradition of our country, which 'should not be matter of debate, as it is well-established'.[1] I now submit that the matter be reconsidered irrespective of any prestige attached to our having a long tradition and that we delink the use of archaeological terms from national prestige. I do not want to enter here into the question of the validity of our traditions—a question that has currently become one of sensitivity. But I would certainly like to emphasize the need for greater precision in scientific terminology, as any looseness therein would lead us nowhere. It is not merely a matter of rose smelling as good by whatever name you call it.

In this matter the historian must have his full say, for the crucial point is: when does the historical period begin in India ? It is the historian who must tell us from which epoch he would like to take charge, leaving the period prior to that to the archaeologist. The historian has to take into account significant changes in the subsistence pattern, modes of production and distribution and general economy, based on literary and other material, including archaeological. Our present-day historians are well-conversant with the problems, and we should like to hear their views. For example, Professor R.S. Sharma once casually remarked in an informal gathering that he would regard the historical period to have begun with the later Vedic age (though at present it may be an archaeologically nebulous period). Perhaps he and his colleagues might some day elaborate this view.[2]

Periodization is in no remote way connected with terminology, for periods must be expressed in nominal terms. I therefore take the opportunity of saying a few words about the terminology of Stone Age archaeology. When, in 1961, the committee set up by the First International Conference on Asian Archaeology recommended the use of the terms Early, Middle and Late Stone Ages, in preference respectively to the then current Lower Stone Age, Lower Palaeolithic and Series I, Middle Stone Age, Middle Palaeolithic and Series II, and Upper Stone Age, Upper Palaeolithic and Series III, 'Neolithic' remaining common in all cases, we thought that the question had been settled at least for some time to come to everybody's satisfaction. But not long afterwards dissident voices started being heard. Not that such voices are not heard even in the better-established terminology of European Stone Age. For example, a British author does not like the term 'Upper Palaeolithic', as it has 'racist overtones of a conquering superior race' and would recommend the term 'Leptolithic'. His reviewer says that the author 'must take the prize for the silliest remark of the year.[3] But in India the situation is more desperate. A single factor that has disturbed the complacence given birth to by the 1961-scheme seems to be the discovery in different parts of the country of blade-and-burin assemblages which cannot be fitted into it. The problem, you will recall, was discussed by a panel in 1972,[4] when divergent views were expressed, including a doubt if all the blade-and-burin assemblages did really belong to the Pleistocene. Unfortunately, the panel agreed to disagree, in spite of the appeal of a student that it should agree to one set of terms at least for the students' sake—an appeal which I would like to repeat here. The present-day trend, to judge from some writings, seems to revert to the European terminology of Lower, Middle and Upper Palaeolithic, with the addition of a succeeding Mesolithic. Whether you consider this as satisfactory, in spite of all the differences between the European and Indian conditions, it is up to you to decide. You may also consider the terminology of A.K. Ghosh – Pebble-Core, Flake and Flake-Blade—which he says is based on cultural-traditional units placed in a sequential framework, both geological and archaeological,[5] but you have to bear in mind Childe's warning: 'No factor of climate or habitat obviously obliges a tool-maker to choose the core rather than the flake detached from it.[6] Whatever terms you choose, let there be no rushing through this time in formulating your recommendations (the recommendations of 1961 were framed in the course of a few hours). At the same time, let us not shelve the matter once more, as otherwise scientific communication between ourselves and with outsiders will be seriously hampered.

Friends, I have fulfilled my Presidential duty by 'saying a few words', though they have been entirely pedestrian and repetitive and have wearied you. Let us now proceed to more serious work, in the course of which I hope to gather knowledge from you. But before that, allow me to thank you for placing me where I find myself today.

[1]H.D. Sankalia in D.P. Agrawal and A. Ghosh (ed.), *Radiocarbon and Indian Archaeology*, Bombay, 1973, 0 pp. 510-10.

[2]Perhaps such papers as R.S. Sharma, 'Class formation and its material basis in the upper Gangetic basin (*c*. 1000-500 B.C.) *India Historical Review*, I, part 2, September 1974, pp. 1-13, may be a beginning of this elaboration.

[3]Desmond Collins, *Background to Archaeology. Britain in its European Setting*, Cambridge, 1973. reviewed by F.H. Thompson in *The Antiquaries Journal*, LIV, part I, 1974, pp. 72-93.

[4]Agrawal and Ghosh (ed.), *op. cit.*, pp. 504-09.

[5]A.K. Ghosh, 'Chrono-cultural perspective on the Palaeolithic industries of India', Agrawal and Ghosh (ed.), *op. cit.*, pp. 23-31.

[6]V. Gordon Childe, *What Happened in History*, Penguin Books, Harmondsworth, 1942, and later reprints, pp. 31-32.

Problems of Indian Archaeology : Planning Ahead[1]

B. B. Lal

I am greatly beholden to you all for having so kindly asked me to preside over the present Annual Conference of the Society. This is indeed a singular honour, but I do not know if I would be able to rise to the occasion. However, I am sure of at least one thing, namely your kind cooperation and willing support. This will be my mainstay during the course of today and the next two days in discharging the onerous duties that you have entrusted to me.

In so far as my Address is concerned, let me tell you that it is going to be rather unconventional. Unlike my predecessors, I am not going to summarize the archaeological discoveries made since the last Conference. Most of the excavators and researchers are present here and, I am sure, they are going mutually to exchange notes. Further, some of the more important topics will naturally come up through the papers that are going to be presented to us. Thus, I shall devote my attention primarily to something which I consider of immense importance, namely the more glaring lacunae in our archaeological studies and how best to cope with them. Later on, I shall present my views on the controversy in which the country seems to have been caught up for the past few months and in which the learned scholars of this place (Chandigarh) have played a notable role: I mean the controversy regarding the historicity and date of the Mahābhārata war. While doing so, I shall also refer briefly to the archaeology of the Rāmāyaṇa sites—a project which I have recently embarked upon.

The Archaeological Survey of India and the State Departments of Archaeology are doing their best, within the limitation of the funds and staff at their disposal, to protect and preserve the cultural heritage of the country, as represented by its monuments and sites. Their efforts in this direction need all praise. Added to this is the work of registration of antiquities which is about to be taken up. It is a tremendous task and we wish the Survey and the State Departments all success in this very important national work. In so far as archaeological research is concerned, here too their output is quite praiseworthy. But it needs considerably to be supplemented as the Survey and its sister Departments cannot be expected to carry loads far far beyond their capacities.

Let there be no hesitation in plainly confessing that, in spite of the advances we have made since Independence in archaeological research, we still lag behind the West in many techniques relating both to field-work as well as laboratory investigations. Let that alone, there are quite a few branches which have not at all been touched in our country. Thus, for example, while several discoveries have been made on European coasts, through under-water archaeology, bringing to light sunken ships with valuable cargo, which tell us so vividly about ancient trade and commerce, nothing of the kind has been initiated in India. One may very well expect Roman ships of the early centuries after Christ or Arab ships of the medieval times under the coastal sea on the west. In fact, one need not be surprised if under the Gulf of Cambay one comes across a cargo-laden boat of the Indus Civilization on its outward journey to Mesopotamia or *vice versa,* for indeed has not Lothal in Gujarat yielded the remains of a dockyard as well as a seal of the Persian Gulf merchants who, as middlemen, were carrying on trade between the towns of the Indus Civilization on the one hand and the contemporary Mesopotamian towns on the other? To embark upon this kind of investigation is not at all a difficult task. Indian archaeologists have to collaborate with experts in the Indian Navy to draw up a scheme and implement it. I am sure most of the equipment needed for the purpose would already be available with the Navy or else it can be manufactured with the assistance of some of the more advanced technical institutes in the country. Should, however, any further technical help be still necessary

[1]Presidential Address to the Indian Archaeological Society, Eighth Annual Conference, Chandigarh, 22 Decembler, 1975.

the same may be obtained by making suitable arrangements with certain European countries who have shown great skill in this kind of work and whose bonafides may safely be depended upon.

Another desideratum is to organize air-reconnaissance of areas which are difficult for ground-operations but are likely to yield important archaeological results. For example, the Rajasthan desert, not easy to traverse, may very well be concealing dried up river-channels on the banks of which prehistoric and protohistoric men may have lived. Amongst the various possibilities there is the existence of many an unknown site of the Indus Civilization, may even of a period prior to it, for has not Kalibangan, in Ganganagar District, yielded the remains of a well-organized Bronze Age culture which was fairly wide-spread in the area even before the arrival of the Indus Civilization itself? It may also not be an exercise in futility to look for a microlithic culture which may have antedated even the pre-Harappan culture. If an approach is made at the appropriate level, I am sure, the Indian Air Force may only be too glad to help us in the matter.

But the most glaring lacuna to my mind is that relating to the study of archaeology of the countries with which India had contacts in the past. Of the Early Stone Age cultures of our country, the one called the 'Madrasian' is known to have had genetic relations with the Stone Age cultures of Africa. On the other hand, the Sohan Culture, dominating the sub-Himalayan regions, seems to have had a lot in common with the Stone Age cultures of south-east and east Asia. Likewise, during the Neolithic times, there seems to have been a migration into India from the north-west on the one hand and south-east on the other.

The well-known Bronze Age Civilization of the Indus Valley, which extended to Gujarat on the south-west and north-western Uttar Pradesh on the east, has had well established trade-contacts as far west as Iraq. Several seals of the Indus style, found variously at Ur, Umma, Lagash, etc. in that country, clearly testify to this trade. It has even been surmised that India exported cloth to Iraq in the third millennium B.C.

Of the early historical times, the connections between India on the one hand and Greece and Rome on the other are too well-known to be recounted here in detail. Archaeology has duly established a good bit of what the Tamil (Sangam) literature has to say about the Indo-Roman contacts. Have not the amphorae discovered at Arikamedu, near Pondicherry, yielded remnants of the resin which had been used in the manufacturing of the coveted Roman wine that these vessels brought all the way for connoisseurs in south India?

In a slightly later period, India itself had a very great deal to contribute to the culture of the south-east Asian regions—Burma, Thailand, Indonesia and the rest. Ancient sculptured panels, depicting scenes from the Rāmāyaṇa, may be wanting, except for a few rare examples, in the home State of Rāma himself, but are profusely available on the temple-walls of Indonesia. It is such factors that bind these countries in a tie which is more lasting than any political one can be.

During the medieval times, India's relations with central and western Asia were so great that they have left an indelible imprint on Indian architecture, art and culture. The admirable synthesis of the Indo-Muslim architecture that one sees for example at Fatehpur Sikri can never be bifurcated, even though the politicians may have bifurcated the country itself. Or, are not some of the Mughal miniatures, with their fairy colours and intriguing subtleties, the pride of the world art as a whole?

But what have we done to study the genesis, growth and other details of these contacts and give-and-take? Do we have specialists—even a single one—in the archaeology of these countries? The answer is a 'No'; yes, a big 'NO'. Should then India, even after completing the Silver Jubilee of her independence continue to be blissfully ignorant of the archaeology of these countries, and take lying down whatever western scholars have to dole out in this respect? Or, could one expect a silver lining (as a gift ensuing from the Silver Jubilee) around the clouds of our ignorance? I am firmly of the opinion that the country should rise to the occasion and take up the challenge in a most befitting manner. But all will depend on what priority the Government gives to this important matter. If there is a will there is no doubt a way. But the will will have to be there first!

The best way to tackle this problem would be to set up a Central Institute of Archaeology which may have the necessary number of Departments, each specializing in the archaeology of a given country, for example Departments of Graeco-Roman Archaeology, Egyptology, West Asian Archaeology, Central Asian Archaeology, South-east Asian Archaeology, Sinology, etc. If there are not enough funds at the moment, at least a beginning can be made with the more urgently needed Departments and others can be taken care of in the course of time.

As mere book-study will not create real specialists, the concerned persons ought to carry out field-work in the respective areas. This, of course, will have to be organized with the concurrence of the governments of the countries concerned. Such expeditions are quite normal and can easily be organised on a reciprocal basis, giving opportunities to specialists of the countries involved to come to India, study its archaeological wealth and do field-work, if desired.

The field-work by Indian scholars in these countries will bring to light new materials some of which, it is hoped, will be allowed to be brought to India for *bona fide* display and teaching purposes. To cite an example, we got a reasonably good collection from Egyptian Nubia as a result of the Indian Expedition's work in that region in 1961-62. Material can also be obtained from these countries on an exchange-basis, for many of them would be interested in Indian exhibits as well.

The Institute thus will not only be creating Indian specialists in the archaeology of Greece, Rome, Egypt, West Asia, Central Asia, South-east Asia, China, etc., who would be able to understand and interpret the evidence of contacts with these countries from the Indian point of view, but would also be acting as a medium for developing museum-collections of the archaeological wealth of these regions, which will be of great use for the general education of the people of India. After all, how many of our people get a chance to see an Egyptian or Greek sculpture or a south-east Asian bronze?

A few years ago, when I was the Director General of the Archaeological Survey of India, I thought of experimenting in this direction and accordingly started negotiations with the Afghan Government for undertaking excavations at Begram, the famous ivories of which place show clear influence of Indian art. I am glad to learn that this year the scheme has brought fruit and actual work has been commenced. However, with the heavy commitments of the Survey in so many other directions, more particularly in regard to the protection and preservation of more than four thousand monuments and sites and registration of hundreds of thousands of antiquities scattered all over the country, it will be too much to expect the Survey additionally to handle the functions of the Institute I have just spelt out. It has, therefore, to be a separate entity by itself, having the suggested wings and complete in itself, with its own library relating to the archaeology of all the concerned countries and a fully-equipped scientific laboratory capable of dealing with the various kinds of archaeological investigations. Any suggestion that different Universities should each have a slice of the proposed Institute would, to my mind, again be a dissipation of energy and resources, of each university will have to build up and additional library and laboratory for the purpose. Above all, the much needed common platform for coordinated planning and for exchange of ideas amongst the scholars involved, and the visualized central collection of foreign antiquities will not be possible to foster. I am not trying to be dogmatic, but these are the obvious disadvantages I see in any kind of fragmentation.

There is no doubt that the establishment of the above-mentioned Institute will not bring back any monetary returns and cannot thus be regarded as an economically viable proposition. But must that be an overriding consideration in the field of cultural developments? How long can India continue to see the historical and archaeological developments in the neighbouring countries through foreign eyes which naturally cannot be expected to do justice to the Indian point of view?

In a booklet of mine, *Indian Archaeology Since Independence*, published in the early sixties, I had briefly touched upon this very issue under a chapter captioned 'Before the bell rings out the Sixties', and had hoped for the best. Not only have the sixties been rung out but in about a week's time half of the seventies also will have been rung out. Should I then caption this part of my Address as, 'Before the bell rings out the Seventies', or as, 'Will it remain a Cry in the Wilderness!'

May I now proceed to the controversy relating to the Mahābhārata and the Rāmāyaṇa? It is indeed our misfortune that these two epics have been inflated from time to time. Thus, for instance, the Mahābhārata which now has 100,000 verses is hnown to have had 24,000 verses at an earlier stage and only 8,800 verses at a still earlier one. What was the earliest or original size no one knows; nor has anybody succeeded so far in sorting out even the 8,800 verses from out of the 100,000 now available. It is to this work that the learned Sanskritists should apply their energy rather than waste it over a controversy based on the eleven-times magnified story.

It is well known and accepted even by the Sanskrit scholars that in their available forms the Rāmāyaṇa and the Mahābhārata are unlikely to be earlier than the 3rd-4th century A.D. On the other hand, if Rāma and Krishṇa were really historical figures, they must have lived earlier than the time of Buddha, which is, in the 6th century B.C. Thus, there is a clear gap of more than a thousand years between the episodes mentioned in these two epics and the finalization of their texts. In such an event, how can one wholly rely on them?

To add fuel to the fire, some people use the evidence provided by still later documents. For example, those who place the Mahābhārata war in 3102 B.C. derive their strength from the Aihole inscription of Pulikeśin II, dated Śaha 556 (expired)=A.D. 634-45, wherein it is stated that 3735 years had elapsed since the Mahābhārata war. Indeed, one wonders how a statement like this, made after such a tremendous time-gap, can form the basis of firm history?

Under the circumstances, there is no better course

than to look up to the direct evidence provided by the sites associated with these two epics. And this is precisely the tool that I have used in my investigations.

In such an archaeological investigation the first and foremost question is: Are the sites of Hastinapura, Kurukshetra, Mathura, Barnawa (ancient Vrāṇavata), Panipat (ancient Pāṛiprastha), Indrapat (Indraprastha), Tilpat (Tilaprastha), Ahichchhatra, etc., the same as mentioned by those very names in the Mahābhārata? If the answer be in the negative, then let us wait till we are able to find out another set of sites bearing the same names. That is to say, let us find out another Hastinapura, another Kurukshetra, another Mathura and so on, with the same *geographical setting* as mentioned in the Mahābhārata. On the other hand, *if we accept the identity of these sites with their namesakes in the epic then we are morally bound to accept the evidence yielded by these sites irrespective of whether it fits into our pre-conceived theories or not.*

Explorations and excavations at the Mahābhārata sites have consistently shown the existence of one and the same kind of material culture in the *lowest levels.* This culture is characterized by the use of a special kind of pottery which has a grey colour and is painted over with geometric and linear designs in black pigment (known to archaeologists as the Painted Grey Ware.) The economy was based essentially on agriculture and stock-breeding. Amongst the domesticated animals particular mention may be made of the horse which was an animal *par excellence* with the Aryans. The major boosting factor in the economy of these people, however, was the use of iron for their tools, as also for weapons. This stands in marked contrast to the use of bronze and copper by the people of the Indus Valley Civilization.

Hastinapura, which stands on the bank of the Ganga, has yielded some very specific evidence about a flood which resulted in the washing away of a big part of the settlement. This evidence has been recovered not only from the toe of the mound but also from the river-bed, at a depth of nearly 15 metres below the water-level, by means of borings which were made into the bed itself. Excavations at Kausambi show a continuity of the culture that prevailed at Hastinapura at the time of the flood. All this fully corroborates the literary evidence which says:

Gaṅgayāpahrite tasmin nagare Nāgasāhvaye
Tyaktvā Nichakshur nagaram Kauśmbyām
sa nivatsyati

"When the city of Nāgāsahvaye (Hastinapura) is carried away by the Ganga, Nichakshu will abandon it and will dwell in Kausambi".

Thus the circumstantial evidence is fairly strong to make us think that there *did exist* some basis for the Mahābhārata story, although, no doubt, most of what is contained in the inflated 100,000 verses is likely to be an exaggeration which, I feel, should be regarded as the normal feature of an epic where poetic imagination always has the upper hand.

As regards the date of the Mahābhārata war, may it be pointed out that amongst the kings who ruled at Kausambi in the lineage of Nichakshu, there is the mention of Udayana who is known to have been contemporary of Buddha. The latter died in 483 or 487 B.C. and therefore the former (Udayana) may be taken to have been ruling around 500 B.C. According to the the list given in the Purāṇas, there were 24 kings between Udayana and Purīkshit who ascended the throne of Hastinapura immediately after the Mahābhārata war. While the estimate for the total region of these 24 kings is anybody's guess, an assessment of the available historical data from the Indian scene is indeed a revelation. There were 47 hings from the time of Qutbuddin Aibak, the first Muslim ruler of Delhi, to Bahadur Shah Zafar, the last Mughal king, the total duration of their reigns being 652 years. This gives an average of 13.9 years per ruler. In the same manner, an assessment made of the more noteworthy dynasties of ancient India shows that the average durations per ruler of the Mauryas was 13.7 years, of the Śuṅgas 11.2 years, Kāṇvas 10.5 years, Sātāvāhanas 14.4 years and Guptas 17.6 years. The average of these averages comes to 13.55 years per ruler. If, however, we take the total number of the kings involved in all the above-mentioned dynasties, which is 100, and the total duration of their reigns, which is 1396 years, the average comes to 13.96 years per ruler. We may thus accept the round figure of 14 as a good working hypothesis. The total duration of the reigns of the 24 kings, from Parīkshita to Udayana, would then be 336 years. Adding this to 500 B.C. which is the time when Udayana was ruling, we arrive at the figure 836 B.C. According to the foregoing evidence, therefore, the Mahābhārata war would be assignable to the second half of the 9th century B.C.

This very date finds support from another computation. The Purāṇas mention that there were 36 kings between Yudhishṭhira on the one hand and Chandragupta Maurya on the other. The generally accepted data for the latter's accession is 322 B.C.*. On the basis of the average reign of 14 years per ruler (as shown above) the total duration of the reigns of the 36 kings would be 36 x 14=504 years. Adding this figure to 322 B.C. we arrive at 826 B.C. which is not very far removed from 836 B.C., arrived at earlier.

That the above-mentioned average of 14 years per ruler is nearer the truth as compared to the averages of 20, 25 and even 33 years advocated by various scholars, can easily be demonstrated from the foregoing Puranic data themselves.

Let us suppose that the date of the Mahābhārata war is represented by the letter M, and the average reign per ruler by A.

From the Puranic data about the Udayana-Parīkshit king-interval we get the following equation:

$$500 + 24A = M. \quad ....(i)$$

where 500 B.C. is the date of Udayana and 24 is the number of kings between him and Parikshit who ascended the throne soon after the Mahābhārata war.

On the basis of the Chandragupta Maurya-Yudhishṭhira king-interval, as mentioned in the Purāṇas, we get another equation, as follows:

$$322 + 36A = M............(ii)$$

where 322 B.C. is the date of the accession of Chandragupta Maurya and 36 is the number of kings that ruled between him and Yudhishṭhira in whose life-time the Mahābhārata war took place.

Re-arranging the two equations, we get—

$$24A = M—500.........(i)$$
$$36A = M—322.........(ii)$$

By subtracting (ii) from (i) we get—

$$-\ 12A = -\ 178$$
$$\text{or } 12A = 178$$
$$\text{or } A = 178 \div 12 = 14.83$$

Thus A, i.e., the average reign per ruler, works out to 14.83 years.

Further, by substituting the value of A in the above-mentioned equations, we get the value of M as 856 B.C.

It would thus be seen that whichever way we assess the literary evidence, namely whether on the basis of the known historical dynasties of India or on the basis of the Puranic cross-lists of the kings themselves, the date of the Mahābhārata war is unlikely to go much before the middle of the 9th century B.C.

Here I would also like to add a word about the Carbon 14 dates of the Painted Grey Ware Culture. The earliest date known so far is 1025±100 B.C., coming from *a middle level* of the Painted Grey Ware deposits at Atranjikhera in District Etah, U.P. Another early date is from Noh in Rajasthan, being 820± 225 B.C. Thi again, is from *a middle level* of the PGW deposits. It is, therefore, clear that the beginning of this culture would be around 1000 B.C. In this context, it may also be stated that the Carbon 14 dates themselves require a correction, known as the MASCA correction. According to the table published by the Applied Science Centre for Archaeology, University of Pennsylvania, USA, the corrected value of 820 B.C. would be 900 B.C. and that of 1025 B.C., 1155 B.C. The MASCA ruler is nearer the truth as compared to the averages correction has been accepted by many scholars in the west and if we in India also accept it (and there is a good case for doing so, because of the discrepancy between the C 14 dates of the Indus Civilization and its dating on historical evidence of contacts with contemporary western Asia), the beginning of Painted Grey Ware culture as a whole may be pushed back still earlier. As to the C 14 dates of Hastinapura, may it be clarified that the laboratory itself has noted that the concerned samples of charcoal were found to be mixed with rootlets, and it is not unlikely that contamination of the samples over the centuries may have resulted in the lateness of the dates.

To sum up. The archaeological and literary evidences combine to show that there was a seed of truth in the Mahābhārata story which, like the famous banyan tree of Calcutta, kept on growing on the fertile Indian soil and in the course of time covered more and more areas under its welcome shade. This seed, as the evidence points out, was sown some time in the 9th century B.C.

To turn to the sites associated with the Rāmāyaṇa story. Here again we have to go by the archaeological data provided by the *lowest levels* of the sites themselves. At Ayodhya, we have excavated in two areas: one near the Saryu, at Jhunki Ghat (as at the beginning, settlements usually hug the river-bank), and the other in a central part of the mound, near Asharfi Bhavan. A few years ago, the Banaras Hindu University had also put two trenches, one near the Janma Bhumi area and the other near the river-bank at Rajghat. The evidence of all the four areas, though located variously from east to west and north to south, is identical, showing that the first settlement at Ayodhya, at least in these four areas, commenced at the fag-end of the Painted Grey Ware Culture. Similar was the evidence from Sringaverapura, in Allahabad District, where Rāma crossed the Ganga on his southward journey. The evidence available at present thus indicates that the beginning of the sites associated with the Rāmāyaṇa story was later than the beginning of the sites associated with the Mahābhārata. And *if Rāma was a historical figure living at Ayodhya,* it only stands to reason that *his period could not have been earlier than that represented* by *the lowest occupation level of the site, viz. the fag-end of the Painted Grey Ware Culture.* For, indeed, *can there be anything earlier than the earliest* ?

That Rāma could have been later than Kṛishṇa is suggested not only by the aforesaid archaeological evidence but also by that from the literature itself. While the Mahābhārata and the Rāmāyaṇa, as already explained earlier, are late works containing a lot of interpolations, the Upanishads are not. They did not have to serve any dynastic ends and, therefore, the historical facts incidentally referred to in them may well be ragarded as impartial. Thus, the Bṛihadāranyaka Upanishad narrates a philosophical discussion in the court of Janaka during which Bhujju Lahyayani asked Yājñavalkya: '*Kva Parikshita abhavan* ?' *i.e.*, 'Where have the descendants of Parīkshit gone ?' The answer was that they had gone to the same place where the performers of horse-sacrifice go. (The central theme of the discussion was that through the performance of ritualistic action, however exalted it may be, one cannot attain Liberation). This discussion very naively lets the historian glean the fact that the time of Janaka was later than that of Parīkshit. Some scholars feel that the Janaka referred to in the above-mentioned episode was not the Janaka of the Rāmāyaṇa. While no doubt the Bṛihadāraṇyaka Upanishad does not mention in so many words that this Janaka was the father-in-law of Rāma, do we not know from several other sources that Janaka, the father-in-law of Rāma, was a philosopher-king who greatly rejoiced in such metaphysical discussions ?

The Mahābhārata and Rāmāyaṇa episodes, broadly speaking, coincide with the eastward spread of the Aryans. The Śatapatha Brāhmaṇa clearly refers to such a movement, as from the Kuru-Pāñchala region (western U.P.), through Kosala (north-eastern U.P.), to Videha (north-western Bihar).

Let me, however, emphasize that I am not going to rest with what has been done so far. I have in mind a thorough exploration of all the sites associated with the Rāmāyaṇa story and excavation of as many of them as possible. Accordingly, it is proposed to excavate at two more places at Ayodhya in the next field-season, namely at the Janma Bhumi mound and the Kanak Bhavan area. These spots are held as being directly associated with Rāma and Daśaratha respectively. We would also take up work at Nandigrāma, associated with Bharata, and at Lakshmaṇa Tila (Lucknow), associated with Lakshmaṇa. The five-year project, called 'Archaeology of the Rāmāyaṇa Sites', for which assistance is being generously provided by the Archaeological Survey of India, University Grants Commission and Government of Uttar Pradesh, would ultimately embrace as many other sites as possible connected with the Rāmāyaṇa story.

Finally, let me add that I would welcome all suggestions regarding the archaeological investigations on hand. For the sake of those who may be feeling uneasy at the possibility of Rāma being later than Kṛishṇa, I offer to dig in their presence the Kṛishṇa *Janma Bhumi* area at Mathura and the Rāma *Janma Bhumi* area at Ayodhya, so that they may see for themselves the outcome Let the spade speak, not me !

Notes and News

Technology and Social Change in Early Indian History: a Note Posing a Theoretical Question

In recent years, a few of our leading workers in the field of early and medieval Indian history have been seriously engaged in analysing the evidence of findings in technological innovations and in interpreting them as having served as instruments of meaningful social change; hence their significance in the history of Indian civilization. That technology is one of the most important instruments for social change and that the history of any technology in any given civilization should, therefore, be of serious concern to any student of history, has long been recognized, more or less universally. The recent studies in regard to the history of technology just referred to, must, therefore, be welcomed and these must receive the attention they deserve.

1

Insofar as early India is concerned the technology which has been receiving significant attention is that of manufacture of iron and use of iron tools and implements.[1] Archaeological excavations in many parts of India, particularly east of the Ghaggar, in the Ganga-Yamuna valley, have been yielding for the last three decades, a good number of tools and implements of smelted, beaten and forged iron, which stratigraphically, by associated objects and by radio-carbon tests, have been dated roughly between 900 B.C. and 200 B.C., confining ourselves to the Ganga-Yamuna valley for the purpose of this note. On this evidence supported by whatever literary evidence is available from Buddhist and Brahmanical sources in the main, it has been argued that the Ganga-Yamuna valley, the Ganga basin in particular, that is, the region which extends from the east of the Ghaggar, in other words, from the Kurukshetra-Karnal region to Bihar, if not farther east to the Ajay-Mayurakshi valley, had emerged from a bronze and/or chalcolithic age to an iron age culture, that iron technology tools and implements were the instruments which cleared the dark and dense forests of the Ganga-Yamuna valley and prepared the land for extensive iron plough cultivation and hence, for a new agriculture (as distinguished from neolithic agriculture) which provided enough surplus to enable contemporary society to bring about a new social phenomenon, namely, of a new (or, a second) phase of urbanization.[2]

One thing leads to another. This new agriculture and this new urbanization, the two together have been interpreted to have led to a new quickening of social impulses (the words are mine but not the implication) which in their turn, gave rise to new social and economic forces that, directly or/and indirectly, helped the rise of such critical and protestant movements as Buddhism, Jainism and Ajivikism and of one of the cardinal principles of all such protestant faiths, namely, of *ahiṁsā*, which was aimed primarily against the slaughter of animals that were used for agricultural purposes.[3]

Let me concede at once that once it is proved beyond doubt that the Ganga-Yamuna valley had emerged into an *effective* iron age culture using *significant* iron implements of a kind and character and of a depth and dimension, that could bring about the sort of great

[1]N.R. Banerjee, *The iron age in India.*, Munshiram Manoharlal, Delhi, 1965, is perhaps the first full-length comprehensive study on the subject. It was worked out as a doctoral dissertation under the general guidance and supervision of the writer of this note during 1955-56; eventually it earned the doctoral degree of Calcutta University. Before publication it was brought uptodate so as to include all archaeological yields till 1964, and their analysis and interpretation.

[2]N.R. Banerjee, *op. cit.*, chaps. 12 and 13; R.S. Sharma "Iron and urbanization in the Ganga basin" in *The Indian Historical Review*, vol. I, no. 1, March 1974, pp. 98-103; Thapar, Romila, *Presidential Address*, Ancient India Section, Indian History Congress, 31st, Session. Varanasi, 1969, *Proceedings*, pp. 15-39.

[3]R.S. Sharma, "Material milieu of the birth of Buddhism", paper presented at the 29th International Congress of Orientalists, Paris, 16-22 July, 1973. For a well-argued critique of this paper, see K. Dilip, Chakravarti, "Beginning of iron and social change in India", in *Indian Studies : Past and Present*, Calcutta, vol. XIV, no. 4, July-September, 1973, pp. 329-338.

social changes which have been claimed to have taken place, I have not much to argue about except in details which are not of much consequence, since I acknowledge that a great deal of the claims made might logically follow, more or less.

I have however reasons to doubt if what has been laid bare by archaeology to date, allows us the very basic premise of the thesis so far advanced. Secondly, and again going by archaeological evidence, I have reasons to doubt if the quantitative and qualitative use of iron technology and iron implements in the Ganga-Yamuna valley before *c.* 321–20 B.C. were such as to induce the sort of great social changes which we are being asked to agree to have taken place. While my first doubt is in regard to facts and their interpretation, the second is somewhat theoretical, that is, what should be the quantitative magnitude and the qualitative depth of a technology which, when applied to a given social situation, should be able to bring about effective and meaningful social change.

2

More than two scores of sites scattered all over the region extending from the east of the Ghaggar right up to the valley of the Ajay-Mayurakshi, by far the large majority being situated in the Ganga-Yamuna valley itself, have yielded, along with iron slags and shapeless lumps of iron, important iron implements of various recognizable shapes, types, and forms, all relatively of *smaller sizes and lighter weights*. All these yields have been found, stratigraphically speaking, in association with what has come to be known to archaeologists as Painted Grey Wares or/and Northern Black Polished Wares, insofar as the region referred to above is concerned. The PG Ware levels are generally dated between *c.* 1000 to 500 B.C. while the NBP Ware levels, between *c.* 500 B.C. to about the beginning of the Christian era, very roughly speaking, the best of the NBP Wares belonging to about the fourth and third century B.C. Radio-carbon tests have more or less corroborated the stratigraphical datings, both enjoying the acceptance of all students of Indian archaeology with but little marginal deviations here and there, which, however, do not affect the argument I am going to present.

The iron implements that have been found associated with the PG Wares include, besides slags and shapeless bits, arrow-heads, spear-heads, knives, nails, spades, knife-blades, daggers, hoes, fish-hooks, tongs, adzes, chisels and scissors. It will be noticed that no iron axe, socketed or otherwise, no iron ploughshare, no iron sickle and no iron implement that could possibly be useful for large-scale forest clearance and land-reclamation and large-scale and extensive agricultural operations which could possibly yield a surplus for rearing up towns and cities and maintaining them, has yet been brought to light at the PG Ware levels, that is at the levels which can be dated between *c.* 1000 and 500 B.C.

The iron implements that have been picked up from their association with the NBP Ware levels, in the region east of the Ghaggar, include chisels, arrow-heads, spear-heads, daggers, nails, knives, hooks, barks, crowbars, spikes, handles, sickles and smith's anvils. It is significant that at the same levels at Taxila one notices a much larger assemblage of tools and implements which include dagger-blades, adzes, bowls, spoons, saucepans, knives, daggers, javelins, arrow-heads, elephant-goads, chisels, tongs, smith's anvils, hoes and nails, but most importantly socketed axes and socketed hoes.[1]

One notices at once that NBP Ware Gaṅga-Yamuna list too, like the PG Ware one, does not include any iron-axe, plain or socketed, no iron hammer and no iron ploughshare. Socketed iron-axes are reported from NBP Ware levels at Taxila as we have just seen, and from chalcolithic–*cum*-pre-NBP Ware levels at Nagda and unsocketed ones from both Nagda and Prakash of the same levels. But Taxila, Nagda and Prakash are all outside the region I am concerned with at the moment. Yet, for argument's sake, the Taxila piece of evidence does not present any difficulty from the point of view that I am going to present in a while. In regard to the pieces from Nagda and Prakash I should think that the evidence is one of chalcolithic survival than of NBP Ware culture proper; at any rate it does not warrant any meaningful and dependable hypothesis. Further, it is significant that even from the NBP Ware levels no iron hammer nor any ploughshare has yet been picked up. Indeed, the earliest iron plough-share reported so far is from Kausambī, and that too, according to the excavator's stratigraphy, cannot be dated earlier than A.D. 200.

How then, in the absence of any find of iron-axe of considerable weight and of any iron plough-share, can we assume that it was iron-technology which effected the clearance of the dark and dense tropical forests of the Ganga-Yamuna valley and extensive agricultural operations which are supposed to have taken place following the clearance of forests ? Vaśishṭha and Baudhāyana say that the easternmost limit of the traditional Aryandom was once Kālakavana, the black forest, which has been identified with the Prayāg region. The *Ayodhyā-kāṇḍa* of the *Rāmāyaṇa* too, states that Prayāg was at that time a clearing in a forest. There cannot therefore, be any reasonable doubt that the

[1]In the compilation of these two lists I have been helped by Dr. N.R. Banerjee and Shri B.M. Pande, both of the Archaeological Survey of India. My grateful thanks are due to both.

Ganga-Yamuna valley was indeed studded with dark and dense forests. Also, one may not doubt that these forests were, slowly and steadily, cleared for habitation and agriculture, but then this clearance could have been done by the well-known traditional method of burning which is practised even today. One may recall in this connection, the *Mahābhārata* legend of the burning of the dark and sprawling Khāṇḍava forest. We may not, therefore, necessarily attribute this felling of huge tropical trees and clearance of forests to iron technology, especially when we have no evidence of iron-axe or iron-saw of any kind. Besides, one may not forget that copper and bronze had not yet gone out of use, and axes of these metals could as well have been used for the purpose. The argument is that at the present state of our archaeological knowledge, there is as yet no *absolute* case for iron technology effecting the clearance of forests even at the earlier NBP Ware levels of culture.

The same seems to have been the case in regard to the assumption of *extensive* plough cultivation, sort of agricultural operations which could provide sufficient surplus for bringing about a new social phenomenon, namely, that of urbanization. It may not escape one's notice that in the two lists given above hoes and spades are all but constant; indeed, almost all the sites have yielded hoes, both at PG and NBP Ware levels, the latter levels yielding sickles as well. There cannot be, therefore, any doubt that hoe-cultivation was relatively the more universal method of agricultural operation. And if tradition can be relied upon, a tradition that persists even today in many heavy flood-washed, rain-fed low-lying regions of the country, wooden ploughs must also have been in use. Can we then, in the absence of any find of an iron plough-share, assume that there was the sort of *extensive* agricultural operations we have been speaking of, knowing fully well that the instruments of hoe and wooden plough cannot achieve that sort of extension ? Assuming that even such instruments could, would we be right in arguing still that it was iron technology which did it ? Assuming further, for argument's sake, that hoe and wooden plough cultivation aided by other iron implements like spade and sickle, for instance, could achieve increased production, can we argue that production would increase to such an extent as to leave a surplus which could provide the new social phenomenon of urbanization?

I am quite conscious that there is in archaeology as in many other areas of empirical knowledge, something called accidence of discovery, especially when there has been no horizontal—large or small-scale—excavation carried out as yet. Had there been a few at least of such excavations, we would have perhaps found the tools and implements, the absence of which I have been using as an argument against large-scale forest clearance, extensive iron-plough cultivation and consequent urbanization. I do not deny the validity of such an objection. But what I have summarized in the above two lists happens to be the yield of about two scores of vertical diggings spread over the entire Ganga-Yamuna valley, not merely the Ganga basin, the totality of which should afford us a fair idea of a wide horizontal area in the region just referred to. Besides, it is the typology of the tools and implements, which is a disturbing element to me. Insofar as this particular region is concerned, this typology is not fundamentally one which we can associate with large-scale forest clearance and large-scale agriculture. Indeed, it is one of a *jana*-life and economy which is struggling to make a break through towards a wider and more meaningful life and economy.

A careful look at the two lists compiled above, would show that by far the larger number of iron implements are those which were presumably used for hunting and warfare: arrow-heads, spear-heads, daggers, big knives etc., and these, from both PG and NBP ware levels. There can be no doubt that hunting was still one of the means of livelihood. But the use of offensive iron implements in *jana*-warfare, which were not too infrequent, if one has to go by the evidence of the *jātaka*-stories and of early Buddhist texts, must have given a sharper and superior edge to certain *jana*-states over certain others, which seems to have had some effect on the existing political order. The reduction of the sixteen *mahājanapadas* in *c.* 600 B.C. to four, and then from four to one by *c.* 321 B.C., that is, the gradual formation from smaller *jana*-states to larger and larger states, may not have been altogether without relatively better and more effective use of iron implements of warfare. Indeed, personally I feel that iron technology did play a relatively more decisive role in state formation in India during these formative three centuries.

Considering the items of finds listed above, none would deny that by far the larger part of India had by atleast about 600 B.C., if not earlier, all but emerged from a bronze/chalcolithic to an iron-age culture. Apart from the finds of iron tools and implements, a couple of sites or more have provided evidence of smelting and manufacturing of iron objects from Ujjayini and Jaderua for instance, both in the Madhya Pradesh of today. At the former place the industry seems to have been fairly at a high level and relates itself to the period ranging from *c.* 500 to 200 B.C. and later. At Jaderua, it is related to the mid-NBP Ware level. Copper and bronze had not altogether gone out of use but these were fast being replaced from *c.* 800 B.C. by iron. This does not however necessarily mean that products of iron technology were being used, if one has to go by the evidence of finds, for the very fundamental functions of society, that is, for increasing economic production which, in the given social situation, could primarily be in the field of agriculture, and only secondarily, in that of certain crafts which were ancilliary to agriculture, the craft of the *kammāra,* for instance. The tools and implements found seem to indicate, more or less clearly, that these were meant for hunting and warfare and for certain domestic purposes. All this means that right up to the end of the upper NBP Waie levels which I would date *c.* 320 B.C., iron technology was not being made adequate use of for any purpose which could bring out any *effective* social change, either in terms of the social structure or even in those of traditional living and behaviour pattern. The fact that Ktesas who lived in the court of Iran in the 5th century B,C. testifies to his being presented with two swords of Indian steel by the Iranian King and his mother, or that Alexander, after his victory over Porus of Taxila in *c.*326 B.C. received from Porus, according to Curtius, a gift of 100 talents (or 30 lbs.) of steel, may prove an advanced stage of iron metallurgy *in the Indus valley and further west* even in pre-Maurya times, but does not alter the hinter-Indian social situation, not in the Ganga-Yamuna valley at any rate. I should therefore think that for the rise of such critical and protestant movements in northern Bihar as Buddhism, Jainism and Ajivikism, for instance, one must look for other reason or reasons than what one finds in the evidence of iron technology as provided for us by hinter-Indian archaeology to date. Incidentally, in regard to *ahiṁsā,* one may not forget that the Buddha himself or the monks of his order, nothing to speak of his lay disciples, were not vegetarians; indeed they were meat-eaters, but they did not *themselves* kill animals for eating. The Theravadins of Burma and Thailand are meat-eaters even today.

3

I have been hinting that from about 320 B.C. or slightly earlier times, that is, from the mid-levels of NBP Ware culture, archaeologically speaking, the situation may have taken a turn for better and more effective use of iron technology, in terms of both quantity and quality. I must confess, I have no direct archaeological evidence to prove this hypothesis; whatever evidence I should be putting forward is, frankly speaking, circumstantial.

What was the metal of the tools and implements that cut out the huge blocks of stone from the hills of Chunar and then shaped and formed the more than forty feet or thereabout monolithic pillars and their capitals which the Mauryas chose to set up ? What was again the metal of the tools and implements that were used to dig out the caves in the Barabar and Nagarjuna hills of Gaya ? Was it bronze/copper that went into the making of the heavy hammers and axes, chisels and borers etc. which must have been necessary for the purpose ? Or, was it iron? One can argue : if the ancient Egyptians could dress their huge boulders of stone and build their pyramids with bronze tools and implements, so could the Mauryas, their pillars and caves, especially when we have the evidence of the copper (not iron) bolt which used to join the capital with the shaft of the Maurya pillars. Yes, it could be bronze or copper. But I would dare suggest that the metal was iron. Why ?

The argument lies in the story of the archaeology of iron in western Asia, especially in Syria, Mesopotamia, Palestine, Iran and the Caucasian world. Since this story is more or less well-known to all professional archaeologists, I reed not refer to any detail except to the fact that all indications of the introduction of iron technology into India are from the direction of western Asia, and this introduction seems to have taken place some time between 1200 and 1000 B.C.[1] That we do not find any tools and implements earlier than 1000 or 900 B.C. may well be explained by the hypothesis that it took some time to locate the iron ores and gain some initial experience of smelting the ore and forging the tools and implements. A second wave of impetus must have also come from West Asia, from Iran and Iraq in particular, which was the heart of the Achaemenid empire, but this wave seems to have been kept confined to India west of the Indus, which was the easternmost, the twentieth, satrapy of the vast, sprawling Achaemenian empire, the largest and the most powerful one of the ancient world. This presumably explains the rich find of the largest assemblage of iron tools and implements anywhere found in India at the early NBP Ware levels, that is, about 600–500 B.C. at Taxila, including the javelin, the straight-bladed and tanged dagger, the elephant goad, the socketed axe, the socketed and plain hoe and the blacksmiths anvil. Still there was a third wave, this time borne on the shoulders of the Hellenistic Greeks led by Alexander of Macedon who had already imbibed the accumulated knowledge of the Achaemenids, including presumably the advanced knowledge and experience of iron technology. That the Mauryas, even presumably from the time of Chandragupta, learnt and put to effective use this advanced iron technology, does not seem to me to be at all imporbable in the context of what we know already of Maurya court culture and

[1]For a short summary and discussion of the archaeological situation in West Asian countries in this regard, see Banerjee, *op. cit* chap. 5.

the impact on it of Achaemenian-Hellenistic cultures.[1] Once this is recognized, one can easily explain the increasing finds of iron tools and implements from the mid and later NBP Ware levels, and may not therefore feel amazed to be told that the repertoire of iron tools and implements may have included heavy iron axes, hammers, chisels and borers etc., even in the Ganga-Yamuna valley, though we have not yet found them. In In a hypothetical social situation of this kind iron plough-share and extensive agricultural operations could not have been distant possibilities. Or, otherwise one would find it difficult to explain what Kauṭilya in his *Arthaśāstra* says about the state departments of agriculture, mining and metallurgy and many other allied activities of the state. The evidence of classical sources too are not only pertinent in this regard, but highly suggestive; indeed, they supplement what Kauṭilya testifies to. It is inconceivable that the *jana*-states of *c.*600–500 B.C. like those of Kāsī, Kosala or Avanti, for instance, had state departments of agriculture, mining and metallurgy which Kauṭilya presumably attributes to the Mauryas.

4

How does one then explain the raising and rearing up of such urban centres as Śrāvastī and Vaiśalī, Kauśāmbī and Kāśī, Rājagṛiha and Ujjayinī, for instance, centres which are supposed to have been in existence in pre-Maurya times, if not from the time of the Buddha himself, the supposition being based on the evidence of early Buddhist canonical and non-canonical texts ? Apart from the argument that all such texts in their extant versions are later than even immediately post-Christian, I am somewhat sceptical about the testimony of these texts in regard to the general picture of these cities which the texts rear up as belonging to the time of the Buddha or even to the two or three centuries which immediately followed. This scepticism originates from the archaeological evidence of the historical period we have before us in regard to the centres referred to above.

Of these urban centres Vārānasī-Kāśī and Rājagṛiha are perhaps the oldest; indeed, these are the two oldest city sites of *historical* times. Traditionally Vārāṇasī-Kāśī has a hoary antiquity as a religious and piligrim centre and hence as a centre of trade and commerce, but the excavations at Rajghat have not laid bare any significant material object which is pre-Maurya. Rājagṛiha, the capital of Bimbisāra and Ajātaśatru, provides the archaeological picture of a hill-girt wide enclosure with massive but shoddy earth-and-rubble fortifications and gates along the entrance-side. Trial digging at places did not reveal anything here which could not be related to any *jana*-settlement of the times. Indeed, Rājagṛiha of the sixth-fifth century B.C. presents the picture of what the capital city of any *jana*-kingdom was like in those days. The excavations at Śravastī and Vaiśālī have revealed nothing to show that they were pre-Maurya *cities*. And whatever remains of proto-historic chalcolithic cultures may have been yielded by the excavations at Kauśāmbī, the site has not yielded anything which one can definitely ascribe to pre-Maurya times. In regard to Ujjayinī, however, the evidence is somewhat doubtful. A circular structure of dressed stone uncovered here, has been ascribed to the pre-Maurya level along with certain other associated objects among which iron figures. Personally, I feel somewhat suspicious, for the simple reason that I have not yet come across anywhere in Indian archaeology, the sort of dressed stone which the Ujjayinī structure is made of, and which can be said to belong to a pre-Maurya date. Be that as it may, the importance of Ujjayinī as a *city*, despite its being once the capital of the *jana*-settlement of Avantī in *c.* 600 B.C., did indeed become effective only when Aśoka or his grand-father Chandragupta made it one of the most important centres of their provincial administration.

What I have said above in general is presumably true of all the other city centres mentioned in early Buddhist literature as belonging to the time of the Buddha and the centuries that immediately followed, for the simple reason that the Ganga-Yamuna valley, particularly the Ganga basin with which this note is immediately concerned, was still (that is, between *c.* 600 and *c.* 350 B.C.) in a *jana*-stage of socio-political development, passing through a long and arduous process of state formation.

But let me put what I am aiming at in a proper historical perspective.

Let us remind ourselves that the Buddha did never stir himself beyond what is now known as the Nepalese *terai*, Bihar and eastern Uttar Pradesh; his immediate and the next generation of his disciples too, are not known to have gone further beyond. The farthest point towards the west the Buddha had ever been to and spent some time seems to have been the Ghoshitārāma *vihāra* at Kauśāmbī. Indeed, whatever dependable evidence pointing to pre-Maurya times we have at our disposal, seems to indicate that the *saddharma* or the *āryasatya* which he propounded and preached, was for a very long time, presumably for a couple of centuries or more, a purely *jana* faith and behaviour pattern confined to small communities of monks scattered over a limited area extending from Bihar in the east

[1] Niharranjan Ray *Maurya and Post-Maurya Art,* 3rd. edn., Indian Council of Historical Research, New Delhi. 1975.

to about Allahabad in the west and stretching as far north as the foot-hills of the eastern and central Himalayas. Not until the great Aśoka Maurya sat on the imperial throne of Pāṭalīputra, became eventually a lay but firm and devoted follower of the faith and took upon himself the task of spreading the universal ethical message of the great master, which he carried out with all the skill, power and organization he could command as the most powerful emperor in the contemporary civilized world, was this local monkish faith and behaviour pattern raised from a simple and local *jana* existence to the status of a national and international socio-religious movement. This was indeed the beginning of Buddhism as a world religion. But to come back to our point. As a confirmed devotee Aśoka seems to have gone out on a pilgrimage as it were to atleast a few of those places which were hallowed and sanctified by their association with the lives and activities of the Buddha himself and his immediate disciples; at these places which were considered sacred he raised *stambhas* and *stūpas,* a fact which is well-known, thus adding to many such *stambhas* and *stūpas* which must have been in existence even before his time, as monuments that marked spots considered sacred. Many of these places must have been, at the time of the Buddha and much later too, just *gāmas* or *mahāgāmas* or at the most, agglomerated and fortified *jana*-settlements or *nigamas*, situated within realms which were headed by *jana*-kings or chieftains. One may remind oneself that even Pāṭalīputra was Patalīgama in the Buddha's time, and so it remained perhaps till the time of the Nandas or, may be, till Chandragupta Maurya. Lumbinī, the birth-place of the Buddha, which could not have been away from the Sākya city of Kapilavastu, was just Lumminīgāma even in Aśoka's time. It is not unlikely that the raising of a few such *gāmas*, *mahāgāmas* and *nigamas* or agglomerated *jana*-settlements (like the one at Rājagṛiha) as were hallowed by their association with the Buddha and his immediate disciples, to city centres, may have been due first to Chandragupta's imperial design and later to Aśoka's pilgrimage to those places. Such pilgrimage centres were perhaps the cities of Srāvastī and Vaiśalī, Kauśambī and Saṅkāsya, for instance. But cities as a social phenomenon cannot be sustained by just the will, volition and direction of an individual, not even of the power and personality of a Chandragupta or an Aśoka Maurya. There must have been weightier social reasons for the phenomenon of urbanization during and after the time of the Mauryas.

Even at the time of Chandragupta Maurya, iron technology must have made itself felt in the society in a relatively bigger way, and by Aśoka's time it must have become a part of Indian life. The process of state formation which had commenced three centuries earlier, had reached its zenith; indeed here was now an imperial, highly centralized, autocratically governed state with far-flung international contacts. Political and economic organization and administration had reached an efficiency which the earlier *jana*-kingdoms or republics knew nothing of, neither in intention nor in extension, and trade, commerce and industry, a net-work which covered a very large part of the country.

The process seems to have started from the time of the Nandas of Magadha in *c.* 400 B.C. It is well recognized that when Alexander's army advanced up to the western banks of the Beas, the Nanda King who sat on the throne of Magadh was presumably Mahāpadmananda who lorded it over Prasioi (Prāchya) and Gangaridae (Gangarāshṭra ?). It seems that the Nanda kingdom extended practically all over the Ganga and Yamuna valleys, westwards right up to the great divide of northern India. If the *Purāṇas* are to be believed the Nandas were immensely rich having amassed huge fortunes; one of their kings was known as Dhanananda. And Alexander's historians and geographers say that they had a huge, powerful army. How did they become so rich and powerful ? Presumably through the participation of their realm in the trade and commerce which was slowly but surely opening up from *c.* 600–550 B.C. in response to the demands of the Achaemenids for such mineral products (among other things) as iron (in the form of iron ores), textiles, ivory and perhaps also precious stones. This trade seems to have been carried on along a trade-route glimpses of which one finds in early canonical and non-canonical Buddhist texts, the route issuing out of, say, Rājagṛiha, passing through Pāṭaliputra, Vaiśāli, Bhandagāma, Hatthigama, Pava, Kusinagara, Kapilvastu, Setavya and Sāvatthi, and thence along the foot hills through the plains of the Panjab to Gandhara in the extreme north-west. It is significant that the route ran through the plains lying along the foot-hills of the Himalayas before it crossed the eastern tributaries of the Indus, and then passing through Pushkalāvati (Peukalaotis), Śakalapuram (Sagala, Sialkot), Takshaśilā (Taxila) and Purushapura (Peshāwar), joined the trans-Asian trade-route somewhere near Kabul, which took one, in stages, right up to the trade centres of the eastern Mediterranean. This seems to have been the route, a good hinter-Indian part of which lay through the oligarchical *jana*-states of the Himalayan *terai* and then through the similar non-monarchical and monarchical states of the Punjab and the North-west, which were made use of by pre-Maurya India to enable her derive some benefit from the Indo-West Asian trade of the times, but only as a secondary or passive partner. But when the Mauryas consolidated their all-India empire and in the process, placed themselves in touch with their contemporaries in West Asia, the small doors and windows were widened up for direct insemination by other cultures than their own. All these inter-dependent and inter-related activities and achievements called necessarily for a wide net-work of roads, towns and cities of varoius nature and character. This was indeed the time when there was a real meaningful quickening of the life-process, the like of which one does not see at any other time between 600 and 320 B.C. or thereabout. This quickened life-process in which iron technology seems to have played a significant role, was really the time for the generation of economic surplus and hence of a new social phenomenon of urbanization.

For a better appreciation of what I have just said as briefly as I could, I would invite attention to a comparative study of what one reads of in early Buddhist texts and sees at Rājagṛiha, a city of the Buddha's time, the capital of the Magadhan kings, Bimbisāra and Ajātaśatru, on the one hand, and of Pāṭaliputra, the capital of Chandragupta, Bindusāra and Aśoka, in the contemporary or near-contemporary accounts left by Greek historians and geographers and in the excavations of Bulandibagh and Kumrahar on the other. To do this objectively and at the same time with some amount of imagination that helps historical reconstruction, is to have two altogether different historical perceptions. Indeed, as one does it, one experiences the wide gulf in terms of urbanization, which differentiates, quantitatively and qualitatively, Pāṭaliputra from Rājagṛiha. Here then is the index of the change in the politico-economic and the socio-cultural situation in India of the Ganga-Yamuna valley, from the pre-Maurya (*c.* 600-500 B.C.) to the Maurya (*c.* 320 B.C.) times. Not a little of this enormous change has to be attributed, to my mind, to the third wave of iron-technology which entered India borne on the shoulders of Alexander and his historical legatees, not on a particular date but spread over a generation or more.

To sum up: Iron makes its appearance in the Ganga-Yamuna valley in association with PG Ware culture, in *c.* 900B.C. (Atranjikhera); in the Indus valley however, it may have manifested itself a century earlier. In the former region its occurrence in association with PG Ware continues till *c.* 600 B.C. when it is seen in association with NBP Ware culture. At the PG Ware culture stage the iron tools and implements are mostly such as were presumably used in hunting and warfare; the tools and implements which were evidently used for agricultural purposes were hoes and spades with which no large-scale extensive agricultural operation could be possible, and hence no urbanization. Iron in association with NBP wares continues to occur till *c.* 200 B.C., and even later. At this stage too, the tools and implements were mostly for hunting and warfare and a couple or two for domestic and small-scale agricultural purposes. It seems, therefore, that at the present state of our archaeological knowledge we cannot attribute large-scale forest clearance and agricultural operations in the Ganga-Yamuna valley to iron technology, though one cannot deny that the region had definitely entered into the iron age since bronze and copper were fast being replaced. But neither quantitatively nor qualitatively the technology was so advanced and diversified as to bring about significant social change, in the Ganga-Yamuna valley at any rate.

But finds at the NBP Ware levels at Taxila, read along with the evidence of the pre-NBP Ware Gandhara graves, seem to indicate that the Indus valley and the region further west were experiencing a somewhat more advanced knowledge and practice of iron technology, from *c.*900 B.C. onwards, which may have been percolating, slowly but steadily, further east, so that by the time of the Nandas, *c.* 400 B.C., the Ganga-Yamuna valley too, began to have some share of the Indus valley experience. But a much more decided advance in iron technology seems to have been made in the Ganga-Yamuna valley itself as elsewhere in the country, when the Mauryas established their empire and brought India into direct contact with the countries in West Asia. It was only then that iron technology could come into full play.

NIHARRANJAN RAY

C-1/, Green Park Extension
New Delhi, 110016

Ancient Gold Workings: Some New ^{14}C Dates

INTRODUCTION

The ear-rings from Tekklakota,[1] the rich jewellery from the Indus sites and such other finds prove beyond doubt that gold has been in use in India right from the neolithic and Harappan times. Though Maclaren, Munn and Foote have reported several ancient workings from Mysore, there were no ^{14}C dates for the famous Kolar

[1]M.S. Nagaraj Rao, *The Stone Age Hill Dwellers Tekkalakota* Poona, 1965), p. 75.

fields so far. We report below the first ^{14}C dates from Kolar gold fields and give a brief review of the geological and archaeological evidence.

GEOLOGICAL OF THE GOLD-BEARING AREA

Gold deposits in India have all along been associated with Sugriva land, consisting of the continental nucleus in Mysore which is composed of the most ancient rocks in India. The gold reefs occur at Kolar, Hutti, Wainad in Mysore and Ramagiri in District Anantapur, Andhra Pradesh. The area is surrounded by peninsular gneisses intersected by basic dykes. Two main types of lodes are found: the quartz lode consists of gold along with galena, pyrrhotite, chalcopyrite, etc. The sulphide lode comprises of gold with pyrrohitite, chalcopyrite, minor galena, etc.

ARCHAEOLOGICAL HISTORICAL EVIDENCE

Allchin in his note on the Mysore gold mines has given extensive evidence of the old workings[1]. Munn[2] and Foote[3] have described the contrivances used to extract gold from the reefs. Iron gauges, crucibles, stone crushers and windlashes appear to be the main equipment.

Near Kolar, some prominent ancient gold mining activity has been traced at Sonnahalli, 29 km south-west of Mysore, at Bellibetta, 32 km north-west of Serignapatam, Kempinakota, 72 km north-west of Mysore, Woolagiri, 32 km south, south-west of Mysore, etc.

In the Raichur *doab,* Hutti and Maski have the main gold workings. In fact, the Hutti workings extended to a length of 1600 m and up to a depth of 200 m. How much labour it would have required to excavate so much of hard quartz can only be guessed.

More interesting is the fact that Aśoka's five rock edicts are found on sites which are located in the gold-bearing fields. "The Minor Rock Edict at Maski is actually on the gold fields: the two Koppal edicts are no more than 30 miles from Gadag band of gold mines; the three at Brahmagiri are equally near to several mines in north Mysore and Sandur; while the other two sites of inscriptions at Yerragudi and near Pattikonda are in the centre of country long famous for its diamonds". The importance of the gold field seems to have been recognized from the Neolithic times, as major neolithic sites like Piklihal, Kotekal, Maski, etc., are found to cluster around the Maski gold fields.[4]

^{14}C DATES

Table 1 gives ^{14}C dates for Kolar gold mines. For the two dates from Hutti, the lab nos. and the half-life used are not indicated. We presume them to be based on 5568 yrs. half-life value of radiocarbon, and have converted them to 5730 yrs. value. (These dates, however, don't find mention in the New Zealand Date Lists I to IV published in *Radiocarbon*, 1963, pp. 118-162).

TABLE 1

^{14}C DATES OF MYSORE GOLD WORKINGS

Site	Sample No.	Locus	^{14}C dates in B.P. base on 5730 yrs.
1. Kolar	TF 1199*	Superficial excavations	1290 ± 90
2. "	TF 879*	Champion reef 50 m depth	1500 ± 115
3. Hutti	S.No. 1	Oakley's shaft 80 m depth	1945 ± 70
4. Hutti	S.No. 2	"	1865 ± 70

The ^{14}C dates in Table 1 show that Kolar gold fields were being exploited from the fifth century A.D. The Hutti mining activity goes back to the beginning of Christian Era.

It will be interesting to explore and date other shafts to locate the neolithic mining activity and to determine if gold was being exported from the neolithic sites to the Harappan centres.

Physical Research Laboratory Ahmedabad, 380009 *and Archaeological Survey of India, Baroda.*

D.P. AGRAWAL AND C. MARGABAND

[1] F.R. Allchin, 'Upon the antiquity and methods of gold mining in ancient India', *Journal of Economic and Social History of the Orient*, Vol. V, Pl. II (1962) pp. 195-211.

[2] L. Munn, *J. Hyderabad Geol. Survey*, Vol. II, PL.1 (1934) pp. 77-104 .

[3] R.B.Foote, as quoted by Allchin, *op. cit.* (1962).

[4] Allchin, *op. cit.*, (1962), p. 209.

*Samples received from Kolar Gold Mining Undertaking.

Comments on Subsistence Pattern of an Early Farming Community of Western India

The excellent paper by Dhavalikar and Possehl[1] is important from two angles. First, it is the only study of its kind in so far as Indian archaeology is concerned, and as such breaks a new ground. Second, by treating the subsistence patterns of the early farming communities, the authors have addressed themselves to the wider perspective emphasized in Binford's words, "the reconstruction of past lifeways" and in this way they have brought their study in line with the modern trends. The paper shows how far the right handling of archaeological data is of determinative value. So far it is customary of Indian archaeology to have Eiffel towers of artifactual typologies and taxonomies in a harshly debilitating framework of space-time continuum. An obstinate preoccupation with chronologically oriented, tailor's dummy-like excavations have led to stereotyped explanations for various aspects of cultural development and transformation. However, while the paper has everything to commend itself, there are a few points that ought not escape comment.

To begin with, the authors have relied too much in their various calculations pertaining to the subsistance analysis on modern data. While analogical approach is in itself useful, it has its limitations as there is always the danger of introducing dimensions which might not have originally existed. Not necessarily the early farming communities practised the same mode of agriculture as are followed today. The yield might have fluctuated from soil to soil, field to field and season to season. Even the soil which goes by the common name of 'black' has a differential rate of yield. Secondly, the role of calories from the hunted animal has been played down on the assumption that the hunting season corresponded with the period of agricultural activities. It, however, needs to be pointed out that more than grains, meat is valued for its fat that has concentrated calorie content. True, not enough food could have been made available for the consumption of all the inhabitants, yet a portion of population could well have survived on the supply even of a very limited nature. Therefore, to this end if some and not all persons devoted their time, is not entirely an unlikely hypothesis. Moreover, the marine food has through the centuries remained a most reliable source of food supply, and for those settlements like Inamgaon, which are situated on the banks of rivers, its importance can hardly be overstated. The authors' excessive emphasis on carbohydrates (grains) has, therefore, led to the calculation of inflated needs and naturally they are at a loss to explain why a stretch of territory extending for thirty-two km should be needed to feed a population of a thousand souls. The authors have also forgotten to mention that the agricultural byproducts in the form of grain husks, leaves and stems after the harvests may provide a good amount of food to the cattle, thus considerably cutting down the acreage assigned to grow fodder. Thirdly, on the basis of mud houses at Inamgaon, the authors have concluded that the occupation of the site was seasonal and the resultant transhumance foi almost half of the year took the inhabitants to the Western Ghats. This, however, is overstating the case. If the same criterion is applied to the West Asian sites at the same stage of economic life with more or less same mode of house construction, it would seem that sedenterism was comparatively a recent and wholly urban phenomenon. However, the available evidence points to the contrary and there are reasons to believe that sedenterism at least in south-west Asia might have preceded the stage of effective food production. To add to this, transhumance involves particular settlement pattern comprising distribution loci of short duration. This, the authors should have taken note of before forming their hypothesis of seasonality. The fact establiahed by them that the black soil can be worked without iron implements contrary to general notion is doubtless of importance. Does this fact, however, indicate that wooden plough and its accessories of either wood or stone were irrelevant to the black soil agriculture?

In the end it needs to be pointed out that while it is easy to comment on the study like this, it need not obscure the inherent difficulties fraught in the formation of valid conclusions. It can be said to the credit of authors that their paper is indeed harbinger of a new atmosphere across the threshold of India's archaeology.

1. M.K. Dhavalikar and Gregory L. Po.sehl, 'Sabsistence Pattern of an Early Farming Community of western India', *Puratattva*, no. 7, pp 39-46

Department of Archaeology
Government of Gujarat, Bhuj

Y.M. CHITALWALA

A Note on the Antiquity of Seal

It is generally thought that in early Vedic literature we hardly have any word to denote seal' or the mode of stamping with a seal. The Harappan sites however have yielded examples of seals and seal impressions.

Attention is drawn here to a passage in the *Rigveda* which sheds some welcome light on this otherwise obscure problem. The particular stanza runs as follows : *indrāvishnū havishā vāvṛidhānāgrādvānā namasā rātahavyā'ghritāsutī dravinaṁ dhattamasme sạmudrah sthah kalash somachanānı*/RV. VI 69.6.

Its translation as given by H.H. Wilson[1] and R.T.H. Griffith[2] is quoted below. "Indra and Vishṇu, feeders upon clarified butter, drinkers of the fermented *Soma*, thriving upon oblations, accepting them offered with reverence, bestow upon us wealth, for you are an ocean, a pitcher, the receptacle of the libation.

"Strengthend with sacred offerings, Indra-Vishnu, first eaters, served with worship and oblations.

Fed with the holy oil, vouchsafe us riches : ye are the lake, the vat that holds the Soma."

The above rendering closely follows the commentary of Sāyaṇa. However, the scholars interpret the last *pāda* of the stanza in an incongruous manner. The two deities Indra and Vishṇu are addressed in dual but the words taken to stand for their metaphorical analogy are in singular.

However, we propose to differ from the traditional interpretation under question. To us this last portion of the stanza appears to denote a pot containing riches which are sought in the preceding statement to be bestowed by the two gods upon tbe votary. Thus, it seems to imply a *somadhāna kalasa* which is (properly) placed (*sthah*), and is (properly) "sealed" (*samudrah*). The last phrase *samudra* is, to my mind, to be understood as *mudrāsahitah* or *mudrā-yuktah* ; i.e. having a seal or *mudrā*. And it is quite possible that here we have an early mention of 'seal' by the word *mudrā*.

1. H. H. Wilson, *Rigveda Translation*, vol. IV, p. 113 (reprint, Poona, 1927).
2. R. T. H. Griffith, *The Hymns of the Rigveda*, Benares, 1896, vol. I, p. 642.

Amethi Kathi Nagwa, Varanasi P.K. AGRAWAL

Origin of the Form of Harappa Culture : a New Proposition

To most of us the origin of the *form* of the Harappa Culture as evidenced in twin-mound system, grid pattern of town-planning, writing, etc., is still shrouded in mystery. To some, 'it is the Cinderella of the ancient world.' Thapar has stated this commonly held view in one of his recently published papers where he has again asked the field archaeologists to find out the place where the actual form of the Harappa Culture developed first; his own feeling is that this place lies below the exposed levels of Mohenjodaro.[1] He also feels that although the mature form of this culture is now known to us, 'the dynamics of this culture still remains to be determined.,[2] The present paper proposes to deal with these two questions afresh.

In 1964, A. Ghosh, for the first time, hinted at the possibility of the origin of the Harappa Cnlture in the Kot Diji-Sothi matrix.[3] In 1970, Mughal thoroughly analysed this possibility in his Ph. D. thesis.[4] As a result of these two attempts most of us have conceded at least this much that the Kot Diji-Sothi complex provided a strong base, achieved by a long process of evolution. Therefore, what has been really mysterious to us is not so much the origin of the basic form of Harappa Culture but the suddenness with which it appears on the so-called pre-Harappan sites.

To us, some of the important Kot Diji-Sothi settlements, such as Kot Diji and Kalibangan' with the elaborate fortifications, use of copper-bronze technology, a variety of wheel-made plain and painted pottery' etc.,[6] appear as the 'First Cities' in India'. They

1. B. K. Thapar, "New Traits of the Indus Civilization at Kalibangan", *South Asian Archaeology* (Duckworth, London 1973) pp. 85; 91-92.
2. *Ibid.*, p. 85
3. A. Ghosh, "The Indus Civilization: Its Origin, Authors, Extent and Chronology", in *Indian Prehistory: 1964* (Deccan College, Poona, 1965) pp. 113-156.
4. M. R. Mughal, *The Early Harappan Period in the Greater Indus Valley and Northern Baluchisten* (c. 3000-2400 B. C.) (Unpub'ished Ph. D. Thesis, University of Pennsylxania, 1970)
6. B. K. Thapar, "Kalibangan : A Harappan Metropolis Beyond the Indus Vally", *Expendition*, Vol. 17, No. 2, 1975, pp. 20-23.

had a strong economic base achieved by a well-knit corporate life functioning under some form of political authority, like the *janapadas* or the republics of early historical India.[1] It means that there was both the technical know-how and the social preparedness for any take-off towards a richer and more complex urban set-up; only an opportunity was wanting.

NATURAL CALAMITIES DESTROYED SEVERAL EARLY CITIES

And, to our mind, this much needed opportunity came first to the people of the Sothi Culture in the lower Saraswati basin where natural calamities, such as the tectonic disturbances, destroyed the entire townships, as it happened at Kalibangan.[2] It may be recalled that practically all the major known sites where the Proto-Harappan and Harappan assemblages have been found superimposed, there is a definite evidence of a major calamity. The entire township of Kot Diji[3] was destroyed by fire, so also of Gumla.[4] Balakot[5] has yielded the evidence of a similar kind: probably floods destroyed the Proto-Harappan settlement. The pre-defence settlement of Harappa[6] was also destroyed by floods. To us, all this could not have been coincidences. This has to be interpreted in either of the two ways: (i) that it was the wanton destruction by the Harappan vandals, or (ii) that the destruction was the outcome of natural calamities. In case we accept the first interpretation, we will have to brand the Harappans as the most barbarous people, but hardly is there an example in prehistory to record that a nomadic barbarous group of people planned new cities of the magnitude and complexity of Kalibangan, Harappa and Mohenjodaro. Also, there is no internal evidence of any kind to show that the early Harappans were vandals or barbarous. Contrary to it, there is ample evidence to show that for quite sometime the Proto-Harappans and the Harappans lived together peacefully. At Kalibangan, Harappan and Proto-Harappan antiquities have been recovered from one and the same house.[7] It, however, appears quite probable that earthquake, flood and fire were natural calamities and not man-made conditions. To us, therefore, the opportunity for the creation of the *form* of the Harappa Culture appeared through such calamities—complete destruction of the settlement by natural forces. But, how?

FORCES GENERATED BY NATURAL CALAMITIES

History tells us that calamities of this magnitude themselves generate, almost all of a sudden, a number of new forces and factors which successfully bring about socio-economic changes of vast dimensions. To begin with, they create the problem of rehabilitation out of which grows national leadership. The emancipator, one or a group of a selected few, becomes the hero, and assumes extra privileges of power and prestige. Herein lies the birth of citadel, the home of the emancipator(s) and the place of his (their) day-to-day activities of planning and execution. The point at issue, therefore, is not so much the birth of citadel (it can arise suddenly along with the natural process of 'hero worship' naturally arising in the period of crises) as the identification of the early form and later forms of citadels. To us, the citadel of Kalibangan was more modest in dimensions and contents than the citadels of Harappa and Mohenjodaro. It had only two parts, one containing four to six mud-brick platforms with ritualistic fire-places and the other containing, at the present state of our knowledge, only about half-a-dozen modest houses along a road, while Mohenjodaro had a big granary, a bath, an assembly-hall, a so-called college of priests, etc. Obviously, we visualize the birth of twin-mound system in the lower Saraswati basin, and its later development in the Ravi and Indus plains.

In this connection a very significant evidence has been tentatively recorded by R.S. Bisht at Banawali,[8] located in the Saraswati basin: two parallel mud-brick platforms seem to have been found in the Proto-Harappan levels. If it is confirmed, by further excavations, it might show two things: first, that the system of a variety of monumental structures had started in the Proto-Harappan times; and secondly, the system of raising mud-brick platforms for constructing State Buildings or ritualistic structures had also begun in the Proto-Harappan times; both in the Saraswati basin. As far

[1]R.C. Majumdar (Ed.) *Age of Imperial Unity* (Bhartiya Vidya Bhawan, Bombay 1960) Chapter I, pp. 1-17.

[2]Thapar, in *South Asian Archaeology*, p. 87.

[3]F.A. Khan, 'Excavations at Kot Diji', *Pakistan Archaeology*, no. 2(1965), pp. 11-85.

[4]A.H. Dani, 'Excavations at Gumla', *Ancient Pakistan*, I differ with the excavator's views that the town was destroyed by the fire set by the Harappans.

[5]G.F. Dales, 'Excavations at Balakot, Pakistan, 1973', *Journal of the Field Archaeology*, Vol. I, no. 1/2, 1974, p. 6 and Fig. 5.

[6]R.E.M. Wheeler, 'Harappa 1946', *Ancient India*, no. 3 (1947) pp. 64 and 93.

[7]Ghosh, *op. cit.*, p. 117.

[8]R.S. Bisht, Cyclostyled copy of a note issued at the time of a Special Exhibition organized at Purana Qila, New Delhi, on the occasion of the meeting of the Central Advisory Board of Archaeology in November 1974.

as the town-planning on grid pattern is concerned, to us even this has the beginning in the Saraswati basin since the 'lower-town' at Kalibangan was certainly not as well-planned as at Mohenjodaro—the roads were not aligned with the fortification walls and the blocks were also not at all symmetrical. According to Thapar, 'the plan of the Harappan fortification followed the plan of the pre-Harappan fortification while the roads followed a new plan'.[1] Why did it happen like this? Obviously, because here was the transition from the Sothi planning to the Harappan planning, a halting process indeed! Nothing of the kind is witnessed either at Harappa or Mohenjodaro; they were very well planned, and planned from the very beginning. Of course, additions and alterations did takepl ace later on.

THE PROBLEM OF THE ORIGIN OF THE HARAPPAN SCRIPT

About script, the less said the better. Script is always an artificial creation for some specific purpose. In China, it arose out of the requirements of the priests, in Mesopotamia for keeping records of the tributes and taxes, and in India, possibly, primarily for stamping bales of goods meant for export. It may grow slowly or swiftly, change quickly or remain static: the Orient gives examples of all kinds. It appears that the Harappan script grew as quickly as the Mauryan Brahmi script, just within a generation or two, without leaving behind the evidence of any so-called formative stage. It remained almost static, somewhat similar to the Chinese script which grew in comparative isolation. We very much doubt if the individual signs, sometimes in groups of two, found on pottery at Amri and a few other Proto-Harappan sites were really parental to the Harappan script, although Lal has put forward this hypothesis in a recently published paper.[2] The Harappan script was never the potter's list of marks; pots during the Harappan times, were not inscribed in a regular fashion. It was, in fact, like the *Mudiya* script of some north Indian merchant groups, evolved by the merchants and for the merchants. The Harappan script, therefore, appears to have been born with the upsurge of the Harappan trade, and it died out with the decline of the Harappan trade. Sporadically, some intelligent potters or copper-smiths also used it, but this was never the regular practice.

[1]Thapar, *op. cit.*, p. 98.
[2]Lal, B.B., "Some Aspects of the Archaeological Evidence Relating to the Indus Script", *Puratattva*, no. 7 (1974), pp. 20-24.

HARAPPAN SOCIAL IDEOLOGY

As far as the Harappan social ideology is concerned, to us it appears that the Harappan ideology was basically mercantile, somewhat analogous to that of the Britishers in the nineteenth and early twentieth centuries. It does not seem to be a priest-ridden society with any extra-mundane social ideology. The absence of elaborate temple architecture and Mother Goddess figurines at sites other than Harappa, Mohenjodaro and Chanhudaro, and comparative rarity of the mythological representations, such as the so-called 'Paśupati' and the 'assembly of priests', and of the ritualistic structures, such as the Great Bath, may indicate that religion was not organized and canonized on a national plane; the pictorial depictions on seals and sealings concerned mainly the local folk-lore and magico-religious practices howsoever popular they might have been. The mercantile ideology is somewhat like the capitalist ideology —people are asked to go for technological advancement and commercial pursuits for producing wealth to lead more and more comfortable life. The phenomenal growth of Mohenjodaro and Harappa as the Great Cities should be viewed in this context. The overall form of the Harappa Culture appears to have been determined by the mercantile ideology whose pace is usually extremely rapid.

ORIGIN OF THE FORM OF THE HARAPPA CULTURE : LOWER SARASWATI BASIN

Our hypothesis is that the *form* of the Harappa Culture originated in the lower Saraswati basin, from where it moved towards the Indus. It is based on two facts: firstly, there is a great concentration of the Sothi sites with Harappan remains in the Saraswati basin, out of about 150 known sites in the Indus System more than fifty sites were located by Stein, Ghosh and others in the old Bahawalpur-Bikaner region alone, and at least three of these are as big as Harappa and Mohenjodaro. Recently, Mughal has re-explored this region and we gather from him that many more sites exist in Bahawalpur region, majority of them being those with Sothi and Harappan remains.[3] Not only that, there are at least two sites which are bigger than Mohenjodaro (and, therefore, may yield better evidence of change from Proto-Harappan to Harappan).[4] Secondly,

[3]Mughal, *op. cit.*, p. 102.
[4]Personal communication from Mughl.

the radiocarbon dates otbained so far, as Mandal[1] has shown, indicate that Harappan Kalibangan and/or a few sites in the Bahawalpur region may be earlier than Harappa and Mohenjodaro. How much earlier we do not know since no samples from the lowest levels of Mohenjodaro have been dated, although in the framework of our theory the difference should not be more than 50 to 100 years.

The trouble is, as Wheeler has rightly observed that urban growth of the Indus kind is usually so sudden and quick that within a generation or two, it may spread over a vast area, but the archaeological tool as applied to our protohistoric sites is too blunt to bring out the evidence of this kind.

AN OBJECTION

An objection may still be raised.[2] How is it that natural calamities occurred simultaneously at so many sites and were followed by basically the same type of town-planning and cultural items which differentiate the Proto-Harappan form of culture from the Harappan There are two points to be clarified in this respect: first, the calamities do not at all seem to have occurred at all the places mentioned above at one and the same time. We do not threrfore visualize any situation which might show that one fine morning the entire Kot Diji-Sothi complex was wiped out only to be replaced by the Harappan complex and, secondly, it is a totally misconceived notion that all the Harappan towns followed the same pattern of planning; Harappa was never identical with Mohenjodaro and Lothal was entirely different from Surkotada and Kalibangan. Once it is clear, it becomes easy to follow our line of approach: the transformation of the Proto-Harappan Culture into the Harappan Culture took place, in all probability, first in the lower Saraswati basin, may be in the Bahawalpur region, as once suggested by Mughal,[3] *primarily* as a result of the challenges thrown by the devastating natural calamities which destroyed one or two of the first cities of the Sothi people While initial experiments in elaborate town-planning, etc., were going on, the Indus System was still in the grip of Proto-Harappan Culture. However, within a generation or two considerable success was achieved which formed a sort of generalized model for others. But this model could not be introduced at all the places at one and the same time; On several occasions the Harappans also occupied virgin lands, but that is a different matter.

This hypothesis completely refutes the theory of Wheeler,[4] Ghosh[5] and others that the genesis of the Harappan urbanism lies in Mesopotamia. It equally refutes the theories of Fairservice[6] and Dales[7] that the origin of the Harappa Culture may eventually be traced in Baluchistan and Afghanistan. It follows to some extent the views propounded by Lamberg-Karlovsky[8] according to which results of the excavations conducted at Tepe Yahya, Shahr-i-Sokhta and other places in south-eastern Iran and Afghanistan, have compelled us to discard, 'both the commitment to a Mesopotamian model of urbanization and the adoption of the diffusion of this model to include the Indus and all intervening areas of the Iraniao plateau."

It also does not subscribe to the opinion given by Dani that one of the coastal Harappan sites holds the key of the problem of the origin of the Harappa Culture. In this respect, at least, the priority of the excavation at Mohenjodaro and Harappa over sites in Bahawalpur—Bikaner region, such as Kalibangan, has been rather unfortunate since the richness of the material that these settlements have yielded often precludes us from thinking afresh on the problem of *first* Harappan cities.

1. D. Mandal, *Radiocarbon Dates and Indian Archaeolagy* (Vaishali publishing House, Allahabad, 1972) He rightly comments: "the latitudinal plotting of these four sets of dates (C 14) demonstrates that they become progressively younger from East to West in the Western Sector, and from north-west to south-east in the Eastern one, ... Does it hint at the direction of the movement of the Harappans and tradition." p. 74.

2. A somewhat similar objection was raised by B. K. Thapar during the discussion on this paper in the Archaeological Conference held in 1975.

3. Mughal, *op. cit.*, pp. 102.

4. R.E.M. Wheeler, *Early India and Paklstan*, (Thames and Hunsom, London 1960) pp. 101-104.

5. Ghosh, *op. clt.*, p. 117.

6. W. A. Fairservice (jr.), *The Roots of Ancieni India*, (George Allen and Unwin, London, 1771) p, 220.

7. G. F. Dales, "Archaeological and Radiocarbon Chronolgies for Protohistoric South Asia", in Hammond (Ed.) *South Asian Archaeology*, pp. 157-170.

8. C. C. Lamberg-Karlovsky, "Urban Interaction on the Iranian Plateau: Excavations at Tepe Yahya 1967-1963", *Proceedings of the British Academy*, No. 59, 1974 pp. 13 ff.

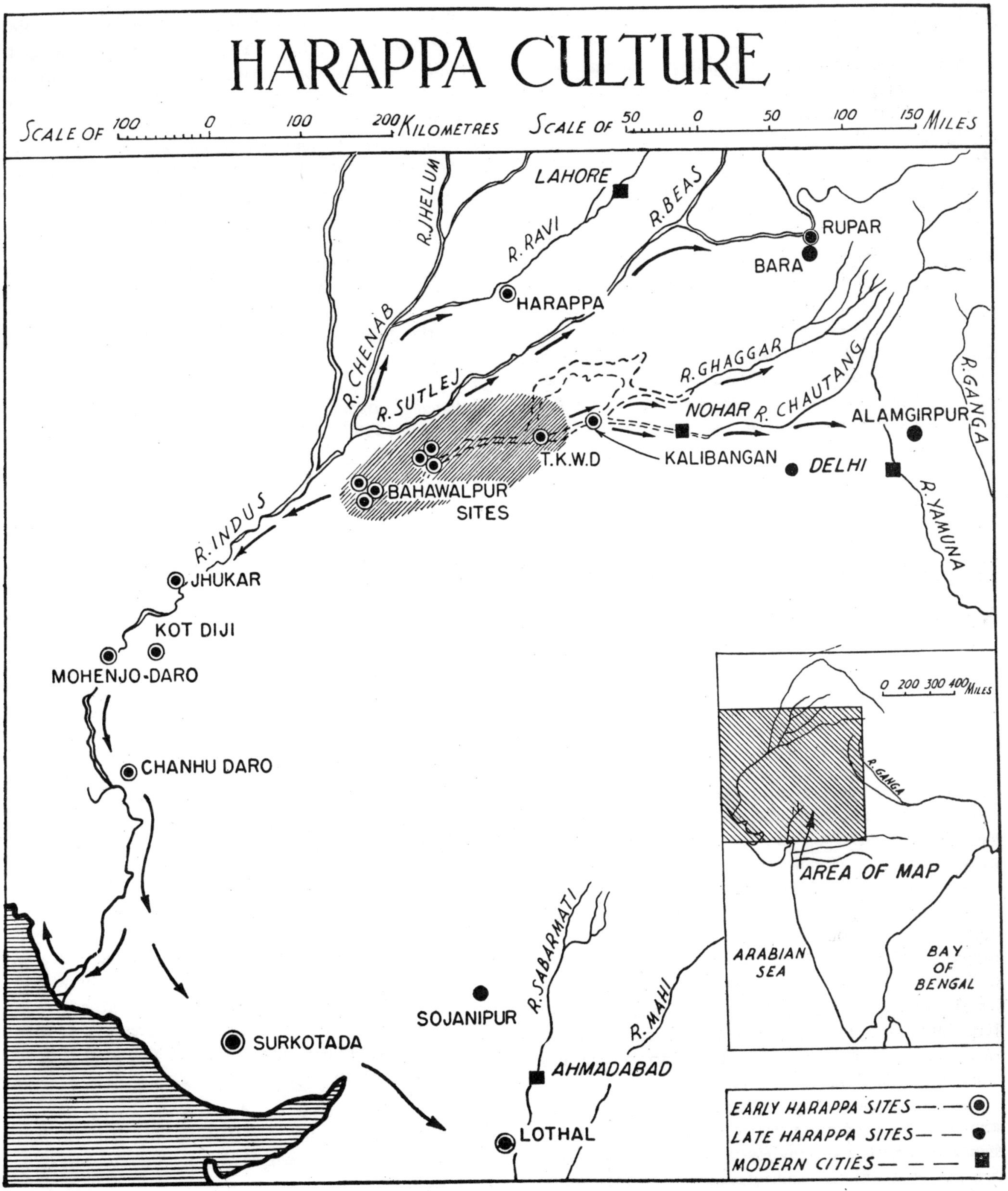
HARAPPA CULTURE
SCALE OF 100 0 100 200 KILOMETRES
SCALE OF 50 0 50 100 150 MILES
LAHORE
R. JHELUM
R. RAVI
R. BEAS
RUPAR
BARA
HARAPPA
R. CHENAB
R. SUTLEJ
R. GHAGGAR
R. CHAUTANG
R. GANGA
NOHAR
ALAMGIRPUR
KALIBANGAN
T.K.W.D
DELHI
BAHAWALPUR SITES
R. YAMUNA
R. INDUS
JHUKAR
KOT DIJI
MOHENJO-DARO
CHANHU DARO
R. SABARMATI
R. MAHI
SOJANIPUR
SURKOTADA
AHMADABAD
LOTHAL
0 200 300 400 MILES
R. GANGA
AREA OF MAP
ARABIAN SEA
BAY OF BENGAL
EARLY HARAPPA SITES
LATE HARAPPA SITES
MODERN CITIES

OUR METHODOLOGY

It may be seen that our methodology combines both the archaeological and anthropological approaches to culture. Thus, although archaeologists define culture as the sum-total of material items (or industries) and the anthropologists contradict them by saying that material-items are the 'products' of culture and not culture itself (culture, according to them, is the sum-total of systems and processes underlying the material items). We feel that in the context of prehistoric societies abstract (systems and processes) can be understood only through the concrete (the material items). The difficulty arises only when we are unable to read the systems and processes through archaeological evidence. We have tried to read them here; how far we have been able to read them correctly, more field work alone will reveal. For the present, we would like to say only this much that the problem of the origin of the *form* of the Harappa Culture is both basic and specific—basic because it involves the problem of 'culture-change', i.e. what factors bring about sudden changes in established patterns of cultures, and specific because we want to understand which one of these factors are likely to have played the decisive role in ushering in what is known as the Harappan *form* of culture. Our hypothesis of 'natural calamities' and 'the processes generated by natural calamities', does not claim to have explained everything. It is only an attempt to understand one of the several factors; to us, a very important factor indeed, which brings us to the thresh-hold of change from the Proto-Harappan to the Harappan *form* of culture.

National Museum,
New Delhi, 110011

S.P. GUPTA

A Note on Cross Contacts of Vedic India with West Asia and Iran

SUMMARY

Recent studies have revealed that cross contacts and synchronisms can be established during the eventful years (2050–1900) B.C, when there was a gigantic mass movement of the Aryans in the ancient world:

In particular, king Divodasa (D.N. 63) is found to be a great king whose diplomatic activities extended not only to Iran but also reached kings of Larsa and Babylon. *Mana,* the international currency, is found to be mentioned in the Rigveda, and Kurusuti prays for the gift of a "mana gold" after a great victory of king Divodasa. Raghu's conquests in Iran were not mere poetic fancies of Kalidasa but apparently had some historical basis, howsoever tennous.

It is further found that Haug's theory that Avestan king Vistaspa lived more than a thousand years earlier than the Achamanean king Hystaspes is perfectly valid: If at all, it is only an understatement. In fact, Vedic Sushraves is found to be the Avestic Hushrava as suggested long ago by Weber and then by Warren & Warren: Hushrava was iso-chronous with Divodasa and consequently, Zarathustra and his Gathas are found to belong to *c.* 1900 B.C. The reasons for Geldner's observation that old Vedic and Gathic are two dialects of the same speech is found to be fully explained by the present chronological analysis.

It is further found that to understand the Rigveda (6th, 7th & the 8th Mandalas, in particular), the whole of Ariana (North western India, Pakistan, Afghanistan and Iran) will have to be taken, of necessity, as one unit as was suggested long ago by Hildebrandt, Brunhoffer and Wilson.

For a proper understanding of the battle hymns of the Rigveda, not only the time horizon but also the geographical horizon will have to be considerably extended.

INTRODUCTION

From a study of the Vedic literature, the following astronomical events and their observers are known.[1]

Event	Date	Observers	Remarks
Autumnal equinox at Rohini purnima	3,070	Nabhanedishtha, son of Manu	Year-beginning under the ordinances of the paramount King Manu.
a. Autumnal equinox at Krittika purnima b. Winter solstice at Magha	2,350 B.C.	Dirghatamas, Viswamitra II, Bharata, Garga	Year-beginning under the ordinances of the paramont King Bharata
Heliacal rising of the Dogstar	2,000 B.C.	Vamadeva	'Twelve days sleep of the Ribhus[3]
Winter solstice at Magha Sukla Panchami	1,630 B.C.	Vagamhrini, King Shruta	Deification of Vagdevi
Winter solstice at Dhanishtha	1,270 B.C.	Lagadha, King Suci	Year-beginning by king Suci of Magadha
K-Draconis as the pole star	1,290 B.C.	Ashwalayana	Marriage rite of showing the Dhruva, the polestar

On the basis of these dates and personalities, the relative chronology of the king list of Pargitar[2] has been converted into a system of absolute chronology.

Dynastic number	Date of birth B.C.	Tristu-Bharatas	Ikshvakus
62.	2,069	Bridhvasva	RAGHU
63.	2,051	DIVODASA	Aja
64.	2,033	INDROTA, Mitrayus	DASARATHA
65.	2,015	Soma	Rama, Bharata
66.	1,997	Sriñjaya	Taksha, Pushkala
67.	1,979	Cyavana	
68.	1,961	SUDASA	

The fourth period (politically, the most important Vedic period) of this system would then read as under:

TRITSU-BHARATAS AND HARAPPANS

According to the Rigveda, Divodasa killed Shambara son of Kulitara, the Asura king, after forty years of grim struggle[3]. Sriñjaya smote the Turnnians (Turvasas)[4], perhaps in aid of Sushrava (Hushrava). Cyavana overran Hariyupia Yavyavati (Harappa, the city of the great granary) in *c.* 1,940 B.C.

Finally, Sudasa foiled the grand alliance of the entire Asura world in their bid to recover Harappa.

[1]S.B. Roy, Chronological Infrastructure of Indian Protohistory (3100–600 B.C.), Journal of the Bihar Research Society, LVIIIth 44–78, 1972

[2]Archeao-astronomy and archaeo-ethnology to-day, comments by S.B. Roy, *Current Authropology*, August 1973.

[3]Pargiter, Ancient Indian Historical Tradition (AIHT), Table pp. 144–148)

[4]Ibid., pp. 116 & 170

[5]Rigveda (R.V.) 4.30.7–14; & also 2.12.11. etc.

[6]R.V. 6.27.7.

[7]R.4. 6.27. 5–6.

In the celebrated battle of the ten kings on Parushni (Ravi river), Sudasa emerged victorious.[1] The Harappan political power ended in 1,930 B.C. thus, explaining the disappearance of the Harappan seals at Sumer around 1,900 B.C. This date tallies with the rectified radio-carbon dates[2].

THE RAGHU-VAMSA

It is possible that Raghu had some connection with Ragha (Avesta) because according to Kalidasa (Raghuvamsa)[3], he went deep into Iran—up to the South of the Caspian sea—the place called Ragha in Avesta being the birth place of Zoroaster. Similarly, King Aja may have some connection with the tribe of Ajas mentioned in the Rigveda[4]. Dasaratha, according to the Ramayana, had fought in the Deva-Asura battle on the side of Divodasa against Shambara—thus showing that the Devasura battle was a battle between two human kings[5]. Bharata received the lands of Kekaya on the Indus as matriarchal property, while his sons Taksha and Pushkala founded Takshasila and Pushkalavati across the Indus[6].

Finally, Dasaratha finds a reflection in the distant Mitanni, in the king Tusaratta[7]; and, Tusaratta says—in his letter to Amen Hotep III (*c.* 1,400 B.C.) that Ramman (Rama?) was his family deity[8].

FOREIGN KING MENTIONED IN THE RIGVEDA

The Rigveda, when examined in the light of the above chronology, reveals certain contemporary Sumerian names which are found to be entered in the Sumerian king lists:

Rigveda	*Sumerian* Iranian	*Place*	*Remarks*
1. Indrota[9]	*Indatu*[10] Inderuta	Ur	Made king of Ur in 1,970 B.C. after the fall of the third dynasty of Ur
2. Emusa[11]	Emisu[12]	Larsa	Yhe second king of Larsa (2,005-1,977) B.C. The Rigveda says that he was killed across seven mountain.
3. Mana[13]	Mana[14]	Sumer	Mana is a Sumerian unit of weight and value (—1/2 Lb) Kurusuti prays for the gift of a mana of gold after the victory over Emusa[19], the Larsa king.
4(a) Sushrava[15].	Hushrava	Iran	Hushrava of the Avesta (and Kai Khusru of the Sahnama) has been identified with Sushrava of the Rgveda[20] Divodasa entered into distant alliance with him[21]
4(b) Istaswa[16]	Vistaspa	Iran	Vistaspa was the patron of Zarathustra.
4(c) Kaksivant Ausija[17]	The Usigas[18]	Iran	7arathustra castigates the Usiges, the war lords, for their rapine. Pargiter[22] says that Kakshivant was junior to Divodasa.

[1]R.V. 7. (18, 33, 83)

[2]S.B. Roy, Harappan, Chronology: an integrated study *Puratattva,* No 7 pp. 65–69.
tattva, No 7 pp. 65–69

[3]Kalidasa—*Raghuvamsa,* 4th Canto (60–80)

[4]R.V. 7.18.

[5]Valmiki—*Ramayana, Aoydhya Kanda,* (9. (11–17)

[6]Pargitar, AIHT, p. 278.

[7]H. Jacobi, On the Boghas Keui Treaty, Journal of Royal Asiatic Society, (JRAS) 1,909, p. 741.

[8]Tell-el-Amarna Tablets, edited by Bezold & Budge (Amarna Tablets): Letter No. 8, from Tuseratta to Amenhotep III, p. xxxviii-comments.

[9]R.V. 8.68. (14–17): On Indrota.

[10]1. Dumont, Indo-Iranian names from Mitamni, Nuzi & Syrian documents, Journal of the American Oriental Society, Vol. 67, pp. 251 & Cambridge Ancient History, vol. 1 part 2 (CAH) p. 654–62.

[11]R.V. 8.77.10; Tait. wamhita, 6.2.4. (On Emusha)

[12]History of Babylon, by L.W. King : Transliteration of the Cuniform Tablets of the Larsa kings by Pro. Clau (*Ibid.* pp. 89, notes)

[13]CAH pp. 654–662.

[14]R.V. 8.78.2 (*mana*)

[15]Amherst Tablets of Cuniforms edited by Pinches p. xxiii etc.

[16]Tell-el Amarna letters, *ibid.*, pp. xxx & xxxi, from Baranhburias to Akhenaton.

[17]See also India—what it can teach us, (for the opposing view).

[18]R.V. 8.77 & 78.

[19]R.V. 1.53.9 20 (a) R.V. 1.122.6

[20]Yasna: XLIV–29; 20 (c) Pargiter, AIHT, p. 160, 192

CROSS CONTACTS WITH WEST ASIA

The proposed identifications are neither isolated nor *ad hoc* but spontaneous and natural. For, contrary to the popular notions, the specialists in archaeology know that there were extensive contacts between India and West Asia in the millennium 2,300—1,900 B.C.

1. PERIOD 2,300—1,900 B.C.

Harappan seals have been found, among others, in Ur, Kish, Lagash, Umma, from the period, at least, of Sargon of Akkad, who ruled in (2,371—2,316) B.C. The cultural contact from 2,371 B.C., is, therefore, established[1].

An inscription in the tenth year of King Gungunum of Larsa (1932-1906) B.C. has been found on an Harappan seal. The contact of 1922 B.C. (very relevant for the period of 2150-1,900 B.C.) now under discussion, is, therefore, beyond dispute[2].

The Harappan political power ended according to the proposed chronology, in *c.* 1930 B.C. (1,7). This explains the sudden disappearance of the seals around this critical period.

Other artefacts like beads, etc., have been found from Iran to Syria in the period 2,000—1,700 B.C.[3]

(The relation between the Harappans and the Vedic people have been already considered in detail. It is only necessary to mention further that the remains of 'horses' have been found in Surkotada (2,300—1,900) B.C.[4]

PERIOD 1900—1300 B.C.

Aryan names have been found in the documents of Mitanni, Nuzi, Khattis (Hittites). At least 81 Aryan proper names (13 from Mittanni, 23 from Nuzi and 45 from Syrian documents) are known.[5]

The Mitannians have king Tusaratta (cf[6]. Dasaratha) who worships Ramman (Rama?) as his family deity (vide letter of Tusaratta to Amenhotep dated *c.* 1,400 B.C. in the Tell el Amarna archives)[7].

The chronological developments of the deity seems to be Rama (Indian)—Ramman (Mitannian)—Rahman (Semetic), in that order.

A treatise on the training of horses has been found in the Boghaz, Keui archives (*c.* 1,400 B.C.). It is written by one Kikuli, a Hittite horse trainer in Sanskritic language[8].

Finally, the Boghaz, Keui treaty (1,380 B.C.) between the Hittite king Subililuma and the Mitannian king Tusaratta, invokes the Vedic gods Indra, Varuna, Mitra and Nasatya as guardians of the treaty. P. Thieme holds that they were Indian and not Indo-Iranian.

GENERAL

It is said that the version regarding the Legend of the great flood given in the Shatapatha Brahmana (*c.* 1,400 B.C.) is of Sumerian origin.

The Chaldeans (*c.* 700 B.C.) show a nakshatra system. It now seems, contrary to the popular opinion, that the Babylonians and the Chaldeans borrowed it from India, because the Indian Krittika system is at least as old as 2,350 B.C.

No documentary evidence of contact with the Egyptians is available but it seems that the Indian Kathopanishad (whose germ is R.V. X-135 composed 1520 B.C.) is indebted to the Egyptian 'Book of the Dead' for a

[1]Warren & Warren, *Shahnama,* Vol. III p. 7; Weber, Indian Antiquary Vol. 3, p. 22

[2]R.V. 1.53.7 (*Sakhya parāvati*)

[3]Sir John Marshall—Mohenjo-daro & the Indus Civilization —Vol. I

[4]Buchanan as quoted in the Birth of Indian Civilization by Bridget & Allchin (BIC) p. 141.

[5]*Ibid*—pp. 142.

[6]J.P. Joshi, Journal of the Oriental Institute XXII—1-2, p. 136.

[7]P.E. Dumont, Journal of the American Oriental Society (JAOS)—Vol. 67—p. 251.

[8]H. Jacobi, *JRAS* 1909 p. 721.

[9]Amarna Tablets the letter No. 8 p. xxxviii comments.

[10]H. Jacobi (JRAS) 1909 p. 721.

sudden interest in the life after death among the Vedic people. It also seems very likely that King Akhenaton (1,406—1,360) B.C. modelled his life on that of King Janaka of Videha (1,470—1,390) B.C. (his senior) and got his inspiration of the Sun-worship from the Aditya sampradaya—the world renowned *Sun school* of Videha (The evidence for these contacts will be subsequently discussed)[1].

In any case, the discovery of the Lothal dockyard makes it almost certain that there was marine contacts. What is a dock for, if not marine trade with neighbouring countries ?

The above brief *resume* shows that there were extensive contacts between India and West Asia during the millennium 2,300—1,300 B.C. In particular, there are specific evidence for the cross contact that existed in 2,050—1,900 B.C.

FOREIGN TRIBES IN THE RIGVEDA

Besides these kings there are other indications also. Certain tribes mentioned in the celebrated hymn on the battle of the ten kings, fought in *c.* 1,930 B.C. when Sudasa emerged victorious. Some of them have already been identified with the Iranians; some more of them are identified now with the West Iranians.

Tribes and mercenaries mentioned in the battle of the ten kings[2]

Rigveda	*Root*	*Iranian names*	*Remarks*
A. *Already identified*			
1. Pakhtas	Pakht	Pakhtoons	
2. Parashus	Parsh	Parshavas	Persians
3. Prthus	Parthas	Parthas	Parthians
4. Dasa	Das	Dahae	
5. Gandharis	Gandhar	Gandarians	
6. Bahlikas	Balkh	Bactrians	
B. *New names now identified*			
1. Turvasas	Tur—	Tur-anians	(See Maxmuller[4]
2. Srnjayas	Srnj—	Zarenkas	See Keith—Vedic Index (Srnjaya)
3. Vaikarnas	Vaikarna	Vahrkanas[5]	Avesta, Darius, Herodotus.[6]
4. Simyus	Sim	Sim-asks	Simars, who overthrew Elan and Ur in 2,005 B.C.[7]
5. Yakshus	Yaksh—	Hyksos	Darivation not known[8] (Brested) They overthrew the Twelfth dynasty in 1,788 B.C.
6. Shigrus	Shigr	Zagrus	
7. Alinas	Alin—	Hellenes	The correct pronunciation of the word Hellenes is '*alinas*' or '*alenas*'. Hellenes appeared in Greece in 2,200 B.C.

[1] H. Jacobi (JRAS), 1909—p. 721.
[2] S.R. Rao—Lothal (1973)
[3] R.V. 7.18, 7.33 & 7.83 (On the battle of tenk ings)

B-20 Sujan Singh Park
New Delhi, 110003

S.B. Roy

[4] Encyclopedia Britanica, Iran
[5] CAH pp. 654–62; also Chronology
[6] Brestead, A History of Egypt, pp. 214–227 (on the Hyksos)
[7] CAH, pp. 772–8; also Chronology, and
[8] S.B. Roy, Ancient India, a chronological study 1500–400 B.C. pp. 79–80
[9] Max Muller, the Science of Language, p. 253.

Bibliograpical Aids for the Study of the Indus Civilization: A Critical Survey

Several new bibliographies on the Indus civilization have appeared recently. It seems appropriate to draw the attention of the readers to them, and, particularly since some of the authors have expressed their intentio to continue this work and have asked for criticism and suggestions.

I have been somewhat surprised to notice that some of the most important works of this kind seem to have altogether escaped the attention of the recent compilers. It will, therefore, be useful to start by listing all the bibliographies that, to my knowledge, deal more specifically with topics related to the Indus civilization.

1. *Annual Bibliography of Indian Archaeology:* published by the Kern Institute, Leiden. Leiden: E.J. Brill. In 4:0. Vol. I, for the year 1926 (1928)through Vol. XXI, for the years 1964-1966 (1972).

This is a very carefully compiled and comprehensive bibliography, giving full details of each publication and of its contents. Its reliability and usefulness is indeed very high. However, the scope is very broad, and it would, therefore, be useful to have all the Indus-related material extracted.

2. Constantin Regamey, "Bibliographie analytique des travaux relatifs aux elements anaryens dans la civilisation et les langues de l'Inde", *Bulletin de L'Ecole Francaise d' Extreme-Orient, Tome* XXXIV, 1934 (Hanoi 1935), p. 429-566. This is, also, an exemplary bibliography, whose scope again is, broader than the bare interest in the Indus civilization, though publications relating to the latter are carefully recorded. The contents, which have been arranged chronologically, span a period from 1856 to early 1934, thus complementing the *Annual Bibliography of Indian Archaeology* (abbreviated hereafter as ABIA) as far as the Indus civilization is concerned; the earliest reference to it is the note on 'Harappa" in *Archaeological Survey of India: Report for the year* 1872-73, by Alexander Cunningham, Volume V, Calcutta 1875, p. 105-108, with pl. XXXII-XXXIII. (Regamey gives under no. 6 the title wrongly as "Report for the year 1971-72" and the other plate as XXII: but these are about the only mistakes that have come to my notice while consulting this bibliography). Also in respect to the subject matter, it complements the ABIA, taking into regard the linguistic and other non-material evidence relating to Pre-and Non-Aryan India as well. The 234 titles are given with full bibliographical details, and their contents are aptly summarized so that the user will know whether the book or paper concerned contains anything of interest for him: in addition, there are cross references, comprehensive lists of reviews, and an 24-page index to the authors, subjects and words of different languages.

3. Louis Renou, *Bibliographie vedique,* Paris: Adrien-Maisonneuve, 1931. (4), V, 339 p.

The section "126. Prehistoire (not., faits de Harappa —Mohenjodaro)" on pp. 140-141 comprises 21 items, with indication of reviews in addition, and mostly with a brief summary also. Almost all titles are relevant, and some of them are missing in the recent bibliographies.

4. R.N. Dandekar, *Vedic Bibliography.* Bombay: Karnatak Publishing House, 1946, (New Indian Antiquary, Extra Series, VII.) XX, 398 p.

The section "XX. Indus Valley Civilization" on pp. 281-303 comprises altogether 199 items.

5 R N. Dandekar, *Vedic Bibliography,* Second Volume. Poona: University of Poona, 1961. XXIII, 760 p.

The section "XIX. Indus Valley Civilization" on pp. 655-685 comprises altogether 205 titles.

6. R.N. Dandekar, *Vedic Bibliography,* Third Volume. Poona: Bhandarkar Oriental Research Institute, 1973. (Government Oriental Series, Class B, No. 10) (8), xxiv, 1082 p.

The section "XIX. Indus Valley Civilization" on pp. 928-982 contains altogether 432 items.

These three volumes by Dandekar continue Renou's bibliography. Dandekar has aimed at giving exhaustive data, i.e. bibliographical details in full, a short description of the contents, listing all the reviews, and an index. Unfortunately, however, some of the data, e.g. page numbers, or the year of publication, and so on, may be missing, or the title is given abbreviated. In an undertaking of this magnitude, this is certainly pardonable, but it does not make the work as reliable as a bibliographical reference work as the previous ones. It may also be noted that not all the items have been checked from the originals, but also uncertain information supplied by scholars has been included, which has resulted in ghost titles, e.g. III 89:8, based on my own communication of a planned publication that has not appeared. Moreover, some titles have been repeated in the various subsections, while others, again, like Anderson's bibliography from 1967 (cf. below, no. 8), are mentioned in other sections (in Anderson's case in "XX. Miscellaneous: 91. Bibliographies, catalogues, collected writings, etc.)."

It may be useful to publish here a survey of the material in Dandekar's three volumes, giving the numbers and headings of his subsections and statistics about the items cited: Subsection no. & heading (varies a little) number of items

II/III	(I)		I	II	III	tog.
85.	(156.)	Indus Valley Civilization (General)	73	109	195	377
86.	(157.)	Script and seals	46	30	111	187
87.	(158.)	Pottery, (figurines,) arts and crafts	18	24	34	76
	(159.)	Agriculture, cattle	6			6
88.	(161.)	People	15	6	20	41
89.	(160.)	Religion	16	26	13	55
90.	(162.)	Relation with other civilizations	25	10	59	94
Together			199	205	432	836

Taking into account the bulk of these books and the standards of printing in India, there are tolerably few misprints (e.g. in III 85:17 civila for civilta, 85:58 Faisservis for Fairservis, 85:135 Posschl for Possehl, 86:5 Bongrad-Levin, etc.).

7. H. Heras, *Studies in Proto-Indo-Mediterranean Culture,* Volume I, Bombay: Indian Historical Research Institute, St. Xavier's College, 1953. (Studies in Indian History, No. 19.) It contains on pp. xxxviii-cix a valuable "Bibliographical introduction" of 1016 titles (of which all are, however, not relevant); Father Heras was assisted in its compilation by B. Anderson.

8. Bernard Anderson, "Indus Valley Civilization: A Bibliography 1954–1966", *Indica* 4:2, September 1967 pp. 107–124. It Comprises 227+6 items, supplementing the bibliography cited above under no. 7. according to Indica 4, p. 132, Mr. Anderson holds an M.A. degree and is Deputy Librarian of the Bombay University. As far as I could check, these bibliographies are, on the whole, rather accurate. They give full bibliographical details, and misprints are relatively few. (In *Indica* 4, e.g., Harappan in no. 1, gennen 4000 AR for the correct gennem 4000 ar in no. 14a, Sovietskve for Sovetskoe in no. 17, Dilshit for Dikshit in no. 67a, Sudhansa Kumar Ray for Sudhansu.... in nos. 175–6).

9. B.M. Pande and K.S. Ramachandran, *Bibliography of the Harappan Culture.* Edited by Henry Field. Miami, Florida: Field Research Projects, 1971. In 4:0, xii, 46 p. Field in his foreword estimates the number of titles collected here to about 1,400 but according to my counts there are only 1117 of them. The arrangement is alphabetical, as in Anderson's bibliography, and the secondary arrangement of the several books by one author chronological. While Anderson's typographical arrangement clearly brings out the anonymous items, they are here very much susceptible of confusion: e.g., on page 13 one could mistake the monograph ***Human skeletal remains from Harappa***(by N.D. Bose and others, not mentioned here) to be a work by Bedrich (read thus) Hrozny, since it is listed immediately after his books and papers, and its year of publication (1962) is later than theirs. A similar case is found on p. 22, where *Proto-Indica:* 1968 and *Proto-Indica:* 1970, written jointly by several Soviet scholars, are listed under M.A. Probst. The reviews have been separated to form a specific section at the end, arranged according to their authors; but it would have been more convenient for the user if they had been incorporated in the main section, with cross references added under each of the titles reviewed. As an appendix, the authors have given a useful list of Harappan and affiliated sites, numbering altogether 258, and a list of available radiocarbon dates. Similar lists have been published elsewhere (cf. e.g. M. Wheeler, *The Indus Civilization,* third edition, Cambridge 1968, p. 138-140; and M. Rafique Mughal, *Present State of Research on the Indus Valley Civilization,* Karachi 1973, p. 24-28), but these most comprehensive lists are very welcome and useful.

In the foreword, Henry Field says that he has deleted transliterations of Russian, Hindi, Maharathi (sic), Urdu, and Czech, while the English translation (which is sometimes missing) has been retained with the words "In Russian" (etc.) added. In a bibliography, one should have expected to get all such details as the original title. The authors, in the preface, confess that they have "relied heavily upon some of the general Bibliographies and other publications", and note that "some titles were also not accessible to us in the original and a number of such publications have been included without our verification and even though in some cases the information is incomplete. An asterisk preceding such entries indicates incomplete information" (p. V). If one examines such asterisked entries, one is left wondering how are such publications as, e.g. *Puratattva* Vol. I (cf. S.P. Gupta on p.11), *Antiquity* 41, 1967, (cf. p.17) or the *Annual Report of the Archaeological Survey of India* 1923-24 (cf. p. 18) inaccessible to archaeologists who have at their disposal the Central Archaeological Library in New Delhi. Whatever be the reason, it is to be hoped that they could spend some more time in checking the entries, also the non-asterisked ones, for the revised edition in several well-equipped libraries. As it stands, the bibliography is entirely unreliable for any bibliographical use, though it, of course, is helpful in locating material for research in a given subject. In the following I shall illustrate this with a few examples.

On p. 3 under Bibby 1957 (non asterisk) we read "..gennen 4000 A.R.", which shows that this item has been taken unchecked from Anderson (cf. above), with one additional error (in Danish ar means 'year', but here it has apparently been understood as parallel to A.D.). p. 29: T [homas], F.W., is credited with having written the paper "Mohenjo-daro—Indus epigraphy" in Journal of the Royal Asiatic Society 1932, p. 466–503, although it is by G.R. Hunter (cf. p. 13), while what Thomas has published ibid. p. 453–466 is a review of John Marshall (ed.), Mohenjo-daro and the Indus Civilization, I-III, London 1931. In the reference given on p. 30: Venis, Arthur, 1913: "Seals from Harappa", JRAS, p. 699–703, the author, the year of publication, and one of the page-numbers are all wrong: it should read Fleet, J.F. (not mentioned in the bibliography), 1912: "Seals from Harappa", JRAS, p. 699–701. p. 13: The 1970 paper by P. Joseph is quoted as "Harappa script decipherment—the Reverend Heras and successors", instead of "....—Father Heras and his successors." P. 21: For Parpola, Asko, 1966, Computing approach to Proto-Indian scripts, 1965: an interim report, Copenhagen", read: Parpola, A. and S., & S. Koskenniemi, [1966], Computing Ap (p) roach to Proto-Indian, 1965: An Interim Report, [Helsinki, stencilled, 6 p.]. p. 3: Bissing, Friederich (sic) Wilhelm (Freiherr) von, 1943, Zu Bedrich Hrozny's (sic for Hroznys) Altester Geschichte Vorderasiens und Indiens, Zweite Auflage, 21, pp. 39–44; but it was Hrozny's book's second edition that appeared in 1943, while von Bissing's review having the above title appeared in Festschrift Friedrich Zucker, Berlin 1954, p. 37–44, as cited in the next item.

In a bibliography, one expects to find full bibliographical details. For instance, it would have been useful to see also the subtitle of Waddell's (whose name is spelt twice as Waddel, p. 30–31) book from 1925, *Indo-Sumerian Seals Deciphered,* since it tells a great deal about the book: "Discovering Sumerians of Indus Valley as Phoenicians, Barats, Goths and Famous Vedic Aryans, 3100–2300 B.C." Sir Max Mallowan's paper "The mechanics of ancient trade in Western Asia" also has an important subtitle omitted from the bibliography (p. 18): "Reflections on the location of Magan and Meluhha". p. 19: Meriggi's paper from 1934 is cited as having appeared in ZDMG XII, but it should have been noted that this number refers to the short-lived Neue Folge (N.F.), while corresponding number of the whole series, now in use, is 87. p. 4; John Chadwick is mentioned as the only author of a paper which on p. 10 is correctly entered as a joint one by Gerard Clauson (read thus for Glauson, which is no misprint of the alphabetic order and John Chadwick, p. 4 and 11. Instead of simply *Studies in Honor of Benno Landsberger,* the full title of the publication should have been cited (..*on his seventy-fifth birthday April,* 21, 1965) and the series it forms part of (The Oriental Institute of the University of Chicago, Assyriological Studies, 16). Under the individual papers of Buchanan (p. 4) and Hallo (p. 11), one should moreover have indicated the common title of their contributions, cited on p. 11 with one wrong page number (204 for 199). p. 14: The title of Hunter's book is incomplete: add *and its connection with other scripts* after *The Scripts of Harappa and Mohenjodaro* (thus instead of *Mohenjo-Daro* in the bibliography); its series has also been omitted: Studies in the History of Culture, No. 1. p. 5 mentions under V. Gordon Childe *New light on the Most Ancient East,* London, as from 1952, but in no way indicates that this is a revised edition of a book that appeared originally as early as 1934 (the first title by Childe in the bibliography is from 1937); besides, not only chapter IX mentioned in the bibliography, but also Ch. VIII is relevant for the Indus civilization. Similarly, only the third edition of Wheeler's book *The Indus Civilization* is mentioned (p. 31), while one could well imagine that some one might consult the bibliography precisely in order tc find out when did the earlier editions appear. P. 31: the two papers by Zide have been entered separately, though that from 1970 is only a reprint of that from 1968.

Misprints and omissions (unmarked by asterisms) are fairly numerous; e.g. p. 18 Mahadevan, Iravathan, 1950....read Iravatham and 1970; p. 19 read Masson-Oursel, P., H. de Willman-Grabowska and P. Stern, for Masson-Gursel (sic), Grabowska and Stern..P. 20: read Doniger for Doninger under O'Flaherty, and add 1969 as the omitted year of publication for Pandit. P. 27: Schmokel's omitted first name is Hartmut. P. 29: read Romila for Ramila under Thapar; Tosi's paper was published in 1968, not 1948; read van Lohuizen-de Leeuw for Van Lohuizhen-De Leeuw: although the original Dutch title of her 1960 booklet has been removed by the editor here, it stays in the review section (under J.F. Staal, who has not written the *following* review), with hum misprinted for hun.

I have gone into all these details, because in their preface the authors say that they "expect that the mistakes and the shortcomings will be pointed out by scholars so that we may be able to improve our present compilation". In private conversation, they have informed me that a second much enlarged edition is soon due to appear. While looking forward to its appearance, we hope that the authors will do more checking, and include all bibliographical particulars, also the number of pages and name of the publisher in the case of books, and if possible, some sort of indication of the contents: Renou's above mentioned bibliography could serve as a model, if a commentary along the lines of the Annual Bibliography of Indian Archaeology or Regamay is too demanding.

10. Robert H. Brunswig, Jr., "A Comprehensive Bibliography of the Indus Civilization and Related Subjects and Areas", *Asian Perspectives* XVI:1, 1973 (1974), pp. 75–111.

The brief general introduction about the Indus

civilization does not inform us about the sources or methods utilized in the compilation of this bibliography, nor supply us with the abbreviations used. The material, comprising altogether 802 titles according to my counts, is presented under the following headings, each arranged alphabetically according to the authors:

(i) General references for the study of Harappan Civilization	129	titles
(ii) Indus-Related Cultures in Baluchistan, Afghanistan, Pakistan, and India	47	,,
(iii) The Indus and Western Asia	115	,,
(iv) Harappan Culture and the Vedic Aryans	17	,,
(v) The origin, decline, and eclipse of the Indus Civilization	28	,,
(vi) Archaeological explorations and surveys	47	
(vii) Towns and cities of the Indus: The Harappan Culture Sites	114	,,
(viii) Chronology of Harappan and related sites	45	,,
(ix) The Harappan Culture: The Artifacts of the Indus Life	65	,,
(x) Peoples, Plants, and Fauna of the Indus Civilization	31	,,
(xi) Form, Structure, and Architecture in Harappan culture	10	,,
(xii) Indus Script	99	,,
(xiii) Religion of the Indus People	25	,,

As a comparison with the other bibliographies listed above (only nos. 7 and 8 are cited) will indicate, this one is not as comprehensive as its title suggests; but neither are others. Put together, we should, however, have a fairly good coverage.

Although the division of the material into different sections has certain advantages, it may lead to serious omissions: the user of this bibliography will, for example, not find Heras's chief work on his 'decipherment' of the Indus script under section 12 at all, because it has been included in section 1. And there are many similar cases. Moreover, it is very inconvenient to find a title by a specific author. For these reasons, I think that an alphabetic or chronological arrangement (in the latter case with an alphabetic index) is preferable, and that a short indication of the contents is almost necessary. Bibliographical information is, here, too, defective although Brunswig tries to record the publisher. Thus, with no indication of the page numbers of the monographs, they are practically put on par with short comments in newspapers, which abound in this bibliography.

The bibliography has been beautifully printed, but unfortunately has so many errors that it is unreliable for bibliographical checking. Here is a collection of errors relating to authors' names: p. 79 Gorden for Gordon; p. 80 D.C. Kosambi for D.D. Kosambi; Makik for Malik; Masson-Oursel, Paul, for Masson-Oursel, paul, H. de Willman-Grabowska, and P. Stern; p. 81 Sankaranada for Sankarananda; p. 82 Würst for Wüst; p. 85 Bibby, Geoffery for Geoffrey; Buchanan, Biggs for Briggs; p. 86 Ehrenfels, O.R. for Ehrenfils, O.R. von, p. 87 Jarity for Jaritz; Karmarker for Karmarkar; p. 88 Paroda for Porada; p. 91 Mughal, Mohammad Rabique for Rafique; Sankaranada for Sankarananda; p. 96 Leshnik, Laurence for Lawrence S., p. 101 Fleet, I.F. for J.F.; p. 103 Quintana for Quintana Vives; p. 105 Von Cappieri for Cappieri (here German von=English by, from the title page); Lohuizen-Leeuw, J.E. van for Lohuizen-de Leeuw, J. E. van; p. 107 Jaroslav, V.P. for Vacek, Jaroslav; p. 108 Liendard for Lienhard; Otto, Von E. for Otto, E. (cf. Cappieri above); Pandi for Pandit; p. 109 Sankaranda for Sankarananda; p. 110 Sutran (after Subbiah) for Autran; Venkalaubbiah for Venkatasubbiah; Waddel for Waddell (cf. above, on Pande & Ramachandran); p. 111 Venlalasubbiah for Venkatasubbiah.

An examination of Brunswig's bibliography shows that it, too, is much based on secondary sources. For example, we have here the same ghost title under Bissing, F.W. von (p. 85) as in Pande & Ramachandran (cf. above), namely, "1943 Zu Bedrich Hrozny's (sic) altester (sic) Geschichte Vorderasiens und Indiens. *Zweite Auflage* 21: 39–44", with that difference, that here the words Zweite Auflage (=second edition) have apparently been comprehended as a journal title, put into italics, and the mysterious number 21 as a volume number. Mistakes in spelling German words are also found on p. 90 Die alteste Volerwanderung for Die älteste Volkerwanderung, and p. 100 Das Alten for Das Alter. An influence of American English is visible. in the recurring replacement of capital by capitol (p. 86 s.v. Glob 1954 and 1957 and p. 95 s.v. Lal 1962) Russian words are also misspelt: Nauke for Nauka p. 82, and Sovetskye Voslokovedenie for Sovetskoe Vostokovedenie p. 105; also Latin: Etruscarium for Etruscarum p. 109; proper names and place names have also been affected: p. 86 Darbar-Kot for Dabar-Kot, and Meluha for Meluhha, p. 91 Hoshiapur for Hoshiarpur, and p. 95 Bhandakar for Bhandarkar. The last example occurs in a journal title; this is wrong also in Kadmus for Kadmos on p. 106, and in Bulletin of the American School of Oriental Research (read Schools) on p. 85. The volume number of a journal is missing from Petrie 1932 (Ancient Egypt, II) on p. 97, and from a monograph reference (Vol. III) in the case of Burnes 1834, p. 92. Wrong page number is found e.g. on p. 108 S.V. Otto 1936: read 109–114. On p. 103 we come across the following title: "Roopa-Lekha (in small capitals, as an author's name), 1955 Indus seals discovered in Ahmedabad. *Marg* [Bombay] VIII. *Mārg*, put into italics like the journals usually, is a journal appearing in Bombay, but this article is anonymous (its title has *seal* for *seals* in the above quotation) and has been published in *Roopa-Lekha*, which is a journal appearing in Delhi (N.S. Vol. 26: Part, 1, Summer 1955, p. 70–71)., In the title of Sir Aurel Stein's book from 1937 (p. 93), read *South-Eastern Iran* for *southwestern Iran*. This first volume of Charles Masson's *Narrative of various journeys in Balochistan, Afghanistan, and the Punjab, including a residence in those countries from* 1826 *to* 1838 (thus in the title page of the first Vol., instead of *Narrative.... Baluchistan, Afghanistan, the Panjab and Kalat* in the bibliography) appeared in 1842, not 1844 as stated on p. 93; moreover, a bibliography should tell us that Charles Masson is a pseudonym of James Lewis (cf. British Museum Catalogue of Printed Books, Vol. 155, p. 180). The full title of Mode's book *Indische Frühkulturen* (p. 80) should have been recorded, instead of leaving off the words *und ihre Beziehungen zum Westen*; the note on Mallowan's 1965 paper made in connection with Pande and Ramachandran applies here, too (p. 88; the last page is 7 and not 8); the series in which for instance Fairservis' papers have been published, should not have been left unmentioned (e.g. p. 92: 1961a Anthropological Papers of the American Museum of Natural History, Vol. 48, Part 1, pp. 1–128; 1961b (sic was actually published in 1959 in the same series as Vol. 47, Part 2, pp. 273–448). The various editions are not mentioned on p. 78 (Childe 1952: cf. above, on Pande & Ramachandran, and note that here only "New York: Praeger" is mentioned as the place of publication, not London) or p. 79 (2nd ed. of Gordon 1953 appeared in 1960). The reference to Ross 1946 cites the pages as 291–315, and makes no reference to Donald E McCown's "Prefatory remarks" on pp. 284-271, or the "Report on Skeletal Remains" by B.S. Guha and B.K. Chatterjee on pp. 315–316, both included in the article.

In conclusion attention might be drawn to some dublets which apparently result from the same title being cited differently in different sources: they have been given as separate items, instead of checking and removing the erroneous one. Thus, on p. 79 we find under Hussaini, N.A.Z. " 1956 *a* River links of the Indus Valley civilization. *Miscellanea Asiatica Occidentalis* XVIII: 78–92. American Documentation Institute microfilm no. 5070", and "1956b River links of the Indus civilization. American Documentation Institute, no. 5200, pp. 78–92"; under De Cardi, Beatrice (p. 83) "1965*a* Anjiri (sic) and Siah Damb. *Pakistan Archaeology* 2: 86–182" and "1965*b* Excavations and reconnaissance in Kalat, West Pakistan—the prehistoric sequence in the Surab region. *Pakistan Archaeology* 2: 86–182" (it should have been easy to check and find out that only the latter is possible and correct); under Stein, Sir Mark (read Marc?) Aurel (p. 93) "1943 *An Archaeological Tour along the Ghaggar-Hakra River*. American Documentation Institute microfilm no. ADI-4861" and "1956 *A Reconnaissance along the Ghaggar (Hagra) River*. American Documentation Institute microfilm no. 4861, 1–194", which obviously refer to the same microfilm. On p. 109 we have "*Preliminary Report on the Investigation of the Proto-Indian Texts* the anonymous book title in the place of the author 1968. Moscow: Institute of Ethnology, Academy of Science of the U.S.S.R." and as the next item "*Proto-Indica:* 1968. *A Brief Report on the Investigation of the Proto-Indian Texts* 1968 Moscow: Institute of Ethnology, Academy of Sciences of the U.S.S.R." Only the latter description is correct, with the following modifications: remove the article "A" from the subtitle, change "Ethnology" into "Ethnography", and "the U.S.S.R." into "USSR"; the cover (but not the title page) of this publication carries, moreover, the words 'VIII International Congress of Anthropological and Ethnographical Sciences (Tokio, September, 1968)". In the case of the pair occurring on p. 96 under Mackay, E.J.H., the latter should have been omitted altogether, a mere reprint being concerned, but only after adding the information concerning the reprint at the end of the title: "1943 *Chanhu-daro Excavations,* 1935-36. American Oriental Series, Vol. XX [read 20]. Boston: Museum of Fine Arts". and "1967 *Chanhu-daro Excavations,* 1935–36. American Oriental Series, Vol. 20. New York: Kraus Reprint Corp." It may be noted that the place of publication and the publisher are not correctly indicated in the first reference; the title page reads:" "Published for American School of Indic and Iranian Studies, and Museum of Fine Arts, Boston, by American Oriental Society, New Haven, Connecticut, 1943".

I want to make it clear that the mistakes pointed out in this paper were not specifically sought for, by combing through other bibliographies and making comparisons, but simply noted or suspected while reading through these compilations. I have no doubt that many

[1]This paper was uot accessible to us when *Materiais for the Study of the Indus Script,* I. by S. Koskenniemi, A. Parpola and S. Parpola (Helsinki 1973) went into press; I take this occasion to clarify the reference 1. 1. 1 on p. viii of that work by noting that the article reports the finding of the first Indus seal (described only as having "a unicorn in from of a 'manger' and one line of 'Harappa' script at the top") from *Lothal*: Ahmedabad refers to the respective District of the 'Bombay State'.

more could be discovered by systematic study. Because it is important that *bibliographies* should be improved upon, it has seemed necessary to me on the one hand to make clear to their authors that they should be more careful, and on the other hand to their users, that they should be on their guard against relying too much on them in their present shape.

University of Helsinki
Helsinki (Finland)
ASKO PARPOLA

Inscribed Harappan Material from Kalibangan : Some Remarks on Methodology and Approach

In the present note, an attempt has been made to indicate certain aspects connected with the analysis of the Harappan script and also the methodology and approach adopted by Lal and the present writer[1] while studying the inscribed Harappan material recovered from the excavations at Kalibangan. At this stage, it would be proper to point out that there are certain basic inconsistencies in the decipherment of the Harappan inscriptions by various scholars, as also in the methodology adopted by them. These inconsistencies emanate primarily from the fact that the entire inscribed material—seals and sealings in different material, graffiti, signs painted on pots or engraved on stone or metal objects—has been taken *en masse* irrespective of their spatial or temporal distribution. Prolonged use of the Harappan signs in a vast area could have led to (possible) changes in the nature of the script itself, implying thereby changes in the phonology, and the reduction in the number and/or regional variations. Unfortunately, these factors have not been considered and the signs occurring on different media, those too from widely divergent sites and levels, have been accepted as having (necessarily) the same values and meanings.

While examining the inscribed material from Kalibangan, an attempt has been made to study the evidence on the basis of stratigraphy and its distribution at the site. The analysis, based on the vertical distribution, has been followed by an analysis based on the distribution of the material in different areas at the site. It may, of course, be addded here that, being portable, the inscribed objects could also have been carried to other parts of the settlement. Subsequently, after studying the distribution of the inscribed material at a particular site, the study has to be extended to other Harappan sites. This study is likely to provide us information about knowing whether certain signs were more common in a particular site or area. For example, at Kalibangan, as many as seven terracotta sealings bearing the same legend were found in the 'Citadel' area.[2] Likewise, twelve sealings having the same inscription were found from the 'Warehouse' at Lothal.[3] In a wider context can be cited the example of the inscribed Harappan material from Surkotada where, in most of the painted potsherds having Harappan inscriptions, the sign..  recurs and, in certain potsherds this sign alone has been drawn.[4] These inscriptions are all found in the citadel area.[5] It would, however not be safe to hypothesize on this meagre evidence; it could perhaps indicate the possibility that in the major sites like Harappa, Mohenjo-daro, Kalibangan or Lothal, certain signs which were in use might not have been common to all or were in use more in one particular site only. For instance, the signs..  and..  are found at Kalibangan alone and do not seem to have been used in other Harappan sites.

The possibilities of the inscriptions or signs being exclusive to particular sites also emanate from the fact that the copper tablets, containing an inscription on one face and an animal/human figure or some symbol on the other, are found only at Mohenjo-daro and have not been found at any other Harappan site.[6] Besides, ins-

[1]The work was jointly conducted by Prof. B.B. Lal of the Jiwaji University, Gwalior, and the present writer as a preliminary to the analysis and study of the inscribed Harappan material from Kalibangans.

[2]B.B. Lal, 'Some aspects of the archaeological evidence relating to the Indus script, *Puratattva*, no. 7 (1974), p. 23.

[3]*Ibid.*

[4]Jagat Pati Joshi, *Excavation at Surkotada 1971-72 and Exploration in Kutch* (in press). Shri Joshi has kindly shown the present author the MS. of the report prior to its publication by the Archaeological Survey of India.

[5]Information from Shri Jagat Pati Joshi.

[6]B.M. Pande, 'Inscribed copper tablets from Mohenjodaro : a preliminary analysis , in (eds.) D.P. Agrawal and A. Ghosh, *Radiocarbon and Indian Archaeology* (Bombay. 1973), pp. 305–22.

criptions, certain animals and symbols occurring on the copper tablets have not been found at other Harappan sites. For example, animals like the hare,[1] animal having a head at each end of the body, and certain symbols[2] as well like, for instance,..  ..are not found in the seals and sealings from Mohenjo-daro or other Harappan sites. In the same context, therefore, it also becomes necessary to find out whether certain animals which occur along with the inscriptions are peculiar to one site alone.

In the analysis of the inscribed material from Kalibangan, these factors have been duly considered and, to begin with, the inscribed material from the 'Citadel' and the 'Lower City' is being separated; this is being followed by plotting the finds vertically and horizontally so that it may be possible to ascertain in which particular house or area the inscribed material has been found.

1 However, a few hare-shaped steatite seals have been found at Harappa; see, Madho Sarup Vats, *Excavations at Harappa* (Delhi, 1940), vol. I (text), p. 328 and vol. II (plates), pl. XCV, nos. 421-25 and pl. XCVII, no. 565. Vats has referred to the representation of a 'running hare with long ears' on a small fragment of a bossed seal (no. 568) from Harappa; *ibid.*, vol. I. p. 324 and vol. II pl. XCV, no. 568. But the hare does *not* occur in the more common larger seals and sealings alongwith the inscription. The hare-shaped seals belong to a differnt class by themselves. See also Earnest J.H. Mackay, *Chanhu-daro Excavations* 1935-36 (New Haven 1943) p. 91, pl. xxxvi 19, Sir John Marshall *Mohenjo-daro and the Indus Civilization* (London. 1931), vol. I (text), p. 22f for the faience hare found at Mohenjo-daro, VS Area, Bl. 2, House X and p. 351 pl. XCVI, no. 9 for a pottery model of the hare recovered from DK Area, Section B, 9 feet below surface.

2 The 'endless knot' design at Mohenjo-daro has an added significance for it occurs without any change of form even during the later periods. See, H. Sarkar and B.M. Pande, 'A note on the knot design from Mohenjo-daro and its occurrence in later times,' *Puratattva*, no. III (1969-70), pp. 44-48.

Archaeological Survey of India, Janpath, New Delhi, 110011. B.M. PANDE

On the Conquest of Meluhha by Rimus (2315-2307 B.C.) a Hypothesis

THE Sumerian and early Akkadian inscriptions refer to Magan and Meluhha as regions to the east of southern Mesopotamia. Since the third millennium B.C. there are definite indications of trade and maritime contacts between the two regions viz., Mesopotamia and Magan and Meluhha. A place known as Dilmun (also spelt Telmun) in the Sumerian and the Akkadian inscriptions, was an intermediate station between the two, and the place is often identified with the island of Bahrein in the Persian Gulf.

The reference to Magan and Meluhha occurs side by side suggesting geographical contiguity of the two regions. Meluhha the homeland of a people of dark complexion speaking a distinctive language[1] exported *via* Dilmun important raw materials like copper ore, ivory and precious stones by boat.

Recently, Romila Thapar has made an attempt, specially on the basis of proto-Dravidian linguistics to identify Magan, Meluhha and Dilmun.[2] She has made out a good case to identify Magan or Makan with Sind and Baluchistan, Meluhha with Gujarat and Dilmun with parts of western India.[3] She has also referred to an allusion in Sumerian records to the conquest of Meluhha by Rimush (2315-2307 B.C.) Significantly, the date of Rimush is close enough to the suggested date of the Harappan settlement at Lothal.[4] If Thapar's

[1]There occurs a reference to an official interpreter of the Meluhhan language during the period of the empire of Akkad. See, A. Leo Oppenheim, *Ancient Mesopotamia* (Chicago, 1964), p. 64.

[2]Romila Thapar, 'A possible identification of Meluhha, Dilmun and Makan', *Journal of the Economic and Social History of the Orient*, vol. XVIII, pt. 1, pp. 1-42.

[3]Kramer identifies Magan and Meluhha with Egypt and Ethiopia respectively, while Dilmun, according to him, is likely to refer to the region of the Indus river or Baluchistan. See, Samuel Noah Kramer, *The Sumerians* (Chicago, 1964), pp. 277 and 281. For his Dilmun—Indus equation, see 'the Indus Civilization and Dilmun the Sumerian Paradise Land' in *Expedition*, vol. 6, no. 3 (1964), pp. 44-52. He also thinks that the Ubaidians, the original settlers of Sumer left Mesopotamia and sparked the Indus Civilization. According to Oppenheim, *op. cit.*, p. 398, 'There exists a definite difference between the second and first millennium uses of the two toponyms (i.e. Magan and Meluhha). In the second millennium they referred to the outmost eastern fringe of the known world i.e. to eastern Arabia and India. In the first millennium they were exclusively used to denote, only in literary contexts, Ethiopia and perhaps the region beyond. A few scholars insist that the early references deal likewise with these African countries supposed to have been in contact with Mesopotamia via the Indian Ocean'. Oppenheim identifies Dilmun with the Bahrein island. Allchin writes in *Antiquity*, XLIII (1969), p. 315 about a sailor's account of how they used to call Kathiawar as Dilmun till recent times. There still exist two villages Dulmāna and Dulmāni, in north-west Rajasthan. See also, Arun Kumar, 'On the location of Dilmun', *Journal of the Oriental Institute*, Baroda, vol. XXI (1971-72), pp. 348-50.

[4]Romila Thapar, *op. cit.*, p. 15.

identification of these regions is correct, the following evidence from Lothal may support the alleged conquest of Meluhha by Rimush. But the evidence is more anthropological than archaeological.

Lothal yielded about twenty-one human skeletons from a supposed burial-ground outside the acropolis.[1] The report by Sarkar on these human skeletal remains has not yet been published but a summary of it appears in his recent publication. Sarkar's findings are as follows.[2]

> Lothal skeletons thus showed an overwhelming majority of males many of which had not yet cut their wisdom teeth.... The population does not indicate a normal population of an area. Then the large number of fractures of the skull and the tibiae, the three headless skeletons and the careless nature of burials, as seen in huddled up skeletons, probably indicate that the place was the scene of a battle field.

Another interesting feature brought out by the anthropological study is the close relationship of the Lothal crania, both in their long-headed and broad-headed forms, with those of Sialk. Further, Lothal dolichocephals are similar to those from Al 'Ubaid, Kish, Sialk and Mohenjo-daro. There are at least three skulls which are close to the brachycephals from Sialk. Incidentally, the autochthonous Australoid ethnic strain is also reported at Lothal.[3]

It is noteworthy that there are no brachycephals in Harappa and Mohenjo-daro except in the Area G at Harappa. It is also absent at Langhnaj, Nevasa and Chandoli. Sarkar is also of the opinion that the skeletons from Area G point to the presence of brachycephalic hordes who invaded Harappa from time to time. Nonetheless, brachycranial element at Lothal is of importance in the ethnic history of India as this racial strain might have been responsible for the occurrence of brachycranials in later times.[4]

There are, thus, some evidences at Lothal of a skirmish that took place, perhaps as a sequel to the arrival of a new people, by about 2300 B.C. or so.[5] This suggestion seems to fit in well with the over-all picture drawn by Romila Thapar.[6]

Archaelogical Survey of India, Janpath, New Delhi-110011 H. SARKAR

[1]S.R. Rao, *Lothal and the Indus Civilization* (Bombay, 1973), pp. 146–147.

[2]S.S. Sarkar, *Ancient Races of the Deccan* (New Delhi, 1972), p.9.

[3]Sarkar (1972), *op. cit.*, pp. 8–9. Chatterjee and Kumar, who have measured eight Lothal skulls, four of which are supposed to be of female, postulate on the basis of preliminary examination the presence of three racial types: mesocranial dolichocranial and bracyhcranial. See, B.K. Chatterjee and D.G. Kumar 'Racial Elements in Post-Harappan Skeletal Remains at Lothal', in (ed.) Bala Ratnam, *Anthropology on the March* (Madras 1963), pp. 104–110. It is a very sketchy study not dealing at all with long bones and other physical features.

[4]Sarkar (1972), *op. cit.*, pp. 202–03.

[5]Rao (1973), pp. 161–67. Period A (I) of Lothal begins by 2450 B.C., while A (II) falls in the period between 2350 – 2200 B.C.

[6]The Rig Veda Preserves the memory of some migrations by sea-route, presumably through the Persian Gulf to the west coast of India. For instance, it has been stated (VI, 20.12 and 45.1) that Indra brought Turvasa and Yadu over the sea, and it is worth noting that in the tenth *mandala* Yadu and Turvasa have been called Dāsas. In all likelihood, the Yādavas were originally settled in Saurashtra or the Kathiwar peninsula wherefrom they spread to Mathura. According to one of the legends of the *Harivamsa*, the Yadava clans comprise Bhaima, Kakkura, Bhoja, Andhaka, Yadava, Dasarha and Vrishni. See Ramaprasad Chanda, *The Indo-Aryan Races* (reprinted, Calcutta 1969), pp. 14–15.

Reserved Slip Ware In The Harappan Context

As a way of surface treatment and pottery decoration the "reserved-slip" technique means that two coatings of colour are to be applied to the pot before firing and then the upper one should partly be taken off by a comb-like object leaving the colour underneath exposed and thus creating a contrast between the two according to any preferred design. One may also apply a single coating of colour and then similarly take it off by making it contrast with the colour of the body clay of the pot. Occasionally, this technique is also described as "combed-slip" technique. This is a fairly simple way of pottery decoration. What, however, lends it interest is its comparatively limited distribution both in space and time.

In the Harappan context it was first taken note of by Ernest Mackay in 1931.[1] Up to 1929–30 only four sherds of this type were discovered at Mohenjo-daro and what was more interesting was that they were glazed. The two sherds which Mackay illustrated in plate CLIX of John Marshall's report on Mohenjo-daro

[1]J. Marshall (ed.), *Mohenjo-daro and the Indus Civilization*, vol. II, (London, 1931), p. 578 (hereafter referred to as *Marshall*).

were "made of a light-grey clay of medium thickness, well-baked and fairly tough".[1] The sherds were first coated with a purplish-black slip which on analysis was found to contain manganese, and then washed over with a glaze. Before firing, this glaze was removed in such a way as to leave a wavy pattern. Details of the third sherd were not given but this also is supposed to be of the same technique and colour. The fourth sherd was not described at all. As the pieces were all in small fragments in no case was the shape of the pot clear. Of the two sherds illustrated by Mackay, no. 1 was found at a depth of 2 feet below surface in the VS area while no. 2 came from a depth of 5 feet below surface in the HR area. The third sherd also comes from the HR area but its depth below surface is not mentioned. There is no information about the fourth sherd.

The first two sherds which were identical in nature were analysed by H.J. Plenderleith.[2] He suggested that the pot was first coated with a colouring clay which was burnished into the surface by a blunt instrument. It was then covered over by a dressing, possibly made from powdered slag, and sun-dried. The wavy pattern was created by removing this in a regular fashion with the aid of a comb-like object. The hard and white character of the body of the fired pot containing traces of translucent" material suggested firing "at a fairly high temperature". In 1938 Mackay reported from Mohenjo–daro four (of which one should be the fourth sherd mentioned in 1931) fragments of precisely the same kind. F.R. Allchin[3] points out that it is not clear from the published description whether the pottery was truly "glazed" or, as seems probable, only with a surface gloss resulting from the fusion of particles of the dressing. There should be a glass surface in a truly glazed pottery and this surface can be achieved through a number of techniques. Accidental fusion of particles of the dressing need not be called a true glaze. Mackay himself points this out : "this glazed ware is so like mosaic glass that one feels that some craftsmen experimenting in this direction perhaps produced a vessel composed entirely of ropy glaze which had not fused throughout and could, therefore, not be truly termed a glass".[5]

Not all the discovered pieces of this type of pottery were, however, glazed. The glazed fragments are possibly only seven or eight. In plate LXVII of the 1938 publication[6] Mackay illustrates two pieces of pottery (nos. 3 and 4) which were basically of moderately thin and light red body. They were covered with a white slip and then it was so removed as to produce a parallel wavy line pattern. Though only two fragments are illustrated Mackay refers to "quite a number of pieces of pottery"[7] of this type, "none found anywhere above the level 31.8 ft. below datum."[8] In 1943 Mackay[9] reported three sherds of this type from Chanhu-daro of which the level of only two were mentioned (15.1 ft. and 15.2 ft. below datum). The pink slip of the first sherd was removed to expose the body colour. The second piece was covered first with a dark, almost black slip and then with another of light grey colour. The upper slip of the third sherd was purplish-black while its lower slip was possibly a cream-coloured one.

Only two other Harappan sites have revealed examples of this ware in stratified contexts: Lothal and Surkotada, both in Gujarat. The finds from Lothal are neither adequately published nor illustrated.[10] Two sherds with pink and white slips are said to occur in Lothal IIA and some sherds are supposed to come from Lothal IIIA also.[11] At Surkotada IA, the occurrence of this ware seems to be more common and it is said to be available in a "meagre quantity" 1 B and IC.[12] The nature of the slips of the Surkotada specimens is not clearly described; the decoration is said to be "in blueish, or sometimes reddish hue".[13] The decoration is mostly in either straight bands or wavy lines but in three illustrated examples at least both these patterns have been used.[14] The most important aspect of the Surkotada finds is that their shapes can be reconstructed. The common shapes seem to be narrow-mouthed globular vase, concave-necked vase and basin with incurved rims. Though J.P. Joshi mentions it,[15] the occurrence of the dish-on-stand is not particularly clear. Apart from these stratified occurrences, five unexcavated sites in Kutch—Kotadi,[16] Pabumath[17], Lakhapar[18], Jhangar[19] and Kotada[20], all

[1]*Ibid.* pp. 692–693.
[2]E. Mackay, *Further Excavations at Mohenjo-daro* (Delhi, 1938), p. 188, Plate LXX, 1,2,3,4. (Hereafter referred to as *Mackay*).
[3]Personal discussion.
[4]*Mackay*, p. 188.
[5]*Ibid.*
[6]*Ibid.*
[7]*Ibid.* p. 45.
[8]*Ibid.* p. 188.
[9]E. Mackay, *Chanhu-daro Excavations* (New Haven, 1943), p. 21.
[10]For an illustration of a few sherds from Lothal, S.R. Rao, Further excavations at Lothal, *Lalitkala*, no. 11 (1962), Plate XIX.
[11]S.R. Rao, *Lothal and the Indus Civilization* (Bombay, 1973), p. 57, pp. 164–165.
[12]J.P. Joshi, Exploration in Kutch and excavation at Surkotada and new light on Harappan migration, *Journal of the Oriental Institute*, vol. 22 (1972), p. 126.
[13]*Ibid.* pp. 125–126.
[14]*Ibid.* Figure, 8.
[15]*Ibid.* p. 126.
[16]*Ibid.* p. 109.
[17]*Ibid.* p. 111.
[18]*Ibid.* p. 111.
[19]*Ibid.* p. 112.
[20]*Ibid.*
[21]*Ibid.* p. 113.

explored by Joshi——have yielded reserved-slip ware on the surface.

On the basis of the present published evidence the information about the reserved slip ware in the Harappan context may be summarized thus: it cannot be tied to any specific phase or level of this civilization; if the present evidence is any indication it occurred sporadically throughout. At Mohenjo-daro, if the sherds reported by Mackay in 1938 came, as Mackay emphasized, only from the lower levels, the glazed sherds decorated in the same technique and reported in 1931 were found far more close to the surface. One of them was found at a depth of only 2 feet from the surface. At Chanhu-daro they, however, occur only in an early level. At Lothal they occur both in Phase II and III. At Surkotada they occur in a comparatively large quantity in IA but are also found in IB and IC. Thus, no strict chronological level can be assigned to this ware in the Harappan context. At both Mohenjo-daro and Chanhu-daro in Sind the number of finds was very limited. This seems to be true also at Lothal. Only at Surkotada a comparatively larger number of finds have been made and this accords well with the recognition of this ware on the surface at five other Kutch sites. On the whole, its wider occurrence in the Kutch area seems to be a distinct possibility. Of the four shapes reported at Surkotada only the narrow-mouthed globular vase seems to be a special feature of the reserved slip ware among the published pottery from this site. The designs in all cases (at all the sites) seem to be wavy lines and straight bands. The colour of the slip varies and in some cases there is no double slip, the exposed colour being the colour of the body of the pot. What is also interesting at Surkotada is that wherever the complete form including the base is available, the entire body is found decorated in this technique.

TABLE 1

RESERVED SLIP WARE IN THE HARAPPAN AND SLIGHTLY EARLIER NON-HARAPPAN CONTEXT

Site	Context	Brief description
Mohenjo-daro	(1) 2 ft. below surface (2) 5 ft. below surface (3) Below the level of 31.8 ft. below datum.	No recognizable shape. Purplish-black slip washed over with a glaze in case of the glazed specimens, and otherwise light red body covered with a white slip. Wavy pattern.
Chanhu-daro	(1) 15.1 ft. below datum (2) 15.2 ft. below datum	No recognizable shape. (1) Pink slip partially removed to expose the body colour. (2) Dark, almost black, slip under a light-grey one. (3) Purplish–black slip over a cream-coloured one. Wavy pattern.
Lothal	IIA, IIIA	No recognizable shape, pink and white slips. Parallel bands.
Surkotada	IA,IB,IC	Narrow-mouthed globular vase, concave necked vase, basin with incurved rims dish-on-stand (?). Slip (?). Parallel-bands, wavy pattern or both.
Periano-ghundai	Throughout the duration of the site	Globular jar with out-turned rim. Thick light brown or buff slip partially remove-to expose the body colour. Wavy pattern and parallel bands.
Moghul-ghundai	Same	Same
Surab	Period IV	No recognizable shape. Grey-buff, self-slipped, wavy pattern.

The data on the occurrence of pottery reported to show the reserved slip technique in a non-Harappan context seems to come only from three sites in Baluchistan—Periano-ghundai and Moghul-ghundai in north Baluchistan, and Surab in the Kalat area of central Baluchistan. On plates VI and VIII of Aurel Stein's *Waziristan*[1] there are four sherds from Periano-ghundai, which very much look like the reserved slip ware specimens from Mohenjo-daro and Chanhu-daro. P.SW.71 illustrated on plate VI suggests a globular jar with outturned rim. The painted decoration on the neck is a series of small arches bounded by a line above. Below this is an incised multiple zigzag and wavy pattern. P. 69 illustrated on the same plate seems to be a similar specimen, though in this case there are only two plain bands at the neck. P.SW.15 on plate VIII exactly resembles P.SW.71. P.SW.37 gives no indication of shape but the multiple wavy bands are unmistakable. No details are available in Stein except that he includes them within "incised or relief-decorated pottery"[2] Stein found some similar specimens at Moghul-ghundai also (plate XI, M.M.E. 1 and 15).[3] The percentage of finds was small at both places.

That Stein's finds deserve to be included within the reserved slip category has been made clear by Fairservis. He found some of these sherds on the surface at Periano-ghundai and he listed them as "Periano Reserve Slip", pottery...". . Its principal characteristic consists of wavy and/or parallel ridges that were formed apparently by grooving, in some yet to be determined fashion, a thick light brown or buff slip so that the buff or brown under slip shows through".[4] According to Fairservis, Stein's evidence from Periano-ghundai falls into two successive phases——Zhob cult phase and Incinerary pot burial phase.[5] The reserved slip ware comes from both the phases. At Surab, the existence of the reserved slip ware was noticed by Beatrice de Cardi in Period IV. The sherd in question was part of a straight-sided bowl with thick walls thinning as they curve into the base. It was grey-buff, self-slipped and decorated with horizontal ribbing with wavy combed incising below.[6]

The Indian data on the reserved slip ware are thus somewhat sketchy. Its occurrence in the Zhobcult phase in north Baluchistan, in Surab IV and in the lower levels of Mohenjo-daro, however, seems to make sense together. The beginning of this technique may be said to have begun in the Indian context in an immediately pre-Harappan period and this may also be said to have lasted throughout the Harappan period, though apparently in a very much limited quantity outside the Gujarat area.

A Mesopotamian analogy for this ware in the Indian context was pointed to by Mackay in 1931, though in that year all he could refer to was one sherd found at Kish in 1929–30 by Watelin, which, unlike the Mohenjo-daro specimens was not glazed.[7] In 1938 he referred to the occurrence of this ware at Nineveh "at the end of the Jemdet Nasr period" and at Ur in its "early levels" and at Warkaf.[8] On this basis he suggested that the Mohenjo-daro examples of reserved slip technique, "all of which were found in the lower strata and in such small fragments that the original shapes of the vessels cannot be ascertained" could be regarded as "having been introduced from outside". He also quoted Woolley's opinion that this technique originated in north Syria or Anatolia. In 1943, in the context of Chanhu-daro he wrote more or less the same thing[9]. After the discovery of this ware at Lothal S.R. Rao referred to its occurrence at Mesopotamian sites like Brak, Kish and Ur and tried to emphasize its significance as an item in the Indus-Mesopotamian interrelations.[10] Joshi has attached the same significance to the reserved slip ware among his Harappan finds in Kutch.[11]

To begin with, Woolley's opinion[12] that north Syria was the probable source of this ware need no longer be considered valid. Delougaz[13] pointed out its occurrence in the Mesopotamian context as early as Protoliterate C at Khafajah. The earrliest occurence in Mesopotamia is perhops in a Protoliterate A level at Nippur[14]. In north Syria and the adjacent region it occurs at a number of sites. In north Syria the main context is early to middle phase G where it represents 3-8 per cent of total collected sherds. The forms indicated by the sherds are mostly large jars and the most usual type of decoration consists of re-

[1]A. Stein, *An Archaeological Iour in Waziristan and North Baluchistan* (Calcutta, 1929).
[2]*Ibid*, P. 36.
[3]*Ibid*, PP. 44–45.
[4]W.A. Fairservis, *Archaeological Surveys in the Zhob and Loralai Districts* (New York, 1959) p. 382, Plate 32, b-g; i-j; Figure 52, c-k, 53, d-e.
[5]*Ibid*. pp. 330–333.
[6]Beatrice de Cardi, Excavations and reconnaissance in Kalat, West Pakistan: the prehistoric sequence in the Surab region, *Pakistan Archaeology*, no. 2 (1965) p. 177, Plate IX A, 4, also p. 179.
[7]*Marshall*, P. 578.
[8]*Mackay*, P. 668, P. 652.
[9]*op. cit*, P. 72.
[10]S.R. Rao, *Lothal and the Indus Civilization* (Bombay, 1973), pp. 164–165.
[11]J.P. Joshi, *op. cit.*, P. 124.
[12]L. Woolley, *The Development of Sumerian Art* (London, 1935), pp. 50–51.
[13]P. Delougaz, *Pottery from the Diyala Region* (Chicago, 1952), P. 133. Donald P. Hansen, The Pottery sequence at Nippur from the Middle Uruk to the end of the Old Babylonian period (3400–1600 B.C.), *Chronologies in Old World Archaeology* (R.W. Ehrich ed.), Chicago, 1965, P. 203, Figure 13.

served oblique radial lines and "some elaboration in the way of bandings," What is important is that the phase G in this area bears evidence of a Mesopotamian contact and the occurrence of the reserved slip ware may be explained by this.[1] At Carchemish Woolley[2] points out that this feature "which is never very common, persists into both the Early and the Late Bronze Age". At Gzōlū Kule, Tarsus, this was more common in Early Bronze Age II when it was used chiefly for pitchers and possibly for jars[3].

TABLE 2

REPRESENTATIVE OCCURRENCE OF RESERVED SLIP WARE IN WEST ASIA

Site or Region	Context	Brief description
North Syria and the Adjacent Region	Antioch Plain: primarily Amuq G level; also at Carchemish Early and Late Bronze Age; at Gozlu Kule, Tarsus, more common in Early Bronze Age II.	Mostly large jars; Oblique radial line and "some elaboration in the way of bandings".
Khafajah and Other Sites in the Diyala Region, Mesopotamia	Protoliterate C Early Dynastic II	Large spouted jar with short flaring neck and slightly rounded base; also solid foot goblets and jars. Oblique lines and horizontal lines, occasionally combined with other designs.
Nineveh	Level 4, towards the top of the stratum	Globular jar with a spout
Kish	Early Dynastic I-III	Fragments only.
Ur	Protoliterate—Early Dynastic	Straight-necked rimless jar with oval belly.
Nippur	Levels XIX-XVI (middle-late Uruk)	Jar with everted rim, tall jar.
Susa	Middle Uruk (?)	No detail
Brak	Sargonid	No recognizable shape. Horizontals, Zig-zag curves.
Jidle	Same	Same
Hama (Orontes, Syria)	Early Dynastic (?)	Radial lines. Goblets and jars.
Bampur	Periods I-IV	Wavy pattern Jars, bowls and basins.

[1]R.J. and Linda Braidwood, *Excavations in the Plaun of Antioch, I, The Earlier Assemblages,* Phases A-J. (Chicago, 1960), PP. 275–277. Figures 218, 219, 220; Plates 88, 1,3,4, 85,1,7.

[2]L.Woolley, *Carchemish, Report on the Evcavations at Jerablus on behalf of the British Museum,* Part III (London, 1952), P. 229.

[3]Hetty Goldman, *Excavations at Gozlu Kule Iarsus,* vol. II (Princeton, 1956), p. 117, Plate 248, no. 207.

In Mesopotamia the occurrence of reserved slip ware in the Diyala region has been comprehensively studied by Delougaz. At Khafajah, a sherd came from a layer of debris below the foundations of Sin temple I, and at a higher level, there were two globular spouted jars from beneath the Small Temple in 043. The characteristics of these jars are: a short neck, flaring sharply at the top; a flat base; and a long spout.[1] Delougaz has described and illustrated a number of this pottery from Khafajah, Tell Asmar and Tell Agrab. From its beginning in Protoliterate C (Jemdet Nasr period) it continues to occur up to Early Dynastic III, though in this period it is "very rare, and in all probability such sherds as were found in ED III levels belong to vessels of earlier periods". A distinctive shape seems to be a large spouted jar with short flaring neck and slightly rounded base.[2] Reserved slip is seldom applied all over the jar; in most cases it is limited to the upper part of the jar and occasionally can be combined with other incised or applique designs also.[3] Solid foot goblets and jars with upright handles also show sometimes traces of reserved slip.[4] The designs are mostly oblique lines and horizontal bands. In one case there is a chequer pattern.[5] At Nineveh in north Mesopotamia, the reserved slip occurs in Nineveh 4 towards the top of the stratum and the earliest example is a globular jar with a spcut.[6] This jar bears such a close resemblance to the Diyala specimens that according to Delougaz "it provides fairly precise evidence for relative dating".[7] In south Mesopotamia, one may refer to the sites of Kish, Ur and Nippur. At Kish, Watelin[8] found numerous fragments of these wares (not illustrated in the report) but their shapes could not be reconstructed. They shou'd belong to Early Dynastic I-III period. At Ur also the stratigraphic occurrence is not quite certain but it occurs on vessels found in the Jemdet Nasr cemetery. As Ann Louise Perkins puts it, "whether the Ur vessels are Protoliterate or Early Dynastic we cannot say".[9] The shape Woolley illustrated is a rather straight-necked rimless jar with an oval belly.[10] Donald Hansen has illustrated a number of reserved slip spec mens from Nippur. The earliest occurrence is in Inanna level XIX (middle Uruk period) in the form of a buff ware jar with everted rim, and decorated by oblique lines in reserve slip below the shoulder.[11] A tall jar with reserved slip on the upper part of the body comes from the Inanna level XVII, also in the middle Uruk or Protoliterate period[12]. In level XVI (late Uruk or Protoliterate B), there is a jar with an incised design on the shoulder and with vertical stripes of reserved slip on the body.[13] The reserved slip ware also occurs in a roughly middle Uruk level at Susa.[14]

In the Sargonid context, reference may be made to the sites in the Khabur and Balikh valleys. From Brak, Mallowan reported and illustrated fragments of reserved slip pottery consisting of a buff clay painted over with a reddish brown wash. No shape could be reconstructed but the design consisted of a series of horizontals, zigzags and curves.[15] Mallowan pointed out that the fabric was of great rarity. Apart from Brak this occurred in 5 level in the Balikh valley.[16] Even here no complete pot could be recovered and the nature of designs was the same. Mallowan also refers to its occurrence at Hama in the Orontes valley of Syria in a somewhat uncertain context.[17]

The following points deserve notice while comparing, the Indus finds with those of Mesopotamia. First there is no specific similarity at all between the early Mesopotamian (Protoliterate to Early Dynastic) and the Indus finds. There is no typical Mesopotamian shape and there is no typical Mesopotamian design of this period among any of the Baluchistan, Sind and Gujarat finds. Secondly, the Indian specimens share only the element of similar designs with the Mesopotamian finds from the Sargonid level of the Khabur and Balikh valleys where, it may be added, they are to great rarity. But the comparison is not of much significance because of two reasons. The Baluchistan and early Mohenjo-daro occurrences are not later than the Khabur and Balikh finds and cannot in any way be said to have been de-

[1]P. Delougaz, *op. cit.*, P. 35, Plate 17 ; P. 37, Plate 19, b-c.
[2]*Ibid.* cf. P. 53.
[3]*Ibid*, cf. P. 60, Plate 51, c.
[4]*Ibid* cf. P. 56, Plate 46, g-h.
[5]*Ibid*, Plate 67, f.
[6]M.E.L. Mallowan *in* the British Museum excavations at Nineveh, 1931–32, *Annals of Archaeology and Anthropology*, University of Liverpool, vol. 20 (1933), P. 167, Plate LII, 12.
[7]P. Delougaz, *Op. Cit.*, P. 134.
[8]L. Ch. Watelin, *Excavations at Kish*, vol. IV, 1925–30 (Paris, 1934), P. 14.
[9]A.L. Perkins, *The Comparative Archaeology of Early Mesopotamia* (Chicago, 1949), P. 163.
[10]L. Woolley, *The Development of Sumerian Art* (London, 1935), PP. 50–51.
[11]Donald P. Hansen, *Op. cit.*, P. 203, figure 13.
[12]*Ibid*, P. 204, figure 19.
[13]*Ibid*. P. 205, figure 23.
[14]R.H. Dyson, Problems in the relative chronology of Iran, 6000–2000 B.C., *Chronologies in Old World Archaeology* (R.W. Ehrich ed.), Chicago, 1965, p. 224.
[15]M.E.L. Mallowan, Excavations at Brak and Chagar Bazra, *Iraq*, vol. 9 (1947), P. 191, Plate XLIII.
[16]M.E.L. Mallowan, Excavations in the Balikh valley, 1938, *Iraq*, Vol. 8 (1946), PP. 111–159.
[17]H. Ingholt, *Rapport Preliminaire sur la Premiere Campagne des Fouilles de Hama* (Kopenhagen, 1934), PP. 17–18. Also, H. Ingholt, *Rapport Preliminaire sur Sept Campagnes de Fouilles Hama en Syrie* (1932–38), Copenhagen, 1940, Plate VIII; goblets and jars. The context seems to be broadly Early Dynastic (loca level J).

rived from that area. The Baluchistan and Sind finds share common designs with the Gujarat specimens and so in the case of the Gujarat specimens also there is no ground to derive them from the Khabur and Balikh valleys.

To explain the beginning of this technique in the context of Baluchistan (which along with its occurrence in the lower level of Mohenjo-daro may be said to mark its beginning in the Indian context) one need not go further west than Bampur. At Bampur, shallow comb incising as a form of decoration persisted in all the periods from I to IV. It occurs on the shoulder of a white-slipped jar in Period I.[1] It is usually used on jars or wide bowls in Period II.[2] In Period III comb incising was in use for jars and large basins. In most instances incising was applied on a cream or thin buff slip.[3] In Period IV, comb incising was applied to cream-slipped as well as red vessels.[4] This rather common use of the reserved slip technique in all the periods of Bampur should have some significance in relation to its occurrence in the prehistoric context of Baluchistan. What is also interesting is that its occurrence in Bampur I makes this technique in south-eastern Iran almost as early as its occurrence in Mesopotamia.[5] The technique seems to occur also at Chah Husaini in the same area.[6] It is probable that when pottery from sites in this area are more fully published more evidence of this technique will be found. In the present context what seems logical is that its occurrence in Moghul-ghundai, Periano-ghundai, Surab and early Mohenjo-daro should be viewed in the background of its occurrence in sites of south-eastern Iran like Bampur and Chah Husaini.

At the same time it must be pointed out that the technique had its own history in India. The present knowledge of this history is sketchy but there is not a scrap of reasonable archaeological evidence to interpret the Indus finds as evidence of any link with Mesopotamia. It is also interesting to note that this ware seems now to be rather common at the Harappan sites of Kutch. Those who find in them evidence of Indus-Mesopotamian contact must explain why of all categories of Mesopotamian objects only this should occur in such quantities at the Indus sites, particularly when the other types of objects are so rare at them. The basic technique of the reserved slip ware, like so many others of the potter's repertoire, is not difficult to learn or apply, and there seems no reason why it should not occur widely and sporadically without giving evidence of direct contact or trade.

Churchill College
Cambridge, U. K.

DILIP K. CHAKRABARTI

[1]Beatrice de Cardi, *Excavations at Bampur, a Third Millennium Settlement in Persian Baluchistan*, 1966 (New York, 1970), p. 279, figure 17,8.

[2]*Ibid*, figure 18, 30–34, p. 281.

[3]*Ibid*, p. 287, figure 22, 133.

[4]*Ibid*, p. 291.

[5]For the position of Bampur I in relation to the Mesopotamian sequence, C.R.H. Meadow, A chronology for the Indo-Iranian borderlands and southern Baluchistan: 4000–2000 B.C., *Radiocarbon and Indian Archaeology*, D.P. Agrawal, A. Ghosh ed. (Bombay, 1973), p. 201, figure 1.

[6]A. Stein, *Archaeological Reconnaissances in Northwestern India and Southeastern Iran* (London, 1937), plate XIX. Hus. 17.

A Channel-Spouted Vessel From Hissar

The specimen in question bears the Tehran Museum number 5198. It does not have any excavation number written on it but, according to the Museum Register of Antiquities, it comes from Hissar and was acquired in 1933. It was obviously found in excavations which ended towards the end of 1932.[1]

It is a coarse handmade vessel, pale buff with a tinge of red and black in places, evidently the result of careless firing. The pale buff surface is not the result of any application of wash or slip; it is just the colour the original clay took after firing. The profile is convex and the base flat. The height is 12 cm and it measures 10 cm across the mouth. The open channel spout is 4.5. cm long. The thickness of the body at the rim is roughly 4 cm. This type of spouted vessel does not occur before Hissar III, and if the number of specimens in the Tehran Museum is any indication, it is more

[1]We wish to offer our thanks to Dr. Gholam Ali Shamlou for facilitating our study of the Hissar collection, and to Dr Firouz Bagherzadeh, Director of the Iranian Centre for Archaeological Research, due to whose kind initial interest it was possible for the second author to have access to this collection.

common in Hissar IIIB than in IIIA or IIIC. What needs emphasis, however, is that all the other specimens (published, or unpublished in the Tehran Museum) belong to the general run of grey pottery and have nothing in common (except the channel spout) with this pale buff, coarse vessel. This does not generally fit in the range of typical Hissar pottery. On this point we feel reasonably beyond doubt.

What lends this vessel further interest is that Rafiq Mughal[1] has reported an identical type—coarse, handmade (as suggested by Mughal's photograph), pale buff in colour and channel-spouted—from Dabarkot, the result of a surface exploration. Mughal[2] has already spoken of a general Hissar-Shah Tepe analogy, and considered the Dabarkot specimen as an imported item from eastern (northeastern) Iran. Mughal, however has not appreciated the fact that a coarse, handmade, pale buff, channel-spouted vessel is not at home in the

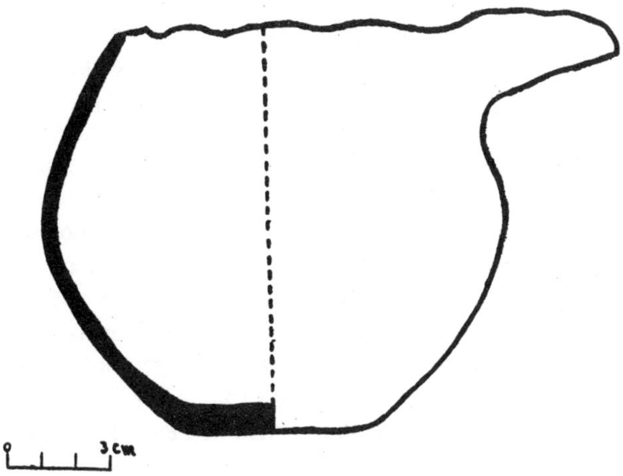

FIG. 1.

Hissar-Shah Tepe ceramic and the Dabarkot specimen is unlikely to be an import from Hissar-Shah Tepe area. On the contrary, both Hissar and Dabarkot might have got it from some other common source. Open channel spout is a general type, hardly useful to dub any piece as an "imported item"; it is the vessel as a whole which should be considered for any specific comparison. We feel that our specimen from Hissar and Mughal's specimen from Dabarkot have enough elements in common to be considered the products of a common manufacturing area.

The question of this common source is difficult to determine but one may draw attention to a similar shape in coarse red ware from Garden Reg Copper site in Afghan Seistan, reported by George Dales[3]. Garden Reg possesses buff ware also but no channel spout has been reported in this buff ware. The date of the site is still unknown but considering some of the positive Hissar analogies (notably the Alabaster objects which are almost one of the type-fossils of Hissar IIIC) Dales has cited for the neighbouring (and possibly related) site of Godar-i-Shah[4] it need not come as a surprise if the Garden Reg Copper site turns out to be prehistoric and contemporary with Hissar IIIC.

Meanwhile, the specimen illustrated by Mughal from Dabarkot becomes positively interesting in view of our illustrated vessel from Hissar, but it may be emphasized that the Dabarkot specimen does not have any bearing at all on the open channel spouts found in different contexts in inner India. Secondly, even in the context of Baluchistan it is no way more significant except the fact that it is an evidence of contact between Baluchistan, Seistan and northeast Iran in about Hissar IIIC period.

Teheran Museum
and British Institute of
Persian Studies, Teheran

PARVEEN MOGHRDAM
DILIP K. CHAKRABARTI

[1]R. Mughal, 'Explorations in northern Baluchistan, 1972: new evidence and fresh interpretation' *Proceedings of the IInd Annual Symposium on Archaeological Research in Iran*, ed. Firouz Bagherzadeh, (Tehran, 1974) pp. 276–286, fig. 3.
[2]*Ibid*, p. 278

[3]G.F. Dales, 'Prehistoric research in southern Afghan Seistan', *Afghanistan* (1972), pp. 14–40, fig. 6.
[4]*Ibid*, pp. 30–36

The Heliodorus Pillar at Besanagar

The famous Heliodorus pillar[1] at Besnagar (fig. I) is so-named because an inscription of the second century B.C. tells that it was erected by Heliodorus, ambassador of an Indo-Greek king, in honour of Vasudeva, god-of-gods. It needs no introduction to students of ancient India. But since our aim here is to break new ground a few preliminary words about its site, the present-day appearance of the pillar, and what has been said and thought about it hitherto, may not be out of place.

Besnagar in central India, where the pillar stands, is the site of the ancient mercantile city of Vidisa, about six miles from Sanchi. This region owed its prosperity in early times to local fertility of soil (still famous for grain-growing), and to its location on the *dakshinapatha* or 'southern trade route' linking the Ganges valley with the Deccan and the seaports of the West coast. The city had been founded at the confluence of two rivers, the Betwa and the Bes, and the pillar stands outside the fork on what must have been the north-eastern periphery of the city (Pl. XIII A.).

Its present height, with crowning emblem missing, is about six metres above modern ground-level, where there is a square platform or *chabutra* of comparatively modern construction' (Original ground-level as we shall presently learn, had been at least one metre lower than it is to-day). Compared with so-called 'Asokan' pillars, the Heliodorus is barely half the size. It is carved in pinkish-brown sandstone, and was originally well-polished, but not to such a high lustre as 'Asokan' pillars.[2] Also unlike the latter, the Heliodorous is faceted and highly ornamented. The shaft changes in form from octagonal at base, to sixteenths in the centre, thence to thirty-seconds, and finally into a smooth round surface near the top. The junction between the octagon and the sixteenths is ornamented with a band of half rosettes; and the junction between sixteenths and thirty-seconds with a conventional garland held up by birds carrying fruit in their beaks. The garland is three-stranded and somewhat rope-like, hanging in festoons. Surviving components of the capital include a 'bell' with rope-moulding above, and a rather heavy, square abacus. The latter is badly damaged (supposedly by lightning), but retains traces of geese-and-honeysuckle decoration, and is edged at the base with necklace ornament (Pl XA and B).[3]

This pillar was first brought to notice by Alexander Cunningham in the 1870's,[4] long before it was known to bear any inscription. It was then under worship by a local Saivite sect calling it Kham Baba, and its surface was thickly encrusted with red-lead paste applied in ritual. Both high and low castes were paying homage, and animals were being sacrificed. The attendant priest or *pujari* lived in a modern house built on top of an adjacent mound, known to be of ancient origin.

Although assured to the contrary, Cunningham suspected that an inscription was concealed beneath the encrustations of paste. He sensed intuitively the monument's historical importance, describing it as one of "the most curious and novel" of all his discoveries. However, he then went on to make a number of false inferences. For instance, he assumed that it was of Gupta origin and that the original crowning emblem had been a fan-palm which he found lying on the ground nearby. So certain did he feel about this that when he came to draw the shaft, he depicted it with this emblem on top.[5] He also rendered inaccurately the ornamental details of the shaft, showing the band of half-rosettes as whole-rosettes, and putting this band in the wrong place (too high up). The shaft's upper band of swag-like ornament and birds he left out altogether. He also omitted the section where the shaft breaks from sixteen into thirty-two facets.

A few yards further off, Cunningham found a second pillar-capital, this time with an emblem in the form of a water-monster or *makara*, No trace of the shaft was discovered; but once again his draughtman's imagination went to work, and he published a drawing of how this particular pillar might have appeared when complete, and in scale relationship to the Heliodorous..[6]

[1] This article originated as a lecture given at the School of Oriental and African Studies' University of London, which was published verbatium in AARP (Art and Archaeology Research Papers) No. 6, London, 1974, under the title "The Heliodorus pillar: a fresh appraisal". In that form it was intended primarily to provoke discussion. Here the material is re-presented with some changes in emphasis, but without alteration to the basic thesis.

[2] The polish has been partly obliterated above ground by the corrosive action of coatings of red-lead paste applied in worship (to be mentioned again presently).

[3] I am much indebted to my colleague Margue Margaret Hall for the drawings published with this article, and also for many helpful comments and suggestions made in discussion.

[4] *Archaeological Survey of India Reports*. vol. x, Calcutta, 1880, pp. 41–42.

[5] *Ibid.* plate XIV, left.

[6] *Ibid.* plate XIV, right.

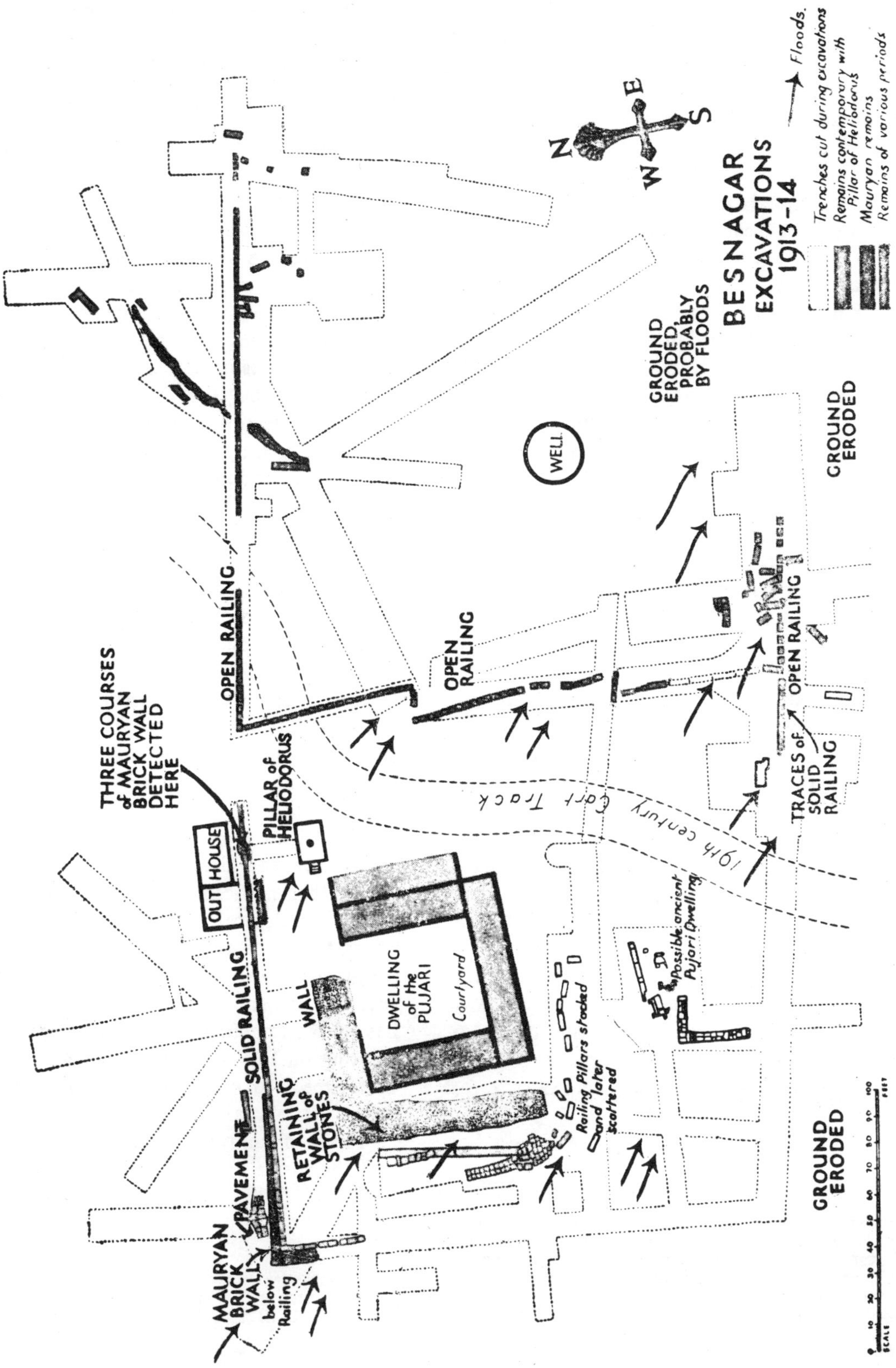
BESNAGAR
EXCAVATIONS
1913-14
Trenches cut during excavations
Remains contemporary with Pillar of Heliodorus
Mauryan remains
Remains of various periods
Floods.
N
E
S
W
GROUND ERODED, PROBABLY BY FLOODS
GROUND ERODED
GROUND ERODED
WELL
OPEN RAILING
OPEN RAILING
OPEN RAILING
TRACES of SOLID RAILING
19th century Cart Track
THREE COURSES of MAURYAN BRICK WALL DETECTED HERE
PILLAR of HELIODORUS
OUT HOUSE
SOLID RAILING
WALL
DWELLING of the PUJARI
Courtyard
RETAINING WALL of STONES
PAVEMENT
MAURYAN BRICK WALL below Railing
Railing Pillars stacked and later scattered
Possible ancient Pujari Dwelling
SCALE
FEET

Half-a-mile away, he found a third pillar-capital of approximately the same size and period-style. This time the crowning emblem was in the form of a *kalpa-druma* or wishing-tree[1] the type of tree popular in ancient Indian folklore as producing from its branches all kinds of material wealth such as money, jewels and clothes. Cunningham thought that all these pillar-remains had belonged to the same site as the Heliodorus, but he did not explain why so many votive pillars should have been concentrated before one particular shrine, not what their precise meaning and function might have been.

Thirty years later, in 1909, the Heliodorus pillar came into the news again with the discovery of the inscription on its shaft.[2] Carved in Brahmi characters, it stated that the pillar was a *Garuda-dhvaja,* literally 'Garuda-standard', erected by one Heliodorus, a Bhagavata, the son of Dion, from Taxila, in honour of Vasudeva, God-of-gods. Heliodorus further described himself in the inscription as having come as envoy of king Antialkidas to king Kasiputra Bhagabhadra.

Antialkidas, well-known from his coinage, was a Greek who ruled between the Hindu Kush and the Jhelum in the latter part of the second century B.C. As to Kasiputra, most scholars have until recently identified him with the ninth Sunga king in the Puranic list; but excavations by West German arachaeologists at Sonkh, near Mathura, have now provided evidence to suggest that imperial Sunga rule at Vidisa did not extend beyond 120 B.C., in which case Bhagabhadra would have been the name of a local ruler.[3]

As to Heliodorus himself, his name being pure Greek he was assumed to have had Greek blood, and this encouraged the further conclusion that he was a foreigner converted to the cult of Vasudeva, the followers of which called themselves Bhagavatas. Although an important cult in northern India in the second century B.C., its history and origins are obscure; but on the grounds that the worship of Krishna and Vishnu were linked with this cult, it has been regarded as a kind of proto-Vaishnavism.

An additional point of interest about the Heliodorus inscription is that its last line includes what seems to be a quotation from the *Mahabharata*[4] an advocacy of the virtues of Restraint, Renunciation and Rectitude. This was interpreted as a rare instance of a Greek being versed in Indian epic literature.

The first serious archaeological excavations were conducted at Besnagar between 1913 and 1915 under D.R. Bhandarkar, who dug a network of trenches shown in the plan at Plate 3B. A number of interesting discoveries were made,[5] but we shall have time here to focus only on those of direct relevance to the history of the pillar. (A severe limitation of the operation was that Bhandarkar was not at this time allowed to dig into the mound which supported the *pujari's* house, recognised as the logical site of the shrine to Vasudeva). Among the facts he did establish was that from the earliest times the site had been subjected to major floods,the direction of the flood-waters being indicated by arrows in the plan at fig. 1.

Bhandarkar dug a trench into the foundations of the Heliodorus Pillar from the north side. The stratification he reported was most telling, yet at the time he did not apparently recognise its full significance, as we shall presently show. Fortunately, his report included a photograph (reproduced here at Plate 5A, and a detailed drawing elaborated at Plate 5B). There are three important details to be noted from these: (1) that the shaft started below ground as an octagon, the first three feet being left untrimmed; (2) that the original ground-level was about 4.5 cm above the junction between trimmed and untrimmed sections of the shaft; and (3) that beneath the shafts were two placement stones, with a layer of stone-metal between. Bhandarkar did not try to draw any historical conclusions from these facts.

Another half-century elapsed, until 1963-65, when the Archaeological Survey of India resumed excavations at the site, this time under M.D. Khare, who had permission to demolish the *pujari's* house and to investi gate the ancient mound underneath. Since no report has yet been published, there is an obvious risk in commenting on this excavation, but as a hint of what we may expect to come, Khare wrote a popular article in the art journal *Lalit Kala.*[6]

From circumstantial evidence, Khare concluded that the shrine contemporary with the erection of the Heliodorus Pillar had stood on top of the mound, al-

[1]*Ibid.*, plate XV, This capital is now in the Indian Museum Calcutta.

[2]J.H. Marshall, "Notes on archaeological exploration in India, 1908–09", Jr. *Royal Asiatic Society*, *London*, 1909, pp. 1053–1056. Also D.C. Sircar, *Select Inscriptions*, vol. I, Calcutta, 1965, p. 88.

[3]The Sonkh excavation report has not yet been published. The information was communicated personally by Dr. H. Hartel. The idea of Bhagabhadra or Bhagavata having been a local ruler was first mooted by A.K. Narain in a footnote to his book, *The Indo-Greeks*, Oxford, 1957, p. 199. However, the same author contradicts himself in another passage where he claims as almost certain the identification of Bhagabhadra with the ninth Sunga king in the Puranic list.

[4]Hemchandra Raychaudhuri, "The Mahabharata and the Besnagar Inscription of Heliodorus", *Journal of Asiatic Society of Bengal*, vol. XVIII, 1922, Calcutta (1923).

[5]D.R. Bhandarkar, "Excavations at Besnagar", *Archaeological Survey of India, Annual Report,* 1913-14, pp. 186 ff; and *ibid* 1914–15, pp. 66 ff.

[6]M.D. Khare, "Discovery of a Vishnu temple near the Heliodorus Pillar", *Lalit Kala*, nos. 13-14, 1967–9, pp. 21–27.

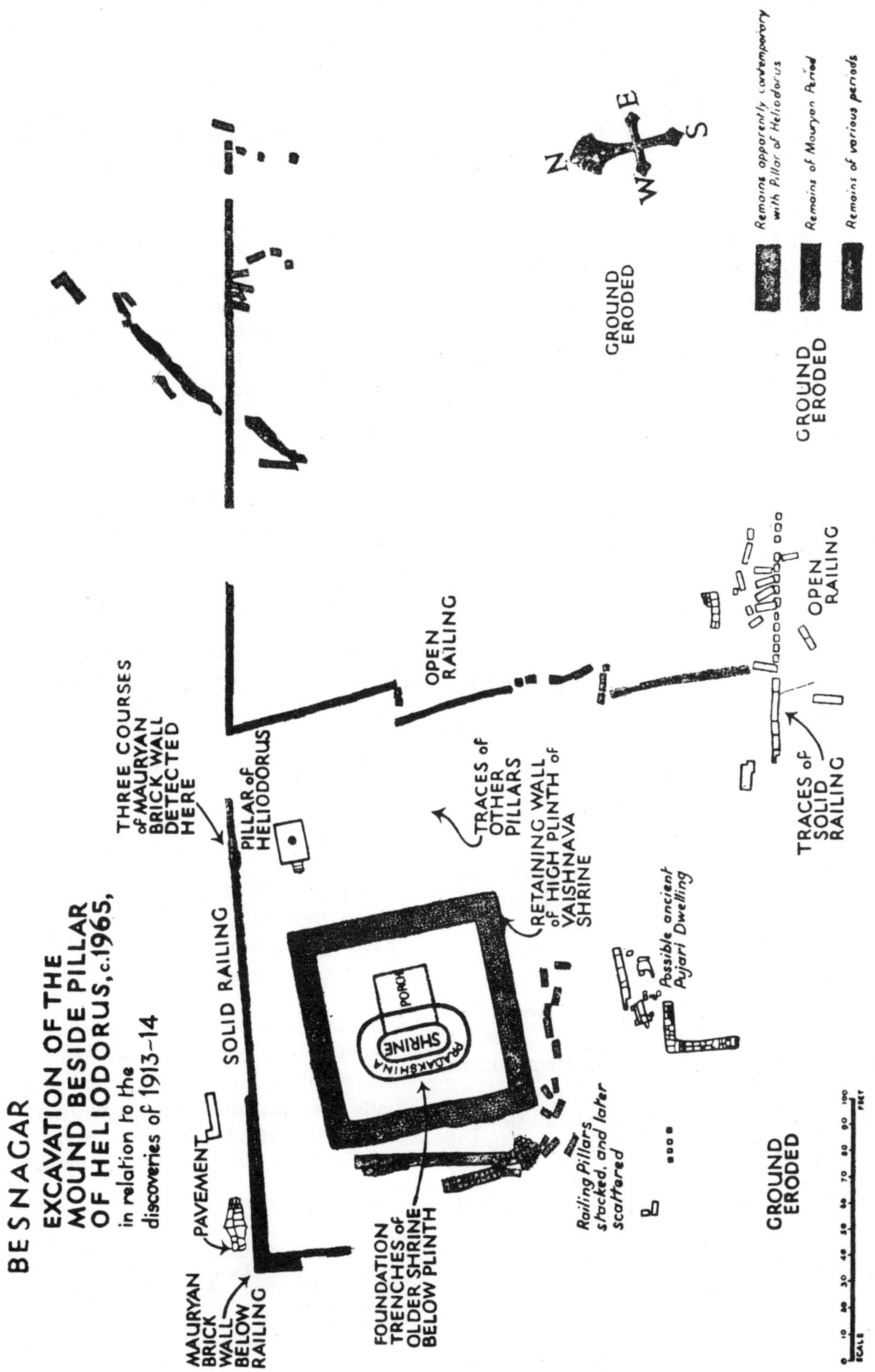
BESNAGAR
EXCAVATION OF THE MOUND BESIDE PILLAR OF HELIODORUS, c.1965,
in relation to the discoveries of 1913–14
MAURYAN BRICK WALL BELOW RAILING
PAVEMENT
PAVEMENT
SOLID RAILING
THREE COURSES of MAURYAN BRICK WALL DETECTED HERE
PILLAR of HELIODORUS
FOUNDATION TRENCHES of OLDER SHRINE BELOW PLINTH
SHRINE
PRADAKSHINA
PORCH
RETAINING WALL of HIGH PLINTH of VAISHNAVA SHRINE
TRACES of OTHER PILLARS
OPEN RAILING
OPEN RAILING
TRACES of SOLID RAILING
Railing Pillars stacked, and later scattered
Possible ancient Pujari Dwelling
GROUND ERODED
GROUND ERODED
GROUND ERODED
GROUND ERODED
N
E
S
W
Remains apparently contemporary with Pillar of Heliodorus
Remains of Mauryan Period
Remains of various periods

though all traces had apparently been expunged by the time the modern *pujari's* house was built. The mound itself was found to have retaining walls of brick, and digging down to the very bottom (that is, to the original surface-level of the site), he reached traces of a still earlier elliptical foundation (clearly visible in fig. 3. These he interpreted as the foundations of an elliptical temple built of perishable materials at least a century before the erection of the Heliodorus pillar. This temple, he concluded, had been destroyed by flood before 200 B.C. whence the mound was raised and another shrine built on top. It was after the building of the second shrine that Heliodorus erected his pillar. Khare then adds the following interesting information:

> That more than one pillar may have been erected in one alignment N - S) out side the eastern rubble wall, is indicated by the traces of several pits at uniform distances with similar filling as that of the Heliodorus pillar, as confirmed by an exposed section cut into a pit with indication of at least more on the plan in the trenches excavated on the eastern side of the mound. .. The plan of the pits, probably dug for the other four pillars. .. is in alignment with the rubble wall only and not with the temple of Period 1

In other words, Khare is here suggesting that all pillar-remains post-date the construction of the second shrine.

Before making our own comments, let us now collate and summarise information embodied in the two reports. We get from them a picture of three phases in the history of the site.

Phase 1 (possibly 4th/3rd century B.C.) At this stage there was an elliptical shrine (said to be a temple) founded at original ground-level. This shrine had been destroyed by flood by 200 B.C.

Phase II, (about 200 B.C.) An earthen mound with brick retaining wall was raised on top of the foundations of the elliptical shrine. On top of the mound is thought to have been built a second shrine to Vasudeva, all traces of which have disappeared.

Phase III (late 2nd century B.C.) Heliodorus appeared on the scene and erected his famous pillar. A number of other pillars were also erected in an alignment running north- south from the Heliodorus.

So much, then, for what has been said and thought hitherto about the Heliodorus pillar. We shall now review the evidence in the light of knowledge more recently gained from re-examination of 'Asokan' pillars.

First, a few observations about the site itself. One thing we ought recognise is that the site of the Heliodorus pillar is first and foremost a *tirtha*. It is a *tirtha*, moreover, which is coincident with the confluence of two streams and a major crossroads. Such sites were pre-eminently the sacred spots of prehistoric and protohistoric India, and the antiquity of this particular one is attested by the discovery of many neolithic and chalcolithic implements, independently reported.[1] From what we know about such *tirthas* elsewhere, we can suppose that the site was also a centre of tree-worship, and probably marked by a sacred grove.

From all this it is obvious that whatever conclusions we are going to reach about the Vasudeva shrine and its accompanying votive pillars, they must have represented a relatively late intrusion into what was already a very ancient religious site or 'sacred centre' associated with the pre-literate cult of the *axis mundi*, universal to the ancient world. It is strange and yet symptomatic of the narrowness of interest and vision of most scholars specialising in the study of material culture, that none writing on the Heliodorus pillar has hitherto bothered to mention that pillar-worship and tree-worship are combined at this site up to the present day.

Taking now a second look at the foundations of the Heliodorus pillar as revealed by Bhandarkar's excavation in 1913, we are bound to ask a question hitherto ignored: why are there *two* placement stones under the shaft?

Those who have followed recent research on 'Asokan' pillars[2] will remember that the use of placement-stones was a relatively late technique. We called it Method 'A', distinguishing it from the pre-Asokan Method 'B' which did not employ them. The fact that there are here *two* placement stones, separated by a layer of stone-metal, suggests that when Heliodorus erected his famous pillar he was replacing an earlier stone votive pillar, the latter perhaps destroyed by the same flood which washed away the earlier shrine.

As we have already noted, the inscription on the Heliodorus pillar calls it a *Garuda-dhvaja*, literally 'Garuda-standard'. This is perhaps the earliest recorded instance of the term *dhvaja* being applied to a monumental stone column, and its use therefore deserevs close attention. In Indian literature, the term *dhvaja* is commonly applied to *portable* standards bearing either flags with insignia, or animal-emblems. They were essentially war-standards, and the custom of carrying them into battle extended wherever Aryan culture spread in Asia and in Europe.[3] Prior to the Aryans, there were

[1] *Ibid*, p. 21, footnote 1.

[2] John Irwin, "'Asokan' pillars: a reassessment of the evidence", Part II, "Structure", *Burlington Magazine*, vol. CXVI, London, December, 1974.

[3] Comte du Mesnil du Buisson, "L'Etendard d'Atargatis et Hadad a Doura-Europos ou la desse Semia", Revue des Arts Asiatiques, tome XI, Paris, 1937, pp 75–87; and J. Prozyluski "Le culte de l'Etendard chex les Scythes et dans l'Inde", *Zalmoixs* (*Revue des Etudes religieuses*). vol. I, Paris, 1938, pp. 13–19.

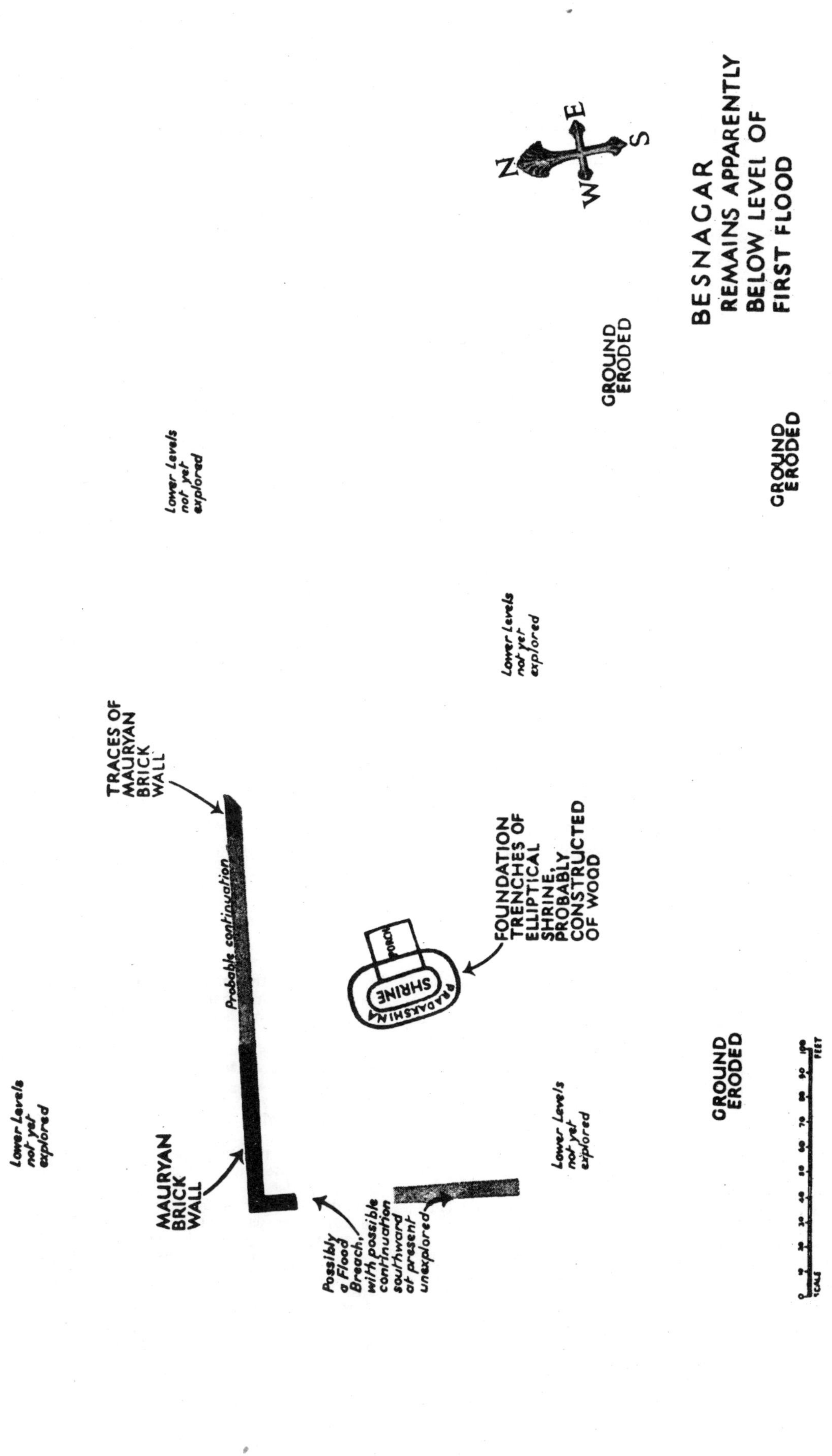
BESNAGAR
REMAINS APPARENTLY
BELOW LEVEL OF
FIRST FLOOD
N
E
S
W
GROUND ERODED
GROUND ERODED
GROUND ERODED
Lower Levels not yet explored
Lower Levels not yet explored
Lower Levels not yet explored
Lower Levels not yet explored
TRACES OF MAURYAN BRICK WALL
Probable continuation
FOUNDATION TRENCHES OF ELLIPTICAL SHRINE, PROBABLY CONSTRUCTED OF WOOD
PORCH
SHRINE
PRADAKSHINA
MAURYAN BRICK WALL
Possibly a Flood Breach, with possible continuation southward at present unexplored
FEET

still more ancient cults of the sacred standard in Western Asia and Egypt.[1]

In India the chief source of evidence is epic literature. In the Mahabharata, in particular, there are many references to show that the first aim in combat was destruction of the enemy's *dhvaja*, because to destroy his standard was to leave him divinely unprotected. What is more, the *dhvaja* was worshipped before battle by the rite of circumnambulation (*pradakshina*) in the belief that the protective deity was actually incumbent in the emblem.[2] In other words, the *dhvaja* was not simply a symbol, but an actual manifestation of the divine. In Vedic texts the term is used interchangeably with *ketu*, implying divine luminosity and equated with the actual godhead.[3] In *Rigveda* VIII. 96.4, for instance, Indra is called a *ketu*. By the same logic, the *Indra-dhvaja*, which was the banner carried by Indra in his demiurgic war against the demons, is also called *Indra-ketu*. Such connections, illustrations of which could be multiplied, leave no doubt that the *dhvaja's* original significance was cosmic. In other words, when carried into battle by the mortal warrior, it partook of the character of the archetypal *Indradhvaja*, which we should now be in a position to recognise as mystically synonymous with the *axis-mundi*—most important of all concepts in the pre-history of religion.[4]

All this helps us to understand the great faith warriors placed in the magically protective power of their portable *dhvajas*, which one passage of the Mahabharata describes as *jayaspadam* (literally, 'seat of victory').[5] The king carrying this portable *axis mundi* into battle felt himself anchored to the unshakeable centre of the universe, and as long as he remained under its protection he was confident that no harm could befall him. Many references show that the moment his *dhvaja* was destroyed, hope of victory vanished. Professor F.B.J. Kuiper has demonstrated,[6] moreover, that in earliest traditions relating to the *dhvaja*, the most important part was not the flag or emblem but the actual staff or pole (*yashti*) — in other words that part which constituted the cosmic pivot, and was variously imaged by pillar, pole, post, tree or mountain.[7]

We know what portable *dhvajas* looked like in the second century B.C. because they are often depicted in Buddhist reliefs of the period. For instance, the relief from Bharhut shows a queenly personage on horseback carrying a *Garudadhvaja*, the staff of which consists of a plain wooden pole typical of all such standards. Garuda seems to have been one of the most favoured *dhvaja-emblems* both in their portable and in their monumental form. Do we know that in the second century B.C. Garuda was already fulfilling his prime role as Vishnu's carrier? To the best of our knowledge, the question has neither been posed nor answered, and scholars have perhaps too readily assumed that Garuda's later role can be read into this period. It is certainly relevant in this context to recall that in Vedic mythology the lower end of the cosmic pillar was supported by *nagas* in the underworld,[8] and that the relationship between Garuda and the *nagas* was clearly the expression of a cosmic dualism (Garuda being a later name of the Vedic *syena/suparna*). These facts are likely to be more relevant to Garuda's place on the top of the cosmic pillar than his later mythological role as Vishnu's carrier.

We have elsewhere pointed out that *dhvajas* of the type reproduced at fig. 10 are formally and aesthetically related to the 'Asokan' pillar, which is virtually an

[1]Henri Frankfort, *Kingship and the gods*, Chicago, 1948, pp. 91–93.

[2]For references, see the appendix to A.K. Mitra's article, "The Mauryan Lats or Dhvaja-stambhas: do they constitute an independent order?" *Journal and Proceedings of Asiatic Society of Bengal*, Calcutta, new series, 1934, pp. 317–326.

[3]Louis Renou, *Etudes sur le vocabulaire du Rigveda*, premiere serie, published by Institut francais d'Indologie, Pondicherry, 1958, pp. 15–18.

[4]The best modern introduction to the cosmogonical aspects of ancient religion, so crucial to an understanding of the origins of religious art and iconography, is Mircea Elade's *Le Mythe de l'enternel retour*, now available in paperback translation under the title, *The myth of the eternal return*, published by Princeton University Press (Bollingen Series XLVI).

[5]Mbh. VIII. 91.36. The critical edition has *urjaskaram*, and another reading is *myasaskaram*. The fact of the fortune or misfortune of the king being linked with the fate of his *dhvaja* reminds one that when the *Indradhvaja* falls down it predicts the death of the king (Vishnudharmettara Purana, 156, 1). For this, and other valuable references, I am indebted to Professor F.B.J. Kuipers' remarks in a book review published in the *Indo-Iranian Journal*, vol. XI, 1969. pp. 154–157.

[6]F.B.J. Kuiper, *ibid*, pp. 156–7.

[7]The fact that sanctity of the *dhvaja* was originally embodied in its staff, rather than in its flag or emblem, seems to be relevant to the history of the Tami ford koti. In medieval literature *koti* means flag or emblem; but *Dr. M.G. S. Narayanan* of Calicut University tells me that in ancient Sangam literature *koti* is sometimes used in a sense which could only mean staff or pole. For instance, in a song by Paranar (*Akananuru*, no. 196) a chieftain's battle-standard is described as netunkoti, literally, 'long, vertical koti'. There also seems to be a mystical connection between the northern kings *dhvaja* which protected him in battle and the southern king's kaval maram or 'guardian tree' which is often mentioned in Sangam literature as ensuring the king's magical protection (e.g. *Patirruppathu*, IV. 10; V. 4, etc.) All sacred posts, poles and pillars are, like the *Indradhvaja*, synonymous with the cosmic tree, which makes one suspect that the *kaval maram* was ot an actual tree but a standard which symbolised the tree, just as the Indra-pole or *Indradhavaja* symbolised the Indra-tree. By a parallel process of mystical identification, the *dhvaja* is sometimes identified with the cosmic mountain. For instance, in Mahabharata VIII. 24, 78, Siva's *dhvaja* is described as Mount Meru – an identification which makes sense only when we grasp the nature of cosmic symbolism and its central place in the pre-history of religion.

[8]Rigveda V. 101.2 , and VII. 69.48.

emblem-bearing pole blown-up and petrified.-[1] The Heliodorous pillar, on the other hand, in spite of being called a *Garuda-dhvaja* in its inscription, is nothing of the kind. Formally, its shaft corresponds more to a post than to a pole.

The first point to note is that the Heliodorus shaft is not tapered as in the case of the 'Asokan' pillar and the portable standard. Whereas the latter remind us of straight, slender tree-trunks shown of branches and pared to a smooth surface, the Heliodorus is faceted. It starts as an octagon, breaking down to sixteenths, and then to thirty-seconds, before a short round section is reached at the top. In other words, the Heliodorus is essentially a *sculpted post.*

Looking next at its ornament, we recognise that its primary explanation is technical rather than decorative. Before lathes were used for fashioning large shafts, the only practicable technique was to start by hewing the log or stone into a quadruple then,as a next stage, to break down the quadruple into an octagon; then from an octagon into sixteenths,and finally into thirty-seconds. From thirty-seconds, it was then easy to break straight into the round.

The advantage of working in these stages was that the sculptor had easy control of the stability of the form throughout all stages of the operation, difficult to achieve in any other way except by use of a lathe. But there was also an accompanying *dis*-advantage in the sense that the shaft inevitably lost bulk or circumference at each stage. These points are clearly illustrated by the drawing at Plate 6C. At the points where the facets are multiplied, there are inevitable 'steps' in the reduction of circumference. In other words, instead of tapering, the shaft extends upwards like an inverted camera-tripod.

What is remarkable about the Heliodorus pillar is the skill with which the craftsman has exploited the limitation of the technique for purely aesthetic ends. For instance, we can now recognise the functional role of the ornamental bands. Their primary purpose is to conceal what would otherwise be awkward to the eye: they serve to disguise the 'steps' which would otherwise have spoiled the lines of the pillar. In short, we are now in a position to recognise the Heliodorus shaft as a sophisticated design, and as aesthetically unrelated to the pole type of shaft. It derives, in fact, from a different tradition. What was that different tradition? The answer, I believe, can be given in one word: the *yupa*.

The *yupa* is of course well-known as the ritual stake of the Vedic sacrifice, though whether in fact it belongs in origin to Aryan tradition we would very much doubt.[2] It was the post to which the animals were tied before blood sacrifice. In fact, the *yupa* was much more than that. It was synonymous with the cosmic tree (*vanaspati*)[3] Most significant of all in our present context, the *yupa* is described in the *Rigveda* (III. 8.8) as "the *ketu* of the sacrifice". Because the *yupa* had to be carved from wood of the sacred tree, it is not surprising that none of the Vedic period now survive. However, in order to commemorate the sites at which major sacrifices, were performed, *yupas* were sometimes (at later periods only, it seems) copied in stone and erected as memorials. A number of these stone memorial-*yupas* do survive,[4] giving a clear idea of what the original wooden posts must have looked like. The drawing at Plate 6B shows a stone *yupa* of the first or second century A.D. discovered at Isapur, near Mathura, and now in Mathura Museum. Analysing its features, we note that about 90·2 cm. (3 feet) above original ground-level is clearly depicted the sacrificial rope to which the animal was tied, and that the rope is wound three times round the shaft as specified in the texts. Near the top is an octagonal projecting band. (This had a symbolic meaning to which we shall be returning in a minute.) Hanging from the projection is a garland, which is probaby the garland taken oft the neck of the sacrificed animal, as suggested by Vogel.[5] At the very top the post curves. From the texts we know that it originally terminated in a wheel-like headpiece, apparently made of perishable material, the exact appearance of which is not known. This wheel-like headpiece was quite definitely a sun-symbol.[6]

[1]John Irwin, *op. cit.*, pp. 712–27. The relationship between *dhvaja* and 'Asokan' pillar was partially recognised by Ram Prasad Chanda, "The Beginnings of Art in Eastern India", *Memoirs of Archaeological Survey of India*, no. 30, Calcutta, 1927, p. 32. The idea was further developed by A.K. Mitra (see above, footnote 17). However, neither of these pioneer scholars grasped the cosmic ymbolism, and the first to draw attention to this aspect was Professor F.B. Kuiper (see above, footnote 5 on p. 172).

[2]This is too big a subject to discuss here. In passing, however, it should be remembered that the *yupa* had to be sited outside the sacred enclosure of the Vedic sacrifice; and philologists have independently noted that some of the key-terms associated with *yupa*-symbolism are obviously non-Aryan (e.g. *cashala*, *tupara*, and *kumba*).

[3]The most important source for this is Rigveda III. 8.

[4]J. Ph. Vogel, "The sacrificial posts of Isapur", *Annual Report, Archaeological Survey of India*, 1910–11, pp. 40–48.

[5]W. Caland, in a note on the Isapur *yupas* published in Actorum Orientalium, vol. III, disagreed with Vogel on the identification of garland and sacrificial rope, but his argument does not seem to us convincing, and we believe that Vogel was correct in his original description.

[6]The sun-symbolism of the *cashala* is particularly clear in the Rewa inscription published by R.D. Banerji, "The Haihayas of Tripuri and their monuments", *Memoirs of the Archaeological Survey of India*, no. 23, 1931, p. 136, line 33.

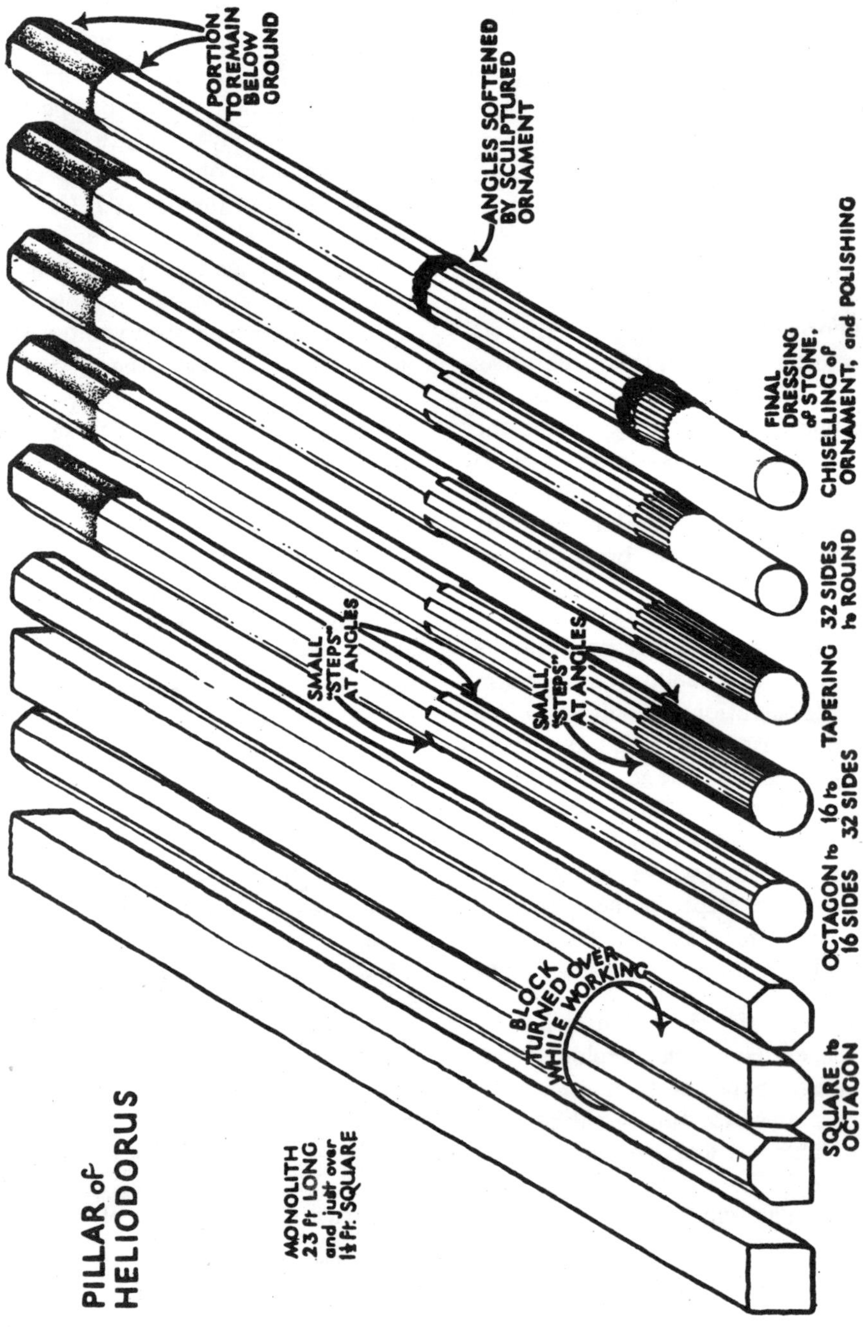
PILLAR of HELIODORUS
MONOLITH 23 ft LONG and just over 1½ ft. SQUARE
PORTION TO REMAIN BELOW GROUND
ANGLES SOFTENED BY SCULPTURED ORNAMENT
SMALL "STEPS" AT ANGLES
SMALL "STEPS" AT ANGLES
BLOCK TURNED OVER WHILE WORKING
SQUARE to OCTAGON
OCTAGON to 16 SIDES
16 to 32 SIDES
TAPERING
32 SIDES to ROUND
FINAL DRESSING of STONE, CHISELLING of ORNAMENT, and POLISHING

Now turning to the symbolism of the different sections of the *yupa,* as described in the *Satapatha Brahmana,* we learn that the section below ground enabled the sacrificer to gain the World of the Fathers – in other words, to maintain contact with the dead ancestors whose spirits were believed to have returned to the earth- in other words to the womb of the Earth Mother. We are next told that the section between the ground and the sacrificial rope represents the human world, over which the sacrificer gains power by the sacrifice. The section between the sacrificial rope and the octagonal ring enables him to gain the World of the Gods. And the final section – the section above the octagonal ring– extends, we are told, into the highest celestial sphere of all. "Whoever knows this", says the *Satapatha Brahmana,* "reaches the most Blessed of All the Gods" – in other words Prajapati identified with the *cashala* or wheel-like headpiece symbolising the sun.

The cosmic nature of the symbolism is enormously extended by rites associated with the carving and erection of the *yupa* – including the actual ritual felling of the tree from which it was fashioned. Priests accompanied the woodcutter into the forest to identify the Sacred Tree, which was then addressed as *vanaspate-deva,* literally "the god who is lord of the forest." The leading priest then declaimed before it: "With thy summit, do not rend the heavens (in other words, do not damage the heavenly vault, *asman,* which it is the function of the cosmic pillar as separator of heaven and earth to sustain). With thy trunk, do not wound the atmosphere (in other words, do not damage the upper sky, which is the region of the rain-bearing clouds)." After the felling, the trunk of the tree is then fashioned into a *yupa* by the sculptor, its form having to be octagonal. After it had been carved, the priest then declaimed to it: 'Lift thyself up, O Lord of theForest, unto the summit of the earth! With thy top thou holdest up the heavens 'with thy branches, thou fillest the air with thy foot, thou steadiest the earth!"

There could hardly be a clearer picture of the *yupa* as cosmic pillar or *axis mundi,* the mystical link between the three cosmic regions. And if anyone is unconvinced about this, there is still the rite of the sacrificer and his wife ascending the ladder to the top of the *yupa,* in symbolic ascent to the sun. When they reach the top and touch the wheel (*chashala*) they exclaim: "We have reached the light, the gods! We have become immortal! We have made contact with the very source of life (*amrita abhuma*):

With this symbolism in mind, let us look against the shaft of the Heliodorus pillar. What, for instance, is the significance of the swag-like ornamental band or garland with birds, flowers and fruit? No student of Indian art is likely to interpret these motifs as inventions of an individual craftsman's fancy. As Coomaraswamy was never tired of stressing, the idea of 'pure ornament' was foreign to ancient India. Instead, every motif originated as a religious symbol, even though it may have continued in use after the original meaning was forgotten, or modified by later doctrine. In light of everything said above, how can we any longer be in doubt as to what the ornament derived from in this particular case? We suggest that the swaglike band or garland with three strands or ropes is none other than a fossilized remnant of the sacrificial rope which (according to the texts) had to be wound three times round the shaft of the *yupa.* Once this hypothesis is accepted, it is not difficult to suggest a possible explanation for birds, flowers and fruits as well, since it was customary in ancient times to decorate the sacrificial stakes by draping them in cloths and attaching fruit and flowers, as attested, for instance, in the account of Risyasringa's sacrifice in the Ramayana (I. 13, 17-21) . In this case twenty-one *yupas* were erected and so adorned. If the cloths were white we can readily understand the imagery of the Vedic poet who likened a row of *yupas* at the sacrifice to "geese flying in a line":

hamsa iva sreniso yatanah sukra vasanah svaravo na aguh
unniyamanah kavibhih purastad deva devanam api yanti pathah[1].

Admittedly the birds depicted on the shaft of the Heliodorus pillar, unlike those on the abacus, have little resemblance to the goose *anser Indicus.* Nevertheless, the possibility that the visual convention shared common roots with the poetic one of equating *yupa* and bird, seems to us a plausible speculation. We do not wish to claim more than that.

We are still left with bigger and more difficult questions to answer. For instance, why was the Heliodorus pillar, which we now recognise as linked with Vedic tradition, dedicated to Vasudeva? Who really was Vasudeva? Should he at this stage in history be identified as well as equated with Vishnu, and what positive evidence or even justification have we for calling this a Vaishnava site (the usual automatic response to seeing an emblem of Garuda, probably not associated with Vishnu as his carrier until a later period)? Was it really an elliptical temple that Khare claimed to have found?[32] And what are the real grounds for assuming that it con-

[1]*Satapatha Brahmana,* translated by J. Eggeling, Sacred Books of the East, vol. XXVI, pp. 162 ff.; also Rigveda III. 8.9.

tained an image of Vishnu or an anthropomorphic image of any kind?[1] It is perhaps too early to attempt anything like definitive answers to any of these questions, which makes it all the more important that we should avoid trying to draw fixed conclusions in the meantime.

Archaeology has not yet provided enough evidence to prove that in the second century B.C. any of the major Brahmanical deities were worshipped in temples in human form, and literary evidence is no substitute. We know that the lesser deities – *yakshas, nagas, bhutas* and suchlike were worshipped in human form at this period, and earlier; but these were terrestial genii who lived in close proximity with men, and whose divine powers did not extend beyond the groves, hillocks, rivers and ponds which were their actual abodes. But the cosmic deities who belonged to the higher celestial spheres are surely another matter? If Vasudeva was a god of this order, one would expect him at this period to have been worshipped in aniconic form – perhaps only as a pair of footprints – one of the forms in which Vishnu was worshipped at a later period.[2] Or are we to regard this as inconsistent with the supposed association between *bhagavata* and the worship of the five heroes (*bhagavat*) in the Mathura region?

[1]The evidence Khare presents with his summary article in *Lalit Kala* (op. cit.) is not in itself sufficient on which to base opinion, and the ecxcavation report with plans and drawings is therefore keenly awaited.

[2]In this connection, see D.R. Bhandarkar's pertinent comments on the famous Vasudeva inscription at Nagari in *Epigraphia Indica*, vol. XXII, 1938, pp. 198–205.

In key inscriptions of the early Vasudeva cult, the words rendered as 'temple' are in one case *prasada*, and in another *mahastana*. At this period, *prasada* could have meant simply a 'lofty seat or platform'. *Mahastana* does not imply a structural building at all: it could mean simply an altar-throne or some other kind of sacred stone (*puja-sila*). Such aniconic shrines we know best in their Buddhist adaptations, but they must have been a common feature of cult-worship independently of Buddhism. Their main line of descent seems to have been from the non-Aryan folk-shrine or *caitya* which from earliest times was expecially associated with *tirthas*, such as we recognise at Besnagar, a typical sacred centre and classic location for the *axis mundi*.

As far as we can see on the basis of present evidence, the cult of Vasudeva was the first popular, unifying creed evolved by Brahmanical tradition in response to the challenge of Buddhism. One might further add that everything we know about the Heliodorus pillar and its site adds plausibility to this. The very design of the pillar seems to unite diverse strands of the Brahmanical inheritance represented by the *yupa* on the one hand, and the *dhvaja*, on the other. If there is more than a hint of truth in this hypothesis, then it is surely time to recognise that the Heliodorus pillar deserves to be treated as something more than a footnote to the history of the Greeks in India. Instead, we should see it as deeply founded in Indian tradition, and as one of the keys to an obscure phase in the history of Indian religion.

Victoria and Albert Museum London. JOHN IRWIN

Comments

The following are the issues raised by Irwin in his article:

1. Do the elliptical foundations discovered at Besnagar belong to a temple ?
2. Was the history of the Bhagavatas, the followers of Vasudeva cult obscure at that time ?
3. Did the elliptical temple contain an image?
4. Could the Garuda pillar be a Yupa?
5. Do all the pillar remains post-date the construction of the second shrine?

The foundations of an elliptical structure at Besnagar, adjacent to the Heliodorus pillar site, do belong to a temple and are associated with Vaishnava religion. It has all the basic components of a temple, viz. a *garbhagrha, pradakshinapatha, antarala* and *mandapa*. That the plinth was of baked bricks and the superstructure of wood, thatch and mud is proved by the availability of bricks, iron nails and post-holes. Various sizes of post-holes are discernible in plan. In addition, there is a wel laid extensive floor.

Every where a temple site has invariably been used and reused in successive periods for the same purpose. Therefore, the sanctity of the site, the availability of the inscription on the Heliodoros pillar and the existence of the above mentioned components, besides the identical structure discovered at Nagari (Chittorgarh) by Bhandarkar, assignable to 350 to 300 B. C.,[1] prove that the elliptical structure was a temple. As a matter of fact, this structure is a full-fledged temple and does not requiire any other corroborative evidence. That the large images like the *Yakshas* and *Nagas* were not found enshrined in the temples, does not prove the non-

[1]D.R. Bhandarkar, *The Archaelogical Remains and Excavations at Nagari*, Memoirs of the Archaeological Survey of India, no. 4, 1920, p. 131.

existence of temples in those days, The early literature provides ample evidence in this respect.

According to Irwin, the literary evidence goe sagainst the existence of a temple of such an early date. Two of the references[1] quoted by hias mare under :

The Vedic altar survives in the *structure* of the body of the temple in its lowest and its highest part. In technique and name the *prasada,* the Hindu temple, shares in the name of the Vedi and Citi. Its *total* structure moreover, when *seen from outside* has the appearance of a massive pile, and is a monument more than a building. The thickness of the walls of the *garbhagraha* and the *often nearly* compact superstructure also reveal that the entire *prasada* is a Citi.

Although, self-explanatory, the underlined words presuppose something more than a 'piled up seat or altar', particularly when '*garbhagrha*' is mentioned there.

Prasada in the sense of 'palace' does not occur until the late Abdhuta Brahmana" (Vedic Index, Vol.II, p. 51).

Since the date of the Brahmanas is between 800 and 500 B. C.,[2] the existence of *prasada* in the sense of a temple and not of a 'Palace' as mentioned in the Vedic Index, after 500 B. C. is in no way contradictry.

Devakiputra Krishna has been mentioned in the *Chhandyogya Upanisada* (3, 17, 6) . In the subsequent literature, Krishna is identified as god of Vishnu (Taittareya Aranyak 10, 1, 6 : Paninis *Astadhyayi,* 4, 3, 98 etc.) Rama's, identification with Vishnu can also be seen in Ramayana, whose kernel was composed before 500 B.C.

Vaishnava religion and Vidisha are very closely related. Vidisha is one of the thousand names of Vishnu (*Vishnu Sahasranam*) and it shows that Vaishnavism was very popular there much before the installation of the Heliodoros pillar. The *Mahabharata* is of vital importance for the history of Vaishnavism. It is in this epic that Vasudeva Krishna is identified with Narayana-Vishnu. Sukhthankar rightly concludes "that Vasudeva Krishna was already recognised as a god at the time of the composition of the Mahabharata and there is not a passage in the whole of the epic which does not presuppose his divinity". In the *Bhagvata- Gita* Krishna is called the son of Vasudeva. As the date of the composition of the Mahabharata is between 500 B. C. - 200 B. C., the recognition of Vasudeva Krishna at the time of the construction of the temple at Besnagar is beyond any doubt. According to Bhandarkar, Vasudeva came to be identified with Narayana as early as the fourth century B. C.[3]

The root words of Vasudeva and Vishnu have almost identical meanings. (*Vasu,* to dwell, reside, the one who dwells in all things and *Vis*' entering into, pervading the universe). That is why Vishnu is called *Virata, Sarvavyapi* (all pervasive), etc.

Regarding the Garuda's association with Vasudeva, Jaiswal's remarks are noteworthy[4]:

We fail to understand that if the worshippers of Vasudeva did not consider their deity identical with Vishnu in the second century B.C. and if Garuda was originally associated with Vedic God, how the same worshippers of Vasudeva could dedicate Garuda-pillars in honour of their deity. In our opinion it is probable that the dedication of the Garuda banner to the god Vasudeva, like the palmyra banner for Sankarsana was an ancient practice, indicating an earlier compromise between the cult of Vasudeva and Garuda".

On the evidence of the archaeological discoveries at Besnagar, Nagari, Mathura, it is undoubtedly proved that *devadevas* Vasudevas was none other than the all pervasive Vishnu of the *Bhagvatas.*

Installation of an image in the temple. No doubt that there had been no such archaeological evidence to show the installation of an image inside a temple, but how many such temples of so early a date have been brought to light so far ? May be, that the images, like the superstructure of the temples, were also made of the perishable material, like wood. The subsequent literary traditions, refering to the making of wooden images, during the life time of Mahabir and Buddha, cannot be ignored. Slightly raised flooring within the *garbhagrha* of the elliptical temple at Besnagar could not have served any other purpose than a low platform for the image.

Heliodors piliar

By no stretch of imagination could this pillar be a *Yupa* (a sacrifical post). The purpose and the forms of the two types have no similarties, whatsoever. Irwin would do well to understand a distinction between a *dhvaja* and a *pataka.* The former is any standard, while the latter is a portable one. Similarly, during period under review *dhvaja* and *Yupa* had distinct definition and uses and therefore it is futile to mix up the two. A temple called *prasada,* had the same magnanimity and grandeur as that of a palace and it was more essentialwhen it was associated with the god of gods. Therefore, the purpose of these pillars, which Irwin could not understand and Bhandarkar did not deem it necessary to elaborate, was not merely decorative but also religious, for each one of them had a capital like *Garuda, makara,* Palm-leaf, *kalpvraksha,* etc. all of which are associatd with Vaishnavism. Further, it is interesting to note that an octagonal pillar is called *Vishnu-Kant.*[5] The Heliodoros pillar is basically an octagonal pillar, its octagonal portion covering more than half of its height. Hence its association with Vishnu.

Irwin is laying undue emphasis on the worship of the tamarind tree adjacent to the Heliodoros pillar. The trees are still worshipped in every part of India. But the reason for the silence of all the writers on the worship of

[1]Stella Kramsch; *The Hindu Temple,* pp. 17—148

[2]*The Imperial Gazetteer of India,* vol. II Reprint edition p.230.

[3]Bhandarkar op. cit. p. 119

[4]Subira, Jaiswal, *The Origin and Development of Vaisnavism* p.72.

[5]Mansaara, An Encyclopaedia of *Hindu Architecture,* vol VIII·

this tree had been that it was never worshipped prior to 1963, when we commenced our excavations. Instead, the pillar was worshipped and the locks of hair, now seen hanging around the tree, were tied around the Heliodoros pillar. It was at our instance that the villagers were stopped from worshipping the pillar and damaging it. Since the devotees from the neighbourhood still come there, the nearest tree has served as a substitute for the pillar.

The two basal slabs of the Heliodoros pillar do not indicate that the lower one was meant for a different and earlier pillar. The consolidation of the layer between the two slabs is not a new feature. From the foundation trenches and the basal slabs of seven more pillars discovered by me at this site in 1965, it can be said with certainty that in more than one case, two basal slabs had been used without any interval. The second slab (lower) served as a subsidiary slab in strengthening the foundation of the pillar. Seven more pits, with similar material like the alternating layers of laterite, black earth, occasionally mixed with brick-bats and small pebbles, and a number of steel and stone wedges placed on the basal slabs, show that there were eight pillars in front of the Vasudeva Temple of the second century, B. C. , Seven of them in one row running north-south the Heliodoros pillar being the first in the north and the eighth in front of the central pillar towards east. A fragmentary inscribed pillar discovered by Lake, mentioning *Prasadottama* (best temple) must have belonged to one of these remaining seven pillars. Moreover, there is no referene of replacement or re-establishment of pillar in any inscriptions.

The sculptural representations of some of the temples are available in the gateways of Sanchi. The roof of the temples depicted there could not have been different from the one conjectured by me in the plan, (*Lalitkala* No. 13.) The continuity of the tradition of erecting pillars in front of the temples can also be noticed there. Besides, the early cave architecture has not been forgotten in this context.

Irwin bases his argument on the non-availability of any archaeological or literary evidence prior to this discovery. But how far such an attitude is justified on his part, is a matter about which less said the better because he has not cared to take complete data from the excavator, even when he came here . Here I am constrained to remember Law[1], who wrote,

> "many western scholars tried to prove as far as possible the comparatively later date of our civilization, and that they picked up the pen" with a questionable motive to cast doubt upon facts which constitute an object of pride to the Indians".[6]

Archaeological Survey of India M. D. KHARE
Bhopal

[1]N.N. Law, *Studies in Indian History and Culture* (1925 pp.), 186-7 quoted from Mrs. Jayswal Suvira :

A Note on the Excavation at Bhagwanpura

Bhagwanpura (Lat. 30·04, Long., 76·57), District Kurukshetra, Haryana,[1] is situated on the right bank of the river Saraswati. A horizontal excavation was carried out by the Archaeological Survey of India, during December, 75 to February, 76. The present note gives the summary results of this excavation particularly bringing into focus the phenomena of overlap between the so called late Harappan and Painted Grey Ware Culture.

The excavation revealed a two-fold culture sequence with a deposit of 2.70 m, the earlier of which in content was Late Harappan (Period IA) and the latter, of the Painted Grey Ware (period I B) using people. The Late Harappans made their first habitation at this site over the rich alluvium of the river Saraswati and built, in two successive phases, solid mud platforms to protect their habitation from the ravages of flood. In one of the trenches was exposed one such platform, measuring 4.25 x 10m, which had also a landing step. After some time (within which there was an accumulation .70 - .80 m. of cultural deposit) the occupation was considerably damaged by a flood. The excavation has

[1]With a view to excavating a site having Late Harappan and Painted Grey Ware Cultures, the author extensively examined a large number of sites in Haryana in August, 1975. Sri R.S. Bisht, Deputy Director, Department of Archaeology, Government of Haryana, Chandigarh, who had earlier discovered the site at Bhagwanpur, kindly showed it to the author. Later, excavations were carried out at this site by the author, assisted by Shri Laxmi Dutt, Sri A.K Sharma, Kumari Madhubala. Sarvasri S. N. Jayaswal, J.R. Batra, S.D. Dogra, Brij Mohan Khanduri, G. L. Narayan and J. Dey.

clearly revealed that the late Harappans continued to occupy the site even after this calamity.

The major ceramic industry of this Period consists of a sturdy red ware having pottery types associated generally with the sites yielding Late Harappan Cultures, like Bara, Bahadarabad, Atranjikhera, Siswal IIB ,Mitathal IIB, Daulatpur and Raja Karan Ka Qila[1]. It was observed at Bhagwanpura that the well-known pottery called Ochre-colour were derived its ochre colour due to water logging. Whenever the pottery of the late Harappan type had come in contact with water it had assumed the so-called ochre-colour. A few sherds of thick grey ware usually associate with Harappan and Late Harappan fabrics, were also available. An incised ware, having pre-Harappan lineage, was found to have been continuing here up to the Late Harappan times and even later. The shapes consisted mainly of dish-on-stand, bowls, drooping dishes, cups-on-stand, high-necked jars, jars with everted or flanged necks, basins and button-based goblets. The design repertoire included thick and thin horizontal bands, criss-crooss patterns, fillele-in triangles, rows of opposite traindes, hatched triangles, arches with obliquely filled lines, leaves, banana tree and *Pipal* leaf.

Amongst the other finds of this sub-period mention may be made of the terracotta bull with long horns and pinched up hump, fragmentary piece showing leg portion of a human figure or a deity, two anthropomorphic figures, potsherds with graffiti marks of Harappan lineage, Copper rods, terracota toy wheels with hubs, beads of terracotta, faience and semi- precious stones, and bangles of faience and terracotta.

The Sub- Period IB which closely followed IA without any break in between marked the continuance of late Harappans and the arrival of Painted Grey Ware using people. It appears that after the Painted Grey ware people had settled at this site (marked by a deposit of ·15 - ·20m.), the entire habitation was once again damaged by a massive flood which washed away a considerable portion of the occupation. However, this calamity could not deter the occupants, and the site was immediately reoccupied by the Late Harappans and Painted Grey Ware using people. Though the Late Harappans continued their influences but their pottery gradually diminished, specially, in the late levels of Sub-period IB, possibly due to the impact of the Painted Grey Ware Culture.

Significantly, the remains of Sub-period IB revealed three phases of structural activity of the Painted Grey Ware people. In the earliest phase, the people were living in round or semi-circular thatched huts. Twenty three postholes, conforming a round or semi circular hut, were noticed in an area of 4·25 x 6·85m. in the south-eastern side of the mound. Inside the hut were found four saddle querns and pestles of different types ; possibly the hut belonged to a corn grinder'.

Associated with this phase came an oval-shaped structure of highly burnt mud wall running north-east to south-west . The structure yielded a few potsherds in sturdy red ware. The burnt earth pieces inside, besides the baked earth-lumps, contained a few pieces which perhaps belonged to a roof of domical shape of the structure. No ash, charcoal or metal came from the structure.

The second structural phase is marked by the building of mud-walled houses. A complete house complex, mud walls, having an average width of 90 to 100 with an extent height ranging from .15 to .40m. had thirteen rooms, a corridor and a courtyard in the eastern side. The size of the rooms varied from 1.60 x 1.60m. to 3.35 x 4.20m. The rooms yielded animal bones, Painted Grey Ware dishes and bowls, associated grey ware and red ware ; *ghata*-shaped terracotta beads, bone styli and copper objects. Significantly 2 to 5 percent of Late Harappan pottery was also available from the rooms of this house complex.

In the third structural phase, the houses were built of baked bricks. Whatever bricks were found *in situ* conform to the following sizes : (*i*) 20x12x8 cm; (ii) 12x12x8 cm; (iii) 29x22/12x7½ cm. (wedge shaped), 20 x 20 x 8 cm; and (iv) 16 x 12 x 4cm. Some of the bricks bore finger-marks.

Two curious oval-shaped structurs, associated with this phase also came to light. One of these was found in the south-eastern periphery of the mound (size : 1·80x .85 m) and the other in the central area of the mound (size : 1·60x92 m) having two phases of construction. Again these have ·5-·7 m. highly burnt wall and contain burnt earth pieces, portions of a collapsed domical shaped roof and a few potsherds. One of these yielded fragments of a dish-on-stand in red ware and some uncharred animal bones, besides a fragment of a horn, presumably of terracotta animal figurine. No metal or any other material, indicating a furnace or a kiln could be noticed. However, a fragmentary legged terracotta was found from the working level of one of the oval structures.[2] Perhaps, these oval structures had some religious functions.

[1]*Puratattva*, nos. 5-6, (1971-72, 72-73). Fig. 15.

[2]*Ancient Pakistan*, Vol. 3, 1967, Pl. LI.

Two skeletons have been found from the habitation area of the Painted Grey Ware Culture. Both the skeletons were found lying in north-south orientation, with head towards the north, and face towards the west. The field study indicated that one of the skeletons belonged to an adult of advanced age while the other was that of a child of eight to ten years of age. Surprisingly, the graves were devoid of any grave-goods.[1]

Besides the continuance of the Late Harappan pottery and antiquities, Period IB yielded Painted Grey Ware, grey ware, associated red ware and a limited quantity of black polished ware. Painted Grey Ware with designs in thick lines is also available from the early and middle levels of the Sub-period. The design-repertoire is very rich in the Painted Grey Ware tradition . For the first time, a maltese cross and intersecting circles giving rise to six or four petalled flower have come to notice. The shapes in this Ware consist of bowls and dishes. For the first time it has been noticed that a few Late Harappan shapes like bowls, basins, dishes, jars, and dishes-on-stand have been copied in the grey waie, showing. the influence of the former over the latter .

Amongst the other important finds of this Period are some terracotta anthropomorphic figures having parallels with similar objects found in the Gandhara Grave Culture I in Pakistan[2].

A good quantity of animal bones have also been obtained from the different levels of the site. The assemblage consists of a large number of charred bones, particularly belonging to that of cattle. Field observations show that bones of cattle, sheep, goat, ram, dog and equus are present in the assemblage. Cattle bones from the lower levels are mostly of massive size. Few of the cattle bones show incomplete ossification. Charred tortoise shells are also present. Cattle bones from upeer levels show weaker and small sized breed. Noteworthy among there are those of *Equus Cabalus Linn* from the Painted Grey Ware levels. A second phalanx of *Eqqus Caalus Linn* is of special significance. Other Equus bones are that of smaller variety.[3]

The prophetic remarks of Sri A. Ghosh, "Even that be the future Consensus the possibiity will remain that the descendants of the Harappans, after the end of their glorious days lived some where in India still holding to theii eulture, if in a modified forms, to contribute its traits to the pattern of Indian Culture either directly or through the Aryans or some other agency.[4] have come true. Such an evidence of overlap, noticed clearly at Bhagwanpur for the first time is perhaps of considerable ignificance so far as the reconstruction of a continuous history of the Kurukshetra from the middle of the second millenium B.C. is concerned. That there was a fusion of two cultures here is evident from the continuity of the tradition in pottery types, painted designs, art of terracotta figurines and burials. Absence of iron and black and Red Ware is another important aspect which perhaps might indicate the arrival of this site of earlier wave of Painted Grey Ware using people, than those met with at Hastinapur .

Archaeological Survey of India
New Delhi.

J. P. JOSHI

[1]Based on field study made by Shri A. K. Sharma.
[2]*Ancient Pakistan.* Vol. 3, 1967, a, i, b, p. LIII.
[3]Based on field study nade by Shri A. K. Sharma,
[4]A, Ghosh, Notes, *Ancient India*, no. 10-11, p. 8.

A Note on the Excavation at Virbhadra

The whole of the mountaineous tract lying between Gangadvara (Hardwar) at the foot of the Himalayas upto Ratnastambha (Kailash) in the north and from Nandgiri (Nandadevi) in the east to Kashtagiri (near source of river Tons) in the west, was known to the ancients as Kedarkhand.[1] It is further subdivided into Kshetras. The area of Mayakshetr of Kedarkhand, that lies between Hardwar and Rishikesh has been assessed as of 12 yojanas[2] (136 Km). The Kshetra has been further subdivided into sub- Kshetras, and the excavated site of Virbhadra falls into Kubjamra Kshetra.[3]

The Kubjamra Kshetra lies between Lakshmanasthan near the present Lakshmana jhoola in the north and the Saptasamudrik i.e. Saptarishi, north of Gangadvara, in the south. It is within this area that Rambha joins Ganga, and, at the confluence of the two rivers, accor-

[1]*Sri Skanda Maha-Purana*, Kedarkhand, Chapter 101. Verses. 30-31.
[2]*Ibid*, Ch. 101. Vs. 10.
[3]*Ibid*, Ch. 115. Vs. 53

ding to the Puranic traditions,[1] lies the temple of Rambheswara Mahadeva.

The area was distinguished by the presence of a Vilvavan,[2] a number of streams joining Ganga on its eastern and western banks, and the temples of Siva and Vishnu at their confluences.

A notable settlement of this sub kshetra was Mayapuri which lies along Rambha. The other settlements like Argalpuri and Vijaypur were located around Hardwar. As for the inhabitants of the area, the original settlers appear to be Bhils[3] and Kiratas,[4] who were nonvegetarians the meat of deer being a favourite dish. They partly lived by hunting. The main weapons were bow, arrow and sword. A solitary reference of the presence of 'Yavana' in this area is also there.

As for the chronological position of Skandapurana, the anchor sheet of the literary evidence cited above is dated to *circa* A.D. 700 by Professor Hazra (R.C.).[5]

Prof. Hazra has also pointed out that certain cahpters were interpolated in the Purana from time to time upto A.D.1400. But the chapters, the evidence of which is used here, have no where been mentioned by him as interpolated. His main argument for interpolation is reference of Tantras in the Purana. The chapters quoted here do not contain any reference to the Tantras. Hence, they have been treated as original chapters, datable to circa A. D. 700.

The archaeological evidence of the region is both positive and negative. The negative evidence relates to the exploration. Exploration along the course of Ganga has not brought forth any evidence of an early Historical settlement along the course of Ganga in the surrounding region. Secondly, there is no evidence of the change of course by Rambha from the early centruries of the Christian era. The lower terrace to the north of the site, probably, served as the flood plain of Rambha as well as of Ganga. The orientation of high terrace along Ganga, on which the excavated site is situated, refutes any idea of the change of the course by Rambha in the early historical times. From foregoing discussion it is evident that the presently excavated site is the ancient Mayapuri, referred to in *Skandpurana*.

The positive results revealed from the exploration, are the discoveries of early historical coins from Rishikesh (Sivanandashrama), the sculptural representations of yakshas and Yakshis' of early centuries of the Christian era at Bharatmandir (Rishikesh), the Bharatmandir of *circa* A. D. 800 itself, and, the evidence of a site at Shyampur Garhi, south west of Virbhadra, which contains the deposit contemporary to that of Virbhadra[6].

More positive evidence is forthcoming from the excavation at Virbhadra[7] which revealed cultures of the period ranging from A. D. 100 — 800, divisible into three phases, namely 1, 2, 3. Phase 1 revealed the remains of the Kushan period. Amongst the remains of this phase are Kushan ceramics, bricks, and Kushan coins. It has also brought forward charred bones of animals, which are conspicuous by their absence in the later phases.

From the early level of middle phase, a saivite sanctum, has been excavated. Within the sanctum is a Sivalinga resting on Bhadrapitha. The Linga is octagonal at base, with tapering sides and round top. The girth of the Linga at the base is 80 cm and at the top, 72 cm. The square "Bhadrapitha" measures 72 cm at the top and 85 cm at the base, with receding courses in the middle. The first and third projecting courses at the base have moulded bricks. Only the eastern well of this shrine has been traced, as the other ones are overlain with later walls. The brick sizes are 23x15x6cm and 22x12x6cms, and 27x12x6cm. The sizes of bricks are shorter than those of period IV at Hastinapur. These bricks of Saivite shrine of Virbhadra may be assigned to the post- Kushan period. The decorative pottery at the site is analogous with the Gupta red ware and painted ware is comparable to the Rangmahal pottery. Phase 2 has also brought to light certain other rectangular brick built shrines. The deity of these shrines is, however, missing.

Similar but larger shrines have been excavated from the phase III. This phase has also yielded certain Gadhaiya coins, datable to circa 800 A.D.

It is evident that the literary evidence supplements the evidence of archaeological explorations and excavations. The area was sparesely populated during the period, and, the early habitants were meat-eating *Kiratas* and *Bhils*.

Amongst the weapons the literary evidence of sword is not supported by the excavation, but the recovered iron arrow-heads indicate the use of bow an arrow. However, the spears were also in vogue.

Archaeological Survey of India N. C. GHOSH
New Delhi R. P. SHARMA

[1]*Ibid,* Ch. 115.
[2]*Ibid,* Ch. 109. Vs.39.
[3]*Ibid,* Ch. 206. Vs. 2.
[4]*Ibid,* Ch. 206. Vs. 4.
[5]R.C. Hazra, *Puranic records on Hindu rites and customs,* Shaka 1940, p. 165-66.

[6]A, Ghosh, *Indian Archaeology* 1963-64—*a Review*, p. 45.
[7]Excavation at the site was carried out in 1973-74 and 74-75 under direction of Shri N.C. Ghosh and reports on the same have been submitted for inclusion in *Indian Archaeology —a Review* for these respective years.

Fallacies of Archaeological Interpretation

Recent trends in India Archaeology indicate that the Indian archaeologist will not be content with mere stratigraphic and chronological reconstructions but, by relying more heavily on scientific methods of distributional analysis in horizontal excavation studies, will try to reconstruct all possible factes of the life and cultuie of the communities to which the archaeological settlements belong. With the competent archaeological techniques available in the country, this would not be too difficult to achieve. But the major problem that the Indian archaeologist will have to solve—and this, I feel, has remained unsolved till the present day—is how would he interpret the essential nature of the culture he has so painstakingly reconstructed.

The limitations of application of 'scientific methods' to the study of the behaviour patterns of human beings, realised in the West with increasing clarity, has only been dimly appreciated in our country. Archaeologists, while studying artifacts, which are the result of human activity, have borrowed the methodology and thought models from the natural sciences. The elucidation of the general problem of human behaviour by the materialistic view of natural sciences, both simplifies the problem and fails to answer it. In consequence of an unprecedented development of traditional methods during the last centuries, knowledge of outward nature has far outstripped, if not wholly eclipsed, knowledge of the inner, with the result that the existence of an 'inner realm' has been denied altogether, or has come to be doubted, or else has been dismissed as 'mysticism'. Even in the case of the external physical realities, the scientist, unable to fathom the essential nature of such basic entities as 'energy' and 'mass' has tended towards the acceptance of the 'operational concept of physical entities'. Meaning thereby, that science is not concerned if it can't go to the root of 'reality' so long as it can accurately measure its compoenents, determine the laws which govern them, operate them and succeed in such amazing feats as sending a man to the moon.

The success of the rational method of science has led to the popular belief that material progress by itself is linked with inner freedom and this belief in its turn forms the root of all socio-political systems of the present day, based as they are on the market industrial society of the Machine Age. The social philosophy of this age explains the individual and social behaviour of a man on two axiomatic statements, viz. (i) the incentives on which the every day life on an individual is organised to spring from material motives, and (ii) all social institutions are determined by the economic system.[1]

Extrapolating the temporally strictly limited drives of the 'economic man' to other ages, the modern academicians, archaeologists, historians and anthropologists have interpreted the cultures of man as arising out of the twin incentives of deprivation and gain which form the basis of the market industrial society of the present day. This can be most clearly seen in the interpretation of life in the Old Stone Age. The Palaeolothic Man has been descirbed as a savage, as one totally occupied with an incessant quest for food. He has to rely on meagre and unreliable natural resources and had an absence of economic surplus. He had no lesiure because of his daily struggle to get food for himself and his family. Braidwood says "A man who spends his whole life following animals just to kill them to eat, or moving from one berry patch to another, is really living just like an animal himself".[2]

The fallacy of the above view is apparant when one realises that the Paleolothic Man has given bourgeois desires and impulses but has been equipped with stone tools and hence his life and culture have been concluded in advance as primitive, miserable and hopeless. It does not come as a surprise therefore, that the earliest agricultural communities were extolled as a 'great leap forwards for mankind' and as the Neolithic Revolution.

From the ethnological studies of Richard on Dobe Bushmen and Woodburn on the African Hadza, a good case can be made that hunters and food gatherers work less than we do, and, rather than a continous travail, their food quest is intermittent, and their leisure abundant,[3] The Stone Age man did not have to work more than 3 to 5 hours a day to procure his daily food requirements and his movements were not conditioned by his quest for food but by his abundant lesisure time. He was neither tormented by hunger nor was he acti-

[1]K. Polanyi, 'Our Obsolete Market Mentality', *Commentary*, Vol. 3 (1947), p.109-17.

[2]R.J. Braidwood, *Prehistoric Man*, (Chicago, 1952).

[3]L. Richard, 'Kung Bushmen Subsistance : 'An Import-Output Analysis', in A Vayda (ed.) *Environmental and Cultural Behaviour* (New York' 1969), also J. Woodburn, 'An Introduction to Hazdo Ecology', in R. Lee and I. Dev. Ore (eds.) *Man the Hunter* : (Chicago, 1968).

vated by a desire for gain. Marshall in her studies of Kung Bushmen found them to 'live in a kind of material on two axiomatic statements, viz., (i) the incentives plenty,[1]. Mair found no destitution under the Kraaland system of Kafirs[2]. Loeb states that no Kwakiutl 'ever ran the risk of going hungry. But the archaeological and anthropological opinion, unable to see through the seeming paradox of the Stone Age Man's unparalleled material plenty with a low standard of living (reflected in his dislike for storing, hoarding and owning of objects), has evaluated him culturally as one with restricted 'wants', retained 'desires', a limited 'notion of wealth' and mentally underdevolped.

The same applies to the stimulus of individual gain. Thurnwald finds "the characteristic feature of primitive economics is the absence of any desire to make profits from production and exchange"[3]. Malinowski states "Gain, which is often the stimulus for work in more civilised communities, never acts as an impulse to work under the original native conditions"[4]. Sahlins in a searching study calls the Palaeolithic society as the 'original affluent society'.[5]

[1] L. Marshall, 'Sharing, Talking and Giving : Relief of Social Tensions Among Kung Bushmen', *Africa*, Vol. 31, (1961), pp. 131—39.

[2] L.P. Mair, *An African People in Twentieth Century* (London 934).

[3] R. Thurnwald, in *Economics of Primitive Communities*, (1932).

[4] B. Malinowski, in *Economics of Primitive Communities* (1932).

[5] M. Sahlins, 'The Original Affluent Society', *Ecologist*, Vol. 4, no. 5. (1974),

The limitations of the use of 'scientific methods' and of temporal extrapolation of impulses of our age in the context of the past cultures of India is obvious. The earliest literary references of India, *viz.* the Vedas and the Buddhist and Jain canons as well as the earliest epigraphic records of Ashoka, emphasise the immediate and the unrelenting concern of the ancient Indian with the knwoledge of the 'inner realm'. With few exceptions, the archaeologists, historians and indologists have approached the ancient texts with the interest of the antiquary or the philologist, devoting themselves mainly to 'textual criticisms' or finding 'internal evidences' which can be correlated with monuments, relics and archaeological finds of India and, in particular, with similar known records of other countries. The truth (or falsehood) of the ideas in the text have failed to attract their efforts. Thus, for correct interpretation of ancient Indian culture, the archaeologist will need to re-examine the ancient texts and explore the ideas and impulses which form the matrix of human behaviour and give real meaning to his artifacts. It is to be remembered, however, that it is not possible to do justice to ideas and impulses if, instead of seeking to understand them in and by themselves, one reduces them to one's own standards with a preconviction of the accuracy of the world of material civilization. This, therefore, is a plea for deeper and more human understanding and reconstruction and then interpretation of our past.

M.S. University of Baroda
Baroda
A.M. THAKKAR

Sociological Framework For Archaeological Research

This paper aims to present, with suitable examples, some glimpses of what may follow when archaeological research is conducted within the framework of general anthropological theory. Old World archaeology is not yet in the service of anthropology. Time has come when some one should present the facts and tell the archaeological fraternity of the Old World that there is an urgent need of a drastic change in the perspective and goal of archaeological research. The term sociological in the title of this paper does not mean 'pertaining to a specific discipline called sociology' because the whole tenor of the paper is anthropologically oriented. Within the context of archaeology a sociological framework is expected to provide something different to look up to for archaeological interpretations and inferences than, say, the historical framework. Further, elaboration will be found in the main body of the essay.

In a substantive sense, the sociological segment of a culture may be said to refer to social relations, social institutions and social stratification, or more broadly, to social structure. With reality (generally called technological or material) culture and value, culture social (or sociological) culture constitutes the third major segment of any culture. By culture, we anthropologists, including the archaeologists amongst us, mean a systematic whole consisting of functionally interrelated parts or sub-systems such that any change in one sub-system should bring about specifiable changes in others.

Due to the nature of cultural materials the archaeologist has for his data, an ecological frame of reference acquires much greater importance in his study of the cultural system than that of a social-cultural anthropologist. The success of a sociological framework lies in producing archaeologcial researches which are notably different and more impressive than those conducted unader a non-sociological framework. The sociological framework discussed in this paper has an unmistakable anthropological imprint.

The archaeologist deals with the imperishable material remains of a people of the past. What can he do with these and how can he do what he wants to depends upon what he thinks archaeology is supposed to do. In the Old World, for instance, archaeological accounts have been concerned primarily with delineating reality culture. While saying so I am aware that Grahamme Clark came out with his famous economic interpretation of the European Mesolithic several decades earlier. The Old World archaeologist is found sometimes to venture hesitatingly to infer some religious belief, ritual and art from his data. Sackett (1968 : 66-67) demonstrates how this interest fits into the overall natural science framework of the Old World archaeologist's 'attribute-cluster analysis'. Little or no account of the behavioural dimensions of prehistoric culture finds a place in the archaeological reports. The difference between the Old World and the New World archaeology is pronounced due to their different conceptual—theoretical orientations and the differences in the academic affiliations sought both inside and outside the university structure. There also seems to be a great difference in the goals of archaeological research in the two hemispheres.

Childe belongs to the school of archaeology according to which one could never know how prehistoric people lived. Since 'fortunately....the bulk of the archaeological record falls within the domain tritely termed 'Material Culture' objectivity demands that the archaeologists keep his inferences to the minimum, Today's archaeological anthropologist will not be eager in joining Childe to say that "archaeologists are constantly finding equally convincing and illuminating explanations for otherwise incomprehensible relics and monuments in the equipment and technology of savage or barbarian tribes still living.............." Unlike Childe, he studies the spatial and temporal distributions of artifacts to find out "how prehistoric peoples actually lived'. He is interested in developing means by which he can know of 'many aspects of prehistoric cultural systems that were formerly considered beyond the limitations of our data and competence. The archaeological anthropologist firmly believes that "the material culture of the extinct system will reveal a structured set of relationships, just as social anthropology has demonstrated these relationships in the behavioural aspects of cultural system"

There are notable differences between the archaeology of the Old World and that of the New World. Sarana has tried to being out the implications of these differences elsewhere (see Sarana 1969 and 1971). It is striking to note that Stone Age archaeology in the Old World, which is also called prehistory, is distinctive for its typologies of stone tools. I do not know if the naming of the major Stone Age periods by the terms 'Palaeolithic' and 'Neolothic', originally coined by Sir John Lubbock, had something to do with the typological rather than culture historical orientation of the Old World prehistory. To mention only a few names, from Gabriel de Mortillet to Abbe Breuil to Denis Peyrony to Francois Bordes many a leading prehistorian have been too often busy working out the sequential schemes dividing Palaeolithic solely on the basis of classification of stone tools. Even America-trained Old World specialist, H.L. Movius, Jr., has not escaped this all-pervading stone-tools typology-building. It is not surprising that typologies have not been a means to answer such basic questions of life of the prehistoric peoples as are given below. They have become an end in themselves: "What precisely were the subsistence techniques of Upper Palaeolithic foragers, what population size and densities might they support, and with what kinds of settlement patterns were they associated? Or again, do the successive Upper Palaeolithic artifact complexes refer to distinct types of economic or social organization, or do they merely reflect stylistic variations within a single cultural tradition?"

Christopher Hawkes makes a very meaningful distinction between *text-aided* and *text-free* archaeology. Text-aided archaeology can be a hand-maiden of history or of the Classics. In both cases archaeology is reduced to merely a technique to be used for additional (or supplementary) information with little creative role of its own. When history does not talk much about the social relations and the behavioural dimensions of people's life, there is not much meannig in discussing the possibility of a sociological framework for research in the realm of text-aided archaeology though its potential utility cannot be denied.

University of Karnataka
Dharwar. GOPALA SARANA

Greek or Yavana Donors in Ancient India

India was undoubtedly one of the earliest civilised countries on the face of the globe. This fact is proved by her sacred writings. The actual records are strongly confirmed by the very fables and traditions of the West, which all point to India as the land of wealth and learning-the El-Dorado of the ancient world.

It was to India that the mythic heroes of ancient Greece,[1] Hercules and Bacchus bent their steps, and from the time of the scarcely less fabulous Semiramis to that of Cyrus, it was the desire to reach her long coveted treasures that called forth the mightiest efforts of the great central monarchies of Asia. Darius and Alexander followed the same path of ambition with better success, but even they could never penetrate beyond her boundaries, never saw her sacred streams, nor the fertile plains which they watered.

But the event which in the popular imagination has, for more than twenty-two centuries past connected India with Europe, is undoubtedly the Indian expedition of Alexander the Great. He came to the throne of Macedone in 336 B.C., and, after having subdued Greece, he crossed over the Hellespont and began the conquest of western Asia in 334 B.C. After the defeat of the Persian monarch Darius III Codomannus, at the decisive battle of Gaugamela in 331 B.C, the Persian dominions in India together with all the rest of the empire came nominally under the sway of the conquerors. The military campaigns which followed, had, as their ostensible object, the vindication of the right of conquest and the consolidation of the empire thus won.

Consecutively, in India, where the Greeks came into contact with an ancient civilisation, which was in many respects, as advanced as their own, it was necessary to effect a compromise. The fact is, the Greeks excelled all other nations of antiquity in the width and depth of their aesthetic sentiments. The blessed teachings of Buddha began to appeal to the Greek mind. The *Milinda Pannha,* is the alliance between the two most dynamic forces in India at that time—the radical reforming creed of Sakyamuni and the thrust of invaders over the Hindukush, which acted as a kind of catalyst to reinvigorate the stagnant society. This is amply justified by the king like Menander, whom we first see as obsessed with doubts and dilemmas[2] about the teachings of Buddha and who himself later became a devout Buddhist ruler and propagated the teachings of the Buddhist religion.

No doubt, Buddhism had a considerable effect on the Hellenistic thought, and it obviously played a more immediate part in modifying the attitudes of Greeks within India itself.[3] It is hard to estimate the number of Greeks who were converted to Buddhism. Through the obscurity in which the details are enveloped, we can perceive that the Greeks in India were men of taste. They were, as was natural, attached to literature and the arts, which reminded them of their distant fatherland.[4]

It would be congenial to emphasize that the Greek settlers in India were not altogether the illiterate military colonists that the anti-Hellenists like Coomaraswamy and Havell would have us suppose them to have been. The traditions of Menander appear to indicate that the Bactrian Greeks were a cultured nation at the time of their greatest prosperity. The description of Greek monarch's capital[5] at Sagala seems to show that he was not a semi-barbarous conqueror, but a ruler, who if he did not seek to rival the great pomp and splendour of the Ptolemies or the Seleucids, at any rate upheld the tra-

[1]When speaking of the Greeks in India, it is customary to give a long excursus on the usage of the term for the Greeks. Three names were in current use in ancient India to refer to the Greeks, viz. *Yavana, Yona,* and *Yonaka.* For our purposer, it is quite sufficient to note that the word *Yavana* is encountered, first in Grammarian Panini's Ashtadhyayi (4-1-49) of the fourth century B.C. And the Prakrit *Yona* is the form of the Sanskrit *Yavana* and it occurs in the 13th rock edict of Ashoka. Hence the occurence of the term prior to the Greek advent suggests a borrowing from the Achaemenids. Darius for example calls the Greeks *Yauna* in his Naqshi Rustam inscription cf. H.C. Tolman, *Old Persian Lexicon and Texts*, pp. 44, 46. However, it is evident that the term goes back to the Greek '*Iones*', denoting the Ionians in Homer. (*Iliad*, XIII, 685)

[2]*Tuccho vata bho Jambudipo palapi vata bho Jambudipo Natthi koci Samano va Brahmano va yo maya saddhim sallpitum sakkoti..............(Milinda Panha,* Trans. by Jagan Nath Pathak, Moti Lal B. Dass, p. 5.)

[3]The resemblances between orphic and Buddhist beliefs have often been remarked, and in ater years Mahayanist influence played its part in the development of Neo—Platonic ideas in Alexandria and even in the early formulations of Christian dogma in that centre. (Woodcock, *Greeks in India*, London, 1966, p. 55)

[4]W.W, Tarn, *Greeks in Bactria and India*, 1951, 2nd. edn. p. 391—93.

[5]*Milinda—Pannha,* Translated by Rhys Davids in the *Sacred Books of the East*, vol. XXXV, Pt. i, (1965), 2-3 also Nilakantha Sastri, (*Ed.*), *Age of the Nandas and Mauryas*, Revised edn., p. 157

ditions of Hellenic civilisation in a not most unworthy manner.

It is fascinating to remark that even during the reign of the Mauryas, the presence of a large Greek population in India[1] becomes increasingly evident. The treaty between Seleucus and Chandragupta was sealed with a marriage agreement by which a daughter of Seleucus entered the house of Chandragupta.[2] Since she could have hardly become the wife of any lesser person than the Indian emperor himself or his son and heir Bindusara. The fascinating possibility arises that Asoka, the greatest of the Maurya emperors, may, in fact, have been half or at least a quarter Greek. He followed the doctrine of Buddhism and the Buddhist traditions are full of the name of Asoka as the founder of viharas or monasteries, stupas or dagobas, asylums and other religious and charitable works.

Asoka was anxious to make Greek converts and in later days there were colonies of Yavana or Greek Buddhists. Hence, it is interesting to note that the converts were made even to the more conservative East among the Greeks.[3] Consequently, it will be a nice endeavour to study the names of those Greeks who played a nice role in the promulgation of *dhamma* and made handsome contributions for the propagation of the new faith.

The names of the Yavana donors of sculptures, cisterns, pillars, etc. frequently occur in the saveral west Indian cave inscriptions. The earliest mention of Yavana workmanship appears to be in the Girnar inscription in Kathiawad, which records that the Girnar lake was furnished with conduits by the Yavana Raja Tusaspa for Asoka,[4] When Asoka became emperor, he began to include Greeks among his officials, and of these, the Yonaraja or Greek prince- Tusaspa, was governor of the province of Aparanta in the region of Saurashtra. The eighth line[5] of the inscription refers to the young alien prince. It runs thus :

> ....*Asokasya Mauryasya te Yavanarajena Tushasphen adhis-Rithaya.*
>
> (*Trans :* For Asoka the Maurya - by the Yavana king Tushaspha while governing, and by the conduit ordered to be made by him, constructed in a manner worthy of a king (and) seen in that breach, the extensive dam.)

It is worthwhile to note that the consciousness of Asoka's own Greek ancestry on the maternal side, if it indeed existed, may also help to explain the particular interest he took in the Yavanas. With one result, the commendable work done by the Greek prince is a nice landmark in the early pages of the Indian history.

Likewise, in the case of the Karle caves, some of the inscriptions date from the second century A.D and point to the continuance of Graeco-Buddhist settlement at quite a late date. Inscriptions No. 7-10 (Bombay Gazetteer, Vol. 18) refer to pillars, the gift of Siladhyay and Dhama Yavanas from Dhanakakata (Benakakata in the Nasik district).[6]

As the places from which the Buddhist Yavana donors come have not been indentified, it is difficult to say whether there existed Yavana-colonies in places like Dhenukakata, Umehakakata. Many donors are Dhenukakatans and the excavation seems today primarily a monument to their generosity. On the strength of what remains on the rock, there is no doubt that Dhenukakata had a settlement of Greeks bearing Indian or Indianised names.

In as much as the donor calls himself a Yavana Dhamma - Dheya from Dhenukakata (Karle 24), that settlement must have contained Greeks in trade contact with Alexandria. Supporting evidence may be seen on right pillar (17th) in the physician's name which Kombai[7] Milimda i.e. Menander. The script is somewhat later and the pillar is quite plain, which shows that the generosity, if not the wealth and glory, of Dhenukakata was on the wane. Milimda, though from Dhenukakata, does not call himself a Yavana; his wife and children bear Indian names.

From a social point of view one gets the impression that Yavanas, whoever they might have been, were ab-

[1] *Ibid*, p. 157.

[2] Appian, *Roman History*, Vol. II, Bk. xi, 9.55, p. 204. also K.H. Dhruva, *Journal of the Bihar Oriental Research Society*, Vol. 16, 1930, p. 35, no. 28.

[3] The Pali texts represent the Greeks as taking part even in missionary activities. We are told that after the conversion of the Yavana (Greek) country to Buddhism, Moggaliputta Tissa went to that country and selected a Greek Elder, Dharmaraksita for missionary work. (Bapat, P.V., 2500 *Years of Buddhism*, 1956, p. 55)

[4] The suggestion that has been advanced by some historians that the Yonaraja Tusaspa was, in fact, an Iranian is in this context singularly inept, since it was from the Iranians that the Indians borrowed the expressions Yavana and Yona to distinguish the Greek; it is unlikely that they would apply either of them to the race among whom they originated. Since Tusaspa is described as a Yona, we can safely assume that he was, infact, a Greek, however he acquired his strange name. (Woodcock, *op. cit.* p. 153)

[5] *Epigraphia Indica*, Vol. VIII, p. 43.

[6] Rapson, *Andhra Catalogue*, XXIX, XLVII.

[7] D.D, Kosambi, Dhenukakata, *Journal of the Asiatic Society of Bombay*, 1955, p. 57.

sorbed by the Indian society, If we can infer from the Buddhist votive inscriptions, these foreigners became also adherents of Indian religinos systems is clearly seen from their own confession. It seems that there existed, according to these early inscriptions, Greek colonies in the last centuries before and in the first centuries after the beginning of the Christian era in India, with social or religious independence.

Besides the inscription[1] dated in the 24th year of Pulumayi refers to Harapharanasa, probably a Persian Greek. It states:

> .... *Upasakasa Haraphranasa Setapharana Puttasya Sovaskasya Abulamavathavasya ima deyadhama matapo.*
>
> (*Trans:*A hall has been given to the adherents of the Mahasanghika (school) the community (of monks) living in the quarters (of the world) by the lay worshipper Harapharana son of Setapharana, a Sovasaka, living in Abulama, in honour of his parents and for the welfare and happiness of all living creatures.)

The two names in this inscription, viz. Harapharana and Setapharana are foreign and most probably Perso-Greek. The former exactly corresponds with Graeco-Persian *Oxophernis* or *Olophernis* and the latter with *Sitaphernis*. Fergusson[2] states that the termination *Pharana* probably contains N. Persian *frana.* (lord) and the *Seta* may be a corruption of old Persian *kshaeta.* Whatsoever may be the name. the meritorious gift of a hall by a Greek donor is indeed commendable.

Similarly, in Nasik cave[3], we find one *lena*[4] or cave owned by Indragnidatta, son of Dhammadeva, a Yonaka (Greek) from the north, from Dattamitra. Here, both father and son appear to have Hindu names. Their residence, Dattamitra, is thought to have been founded by Demetrius. The inscription runs thus :

> *Sidham otarahasa Datamitiyakasa* (1) *Yonakasa Dhammadevaputasa Idragnidatasa* (2) *dhammamana* (3) *imam* (4) *lenam pavarte Tirammhumhi Khanitam*.................
>
> (*Trans :* Success. The gift of Indragnidatta son of Dhammadeva, the Yavana, a northerner from Dattamitri. By him, inspired by true religion, this cave has been caused to be excavated in mount Tiranhu........)

It will be interesting to remark that Dattamitri would be an Indian adaptation of the Arachosian Demetrias, a name mentioned by Isidore of Kharax.[5] In that case a metathesis of syllables had taken place which is not found in other forms of that name Besides, as pointed out by Tarn, there is litlle evidence for Demetrias in Sind,[6] and the references to the battles of the Mahabharata to a brave Yavana king Dattamitra is now shown to be a later interpolation and the passage has been ommitted from recent critical editions[7] E. Senart.[8] while editing the inscription prefers to take the first words as far as Indragnidatasa as a complete clause, meaning a 'gift' or 'cave' of Indragnidatta....... It becomes clear that the donor had undertaken the work and made that grant under the impression of his recent commission to Buddhism. Be it as it may, the Yonaka, though aware of his paternal home, perhaps from Arachosia, uses Indian forms for his family names as well as for his relatives. Perhaps, it is not hazardous that he again is a Buddhist, for the teaching of that faith has cancelled the barriers of racial and social groups.

Likewise, in the Junnar caves[9] we have three inscriptions referring to the Greeks. The first deals with a donor named *Irila,*[10] which sounds suspiciously like a Greek name, perhaps Euryalus or something of that kind. It runs thus :

> *Yavanasa Irilasa Gatana deyadhama be podhiyo* (*Trans :* The meritorious gift of two cisterns by the Yavana Irila of the Gata country.)

It is interesting to note that *Gata* corresponds with the Sanskrit Garta, which is the ancient name of a district (a part of Trigarta or Kangra) in Himachal Pradesh.

1Vide. Karle, No. 21; Fergusson, *Cave Temples and their Inscriptions,* Vol. IV, p. 113.

2*Archaeological Survey of Western India,* Vol. IV, 1964, p. 113.

3*Epigraphia Indica,* Vol. VIII, no. 18, Pl. V, no. 3

4It is very interesting here to note the word *lena* for a cave. Normally in Sanskrit and particularly in *Amarkosa,* a cave is termed as *guha, gumpha, dari* and *kandari,* but in Greek the world *lainos* or *laini* means *taphos* or *mnima* ie made either of stone or marble. Some scholars tried to derive it from sanskrit *—Li—lyut—Layanam*; but this derivation does not seem to be very popular. I feel quite certain that the west Indian caves must have been within the jurisdiction of the colonial *Polis* of the Greeks and they being the chief donors preferred to give the name of their own language and steadily it became popular in the common Indian folk and till now every cave in Maharashtra is called *lena.* Hence, the parallel Greek origin of the word here is quite startling and convincing as well.

5*Parthian Stations,* translated by Shoff, W.H. (1914), p. 8ff.

6W.W, Tarn, *The Greeks in Bactria and India,* pp. 142, 526.

7E.H, Johnston, Demetrias in Sind (?) *Journal of the Royal Asiatic Society*, 1939, pp. 217—40. and Hopkins, *The Great Epic of India,* p. 392.

8*Epigraphia Indica,* Vol. VIII, p. 91.

9*Archaeological Survey of Western India,* Vol. IV, no. V, pp. 93.ff.

10*Indian Antiquary,* 1911, pp. 11—14.

Hence Gatna may be translated 'of the Garta[1] Country or' of the Gartas.' It is intelligible how a Yavana might have in Trigarta, where Greeks and Persians his home in resided from earlier times.

Moreover, it is for the first time that in these votive inscriptions, besides the word Yavana, a personal name occurs, and further the genitive plural of a noun. The strange appearance of the personal names, especially that of Irila, has led some scholars to see foreigners of the Gartas, i.e. the Goths a Germanic people.[2] However, Luder explained the ethnicon as corresponding to the sanskrit Garta.

Similarly goes the inscriptional line in cave 67 on Sivaneri hill[3]

> *Yavanasa chitasa Gatanam Bhojanamatapo deyadhama saghe.*
>
> (*Translation*—The meritorious gift of a refectory for the community (samgha) by the Yavana Chita (Chaitra) of the Gatas (or of the Garta country.)
>
> Likewise runs the third inscription.[4] *Yavandsa Chandanam deyadhama........* .
>
> (*Translation*—The meritorious gift of a hall front by Chanda the Yavana or Greek.)

Here, the yavana bears undoubtedly an Indian name Chandra. It seems that the genitives must be taken as family names. There are other instances of that in the Nagarjunakonda inscriptions. The clans or families of the Kulahaka of the Dhanaka of the Hiramnaka occur there.[5] Incidentally, in the Nagarjunakonda inscriptions[6] the yavana seems to belong to the countries which have been converted to Buddhism as told in the literary sources. As far as the material at disposal allows it, these are the early inscriptions in which the term yona, respectively yavana, occurs. But there are some epigraphs where that term indeed is not found but personal names at least of Greek make.

Thus, frequently the west Indian cave inscriptions give us the names of the private yavana individuals, who made gifts to the Buddhist *chaityas* or monasteries and consequently were unquestionably Buddhists and not only did they embrace Buddhism but borrowed Indian names ; 'in short' says an eminent Indianist,[7] "if the word Yavana had not been mentioned in these inscriptions, their foreign extraction would have remained undetected".

Besides, all these inscriptions, a reference to a Yona in the Sanchi inscriptions is also of immence value. Buhler[8] believed that the inscriptions at Sanchi belong to the third century B.C. However , it is not possible without any reproduction to say to which age each inscription may belong. One of the inscriptions[9] announces the gift of the Setapathia Yona - *Setapathiyasa Yonasa danam,* i.e. the gift of Yona, inhabitant of Setapatha.

The word yona can't be here anything, but a Greek donor. Whether he was really a yona or an Indian by nationality , it is hardly possible to decide. May be that the foreigner, a yavana by birth, became a Buddhist and settled down among his Indian co-believers ; for them he was the yona that became his personal name.

After having discussed about the cave inscriptions, there are other inscriptional evidences also, which partake the formidable part of the contribution made by the Greek in India. Of utmost importance is the Besnagar pillar, which is a living insignia of Indo-Greek unity (pl. 1)

The Besnagar pillar inscription is unique, because it is one of the few contemporary Indian records of the Bactrian Greeks. Antialcidas is the only Indo-Greek king other than Menander to be mentioned by name in an Indian source. The inscription engraved on a Garuda pillar was discovered by Sir John Marshall[10] at Besnagar near Bhilsa. It records the name of an inhabitant of Taxila, Heliodorus son of Dion, coming as an envoy from Antialcidas to the court of Kashiputra Bhagabhadra (c. 100 B. C) and presented this marvellous gift. It thus states :

> (*De*) *Vadevasa va* (*sude*) *vasa garudadhvaje ayam Karite i* (*a*) *Heliodorena bhagavatena Diyasa putrena Takhkhsilakena Yonadutena* (*a*) *gatena maharajas Amtialikitasa........*
>
> (*Trans*.- The Garuda pillar of Vasudeva, the god of gods, was erected by Heliodorus, a

[1]For Gartas see Wilson, H.H., *The Vishnu Purana*, Calcutta 1961, p. 159; Cunningham, *Archaeological Survey Reports*, Vol. V, p. 148 ff.; *Indian Antiquary*, Vol. IX, p. 252.

[2]Sten Konow, *Journal of the Royal Asiatic Society*, 1912, p. 379 ff. and A.V. Premerstein, *Zeitschrift fur. deutsches Altertum und deutsche Literatur*, 60, 1923, 72 f.

[3]*Archaeological Survey of Western India*, Vol. IV, no. 8, p. 94.

[4]*Ibid*, no. 6, p. 94.

[5]*Epigraphia Indica*, XX, p. 18.

[6]*Ibid*. p. 22.

[7]D.R, Bhandarkar, 'Foreign Elements in Hindu Population' *Indian Antiquary*, Vol. 40, Jan. 1911, p. 13.

[8]*Epigraphia Indica* Vol, II, p. 395.

[9]*Epigraphia Indica*, II, p. 395; Luder's List in *Epigraphia Indica*, Vol. X, *Appendix*, No. 547.

[10]*Journal of the Royal Asiatic Society*, 1909, pp. 1053–56 Chanda, *Memoirs of the Archaeological Survey of India*, No. I. Sarcar, *Select Inscriptions*, p. 102. Luder's list in *Epigraphia Indica*, X, Appendix, 669 Bhandarkar, D.R; *Journal of the Bombay Branch of the Royal Asiatic Society*, Vol. XXIII, 1914, 104—6.

Bhagavata, the son of Dion and an inhabitant of Taxila, came as a Greek ambassador from the great king Antialcidas........)

The inscription, though in the Brahmi script, throws a much valued light upon the most controversial pages of Indian history, when the Greeks and the Indians were in close contact with each other. It shall remain for ever as a living replica of the unity of the two mighty cultures of the ancient world.

Of equal value to the Besnagar pillar inscription is the Bajaur Casket inscription. The inscription consists of two groups of small epigraphs of different periods, the first mentions the name of Maharaja Minandra and can be dated in the middle of the second century B. C. while the second refers to the reconstruction of the casket in the time of certain Vijayamitra,[1] who has been identified with the Vijayamitra named on certain Indo-Scythic coins.[2] Unfortunately, the portion of the lid of the casket which may have contained a date is broken. Nevertheless, this small and fragmentary inscription is of great value.[3] It is in Kharosthi and runs as follows -

....*Minendrasa maharajasa Katiasa divasa* 44411 *pra (na) --Sameda ......(pra) (thavi) ta.* (*Trans :* ....on the 14th day of Karttika, in the (reign) of Maharaja Minedra, (in the year), (the corporeal relic of the Buddha), which is endowed with life ....has been established).

This inscription proves beyond doubt that king Menander helped in the propagation of Buddhism in the region between Hindukush and Sindh.[4] Plutarch says that as a ruler Menander had a keen sense of justice and was dearly loved by his people. Though the power he had established in India disappeared with his death, the memor y of this just and wise ruler shall for ever remain enshrined in the pages of the *Milinda pannha*. It is interesting to note that at his death, he was given funeral as was given to lord Buddha[5] and a dispute arose over the disbursement of the ashes.[6]

Apart from Bajaur—casket, the Swat relic vase inscription (pl. IIA) is one of the oldest, perhaps the oldest of all Kharosthi inscriptions, with the exception of those of Asoka, and it can hardly be later than the middle of the lst century B. C. The whole inscription accordingly runs :

Theudorena meridarkhena pratithavid (r) a ime sarira Sakamunisa bhagavato bahujanastitiye. (*Translation:*By Theodoros, the meridarkh, were established these relics of the Lord Sakyamuni, for the purpose of security of many people).

The name Theudora is Greek. Theudoros is no less Greek than Theodoros. However, Theudora is a correct writing and not only the name, but also the official title which occurs once more on a Taxtila Copper plate point to a Greek individual. Meridarkhena is the Greek title *Meridarxis,* which belongs to the Hellenistic and Roman period. (plate IIB)

From this inscription, it is clear that Theudoros was officially a *Meridarxis* or District Officer. He was most probably in-charge of a part of the Kabul territory (the Paropamisadae) or of Arachosia or Gandhara. Obviously, the donor is a citizen of a Greek state or at least a state, organised according to Hellenistic norms. It is interesting to set how far Buddhism had influenced the foreigners in their own territory when high administrative officers professed Buddhism.

The name Theodoros is met again in the Kaldarra inscription[7] of the year 113. It records the laying out of a tank by Thaidora, the Datiaputra. Though the name of the devotee is Greek, his father's name is some way strange. It is curious that among the many names of Greek rulers in India, the name Theodoros is not found, while it occurs a third time on two silver cups from Taxila.[8]

However , it is interesting to note that how such staunch converts were made even among foreigners. Not only the Greeks, Indo-Parthians and Kushanas also followed the same path. Ultimately, Buddhism reached its zenith in the reign of Kanishka, who was obviously a phil Hellenic ruler.

Indeed, peculiarly beautiful example of Graeco-Buddhist workmanship is the priceless reliquary (pl.III) discovered by Dr. D. B. Spooner[9] in the remains of

[1]Sten Konow, *New Indian Antiquary,* 1939-40, p. 642.

[2]N.G. Majumdar, *Epigraphia Indica,* Vol. XXIV, p. 6.

[3]Minamdra as the name of a donor is noticed on a piece of culpture of the Peshawar museum, representing two wrestlers. But the style of the characters points to the later Kushana period. Sten Konow, *Corpus Inscriptionum Indicarum,* Vol. II, p. 134.

[4]Ray Chaudhury, *Political History of Ancient India,* 6th edn.; 1953, p. 382.

[5]Plutarch, *Praecepta gerendae Reipublicae,* Morala, 821, D.

[6]*Sacred Books of the East,* Vol. XI, p. 131

[7]*Corpus Inscriptionum Indicarum,* I, Vol. XXIV, p. 65. f; Buhler, *Indian Antiquary,* Vol. XXV, 1876, pp. 141 ff. Banerjee, *ibid.* Vol. XXXVII, 1908, pp. 31, 66 ff. with pl. opp. p. 66.

[8]*Corpus Inscription Indicarum,* II, i, no. XXXVII, i & 2, p. 97.

[9]*Journal of the Royal Asiatic Society,* 1909, 1058 p. II; *Archaeological Survey of India, Frontier Circle,* 1907-8, 1908-9, pp. 14 ff. *Archaeological Survey of India, Annual Report* 1908-9, pp. 38 ff; 1909-10, pp. 135 ff.

great stupa of Kanishka, near Peshawar in 1908 and 1909. This again is the contribution of a Greek artist, for it bears an inscription to the effect that it was made by *Agasilaos* - an overseer at Kanishka's *vihara* in the Sangharama of Mahesana.[1]

The occurrence of the Greek name Agisala found in the inscription on the casket, (*Dasa Agisal navakarmia kanashkasa vihare mahasenasa Sangharame*) is a interesting point. The form Agesilas occurs in the last paragraph of chapter XVIII of the VIIIth Book of Pausanias, where he is mentioned as a man of Lusi, who was a victor in the Pythian festival held by Amphictyons. The forms Agesilas and Ageisilas also occur, the latter in a Boeotian inscription from northern Greece (vide Liddle and Scott, *Greek English Lexicon*).

It may be pointed out that the inclusion of this name in the casket semes to be a parenthetical addition, and it seems that the casket was not for public exhibition. Anyhow, there is every possiblity that the artist had been a westerner. The decoration on the casket shows a curious blending of classical and Indian elements. It points to a time when the graceful plant of Greek art transplanted on the Indian soil had become choked by the luxuriant growth of indigenous culture.

Thus, plenty are the inscriptional evidences to show that the Greeks shared a good amount in the development of the architectural and artistic wealth of India. Besides their contribution for centuries in succession in the enhancement of the prolific faith of that time shall ever remain enshrined in the cultural heritage of India. It is a curious fact, besides that a few races have disappeared so utterly in India as the Greek. However, I would deem it fit to remark at this juncture that capital data are possibly waiting there underground - the Kabul valley for instance, which was almost a sand-laden soil for archaeologists and a wonderful mirage for W.W. Tarn for forty years, is making us to arrive at certain conclusions now. For the last one decade, it has brought to light many valuable materials which are compelling to modify considerably the views of the anti-Hellenists upon the history of the Greeks in ancient India. The thick mist of obscurity, which was unhappily hanging like a pall upon the early history of India, atleast for the period of the Indo- Greeks, was not making anything approaching to certainty possible. But the recent discoveries at Ai - Khanum and Surkh Kotal in Afghanistan are going to open the door for finding out the settlements of the brethrens of the Greeks of the Indian inscriptions. Here for the first time the French Mission has come upon a Graeco-Bactrian city. The published finds include Corinthian capitals of a debased type and many sherds of Greek pottery. Reports of more recent discoveries include important Greek inscriptions, the tomb of a magistrate, a portico of giant Corinthian columns, and, in the gymnasium, a harem of Herakles. One can only hope that the completion of these excavations may unearth evidence of Hellenistic art comparable to the Russian finds at the old Parthian city of Nisa to present us for the first time the basis for understanding the penetration of Hellenism in the region. Thus, it may explicitly be emphasized that this would certainly be a remarkable new chapter not only for the history of the Indian sub- continent but a nice addendum to the history of the Greek world.

The paucity of Greek remains and material in present day India is due to the fact that the study of the Indo-Greeks is still in its infancy. The coastal region of western India, where we had the colonial stations of the Greek merchants and the hilly terrains of north India along with the shady haunt of Menander are yet to produce palpable evidence of active Hellenism and are awaiting the spade of the archaeologists.

But in any case, the fascinating story of the Greeks in India is not only full of suggestion but is also a most interesting chapter in the history of development of ideas. The question does not interest solely to the Indianist and the Hellenist, but likewise to all those who occupy themselves in tracing the evolution of general history, and to those who, above all, love to follow, even in their more remote expansion, the antecedents of our modern culture and civilisation, the different phases of our national development and progress.

New Delhi. S. D. DOGRA

[1] Sten Konow,; *Corpus Inscriptionum Indicarum,* Vol. II, ii. and p. 135 ff.; *L*; Foucher, *Art Graeco, Boddhique Du Gandhara,* II, p. 531 ff.

Book Reviews

H. D. Sankalia : Prehistory and Potohistory of India and Pakistan. Poona. Deccan College Postgraduate and Research Institute, 1974 (New Ed.); pp. xxiii 592 (including 5 Appendices, Bibliography, Index and 340 line - drawings, half-tone plates, maps, charts, etc). Price : Rs. 120.

The book under review is a new edition of the 1962 edition which was presented as a series of lectures at the University of Bombay. Professor Sankalia was awarded in 1968 the Jawaharlal Nehru Fellowship. He utilised this Fellowship not only for carrying out further work of exploration and excavation in areas hitherto little worked but also to completely rewrite the first edition in terms of new information which had since accumulated due to the efforts of several research scholars, specially the Deccan College team, and by incorporating other concepts which have since emerged in archaeology all over the world. As the title indicates the book covers the entire range of material beginning from the lower palaeolithic culture to the protohistoric sites, including both Harappan and other Chalcolithic cultures of the sub-continent. This book is both voluminous and encyclopaedic. Hence, it is not possible to even list the various sections which have been discussed, for this would involve writing, a monograph by itself. However, it should suffice to mention that in the new edition information has been brought up to date by recording the new discoveries in Kashmir, Konkan, kutch, Saurashtra, south Gujarat, south Uttar Pradesh, south Bihar and West Bengal. For example, the chapters on the Lower and Middle palaeolithic have been much more fully and exhaustively covered, so also the Upper Palaeolithic Chapter which is a new one beocause of several new discoveries of similar types made in the Peninsular regions. The Mesolithic sites of Rajasthan, Karnataka, Maharashtra and Uttar Pradesh have also been dealt with in detail. Incidently, the old terminology of early, Middle and Late Stone-Age has been dropped, and the European one, adopted due to various new disco veries. But is this adoption possibly not because somehow we are always keen to seek European parallels in the Indian subcontinent despite the fact of totally different geography, culture- orientation and other factors? This is true for history, sociology, science and even art. Are we not prisoners of colonial consciousness, and a captive mind ? We must be fully aware of these factors of intellectual growth in India, whereby the West for almost everything has become the point of reference.

At any rate, the sections on the neighbouring areas of Pakistan, Baluchistan and Afghanistan have been completely rewritten and of course the spread of Harappan Civilization in the Indian areas has been thoroughly discussed, such as the excavations at Kalibangan and Surkotada and so on. The Chalcolithic sites outside the Harappan spheres and specially in the Maharashtra regions where the Deccan College is carrying out the horizontal excavations are extremely important, such as the sites of Inamgaon, and the fresh excavations of the neolithic sites at Sanganakallu and Tekkalakota. The appendices in the book cover the C-14 dates in the sub- continent as well as the antiquity of grains in Western Asia, South-East Asia and the sub-continent.

In short, as the blurb indicates, the book discusses all the various discoveries, and the main lines of development of various cultures in India by means of a critical appraisal of existing information which is available for the knowledge of the past, as obtained by archaeological means. The book is undoubtedly, as was the first edition, of great significance for all those who are interested in gaining knowledge about the prehistory and protohistory of South Asia. While this monumental work is praiseworthy and incomparable, for no other attempt has been made to present so ably the discoveries made on this sub-continent, it would not be out of place to offer certain general views which are different to these that reflect the general trend in India.

I had on an earlier occasion (*Indian Civilization : The Formative Period*, 1968, Simla) criticised the approach of Professor Sankalia. In many circles this criticism was construed as an indication of an attempt to minimise the contribution which he has made to the growth of Indian archaeology. This was far from my mind. In the world of scholarship there must be room for free critcism and scope for the discussion of new ideas, and as Professor Sankalia himself does not mind the spirit of free enquiry, and of raising new issues, others should also encourage this despite constrainsts of the Gura-India tradition. The present criticism of the approach is being made in the same light.

In 1968 , I criticised the definitions given by Professor Sankalia ; these were about archaeology, prehistory and so on. Unfortunately, these definitions remain unchanged in the new edition. In these circumstances if Professor Sankalia continues to lament that the work here is far from being complete and is scanty, specially when compared to Europe and America from the socio logical viewpoint ; then the fault is nobody's but our own. If we do not pose the right questions or raise the relevant problems, then the information which we are looking for will not be obtained. If archaeology is defined, for instance as is done by him (p.7) to mean primarily the study of antiquities, it is no wonder that the sociological background is not available. Again, when discussing the spread of lithic industries, to use the word culture, and to suggest that there is a uniformity of cultures all over the sub-continent is very misleading. This kind of "cultural unity" is misleading because the use of similar tools, specially the surviving lithic tools, is no indication of a uniformity of cultural patterns. But more than this, at the early stages of human development, recent work in behavioural studies of non-human primates indicates that a certain basic functional pattern such as that of tool-using and even elementary toolmaking is a fundamental part of primate behavioural patterns.

It is often said that theoretical developments and discussions are out of place in any discussion of archaeology. It is also suggested that science means empiricism. But this is a nineteenth century concept of science which is not being followed today by scientists themselves. We continue to believe in India that 'factual' knowledge is somehow more basic, solid and reliable. But howsoever objective one may be, only those discoveries or materials become 'facts' that are relevant to the conceptual framework within which we are trying to explore and excavate the evidence of the past. It is very clear to the philosophers of science on both logical and psychological grounds that 'facts' never speak for themselves or exist by themselves. But since the empiricist-inductive approach believes that each trait is a discreet entity with its own inherent meaning, somehow material remains are taken to be 'real' cultures. From this arise the common theory of culture variability and change ; i. e. since cultural norms are represented by artifacts, changes are as a result of new ideas or norms as represented by newer material changes. These are introduced usually by means of 'influence' or 'diffusion' from other cultures mainly by migration, though sometimes by innovation. Hence, the major problem becomes one of finding the origin of cultural traits. This is why archaeological cultures are described in terms of lists of traits. The next step is to compare assemblages and explain similarities and differences in terms of differential diffusion, sometimes by environmental changes and influences and so on. The orientation of field-work also follows these goals, i. e. the goals are to locate the distribution of material traits, representing cultural norms, specially the most diagnostic features, which for each archaelogist become the most important or unique—often a projection of the self.

The emphasis is thus on the observation of cross-stylistic variabilities rather than the functional or adaptational one, so that analytical techniques also value this orientation, effecting sampling techniques. As a consequence what has happened is that despite the increasing amount of overwhelming socalled factual evidence, problems are not getting any nearer to solutions. In fact, such an approach has acted as a deterrent rather than as a stimulant for better information, leave aside even providing a body of reliable knowledge about various socio-cultural phenomena. All this does not mean that sophisticated field research has a second place. But since empirical research requires verification by the use of comparative methods, and generalizations require theories and hypotheses, this is the only way to avoid the confused intellectual state in which Indian archaeology is today; viz. at the conceptual level, there is no clarity and this is reflected in the confused state of field research and of the mixed bag of terms and definitions which are used differently by each worker whereby unnecessary controversy is created. Consequently, it is very essential to be self-conscious of *how* and *why* of *what* we are doing.

In short, the basic approach in India is the inductive approach in which the data, the method of analysis the interpretations and hypotheses formation are carried out separately, such as (1) excavation, exploration or collection of data, (2) classification and placing of data in a chronological order, (3) analyses and (4) interpretation. This method is grossly inadequate and misleading. The objection to this traditional approach is that it allows one to collect indiscriminately all data as if field work can be adequately carried out without technological expertise, specially without any interest in theories and problems as such. Contrarily, according to the deductive approach material evidence which exists in the world has no meaning by itself; its meaning is given by the framework of concepts. This is why problem-orientation and long term plans are necessary, for they avoid a great deal of widespread duplication. In this way great deal of waste may be avoided if some basic issues are discussed with explicit awareness, specially bearing in mind those questions about culture that we ask for this subcontinent, that are common to archaeology, anthropology, sociology and history; all of which deal with the phenomenon of man. All this does not imply that since we have a problem in hand, that the obvious in the field will be ignored since it does not fit in the set of problems and hypotheses. Ideas will be modified when faced with new or unexpected kind of obseravtion. It is crucial to remember this interaction that is an essential feature of the new approach to archaeology.

Thus, if we look at the changing perspectives of archaeology which have been taking place during the last decade, and view this book in this light, it will be noted that in India we are just about completing a pre-paradigm state when there are many views and schools of thought competing for prominence. At this state, in the absence of any common body of beliefs and concepts,each researcher thinks about building the foundation of his discipline. We have yet to emerge from this first stage to that of forumulating a set of theories as are part of normal science when paradigms are logically explored, tested and discarded. But if a tremendous amount of information has been obtained today, it is not because of the approaches in India but because of the increasing use of scientific techniques which have been borrowed from the natural and physical sciences. However, even though there is an increasing quantitative representation of data by means of tables, histograms, graphs, etc., these are insufficient in providing adequate analytical techniques that yield clues to problems. The various analytical techniques which are being used today, with the use of computers, etc. have developed against the background of 'new' archaeology. It is this perspective which should be borne in mind both in terms of the approach and for using recent analytical techniques. Ultimately, what we are trying to understand is socio-cultural phenomena in terms of group activities; their settlement patterns and mobility during various sessons, the territorial range and its extent; economic patterns and subsistence or diet; and both macro and micro patterning which forms the basis of typological and taxonomic problems whereby we are able to categories intergroup differentials, diffusions, cultural contact situations and so on.

It is to the credit of Professor Sankalia that he is open to new ideas and he is no hesitation in adapting to new discoveries. This is indeed a natural course for an intellectual, which most of us academics cease to be when past our prime. He has discussed in the book though insufficiently for me 'new' archaeology and adopted some new approaches with which he differed earlier. This is a far cry from the time when he reviewed any book in the *Times of India,* stating in the context of my approach that "Malik is in a Formative Stage". At another point he had criticised my suggestion of a division of labour in early societies on the basis of sex, viz., men hunting and women gathering and collecting food. This is logical and valid on both theoretical and empirical grounds of studying human societies Every evidence cannot be obtained through material terms, for the intangible has to be shown, to be probable, through logical statements. This is what indicates its validity; this is what science and scientific statements imply not mere empiricism.

Based on the above briefly mentioned general views, I would take up specific chapters for criticism. But that will be a lengthy process and not quite necessary. There are also proof and typographical errors in the book, which may be avoided next time. Needless to add, the book is worth every shelf in the library, and at home if one can afford it, for the wealth of information.

Indian Institute of Advanced Study S.C. MALIK
Simla.

Shashi Asthana, with a foreword by S.P. Gupta : History and Archaeology of India's contacts with other countries from earliest times to 300 B.C. Delhi : B.R. Publishing Corporation, 1976; pp. xii & 275, with a msps and illustrations. Price : Rs. 120.

Since I took to archaeology, I have always been struck by similarities in style or expression between terracotta figurine and architectural styles found in different parts of India. So special sections were devoted to these topics in my books on *University of Nalanda* and *Archaeology of Gujarat,* for this was the fashion among old scholars like Bernet Kempers, Kramrisch, Vogeal and others. Of course, while attempting this comparision one had always to remain within the framework of time and space. Later, the same method was followed in my book on *Investigations into the Prehistoric Archaeology of Gujarat,* basing my comments, as far as the Indian material was concerned, on a prolonged study of the Foote collections in the Madras Museum. This kind of comparision of data, from specific regions in India and outside, always helped me not to be parochial but appreciate the good points in each.

Later on, when I handled evidence from stratified sites in India and found very close similarity *but not identity* between objects from Central India and Iran, the same kind of culture contact was postulated. While postulating this contact I was more than careful in

India and Western Asia, and the vast areas that separate them.

As we excavated more and more sites in Central India and the Deccan, the evidence grew, but unfortunately scholars like the late Sir Mortimer Wheeler always treated these questions sceptically. However, doubts regarding the much earlier antiquity of such vessels as the channel spouted bowl were dispelled when I studied these and other things in the Iran Bastan Museum in Tehran. Even now, I think, if a scholar like Shashi Ashthana with all her background of Indian evidence, has a chance of visiting Pakistan, Afghanistan, Iran, Iraq and Turkey, she is bound to find objects exhibiting close identity in shape and treatment, and sceptics like Dilip Chakrabarty will be satisfied.

During the First International Conference on Asian Archaeology, held in Delhi in 1961 Prof. Max Mallowan who held views similar to those of Chakrabarty was indeed struck by the identity of the zoomorphic vessels from Nevasa, Chandoli and Western Asia. We must remember that all these are locally made in the Jorwe fabric. Why? The obvious and the only answer is that the people in the Deccan were influenced in some way or the other, which we cannot understand fully at present, by the religious ideas prevailing in Western Asia.

The same is true of Inamgaon mother-goddesses. These goddesses, as one participant in the Tata Institute, Bombay, Symposium held in 1972, thought, are not like any other nude, to be found at any time throughout the historic past, but belong to a cultural milieu. This, I have pointed out in an article .

Shashi Asthana stops in her survey at 300 B.C. but had she extended her sweep she could have cited our Smiling Boy from Nevasa and explained how it is an exact copy of the Greek child god Pluto. Inspite of the correct hesitation in looking for foreign or outside influence to explain the few such objects one finds right from the Lower Palaeolithic through the Middle and Upper Palaeolothic to Neolithic in India, what has happened in historical times and what is happening on a mass scale today—drain pipes followed by bell-bottoms-has to be kept before the mind. Our love for "foreign" is very old. And that is why the little evdence of the Upper Palaeolithic points to such culture-contacts. We are certainly becoming wise (p. 11) and learning more about the culture its specific tools, both bone and stone, its art, and its time span. The C^{14} date for the ostrich shell given by Groningen Laboratory about 20,000—25,000 B.C. is quite consistent with the dates from Western Asia and Europe. But while the date, and some culture traints, agree fairly well, one should not expect cent per cent identity, because the environmental conditions in Europe and India were markedly different. Hence, what little is found is indeed significant.

I am glad, that all these and many more issues of culture-contacts have been handled by Shashi Asthana with exemplary care, she has documented all evidence and drawings in each case, and arrived at very provisional conclusions, Thus, all true scholars should be masters of evidence and judgement. These twin qualities help her to avoid fancilful theories, though these are becoming fashionable and are even applauded. Hence, Shashi Asthana's work has become a reliable reference work but at the same time it is eminently readable. The illustrations are numerous and excellent. Both the *guru* and the *Shishya*—Dr. S.P. Gupta and Dr. Shashi Asthana—and the publishers deserve our congratulations.

Poona H.D. SANKALIA

Purshottam Singh : Neolithic Cultures of West Asia. London: Seminar Press, 1974; 240 pp., 74 figures and plates. Price : Rs. 4.

Anybody would be tempted to buy this elegantly published book, printed fully in art paper, by a prestigious publisher and at such a modest price. It's not only the get-up but also the contents that make this book a valuable work.

Dr. Singh is very well-known in Indian archaeology for his numerous learned articles and a book. What is less known is that within his short stay in U.K., he mastered West Asian archaeology, under the able guidance of Prof. David Oates. In fact, by producing this scholarly work on West Asian Neolithic cultures during his stay in U.K., he has put other scholars who spend long periods abroad in an embarassing position. The book is extremely valuable to us in India as a ready reference work with up-to-date and exhaustive data on all the known sites. Even the critical British archaeologists have strongly recommended it to their students of West Asian Archaeology.

After explaining the scope and approach of the book the author describes the neolithic sites under the Levant, Turkey, Iraq and Iran. He has deliberately chosen these modern geopolitical regions for ease of comprehension, though the neolithic cultures discussed to not respect these boundaries. The book is based on primary and latest reports scattered in a multitude of journals. It will not become, therefore, obsolete for at least some years to come. Moreover, the data are not simply called from the reports. The author toured extensively many of these sites and studied the material first hand. of Course, the famous sites of Jericho, Hacilar, Catal Huyuk, Karim Sahir, Shanidar, Jarmo, Hassuna, Nineveh, Tell Arpachiyah and Tepe Yahya are discussed in detail. But these are not all; a total of about fifty sites are described. The well reproduced maps make it easy not only to locate the sites but also to study the obsidian trade (fig. 74) and 'early domestication and spread of einkorn wheat and barley (figs. 72 and 73).

Dr. Singh has taken care to cover not only traditional archaeological assemblages but also faunal and floral remains. The chronologies are based on a critical study of the available ^{14}C dates. To steer clear of the controversies pertaining to different ^{14}C half-life values and $^{14}C/^{12}C$ variations, he gives his dates on the Libby value (5568 years). This is definitely a more scientific approach than indiscriminately using calibration curves of one's own choice and then making far reaching archaeological inferences. An appendix gives the total available ^{14}C dates of the West Asian Neolithic.

No book on archaeology can be of much use without illustrations and here lies the chief strength of the book. It is profusely illustrated with plates and line drawings and maps (total 74 figures). For this, naturally the author had to depend upon the excavators. As a result some of the illustrations are not clear (e.g. fig. 28) and many are without scale. For example, the wooden dish in fig. 39 looks, without a scale, like a crater.

The limitations of space naturally could allow only brief summaries of reports, but for further information a rich exhaustive bibliography is given, which incidentally shows how thorough a study the author has made. It would have been better if the author had also given original references to the ^{14}C dates used. Three indices make it very easy to locate topics, authors and site's.

In the summary, the author has chosen to summarize only the evidence on architecture, domestication of plants and animals and obsidian trade. Of course, these are the main neolithic traits. But one fails to get a general picture of the neolithic cultures from the summary.

One could point out a few proof-reading errors and some minor errors of statements (e.g. the claim that the earliest bricks used were at Ganj Dareh is wrong). But such minor errors have a way of creeping in, despite one's efforts.

A book is rarely a pure research work of an individual. A book generally is a critical review of the available data including the author's, if any. The author in this case candidly defines his book as "a synopsis, without pretension to original research". In fact, Dr. Singh need not be apologetic about it because this learned synopsis of such a vast and scattered data is itself a gigantic task which the author has so competently performed. I only wish that some other university colleagues could do the same in their fields of study for the benefit of the lay and the scholar alike.

This is a factual book, therefore no theories need be criticised. One of course, expected the author to include some sites nearer the Indo-Pak sub-continent so that we could connect the West Asian evidence with ours. Though the author has chosen the term 'Neolithic', at times he has reverted back to Braidwoodian terms. One perhaps also expected a synthetic picture that emerges from this vast range of data. But the author has scrupulously avoided involving himself in any controversies and such a synthesis would have betrayed his bias.

To conclude, Dr. Singh has done a great service to the archaeological world by producing such a factual, lucid, well illustrated synopsis of the West Asian Neolithic.

Physical Research Laboratory D.P. AGRAWAL.
Ahmedabad, 380009

K. Paddayya : Investigation Into the Neo lithic Culture of the Shorapur Doab. South India. Leiden: E. J. Brill, 1973; XXIII+98pp., 29 figures and 9 plates. Price: not mentioned.

In the monograph, which is a part of the author's Ph. D. dissertation, Dr. Paddayya has given a regional survey of the neolithic culture of the Shorapur Doab, based mainly on the stratigraphical scraping at Kodekal, and secondarily, on the surface explorations of various sites. Basically, it is an investigation into the origin and authorship of the ash-mound culture, belonging to the southern neolithic complex. None the less, Paddayya has tried to extend the scope of his study further by a discussion on the chronology, external contacts of the southern neolithic culture and reconstruction of the life and times of the people. Based on the data, easily available to him, he has postulated the existence of several regional variants in the southern neolithic complex.

He has divided the book —indeed written in a lucid style with neat presentation of facts — into seven chapters. In Chapter I has been given the account of the geographical features of the Doab, while four successive chapters deal with the study of various artefacts like pottery, pecked and ground stone tools, blade industry, miscellaneous objects and rock-bruisings. The most important of the chapters is Chapter VI devoted to the stratigraphical scraping in the Kodekal ash-mound. Apart from an Introduction, the book has a preface by Professor J. E. van Lohuizen-de Leeuw who has edited the series 'Studies in South Asian Culture' for the Institute of South Asian Archaeology, University of Amsterdam. The appendix deals with the 'Animal Remains from the Kodekal Excavations by D. R. Shah. It is a fairly well-illustrated book if it is viewed from the point of view of printing and get-up. An index would have certainly enhanced its value.

As already stated, Chapter VI is undoubtedly a contribution to the study of the southern neolithic culture in general and the problem of ash-mounds in particular. The stratified section of the Kodekal ash-mound, divided into seven layers, disclosed three occupation phases and two burnings. Paddayya is of the opinion that layers 1 and 3 are composed of burnt cow-dung. This is a conclusion that confirms the earlier findings at Utnur Palavoy, Kupgal and a few other sites. Significantly, layer 4 at Kodekal has yielded charcoal sample that has been dated to 2335 B. C., a date earlier to Utnur (2170. B.C.) by a century and a half.

Now the question arises whether the eleven-feet deposit at Kodekal belongs to one and the same period. According to the author, layer 6, measuring about 10 inches in thickness, is an occupational deposit, even bringing to light traces of structural activity represented by a series of granite-gneiss blocks. All types of pottery except incised and rusticated coarse grey ware came from this stratum ; in layer 4, only rusticated pottery is absent. Thus, by and large, both the strata, though separated by a rammed flooring, are ascribable to the same phase. The paucity of antiquity in layers 1 to 3 clearly demonstrates that the site was no longer occupied for the purpose of dwelling or habitation. Instead, it was chosen to be the venue of bonfire or cow-dung burning, a ceremony observed at some regular cycle. The findings of Kodekal, coupled with the evidence from Utnur, establish the fact that some of the ash-mounds are datable to the neolithic times. At the same time, there is ample evidence, particularly in the Upper Krishna valley, that some of the ash-mounds belong to the Iron Age cultutre; mounds there represent ovens for iron smelting.

Though he has concentrated more on Kodekal, Paddayya revisited the already-known sites in the Doab and also explored some new ones. The result of his exploration has been incorporated in the first chapter. He has classified the archaeological sites into (a) ash-mounds, (b) habitation sites and (c) ancient gold workings. As per his statement (pp. XXII, 60 and 80) there are eleven ash-mounds in spite of the fact that he has listed thirteen of them, viz., (1) Budihal, (2) Mallur, (3) Thanmandi, (4) Thanda, (5) Kodekal, (6) Budihal-S, (7) Tirth, (8) Kakkera, (9) Benkanhalli, (10) Shakapur, (11) Rajankolur, (12) and Dimanhal, (13) Once there existed circles made up of ash-mounds at Rajankolur and Dimanhal but the author has ascribed them to the iron age culture ; and this may be the reason for counting the total number of ash- mounds as eleven. Whatever may be the actual number, there are, in all, eleven sites, in the Shorapur Doab, associated with ash-mounds, ascribable either to the neolithic or the iron age periods. The number of habitation sites briefly described by the author is eight. Whereas his map shows more than a dozen of them because a few other sites are associated with stray finds (p. 11) of comparable age.

In the absence of the list of antiquities at the end of the description of the respective sites, it is not easy for a reader to visualize the cultural assemblage of a particular settlement. As different types of antiquities have been dealt with collectively, one gathers an impression of their having no context at all. At Bijaspur, more than one cultural deposit has been encountered, yet the finds from their respective periods remain undefined. The author seems to have been guided by *a priori* conclusion that all the sites constitute a homogeneous cultural group ; hence, may be treated as one entity. It would have been more scientific to deal the antiquities of the each site separately before building up an over-all picture of a particular industry or tradition.

To return to the evidence of Bijaspur (BJP) , it has yielded 6 ft. deposit, shared by the neolithic, iron age and early historical cultures ; a few sherds of the Jorwe Ware have also been picked up. But Table I (Distribution of pottery according to site and ware) does not show any Black-and-red Ware or Iron Age pottery ; as a result, we are in the dark about the cultural components of this phase. Surprisingly, he is very particular in dealing with the early historical pottery under a separate sub-section. Then, how could he arrive at the conclusion regarding the existence of iron age (megalithic) phase at Bijaspur ?

We are very much disappointed in not having any glimpses of the ceramic tradition from Rajankolur and Dimanhal ; a reassessment of the earlier material from these sites would have given a clear picture about different cultural phases of the region. Such a study is all the more imperative as some of the ash-mounds are clearly of the megalithic association (p. 62). On the Whole, he has not given due emphasis to the iron age culture of the Shorapur doab, his intention being to focus all attention on the neolithic elements.

The pecked and ground stone industry as well as the blade industry (what others call microlithic) have also been dealt with collectively, with the presumption that the entire collection partakes of one culture. A reader is considerably handicapped by the absence of description of tools or drawings of individual specimens. Viewed colle ctively, the industry appears to have lacked variety unlike other neolithic sites of the Deccan. But it is certain that it is accompanied by a flake-tradition as established by the present reviewer on the basis of the neolithic industry at Nagarjunakonda.

So far as the blade industry is concerned it is marked by a high percentage of retouched tools, including re-touched blades, and it is a phenomenon not typical of the neolithic stage. Does it mean that he is dealing with a mixed surface collection ? If all the explored materials were studied sitewise, perhaps he could have avoided any probable misconception and also arrived at some relative chronology, based on typological study, of the different sites and their variable levels of cultural attainments.

Paddayya's attempt on the reconstruction of the life and times of the people is an exercise in futility. His Procrustean endeavour to tailor borrowed facts to fit into his imaginary picture of the ash-mound culture is undeniably brave, specially considering the meagre data available to him from the Shorapur Doab, but it is premature and unscientific. He has not encountered any dwelling except some stone-alignments and bamboo-impressed clay clods from Kodekal yet he postulates that the people led a sedentary life and lived in circular huts. His own research has shown that the 11ft. thickness of the deposit at Kodekal does not signify any long span of time . Further, he must be well-aware that the ash-mound people, specially those of neolithic times, were possibly pastoral and had to move from one place to another. It is equally well-known that some form of agricultural nomadism was inherent in early neolithic economy in different parts of the world. Now about the circular huts. There are none from the Shorapur doab. Then, how could we presume that the evidence of Tekka-lakota, Sanganakallu and Hallur will repeat at Kodekal or other sites of the area ? Brahmagiri has yielded traces of postholes and low walls of rough granite blocks, sugg-esting the occurrence of houses of timber and stone. There were huts of oblong plan at Nagarjunakonda alongside the semi-subterranean dwellings. It is, then certain that there was no uniform pattern of dwelling in the neoli-thic culture of the south, and it is quite unsafe to fill in cultural lacunae from the evidence of other sites without analysing all available data. Similarly, to superimpose the picture of burial custom of another place into his own canvas may be a good collage but is hardly scientific. House-burials of Tekkalkota are absent at Brahmagiri while Negarjunakonda had a regular cemetery with two strata of burials associated with extended inhuma-tion and post-excarnation burials. There is no use multiplying instances, for it is evident that he has not gone through all available collection of materials as well as literature. It is inexplicable how he can overlook V. D. Krishnaswamy's paper on the 'Neolithic Pattern of India', which is a Presidential address in the Anth-ropology & Archaeology Section of the Science Congress and also published in *Ancient India*, no. 16, specially when he discusses the problem of the origin of the southern neolithic traditions and its various regional variants. He does not, however, take into account cultures in the lower Krishna valley, Orissa and Singhbhum plateau as distinct variants. Nevertheless, despite all these, the monograph may be considered as a valuable addition to our knowledge of the ash-mound culture of the Deccan.

Archaeological Survey of India
New Delhi, 110011

H. SARKAR

M. Hanumantha Rao & S. Nagaraju : Excavations at Hemmige. Mysore Directorate of Archaeology and Museums in Karnataka; 1974; pp. 80, plates 14, figures. Price : Rs. 30

Years ago the site of T. Narsipur on the Kaveri was excavated by Prof. M. Seshadri which brought to light, for the first time, the extension of neolithic-chalco-lithic cultures in an area which was basically taken by Foote, Krishnaswamy and others to be as purely neolithic. Unfortunately, the work could not be expanded due to the sudden demise of Prof. Seshadri. The present report of the excavations at Hemmige by his close associates M. Hanumantha Rao and S. Nagraju, has shown that T. Narsipur was not an isolated site of a culture complex which spread as far south as the southern most boundary of the present Karnataka state, The excavated material however, has not added anything new to knowledge.

The site has yielded rich material of the Satvahana period which goes well with the material earlier discove-red at Brahmagiri. The printing of the report is clean and the illustrations fairly good.

National Museum
New Delhi, 110011

AMARENDRA NATH

A. V. Narasimha Murthy : The Coins of Karnataka. Mysore: Geetha Book House, 1975; pp. 254. Price : Rs.50

Consisting of twenty chapters, the volume under review is basically a survey of the dynastic coinage of Karnataka. Its coverage is quite comprehensive in that the survey continues down to the most recent dynasty that ruled in Mysore till a few years back.

Not all the dynasties included in the book originated in Karnataka although their power is known to have extended to this region ; besides, several dynasties originating in present Karnataka expanded beyond its borders These, apart from other considerations such as the circulation area of coins, make it somewhat difficult to view the coinage of any particular State strictly in terms of its dynastic coinage. In fact, many of the coin series incorporated in this book will surely be included in similar studies on the coinage of Maharashtra or of Andhra. In the absence of precise information about mints, particularly of the early period, the coinage of a present political area can be studied only in terms of the various series in circulation in that area, despite the fact that information on the findspots of coins is often regrettably poor. That Dr. Narasimha Murthy is to a certain extent aware of this criterion emerges from his treatment of the punchmarked coins found in Karnataka and also from his comments on their chronology. The Roman coins found in Karnataka have also been assigned a separate chapter, thus indicating that although the accent is on local dynastic coinage, other coins found in the area have justifiably been considered to be of relevance for a study of its currency history. Unfortunately, the lengthy introduction, except for its sketchy bibliographical part, as well as the general remarks on punchmarked coins are totally redundant for the purpose of this book. Similarly, the details regarding the Yadavas, although highlighted as a 'Karnataka dynasty' in this book (p. 106) are really irrelevant, considering that the major findspots of Yadava coins lie outside Karnataka.

While the survey attempted in this book is generally competent and up to date, there are certain lapses which could have been avoided with a little more thoroughness. Any conclusion of the antiquity of coinage in India has now to rest upon archaeological evidence and there is at the moment nothing in archaeology that can warrant such a statement, as "Indian coinage originated .... somewhere around 1000 B. C. , possibly even earlier' (p.23). On p. 129 the author describes a silver coin which he, following V. A. Smith, attributes to the Goa Kadambas. It was shown as early as 1923 by N. K. Bhattasali that the coin was actually struck by Govinda Manikya of Tripura at a much later date (*Journal of the Asiatic Society of Bengal. Numismatic Supplement,* 1923 the most recent note on this coin is published in the *Journal of the Numismatic Society of India,* XXXIII, pt. II, 1971, pp. 69-72).

As the book is nothing more than a survey, one should perhaps not look for any kind of analysis in it. But lack of analysis also implies a failure to question existing views, which in turn affects the quality of a survey to a certain degree. The author does not distinguish between different stages of coinage in Karnataka, although the profusion of references to coinage in epigraphs of the early medieval and medieval periods would have led one to suppose that at least in terms of quantity, coinage in those periods was substantially different from what preceded it. The author has questioned the present review's suggestion regarding the chronology of Kadamba coinage (p. 61), but the so-called *padmatanka* coins which he, following earlier writers, assigns to the early Kadambas, were more akin to other similar series of the early medieval period in terms of metal, typology and weight standard. The silver punchmarked coins of the early historical period and the gold 'punch-marked' coins of the early medieval period represented two historical contexts ; the chronology of one series cannot thus be determined in the light of the other. The author has in fact failed to grasp that there was a significant break in the coinage of Karnataka between the early and early medieval periods, as of other areas of south India.

There are two major technical flaws in the book. The reproductions of coins are in the form of line-drawings, which do not do justice to the subject. The Bibliography is unsatisfactory and unlikely to be of any help to future investigators.

Centre of Historical Studies B. D. CHATTOPADHYAYA
Jawaharlal Nehru University
New Delhi, 110057

M. K. Dhavalikar : Ajanta : a Cultural Study. Poona - University Press : 1974, V+ 144 pp. 12 plates 31. Figs. Price - Rs. 75.

At long last , there is a book in which Dr. Dhavalikar has made a bold attempt to study the entire wealth of material-culture that is depicted in the famous Ajanta murals in the light of actual specimens found in archaeological excavations, parallels occurring in plastic-representations, literary references and accounts of the foreign travellers. Besides the usual preface and introduction, it has twelve chapters dealing with architecture, costumes, textiles, coiffure, head-dresses and ornaments, vessels and house hold articles, arms and armour, musical instruments, conveyances, royal insignia, flora and fauna. The approach and the plan of the book is the same as that of *Amaravati Sculptures in the Madras Museum* by. C. Sivaramamurti and in *Harsacharita Ek Samskrtika Adhyayana* by V. S Agrawal, and, to that extent, it follows only an already trodden path.

Dr. Dhavalikar's study shows that the representations of religious-architecture at Ajanta are very few whereas we get a fairly good idea of the secular architecture of the time, for example, various *salas* and *agaras*, like the apanasala, sangitasala. He justly remarks that most of the architectural depictions come from the later group of paintings. Among these are secular apartments. However, the literary references cited in this connection are more or less the same as we notice in the studies of Harsacharita and Kadambari made by V. S Agrawal.

The Chapter dealing with the costumes is full of references to *dhoti* or *ardhornka, antariya* (the lower garment) and *uttariya* (the upper garment) of the kings, ministers, soldiers, monks and laymen but without telling us sufficiently in details how the costumes as a whole differed in every case. Regarding the textile and foot-wear, Dhavlikar has rightly arrived at two major conclusions. One is that although the identification of different types of fabrics, such as cotton and silk, is difficult to make, yet we can presume that the higher strata of the society mostly used silk and fine white muslin while the lower classes had to be contended with coarser varieties of cotton, The other is that the women did not wear shoe at all, and the men also used it rarely. (p. 41 ff.)

As regards the chapters on coiffure and head-dresses, and ornaments the material has been well sorted out and nicely catalogued, The treatment of vessels and other house-hold articles is certainly much better than the treatment of similar objects by Sivaramamurti and Agrawal, since it takes into account the archaeological findings from Taxila, Kasia, etc. (p. 82). The chapter on furniture makes evolutionary study of various types of thrones (*Simhasanas*) - those with animal supports (*paryanka*) etc. and those with arms and without back, etc. ; which brings an extra credit to the book. Dhavlikar's remarks (in the light of the facts he has put forward) that 'during the Vakataka-Gupta period, the art of furniture -making had reached its zenith' is somewhat a bold challenge to the future art-historians since field-archaeology and literature have very little to support it.

Looking into the chapters on arms and armour, musical instruments, conveyances, royal insignia and the flora and fauna, we feel bound to appreciate the pains Dhavalikar has gone through in sorting out the information from a bulk of Ajanta murals, though we cannot help in repeatedly being reminded of the works of Sivaramamurti and Agrawal, which is , of course, perfectly in agreement with the introductory remarks of the author.

The monograph ends with 'The World of Ajanta' in which the author has shown with absolute clarity and brevity the life of a *nagaraka* or city-dwellers of the Gupta period which was extremely colourful within a set-up of very rich material achievements.

It is a nicely brought out publication with beautiful photographs and line drawings. However, there are a large number of proof-mistakes which, I believe, the author would rectify in future editions.

Institute of South Asian Archaeology S. P. TEWARI
University of Amsterdam.
Amsterdam.

D. Desai : Erotic Sculpture of India. Calcutta : Tata McGraw. Hill, 1975; 269 pp, 26 drawings, 155 photographs. Price : not indicated.

Erotic art is a hot favourite of the publishers and there is a plethora of books on this theme available today. In fact, Khajuraho and other such monuments have been so vulgarly advertised by such art publishers, picture-post- card dealers and the tourist agencies that these elegant monuments are treated just as erotic albums. No wonder that I saw only two Indians and the rest-foreign tourists in the Boeing that landed at Khajuraho on a November morning this year. These tourists- Indians and foreigners alike-hunt for the erotic scenes and forget the over all beauty of the architectural and sculptural art. To a great extent this is due to the commercial exploitation of such art by various publishers who emphasize the erotic themes completely out of context. For the first time, Dr. Desai's book breaks new ground and places the Indian erotic motif in its proper socio-cultural context. Tata Mc Graw-Hill publishers deserve all praise for promoting such an academic book on this theme.

Indian erotic art is a much debated topic. It has been condemned as profane and obscene by some, while others have idealized it as the Union of the individual with the cosmic spirit. Even the materialists like Mulkraj Anand seem to be trying their best to disguise such art in a spiritual garb: "seldom do the faces reflect mere animal lust, as though the artisan always remembered the spiritual values of which the naked physical connection was merely the expression". One may recall here a small note by Chakrabarti and Glantz on the erotic terrecottas in which they began the process of stripping the studies on erotic art of its spiritual mumbo-jumbo. Devangna Desai has completed this rational process by providing a logical analyses of the multiple causes that went into the development of Indian erotic motif. In this respect, she has de-mystified the Indian culture of its metaphysicl aura.

Devangna's attempt is revolutionary in more than one sense. Firstly, she has ventured into a field which is traditionally a taboo to Indian women researchers. Secondly, for the first time she has brought to bear an interdisciplinary and evolutionary approach to this vexed problem. Lastly, she has used a scientific approach in dealing with the erotic motif as it occurs on the temples, as an empirical reality, bereft of its idealistic accoutrements. She does not condemn or rationalize anything but tries to objectively analyse the genesis and efflores cence of the erotic motif. The result is a most valuable book which takes into account the primitive cults, the later religious practices, the feudal society, the art forms, the literary evidence and the secular life too.

Dr. Desai has discussed the erotic art in three periods : Early period ; A.D. 500 -900 and A.D. 900-1400. The Early Period covers a very big time range and is a subject by itself. Its treatment is cursory and introductory to the other two sections. Chapters III and IV deal exhaustively with A. D. 500-900 and A. D. 900-1400 periods respectively. She does not give just her conclusions but presents the whole array of the interdisciplinary data collected by her. Magico-religious problems are discussed in Chapter VI, and Tantrism and Erotic Sculpture in VII. The social setting of the Hindu temple is explained in Chapter VII and the sexual modes of the society inIX. Literary data on the subject is marshalled in Chapter X. Dr. Desai is primarily a sociologist and therefore her approach is informed by such a broad perspective. Its not an eclectic assortment of data either. Every bit of the work reflects the painstaking work of seven years that has gone into its making. The last chapter summarizes and synthesizes the vast data collected by her. The book is marked by its coherence and forthrightness. The author first gives a survey of the evidence as available, then discusses the other relevant data on the contemporary art, society and religion. Explanations are based on the erotic motifs as found on the temples and its emplacement on the architectural scheme of the temples of various regions.

Her refutations of the existing theories are always based on hard facts and not merely on subjective arguments. Such a scientific treatment is something rare and refreshing in such art books :

I will quote some instances of how she refutes the existing theories. Some scholars see the sublime union of the individual and the cosmic spirit in the conjugal scenes. She asks but how can one explain the scenes of bestiality and orgies. Others have dismissed this phase as an aberration. But the presents a survey of Central India, Gujarat, Maharashtra, M. P., Orissa and South India to show that it was a widespread movement and not a localised aberration. Nor does she agree that it was merely a Tantric cultic manifestation. Tantrism was an esoteric religion and its art was not decorative but cultive. Nor were the depicted postures sexo-yogic. The erotic "art was influenced by Tantrism without being functionally related to Tantric *Sadhana*. Tantrism only helped in fostering a general attitude of permissiveness towards sex" and recognition of the need of bestowing love and care on the body which was denied earlier. Tantric practices also sanctified short-cuts to acquiring virtue (punya). Temple building got a fillip as the feudal aristocrats found it an easy way of achieving *moksha*.

She has shown how the fragmentation of political power was catalysed by the feudal self-sufficient economic units. This led to regionalization and conventionalization of art forms. In the A.D. 900-1400 period, each region interpreted the erotic motif according to its own cultural beliefs and conconized art patterns.

She thus gives several factors for the development of Medieval erotic art such as magico religious significance of erotic themes engrained in the public mind ; old practice of decorating monuments with *mithuna* which degenerated into *maithuna* and orgiastic figures under the Tantric influence ; the sensual atmosphere of the Medieval temple ; the tendency of feudal lords to accrue virtue by short-cuts such as temple building ; the widespread prevalence of *devadasi* institution ; and the socio-cultural conditions of the degenerate feudal states.

Her book analyses the processes which brought about the fusion of the magico-religious and secular interests in sex. This fusion in fact is represented in such erotic motifs of the Medieval period. In a feudal system, with its independent land grants and management, the temple itself becomes a feudal lord with its *devadas is* and other manifestations of its sensual atmosphere. In this perspective, the erotic motif appears as a natural product of the Medieval feudal society. Summing up, Dr. Desai says, "our study of sexual representation in Indian culture convinces us that there is no philosophical or rational motivation behind it. Its presence in religious art is a pointer to the continuity and persistence of primitive and popular cultural elements in a civilized society. Far from being an anomaly in Hindu culture, erotic motifs were in harmony with the religious environment to which they belonged and with the majestic, courtly and artistic temples they decorated. They were *alankaras*".

It is no wonder that the book has been unanimously acclaimed by art-historians and sociologists alike. Devangna Desai's this *magnum opus,* I am sure, will become a trend- setter in such studies. Not all photographs are upto the mark ; some are poor. Except for such minor flaws, the book has a beautiful get-up and very well printed. It is a book that will not only adorn a bookshelf but will also make an enlightening and interesting reading.

Physical Research Laboratory
Ahmadabad, 380009

D. P. AGRAWAL

A. Narrow elongated handaxes of the Acheulian industry from Bhimbetka.

B. Ovate handaxes of the Acheulian industry from Bhimbetka.

[See p. 27] [Photos : Deccan College, Pune.]

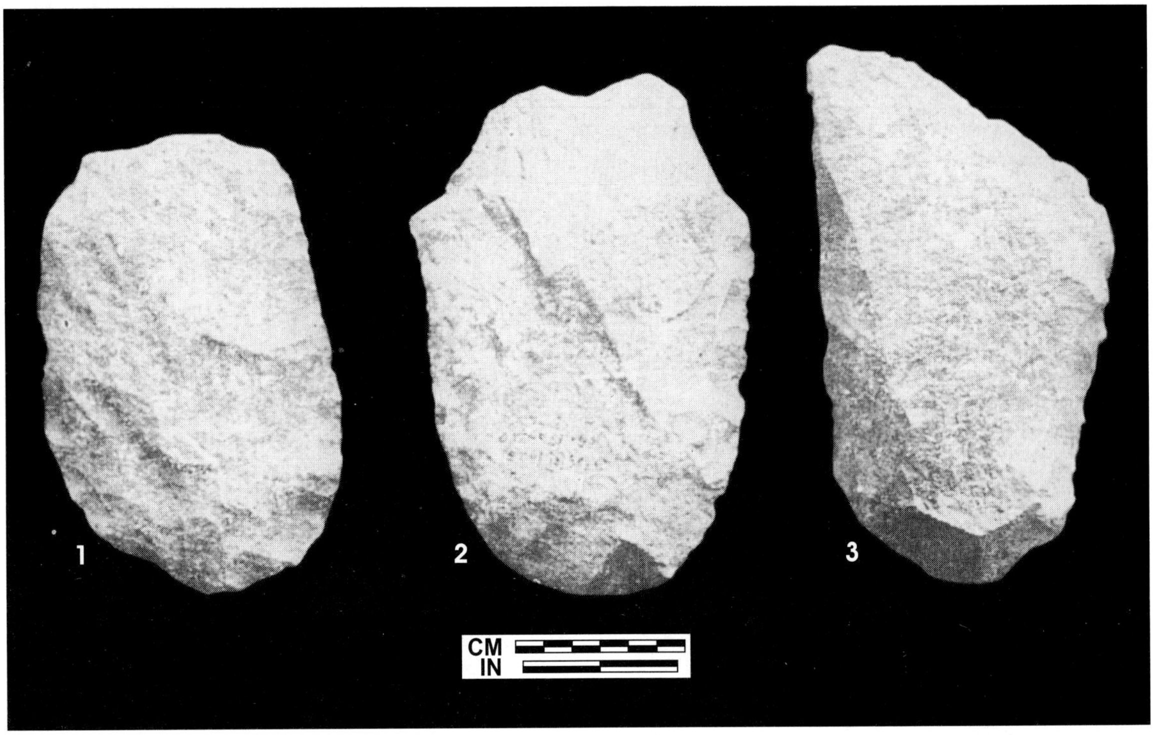

A. Rounded butt cleavers of the Acheulian industry from Bhimbetka.

B. Pointed butt cleavers of the Acheulian industry from Bhimbetka.

[See p. 27] [Photos : Deccan College, Pune.]

A. Levalloisian flakes of the Acheulian industry from Bhimbetka.

B. Levalloisian blades of the Acheulian industry from Bhimbetka.

[See p. 27]

[Photos : Deccan College, Pune.]

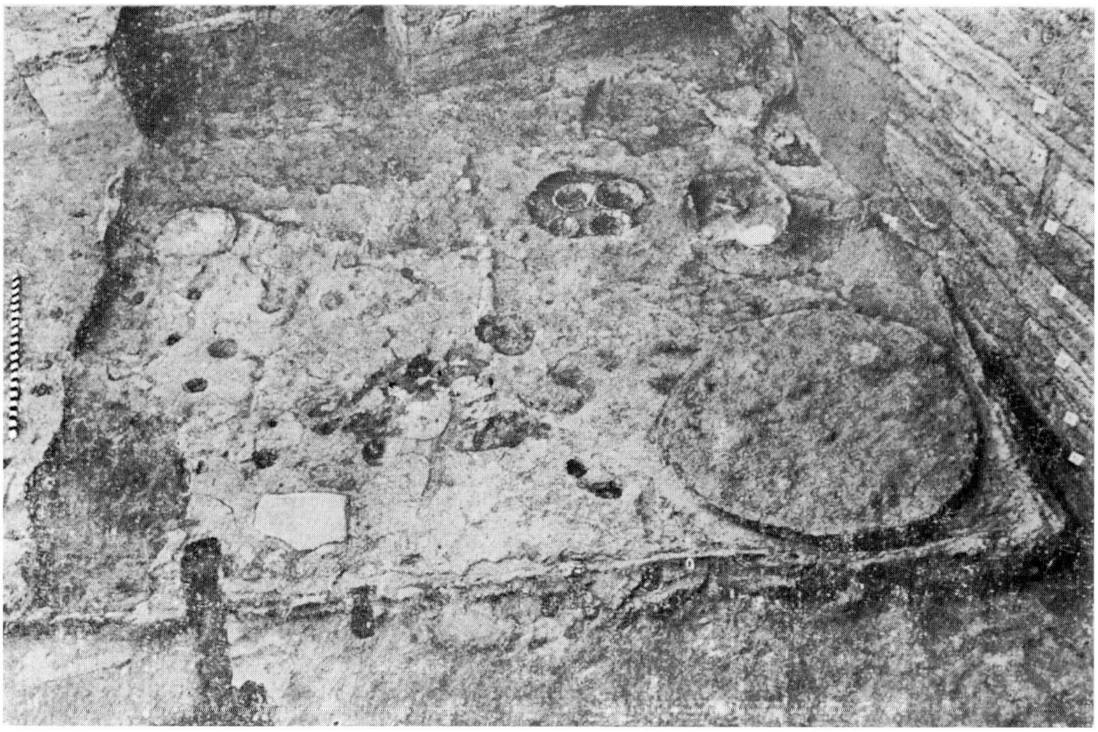

A. House-remains of Period I at Inamgaon.

B. Pottery kiln of Period II at Inamgaon.

[See p. 51] [Photos : Deccan College, Pune.]

A. Close view of a part of the granary of Period II at Inamgaon.

B. House-remains of Period III at Inamgaon.

[See pp. 49 and 51] [Photos : Deccan College, Pune.]

1. Carbonized grains of hulled barley *(Hordeum spp.).*

2. Carbonized grains of larger hulled barley *(Hordeum spp.).*

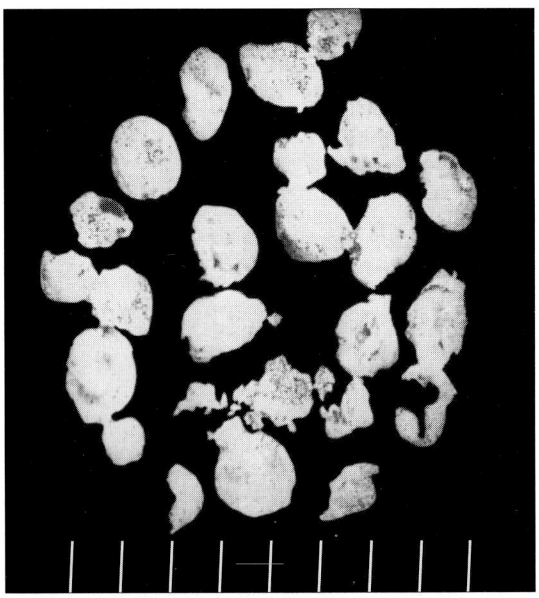

3. Burnt grains of Sorghum vulgara Pers.

4. Carbonized grains of wheat (*Triticum spp.*).

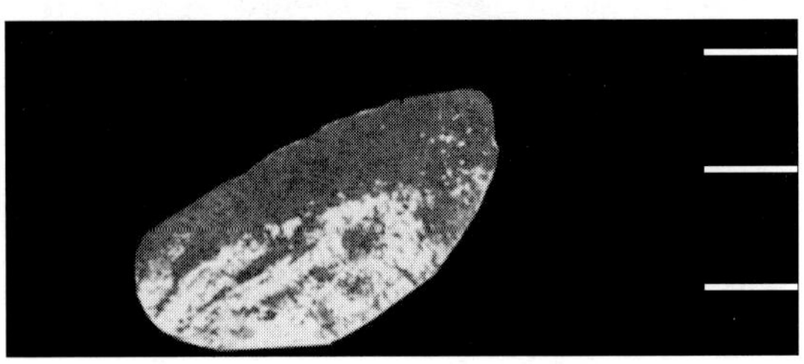

5. Single carbonized kernel of rice (aryza sativa).

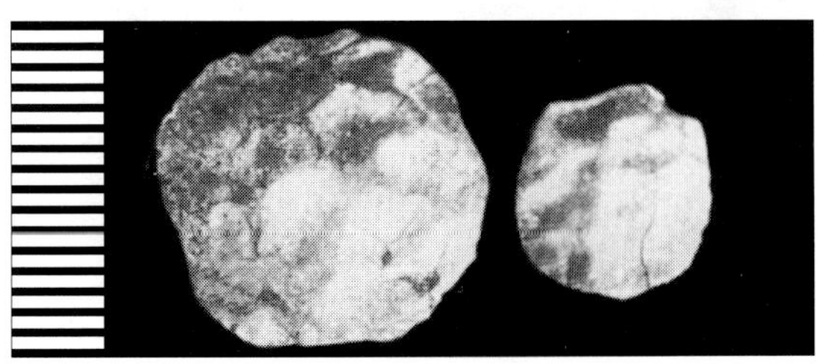

6. Unidentified fruit.

[See pp. 56-61]

[Photos : Birbal Sahni Institute of Palaeobotany, Lucknow.]

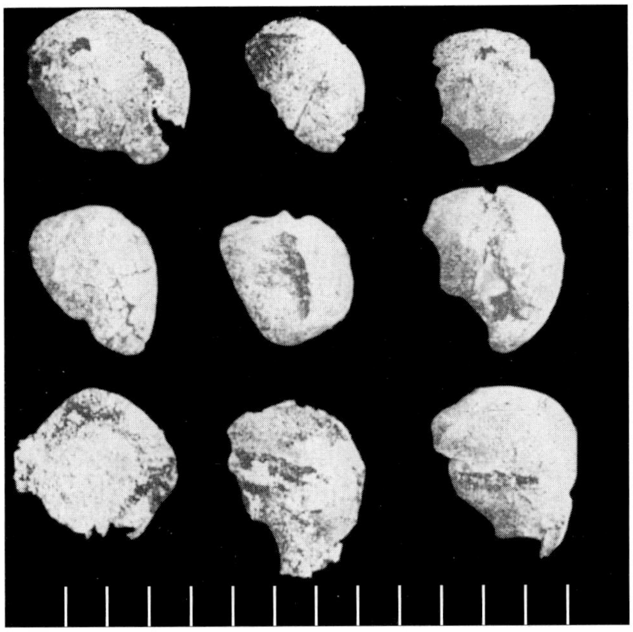

1. Carbonized seeds of *Pisum sativum Liun.*

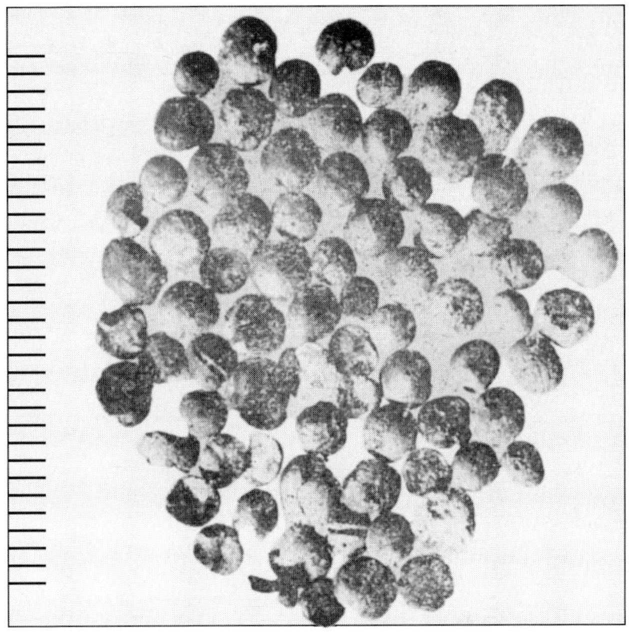

2. Carbonized seeds of *Lens esculenta Moench.*

3. Carbonized seeds of *Dolichos Lablab Lin.*

4. Carbonized seeds of *Phaseolus radiatus willd.*

5. Carbonized seeds of *Lathyrus Sativus Liun.*

[See pp. 56-61]

[Photo : Birbal Sahni Institute of Palaeobotany, Lucknow.]

1. Carbonized seeds of *Dolichos biflours Liun.*

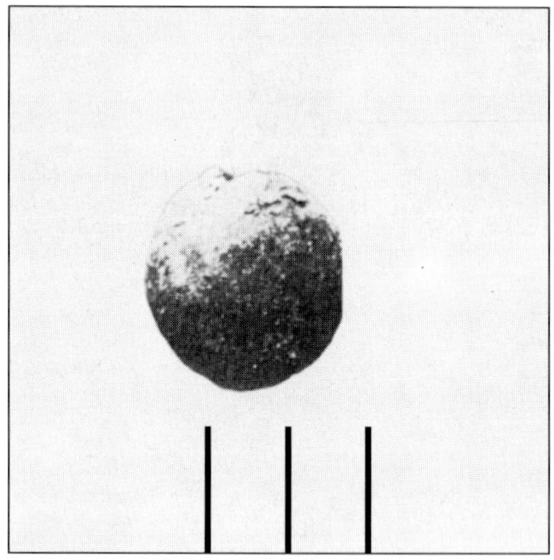

2. Carbonized seeds of *Vicia sps Liun.*

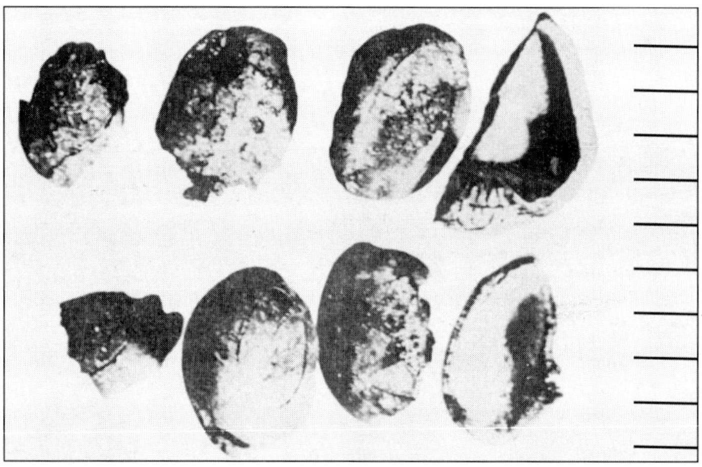

3. Carbonized nuts and shells of oil seeds — *Buchanannia angustifolia Roxb.*

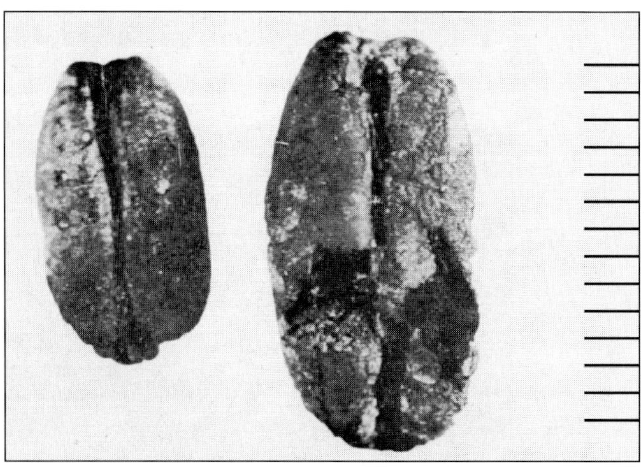

4. Carbonized fruit-stones of *Phoenix sylvestris Roxb.*

5. Carbonized fruit-stones of *Ziyphus nummularia W & A.*

[See pp. 56-61]

[Photos : Birbal Sahni Institute of Palaeobotany, Lucknow.]

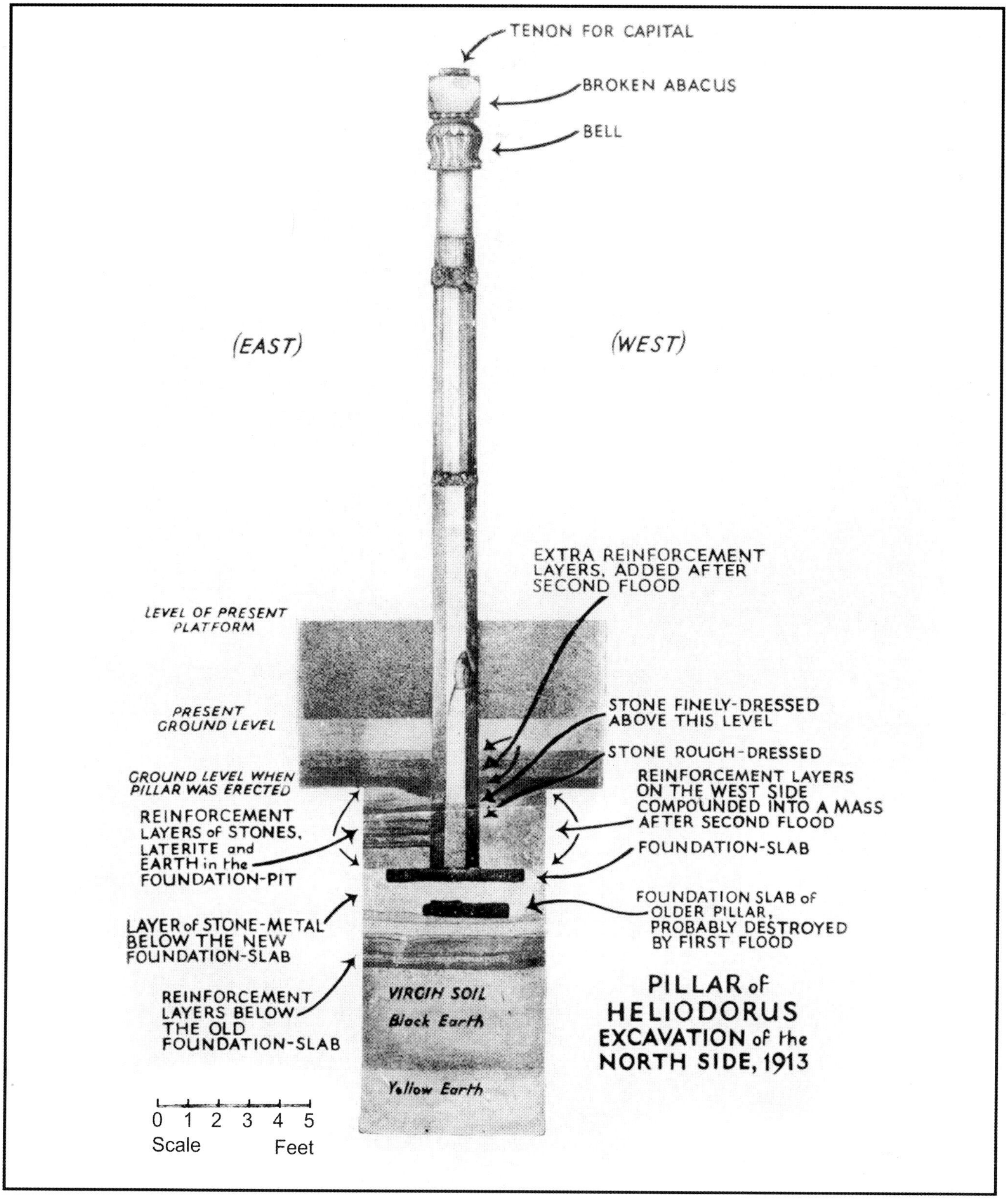

[See pp. 166-76] [Drawing : Archaeological Survey of India.]

A. Details of ornamentation. Drawn by Margaret Hall.

[See pp. 166-76]

B. Column of Heliodorus (detail).

C. Heliodorus pillar at Besnagar.

[Photos : Archaeological Survey of India.]

Details of the shaft of the Heliodorus pillar at Besnagar.

[See pp. 166-76]

A. Memorial yupa in stone. Drawn by M. Hall, after J.P. Vogel.

B. Lower portion of the pillar after excavation.

C. Horse-rider carrying a garuda-dhvaja.

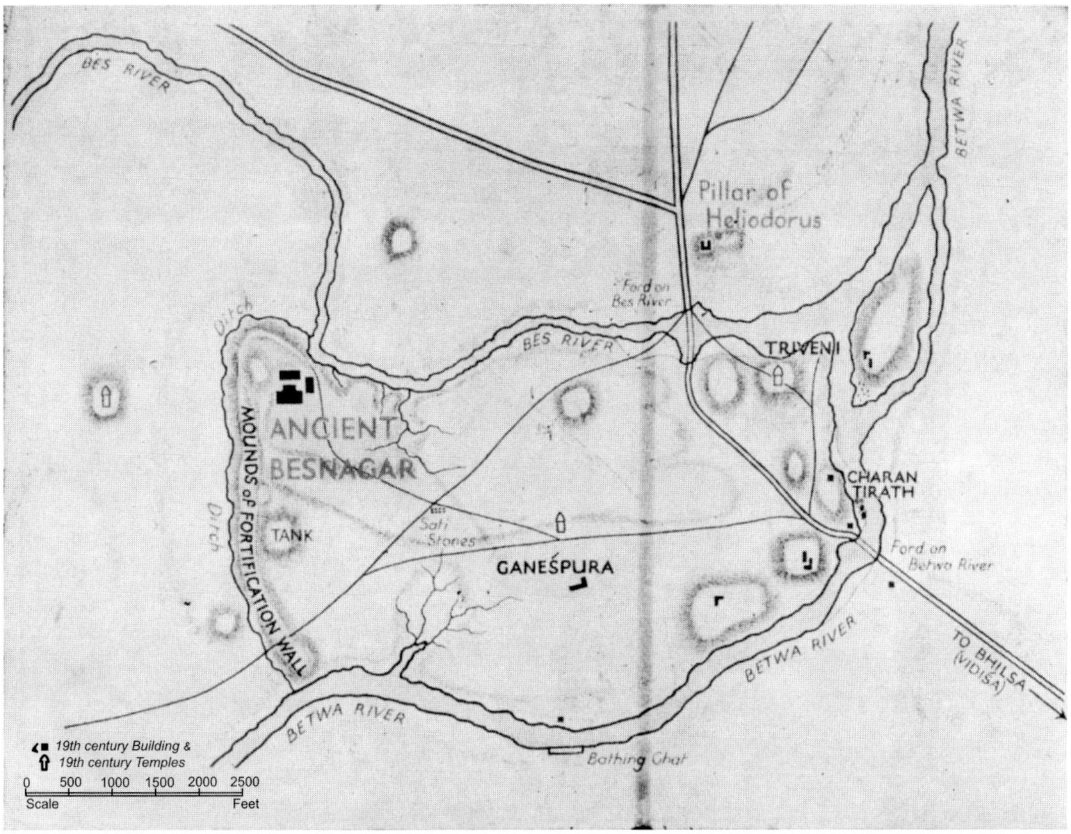

A. Site plan of ancient Besnagar.

B. Elliptical plan of the Vasudeva shrine, as revealed by Khare's excavation of 1963-65.

[See pp. 166-76] [Photo : Archaeological Survey of India.]

Relic casket of Kanishka from Saraneri.

[See pp. 185-90] [Photo : Archaeological Survey of India.]

A. Remains of the temple and monastic establishment of Phase III at Virabhadra.

B. Remains of successive shrines of Phase II at Virabhadra.

[See pp. 180-81]

[Photos : Archaeological Survey of India.]

Close view of the deep digging, showing successive structures at Virabhadra.

[Photos : Archaeological Survey of India.]

[See pp. 180-81]